# RECORDS OF THE INTELLIGENCE DEPARTMENT

## OF THE GOVERNMENT OF THE NORTH-WEST PROVINCES OF INDIA

## DURING THE MUTINY OF 1857

# RECORDS OF THE INTELLIGENCE DEPARTMENT

## OF THE GOVERNMENT OF THE NORTH-WEST PROVINCES OF INDIA

## DURING THE MUTINY OF 1857

INCLUDING
CORRESPONDENCE WITH THE SUPREME GOVERNMENT
DEHLI, CAWNPORE, AND OTHER PLACES

WILLIAM MUIR
THEN IN CHARGE OF THE INTELLIGENCE DEPARTMENT,
AND SUBSEQUENTLY LIEUTENANT-GOVERNOR, NORTH-WEST
PROVINCES

EDITED BY
WILLIAM COLDSTREAM

IN TWO VOLUMES
VOLUME ONE

GYAN

*Published by*

Gyan Publishing House
5, Ansari Road
Daryaganj, New Delhi-110002
Phone: 011-47034999, 9811692060
E-mail: books@gyanbooks.com

*Distribution Network*
gyanbooks.com
India, USA, Canada, UK, Australia, France



ISBN : 978-81-212-3947-9 (Set)
ISBN : 978-81-212-5035-1 (PB)
First Published, Edinburgh, 1902

2nd Impression 2020

*Printed at:* Gyan Press, Delhi.



**Records of the**
**Intelligence Department Vol. I**
Author: William Muir

# RECORDS OF THE
# INTELLIGENCE DEPARTMENT

OF THE

## GOVERNMENT OF THE NORTH-WEST PROVINCES OF INDIA

DURING THE

# MUTINY OF 1857

INCLUDING

***CORRESPONDENCE WITH THE SUPREME GOVERNMENT, DEHLI, CAWNPORE, AND OTHER PLACES***

PRESERVED BY, AND NOW ARRANGED UNDER THE SUPERINTENDENCE OF

SIR WILLIAM MUIR, K.C.S.I., D.C.L.

THEN IN CHARGE OF THE INTELLIGENCE DEPARTMENT, AND SUBSEQUENTLY LIEUTENANT-GOVERNOR, NORTH-WEST PROVINCES

EDITED BY WILLIAM COLDSTREAM, B.A., I.C.S.

VOL. I.

EDINBURGH
T. & T. CLARK, 38 GEORGE STREET
1902

# TABLE OF CONTENTS

## VOLUME I.

### *INTRODUCTION:* FAMILY LIFE AT AGRA, AND PRIVATE CORRESPONDENCE



### RECORDS OF INTELLIGENCE DEPARTMENT

# AGRA IN THE MUTINY
AND
# FAMILY LIFE IN THE FORT.

A SKETCH FOR THE FAMILY, 1896.

[*Extracts from the above.*]

FOR some time I have been pressed to give the family an account of our experience during the Mutiny of 1857. I shrank at first from the idea, and put it quite aside. By and by, however, the reasonableness of the request grew upon me. Five of our children were for several months shut up with us in the Fort, and for the whole family it was a time of great anxiety. Anything of a literary or historical character was, of course, out of the question; but it appeared on consideration quite possible, and for the above reason right and proper, that I should give a simple outline of that eventful period, in so far as it affected us personally.

Musing thus, I was led to look over the half-dozen volumes of Mutiny records which I kept up in 1857 when in charge of the Intelligence Department, and which I had cast aside amid other old documents relating to my work in India. And I turned also to Kaye's account of Agra, in his *Sepoy War*, where I was startled to read this long-forgotten passage:—

"We had wisely organised an Intelligence Department, of which William Muir had the chief direction. It was highly important at such a time that reliable information should be obtained from the Officers of Government themselves, in place of the gossip of the bazaars, or the confused statements of frightened messengers, and no man could have done the work better than Muir. The semi-official or private correspondence that came in from day to day was full of the most instructive and suggestive details. It was said that he was a little over-chary in the dissemination of the intelligence he obtained. But this can scarcely be regarded as a fault, when we consider how likely it was, amid such a population as that of the Agra Fort, a story once floated would be exaggerated or distorted, and might rather add to the anxieties than strengthen the confidence of our people. There was, in truth, little or nothing of an exhilarating character to be communicated, so, perhaps, silence at such a time was of better metal than speech."—Vol. iii. p. 406.

Reading thus, it dawned upon me that these same old neglected books, containing as they do the result of my daily correspondence with the officers of the Company throughout our beleaguered districts, and still more the often hourly record of reports taken at the mouth of messengers and spies, might have a special interest and value not only for the family, but for others desiring to consult them. Besides much personal information, they present a vivid picture of our insulated position at Agra, and of the reeking flood of mutiny that poured around us. These records had been made over to Kaye, and were used by him till, on his untimely death in the middle of his great work, they were returned to me and put aside. I have now gone carefully over them. How they carry one back to those terrible times, and to the singular experience of the Agra Fort when we, with five or six thousand souls, were segregated for months within its walls from all the world!

I mention these Volumes here, simply because they led my thoughts back to the days of the Mutiny. In using them for my little story, I have only referred to such occasional details in them as bear upon our life at Agra, and the dangers that beset us. There is no attempt at following the Mutiny elsewhere. I will notice at the end of this sketch how I propose to deal with the Volumes themselves. Meanwhile I proceed to the rough-and-ready outline which I have promised to the family, of our life and experiences at Agra.

In January 1857 we (your Mother and I) set out on a circuit, which, as Member of the Board, I had to take throughout the upper districts of the North-West Provinces. And so we travelled in camp with the children up the Doab by Meerut and Seharunpore, and round by Kurnaul and Delhi, returning home again by the Goorgaon and Muttra districts on the left bank of the Jumna;—that is, through a Country and Cities which shortly after were convulsed with outrage and rebellion. How quiet and peaceful it all was then! During our tour, however, the cartridge trouble had transpired. In February the Pandy regiments at Barrackpore began to show disloyalty; and from thence, as a kindling centre, factious emissaries were being sent all over the land to infect the Hindoo regiments. And they felt their power; for India had been drained of its European troops for the Russian War. From Meerut to Calcutta, say over 1000 miles, there were but three European corps,—one with us, one at Lucknow, and one at Patna; while the cities teemed with native regiments. No wonder that the Pandies saw the game to be all in their own hands. It was at the close of March that Mungal Pandy was shot, and immediately after the Nineteenth Regiment was disbanded.

About the middle of March, on our return, I met Sir Henry Lawrence as he passed through Agra from Rajpootana to Lucknow; and about the end of the month, Sir Henry Durand rested with us as he journeyed to take Lawrence's place at Indore. I remember conversing with him on the outlook of affairs. There was anxiety as to the spread of discontent, but no immediate sense of the volcanic ground on which at the moment the Company's rule was standing. As the result of his observations, he wrote while with us to Lord Canning, noting especially that our General, Polewhele, discountenanced as unwise the anxious views of the younger officers, who felt that the Sepoy corps generally were sympathisers with the Nineteenth Regiment.[1] But it was all too true; and April passed sullenly away, while mutinous messengers were secretly spreading treachery among the Pandy regiments everywhere.

At last came the crash; and on Sunday the 10th May, as the Europeans were preparing for church parade at Meerut, the great Mutiny broke out. On Monday, 11th, a message was received from a lady at Meerut, by her aunt at Agra, warning her not to start for Meerut, as the cavalry had risen, set fire to the houses, and killed all European officers and soldiers they could find;—a message, as Kaye says, scanty in words but of tremendous significance.[2] It was the last message the broken wires conveyed. For one or two days we were left in ominous gloom, till, by degrees, the awful truth transpired with the terrible addition of the fall of Dehli and slaughter of every European there. During the month, there was mutiny all around. The regiments at Allygurh, Mynpoory, and Etawah, one after another, went the way of their wild bloodthirsty brethren, and the consternation at Agra was intense. People rushed to the Fort with all their goods and chattels; but permission to enter was shortly after withdrawn, and then R. Drummond's policy

[1] Kaye, iii. p. 239. [2] *Ibid.* p. 595.

was rigidly adopted of avoiding even ordinary precautions, lest the people should construe them into signs of fear and of alarm. Had reasonable arrangements been allowed, how much might have been saved, not only for the convenience of all who eventually took refuge in the Fort, but of valuable records, literature, etc. At the end of May, Muttra, some thirty miles off, went like the rest, and then arose with us the panic of sudden attack from its rebel Sepoys. There were at this period times of intense anxiety, when a day seemed to hang upon one like a year, and the thought was of nothing but the danger to the dear ones about us.[1] Driving through the streets, I remember the singular feeling as if we had suddenly become strangers in a strange land, —as if, in fact, the people were pitifully regarding us as shortly, like all around, to be swept away. While the road down country was still open and regarded safe for carriage Daks, I at one time thought of sending off your Mother and the children to Calcutta, escaping thus the danger that was louring upon Agra. Indeed, the carriage had been ordered. I dare not think upon it but with a shudder, as they would almost certainly have been stopped at Cawnpore,—a terrible thought! Thank God, the danger was apprehended in time, and the idea dropped.

As time went on, Volunteer companies were formed. To encourage the movement I joined it at first on the dear old brown mare, though my duties lay in another direction; and I remember Charlie, then a little lad of seven, following us in play with boyish delight, clad in his little uniform, with red kummerbund and turban round his sola-topee, on his small white pony. The Gwalior Bodyguard was a great help to us; and indeed the countenance of Scindia, supported as he was by that grand man, my friend Dinkur Rao, was invaluable. But they failed to curb their heavy Contingent, which at last, in the middle of June, mutinied and massacred our people at Gwalior, of whom but a small portion escaped to Agra. Major Macpherson, the Agent, was immensely serviceable, keeping us ever *en rapport* with Scindia, and helping us with information from that quarter.

I have no clear recollection whether I was present in Cantonments (some two or three miles off) when Mr. Colvin, on the 15th May, addressed the two Native corps, and was received by them with a hollow cheer. But I have the most vivid picture before my mind of the night of the 30th May,

[1] At such times one did not think even of meals, and the only thing that flourished was the beard. With me, as with many others, it was the beginning of that luxury.

when, in consequence of the sudden intelligence that the Bhurtpore troops, who, on the farther side beyond Muttra, were escorting Harvey to Dehli, had mutinied and might at any moment come against us, it was determined next morning to disarm our Sepoy regiments. At midnight a notice went round for all families to betake themselves, by early dawn, to the several rendezvous already appointed as places of resort in case of danger. Your Mother at once went up to ours ("Loyd's Kothee," at top of a hill close by), and slept there with the children; by the morning this house and all about it had become a strange scene, crowded with women and shrieking children. Meanwhile, Farquhar and I had volunteered to carry the warning of the danger over that quarter of the Station that lay next the city. It was a singular sight and marvellous lesson that night's experience. Some even of the ladies were brave and prepared for all risks; others least expected, even of the other sex, trembled and almost fainted for fear. From the Convent to the Mission House, we warned every one; and by the dawn we, like the rest, were at our rendezvous. It overlooked the Jail, where part of the disarmament was being carried out under our eyes. Fortunately, both there and in Cantonments, all was safely and well accomplished. The Sepoys generally went off to their homes, and for the time Agra was relieved of immediate danger.

And so we entered June. The story of this fateful month at Agra is told with wonderful truth by Kaye, whose vivid description of scenes, and of the character of those concerned, comes to my recollection as marvellously accurate and sound. But I have not a single note or memorandum of events till the following month. Harington, Reade, and I, had been nominated, in a sort of informal way by Mr. Colvin, to keep the wheels of Government in motion, Judicial, Financial, and Revenue, respectively. But as tract after tract fell out of our hands, the administration collapsed, and the labour of conducting it shrank to nothing; there was in fact no Government to conduct. This was especially the case with my department. Every now and then, as things seemed to brighten, a little revenue might appear. But at last all came to an end, and my occupation was left high and dry; for otherwise I rather kept aside from the Lieutenant-Governor's councils, in which a good deal of feeling sometimes transpired.

And thus the month of June wore away, till towards its close the Mutineer body from Nemuch and Nusseerabad, instead of, as was expected, crossing over to Dehli, were found to be marching direct upon us. Then, as they approached, things began to look so threatening that the women and children were warned (it might well have been before) to take refuge in the Fort at once. The chamber allotted to us was a long, bare, stone room on the lower floor on the east side of the Dewan-Khas, or Palace Square, with windows looking into the square. It served, when fitted with a few simple pieces of furniture, for all purposes of the day, and for the numerous neighbouring friends who took their meals with us. At night the farther end, when curtained off for our beds, was suitable enough for ourselves and the children. Beyond the actual necessaries of life and reasonable comfort, we could bring in nothing to our room; but we managed to save and store away what things we chiefly wished to keep.[1] It was Wednesday the 1st of July that your Mother, with our five children, left the dear old house at Hurree Purbut, where we had lived so long, and occupied this room. A curious incident here occurred. The Dhai who nursed T. . ., shut out by the European guard at the Ummer Singh Gate, in terror of her life took refuge under one of the Fort bridges, and feared to enter again. But most fortunately for the poor child, and for us all, after two days she saw a company of native women working at the Fort gate, and, getting one of them to let her change clothes with her, thus managed to get in as if a cooly woman, and in joy so reached our room.

I myself, with Thornhill and Farquhar, slept out for the rest of the week at the Mofussilite Press, close by the Magistrate's house, ready for any emergency. The Mutineer force steadily advanced upon us, and our troops were held in readiness to meet them. On Sunday morning the 5th, after breakfasting in the Fort, I rode down to the General's house in Cantonments, where the leading officers were assembled, to see what was going on. At last, after much indecision, General ——, finding that the enemy were already within two or three miles of us, had resolved on meeting them at once, and I was deputed with a message to see that the Company guarding the Jail were forthwith despatched to join the rest of the regiment. It was a trying ride, for every creature, man, woman and child, had fled; and all along the deserted road, for a couple of miles or more, I met not a single soul. Especially as I passed the Ajmere Gate, by which lay the enemy's road, I felt, keeping hand on pistol, that at any turn their scouts might have been down and had a shot at me. But

[1] I remember the first thing I sent into the Fort for preservation was the precious MS. of Wackidi, which, after having used it for my *Life of Mahomet*, I eventually made over to the India Office Library. A beautiful copy made from the same MS. is now in our University Library.

my good old mare carried me swiftly along. After reaching the Jail, which was all in confusion while the prisoners were being released and led across the river, I delivered my message and returned to the Fort. My way now lay through the main street of the city, which was in a strange state of excitement and alarm, knowing well as the people did that any reverse would plunge the whole place into uproar, and put both loyal and disloyal at the mercy of miscreants and rebels everywhere. But I got safely through, to your Mother's intense thankfulness and relief. The Durzie afterwards told her that when he saw me riding along the street, he felt as if he would never see me again.

Then followed the anxious watching from the ramparts of the Fort, the first intelligence of our force being obliged to retire, and the sad sight of the wounded brought in with the re-entering troops. Beyond one or two shots to keep the immediate neighbourhood clear, there was no firing from the Fort; all were now within the walls; beyond them, everything was in the insurgents' hands. From the ramparts we could see the bungalows far and near—the thatched roofs giving every facility to the incendiaries—in a vast blaze during all the night, and the savage Sowars cantering round our flaming homes. Thank God for the Fort of Agra! What would it not have been for our dear ones on that dreadful night without it, but a place of awful peril! I find that on the Monday I began letters to Sir H. Lawrence, and also to the *Bombay Times*. As the Bombay letter records in detail our position at Agra, before and after the battle, and the battle itself, I think it will be of interest to quote the greater part of it here.[1]

After describing the composition and advance of the Nemuch force, the report continues:—

"Our position at Agra was in some degree complicated by having to guard our monster Jail[2] by European troops, for the Jail nujeebs (armed guard) had gone off in a body towards the end of the month. If the 3rd Europeans should be required in the field, it would be necessary to draw off the men employed on this duty, and the only resource left was to make over the custody of the Jail to the Sikh prisoners, who were to be released and armed for the purpose.

[1] I subsequently found two previous letters, dated 13th and 16th June, addressed to the *Bombay Times*. These will be found below in the Intelligence Collection, No. XI., see p. 24.

[2] It was the Central Jail for the North-West Provinces, containing a vast collection of the worst prisoners in the land.

"The Kotah contingent—a small force consisting of about 600 men of all arms, with two guns—reached us in the early part of June. It remained encamped for some time between this and Muttra, and was then marched across the Jumna to Sydabad, sixteen miles on the Allygurh road, where it did good service in quieting the country, to such an extent that the revenue balances were beginning to come in. As danger began to threaten us from the Nemuch troops, this corps was gradually drawn in towards Agra, and was marched into the native lines of our cantonments on Friday the 3rd July. It was generally believed to be sufficiently staunch to hold this position with European guns and bayonets close at hand. But some little symptoms of disrespect to British officers, and the suspicion of them prevalent in the city, were symptomatic of disaffection, especially among the Sowars. Syfoolla Khan's levy of Keraolee horse and foot continued up to this time to be of the utmost service to us in keeping the Agra district peaceful. It was now brought close to the city, and encamped on the enemy's road.

"Besides these purely military forces, we had an organised body of Militia, consisting of unattached officers, civilians, and clerks. It numbered 50 or 60 horse and about 200 foot. They had been under drill for only two or three weeks, and were generally raw and imperfect in military evolutions. The effect of the Contingent mutinying at Gwalior, was slowly but surely to draw off the Contingent of horse which had been hitherto assisting us in various quarters. About the end of June or beginning of July, accordingly, Raikes' horse at Mynpoory, Alexander's at Hatrass, and Burlton's at or about Allygurh, became disaffected, not without violence. Pearson's battery of nine-pounders followed them. The result was the arrival of all the European officers of those troops at Agra, and the withdrawal of the magistrates of Mynpoory, Allygurh, and Muttra from the positions they had hitherto been occupying. Such was our situation when the Nemuch mutineers came down upon us.

"On Wednesday the 1st of July, we had intelligence that they were at Futtehpore Sikri, distant twenty-two miles, and had seized our officials there, some of whom went over to them. The Tehseeldar seems to have been carried off and maltreated, and his arm broken. The Moonsif was made Tehseeldar by the mutineers, and the Thannadars and Resaldar maintained in their posts. Arrangements had been in progress for some days, judiciously directed by the Lieutenant-Governor, for bringing the more helpless classes, schools, etc. into the Fort. Almost all the ladies who were yet outside, now betook themselves to the Fort; the gentlemen slept in rendezvous outside.

"A picket of our Militia horse was posted at Pithoulie, three or four miles out of Agra. On Saturday the 4th, they brought in accounts that the enemy was picketed half-way between this and Futtehpore Sikri, and that their advance guard was coming on. Upon this, it was resolved that our forces should proceed to meet them. The Kotah contingent was to move out in the afternoon, and the European regiment at eight in the evening. Syfoolla's Keraolee levy was already in that direction. In the afternoon, the Kotah contingent moved and halted outside the town, but had hardly done so when they mutinied, the cavalry taking the lead, the infantry and artillery passive. They shot at their officers, but killed only one sergeant. The corps went off towards the enemy. Our Militia pickets happened to be near, and, in the midst of a thickening storm, followed up the retreating troops, cutting up some, and, what was of more importance, bringing back the guns and all the ammunition.

"Two of our guns, which had been placed with Syfoolla's force, were precautionally brought in the night before. The force was discontented at this mark of suspicion; and, on the ground of being unsupported, asked leave to go home. This was granted, and Syfoolla led them off towards Jugneyr on Sunday morning. Some of the horse probably seceded to the enemy. We heard nothing more of the Ulwur Durbar troops, who promised great things in harassing the mutineers. So we were left alone with our 3rd Europeans, the Company of artillery, and the Militia.

"A little before midday on Sunday, our picket came in with the intelligence that the enemy was within two or three miles of Agra; their advance guard even pushing in from Shahgunge, a suburb close to Government House. Immediate measures were taken for an advance by us. The Jail guard of fifty soldiers was called in to join the main body,[1] and all marched off about one o'clock P.M. Two hundred of the 3rd Europeans and a portion of the Militia were left behind to guard the Fort. Only about five hundred of the former were thus available for the field. The Company of artillery, considering that it had only lately been horsed, was in an efficient state, and was officered by gallant fellows, D'Oyley, Pearson, Lamb, and Fuller. The troops halted at Shahgunge for half an hour, to allow the party from the Jail

[1] It was at this time I carried the message to the Jail.

to come up, and to refresh themselves. They then moved forward, and, believing the enemy to be in force with their artillery commanding the Futtehpore Sikri road, defiled to the right of it by the back of a high-walled garden, and took up a position beyond. The regiment then formed into line and advanced in échelon with their front bearing obliquely on the road, and facing the village of Bhondagaon, in and about which, at the distance of one and a half or two miles, we subsequently discovered the enemy to be posted. The European infantry formed the centre, flanked on the right by half our battery, under D'Oyley, and the left by the other half, under Pearson. The Artillery, again, was protected by the Volunteer horse and foot to the extreme right and left of our position. In this order we advanced till we again approached the road, our extreme left nearly resting upon it. Between two and three o'clock, when we were about half a mile from Bhondagaon, the Mutineer artillery unexpectedly opened upon us from their right. We found it to be planted on either side the village, and there are believed to have been as many as eleven or twelve guns (six and nine-pounders). The Mutineer infantry, some two thousand strong, occupied the village; and large bodies of our well-trained cavalry—some six or eight hundred—were scattered around.

"Our artillery lost little time in replying to the enemy's fire, and a fierce cannonade was kept up,—our line advancing till the left guns had well crossed the road. The advance continued till our infantry came up to the village. About this time the cannonade was so hot that they were directed to lie down and take such advantage as they could of the shelter of the walls or trees to fire upon the village. Meanwhile, two of our tumbrils on the left blew up from the enemy's shot—for their guns were well served; and one of our cannon had its carriage destroyed. The remaining two guns with their tumbrils executed a rapid movement about 60 yards backwards to avoid the contact of exploding ammunition, amid the cheers of the enemy; but they soon turned, unlimbered, and were at work again.

"The enemy's horse now appeared in great numbers on our left, and at one time made a charge which threatened our guns on that side. They were met by our left flank volunteer horse, twenty-five in number, who made a brave counter-charge, and checked their advance. The Mutineer horse were, however, so greatly superior in numbers that, though obliged to stand at a safe distance, they crept round our team, and began to harass our infantry, but a volley obliged them to retire. If that immense body of horse had shown any courage, or had been at all efficiently handled, it would have seriously affected our position.

"The battery on our right continued to advance; and our infantry, having entered the village and set fire to it, were now in a position to have stormed and entirely dislodged the enemy, when, to the dismay of all, it was announced that our ammunition, owing to explosion of the tumbrils and our rapid firing, had been entirely expended. There was now no alternative but to retire; and the retreat, in the face of artillery and clouds of horse, was executed in an admirable manner. The troops in fact retired with all the order and steadiness of a parade, and reached the Fort at about 5 P.M. The action lasted full two hours. We had 30 killed and about 80 wounded. The enemy's loss we do not know; but although they were under cover of a village, their casualties were probably greater than ours. Their brigade-major lost his two hands, and is said to have died afterwards. The result certainly has been that, although the field was left in their hands for a time, they decamped without delay, towards Muttra. The fact is that their ammunition was nearly as low as ours; that we were on the eve of a great victory against tremendous odds; and that if we had gone out again the next day, well supplied with ammunition, we must have driven them from their post. Various circumstances, however, prevented this; among others, the disorganisation of our field battery from the desertion of the greater portion of our native artillery drivers, so that the day after the fight we could only have effectively equipped two guns of horse artillery.

"In criticising the battle, it is the opinion of some of our authorities that the ardent European infantry should have been led earlier to a dashing charge at the village, which might have been carried and the enemy routed before our ammunition ran so low. I do not pretend to judge this point. I am satisfied with the final result. Against immense odds we held our own ground and pushed forward. All our ammunition was used up. Then we quickly retired, and the result was the disappearance of the enemy next day.

"Although no large body of the enemy ventured from their camp, the loose cavalry that harassed our rear prowled around the outskirts of the City and Station, firing the bungalows and cantonments, and giving the signal of licence and plunder to the too ready villains of the town. In sight of our retreating column, the Normal School—an elegant building, erected by the late Lieutenant-Governor—was set on fire, and the wild Sowars could be discerned from the Fort galloping savagely round it. All night the lurid flames of burning houses lighted the heavens. Fortunately, by the foresight of the Lieutenant-Governor, the whole of the Christian population, with exception of a few too venturesome,[1] were safe within the Fort. Beyond one or two guns, fired in defiance as well as to protect buildings within easy range of the Fort, nothing passed that evening. Next morning, the Mussulmans of the city, on a rumour that we had almost all been killed, were debating whether they should not proceed to the enemy's camp and make their peace, when the disaffected were confounded and our adherents overjoyed by tidings that the Mutineer army had gone. We did not know this for some considerable time, and were preparing ourselves for an attack which was noised abroad, probably by the mutineers themselves, to cover their departure. But we were ready for any attack; and even if shut in by a siege train—which they had not—possessed two months' provisions in the Fort.

"Monday and Tuesday were passed inactively. We kept ourselves shut up in the Fort, though we had positively not a man to oppose us. On Wednesday (8th) a demonstration was made by marching a column through the city, and (I regret to say) by plundering the shop of a large Mahometan merchant in the military bazaar. Our friends from the city now began to come in, and arrangements were set on foot for the reorganisation of the police.

"20th July.—Our magistrate, the Hon. R. Drummond, had preserved an admirable front throughout the disturbances, and had maintained the city in perfect peace and security up to the time of the appearance of the enemy before our walls. Then, of course, when the inhabitants of a town, open and unprotected, saw themselves exposed to the ravages of the enemy if he chanced to drive back our so much smaller force, the reins of ordinary authority were cut asunder. The civil administration gave place to the military.

"At this point, moreover, a peculiarity in the system, pursued by Mr. Drummond, was felt to be a serious defect and embarrassment. He had not only trusted mainly to the respectable Mahometans for information and advice, but had employed them almost exclusively in the Government service, both revenue and police, both in high and in low office. However excellent

[1] About twenty, I believe, lost their lives that night by not retiring to the Fort.

and trustworthy these men under other circumstances might have been, they were now placed in a peculiarly trying position from the religious and Mahometan element at this time dominant in the Mutineer movement. The whole police officers and men (almost all Moslems) quitted their posts. The Burkundazes are said to have been forward in committing enormities against us in the city, and in plunder; while some of the influential Moslem citizens, both in and out of office, are suspected of connivance. A few joined the enemy. Many respectable and, I believe, strictly loyal men, who in our rearrangements would have been of essential use to us, were repelled and alarmed by the fierce anti-Moslem feeling which they knew pervaded most Civilians and almost all the Military leaders. Mahometans therefore, both high and low, fled in multitudes from Agra, partly, no doubt, conscience stricken, partly through apprehensions just described. Crowds, it is said, repaired to the Mutineer camp at Muttra, complaining against imaginary cruelties and excesses committed by us against them, to whom the General commanding the enemy promised to send a detachment for their assistance.

"Our police having thus vanished, it became necessary, on the return of tranquillity, to make new constabulary arrangements. The Lieutenant-Governor (who for a week had been entirely prostrated by illness, but was now able partially to resume business) determined on the judicious plan of working mainly through the Hindoos, whom alone we can, at this juncture, as a body depend upon, without displaying any antagonism against or any active distrust of the Mahometans. This policy, however, ran so counter to Mr. Drummond's previous system and agency, that the Government was obliged to supersede him, and appoint another officer to his post. The arrangements for the security of the city have been thus peacefully and effectively carried out.

"[The correspondence with Bombay here ends by saying that the Nemuch troops, being now bound for Dehli, everything was quiet at Agra, and our only apprehensions were in regard to the mutinous body at Gwalior.]"

As our troops returned from the battle, the wounded were at once carried into the Motee Musjid, the beautiful Mosque of the Fort,[1] which made a most comfortable hospital.

[1] There is also, if I remember rightly, another small Mosque for the more private worship of those of princely rank.

D'Oyley was so badly struck in the stomach that the uniform could not be removed from his poor body; and it was sad to see him, as I did, without even the comfort of being able to lie down in peace. He did not long survive. Kaye gives a charming account of Mrs. Raikes' hospital, which Dr. Farquhar got her to establish for the sick of the non-military inhabitants; the description also of the other ladies by the same correspondent, I may quote here, specially for its touching notice of your Mother:—

"Here was Lady Outram discussing the thousand and one rumours of the Fort, always cheerful, lightly treating the adventures of her walk barefooted for many miles on escaping from Allygurh, . . . sometimes borne on her *Taunjon*, her son, Frank Outram, walking beside her. It was a delight to the European soldiers, scattered about Arsenal Square, to see her with her serene face, always ready with a kind smile and a kind word. In Palace Square was Mrs. (now Lady) Muir, with her five children, cheery as a sunbeam, energetic in promoting the employment and welfare of the native Christians, with her neighbour, Mrs. C. B. Thornhill, enlisting other ladies in good work, stirring up the subscriptions for the wounded and destitute of the North-Western Provinces. She and those above-mentioned leaders in the social scale, were leaders also in the multiplied tasks of urging the well-disposed to active usefulness, relieving the poor, providing guardianship for waifs and strays of humanity, visiting and supporting schools, soothing vain alarms, repressing the vindictive feeling against the natives of the country, promoting charity among all."[1]

The picture is by no means overdrawn. The native Christians, several hundreds in number, after some doubt as to whether there was room for them in the Fort, had all, thank God, been allowed to enter, very much at French's hands, for otherwise he would have stayed out with them, and have surely shared their fate.[2] It was a noble act, which few but he would have attempted. Our servants were, with one exception (the Mahometan Bheestie), faithful to us; but, of course, were not

[1] Kaye, vol. iii. pp. 400–402.

[2] French and Stuart came out together a few years before, and on their arrival in Agra, during the summer and autumn, stayed for weeks with us in the "Library" by our house—there being no other place available for them in the Station. Stuart had before the Mutiny left for Calcutta, where he was for long Secretary to the C.M.S.; but French was still Head of the C.M.S. College at Agra. Years after, they were both consecrated Bishops (Punjab and Waiapu) in the same week.

then allowed into the Fort, and in their absence the native Christians were of great use. But it required all the influence of your Mother and her friends to keep them from being harshly treated, for the unkindly feeling towards Natives had already begun to spread. Among other services of your Mother's was the appointment of a little room we called "the Hospital," close by us, where she tended Jim Power then sick, and Colonel Eld, who came in wounded from Allygurh.

So far as our surroundings went, the spacious Square in which we lived was well kept, and in seasonable weather afforded pleasant range for strolling about; as well as the bigger Square —*Dewân-i-âm*—beyond it, and the ramparts on the city side. At the farther end of our Palace Square was the *Dewân-i-khâs*, or royal room of reception, with a charming look-out across the Jumna River, over which it stands loftily. This palatial hall served as our Church for the English service, and indeed for the worship of Presbyterians, Roman Catholics, and all others; so that on Sundays there was a continuous succession of services, the vision of which would somewhat have startled the Imperial assemblies of ancient days.

And so we settled down, most of us with something, however small, to do, in an otherwise listless life, cut off from all the world, in a little world of our own, with no concern beyond the ramparts of our Fort. One remembers the strange feeling, as, looking across the river, we felt that even the other bank was, one might say, not our own but foreign land. Yet, with a family and surroundings such as ours, there still was work (as Kaye says) for busy hands to do. It was during the worst hot months of the year that we were thus incarcerated, and it may well be imagined that, with none of the accessories to moderate the heat, or avoid the floods of rain, it must often have been in our little quarters a wearisome time, especially for the little ones. In the lack of servants, we had not even bearers to pull the punkahs, and so, with musquitoes and the other annoyances of the hot and rainy months, the surroundings were often stifling. But, thank God, we were upon the whole kept well. There was at one time a serious threatening of cholera epidemic, and we lost by it our nephew, James Wemyss, who had taken refuge with us from Muttra, and had a berth in the side of the Square opposite to us. But, otherwise, we were spared from this dread malady, thank God. And last, but not least, we regard it as one of our special mercies that we had so loving and affectionate a friend in Dr. Farquhar. . . . In fact, to all around he was one among a thousand, night and day going about and doing good; carrying his heart in his hand, without a thought of himself, he was ever ready in the thought of others. It was the beginning of a binding love and friendship between him and us. Ah! how one misses now his bright, wise, and loving life; and the graphic tales of the Mutiny that used to flow from his ready lips—a living portraiture—which he was never weary of recounting. French too was a dear friend to us. He not only devoted himself to the service of the native converts, who owed their safety to him; but was unwearied in his pastoral care of all, and attendance on the sick and needy.

It must have been a couple of days after the battle, that the Lieutenant-Governor placed me in charge of the Intelligence Department. This involved the very serious responsibility of keeping myself, by means of spies and informers, *au courant* with the progress of the revolt in every direction. For this end, a body of confidential messengers had to be entertained and highly paid. Where the road was dangerous, as towards Cawnpore, they had to carry little letters written on the thinnest paper, thrust sometimes into a quill or secreted in any part of the body. The risk was great, for they were often searched, and if any letter was found upon them, they were killed or even blown from guns; and it took from a week to a fortnight for a letter to get through to Cawnpore.

Among these tiny scrolls I had several from Havelock, on his march to Lucknow, in my collection, which were sent to Kaye; other little specimens of the same sort will be seen in the respective Volumes. As the spies and informers came in at any hour of the day, and sometimes of the night, I used to take down their depositions from their lips at once; and the news, if important, was communicated to Mr. Colvin or other of the authorities. For some weeks that grand old man, Choubey Gunshâm Doss, blind as he was, waited on me daily as my chief informant. Eventually he went away to watch matters at his Etah Tehseel, and there was killed, being surprised by the rebels. His brother, Jye Kishen Doss, was granted, both for his own services and in recognition of his brother's, the title of Rajah and C.S.I. For some time I had only such loose sheets to write upon as are at the beginning of Vol. I. I had also to maintain daily correspondence with the authorities in both quarters, East and West, keeping each informed of what was going on elsewhere;—chiefly thus, with Greathed at Dehli,

Sherer and Havelock at Cawnpore, and many others besides. As the country below became clearer, I began to correspond also direct with Calcutta. Copies of all my letters were at once entered in the several books by Oldfield, Outram, Farquhar, Thornhill, and Lowe; and much in your Mother's own hand.[1] At first, and from time to time as Mr. Colvin was well enough, and able to dictate, many of the letters were written as from him; and I consulted him regularly in his apartments just beyond ours, in the north-east buttress of the Fort, looking out upon the Taj. For months Rajpootana and Bombay was the only route by which ordinary posts could be sent to Calcutta and England, and that with some difficulty and delay. It was not till the beginning of 1858 that the road *via* Cawnpore to Calcutta began to be open. This Intelligence work gave me regular, often unremitting, employment for hours, which, cut off as we were from all else, must otherwise have fallen wearily upon me.

As may be supposed, the inhabitants at large, with nothing to do, besides the tittle-tattle of the day, allowed all sorts of reports to fly about, seldom true and often alarming. To place important news as it came in at their command, I began, after a month or two, to circulate printed sheets of intelligence. The first of these dates at the beginning of September, and the last issue in my collection is that of the 5th January 1858, when the posts, being more or less open, and the local papers partly re-established, they were no longer needed. The collection is with the other papers.

There was, and I fancy still is, a little bungalow within two or three hundred yards from the Taj Gate of the Fort. Being so close to our guns it escaped the destruction of the 5th July, —the only bungalow indeed that did survive. To give the children . . . a reviving change of scene and air, we were granted the privilege of occupying it. How charming it was, after long confinement within battlements, to get out into open space, and into a house with all its free surroundings, one can well remember. When we first had this pleasure I forget; and for long it was only in the daytime we could with safety stay outside, returning always before the gates were closed at night into the Fort. But in a letter to Harington (who had gone *via* Rajpootana to Calcutta), I find this notice of it: "We have moved out again into a bungalow; this time, I trust, per-

[1] When any very secret news had to be mentioned, it will generally be found written in Greek lettering, occasionally also in French, lest it should fall into the enemy's hands.

manently. I am going to have my double-storeyed house re-thatched." This letter is dated 5th November, several weeks after our second attack; but we had probably ventured out some little time before that date. Eventually, when it became safe to sleep in this bungalow, Farquhar and others of our party used to come out also, and sleep in the verandah. We had also our carriage there.

The attack of the Nemuch mutineers from Gwalior, just adverted to, was the last that threatened Agra. The Gwalior Contingent had long been a source of uneasiness to us, but (as already mentioned) was kept back from any hostile movement, even after it had mutinied, through the influence of Dinkur Rao, by whose wisdom and strength of purpose Scindia was guided. The Contingent itself, eventually taking the route along the Jumna, attacked Cawnpore; but a mutinous body from Nemuch and Indore, with the riff-raff of rebels and deserters about Gwalior, now made Agra their object. Throughout September, reports kept coming in every day that this body was on the eve of marching against us. At last, well on in the month, they did start from Gwalior; but they loitered on the road, and spent several days at Dholepore, some thirty miles from us, endeavouring to treat with the Rajah there. As they approached Agra, Macpherson [1] and I had daily, and latterly even hourly, intelligence from our spies of their progress and of their design to storm our Fortress, which were laid at once as they came in before Colonels Fraser and Cotton. The news at last became so alarming, and the approach so close, that on the evening of Saturday the 8th October, I urged on both the immediate need of sending out "a reconnoitring party, and continuous military pickets." By great good fortune, a strong column under General Greathed was just on its way from Dehli to Cawnpore; and when the danger threatening us became known, it was turned aside from Allygurh to relieve us. To hasten therefore their march, mounted messengers were every few hours despatched to tell Greathed of the pressing danger, and of the urgent need of help, and desiring him to come on by forced marches, so as to prevent any surprise. The imminence of the attack is mentioned in several places of my correspondence; for example, on the 9th, Sunday, the day before the battle, I find this in a letter to Sherer: "The Indore force is moving steadily on this. It is to-day at Tehree, and is making preparations for bringing its guns across the Kharee River, about ten miles distant. Some

[1] Major Charteris Macpherson, Political Agent at Gwalior.

hundreds of Sowars have already crossed, and are prowling about the country and obstructing the road. A reconnoitring party of our Militia cavalry went out this morning. It was fired on at the river, and followed, though at a respectful distance, by the enemy's cavalry to within a few miles of Agra."

To watch its advance and guard against a surprise, had thus become no longer a matter for unarmed and helpless spies. It had passed into the hands of the Military. Why reconnoitring parties and pickets, as I suggested, were not kept out all night till Monday morning to prevent surprise, I never could understand; but so it was. On Monday morning, Greathed's column arrived, and marched through the streets amid crowds of applauding citizens. So little danger, indeed, was apprehended, that we drove out in our carriage with Farquhar to meet the force as it crossed the bridge of boats, and get hold of Anson, who had ridden in the day before to see us and had then returned to camp. Coming up when he saw us we took him in our carriage to see our ruined bungalow, and then back with us to the Fort. The column had meanwhile marched on to the Cantonment, but no sooner had they begun to pitch their camp on the Gwalior side of the Station, than suddenly the enemy's guns opened fire upon them. Trusting to the military outlook already mentioned, I had so little anxiety myself at the moment, that, as we were sitting quietly at breakfast on Monday the 10th, with Anson and Norman (who had just come up from the camp) at our table, we were suddenly startled by the guns of the rebel force, and both hurried off to the fight. But the enemy had already been driven back, and was in full flight; and doubtless, as was said at the time, the surprise was more on their side than ours. But our helpers judged us severely, and reasonably so. The following passages may be of interest, as showing where the blame lay. [I omit them here, as they will be found in the correspondence.]

This danger over, Agra no longer felt anxiety from any quarter. The Contingent left Gwalior, as before stated, some two or three days after this fight, and marched towards Cawnpore. Next month, Dinkur Rao came over to see us; and at Christmas, Scindia himself honoured us with a visit. To the West and South, the country was quite peaceful, and communications open as in time of peace; so much so, that Mrs. Harington and other ladies were able before the end of the year to leave us (by Bombay) for Calcutta or England. But to the East, the roads continued as before, absolutely closed; the only mode of communication was still by Cossids, who took at least a week or ten days to get through to Cawnpore. Things continued so till Futtehgurh was taken by the Commander-in-Chief, 27th December, after which the Trunk road to Cawnpore and Calcutta, on the right bank of the Ganges, was freely open to travelling and traffic; though rebellion still raged in Oudh on the opposite bank.

With the return of tranquillity people began in numbers to leave the Fort, as quarters became available outside, in town or cantonment. A double-storeyed house—the "Library" as we used to call it—within our compound, and close to our ruined bungalow, being built of masonry, had, excepting its roof, pretty well escaped, and so we early set about repairing it. It must have been about the beginning of the New Year that we quitted the little bungalow at the Fort gate, where we had found such rest and comfort, and took up our residence in the "Library." Here, then, we should have remained, resuming our old habits of life, had I not towards the end of January received a summons from Calcutta to join the Governor-General at Allahabad with part of the Secretariat Office. Lord Canning had arranged to make that his headquarters during 1858, carrying with him the Foreign Office, and at the same time to assume immediate charge of the North-West Provinces in place of appointing a new Lieutenant-Governor; and as the country was gradually reoccupied, so to restore it to order. It was accordingly to join Lord Canning as Secretary to his Government of the North-West Provinces, while as Member of the Board I at the same time took revenue charge of the lower districts, that I was called to Allahabad; while Reade, with Thornhill as his Secretary, remained at Agra for the revenue administration of the upper districts.

Thus, on the 7th February 1858, leaving your Mother with the family at Agra, I travelled by carriage dak to Allahabad; and can well remember the lonely feeling of driving along my old haunts, now so sadly changed, through the Cawnpore and Futtehpore Districts, scenes of such tragic events, and in such close proximity to the still rebel border of Oudh. It was two or three months later that I was joined by your Mother and the children. We at first had rooms—for accommodation was still hard to get—in an out-building used for the Secretariat Office; but eventually in the large and comfortable house behind the Cucherry at the Kuttra. To carry on the Secretariat work, I gradually got down the greater part of the native Christians, who had by this time returned from the Fort to the Secundra Orphanage. The Rev. David Mohun, of the C.M.S. at Chunar, took the pastorate charge at Allahabad. I helped him sometimes, and eventually settled the community in a piece of land beautifully overlooking the Ganges, where the Christian village has grown up, and which is now called "Muirabad."

The children went up in the hot weather to Mussoorie; excepting two, K. . . and T. . ., who remained with us. And we remember how sweet and kind Lady Canning used to be to K. . . . A little girl then of but four or five, she used to go over to Lowther Castle to interpret Lady Canning's orders to her servants, and to feed four black swans swimming in the pond hard by—a gift by Lord Clyde, the only booty (he used to boast) he had brought away with him from Lucknow. Lord and Lady Canning lived very simply in this unpretending house,—the best, however, that was available in the Station. It served them for all purposes, both private and official, Lady Canning having but a single room for herself. Lord Canning was equally homely in his wants. I admired his self-possession and strong sense of justice. The wild hue and cry against all Natives good and bad, was checked by his firm resolve to protect the unoffending, and confine punishment to the guilty. He had strong control over himself; and I can remember how he would simply bite his lip when tidings of reverse came in. But he had also a singular habit of procrastination, the same which led to such an unfortunate issue at the Barrackpore Mutiny. He would keep the boxes of despatches sent to him by his Secretaries for disposal days and days, and then return a whole heap of them at once, so that urgent matters might easily have escaped orders till evil had ensued. On my stated visits to his official room, I used to find his table with a whole battlement of undisposed boxes around him. But with it all, he was a grand man; and the nick-name, "Clemency Canning," with which our people used to abuse him, was in effect the highest praise that could have marked his just and noble life.

It was the beginning of the following year that C. . . (our eldest daughter) arrived in Calcutta, and your Mother went down in a steamer to meet her there. Returning with her by dak carriage, there happened one of the most merciful escapes the Family ever had. Just then occurred the inroad which the rebel Kunwar Singh made from Bundlekhund into Jounpore.

In doing so, he must cross the Trunk road somewhere between Patna and Benares. Alarmed at the news of his close approach just about the critical moment when your Mother would be passing up the same way, I started off in company with Farquhar for Benares. Arrived there we found, to our intense relief, that your Mother had already passed the spot—thank God, safely—just after the savage horde had crossed the road, and that she was already on her way to Allahabad, having passed us without our knowing. But how great the deliverance! for at the point where the Rebels had passed by the day before, were found the broken remains of a dak carriage, which the Rebels had seized, and murdered the Baboo passengers in it. When your Mother next day came up to the spot, it was still being patrolled as dangerous by mounted pickets. For a little way off, by the Trunk roadside, there was fortunately a Dumdumma (small fortress) occupied by an Artillery detachment. The carriage was stayed there by the Officer in charge for the night. Your Mother and C. . . were kindly invited to go into their Mess for dinner, but remained on in their carriage till the morning, when, the road being declared safe, they were allowed to pass on to Benares. And so it was that Farquhar and I, with thankful hearts, found that they had gone ahead of us to Allahabad. What the difference of a few hours might have caused! Thank God for the deliverance. This must have happened about the middle of March, as I find that Kunwar Singh defeated Milne in Jounpore on the 22nd of that month.

And so ends our personal interest in the Mutiny. I have confined myself strictly to matters immediately affecting Agra and the Family. And one cannot close the brief review without an earnest thanksgiving to our Heavenly Father for sparing your Mother and the children from dangers which overwhelmed so many of our fellow-countrymen elsewhere, to which we were ourselves for so many months exposed, and crowning us throughout with His loving-kindness and tender mercy.

---

*Note.*—I must have mistaken the occasion of the Trunk road adventure given above, as I find it occurred some months earlier, about the end of November 1858.

The volumes of Correspondence spoken of at the beginning of this little story are full of matter which, well digested, should not be wanting in historical importance. I have, therefore, committed them into the hands of William Coldstream, who promises to select and arrange the more valuable of the materials in such a way as to allow of their being printed. There are many passages throughout of the deepest interest, such, for example, as the account of the overthrow of Dehli, by a native; and also of its reoccupation, by another.

When Mr. Coldstream has done with these records, they will then be placed for safe custody in the Library of the University, where they will be available for reference to any who might wish to consult them.

A descriptive list is subjoined.

---

*Description of the Records belonging to the period of the Mutiny, as kept by me when in charge of the Intelligence Department at Agra,—from July* 1857 *to January* 1858.

*Volume I.*—Correspondence after the battle of 5th July to 30th September 1857.

One side contains mainly letters sent to the Authorities down country,—Cawnpore, Lucknow, etc.; the other to those up country,—Delhi, Meerut, etc.

[The correspondence at first was largely by direction of the Lieutenant-Governor when he was sufficiently able to attend to it; but he was often disabled by illness, and died 9th September.]

*Volume II.* contains letters from October to 19th November 1857, addressed down country to Cawnpore, Allahabad, and Calcutta; chiefly to Mr. Sherer, with intelligence for Lord Canning of affairs at Delhi and elsewhere in the Upper Provinces; and telegrams for the Governor-General at Calcutta.

*Volume III.*—Same as No. II., from 20th November 1857 to end of January 1858.

On its other side is an important document, drawn up by me at Lord Canning's request, on the alleged dishonour of European women by the Rebels at the several mutinies and outbreaks; with the opinions of the several able Officers whom I consulted. The almost universal opinion was that the attacks were purely murderous, with no attempt anywhere at dishonour.

*Volume IV.*—Letters to Colonel Greathed's column, and other up-country authorities, from 1st to 16th October.

*Volume V.* — Epitomes of Notes of Correspondence from other stations, received by myself and others, in order to keep ourselves *au courant* with what was going on elsewhere, and the opinions and views in other quarters,—during August and September 1857. One side relates .to correspondence of Officers at Delhi and up-country stations; the other to letters from stations below, — as Cawnpore, Allahabad, Calcutta, etc.

[This volume contains also a few native (Urdoo) documents of interest, including copy of a Lucknow paper published in March 1857, and an original copy of the Nana's proclamation put forth at Cawnpore against the Company's government.]

*Volume VI.*—The Notes of Intelligence collected, and depositions of informers, spies and messengers,—commenced three days after the battle of 5th July, and at first written on loose slips, the only thing available at the moment. The last entry is dated 11th December 1857. Some of the narratives by natives who had fled from Delhi, and other depositions, will be found intensely interesting.

*Volume VII.*—Continuation of Volume IV., being letters written to Delhi, from October to December 1857, chiefly to Saunders, who succeeded as Commissioner on Greathed's death. It contains intelligence from down country, remarks on the treatment of natives in Delhi, news about the battle of 10th October, and other local matters.

*Volume VIII.*—Unbound. Private letters, chiefly to Havelock, copied by Lady Muir, from 6th August to 9th September 1857.

*Book IX.*—Printed sheets with the news of the day, circulated in the Fort,—September 1857 to January 1858.

[1] *X.*—Envelope containing original correspondence, chiefly from Sherer at Cawnpore, during the autumn of 1857, giving daily accounts conveyed in light and tiny sheets by Cossids of events there and at Lucknow.

[2] Also printed Census of Inhabitants in the Fort. List of Officers who lost their lives in the Bengal Presidency from May to December 1857,—so far as then known at Agra.

[1] *XI.*—(1) Envelopes with Letters from Sir John Lawrence to W. Muir and Colonel Fraser. (2) Letters from W. M. to *Bombay Times*, dated 13th and 16th June and 7th July 1857. (3) Letters from Mr. Commr. Alexander to Mr. Colvin.

[1] See Introductory Note to Thirteenth Series, vol. ii. p. 239.—W. C.

[2] The "Census" and List of Officers here mentioned are printed in Fourteenth Series, vol. ii.—W. C.

BEFORE PASSING TO THE "INTELLIGENCE" RECORDS I PREFIX EXTRACTS FROM CORRESPONDENCE HAD WITH MY FAMILY AT HOME; AS WELL AS OF LETTERS FROM ALLAHABAD AFTER JOINING LORD CANNING THERE EARLY IN 1858.

W. M.

# PREFATORY NOTE

## FOR THE FAMILY.

The following Letters . . . were written from Agra to give our Family at home information regarding the Mutiny on its outbreak and during the following months, before I left to join Lord Canning at Allahabad. . . . We had five of our children in the Agra Fort. . . . The MSS. are in a few cases incomplete.

To the above is added a second series, which I wrote to your Mother at Agra after reaching Allahabad, in February and March 1858. Many are wanting and imperfect; but what I have quoted from those that remain, will, I trust, be of interest, giving an idea of the state of things around us at the time.

. . . . . . . .

It was the beginning of February when I left Agra for Allahabad at the call of Lord Canning, to take charge under his orders of the recovering administration of the N.W. Provinces. On first arrival I lived for a short time in the Governor-General's camp in the Fort, but afterwards in tents in the Civil Station, chiefly with my friend Cnd. Thornhill. The houses throughout the Station had all been burned down by the Mutineers, excepting one or two of solid masonry. But by and by I got one repaired, in which, eventually, we lived comfortably enough. It was then that W. . . . and C. . . . (our two eldest) joined us.

W. M.

# LETTERS FROM AGRA

## TO MY FAMILY IN EDINBURGH.

AGRA, 18*th May* 1857.

MY BELOVED MOTHER,—I write to you a general account of the proceedings of the last week. . . .

The week has been one of perturbation, if not of real danger; and the barbarities which have been enacted in it, make the blood run cold. But I must begin at the beginning.

It has long been known that our Native army—the Sepoys especially of the Regular line—was in an alienated state of mind, discontented and suspicious. This feeling, as you know, showed itself, at Barrackpore and elsewhere, in the refusal to use cartridges believed by the Sepoys to be made up with some objectionable stuff that would affect their caste. It has been doubted whether this was felt to be a real grievance, and not a mere blind to cover other objects or causes of discontent. I see no reason to doubt that it was felt to be a real grievance, and that the Government should have quietly and discreetly given in. The Sepoys are children. It was no use reasoning with them to show that there was nothing harmful of caste in the cartridges. They had made up their minds, and would not be persuaded.

The feeling spread abroad. At Lucknow one regiment mutinied, and was disbanded by Sir Henry Lawrence. At Meerut the 3rd Cavalry refused the cartridges, and a large number were put under arrest. About nine or ten days ago the orders arrived from headquarters at Meerut, sentencing *eighty* of that corps to imprisonment in the Jail here. They heard their sentence with emotion on Saturday the 9th. On Sunday a general Mutiny seems to have been resolved on (at Meerut). While the European troops were at church for the afternoon Service (the 10th), the Cavalry and Native regiments issued forth, killing their Officers, and all Europeans (even women and children) whom they met, and firing the bungalows. The European troops were not long in bringing the Mutineers to account, and repressing their attack. But the confusion and alarm—what with burning bungalows, and riotous bands of plunderers and Sepoys—must have been fearful. The Mutineers were at last expelled the Station.

The Cavalry made off with their horses, and a large party probably took the earliest opportunity of getting away, for they were at Dehli (about forty miles off) by 8 or 9 next morning (Monday).

On reaching Dehli, our Cavalry Mutineers demanded admittance at the gate of the Fort by twos and threes. They got inside on pretence of wishing to see the commandant, Captain Douglass. He was in his rooms over the gateway. When he came down, he was killed by a pistol shot. They then went upstairs. With poor Douglass the Rev. Mr. Jennings and his daughter were living, and they were all at breakfast about 9 a.m. Miss Clifford, sister of a young Assistant at Goorgaon (who had left the party only two hours before), and Fraser, the Commissioner, were also there, with one or two others. It is not certain whether Charles Thomason, lately engaged to Miss Jennings, was there or not. The Mutineers broke in, and killed them all. After possessing themselves of the Fort, they set to to kill every European in the city. All the Civilians were slaughtered: Hutchinson, the Magistrate; Galloway, the Assistant; Chimmun Loll, the Christian Sub-Assistant-Surgeon. They gained over the two Native regiments and artillery. A few Officers effected their escape to Meerut, and to the Raja of Bullubgurh. The rest were murdered, and the insurgents left in sole possession of the city. This was probably all done by Monday afternoon.

Now for the effect of these proceedings on the country.

A telegraphic message reached us on Sunday night saying that the 3rd Cavalry had mutinied, and were killing their Officers and burning bungalows. So little excitement, however, did this produce, that I myself did not hear of it till Tuesday morning. On Monday the Sunday's dak of Meerut and Dehli reached this, I believe,—but am not quite sure. However, from that time, at any rate, our communication with both Stations ceased: neither dak nor telegraph was open. We were left to bare conjecture, aided by the darkest and most fearful rumours. Things went on thus till Thursday morning, when we were relieved by an express from Meerut assuring us, at anyrate, that our European force was safe.

Meanwhile, in the absence of all information from Monday

till Thursday, rumour represented that the insurgents, having taken Dehli, were marching down on Agra. Mr. Ford, Magistrate of Goorgaon, about thirty miles on this side Dehli, held his ground for some days; but sent us accounts of marauding parties prowling over his district. On Tuesday Mr. Colvin, putting all his information together, came to the conclusion that a movement was intended in this direction. Our difficulty was now regarding our two Native corps. Were they to be trusted? Providentially we have a European regiment the 3rd E.I. Company's, and European artillery here, or it is impossible to say what the Native corps would have done. The general impression was that they would not show any overt acts of mutiny, but that they would not actually fight for us in case of emergency.

In this difficulty we had a council of war, and Mr. Colvin—who has throughout maintained an admirably firm front, and taken on himself the responsibility of all movements—announced his resolution of sending all families into the Fort the next day, and moving out to Secundra with the troops, to give battle to the insurgents. There certainly was not evidence that insurgents were on the march upon us; but supposing it possible they might have been (and with no tidings from Dehli itself, either along the right or the left bank of the Jumna, such a movement was *possible*), no doubt the plan laid down by Mr. Colvin was the only thing we had left to do. In order to test the feeling of the Native troops, and give them security on the cartridge question, a parade was ordered for Thursday morning (14th), when Mr. Colvin addressed each regiment separately. Almost all the Civilians accompanied him. He gave his word to the Sepoys that the cartridges would not be forced on them, and asked them if they were satisfied. There was no dissent, and an occasional assenting response; and as we left there was cheering.

That night, as I said, had brought us better news. We knew that our European troops were safe. A flying telegraph-machine had been sent to Allygurh, which (not a repeating station before) was thus placed in immediate communication with us. The Magistrate there (W. C. Watson, who has done admirably) and the Magistrate of Bolundshuhur, Mr. B. Sapte, ably seconded by Turnbull the Judge, kept open the communication, and assured us that all was quiet up to Hauper. From Hauper westward, however, the wild Goojur zemindars were taking advantage of the emergency to recur to their ancient habits of plunder and violence; and it was they apparently who had broken the telegraphic wire and destroyed all our postal arrangements, carrying off the horses, etc.

On the Thursday there was again a panic. Muttra was in excitement, and it was doubtful whether we could hold our ground there. More rumours came in of an advance from the Goorgaon quarter. The Allygurh telegraph gave no reply from Mr. Watson. Parties *might* be coming down either bank to try here the same game they had so successfully played at Dehli. Mr. Colvin was so weighed down by these ideas that he directed all families to retire into the Fort, and a general patrol to be kept up at night by the Civilians. Drummond, our Magistrate (an admirable, cool, intelligent fellow), persuaded Mr. Colvin that there was no immediate danger, and had the order for sleeping in the Fort withdrawn—but not in time for some. Among others, we did not get the counter order till I had deposited the whole family in the Fort. J. . . will know what a place it is for stifling heat, and what a night dear B. . . and the five little ones must have passed there. The Thornhills (he is Acting Secretary to Government) have been with us since the tumult broke out; and another dear friend, Mr. Lowe, Secretary to the Board. Mrs. Thornhill was with B. . . in the Fort all night. The rest of us met together at Candaharee-bagh, and relieved each other patrolling the roads. Early in the morning I went to the Fort, and brought away the party, half dead with heat and thirst.

We had better news that morning, but I did not hear of it till midday; and in the meanwhile felt very low. It was the worst time to me. The telegraph had apparently ceased working at Allygurh, implying that things had gone wrong there, and that we had no certainty that a movement might not be in progress, on either bank, upon Agra. The only solution, it seemed to me, would be to secure the families in the Fort more comfortably, and be prepared for surprise and the field.

From that time things have brightened up. The stoppage of the telegraph with Allygurh was only accidental. Bhurtpore sent us horse (1400 were promised) to guard Muttra. Major Macpherson sent us over a portion of the Gwalior Contingent with guns, now encamped near Government House. Scindia has promised half his bodyguard. Telegraphic communication was reopened with Meerut on Friday evening. An advance on Dehli has been organised from Umballah and Meerut. But when it will take place we do not know. Proclamations (which I have had the task of translating) have been issued, and general confidence is gradually replacing the terror of last week.

As yet the news from out-stations is good. Bareilly was in

great excitement for two or three days. But the last accounts from Alexander (Commissioner) were that it was quiet, and it was hoped the crisis was over. Moradabad was also excited, but Saunders, the Magistrate, an able man, is keeping things quiet, and the 29th Native Infantry is thought to be satisfactory. Wilson has gone over to Rampore, to raise irregular horse.

For two things we cannot be sufficiently grateful to Providence.

First, that this calamity did not overtake us when our hands were full with external war. The crisis, grave as it is, would in that case have been fearfully critical.

Secondly, that the country keeps quiet and contented. The character of the affair is that of a Military mutiny,—a struggle between the Government and its Soldiers, not between the Government and the People. After such a stroke at Dehli, the prescriptive Capital of India, it is astonishing that there is so little excitement and rising, throughout the country. The general conclusion is that there is something radically wrong in the constitution or management of the Native army, while the Civil Administration is shown to be at least not unpopular or unsuccessful. And in this state of the Sepoys' feeling, conceive a place like Dehli having been left with only Native troops! I conclude one of the first effects of the movement will be to lead to the despatch of strong reinforcements of European troops. What trust can we henceforth place in our Native troops unsupported by European ones? It will, at anyrate, take many a long year to eradicate the feeling of mistrust of their allegiance, not only in our own minds, but in those of the native Rajas and Chieftains; and we shall not be able to lean on our Sepoys without weakening ourselves in their estimation.

It is said that the insurgents have placed the son of the old King (who himself declined to join them)—the son lately acknowledged by us Heir-apparent—on the throne, and have issued calls of allegiance in his name. It is not to be expected that the excitement throughout the country will subside until Dehli has been reclaimed by us. We are waiting patiently for this. They are strong in European troops at Meerut, and there is a feeling that more might have been done by them. But after all it may be best that the advance should be made simultaneously from Umballah and Meerut.

By the way, our immense Central Jail here has been a cause of additional anxiety to us. We have nearly 4000 criminals there—some of them the most desperate characters in the provinces. They, of course, got excited when they heard what was going on, and then rumours of a rescue. This added very considerably to the unsettled feeling in the town; and as our house is close at the gate of the Jail, we had our full share of the feeling. It was feared that the mutinous Sepoys might tamper with the Jail Guard. Late events will no doubt lead to a complete reconsideration of the system of Central Jails on this large scale, which certainly contain elements of danger in them.

There has been hardly an exception to the finest and bravest devotion displayed by all the Civilians, both in Agra and elsewhere.

Poor young Clifford is sadly cut up at his sister's murder, as you may imagine. The Khidmutgar fled to Goorgaon, and told him all the particulars of the tragedy at breakfast over the Fort gate.

Amid all these distresses we have, I trust, had our hearts stayed upon the consolation that "the Lord reigneth"; the same God who is our Father reconciled to us in His dear Son; and in Him we seek to confide. May He bless and keep you all.

W. Muir.

*P.S.*—19*th May*.—We have just had intelligence that no fewer than fifty persons escaped from Dehli, and among them Lebas, and our dear friend Dr. Balfour.

Agra, 2*nd June* 1857.

To my Brother,—

My last letter brought down the proceedings of this eventful month to the 20th ult., I think. Since then we have had another weary fortnight chequered with various incident, but, upon the whole, with less of reverse than might have been looked for from the extending defection of our Native troops, and the continued occupation of Dehli by the Rebels.

The day after I wrote, the headquarters of the 9th Native Infantry stationed at Allygurh, finding the temptation of the Treasury and the overtures from Dehli, too strong for them, mutinied, plundered the treasure, and made off for Dehli. All our Officers escaped and retired to Hatrass, about thirty miles from this. This misfortune again cut off our communication with Meerut, either by post, telegraph, or messenger.

The other portions of the 9th Native Infantry were posted at Mynpoory and Etawah. No sooner did the emissaries of the headquarters from Allygurh reach Mynpoory than a mutiny took place there also. This, I think, was on the 22nd, a day or two after the affair at Allygurh. Your friend John Power has behaved nobly there. He is the Magistrate and Collector. So did a young officer, a German, named De Kantzow, who stayed with the Mutineers at the peril of his life, and was so well supported by half a dozen staunch Sepoys that the treasure and jail were kept secure. By this intrepid and gallant conduct, —although pressed to the verge of defeat and obliged to entrench themselves in the Cucherry,[1]—Mynpoory was prevented from falling into hopeless anarchy, and our communication with Calcutta by dak and telegraph was preserved.

As was to be expected, the other detachment at Etawah followed in the same manner. Hume, the Magistrate, was able to retire across the Jumna with the inhabitants; but the Station was plundered and the Treasury robbed.

While our communications with Meerut were closed, Bolundshuhur also fell, and its treasure was carried off to Dehli, but under what circumstances I am not fully cognisant. The Station has since been regained, and is occupied by Goorkha troops. The impression here is that the Meerut force has *not* been sufficiently active; so large a body of European troops to remain so long on the defensive under such circumstances is unintelligible. Rohtuck has been also plundered from Dehli. Tidings have been received of the mutiny of the regiments at Nusseerabad, but without details. It is hoped that the Treasury at Ajmere may have escaped. The Mozuffernugger Treasury also went; but in consequence of the attack, I believe, of robbers and not of Mutineers.

Thus you will see that these treacherous Sepoys have gained immense booty. From three to seven lacs of rupees were in the several Treasuries.

Our last reverse has been at Muttra. On the 30th, a Company of the 44th Native Infantry from this went to relieve the Company of the 67th, which has been hitherto in charge of the Treasury there, and which it was intended should bring in here a portion of the accumulating treasure. Both Companies united (notwithstanding there had been a bad understanding between the two regiments before), attacked their Officers, shooting one, plundered the treasure, and went off towards Dehli. The Officers and Civilians (Dashwood and young Colvin) got off

[1] Magistrate's office.

on horseback to Mark Thornhill, the Magistrate, who was at Cosee, some twenty or thirty miles on the Dehli road.

Tidings of this event (which occurred about 4 p.m.) reached Agra about 11 at night. Mr. Colvin, finding that Companies of both the Native regiments here had thus committed such enormities, promptly determined that no confidence could be placed in them, and that to appear to show confidence would be weakness; it was therefore at once resolved to *disarm* the two regiments next morning, leaving them, however, still organised corps, but for the present unarmed with guns.

This determination was communicated to the inhabitants at once. I was awoke from sleep at 1.30 a.m. on Sunday the 31st, and went round to warn the people at our end, to be at their various rendezvous in case of disturbance.[1] The disarming was accomplished on the parade quietly. The Company on duty near the Jail made some demur, which we saw from our position at the top of Boldero's Hill, whither we had all removed for safety, and ran off with their arms,—but eventually all laid down their arms quietly. A great number of the men, especially of the 44th, have since slunk away, and many of the 67th (supposed to be better affected) have taken leave to their homes. This measure was a critical one; it has anticipated a possible real danger from a portion of these regiments, and it has, I believe, given satisfaction and, in some measure, restored confidence to the better disposed part of the population.

A further untoward event has occurred in the train of the Muttra Mutiny. The Bhurtpore and Ulwar forces were at Hodul (a little north of the Muttra frontier and in the Goorgaon district), with Harvey the Commissioner, Captain Nixon of the Bhurtpore Residency, and other European Officers. This force was intended to co-operate with the Commander-in-Chief's force and check fugitives from Dehli. But the Muttra Mutineers with their treasure marched right up in this direction. Mark Thornhill, the Magistrate of Muttra, was at Cosee, some eight miles on this side Hodul, with a small body of Bhurtpore horse. When the Mutineers appeared with the treasure, the Bhurtpore horse would seem to have fraternised with them; and Thornhill made off to the force at Hodul on the 31st. By midday the Mutineers had come up, and the whole force was a mass of confusion. Mark

[1] Dr. Farquhar and I went together on this occasion; and it was interesting to observe the various effect of the news on different people: in one house the husband was craven, and the wife most bold. We had to warn the Roman Catholic ladies in their Convent.

Thornhill fled back towards Muttra, and got in here yesterday. It is not quite clear from his statement what the Bhurtpore horse intended to do, but his accounts imply that the Ulwar troops had fraternised with the Mutineers, and that the Bhurtpore men would not act against them.

Meanwhile, every Cantonment throughout the country has been severely agitated. Where there have been no European troops, the trial has been one of the most delicate and critical nature that can be imagined. The wonder is that such stations as Cawnpore, Moradabad, Allahabad, Benares, Azimgurh, etc., have stood at all. Here it was simply the presence of our 600 Europeans and European artillery that enabled us to do what was done,—otherwise we were entirely at the mercy of the Sepoys.

At Lucknow matters are in a critical state. Sir Henry Lawrence is acting admirably. But he weakened himself by sending over a portion of his European regiment to Cawnpore. European troops are, however, coming up to Cawnpore by the dak carriages in forty or so per day; so that the position in that quarter should be strengthening.

But *everywhere* the fact of Dehli still being in the Rebels' hands is an element of strong insecurity and incendiarism. It is in the very nature of the Mahometan faith to seize on such an incident as a religious principle, impelling the more devoted or fanatical to an attempt for re-establishing the ascendency of Islam. Everywhere, therefore, the cry has been for the Commander-in-Chief to retake Dehli.

Our communications on the Meerut side have lately been reopened for the post (the electric wire is cut and mangled for miles) by the admirable exertions of a band of Volunteers from Agra, headed by Cocks and Lieutenant Greathed of the Engineers. They found no opposition, and were *welcomed* by the people both of Hatrass and Allygurh. Indeed, every incident tends to show that this is no controversy between the *People* and the Government (excepting in so far as the Mahometan religious feeling above referred to is called forth by the occasion, and in so far as the present weakness of Government has encouraged the wild and pillaging part of the population to rise against authority), but simply *between the Government and its Native soldiery*.

Our position has been greatly complicated by the cutting off of our communications with Meerut and the Commander-in-Chief, by the Mutiny at Allygurh. It was only on the 31st that Mr. Colvin got the Commander-in-Chief's letter of the 16th May!

But now that Allygurh is clear, we may hope for better communications. Last night brought a letter from the Commander-in-Chief at Kurnal, dated the 23rd, explaining his arrangements, and saying he would be before Dehli by the 8th. The delay has occurred in consequence of the siege train, etc., having been lost with the magazine of Dehli, and the necessity of getting heavy artillery from Phillore, near Ferozepore. It is a good deal canvassed whether this delay was warranted, and whether an immediate attack with the available field-batteries should not have been made. On the one hand, Dehli's walls are notoriously weak, and no resistance would probably have been made; while every day's delay to retake Dehli involves an increasingly serious Imperial risk, and the defection of Native troops. On the other hand, any check at Dehli would have been worse than delay, and been next to fatal.

Simultaneously with the above despatch came news of the *death* of the Commander-in-Chief,[1] of cholera, on the 27th, at Kurnal. This event is startling, and, at the juncture, very remarkable; but it will not, I conclude, have any effect in keeping back our movements.

To-day brings tidings of the first actual success which we have met with. The European troops at Meerut moved over to Ghazeeooddeen-nugger,—a Tehseeldaree on this side the Hindun, some ten miles from Dehli. The Rebels came out,—whether with the view of escaping elsewhere or not we do not yet know. They were attacked by our troops, and thoroughly discomfited, their artillery being taken.

Accounts of the Nusseerabad defection have since come in, and show that the whole force, artillery and all, has seceded from its Officers (excepting a Bombay Cavalry regiment), and left with the intention of going to Dehli.

Amid all these events Agra holds a very marked and distinguished position. Between us and Dehli is anarchy and confusion; between us and Meerut is the same, but being gradually reclaimed by our Agra Volunteers at Allygurh, and by the Goorkhas at Bolundshuhur. The defection of the 9th has thrown the Dooab to the north of us into the same state of wild disorder. If we had had Police battalions, as proposed by Lord Ellenborough, we might have had a force to fall back upon when our Sepoys failed us. But we had *nothing*; our Police had been cut down to the smallest amount, and were scattered in bodies of ten and fifteen men at the several Thannahs. When

[1] General George Anson.

the Sepoys went off, and the turbulent and predatorily inclined saw that we had no reserve force to back our orders with, they burst forth into all manner of excesses; and one's heart bleeds for the cruel injuries to which the poor defenceless villages—unaccustomed for fifty years to anything but profound peace—have been exposed. The authority of Government, wherever the Sepoys revolted and our Officers were forced to abandon the Stations, thus slipped through our hands; and the country, over-run by banditti, was in a flame.

Meanwhile, there is no prospect of material improvement, while there are serious risks at every point throughout the country, till Dehli is retaken. It is wonderful that Rohilkhund and all below this has kept so quiet. If Agra had failed, I do believe all from here to Calcutta would have gone. The surge of insurrection beats as it were all the way from Dehli to this unopposed; but here it is met and repelled by a hitherto steady and immovable barrier. God grant we may hold on and weather the storm.

You may imagine it has been a time of acute domestic anxiety. After the Allygurh defection, I had resolved to send B . . . and the children to Calcutta, and had actually got the dak carriages here. After consulting with Mr. Colvin and others, I abandoned the idea,—partly because the example would have been bad, and might have led to want of confidence,—partly because of the risks of the way.[1]

W. MUIR.

J. MUIR, ESQ.

AGRA, *5th June* 1857.

TO MY BROTHER,—

I WROTE two days ago. I have not much to communicate further, besides what you will learn from the paper and extras I am forwarding to you. The main points are that the defeat of the Mutineers at Ghazeeooddeen-nugger on Saturday the 30th was followed up the next day by the defeat of an apparently large body of the Mutineers who came out (from Dehli) with guns to attack our force. The action is said to have lasted four hours, but we have not yet the details. The enemy made no further demonstration the next day. Our troops there were subsequently strengthened by the Goorkha regiment from Bolundshuhur, and also by a small addition of Europeans.

[1] The fate of Cawnpore made me afterwards tremble at the thought of what might have happened to them.

Meanwhile, we have at last authentic information of the advance of the Umballah force. The advanced brigade would be yesterday within two marches of Dehli; and the whole seems well equipped and, with God's blessing, fully equal to the work before it. Should there be any difficulty in reducing the Fort without siege guns, they are on their way behind the force; having left Phillore on the 21st ult. Moreover, the Punjab Guides will be at Dehli by the 9th, so that they will be able to relieve our European troops of a part of the ordinary duties which at this season of the year must press severely on them.

Meanwhile, as was to be expected from the spirit of the soldiery, the disaffection proceeds. A large party of Mutineers from Lucknow marched towards Seetapore, which is said also to have risen. These insurgents then turned towards Dehli, crossing the Ganges at Canouj, and imperilling our little body of men which still manfully holds Mynpoory. They seem to have committed outrages on the Grand Trunk Road, and waited at Bhowgaon (the fork between the Allygurh and Agra roads), breaking the telegraphic communication, and destroying our Postal establishments. We are therefore at present cut off from direct communication with Cawnpore and Calcutta. These ruffians eventually passed Mynpoory and went on towards Allygurh.

A body of irregular Cavalry, which had volunteered for service against the Mutineers, was stationed at Goorsahaigunj between Furruckabad and Cawnpore. These, from what cause we do not know, rose on their Officers (among whom was Fletcher Hayes), killed them, and went off to Dehli.

There are reports as to similar proceedings at Shahjehanpore, but, I believe, not yet authenticated; and at Furruckabad and Futtehghur they live in hourly expectation of an outbreak from the Sepoys.

The 29th at Moradabad is believed to be staunch. I am not sure whether I mentioned that it had pursued some Sapper Mutineers from Roorkee and forced them to lay down their arms. But such conduct is almost unexampled just now.

At Agra we continue quiet. The Mutiny at Muttra we cannot but look upon as a providential warning to us; and it afforded a sufficient reason—which the 44th and 67th must themselves have felt to be sufficient—for disarming them. The men are now going home on leave. And so we get rid of that domestic source of anxiety and apprehension.

We trust that the early effect of successful measures at

Dehli may be to stop the progress of defection in the army. If, as Mr. Colvin desires, two columns can then be marched, one down the Dooab, the other down the right bank of the Jumna, the most troubled portion of the country would be quieted. But there are immense bodies of Mutineer troops abroad throughout the country. Some 15,000 or 20,000 men must have mutinied. Great numbers of these have no doubt slunk away, both from the scenes of their disorder, and from Dehli itself, towards their homes, but there are still more than enough to do fearful damage to the country.

Muttra has been reoccupied by Mark Thornhill and a few servants, and Volunteers. All is quiet there; but advantage was taken by the bad characters about, on the mutiny of the Sepoys, to burn the bungalows and plunder all unprotected property. The ease with which a Magistrate and Collector with a handful of men recovers his authority *after the Sepoys have gone*, shows the nature of the rising as a Military one, and the source of our difficulty. We have not even a handful of men to give to our Magistrates and Collectors ordinarily to reinstate them. We have been hitherto so utterly and entirely dependent on our Sepoys.

Mr. Colvin holds a fine bold front. He found he could not get on with the ordinary business of the Government and attend to these grave matters also. So he has appointed a Commission, of Harington, Reade, and myself, to discharge the current duties. Reade takes the Revenue, Harington the Judicial, and I the Public Works Foreign and General Departments.

W. MUIR.

J. MUIR, ESQ.

AGRA, *6th June* 1857.

TO MY BROTHER,—

As Mr. Colvin's despatches for the E.I. Court [1] are going off, I send a line in hopes to get it with the express.

Rohilkhund has gone also. Bareilly and Moradabad and, report says, Shahjehanpore also,—certainly the two first. So, after all, the 29th which I was praising has proved treacherous. But it so far did well that it took no life, and guarded its Officers to Nynie Tal. Guthrie at Bareilly has escaped. Alexander, I hear, wounded. It is thus all one sea of anarchy to the foot of the Himalayas.

On the other hand, the news from the Headquarters Army is all of the best kind. They must be by this time hard upon

[1] *East India Court*, as we used then to call the Home Government of the India "Directors."

Dehli,[1] and in two or three days, by God's blessing, we may confidently look to its being ours. The force at Ghazeeooddeen-nugger has been removed to join the main Army, and it is thought the Mutineers will take the opportunity to effect their escape that way.

We keep quiet here; and there is no element of mischief within, and we pray God to keep away any from without. Hitherto the Mutineers have had no combination, excepting to go to Dehli,—so when discomfited we hope they will break up.

Julius Denny is here in command of the Kotah Contingent, which is encamped at Furrah, twenty miles on the road to Muttra.

W. MUIR.

*P.S.*—I have not in my present letters corrected the errors in my first as to the reports of killed in the outbreak at Meerut, as this is all in the papers.

AGRA, 17*th June* 1857.

TO MY BROTHER,—

As it is not improbable that the direct route to Bombay may be closed,—if it be not already closed,—I send a few lines by a route opened out by Jeypore, the post through which now despatched will probably be in time for the mail. Events have thickened upon us since I last wrote. First, all Rohilkhund went, as our Officers were forced to fly from the mutinous troops at Shahjehanpore (where I fear poor Ricketts, the Magistrate and Collector, was killed), Bareilly, and Moradabad. Then the regiments at Nusseerabad (Ajmere), Neemuch, Jhansi, and Nowgaon rose. Then at Benares, Allahabad, and Cawnpore. The Mutineers were defeated and expelled from Benares, but we have no distinct accounts as to the two latter Stations. Last of all, the Contingent troops in Gwalior have gone; and the Maharajah declaring that from the spirit of his own troops he could not answer for the safety of our Officers, they have all come over here. Even the Political Agent, Major Macpherson, has come. Ordinarily this would involve hostilities with Scindia, but one cannot imagine it probable that Scindia would risk his present position by any inimical demonstration.

Meanwhile, the mutinous regiments are abroad in parties all over the country; and excepting in the positions where our Officers have been strong enough to maintain their ground, anarchy prevails. We have had intelligence, though not official,

[1] The Umballah force arrived before Dehli on 8th June.

of the fall of the city of Dehli;[1] and we trust that the Fort (Palace) will soon follow. The European troops there will then be partially freed and able to move down the Dooab and restore confidence. We have hitherto been graciously preserved in peace and quiet here notwithstanding constant rumours and apprehension; and we trust that God will still protect us. The Mutineers have not as yet shown any symptoms of combination. What phases of events may spring up in the future, one cannot say. We hope the rains will soon begin—which will impede the movements of the scattered bodies, and give time for the collection of European troops. We trust that already reinforcements are on their way from England; and that Lord Canning will be able to secure the troops on their passage to China.

I still trust that the Gwalior route may be open for a letter by the regular line.

W. MUIR.

(Added by your Mother.)

I cannot write. Please let our darlings hear we are well, and through God's great mercy have been hitherto preserved, and we trust Him for the future. Our anxiety has been truly sad and harassing. God bless you.—Ever your affectionate sister,

E. H. MUIR.

[*To Mr. H. C. Tucker at Allahabad, after the battle of* 5*th July.*]

AGRA, 15*th July* 1857.[2]

MY DEAR TUCKER,—These two men took above a month to deliver your letter (from Allahabad) of the 10th June. They have therefore got only 3 rupees each here as subsistence money. If they take this back quickly you can give them such present as you think proper. I trust the letters we have been sending lately have reached, giving an account of the indecisive action of Bhondagaon on the 5th inst., two or three miles from Agra; of the withdrawal of our troops from the field, in the face of the Neemuch force vastly superior to us in numbers; of the subsequent retirement of that force to Muttra; of the destruction of the Station by fire and plunder on the part of the ill-disposed portion of the lower classes; of the entire body of Europeans and Christians

[1] This turned out a mistake.

[2] This was written on the thinnest kind of paper, to be wrapped close and secreted on their persons by the Cossids or secret Messengers, in case of their being discovered and shot; the road to Allahabad being then in hostile hands.

being shut up in the Fort; and of the measures subsequently taken for the reorganisation of our City Police. We are all right here now, and shall continue so unless an enemy from without come upon us. But the loss in property, and *material* for civilisation, is sad. I rode out to Secundra this morning; the sight was sickening. Of all that noble establishment, reared by the labour of near twenty years, not a *single* Press remains. The place is strewed with bits of broken printing-presses, leaves, and masses of black rubbish—the unrecognisable remains of thousands of volumes! Alas for education! Alas for the regeneration of India! And yet I would look forward in God's good providence to even this eventuating in real benefit to India. It may be His means of placing us in a better position hereafter for our work.

Things around remain much as before. The Mutineer force at Muttra continues there. Some say they have had reinforcements, but, except it be some of their party that remained behind from Mehidpore, etc., I do not see where they were to come from. On the other hand, having got money out of the Seth, many are going off to their homes. They have no ammunition, and talk of getting some from Dehli; but at Dehli itself they are said to be hard up for ammunition: they fill their shells there with kunkur![1] Gwalior at present keeps quiet. The Gwalior horse that was over the river has partly broken up, having been attacked by the villagers in crossing the Jumna, and has partly gone to Gwalior. Pearson's battery of six guns is said to be in the villagers' hands, and we are trying to get it in. We have Dehli news up to the 8th. General Barnard died of cholera on the 7th or 8th. But the feeling of confidence was not impaired by the event. It was not mentioned who had taken command. On the 9th we know from Harvey at Cosee, that there was the heaviest and longest continued firing yet heard. Native report says there was fighting all day. The Bareilly Mutineer reinforcements were no doubt having their turn, and we doubt not the result was that of all previous actions,—great loss to the Rebels. The feeling in the City[2] is that of disheartenment; they begin to think of aid from Dost Mohammed, etc. Sikhs, Goorkhas and Guides fight well. The 600 Sikhs in Dehli will no doubt turn in our favour when it comes to the assault. Meanwhile, we are wasting away their numbers and resources. What a mercy that the Fort of Allahabad has been preserved! We were long in great anxiety

[1] Small stones or gravel. [2] *i.e.* Dehli.

about it. The inability to replace their expended stores will, we may trust, prove a source of speedy weakness to the Mutineers. *Σενδ υπ πλεντι οφ καπς. Ουρ στωρ ις ςυφισιεντ φορ ουρσελυες: βυτ νοτ φορ ινδεντς φρομ οθερ κυαρτερς. Τοο μονθς προυισιονς ιν θε Φορτ ἑρε.*[1] Mr. Colvin keeps improving, and can attend to business now without further apprehension to his health. Though the Allahabad force can not now be of use to the Cawnpore gallant band, we look to its advance with anxiety. Please God, with what pleasure shall we again renew regular postal communications! It is a strange feeling to be cut off from the world on all sides.

W. MUIR.

H. C. TUCKER, ESQ.

*P.S.*—Pray write to Calcutta that we need medical stores in abundance. The Cawnpore depôt has gone, and a number of the indents have not been supplied, or have been plundered by the way. We shall specially need Quinine, so send up this as well as medicines generally. From Umballah they write that stores of tea, port, etc., are falling short. It would be well to think of this also; for we are *quite* cut off from all income of European goods. Much has been plundered by the way, as well as in depôts, shops, etc., and the remainder is being fast consumed.

AGRA, *1st Oct.* 1857.

TO MY BROTHER,—

I SEND a few of our Intelligence slips. You may imagine this has been a week of tolerable excitement. Dehli has fallen —the thundercloud has burst (alas for the loss! it cost us above 1000 men), and the horizon begins to clear all around. We are in hourly expectation of hearing that Lucknow has been relieved. I do trust it will not now be abandoned. The instructions are, I believe, that when the garrison is withdrawn, the City is to be relinquished. The orders to that effect must have been given some time ago, when things were looking blacker. *Now*, I cannot see that the retention of a garrison there, after the Oudh Mutineers have been fairly discomfited, would dangerously weaken our field force; while, if it be given up, the City will be immediately reoccupied by the Mutineers, and form the focus of rebellion, with a new king for its head.

[1] Send up plenty of caps. Our store is sufficient for ourselves; but not for indents from other quarters. Two months' provisions in the Fort here.

I am kept very busy now. I maintain daily correspondence with Dehli and Cawnpore by Cossid, besides attending to Intelligence as to the movements of the Mutineers all around us.

The fall of Dehli has struck terror into the hearts of them all. The fugitives at Muttra from Dehli have hastily constructed a bridge, and hope to effect their flight to Rohilkhund and Oudh before the pursuing column reaches. That column would have already been down upon them, but it has been detained two or three days by having to attack Malagurh near Bolundshuhur, where the rebel Nawab Wuleedad Khan has so long been troubling us, and interrupting our communications with Meerut. The Native report of an action near Bolundshuhur has just come in, stating that we completely defeated the Nawab backed by the Jhansi brigade, on the 28th, taking five field guns—all they had. Wuleedad Khan had fled.

The Indore Mutineers left Dholepore, it is thought, last night, on their way to join the Muttra host, and are now only eighteen or twenty miles from us. They pass through Futtehpur Sicri.

The Gwalior Mutineers have been long held in check by Scindia. They are now supposed to be about to move towards Cawnpore to retrieve the ruined fortunes of the Nana. There is now no force of the enemy in the field which can, humanly speaking, stand before a British column for a day. The difficulty now lies in the number of the opposing parties in various quarters. They will no doubt soon collect towards Bareilly, where there will likely be a decisive action. There will also probably be a tedious campaign in Bundlekhund, from the number of Forts and independent Thakoors, etc., who have been seeking to make hay while they thought the sun was shining. I trust that the Dooab will be cleared within a fortnight. But it is doubtful when a column will be able to advance into Rohilkhund. I have *no fear* for the country speedily settling down as soon as these Mutineers are out of the way. The Mahometans have lost all excuse for opposition on religious grounds, as their King is gone.

Colonel Fraser has been appointed, temporarily, Chief Commissioner here. It is, I suppose, on the ground that it was advisable there should be a combination of military and civil authority at this juncture in the hands of one person. I fear our last mail from home has been quite lost. We got some papers, but no letters. W. M.

AGRA, 15*th Oct.* 1857.

TO MY BROTHER,—

THE enclosed printed slips of official intelligence will put you in possession of all the news. So I need not recapitulate. We are all in capital health. And the sight of the moveable column, after being cut off from the world for three or four months, was like new life to us. It was like the arrival of the man Friday to the solitary Islander. And, as you will see, they were not an hour too soon. For two days previously we had been sending the *most urgent* summonses to Greathed to hurry on, and at the last they did hurry most nobly. Greathed, in his official report of the action of the 10th, says, "the cavalry and artillery marched over at least sixty-four miles, and the infantry fifty-four miles of road, in less than thirty-six hours. Captain Bourchier's 9-pounder battery had marched in during the night from Haṭrass, thirty miles, without a halt." And an hour or two after they were all under arms again, and pursuing the Indore army to the Kharee,—there and back another eighteen miles. Splendid fellows they are, those Sikhs and Europeans. It was so odd to see Native soldiers about one again, and Native Sirdars. The first feeling was to shrink from them as deadly enemies, but it was only a passing feeling called up by the memory of the enormities of our mutinous Bengal Army. The open, smiling countenances of the Sikhs and Punjabies at once dispelled all such ideas. They are noble fellows.

The *surprise* was an odd event on the 10th. The Military authorities had ample warning from the Intelligence Department; indeed, otherwise, Greathed's column would not have been in to take part in the business at all. On the preceding day a reconnoitring party had, at my recommendation, gone out to the Kharee to see what the enemy were doing. Our party was fired on, and pursued back again close to Agra. Why after this, military precautions were not taken to prevent a surprise, I do not know.

The battlefield was a miserable sight. It was the first *fresh* battlefield I had seen. The dead bodies of the enemy were left on the ground, and they were in such numbers within two or three hundred yards of the burial ground, that in a couple of days the place could hardly be visited for the stench.

Now that the Indore people are dispersed, the only local danger we have is from the Gwalior Contingent. The rumour is that it marches to-day, *via* Jhansi, towards Cawnpore. But one can never be certain that they won't come this way until they have actually left. Colonel Greathed's column will, however, be within reach of recall should they move towards Agra within the next few days.

If the Gwalior people move away, then, I believe, the whole of this part of the country will settle down. Reasonable Mussulmans, who have not already compromised themselves irretrievably, see that there is no chance of eventual success for the establishment of Islam, and they can conscientiously quiet down under our rule. The most remarkable proof of the people being not opposed to us is to be found in Muttra and Bindrabun, with their nearly 100,000 inhabitants. Our Native Officers, under charge of Imdad Ally, Deputy Collector and Deputy Magistrate, have regularly maintained authority there whenever not driven out by the enemy in strength. Over and over they have retired when the mutinous forces occupied the place, and as often returned to rule over a willing and obedient people. The last time, a few days ago, the fugitives from the Indore force arrived in considerable numbers at Muttra; some penetrated the town, attacked the police, and demanded supplies. The Deputy Collector, aided by the inhabitants, repulsed these men; musketry was fired by both parties for a couple of hours, and at length the whole party of Mutineers were obliged to retreat. Both at Bhurtpore and Dholepore, the Officers of those States have pursued the fugitives, killing some. All these facts are encouraging, and show that when the Rebel forces have once lost the prestige of victory and supposed supremacy, and break up into parties sufficiently small not to compel respect, the people are prepared to act offensively against them. In many places, however, it is not so, because the Mussulmans, while they thought their cause had a fair chance of final success, have frequently compromised themselves by flagrantly traitorous acts. At Allygurh, for instance, the Mussulmans were for a considerable time dominant; they forcibly converted many Hindoos; they defied our Government in the most insolent manner; all the ancient feelings of warring for the Faith, reminding one of the days of the first Caliphs, were resuscitated. Few of the families who were otherwise strongly loyal to us could resist this influence.

I think I told you before that our little party under Cocks retook Allygurh and expelled the Naib Sooba, in August I think. We placed a Hindoo Talookdar, Gobind Singh, as our Administrator in Coel, and (as our detachment could not remain so far off) fell back on Hatrass. This arrangement did admirably till one day about three weeks ago, the Mussulmans of a fanatical village fell treacherously on Gobind Singh, and forced him to flee with all our Officers who were there. Since that time the rage and fanaticism of the Moslems at Allygurh has been poured forth against the unfortunate Hindoos. The Mussulman party soon were swept away by Greathed's column, and the place is now reoccupied by us. But from this brief narrative you will see that there are dangerous elements in that district, which has been subjected to the most severe trial which loyalty could be subjected to; and that the utmost delicacy of treatment will be required in its resettlement. Dera and Seharunpore are quiet enough, and the country immediately about Meerut; but Mozuffernugger has been kept till lately in constant agitation by Mahometan fanatics, and Bolundshuhur has been occupied by the rebel Wuleedad Khan at Malagurh. Advantage was thus taken of our weakness, while every available soldier was drawn to Dehli, to work upon the feelings and religious convictions of the Mahometans, and to excite to violence all the rabble of our towns and villages, who were not slow in seizing the opportunity. But no sooner was Dehli fallen, than both Mozuffernugger and Bolundshuhur were speedily reduced to order. The Dehli division is also quieting down—of which there can be no stronger proof than that Mr. Saunders, in his last letter, said he had no news whatever to communicate. But the exiled population of Dehli city (the Military authorities have not felt themselves strong enough to allow of its reoccupation yet) must be hiding somewhere, and there are numerous Native chiefships, as Jhujjur, which have yet to be brought to their reckoning for the aid given by them to Dehli. In Rajpootana the only present cause of anxiety is the Joudpore legion which, at Awa, defied General Lawrence, and is still there. Rohilkhund has not yet been attempted to be reclaimed. Khan Bahadur reigns at Bareilly, oppresses the Hindoos, and with his staff daily proceeds in Zeearut[1] to salute the flag of Crusade planted in the front of the Cotwalee. But, south-west of the Ganges, the Upper Dooab and the right bank of the Jumna may now be regarded as in a fair way of settlement. And if the Gwalior Contingent move eastward, the whole wave may be said to have passed below this.

But eastward and northward there is a great work remaining yet. Havelock has relieved Lucknow, but, from the myriads of opposing hosts, is unable to return to Cawnpore with the women and children. To swell those hosts the Dehli fugitives are

[1] Pilgrimage.

rapidly on their way. The great fight will be in that quarter, and providentially our reinforcements are coming. Greathed's column is hurrying down to their aid. He has Cavalry and Horse Artillery, which will be a great help to them. And from below, the European troops should soon be showing themselves. But I must stop. It has been a glorious struggle for Englishmen this. Neither you nor I could have spoken more strongly than did old Asadoollah,[1] of the courage of the little bands of Foreigners, holding their ground every here and there, at the distance sometimes of two or three hundred miles from any other garrison, and in the end beating off their foes. God has been our Helper, and to Him be all the praise. There is still cause for anxiety eastward, but, on the whole, things are rapidly clearing, and the North-western districts and the Punjab are thoroughly relieved.

We are having even a carriage post to Meerut. Towards Cawnpore we still send by Cossid only.

W. MUIR.

AGRA, *20th Dec.* 1857.

TO MY BROTHER,—

As the telegraph is open between Cawnpore and Calcutta, you will probably have later news that way than I can give you. From the beginning of the month to the middle of it, we were *completely* cut off from all communication with Cawnpore and the eastward. Our first news of the discomfiture of the Gwalior Contingent was through Scindia's messengers. This you will find all in my bulletins.

The Futtehgurh insurgents were beginning to press rather uncomfortably on Allygurh when Seaton's column proceeded to dislodge them. This, as you will see, has been done in the most successful manner. The column will now move on towards Mynpoory, and will, I hope, soon open direct communication with Cawnpore. Whenever the road is safe, we have large supplies of carriage—which they grievously stand in need of towards the East—to send down.

All is quiet to the North-west; and in Rajpootana, excepting Kota where the troops of the Durbar have made an emeute. They must be conscious that punishment will fall upon them, sooner or later, for rebellious and dastardly proceedings in the murder of Major Burton and others.

It would seem that Rajpootana, at least Western Rajpootana, was not so much affected as I anticipated by the late proceedings

[1] A native Judge, a very special friend.

at Cawnpore and Lucknow. Rajpootana *hung* upon Dehli. It was long before its fall was thoroughly believed, but, as soon as the fact was accepted, the game was considered ended.

The great difficulty now in the tract around Lucknow, say with a radius of from one to two hundred miles, will be the vast assemblage of troops, and of others, who have compromised themselves beyond the hope of pardon by mutinous and rebellious proceedings. What fixes the brunt of future operations there, is that the great majority have their homes in that vicinity. Rohilkhund it is not expected will give much trouble. Bijnore could be occupied by a small column. Moradabad, as you know, is administered for us by the Nawab of Rampore. Excepting some local opposition from the Fanatics, nothing need be anticipated there. Bareilly will give a battle, and Budaon and Shahjehanpore will subside with it. All that is now needed to perfectly settle and quiet the Dooab, is the fall of Furruckabad. There are a couple of thousand, mostly untrained, Rebels at Etawah with six guns. But these will not stand after the capture of Furruckabad; and the capture of Furruckabad will, I trust, be the Commander-in-Chief's next operation.

Mynpoory, as I said above, will be occupied by Seaton's column, and I believe without much, if any, opposition.

The death of Havelock is a sad cloud. We have now ascertained beyond doubt that our nephew, J. Bensley Thornhill, died from the wounds he received in the early part of the siege. M. . . . (his widow) must have gone down with the ladies, *via* Cawnpore, to Calcutta. They must have been in a state of miserable discomfort in the Baillie Guard at Lucknow. John Power was with the Commander-in-Chief there, and saw the 1800 *Pandies* killed at Secundrabagh. Conceive a heap of 1800 counted as they were cast into a pit! A just but terrible retribution. The Government continues here in the same abnormal state. Fraser, the Chief Commissioner, takes counsel from the Board and Court. His intentions are good; of course his position is difficult as that of a combined Military and Civil Governor, with no experience in the latter Department. We are all, I am thankful to say, quite well. Poor M. . . . at Mussoorie, is of course greatly cut up by the Lucknow news and the long suspense. From Anson I have not heard for a long time; he must be at Cawnpore. From Brigadier Hope Grant I have had several letters. I am making inquiries for Lord Canning about the tales of females being dishonoured in the massacre. *All* the evidence is *against it*.

W. M.

# EXTRACTS OF LETTERS

## FROM ALLAHABAD TO AGRA.

### February–March 1858.

*Fort Allahabad*, 11*th February* 1858.—Lord Canning's Camp, 6.30 a.m.

Just going out to my ride. But before doing so I sit down to write a few lines. . . .

Near 10 a.m. I went out and had a charming ride on Lawrence's pony. Went to the Jail-house. Some thirty or forty prisoners have already begun work there—clearing away, etc. Met Leckie (Lord C.'s Doctor), and had a long walk with him up and down before the Governor-General's tents. He described a scene in which Lady Canning, before he left (Calcutta), with tears begged him to promise he would write twice regarding the welfare of her Lord. He has been better since he came up here than ever he has been since he came to the country. . . . I dine at the Governor-General's to-night. A book goes round for "yes" or "no." But I don't think I shall dine there often. Was in at the Governor-General's with Gubbins about the rebuilding of bungalows here.

13*th, The Fort.*—Was called over by Talbot (Private Secretary) to see the Governor-General. I took over the papers I had to show him. He was going out in the carriage, and had a white hat on. I talked with him some time, and gave him the names of candidates and eligible men for the Commissioner-ship, etc. . . . I read him a letter from Clifford about Muttra and some other things. Then went to the Trench's. Bid Mrs. Trench an affectionate farewell. She sent her love, and he his affectionate remembrances.

Found Grant in my tent: took him to the Mess; three or four strangers. Returned at 9, and have had two hours' hard work in vain attempt to clear my table: I sent you . . . a message by a Sowar the moment I arrived on Friday;[1] but the Collector's people were wretchedly stupid about it.

*The Fort*, Sunday morning, 14*th.*—When I was ready, E. . . . came in and stayed a bit: talks wildly about

[1] 5th February: the day I arrived from Agra.

hanging. But he came a little round, and admitted that hanging a man for recovering possession of his village and collecting rents, might be wrong. [Such was the wild talk of the day.]

Church at 10. Young Johnston came to my tent, and I walked to Church with him. The Governor-General there, and most of the young Civilians from Court's house, Edmonstone from Calcutta, young Outram, etc. . . . Mr. Harris preached and referred in appropriate terms to the war. . . .

I expect that the road between Cawnpore and Mynpoory will be unsafe, and crossed at many points by the Rebels flying from Oudh. It is possible the Upper Doab may also be threatened until the Punjab force is ready to advance N.E. of the Ganges. So I should prefer your remaining quietly at Agra until we see the course things will take.

(Afternoon).—Church is at 4 here, and 4½ at the big Church ; I am going here. . . . I have had two or three messages to-day from Futtehgurh and Agra, which I have sent to Lord Canning. I also sent him John Thornton's letter about the religious treatment of the Natives, which I thought he might like to see. The quiet and peace of the day, even in the midst of this Camp, is an intense relief after last week. . . .

(Same night).—I went to Church at 4. Very full both morning and evening. Talbot and Colonel Stuart there ; Lord C. seems only to go once a day. . . . Then went out and walked round the ramparts taking a cheroot, and just returned. Looked in at Leckie's, and proposed that the Relief Committee should move in the matter of pension for Mrs. Glen, if nothing else has been done in this matter at Agra. . . .

8 p.m.—. . . I have no doubt that the road will be quite clear within two months. Don't be alarmed by V. . . .'s vaticinations.

(Next morning).—The Court have sanctioned two Assistant Secretaries. . . . I am thinking of young Daniell and Macnaghten. But Lord Canning allowed me to keep on E. C. Bayley (who is Magistrate and Collector of Azimgurh) temporarily, so that only one will be at once required. . . . I hope to get up to the Jail-house to-morrow, where I shall be less liable to disturbance.

18*th February*.—In tents by the Civil Station. Yesterday evening, was just thinking of going out when the Agra dak came in with a heap of letters, and yours which was soon fished out. I went and sat outside (the tent), and as it began to get dark got a candle and read your . . . About that time also came an invitation for Williams (of the Police) to go to the Governor-General, with a private note from Talbot. Williams was to have gone in the daytime, but we had no buggy (the "General"[1] not come yet). He was on the point of starting in the sun on a Sowar's horse, when I persuaded him not; and wrote to Talbot. The result was this invitation. Well, after getting through the letters, . . . we dressed and were off at 6½ in a buggy to the Fort. I introduced Williams to Lord C., who received him very kindly. After about ten minutes' talking about things, dinner was announced. There were fifteen or sixteen. I was speaking to some one else, when Lord C. tapped me on the shoulder, and also the Colonel of the 80th (Lord Carr, I think), and motioned us to go on before or with him into the dinner tent. I sat, as before, on the Governor-General's left; Williams opposite me; on my left, the Queen's Superintending Surgeon (Gaiger, I think his name); Talbot opposite the Governor-General, etc. The latter part of the dinner I talked a good deal to the Governor-General about the Tuckers; also about Mr. Colvin and Mr. Thomason. Dr. G., who had been wrecked on the Andamans, gave me a long, interesting account of his adventures. . . . Williams evidently made a good impression on Lord C. Sat a long time, when we retired. Got home about 10.

*23rd February* (Tent in Civil Station).—Last night Williams and I walked as far as the Cucherries and Kinloch's house (the one I was getting restored for ourselves). It is not getting on well. . . . Only 20 coolies on the house! . . . Drove back.

. . . Up at 4½ morning as usual: reading, and work. Then walked to the Fort, where met Temple and Simson. Accompanied them to the terminus, where Temple starting begged again to be most kindly remembered to you. Rode home.

4.30 p.m.—It has been a quiet, pleasant, working day to-day. Getting through work. I begin to feel more master of the position. I enclose a note from Outram, who likes the Junior Secretaryship.

*24th January.*—Worked away till 5½ or 6 a.m. Then in the buggy to the Fort, and called at the tent where Lady Wilson, Mrs. Greathed, and Mrs. Trench were. Had a long talk with her, and felt much for her. She shook my hand so warmly, and I had a long chat with her. Then we left. . . . They go off they say on the 26th. . . .

I must write to Farquhar about the journey (with the children to Mussoorie). It is such a comfort he is going with

[1] My riding horse.

you. . . . Active proceedings will now commence all along the country from Bijnore to Fyzabad; and when the pressure is felt, escape will probably be attempted at many parts across the Doab. It is necessary, therefore, to take all precaution beforehand to see that the road is not threatened by any such attack. By the time you return to Agra we shall, I trust, see definitely the state of things, and the prospect for the Agra and Allahabad road. . . . Williams has just returned from a long conference with the Governor-General, in which everything has been satisfactorily arranged about the Police Battalions. I am very glad of this.

*Friday*, 12*th March*.—. . . You will have heard from Sherer that the (down-country) road is not safe at present. But it will not, D.V., continue long so. Worked till near 6. Table clear. Drove out with Cud.[1] round the Commissioner's office, and back by the Fort. An immense encampment of Madras Cavalry on the plain before the Fort. A great body of them is going over to protect the Azimgurh and Goruckpore districts. A new European regiment come in, and the 80th gone to Futtehpore, which will check the movement at Humeerpore. . . .

9 o'clock.—G.-G.'s dak come in while I was at dinner, with your . . . of Wednesday. . . . A message from Batten gives a better account of the country generally,—so that I do hope, when the blow has been finally struck at Lucknow, and our troops can be spared a little to return to the Doab, there will be no difficulty . . . in your coming down. . . . I have not seen the G.-G. since last Saturday. I dispose of everything by boxes. . . . Will write to Mrs. Glen about her pension.

13*th*.—Got up early. . . . About 5 set to to the boxes. Rode out about 7. Such a fine, fresh morning! I thought how much . . . you would have enjoyed it. It was one of those fresh mornings we only have in the spring. Back by 8½,—to work again; by 9½ had cleared my table. . . . Good news from Lucknow. The business apparently will soon be over there. . . . I went to see Lord C. before 2, and he received me exceedingly kindly. I did not stay long. Cud. and I, I am sorry to say, dine there this evening. . . .

13*th* (Saturday night).—Worked away this morning till 5½, when went out with Cud. to see Kinloch's house and an Agent I am getting to look after it. Young Johnston and Cottenham, R.A., came to see us. Walked over the Cucherry with them, to see how the work was going on. Then drove with Cud. (our

[1] *i.e.* Cudbert Thornhill.

buggy and his mare) to the bungalow. . . . Went to dinner: Lord Carr, etc., there. Colonel Bradford was on Lord C.'s left; I on his right; on my right a Madras officer. Bowring was next Thornhill, whom I heard discussing the 10th October (the relief of Agra). Pleasant evening; rather. Lord C. agreeable. Got home 9½. . . .

*Saturday*, 14*th*.—About coming down, I quite leave to you the discretion to set out on the journey so soon as the road is clear and you have a proper escort. But the road is, by the last accounts, still threatened, and Cawnpore is very imperfectly defended. It will be far better to wait a few days till Lucknow falls completely, and then considerable masses of our troops will be brought again into the Doab, and there will be no fear. I find the railway is not open *for trains* or engines to Futtehpore. The train still does not run beyond Khaga. It is not to be open till the 25th,—when Lord Canning opens it in person. If you cannot get down before that, I shall try and come out to Futtehpore to meet you. . . . If you came before that, you would have to come on to Khaga, above 20 miles this side of Futtehpore, and I could come out to meet you. By the way, a few days ago, Duryao Sing, his son Sojan Singh, and nephew Narmul Sing, were all hanged at Futtehpore. . . .

Farquhar's message just come in. I am so thankful that he has accepted the Jail appointment, and will be able, as I confidently trust, to bring you down. There is no violent hurry about his journey. . . . I do trust the road will be open, so that you may soon be able to come, as you will find it very warm travelling.

15*th*.—Up before 4½. To work a little after 5. Dressed 6½. Had a nice ride. The General capers about now in the most frisky style, like a kid. Worked till 9, when dak with your . . . letter came in.

The news from Cawnpore is all better. The road does not appear to me just now to be threatened, but you had better wait a bit. At Cawnpore they do not yet think the road safe. . . . The Lucknow news I enclose. The Chief congratulated the Governor-General on the result; and I do trust the termination is near. . . . Things brighter in the Doab; and, if these men who threaten Etawah keep quiet, I don't see why you should not leave.

18*th*.—Brigadier Bradford came up and talked with us some time. He has sent out some troops to help Mayne in driving back the Oudh people, who are pressing rather down again. . . .

I worked away till near 6, when I walked out to the Jail, to see the Native Christians and the progress making with the Jail barracks. One barrack will be ready for the Writers in about a week, I hope. There are now some 8 *families* here of the Writers, and the weather is getting very hot for them in tents. The houses for the Native Christians will, I fear, not be ready for a long time. . . .

19*th*.—Rode to Mr. Owen's, and walked with him down to the entrenchments near the Fort. It reminded me of the time in 1855–56, when we were going down the river, . . . As I was bathing before breakfast, a Shootr Sowar came with an *immediate* summons from his Lordship; so I got the buggy and was off by 9½. It was about instructions for Mr. Mayne (on the Oudh frontier). . . . About midday came your most agreeable message that you were at Meerut yesterday, . . . and trust you will be at Dehra to-morrow. . . .

20*th*.— . . . The weather is getting hot, which, besides . . . , is also a cogent reason why I am anxious for your journey to be over. . . . The news is good from Lucknow to-day: Moosabagh taken, and no Rebels left. Mrs. Orr and Miss Jackson brought in; and they had been honourably treated. . . .

21*st*.—Cud. and I drove to Kinloch's house. It is getting on very slowly indeed. But there will be plenty of shelter in this house for the present. A third room, with bathing-room, will be ready in 2 or 3 days, etc. etc.

22*nd*.—I fancy you will arrange to get back to Agra by Friday or Saturday.[1] . . . I do trust that the road will be all clear, and that you will be able to come down at once. . . . About ¼ to 4 (on Sunday) they told me the (native) Padree had come to have service with the Native Christians; so I walked over to the Jail hospital, where they were all assembled,—some 30 Christians present. Sang hymns, read the Bible, then gave us a sermon. Back by 5. . . . Had a summons to go to Lord C. in the evening about Mayne, who has got into a scrape by getting the troops into a misfortune before a village.

23*rd*.—Everything is quiet now; and this is the time I expected you would have come down had not . . . A. fallen sick. I do trust the road will still keep open; but there is no calculating what these flying Rebels may take into their head. However, Farquhar is "awfully safe," and I can trust fully to his discretion. Things are a little gloomy just now towards

[1] One of the children had fallen sick, which involved another journey to Mussoorie.

Azimgurh. All the troops having been removed away to Lucknow from the Oudh border, has encouraged the Rebels to come on, and our troops in the Azimgurh district may be obliged to fall back on Azimgurh. The troops with Mayne over the river met with a nasty repulse at a village which Mayne should not have attacked, as it was beyond his border. The G.-G. is very angry with him about it, and with reason; for, only the day before, he got instructions not to cross the border. . . .

[Then follows an account of Lord Canning's triumphal journey to Futtehpore.]

Cud. came in about 5½ this morning, going to the railway. I worked on till 6; then dressed. I rode off to the railway station, expecting to find that the party had started. After wandering about a little on the General (my horse), I found that the train was still there. Scene gay; a triumphal arch with "The way to prosperity" on it; banners, etc., with other devices. When I got up to the station, I found that the G.-G. had not arrived, so I talked with the crowd there. Almost every one has gone. I wrote to Bowring last night to say that I had such an overwhelming press of business that I would be glad to remain and not go, unless it were *proper* I should. Bowring replied he would let me know last night if I was required. I asked him this morning about it; and he said when he mentioned it to the G.-G., he said he was glad I would stay, as he had work for me. He has not, however, sent any. But he may have alluded to its being better I should stay in case of any emergent messages, etc.—The only place threatened just now is Azimgurh: our little body of troops was obliged to fall back on the town, and were expecting to be attacked there.—I had been about 10 minutes at the platform when the G.-G. arrived. All then moved along the platform by the railway,—when I found that a Service was to be performed. Mr. Spry was there in his surplice, and read a very appropriate service,—the same as used by the Bishop, with some modifications. It lasted say 10 minutes,—something like the service at Roorkee. I am so glad I was present. Shortly after, the party entered the railway carriages,—the band playing "God Save the Queen." Some 50 Europeans went also, and the band. . . . I am glad I did not go. . . .

26*th.*— . . . I am very glad I did not go yesterday to Futtehpore, as Cud. did not return till late, and had rather a stupid day. They got up to Futtehpore quickly—by 9½—and breakfasted about 10½, in Edmonstone's house. No ladies went. . . . After breakfast, Cud. retired to smoke and Lord C. went away, and then Mr. Purser proposed Lord C.'s health; that was all. They had a salute on arriving and leaving. They came back very slowly. Altogether, I did not miss much. I saw the chief part in the Service at starting. . . .

I do not see why you should not leave next Tuesday morning, if the weather be cool: the mornings are very cool here. If the road continues as at present, you could travel at night to Cawnpore; but Cocks will be the best adviser on that point. . . . A message on your reaching Cawnpore would be sufficient warning . . . , for arranging to go up to Futtehpore next day. May the Lord guide you into the best and safest and least exposing plan of travelling! . . . French, with his Missionaries, arrived. . . . I have persuaded them to come up here and stay till Monday. . . . They are in tents, and won't come into the house.

*27th March.*— . . . Have had no letters for 3 days, and am anxiously looking for the dak. . . . Had a pleasant evening at dinner with French and his two associates. They are both College men: one Clinton, a pleasant, intelligent man; the other Shankey, a good mathematician, from Cambridge. . . . French is determined to have 5 Missionaries for Agra, and none here!! . . . Rebels within a few miles of Azimgurh. There will, I expect, be a fight there soon. . . .

3 p.m.—To my great joy, Lowe's message from Meerut came in reporting your arrival there yesterday. I do feel so thankful to our Heavenly Father for this news; and for the statement of A. . . . being better. By this time you must be quietly at Agra again, and I trust you will start early next week.

Near 4.—An immense dak with your . . . letter of Sunday. . . . I think, so far as I know, the road is quite safe just now, and that you might leave at once with perfect safety. All that is required is for Dr. Farquhar to inquire as you go along, and see that it is smooth ahead.

INTELLIGENCE DEPARTMENT, AGRA.

MSS. VOL. I.

*FIRST SERIES.*

# MR. COLVIN'S LETTERS

AND

# LETTERS DOWN COUNTRY.

# AGRA CORRESPONDENCE, 1857.

## NOTE PREFIXED TO VOLUME I.

Preface, describing plan of Vol. I.

THIS Book, Vol. I., contains the official and demi-official letters relating to Intelligence, etc., written by the Hon^ble J. R. Colvin, Lieut.-Governor N.W.P., or by his order, after the action of the 5th July, which ended in our being obliged to retire into the Fort of Agra.

From the 10th of August this side of the volume was kept for correspondence with the authorities *down* country: the other side [1] being reserved for letters *up* country, Delhi, Meerut, etc.

Mr. Colvin's death.

On the 9th of September 1857 Mr. Colvin died, and after that date the correspondence was carried on by myself as in charge of the Intelligence Department.

From the 1st October the correspondence is contained in another Book, Vol. II.

S^d. W. MUIR.

ALLAHABAD, *14th June* 1860.

---

(Please see page 23 *ante.*) *Note*—In the present Collection a few of the less important documents or parts of documents have been omitted. Each letter or document here printed bears its serial number, as affixed in the original. The remaining letters, however, have been all numbered in the same series, and have, along with those here printed, been copied in typograph, and in that form, as well as in the original, constitute part of the record to be preserved.

The spelling of names has generally been retained as in the original. This explains the variations in the spelling of Native names and words found in the following pages.

W. COLDSTREAM.

[1] Printed as "Second Series," p. 135 *et seq.*

# INTELLIGENCE DEPARTMENT, AGRA.

## MSS. VOL. I.

### *FIRST SERIES.*

# MR. COLVIN'S LETTERS

AND

# LETTERS DOWN COUNTRY.

## XVI.[1]

### GEN^L WILSON TO MR. COLVIN.[2]

CAMP BEFORE DELHI, *July 30th*, 1857.

General Wilson states his determination to hold his position to the last.

MY DEAR SIR,—It is my firm determination to hold my present position and to resist every attack to the last. The enemy are numerous and may possibly break through our entrenchments and overwhelm us; but the force will die at their post. Luckily the enemy have no head and no method; we hear dissensions are breaking out amongst them. Reinforcements are coming up under Nicholson. If we can hold on till they arrive, we shall be secure. I am making every possible arrangement to secure the safe defence of our position.

A. WILSON, Brig.-Gen^l.

TO THE HON^BLE J. R. COLVIN,
L^t-Gov. N.W.P.

(*Note by W. Muir in pencil*)—A grand letter from Gen^l Wilson, Comm^g Delhi Brigade.

[1] Inserted here out of its order on account of its importance.

[2] This letter was in *Greek* character (*i.e.* in the original; not in the copy from which this is taken).—W. C.

## I.

### MR. COLVIN TO H. H. GREATHED.

FORT AGRA, 10*th July*.

MY DEAR GREATHED,[1]—I received yesterday your letter of July the first. A mere acknowledgment of it went in reply. I can add little more now. We have had our turn of burned bungalows and Cucherries at last; and though the city, etc., are now quiet, and supplies come in, our situation needs all the help the General can give us. I need not say more on this, as you have full knowledge of the facts. You can show this to the General. Our action of Sunday afternoon the 5th was fought with gallantry, but we were largely outnumbered in men and guns; and we had *no cavalry* against their 800 or 900. I am extremely sorry that Saunders[2] had not been able to reach you from Meerut. I think that it would be a good arrangement at present to annex the Pergunah of Kurnal to Thuneisur. As to Meerut I have left Williams in charge of the Division till further orders. He should be employed, and you have enough on your hands at Delhi. I have no doubt that he will agree with you as to B. Sapte and Turnbull; the latter has come out remarkably well in this serious disturbance. We may be quite at ease as to the safety of the Fort of Allahabad. A good deal of money may have been plundered at the Station, but we have no exact particulars.

*Action at Agra on 5th July 1857, description of.*

*Recommends Kurnal Pergunah to be annexed to Thanesar.*

I have been glad to see that Sir J. Lawrence has agreed with me in the propriety of offering more lenient terms to the Mutineers; though all move in that direction has yet been fruitless. The thing has gone beyond that. But it was, I am still satisfied, the true view at starting. Pray write too to Sir J. L. to tell him that I have entirely shared in his views in a letter of some 5 or 6 weeks back to me of raising a Police body of horse and foot, at proper rates of pay, for service in each district. The attempt was made by the M(agistrate) of Agra under my sanction; but his selection was too exclusively of one class, and events have baffled it. Please write all this for me, and to Barnes at Umballah, and that his message by the telegraph of June 29th has been received by a Cossid, and its purport sent on. My regards to your brother of the Engineers and remembrances to C. C. G.—Yours, J. R. COLVIN.

*Offer of terms to Mutineers. Sir John Lawrence's views.*

*Proposal to raise Police approved.*

[1] H. H. Greathed, Esq., C.S. Agent to the Lt.-Governor, Delhi.

[2] Charles Saunders, Esq., C.S.

## II.

(*Note in W. Muir's hand.*)

[This is Mr. Colvin's first letter to Havelock, who reached Cawnpore on the 17th July.]

AGRA FORT, 28*th July* 1857.

SIR,—We have received last night authentic information from a private source, of the arrival of your force at Cawnpore, and anxiously look for letters from yourself. **Havelock's arrival at Cawnpore.**

We are endeavouring to lay a regular dak for light packets to you, but meanwhile Cossids can pass up regularly, and in a few days. It is of the utmost importance for us to know your position and plans, and those of Sir H. Lawrence at Lucknow.

Pray write us fully and at once. The state of things above Cawnpore is as follows:—

DELHI: Latest date of English letters 19th, but strong and probably reliable reports down to the 23rd; place not taken, and no immediate intention of an assault. Our troops strongly posted on the ridge constantly attacked by the masses of the Mutineer troops in the City; whom they always beat back, though of course with some loss. **State of Delhi.**

Troops cannot be detached from Delhi downwards as yet. There is an *earnest* wish on the part of the Commander there that your Brigade should march up to reinforce their position. There had been some cholera in camp, and the sickly fever season of August is at hand.

MEERUT: This position is safe, and above it to the Hills in fair order. **State of Meerut.**

PUNJAB: Quiet, and Sikh troops loyal. **State of the Punjab.**

AGRA: We are here living in the Fort after an action on the 5th with the largely superior Force from the Neemuch Camp. This Force has gone on to Delhi. **State of Agra.**

Our Garrison consists of the 3rd European Regt and a Battery of European Artillery, both much weakened by the late action. The Battery indeed could not horse more than two guns. **Agra garrison.**

We have the whole Christian population of the Station within this Fort.—To relieve and secure this Arsenal is of the very first consequence.—*It is the last stronghold of our power up the country.*

Urges Havelock to march up towards Agra.

On all these points you will see how essential it is that you should march up towards us. There is no hostile Force of any strength whatever on the road. My wish and request are that you should come up towards Mynpoory, in your progress to which constant advices would reach you to guide your further movements; we would give you ammunition, supplies, and some carriage. Pray send an answer to this requisition at the earliest moment.—Several letters of the same purport have gone before, General Havelock's name being on the address.—I am, Sir, your obedient Servant, J. R. Colvin,[1]

(Lt.-Gov$^{r}$, N.W.P.).

## IV.

*(Draft Letter in W. Muir's writing.)*

From the Lieut.-Govr: to Com$^{rs}$ of Allahabad, Benares.

*29th July.*

We have had no communication from the East for many weeks, excepting Mr. Charles Chester's[2] of the 11th inst., in Greek, with a message from the Governor-General.

Calcutta papers up to the 22nd June have come lately *via* Bombay and Ajmere.

Let the Governor-General know that the triplicate copy of Mr. Beadon's despatch of the 30th June has just been received through Kurachee. There has been no defect in forwarding reports by every available channel from this. There has been a regular Cossid communication from Delhi, until lately, when it has become interrupted:—the cause we do not know. Copies or important extracts of every letter of interest have been instantly sent on to the Agent Governor-General for transmission to the Governor-General. Full narratives of events down to the 16th ins$^{t}$ have also been uniformly sent; and a continuation is following.

Postal arrangements by Cossids.

We have learnt by native report of the success of the troops at Futtehpore and Cawnpore, and even hear that they are advancing upwards to Furruckabad or this: but not a line has yet reached us from the Army. We can only account for this by supposing that our Cossids as well as yours have been somewhere intercepted. Let us hear from you by Cossids sent from Cawnpore.

[Draft Letter ends here.]

---

[1] Signed by Mr. Colvin himself.—W. C.

[2] Mr. Charles Chester, C.S. Commissioner of Allahabad.

The following is an abstract of the Census taken the other day. It shows the total number of people of all classes who slept in the Fort of Agra on the night between the 26th and 27th of July 1857 to have been 5844. Census of Fort of Agra.

| | Adult Male. | Adult Female. | Juvenile Male. | Juvenile Female. | Total. |
|---|---|---|---|---|---|
| Europeans . . | 1065 | 289 | 344 | 291 | 1989 |
| East Indians . . | 443 | 331 | 429 | 339 | 1541 |
| Native Christians . | 267 | 177 | 205 | 209 | 858 |
| Hindoos . . . | 942 | 49 | 162 | 4 | 1157 |
| Mahommedans . | 244 | 10 | 42 | 3 | 299 |
| | 2961 | 856 | 1182 | 846 | 5844 |

## V.

To Mr. C. Chester, Commissioner, Allahabad.

*July 30th*, 1857.

. . . . . . .

Our latest dates from Delhi are July 24th. Our position there is still strongly held. There had been a severe fight on the 23rd with the usual result. Nine hundred European Infantry and three Punjabee Belooch and Goorkha Battalions expected from the Punjab as a reinforcement. The Camp well supplied with provisions.

Things now quiet here, but we are still living in the Fort, as the bungalows are all burned.

## VII.

Mr. Colvin to H. H. Greathed, Delhi.

Fort of Agra, *July 30th*, 1857.

My Dear Greathed,—I have this morning yours of the 23rd, with letters to others of the 24th, mentioning an affair which seems to have been rather a heavy one, on the 23rd. I send this that the course of our correspondence may have no interrup-

Proposed destruction of Jumma Musjid in Agra.

tion. *ι αμ ανξιους αλσο το ἀνε γουρ ρεπλγ οφ θε εφφεκτ ον θε μαὁμμεδανς οφ γουρ πυνjαβ φορσε οφ ουρ δεστρογινγ ιφ νεσσεσαρy θε Jυμμα μυσjεεδ ἑρε φορ δεφενσιυε πυρπωσες.*

Relief of Cawnpore.

All keeps quiet here, and well with us. Cawnpore triumphantly reoccupied by British troops on 18th, some of which have no doubt gone to relieve Sir H. Lawrence at Lucknow; and a portion moved on probably to Futtehgurh. We have not yet direct letters from the Commanders, but hope to see them this way soon, and shall be ready for them with supplies, etc. The account of the reinforcements coming to you from the Punjab is very satisfactory. It is not believed that the Neemuch men took away much money from Muthra. You will have one sharp action with them, no doubt. It is quite right that Sir John Lawrence should control Hissar at present. The 23rd from Mhow and one or two of Holkar's Battalions have probably reached Gwalior by this time; you shall have warning of any further movement. The large China force must have been now 2 or 3 weeks in Calcutta. I repeat my desire that the families and children should go up from Meerut to the Hills: and that Force be made thoroughly disposable. *μαλαγυρ῾ σδυλδ βε σωεπτ κλεαρ.*

Approves Sir J. Lawrence controlling Hissar.

Arrangement for women and children.

Malagurh.

Administration of justice.

Your rules for Criminal justice will probably work easily with Brigadier Wilson; justice should now be severe and summary.

Special laws.

By a recent law passed in Calcutta death may be awarded against persons convicted of any heinous crime against persons or property in disordered districts. Some of my despatches from 10th to 18th do not seem to have reached you. *ι ἁνε αδυισεδ γου το γετ ινδεπενδεντ κασιδς φρομ μεερυτ κυρναλ ορ οθερ παρτς.*

Arrangements for Cossids.

Write constantly. Your message from Captain Firth to Captain Alexander delivered.

J. R. COLVIN.

Victories at Cawnpore, Pandoo Nuddee.

*P.S.*—A letter from Sherer dated Cawnpore, 23rd, confirms the intelligence that Cawnpore was taken on the 18th and is now held as a garrison; "Nearly 2000 men were to march immediately for Lucknow. Troops daily arriving from Allahabad. When the force returns from Lucknow an advance will be made northwards." The troops stated to be very healthy. A previous letter from Brigadier-General Havelock reported his successes at Futtehpore, Aoung, and the Pandoo Nuddee. 23 guns taken. (*The following in Greek letters.*) Sir H. Lawrence died on the 4th, of wounds received on the 2nd.

## VIII.

To Mr. J. W. Sherer, Collector and Magistrate.

Camp, Cawnpore.

. . . . . . . . .

*P.S.*—1*st August* 1857.—The latest news from Delhi is of the 27th. Mr. Greathed writes: "The Neemuch horde has arrived at Delhi, and to-morrow, weather permitting, a general attack is to be made in front and rear." They had heard of General Havelock's successful advance to Futtehpore. Will you tell Mayne that I have received within the last few days his letters of Jan. (July ?) 19th from Nagode, and 24th from Rewa: but nothing of the actual outbreak which compelled him to leave Bandah. I should be glad to hear from him, where and how he is. The duplicate of a letter to Chester is enclosed; please forward it to him.

J. R. Colvin.

. . . . . . . . .

There is also enclosed a letter for Sheikh Bahador Ali, Naib Rissaedar of the 8th Irregular Cavalry. This man has continued faithful. Please have the letter delivered. Send please a copy to Tucker of our news. Please tell Dr. Hutchinson of Futtehpore that his letter to Thornhill of June the 22nd from Rewa has been safely received, and that he must get his leave from Calcutta.

W. M.

## IX.

To Meerut.

Fort Agra, 1*st August* 1857.

My Dear Williams,[1]—It is important that you should know that Wulee Dad Khan of Malagurh has sent one of his relations to take possession of Allygurh: with the object of establishing a regular Government, and collecting revenue to be sent to Delhi. This adds to the extreme importance of crushing Wulee Dad Khan. Funds will soon be running short at Delhi, and to stop a supply of these is of vital consequence. Pray represent this to the Officer commanding, and do what you possibly can. Send the enclosed to Ramsay at Nainee Tal. Latest Cawnpore news 23rd June. General Havelock has gone over with about 2000 men to relieve Lucknow. He had captured on his advance 23 guns. That noble fellow Sir H. M. Lawrence died on the

**Wullee Dad Khan's efforts.**

**Death of Sir H. Lawrence.**

[1] The Commissioner.

4th of July, of a wound received on the 2nd.—Yours very truly,

J. R. COLVIN.

You can tell all this to Ramsay:

Proposed moving of women and children to hills.

Public letter goes on the question of moving the women and children up to the Hills. A letter from Greathed received last night showed that this project must be dropped. But the importance is every day becoming greater that Malagurh should be swept clean.

Malagurh.

W. M.

## XI.

### TO DELHI.

FORT AGRA, 1st *August* 1857.

MY DEAR GREATHED,—Both your letters of the 27th received. We shall be delighted indeed to hear of the reinforcements from the Punjab having reached you. The sickly season of this and the next month is of course a bad feature. Your advice about the Jumma Musjid shall be implicitly followed. No further news of General Havelock's force to-day. It has gone over to Lucknow, and we must wait a few days before hearing of it. Sir H. Lawrence's death from his wound is a public calamity. On what you say regarding the families at Meerut that point must be dropped. Richardes has done well in sending his Rs. 60,000. I have said that I quite concur in placing all the Hissar and Rohtuck country under the Punjab Government, just now. You are the agent for the Lieut.-Governor at Delhi, with the reversion of Meerut of course when the time comes. No fresh local news here to this date. Wullee Dad Khan is said to be trying to bring Coel under his power. His aim will be to collect revenue. He will be attacked I trust as soon as Meerut has a new Corps.—Yours very truly,

Jumma Musjid at Agra.

Approves of Hissar and Rohtak being administered from the Punjab.

Wullee Dad Khan's movements.

J. R. C.

H. H. GREATHED, ESQ.,
Agent to the Lieut.-Gov$^{r}$, Delhi.

## XII.

### TO HAVELOCK (?) OR NEILL (?).

AGRA, 2nd *August* 1857.

MY DEAR SIR,—I was glad to receive your letter of the 25th. . . .

Reinforcements necessary.

It will be seen from the tenor of all that I have written, that the march of reinforcements upwards is of primary importance. As the advancing troops near Mynpoory, our advices will show where the need of them may be most urgent. . . . Our strength only enables us to hold our own. . . . Things continue quiet up to this date here; the Indore Mutineers have however reached Gwalior, and we wait to see what the plans of that force and Durbar may be. . . . I cordially approve the course you are taking to introduce order and police at Cawnpore. It is most essential this should be done. Our presence should give protection and not bring plundering; although villages or Mohullas known to be inhabited by very bad characters might under military direction be put to the flames and signal examples made. Pray give details of the reinforcements of troops expected, with dates. Pray send copy of this to the G.-G.

Indore Mutineers have reached Gwalior.

Treatment of refractory villages.

## XIII.

FORT AGRA, *3rd August* 1857.

MY DEAR GREATHED,—Yours of the 29th reached last night. The accounts are cheering to us. I have no doubt the Neemuch people will give you one good fight, and that you will punish them as usual. One general matter you are in a good position to prove, and it is of great consequence. What was the real beginning of all this Rebel movement in the Army? what mainly fed the discontent? Prisoners, deserters might tell about this, and the information would be eagerly wished for. The Mhow regiment with some Indore troops has reached Gwalior. We watch their further plans. Saugor said to have mutinied, but Brigadier Sage safe. General Neill of Cawnpore says in a note of the 27th that they crossed the Jumna at Calpee three days before, marching to Delhi, or perhaps to Lucknow. Nawáb Raees said to have sent some troops down to molest Cawnpore; copy of General Havelock's letter shows his position. We do not know his instructions. General Neill writes that Havelock had 4 regiments of Europeans, viz., 1st Madras Fus:—64, 78, and 86th with half a regiment of Seiks, a squadron of Eur: vol. cavalry, and nearly two batteries. He was pitched on the left bank of the Jumna and expected to march on to Lucknow that evening (27th). General Neill adds that then there were good accounts from downwards—about 1600 troops of China expedition had reached Calcutta and would be sent on; 5th Fusiliers would be at Allahabad in 8 or 10 days.—Yours very truly,

Inquiries as to "real beginning of all the rebel movement in the army."

Movement of Indore troops.

Havelock's strength and position.

China troops.

(J. R. C.)

H. H. GREATHED, ESQ.

*P.S.*—Guthrie in an old letter from Nynee Tal very lately received says that he would wish to be transferred to the Delhi Territory, where he has had all his experience. I have encouraged him to make the best of his way to Mussoorie, and thence to report to you. If you have wants for him you can get him *via* Umballa. He knows the Delhi Districts well. (*The following in Greek characters.*) I should explain about the Jumma Musjid, that beside the mass of the building itself, which is close to the Fort, it has parapets, round the Courtyard and Dome, from which much execution might be done by musketry on the lower defences. If we hear that the Gwalior Corps are coming this way, even without many guns, I shall sanction the removal of the parapets; this will be obviously necessary, as a precaution, and if needed this can be explained to your Punjab Mahommedans. The Malagur man has sent a deputy to Allygurh, where he is collecting revenue, and raising troops. This shows the importance of clearing Malagur even more strongly.

Agra Jumma Musjid, proposals for destruction of.

Malagurh.

## XIV.

### To General Neill, Cawnpore.

**Fort Agra, 3rd *August* 1857.**

My Dear Sir,—Yours of the 27th with a few lines from General Havelock of the 26th arrived last night. It is necessary that General Havelock and the Supreme Government should know of *what extreme importance* it is that, if possible, a strong portion of the brigade should march up in this direction. We ourselves may be attacked by the Gwalior troops, but it is not so much that, as the state of things in the Doab, that requires instant vigour. A Nawáb, Wulee Dad Khan, has established himself at Malagurh, near Boolundshuhur, and has now pushed on a Deputy to Allygurh where he is forming a Force, and intends to collect revenue, for the Rebels at Delhi. I have stated this to the Brigadier here, and asked him to do all he can, but he may not feel áble to send away the needful detachment. To crush rapidly this attempt to raise a hostile Government in districts is of an urgency which I need not explain to you. Pray send copies of this to General Havelock, and also to the Governor-General, that he may give any orders that may be thought fit. We do not know here what General Havelock's instructions are. You will send us of course also the earliest tidings of what is done at Lucknow. The bridge of boats here you will find all right and under the walls of the Fort. We

Urges advance of troops towards Agra.

Wullee Dad Khan at Malagurh.

are well provisioned, etc., but *θε πλασε ις α λαργε ονε ανδ ιουλδ ρεκυιρε μορε αρτιλλεριμεν ανδ οφισερς βι φαρ θαν ιοη άνε. ιφ ιου κουλδ σενδ υς αρτιλλερι οφισερς*, they would *βε οφ θε γρεατεςτ ἐλπ.*

Asks for artillerymen for Agra.

Any strong escort of Europeans passing up here would have the best effect, and might take away some ladies and children. I can only ask you to mention all this to General Havelock. Our number of helpless persons, women and children, within the walls is very great. Letters last night from Delhi to 29th of cheerful purport. No new action. Tell me of the restoration of Civil order in Cawnpore. Does Mr. Sherer act under your orders, or how? Where is Mr. Mayne of Bandah? Mention also details of the arrival of fresh troops at Allahabad. You will be on your guard against attack of troops at Futtehgurh. We received information yesterday that the Nawáb Raees had sent a Force towards Cawnpore consisting probably of two Sepoy regiments and an Oudh Irregular Cavalry regiment. Nothing new from Gwalior.—Yours faithfully,

Ladies and children.

J. R. Colvin.

Brigadier-General Neill,
Command$^{g}$ at Cawnpore.

*P.S.*—*5th August* 1857.—The Brigadier has stated himself to be unable to send any troops to Allygurh. Pray let this be known. The messenger has been paid 250 Rs.* (payment of Cossid, W. M.).[1] But it will be well that you should arrange to pay your Kasids, however liberally, when *they take an answer back to you.* We always do this. We sent a letter down to Allahabad by a fast boat some 2 or 3 weeks ago. Did it arrive?

Payment of Cossids.

## XV.

### To Delhi.

Fort Agra, *4th August* 1857.

My Dear Greathed,—Your letter and Brigadier Wilson's of the 30th ult. received. I cannot too strongly express my admiration of the noble gallantry of the Force before Delhi; what they have already done in so many hard combats will gain for them the highest applause; and no one doubts that their endurance and efforts will in the end be successful. To see corps after corps crowding on Delhi without adequate means of arresting them has been deep grief to us all; but we all in our places do our best. The help lent from the Punjab is quite

Delhi force praised by Mr. Colvin.

Punjab helps.

[1] Payment of Cossid (these words and asterisk (*) in pencil by W. M. in the margin).—W. C.

Colvin's tribute to Sir J. Lawrence.

wonderful. The thanks of all India are due to Lawrence for his energetic and unstinted aid. Please send him a copy of this note, and of course show it to Wilson. Nothing new here to-day. At Etawah the Saugor mutinous regiment is expected to pass that way, and may go on to Delhi. It is said to be some 700 strong.—Yours very truly, J. R. COLVIN.

Extract of Beadon's letter, regarding 25,000 troops from England, sent.

## XVI.

(*Inserted at the beginning of the Series on account of its importance.*)

## XVII.

TO THE OFFICER COM$^{G}$ AT ALLAHABAD.

FORT AGRA, *August 5th.*

MY DEAR SIR,—Letters of the 27th ult. received last night. The order of the Gov$^{r}$-Gen$^{l}$ communicated to Brigd$^{r}$ Polwhele and Lt.-Col. Cotton. Lt.-Col. Cotton assumes charge this day.

Cols. Cotton and Fraser of Engineers.

Of course it is known that Lt.-Col. Fraser, Engineers, who is senior to L$^{t}$-Col. Cotton, is with the rest of us in the Fort. He has been acting as second in command and Chief Engineer of the Fort. He will continue to act in the same manner. I send a copy of a letter lately written to Gen$^{l}$ Neill at Cawnpore. It shows the urgent call for the early advances of troops up the Dooab. . . . I now annex copy of the latest report from Brig$^{r}$ Wilson, comm$^{g}$ at Delhi. . . . They will no doubt hold out well and will soon have strong reinforcements from the Punjab. *βυτ θε ποωερ οφ τακινγ Δελι μαι στιλλ βε ναντινγ υιθουτ ιετ φαρθερ μεανς.*

Death of Genl. Barnard.

Sir J. Lawrence has written on this to the Gov$^{r}$-Gen$^{l}$. Gen$^{l}$ Barnard died on the 4th of July. The messages forwarded

Delhi force: its composition and strength.

by you will, however, be sent on to Brig$^{r}$-Gen$^{l}$ Wilson; the latest returns of the 27th from Delhi fix the effective force there as follows:—

| | *ινφαντρι* | *καναλρι* | *ιν αλλ* |
|---|---|---|---|
| *Ευροπεανς* . . | MML | DIV | MMDLIV |
| *ινδοσταντιες* . . | MCCCCXXV | CCCCXCV | MDCCCCXX |
| | MMMCCCCLXXV | DCCCCXCIX | MMMMCCCCLXXIV |

besides *αρτιλλερι* & *Σαππερς*

*Σιcκ* in camp, DCCLXV Blessés Do. DLI

Constant communications are held with Delhi. On this point I refer to my former, and especially to one to Mr. Chester. A full despatch too has gone by Rajpootana showing how steadily intelligence has been sent. The latest date from Delhi is that of which copy now goes. On carriage I sent a letter of which also a copy is attached. We can help as troops approach here, but not to any sensible degree before. We have laid up stores largely, *βυτ ουρ φυνδς αρε βεκομινγ νερι λιμιτεδ, ωε ὁλδ νο κουντρι ανδ σκαρσλι κολλεκτ ανιθινγ. θερεφορε ιτ ις εσσεντιαλ θατ φυνδς κομε ωιθ θε φορσε ιν σομε δεγρεε φορ ουρ οων ἓυσε ἑρε—ουρ ωαντς μαι βε τακεν ατ* 1½ *λακς* (besides an almost equal sum for bills, in all 3 lakhs) *α μονθ. Ωε καν σκαρσλι καρρι ον βειονδ θρεε μονθς μορε.* Want of funds at Agra.

We raise money by small local loans at high interest, ten per cent. On the whole what is needed is an advance with strength and means. This would clear all around us, and make the road open to Meerut. The Gwalior and Mhow mutinous reg[ts] are collected at Gwalior. They talk of coming this way, but the rivers are very high, and we do not look for them just now. It is not known how far they have espoused the distinct cause of Gwalior, or have coerced the Maharajah and are acting with their Delhi comrades. The Maharajah has certainly taken them into his pay. Rajputana so far quiet, if not actively useful. Our Calcutta and Bombay daks come that way, but irregularly. Pray send all this to the Gov[r]-Gen[l], and I again add that Delhi news has been constantly received, and instantly forwarded by Ajmere and Neemuch, and now we shall write it to Cawnpore to you. Loans raised at Agra at 10 %.

J. R. COLVIN.

I enclose a *Delhi Gazette* just now from the press.[1] The news is authentic. Pray send this on to the G.-G., and say that the letter from Mr. Beadon of July the 19th has reached me.

## XVIII.

TO B[R]-G[L] NEILL, COM[G] CAWNPORE.

(*8th August.*)

. . . . . . . . .

*P.S.*—We have no Enfield rifles or ammunition here. Our cash balance at present is only about 6 lakhs of Co:'s Rs. Mr. Reade as Financial Commissioner has borrowed money on high terms Financial position at Agra.

[1] Printed at Agra.

Funds needed. in last month, but further success in raising money in this way must depend upon events. The cash disbursements of each month may be taken at 1½ lakhs, if 1½ lakhs more can be raised by supply bill; the whole monthly demand 3 lakhs. We shall continue to borrow, if we can, but this must be uncertain. From the 6 lakhs in hand 1½ must be paid out from the past month, July.

This shows how pressing our money needs are; the cure is in the most prompt advance in strength and with means.

This has been written several times before, but should again be made known to Calcutta, by every opportunity.

## XIX.

### To Greathed, dated 9th August 1857.

. . . . . . . . . . . .

We had 3 fights on the 29th. Gen[l] Havelock lost 1 officer, his aide-de-camp, L[t] (*blank in original*) Madras Army, and but 3 wounded. The 42nd N.I. from Saugor had passed within 18 miles of Cawnpore, killed a Thanahdar and destroyed a bridge, and then moved towards Futtehgurh. They will doubtless have joined the Futtehgurh Rebels and give annoyance to Gen[l] Neill, who is however very strongly posted at Cawnpore with an armed steamer. Nothing new from any other quarter. Holkar staunch, and Mhow secure. We get letters and newspapers by Nágpore. Latest date from you, evening of the 2nd in a letter from Col. Becher. Three steamers and gunboats coming up armed to Allahabad and Cawnpore.

Position at Cawnpore.

## XXI.

### Brig[r]-G[l] Neill, Cawnpore.

Fort Agra, *9th August* 1857.

My Dear Sir,—

. . . . . . . . . . . .

Latest Delhi date evening of the 2nd, when there had been another of the usual actions with scarcely any loss on our part. We can only repeat again and again that the advance of a Force in this direction is of the most urgent consequence to prevent the country being organised against us and funds being levied by the Rebel power at Delhi. You

Urges advance of force towards Agra.

can say this in all your letters to the Govr-Genl. In the Fort itself we should be especially glad to have more Artillery officers and men. The provisioning, etc., have all been well cared for. *But as we are running very short of funds.* Attached is a memo on this essential point of which copies have been already gone, but every occasion should be taken of informing the Supreme Govt. *The Gwalior Mutinous Troops are 5 or 6000 with some 30 guns besides a 3rd class Siege Train. At this moment we are not in a condition to beat them in the open. We could scarcely man more than 3 Battery guns, effectively. But from the inside,* if they came, they should have a thorough peppering. The copy of the letter at the beginning speaks of camels. Turn back all Sepoys coming up here after their two months' leave. None can be trusted now. About . . . I will mention in my next letter.

**Artillerymen required.**

**Funds required.**

**Number of Gwalior mutinous troops.**

**Weakness of force in Agra Fort.**

. . . . . . . .

## XXII.

FORT AGRA, *July* 24, 1857.

MY DEAR CHESTER,—If a steamer could be pushed up the Jumna with troops in the present fall of the rains it would be *most welcome* succour in men here or for reinforcement of Delhi, and take away the many English ladies and children collected here, an object of vast importance, for our position is obviously very critical. Think if this can be done and consult Calcutta by telegraph, and do it if it be possible. If only troops enough could be brought to protect the steamer, and cover the Lascars in getting wood on the banks, it would be an immense relief to our families.

**Ladies and children, removal of, from Agra Fort necessary.**

J. R. COLVIN.

## XXIV.

FORT AGRA, *August* 12, 1857 (?).

MY DEAR GREATHED,—. . . Malagurh is not only an evil in itself, but it sends its shoots down to Allygurh and Hattrass. The fellow at Allygurh, Ghaus Mohammed, is an especial savage. If money is offered to Williams at 6 per cent. purely as a local loan, principal and interest claimable only at the Meerut Treasury, I see no objection to his raising moderate sums in that way. His rule should be to get as much as will meet each month's cash consumption, by loan or supply Bills, the purpose being only to keep the Station-chest from wastage, and not to make any financial operations which would affect the

**Malagurh.**

**Ghous Mahomed.**

**Loans at Meerut sanctioned at 6 %.**

money market. In an isolated position here we have to pay 10 p. c. for such advances, but then we only took 29,000 Rs. in cash, and our terms are that we have liberty in 15 days' notice to pay the principal with interest when we may wish. Such terms of course are only to be submitted to in an extreme necessity, and for absolutely requisite amounts. Williams need not be in too great a hurry as he has the country open to Seharunpore and Umballah; but if cash is easily to be got by him at 6 p. c. in a local transaction, it would I think be permissible. No new local fact here.

Loans taken at Agra at 10 %.

J. R. COLVIN.

*August* 12, 1857.

## XXVI.

TO COMMISSIONER, ALLAHABAD.

*15th August* 1857.

. . . . . . . .

Bhurtpore Durbar's action.

The Bhurtpore Durbar has sent away the British Agent: and no formal communication can now be carried on. The Durbar, however, continues to aid us in various indirect ways by daks, elephants, etc. Messages regarding these are managed by Capt[n] Nixon.

. . . . . . . .

*P.S.*—The latest Delhi date August 9th.

The only new fact that the Mutineers had established a new 8 or 10-gun battery under our right batteries, which was causing annoyance of course. A letter just come in to 10th. Nothing new. Infantry attacks ceased, much annoyance attempted by Artillery and Rockets.

## XXVIII.

FORT AGRA, *August 16th*, 1857.

Promises attention to General's wishes as to correspondence with officers under General's command, and asks for prompt intimation of General's movements and intentions.

SIR,—I have received your letter of the 10th this morning, and have communicated it to Lt.-Col. Cotton, commanding here. I shall of course attend to your wishes as to correspondence with Officers under your orders, and shall rely upon your informing me promptly of your movements and intentions, as far as you may feel yourself justified in doing so, for our own information at this place and for communication to the authorities at Delhi and Meerut.

BRIG[R]-GEN[L] HAVELOCK.

## XXIXA.

MY DEAR MUIR,—I send J. Lawrence's letter. Sherer's is now with Col. Cotton. I wish I could see my way to acting on Lawrence's suggestion, but he has obedient districts, trustworthy tribes, a real Gov$^{t}$, and money coming freely in. We can scarcely pay our way, and this late Eastern news will not mend our position. Herewith I send three letters of yesterday which came to Nixon. You can take notes of them in your book, which certainly will be useful. The letters have just come in from Colonel Cotton. I send them. Pray send them all back after breakfast, when I must prepare a letter to Gen$^{l}$ Havelock.—Yours very truly,

**Mr. Colvin contrasts his position at Agra with Sir J. Lawrence's at Lahore.**

**Approves of plan of Intelligence book kept up by Mr. Muir.**

J. R. COLVIN.

## XXX.

FORT AGRA, *August* 16, 1857.

MY DEAR SHERER,—

. . . . . . . .

Let me hear from you frequently, as I may hear less from General Neill in consequence of the wishes of General Havelock regarding correspondence.

**Refers to General Havelock's wishes as to correspondence.**

. . . . . . . .

Your arrangements are now carried on under the direct orders of the Supreme Gov$^{t}$, so that I need only say that your appointment of a Sudder Tehseeldar for Cawnpore seems to me likely to do good. The safety of the greater number of the Tehseelee records is a matter of congratulation.—I remain, yours very truly,

**Adverts to the Cawnpore administration having passed under the direct orders of the Supreme Government.**

(J. R. C.)

M. SHERER, ESQ., Cawnpore.

## XXXI.

FORT AGRA, 17 *August* 1857.

MY DEAR CHESTER,—

. . . . . . . .

I repeat that troops at Allahabad cannot look for carriage from here, as we have no escort to send. But when troops come near here, and send an escort, carriage and supplies can be given.

**Cannot send carriage for troops from Agra.**

In want of funds; collecting next to nothing.

Mentions a proposal by Sir J. Lawrence for raising levies, but cannot do so at Agra for want of funds, while Chester controls several districts.

We are in urgent want of funds, having scarcely enough for two months more, and collecting next to nothing. Sir. J. Lawrence has sent a suggestion for raising levies of Native troops, horse and foot, for future employment. This suggestion is more important to you and to Tucker than to us in our present circumstances; for we could not pay for large levies. You have possession and control of considerable districts.

## XXXIV.

### To Allahabad.

Fort Agra, *August 27th*, 1857.

Refers to overtures made by the King of Delhi to his besiegers.

Begum sends emissary.

Women and children in Delhi.

My Dear Sir,—Your letter of the 21st just received. Pray send tel: answers on my part to Calcutta to following effect, "Tel: orders of 20th inst: received." There was a hollow pretence of negotiation entered into by the king of D(elhi). It was noticed in the L[t]-Govr's private letters to the G.G. of July 30th in these words: "The overture to which Mr. Greathed alludes was one from the old king, made no doubt in fraud. Your orders against any terms with the family have been sent on, and accommodation of any sort is now out of the question."

Nothing further has been heard of any overtures from the Palace until a letter of the 22nd from Mr. Greathed this morning. In it he says, "Yesterday an emissary came in from the chief lady of the Palace offering her good offices. He was told we were highly anxious for his personal safety and for that of all women and children, but that no communication could be received from inmates of the Palace." Copy of the order. "The present message will now be sent on at once in continuation of former orders."

Position at Agra Fort.

I don't know what I can have said to have led to the supposition of an early advance of the Gwalior people by Calpee. Our latest information is that they are not moving from there at all just now. We have Delhi news of the 22nd all well. We have a small party out towards Hattrass and Allyghur just to show that we are not helpless in the Fort. There was a smart little action some three or four miles from Allyghur on the 24th in which we had a decided success, but affairs of this kind are only partial and may be but temporary.

(Signed) J. R. Colvin.

Brig[r]-Gen[l] Neill.

## XXXV.

### To Allahabad.

Fort Agra, 27 *August* 1857.

My Dear Chester,—

. . . . . . . .

Foot Police of different Tribes we could get here, but any large number of trustworthy horsemen not Mahom[dns] would be a hard battle. Have you any reality of Gov[t] in the interior of the districts? for instance, what revenue do you collect in Allab[d]? It is remarkable that *burning of Catcherries and Bungalows* and the ravage of property, release of Prisoners, etc., which have happened universally on the occurrence of Milit[y] revolt in our upper North-West Stations, do not appear to have been as common in the Benares Division or at the Behar Stations. Have you heard of any of these Stations particularly in Behar where outrages and plunders of that kind have been permitted? I hope Mayne with his party have given a good account of the men from Oudh who attacked the Moorutpore Thannah.

Remarks that burning of bungalows and ravage of property less common in Benares Division and Behar.

You will send all my letters of course to J. P. Grant.

(Signed) J. R. Colvin.

## XXXVII.

### SERVICE MESSAGE.

From the Hon[ble] J. R. Colvin to Right Hon[ble] the Gov[r]-Gen[l], Calcutta.

Agra, 31*st August* 1857.

Since writing yesterday on the clearance of the Dooab, I have received a statement of the Force that will soon be before Delhi, of which copy is subjoined.

"We shall have before Delhi 7 companies of H.M. 8[th] Foot, and the 52[nd], 60[th], and 61[st] Reg[ts], also the 1[st] and 2[nd] Bengal Fusiliers, the 9[th] Lancers, and a squadron H.M.'s 6[th] Carabineers. The Native Reg[ts] are the Sirmoor and Kumaon Goorkha Battalions, the 1[st] and 2[nd] Punjab Infantry, the 4[th] Sikh Reg[t], the Guide Corps, and wings of the 1[st] and 2[nd] Punjab Cavalry. There are 6 troops of H. Artillery, 3 reserve companies Europeans and Sikhs, a 3[rd] class siege train in Camp, and a 2[nd] class siege train on the road. The Rebels have 24 Reg[ts]

Statement of the force assembling before Delhi.

Regular Infantry, 3 Reg[ts] Regular Cavalry, 3 Reg[ts] Irregulars, 400 Miscellaneous Horse from various Reg[ts] and Contingents, and an armed rabble of fanatics. They have also 30 H. Artillery Guns, with the Delhi Fortress, and Magazine."

Rumour of Nicholson defeating the Bareilly Brigade.

News was received yesterday that Brig[r] Nicholson on the 25th inst. defeated the Bareilly Brigade, which was attempting a movement to our rear, and captured 12 field-pieces, and all their ammunition and baggage. The siege train was expected there about to-morrow the 1st. It is reasonable to look for an early assault, and in that case some superior authority on or near the spot, empowered to direct the employment of troops in whatever direction, seems very necessary.

Suggests the provision of a controlling authority on the spot to direct troops after assault.

. . . . . . . . .

(Signed) J. R. Colvin.

## XXXVIII.

### Message from Major Macpherson, Pol. Agent, to G. Edmonstone, Esq., Foreign Sec[y] to Gov[t] of India.

*Septr. 2nd.*

Major Macpherson (Political Agent at Gwalior) reports Scindia's good services, and asks Governor-General to acknowledge them.

I have reported in my letters of the 1st and 15th July and 7th of August that Scindiah has rendered most important aid by preventing the movement of the Gwalior, Mhow, and Indore Mutineers upon Agra or Delhi, and that I have led Scindiah to expect that such conduct would be acknowledged as good service by the Gov[r]-Gen[l]. Scindiah is distracted by intelligence, possibly erroneous, from his Vakeel that the Agent at Indore is disposed to view his conduct unfavourably, and that the Officers there blame him for giving pay to the Mutineers, one of the devices I sanctioned, if it should be, as it has proved, essential to their detention. This may lead Scindiah to cease to oppose their movement. An expression of the Gov[r]-Gen[l]'s approval of Scindiah's friendly policy would greatly strengthen my hands. I have not heard from the Agent at Indore since the 10th of June, and do not know if my letters have reached him.

## XXXIX.

### Added from the Lieu[t]-Gov[r], N.W.P.

Lieutenant-Governor adds his concurrence.

The Lieu[t]-Gov[r] has seen this message. He would submit on his part that it cannot be doubted that by his active endeavours, which have been so far successful to keep the Gwalior Mutineer Corps on the other side of the Chumbul, Scindiah has hitherto rendered us a signal service. A continuance of the like service, now that the rains appear to have ceased in the Upper Provinces, must be still more valuable. Events cannot be predicted, but the advance of so powerful a body, about 6000 men with 5 Batteries, a 3rd class siege train, cavalry, and munitions of war, would be a very serious complication. The tranquillity and safety of all our Upper Provinces would be gravely imperilled, and Agra might be placed in a state of siege when no means of relief are at hand. As long therefore as Scindiah acts as he has hitherto done, the Lieut-Govr would strongly recommend that the line towards him be that of a confident assurance as to his friendly purposes.

*2nd September* 1857.

## XLI.

### To Gl. Neill, Cawnpore.

*4th September.*

Pray send on in the quickest way to Calcutta the subjoined copies and extracts of letters received from Delhi of the 29th and 30th. The important message from Genl Wilson contained in the letter of the 30th is an answer to a letter of mine of the 25th in which the importance of acting against Malagurh was urged, if there should be a prospect of a long halt before Delhi. The letter to Capt Nixon from Col. Becher gives details of the action at Nujjufgurh, in which Genl Nicholson captured 12 of the enemy's guns. No local news here except that the 23rd Regt from Indore now at Gwalior is said to be somewhat restless and calling on the Gwalior Corps, and we watch what is being done in that quarter. Our detachment in the Allygurh district is doing well; its headquarters are now placed at Hattras.

**Notes importance of acting against Malagurh.**

**Refers to Nicholson's victory at Nujjufgurh.**

**Restlessness of Indore troops.**

**Detachment at Allygurh doing well.**

(Signed) J. R. Colvin.

*P.S.*—I have said to Mr. Greathed in reference to the petition for pardon of the 2000 Ranghurs of the Rhotuck district, that I think that if none of them have been guilty of heinous crimes, especially against Christians, and their submission should be an important step towards the pacification of the District, strong recommendations to the G.G. might be promised to them with much safety on their laying down their arms. At all events, pray bring the circumstance on my part to the notice

**Recommends clemency towards 2000 Ranghurs of Rhotuck.**

of the G.G. in C. Pray too write to Mr. Chester at Allahabad that his letter to Mr. Thornhill of Aug. 27th has arrived, but that I shall be happy to continue to hear from him direct.

Note by Mr. Muir. Illness of Mr. Colvin.

[In Mr. Muir's hand here occurs this pencil note: "Here Mr. Colvin fell seriously ill, and could no longer attend to business."]

## XLIII.

### To the Officer commanding at Cawnpore, or the Magistrate.

Agra Fort, *Sept. 8th*, 1857.

Dear Sir,—Will you kindly transmit the following telegraph message to the Gov.-Gen., and communicate it also to Mr. J. P. Grant.—Yours faithfully, C. B. Thornhill.

## XLIV.

### Telegram: Mr. C. Thornhill, Offic^o Sec^y, N.W.P., to Gov^r-Gen. in Council.

Serious illness of Mr. Colvin.

Mr. Colvin the Lt.-Gov^r is very dangerously ill. He had been suffering from bowel complaint for some time, but yesterday the disease took an unfavourable turn, and the medical attendants consider his situation to be most critical, and have strictly prohibited him from attending to any business. Under these circumstances, pending the receipt of your Lordship's orders, Mr. E. A. Reade, the Senior Civilian, will conduct the duties of the Government.

Gwalior Mutineers at Dholpore.

The latest authentic news from the Chumbul up to this hour is that the Chumbul has risen, and the main body of the Mutineers' infantry, cavalry, and guns had not yet crossed. Their advanced guard continues at Dholepore with two guns. At present, of two streams between Agra and the Chumbul one is certainly unfordable and the boat has been destroyed.

Delhi news.

Latest news from Delhi the 3rd inst. Siege train in course of arrival and expected to be in position by the 6th. Fugitives from Delhi increasing daily.

Account from the detachment in the Allygurh District highly satisfactory. C. B. Thornhill.

## XLIVa.

Continued dangerous illness of Mr. Colvin.

*Sept. 9th*, 8 a.m.—Reported by telegraph to Calcutta, the continued dangerous illness of the Lt.-Gov^r, and mentioned that it was by his special desire that Mr. E A. Reade had assumed charge.

XLV.

*Sept. 9th*, 5 p.m.—Announced the demise of the Lt.-Gov. at ½ past four of the afternoon of the 9th Sept. **Death of Mr. Colvin.**

[Here occurs the following pencil note in Sir William Muir's hand: "Several days before, Mr. E A. Reade (Senior member Board of Revenue and in Financial charge) had taken supreme charge. The correspondence subsequently is in my own name, but always in communication with Mr. Reade, and subsequently under Col. Fraser, who took over charge."—W. M.]

XLVI.

[A pencil note by Sir Wm. Muir to the following effect: "My correspondence with Sherer begins here, immediately after Mr. Colvin's death; it was regularly forwarded by him to the Gov.-Genl, Calcutta."]

MY DEAR SHERER,

. . . . . . . . .

I have little new to add to-day. Nothing new from Delhi by English letters. But the Gwalior news-writer at Delhi has sent reports to Macpherson up to the 7th. These are gradually becoming more and more truthful. The Bankers complain in Durbar of the excesses and cruelties of the Sepoys. The latter are clamorous for their pay, and the King refers them to the Bankers over whom guards are placed, and every means resorted to for extorting money. They are graphically described, poor people, as "bisyar tung wa hairân."[1] Deserters were brought up in Durbar, who taunted the King with giving them no pay for two months; they were going for service to some prince or chieftain elsewhere. The unfortunate monarch could say nothing in reply. **Events at Gwalior.**

The confusion in the City was so great that labourers could not be got for the powder manufactory.

The King is evidently in consternation, for he has addressed an urgent "Perwana" to the Indore and Gwalior Mutineers to proceed at once to Delhi. This was to be carried on the 7th or 8th in person by Golam Hyder and Jehangeer Khan, the latter believed to be a deserter from Gwalior. We shall see what effect the message has upon those for whom it is intended. Our *Ινδωρ* **King of Delhi Indore Mutineers.**

[1] Terribly pressed and in fearful straits.

Dholpore. friends are still at δ'ωλπωρ, and indeed it is uncertain whether they have all of them yet κροσσεδ the χυμβαλ. The Contingent

Scindia. remains staunch to Sindia.

Our Hattras detachment going on well.

Mr. Harington, C.S. Harington and your friends here are all well. He is most useful, from his admirable judgment and sagacity. Everything going on steadily under Reade.

W. MUIR.

J. W. SHERER, ESQ.

XLVII.

AGRA, 12 *Sept.* 1857.

Major Macpherson. MY DEAR SHERER,—Major Macpherson's news from Gwalior received this morning is very serious. The plot appears at last

Mutiny at Gwalior. ready to burst. The Contingent Regiment seem to have demanded carriage of the Maharaja, and to have raised the green flag somewhere about the 8th or 9th. The Maharaja remonstrated with them, and he has succeeded in detaching the $5^{th}$ Regiment, and the remains of the $6^{th}$ with the 2 Mehidpoor guns, and the Cavalry (say 600), from the rest, and they are apparently at present amenable to his orders. The remainder comprising four full Regiments and 5 Batteries openly resist his

Indore troops. authority, and demand carriage. The departure of the Indore troops has probably precipitated this movement. It is to be

Scindia. feared that Sindia will no longer be able to stay the departure of these rebels: and that they may be able to force him to furnish them with carriage. Macpherson says that Sindia has nothing to oppose to their shells; that his Lushkur is entirely open, and that the powerful Artillery of the Contingent could at once

Dinka Rao. coerce him. The messenger who brought Dinka Rao's letter said that the rebels had planted guns on the roads leading to the Lushkur.

This movement may gravely complicate our position here. Unless we have succour from Delhi or from you, before long we shall be exposed to the chances and risks of a siege. Macpherson is sending a message on the subject: it is of serious moment.

Nothing fresh from Delhi. I send you yesterday's printed budget.

The Indore troops remain at Dholepore. It seems almost certain that they are watching for their Gwalior friends.

. . . . . . . . . . . .

W. MUIR.

J. W. SHERER, ESQ., Cawnpore.

## XLVIII.

### Epitome of Financial Commissioner's Report for August.

Cash Balance 3rd July was Rs. 7,27,066, and 31st August was 7,34,388. Income has thus exceeded expenditure, though there has been a much larger expenditure in August, 2,09,780, against 1,43,995 in July. Funds, state of, in Fort.

Increased Military Charges are owing to the completion of supplies to the fort, large outlay in engineering operations within and without it, in strengthening, and enlarging accommodation, and clearing circumjacent space, to European troops maintained as usual without drain on the supplies of the Fort, and lastly in the ordnance making up 200 tents for the European troops when they arrive.

On the Civil head, old accounts adjusted prior to 1st July. Subsistence allowance doled out to all persons, and no complaints.

Under Miscellaneous, the Pontoon bridge across the Jumna completed under the guns of the fort. Portions of the aggregate amount of Treasury drafts held by the local banks liquidated, which enabled many depositors to obtain their subsistence. Period of paying interest on Gov^t Notes having supervened, the public credit has been sustained by discharge of all minor claims, and part payment of larger sums due.

Under Intelligence, increased expense is owing to constant, continuous, and effective communications by Cossid.

Receipts of all branches of revenue indicate restored authority and confidence. The collections are from Agra, Muttra, and Allygurh; 50,000 Rs. tribute safely received from Jeypoor; Bill transactions in the town of Agra have been small. The confidence of the citizens has been much restored. Total receipts 2,17,000. Expenditure of September will be less than in August. Revenue improved.

E. A. Reade.

From E. A. Reade,
To Financial Secretary.

## XLIX.

### To Foreign Secretary.

Active operations commenced before Delhi on the evening of Monday the 7th, when the Koodsia Bagh (old Custom House) and Ludlow Castle were occupied.

Delhi, operations at.

During night, 2 Batteries were constructed on our right front, 700 yards from the Moree Bastion—unknown to the rebels—whose fire was attracted by our guns on the ridge.

Moree Bastion. Koodsia Bagh. Ludlow Castle battery.

On the 8th, 10 guns opened fire: opposing fire at first heavy, already reduced. Moree Bastion damaged. Heavy guns and mortars to open on the 10th from Koodsia Bagh, 300 yards from city walls; also on same day, 16 heavy guns from Ludlow Castle, where is a strong picket. Firing, effective and steady.

Khoorja.

At Khoorja, 50 miles from Delhi, very heavy firing heard about the 9th and 10th.

Cashmere troops arrived in good order at Delhi on the 8th.

Outbreak at Murree.

All quiet in Punjab, excepting a petty local disturbance at Murree caused by plundering villagers.

Delhi expected to fall on 12th.

W. M.

## LI.

AGRA, *12th Sept.* 1857.

MY DEAR SHERER,—Thank Gen[l] Havelock for his note to me of the 9th, which with that for Col. Cotton reached this morning.

Events at Delhi.

The enclosed printed slips gave all our news from the West. I add the following from Lieut[t] Greathed's letter of the 6th:

Account of Baird Smith, R.E. Alec Taylor, R.E. Stewart, Genesti, Lindsay, Carnegy, R.E's.

"Baird Smith is a great invalid, living on medicine by whose aid he bears up against his work capitally. This is limited however to polishing the plans, schemes, and arrangements of Captain Taylor, a most capital officer, of great military capabilities. We have several such men. Several Engineer officers are *hors de combat* from sickness, as Stewart, Genesti, Lindsay, Carnegy. All who could possibly quit their beds were eager to be at their posts in the trenches."

Greathed brothers.

All details I think will be found in the printed paper. Greathed in his letter of the 8th says of his two brothers in the 8[th] and (blank), they do not return to Camp till the siege is over.

We are eagerly looking out for more news, but must not expect to hear of the final event for a couple of days yet.

Indore and Gwalior Mutineers.

I enclose a copy of my letter of Saturday about the Indore and Gwalior troops. We have intercepted letters from Gwalior to Delhi, which leave little doubt of the intention of the Contingent to move on the dix-huitieme jour of this month.

They seemed fixed in their determination to form a junction with the Indore Force at Dholepore, and then, after taking Agra, moving to Delhi. But we trust that long before all this can be effected, we shall be relieved by a strong column from Delhi.

Operations at Delhi.

We have messengers from Gwalior up to the morning of the 11th, who confirm the account of the differences between Scindia and the Contingent, and add that each party had guns out against the other. The Mutineers demanded carriage and 25 lacs of rupees; the Maharajah declined the carriage, but said he would give 5 lacs. These Mutineers look on the treasure of the Residency (?) chest as their own, and it is this I suppose Scindia is prepared to give up under this pressure.—Yours truly,

Scindia's attitude.

W. MUIR.

J. W. SHERER, ESQ[RE].

All well at Hattrass. About Wulleedad Khan, another report is that he had gone out with a Force towards Golasti. The present demonstration is however undoubtedly having a good effect.

## LII.

AGRA, 12*th Sept.* 1857.

MY DEAR SHERER,—I enclose a printed slip of the news of the 9th from Delhi. Letters of the 10th have come in to-day, but I fear the proof will not be ready before evening, and I therefore, in order to secure for the Governor-General the earliest information of the progress of events, note the following particulars.

Operations at Delhi.

Greathed encloses copy of a letter from Gen[l] Wilson to Sir J. Lawrence, dated 10th instant. In it he says: "Our advance battery, No. I. four 24-pounders and six 18-pounders, have done good service against the Shah and Cashmere Bastions, the former of which is much battered. A battery of 18 heavy guns in front of Ludlow Castle, and one for 10 heavy mortars, were armed last night, but contrary to my advice the Engineers have objected to their opening fire until they complete another battery on the left rear of Smith's house (the Custom House), which they expect to complete to-night; but I doubt if it will be sufficiently completed to enable the guns to be put in. This will cause delay, which is very vexatious."

Letter from General Wilson.

Battery at Ludlow Castle;

At Custom House.

"The rebels made a sortie upon these batteries about an

Operations at Delhi.

Coke's Regiment.

hour and a half ago, but were quickly driven in again with loss. Coke's men made a rush at them. There is no restraining these men, or making them keep cover on such occasions. It had however a very good effect. All our men are in excellent heart and spirits, and enter into the business *con amore*. They all work most readily and cheerfully in the trenches, natives as well as Europeans. I regret however to say that my hospitals are filled with men prostrated with fever; I have nearly 2500 sick and wounded."

Koodsia Bagh.

Greathed himself writes: "The progress of the operations has been a little retarded by the discovery that the Koodsia Bagh was not suited for a breaching Battery against the Water Bastion. There were obstacles in the way of the guns that were not known of, so a spot had to be selected farther on, within 180 yards of the wall. This is rather an audacious move, but it will be successful, and the bombardment will commence to-morrow morning, whether the Battery be completed or not.

Moree Bastion.

The battering of the Moree (Bastion) continued all yesterday, and still goes on, and salvos are fired into it, which tear it to pieces; some gunners still work a gun or two on the bastion, but their fire is wild and merely out of bravado. They tried rockets again last evening from the walls; they did no damage.

Casualties at Delhi.

"The actual number of casualties on the 8th were 18 killed and 57 wounded. Yesterday the number is said to be under 10, and no officer. To-day Eaton (Rifles), Randall (Coke's), Murray (Eng[rs]) have been wounded.

Eaton (Rifles), Randall (of Coke's Regiment), Murray (R.E.).

"I do not see any indication of a flight. There is at present some bewilderment at the nature of our attack, but the full effect has not been developed.

Goojurs.

"The Goojurs of Meerut and Mozaffernugur are becoming very troublesome, and intercept the post between Meerut and the Camp, but these smaller considerations must give way for a little to the greater aim."

Anson, letters quoted from.

Anson (Lancers) writes: "The working and covering parties have been most zealous and assiduous, and have elicited a complimentary order from Gen[l] Wilson. The place, Delhi, will certainly fall by the 15th, if not sooner. Poor Hildebrand had his head nearly taken off by a 3-p[der] from the walls. The enemy's fire is not destructive, for they fire without aim or tangible object. They say Sunday 13th will be the day of dire retribution. Bull-dogs en avant, and looting gentry behind. Thermometer 96° now at noon."

Hildebrand killed.

Dickens, letter from.

Capt[n] Dickens writes that he has "been in Camp since the 2nd, and is equipping a Flying Column, which will start in pursuit directly Delhi falls. He says the Cashmere and Moree Bastions have been much damaged. On the former the heavy guns had been dismounted. The Moree still occasionally fires a gun, but it is few and far between." Operations at Delhi. — Cashmere Bastion. Moree Bastion.

"The firing is incessant at present, a great deal of musketry is going on."

"Day before yesterday, Pandy made a feeble attack on our right, which ended in the usual result, utter discomfiture. He has light guns out in the direction of Kishen Gunge, endeavouring to enfilade our right and advanced Batteries; but they don't do much harm.

"The Cashmere Levies made their appearance on the 8th. They are not bad-looking Irregulars, but have a downcast, dissatisfied look about them. Cashmere levies.

"On the 8th we had an explosion in Camp of waggon with loose ammunition and five shells. It killed 6 drivers and wounded 3 Europeans. Yesterday our casualties were fewer, 4 or 5 in all. It is surprising that with so much firing the loss is so small. Everything shows we are approaching the end of the last act, and that Pandy's reign is coming rapidly to an end. Strange to say he does not even molest us in constructing batteries. He volleys away in feeble style with musketry, which does little harm. Casualties.

"I believe our column will make its way down to Agra. I fancy it depends upon which direction the rascals take."

You may fancy with what earnestness all eyes are now looking out for Cossids from Delhi. Indeed the safety of (blank)[1] greatly depends on the speedy termination of the business.

Daily information and messengers from Gwalior confirm the intelligence that the Contingent keeps to its determination of marching on the dix-huitieme de ce mois ci. Gwalior Contingent.

They also keep to their plan of intending to attack Agra first, after meeting with the Indore men. But long before they can take any effective steps, we look for the moveable column or flying brigade to come in sight. Indore troops.

Hathrass party all right.

Colonel Cotton projects an attack on some refractious villages to-morrow morning. He is admirably active and decisive in all his movements. General Cotton.

The presence of the Indore troops at Dholepore disturbs our frontier to the south and west, and has to a great extent

[1] Probably "Agra."—W. M.

unsettled all the Mofussil arrangements of Thannahs and Tehseels in that direction which had been so successfully restored and maintained.—Yours, etc. (S[d]) W. MUIR.

J. W. SHERER, ESQ.,
Collector and Magistrate, Cawnpore.

Scindia and the Contingent.

*P.S.*—It seems that Scindia and the Contingent had an altercation on the 9th and each had out their guns; it is probable that Scindia under pressure of the Contingent has agreed to furnish carriage.

Defeat of the Marwar army. Joudhpore Mutineers. Lieutenant Heathcott. General Lawrence.

A letter has just come in from General Lawrence, dated Beawr 10th September, who reports the discomfiture of the Marwar Army said to be 3 or 4000 strong, by the Joudhpoor Mutineers near Mhow, where they were signally surprised and defeated with the loss of their Commander-in-chief Arrar Lyl (*sic*) Killadar and others and all their guns (8), tents, etc. Lieut. Heathcott,[1] Dy. Asst: Qr: Mr: General, escaped from their camp with difficulty. General Lawrence was to march on Awa that night and expected to reach it in four days; and hoped, if they only gave him an opportunity, to settle them. He had sent for 2 more guns and 50 of H.M. 83[d].

. . . . . . . . .

Alexander. Bijnore. Bareilly. Furreedpore. Rampore Nawab. Mahommedans. Saugor. Khan Buhadoor Khan.

A letter from Nainee Tal dated September 6th has just come in from Alexander, who attributes the defeat of the Hindoos after their first success in Bijnore to want of combination on their part. He attributes their failure at Bareilly to the same cause. There too they had obtained a victory at Furreedpore, but, not being supported by the help they expected from Rampoor and Budaon, they had to retreat to Shahjehanpoor. "I have only learned (?) this to-day," says Alexander, "by the mouth of some men who have brought me up Rs. 2000 and 100 Gold Mohurs from Bareilly." Alexander has no anxiety about resources. The Nawab of Rampoor would assist. He adds: "I am now hearing from Mahomedans, so the lesson at Cawnpore has taken effect. I hear 150 of the Irregulars from Saugor had arrived at Bareilly, but undecided yet as to taking service with Khan Buhadoor Khan."

Bareilly Hindoos oppressed.

The Hindoos of Bareilly had suffered great exaction and oppression. They had begun to leave the town in which their houses and property are confiscated.

(Signed) W. MUIR.

[1] This officer was a Lieutenant in the Bombay Army,—Deputy Asst. Qr.-Mr. Genl. in Rajputana.—W. C.

## LIII.

### Telegram to Gov^t of India, from W. Muir.

16 *September* 1857.

Bombardment of Delhi advances rapidly and favourably. Last letters dated 11th inst. Operations at Delhi. Preparations for assault.

Moree and Shah Bastions battered on the 9th and 10th from No. I. Battery.

No. II. Battery, and one of heavy mortars, opened on 11th. Rebel gunners retired, unable to withstand combined direct and vertical fire on Cashmere Bastion, which greatly ruined; shells being thrown into and beyond the main guard.

Evening of 11th or morning of 12th, remaining battery to open fire only 180 yds. from walls and near Koodsia Bagh, and will play on Water Bastion.

Bombardment expected to continue two or three days, and then assault without much loss.

Troops in splendid spirits, native and European working heartily together in trenches.

Rebels do not talk of retreat, but of fortifying an entrenchment near the Magazine.

All quiet in Punjab.

Indore Force still at Dholepore, supposed to be waiting for Contingent.

Pursuing column being formed at Dehli to be commanded by Nicholson, will probably come this way.

## LIV.

Agra, 16 *September* 1857.

My Dear Sherer,—

. . . . . . . .

Greathed writes: "It was certainly an audacious step to erect a battery at such a short distance" (as the one near the Koodsia Bagh, only 180 yards from the wall), "without first destroying the defences. The whole plan is an audacious one suited to the occasion, but contrary to rule. Baird Smith is cool, clear, and determined, and he has good aids in Taylor [1] and my brother." Delhi operations. Baird Smith. Alec Taylor. Greathed.

"Dunlop writes in good spirits from Meerut. The bands Dunlop.

[1] Now General Sir Alec Taylor.—W. C.

that were to have attacked Sirdana have been driven back by the Police."

In reply to letters which I wrote on the 5th and 6th stating our position with reference to the Indore and Gwalior Mutineers, and submitting for General Wilson's consideration that this was an additional reason, if any were needed, for expediting proceedings with a view to our relief, Greathed writes: "You will see that the pace of operations here can scarcely be quickened. No Force could be inspired with higher zeal."

Spirit of Delhi troops.

Plundering habits of Punjab troops.

Greathed complains of the plundering habits of some of the Punjab troops. "The appointment of prize agents," he says, "will, I hope, prevent an indiscriminate pillage. But the Punjab troops are inveterate plunderers. One of Coke's men shot a "Pandy" yesterday, and a number rushed out to plunder the corpse, and a volley from the City knocked over most of them. There is no restraining these fellows, and the sooner they go back to the frontier when the work is over the better. The Guides Infantry have only 160 left out of 600 who came down. They have been all along on the advanced posts." I hope Greathed over-estimates the original number.

Coke's Regiment.

Guides Corps.

Scindia's action.

Things Southwards remain very much as before. The Contingent are getting carriage, some say by Scindia's aid, who is glad to get rid of them, Macpherson says, in spite of his prohibition. Anyhow they are getting it together, and may move on, or any day after, the dix-huitieme. We are looking towards Nicholson's pursuing column.

A small demonstration was made this morning some 10 miles on the Gwalior road with Infantry and guns against a bad village. This will do good.—Yours truly,

W. MUIR.

J. W. SHERER, ESQ.

Nawab of Rampore.

*P.S.*—The Nawab of Rampoor has informed Mr. Alexander that rookahs from the King of Delhi have been received by Syad Mahomed Shahee, investing him with the Government, who is reported to have immediately set up Thannas and Tehseelies, and by Goolam Russool Khan, a former Kotwal of Delhi, investing him with the Government of Sumbhul; and a third was addressed to Mujeedooddeen appointing him to Moradabad. There are also intrigues going on at Rampoor on the part of Mehndie Ali Khan's wife, and others.

Reported action of the King of Delhi.

Rohilkhund.

Alexander fears that persons armed with authority from

Delhi may be able to organise dangerous combinations and to become firmly established so as with difficulty hereafter to be eradicated, and he urges this as a reason why an early military movement be made in the Province of Rohilcund.

The longer such a movement is delayed, of course, the evils of the rebellion will the more develop themselves, and the rebels (unless successfully opposed by the Hindoos) gain strength. But the day of reckoning will come soon now, and they will all be swept away. When the column can enter Rohilcund, will, I imagine, a good deal depend on the course of the fugitives from Delhi.

W. MUIR.

## LVI.

FROM AGRA—FROM W. MUIR,

TO CALCUTTA—TO FOREIGN SECRETARY.

AGRA, *17th September*.

BOMBARDMENT kept up steadily on the 12th at Delhi. All the batteries expected to be in play on the 13th, and the assault soon after.

Sickness less. W. MUIR.

## LVII.

AGRA, *18th September* 1857.

MY DEAR SHERER,—The printed slip gives all our Delhi news, and you will see that a native report which bears some signs of likelihood on it has also been printed. There is nothing new in our own position. The Gwalior Contingent was *το μαρχ λαστ νιγτ*, but the heavy rain which has been continued during a great part of to-day may probably have arrested their progress. I give daily accounts of our position and exigencies to Greathed at Delhi, so that General Wilson will no doubt send down a strong column this way so soon as Delhi falls, and the other more immediate military requirements have been met. **Gwalior troops.**

While I write, Greathed's despatch of the 13th has been received; as it will be late for the Press, I give the substance in this letter.

No. III. Battery opened on the evening of the 12th on the Water Bastion and Curtain, with one gun bearing on the causeway to the bridge, and continued in full play. It had to endure a warm musketry fire from the walls, and shot and shell from Selimgurh and from across the river. Captain Fagan, Arty., was **Operations at Delhi. — Progress of siege.**

Operations at Delhi.

killed by a shot through the head in exposing himself above the battery to watch the line of our fire. Greathed pays a high tribute to this admirable and gallant officer, whose fine spirit and daring appear to have been unrivalled. Earle, Arty., and Chancellor, 75th, wounded; loss amongst the men moderate. The centre batteries maintain unceasing fire against the Cashmere Bastion and Curtain, and the mortars play searchingly in its neighbourhood. The right battery still batters the Moree. The enemy have mounted in two places in half-moons on the wall a heavy gun; are persevering in their enfilade from the right and doing their best to defend the place. "It is very arduous work; there is only a partial relief for the Artillery men, and the officers never leave the batteries, which are open to the sky. But the only men who are dispirited are those whom sickness or wounds keep in Camp." The assault, it is said, will take place on the morrow (14th) or the day after, or possibly later. Greathed had had no intelligence from the City since the 11th.

It is remarkable that the Gwalior Durbar news from Delhi have stopped. The confusion in the City may be imagined. The messengers describe that parties leaving the city made up on them on the 14th. There is nothing in the letter to discredit the Hattrass report that the assault may have occurred on the 14th.

Writing at 4 p.m.,[1] Mr. Greathed adds: "The expense Magazine on the Water Bastion has blown up and an ammunition waggon on the right flank has also been destroyed. The battering has been very steady all day. Pray let the enclosure with this letter go on direct to the Governor-General, and forward the enclosed message giving an outline of the news.

W. MUIR.

TO J. W. SHERER, ESQ.

## LIX.

### TELEGRAM TO CALCUTTA.

AGRA, 18 *September* 1857.

LETTERS from Delhi to 14th received after despatch of to-day's report.

Delhi taken by assault.

Assault made on morning of 14th. Ramparts from the Water Bastion to Cabul Moree Gate in our possession, and in City as far as College. Preparations to turn the guns of

[1] *i.e.*, on 13th September.

captured bastions on rest of city and bring up other guns and mortars.

Lahore and other bastions, Palace, and chief part of city, still in enemy's hands, but our position made good.

Bradshaw (52nd), Fitzgerald (75th), killed; wounded numerous, including Nicholson, Col. Campbell (52), Reid (Sirmoor batt^n^).

Chief loss in attempting to reach Jumma Musjid.

W. M.

## LX.

AGRA, *19th September* 1857.

MY DEAR SHERER,—It was late last evening when the Delhi despatches of the 14th, relating the circumstances of our first entrance into the city, came in, and I had only time to give Greathed's bulletin. I now send a printed paper giving Col. Becher's account in addition to Greathed's. I also append the following, which is private, and for communication only to the Governor-General. Colonel Becher.

The programme of proceedings for the assault was, that the whole city should have been occupied from the Water Bastion to the Delhi Gate, including the Jumma Musjid. Complete success was contingent on every column carrying out its part. To the right column under Major Reid was assigned the duty of sweeping Kishengunge, entering the Lahore Gate, and supporting the column that was penetrating the heart of the city from the Cashmere Gate. Reid's party "had the Cashmere troops attached to it, and they were not accustomed to the severe style of fighting they met with, and the gallant Reid was wounded (badly, I am afraid), so that movement failed." The advance on the Jumma Musjid was consequently unsupported. "Under the pilotage of Metcalfe it reached the foot of the Musjid, but had finally to retire." Description of assault. Cashmere column. General Reid wounded.

"The other column," writes Greathed, "under General Nicholson met with great difficulties, and the General is I fear mortally wounded. But a great deal has been gained, and if General Wilson's life is spared, I have no fear for results. Nicholson wounded.

"I have just ridden back from the city to my tent, and speak from personal observation."

Greathed's brother in the Engineers was shot through the arm, but not seriously. "Poor Pogson was lying in the moat with his thigh badly smashed." Greathed. Pogson.

I send a copy of yesterday's message for the telegraph; and

also a supplement:—the latter of course alone to be sent if the former has gone.

Allygurh. The native report in Allygurh yesterday was that we had possession of the City, and that the rebels had retired into the Palace.

W. Muir.

## LXII.

Agra, 19*th Sept.* 1857.

My Dear Sherer,—By this Cossid I send copy of the letter and message I despatched this morning. But I trust before this letter goes, there will be fresh news from Delhi to communicate. We do not get regular letters from you. I do not know what is at fault. Do you not send us daily despatches with our return Cossids? I was sorry to see that Mr. Grant had disapproved Chester's idea of working through Duryao Singh. I knew him well, and the worst part of his career—at least the time when he first began to get rebellious—was when I had charge of the District of Futtehpore in 1845. He *then* offered to go with 500 of his followers to fight with us against the Seikhs, and it would have been an excellent cure for the bad blood of Khaga. We had no need then of such irregular aids, but (unless he has irretrievably compromised himself) I do not see why his aid should not now be taken advantage of in settling Futtehpore. Harington I believe is of the same mind with me in this matter.

Duryao Singh.

As a proof of our recovering influence, I may mention that Rao Bhowaney Singh of Mynpoory has written in here to say that he has still our treasure all safe in his Fort ready to deliver up to us!

Rao Bhowani Singh of Mynpoorie.

5 o'clock p.m. Nothing in from Greathed. Macpherson has his news from the Gwalior Durbar writer at Delhi, from which I gather that a regular advance was made by us on the 15th and 16th, and we were then in possession of the Lahori Gate; that the walls and gates of the Palace were battered; that our entrenchments were working onwards; that the Bareilly Brigade made an attack on our Camp on the heights, but was driven back with fearful loss by our guns charged with grape; and that the rebels contemplated either retirement into the Palace or a desperate stand, or flight. Many of them have already gone. The following is an outline of the news. It will be understood that it is written in a loose manner by the news-writer, and in some places greatly coloured in favour of the rebels; in others accurate—it is, in fact, *the news about Court.*

News as to operations at Delhi from Gwalior news-writer.

Native news-writer's description of the progress of troops inside Delhi after assault.

"15th. 500 Europeans came on to the Lall Diggee (Lord Ellenborough Tank), they attacked the sepoys and drove them into the Fort (Palace), then the sepoys issued in strength from the Fort and drove the Europeans away: the few Europeans who survived fled into the houses of the Bankers. Gates of the City closed and nobody allowed to go out. The Europeans are making their entrenchments on the wall. Great confusion in the city. H.M. ordered great vigilance in the Fort defences. It was reported to H.M. that the Europeans were hiding in the houses of the Bankers and in the Church. H.M. ordered them to be brought out and killed. The rebels have erected an entrenchment with 1 gun on the house of Goolab Chund and Meer Chund, Bankers. No supplies come into the city from Bullubgurh: a purwanuh sent in consequence by H.M. The Bankers have given some lacs of rupees to the English: order issued to imprison them. The entrenchments and batteries of the two contending parties are close up one to the other.

**Bankers assist the British.**

"16th. Wednesday, early in the morning. The English came on to the attack from the Cashmere, Moree, and Lahori Gates, which they found open. They advanced to near the Lal Diggee. Nearly 300 Europeans were killed. (This is the style of their narratives of all our movements.) The rest defeated and driven back to the Church and *Magazine*—(which would thus appear to be in our hands); the Cashmere, Moree, and Lahori Gates are in the hands of the Europeans, and they hold the position of Nahir Shuhadut Khan[1]—Bhawulpoora and Illaka Loharu[2] Durwaza (*i.e.*, the quarter in the vicinity of that gate).

"Two Bareilly Regiments went out to attack the English Camp on the heights, and when they got near forty guns opened upon them with grape, 500 were killed and the rest fled back to the City.

"Of 200 Sowars who came with the 'nubeera' of Doonda Khan, 100 have fled, and a number besides were drowned in endeavouring to cross the Jumna. The Rebel Army holds its position under the Fort, and about the Lal Diggee, and outside the Turkmani and Ajmere Gates (*i.e.* the South Gates)—the King sits concealed in the Palace—the Gates of the Fort are demolished—no supplies come into the City, great scarcity and dearness, the Goojurs plunder the roads which are no longer passable; they kill hundreds of the fugitives horse and foot.

**King's attitude.**

**Goojurs plunder.**

[1] Nahar Saadat Khan, the section of the city which lay on both sides of the canal, from the Cabul Gate to the Queen's Garden. The north side has been cleared away for the railway; the south side is still known by this name.—W. C.

[2] Lahori.

Goolab and Bankers (*sic*) are in confinement. Guards are placed over them. Kotwal reported that the Goojurs had forced H.M.'s Police to abandon the Budderpore[1] Thanah. Hundreds of the inhabitants and sepoys fly. Others say they will yet fight; we shall see. The Europeans are in the Siah Boorj (I understand this to be a bastion by the river side),—400 tumbrils with ammunition have reached the English Camp from the Punjab. The Sikhs at the fight ran away from the English Army towards Thanesur (this may allude to the check sustained by the Cashmere troops?)—*the Europeans are clearing away the houses towards the Lahoree Gate.* The 4 Companies of Sappers sent to mine the Fort of Agra (this had been previously reported) have been plundered and dispersed by the villagers at Pulwul."

In the absence of authentic intelligence, I have thought that the G.-G. would like to have this abstract of the news-writer's statement. I have been used to read over his reports regularly with Macpherson, and the impression on my mind from the whole style of the report is what I have before stated. The Rebels are making a stout resistance, far stouter than we had anticipated, but by the blessing of Divine Providence we are working surely and steadily onwards.

. . . . . . . .

W. MUIR.

## LXIV.

*20th September* 1857. Sunday, 3 p.m.

MY DEAR SHERER,[2]—The above is a copy of my letter of yesterday. No Cossids come in yet from Delhi, or any letters later than the 14th. But the native reports continue favourable. Cocks from Hattrass writes to-day: "To-day's native reports say the whole city is in our possession. Guards on all the Gates, and the rebels shut up in the Palace and Selimghur, where there is one gun left to them. 2000 Pandies are said to have bolted down the Allyghur road with muskets only, no guns; they have gone to Khoorja most probably. The Raja of Bulubghur has sent an English address for the Governor-General protesting friendship, etc., which is also significant."

**Native reports of fall of Delhi received at Agra.**

Imdad Ally, Deputy Collector, writes a roobakaree from Muttra, saying that his messenger, who left Delhi on Monday, reported that we had gained possession of the Church in the

[1] Badarpur is still a police station, eleven miles from the Delhi Gate on the Agra road, half-way to Balabgarh.—W. C.

[2] In the handwriting of Dr. Farquhar.

City; on Tuesday we got on to the Ellenborough Tank; on Wednesday and Thursday the (whole) city was carried by assault. He says he has this from messengers too numerous to specify, and he adds that the Company's rule was re-established by proclamation on Wednesday. On the strength of this, Imdad Ally has proclaimed the fall of Delhi in Muttra.

We must not of course be too credulous in receiving native reports. This is the same Imdad Ally whose over-sanguine report led us to believe that Delhi had fallen in the middle of June. Still, the reports are from such various quarters, and all converge to the same conclusion so closely and naturally, that they afford a fair ground of confidence. They also bear out the statement of the Delhi Gwalior news-writer.

Something more certain may come in before the evening. Meanwhile I think it right to send off this, as every step of these momentous proceedings must be watched with intense anxiety by the Government.

I append a short additional message, which please send by telegraph, and this by post to the Governor-General.

W. MUIR.

## LXV.

### MESSAGE TO GOVT OF INDIA.

No Cossid yet from Delhi later than 14th, but native reports agree as to our progress in gaining possession of the City and the continued flight of the rebels from it.

## LXVI.

AGRA, 21 *September* 1857. 1 p.m.

MY DEAR SHERER,—After a weary suspense of two days, without direct news, intelligence dated the 15th came *via* Jyepore this forenoon, and subsequently Greathed's regular despatch to my address of the 15th arrived, and a little time ago a further one of the 16th. The delay is occasioned by the infested state of the roads, Goojurs and Mewatties obstructing the progress of travellers. The news is highly satisfactory, and bears out in almost all respects that which I have for these two days ventured to give from native sources. The report of the 15th is in the Press; I have printed it almost entire, so it need not be repeated here, as I hope to get a copy of the proof in time to send. Keith Young is the writer of the letter in the Extra from "Head Quarters." I add the following from his letter, which has been omitted from publication.

Goojurs and Mewattis infest roads.

Description of assault of Delhi.

"The attack yesterday was in three columns with a reserve column; and another strong column under Reid of the Goorkas

Reid's column.

was to have cleared out the suburbs of Kishengunge and marched into the City by the Lahore Gate. But this movement was unfortunately an entire failure, owing to the cowardice of the

Cashmere Contingent.

Cashmere Contingent which formed part of the column. They fled disgracefully on the first round from the enemy's guns, leaving three of their own. Had it not been for this contretemps we should in all probability have been in entire possession of the City, as the enemy were all ready for a bolt; but their success outside gave them heart to hold on at the Lahore Gate, and Reid being unable to advance as was intended, our other columns were unable to push on so far as was intended."

So much for preceding operations—now for our advance, and

Capture of Magazine.

capture of the Magazine on the 16th. Writing on that day, Greathed says: "I reported yesterday that a battery had been opened from the College Garden against the Magazine. The breach was completed during the night, and this morning the Magazine was carried with the loss of three men wounded, the enemy abandoning the post as soon as the column appeared over the crest of the breach. One hundred and twenty pieces of heavy ordnance and a vast supply of shot and shell were found in it. A battery is now being constructed at the Palace end of the Magazine; and the embrasures of battery in the College Garden are altered so that the guns may bear on Selimgurh and on the Palace. A great number of dead Pandies in various states of decomposition were found in and about the Magazine. Mortars will now play from the Magazine into the Palace.

Remaining opposition of native force.

"The capture of this important post has secured our possession of that portion of the town. The chief annoyance now is from musketry from the Palace walls, from a light gun that moves about the foot of the Palace walls, and from Selimgurh.

Occupation of part of the town.

"The road from the Cashmere to the Cabul Gate is now quite safe; that quarter of the town up to the street leading from the Cashmere Bastion to the Jumma Musjid is entirely evacuated by the inhabitants. Some few old women are found here and there, and are treated kindly by our men; there is only one instance of a woman having been killed, and that was by accident.

"The Force at the Cabul Gate have extended their occupation along the Canal to the point where the road leads from the direction of the Palace to the Lahore Gate, and their outposts are in communication with the outposts from the Magazine side. The troops are now more collected and under better control.

They get their rations cooked on the spot, and they are being reinforced by recovered men from Hospital. The 52[d] were rejoined by 25 men to-day. The enemy's force in Kishengunge made a reconnaissance on the right flank of our Camp yesterday to ascertain apparently the strength left to defend Camp. Finding the picket posts all occupied they retreated, and the camp has remained unmolested." (This is perhaps the Gwalior news-writer's attack of the Bareilly Brigade.) "It is said they are now evacuating Kishengunge. It is impossible to get information from the City. The enemy's cavalry cut off communication outside the town to the right, and no messenger can penetrate from the side in our possession. It is believed the troops are deserting the City, but the Palace is still strongly occupied."

Enemy advance on camp.

Palace still occupied.

Greathed then refers to a requisition of Major Macpherson on General Wilson to send down 500 Sikh horse. The reply, as might have been expected, is that none can be spared till the capture of Delhi is complete.

"The most critical period," Greathed adds, "has, I hope and think, passed, but you will have seen that it has been hard work, and the safety of the Camp was much compromised by the failure of the attack on Kishengunge on the 14th. The Jummoo troops were to take a part in that operation, but they broke and fled, and left four of their guns in the hands of the enemy. This exposed the flank of Major Reid's line and rendered success impossible, but I have not heard about them since. It was this failure that compelled Colonel Campbell's column to retire from the Jumma Musjid, for Major Reid's column was to have entered by the Lahore Gate and supported it.

Major Reid's column.

Colonel Campbell's column.

"General Nicholson's column reached the Lahore Bastion, but their ammunition failed and they could not hold it, and had to fall back on the Cabul Gate.

General Nicholson's column.

"The Cavalry and H.A. (Major Tombs' troop and part of another) were exposed to a very heavy fire from the walls and from the enemy's enfilading battery in Teleewara, while endeavouring to assist the movement in Kishengunge. They bore it most nobly, and succeeded in spiking the guns in battery. Major Tombs lost half his men killed and wounded, and the Cavalry suffered heavily.

Cavalry and Horse Artillery.

Major Tombs.

"Baird Smith has sprained one of his limbs badly by a fall from his horse. Lt. Taylor is the Director of the Engineer Department. We all look to the complete occupation of the City and Palace as a certainty.

Baird Smith, R.E.

Alec Taylor, R.E.

"Metcalfe's conduct on the 14th is highly praised. He entered after the explosion, through the Cashmere Gate, with

Metcalfe.

Colonel Campbell's column, and guided it up to the Jumma Musjid. It was desperate work, and I was thankful when I saw him return in safety."

Officers wounded. List of Officers wounded. Greathed says he is afraid it is not quite complete.

STAFF.—Brigadier Nicholson. Capt. Anson, A.D.C.

ENGINEERS.—Lts. Greathed, Salkeld, Maunsell, Home, Pemberton, Medley.

ARTILLERY.—Lts. Lindsay and Elliot.

CAVALRY.—Lt. Cuppage.

*H.M. 8th Foot.*—Major Brooke, Major Baines, Lts. Pogson and Stebbings.

*H.M. 52d.*—Col. Campbell, Capts. Bailey and Atkinson.

*H.M. 60th.*—Lts. Curtis and Waters.

*H.M. 61st.*—Col. Deacon.

*H.M. 75th.*—Col. Herbert (slightly), Lt. Armstrong.

*1st E.B.F.*—Capt. Greville, Lts. Wemyss, Owen, and Lambert, Speke, Caulfield (3rd N.I.), Grayden (last three doing duty with 1st Fusiliers).

*2nd E.B.F.*—Capt. Hay (60 N.I.), Lt. Elderton.

SIRMOOR BATTALION.—Major Reid, Capt. Boisragon.

1ST PUNJAUB INFANTRY.—Lieuts. Nicholson and Gambier (38 N.I.), and Gustavinski.

Evacuation of Kishengunj. As a P.S., Greathed adds: "Kishengunge has been evacuated. The enemy left 4 heavy guns and mortars which are being brought into Camp."

Captain O. H. St. G. Anson. *Capt. Anson of the Lancers* writes [1] on the 16th: "We are now inside the walls, pounding away at Selimgurh and the interior defences. There is a good deal of musketry fire going on from houses and the tops of houses, and now and then a round shot and shrapnel play amongst our devoted Infantry, who, aided by the Artillery, are working their way solidly on to the occupation of the vast city. We hold now all our side of the Canal except the Lahore Gate (which will probably fall in the course of the day). The Magazine was taken this morning with a dash and cheer, the latter of which carried such terror to the hearts of the Pandies that they dropped their *lighted* port fires, leaving their *loaded* guns an easy prey to us. One hundred and twenty-five guns besides a vast amount of ammunition fell into our hands. The King is in the Jumma Musjid, determined to die with his fanatics." (Other reports say he is in the Palace, which is likeliest.)

Capture of Magazine.

King of Delhi.

[1] To Mr. Muir.—W. M.

"We have met with considerable opposition, principally in consequence of the repulse that our force under Major Reid sustained in attacking the suburb Kishengunge on our extreme right. Reid hoped to effect an absolute surprise, but found the enemy too strongly posted for him. The Cashmerees lost their 4 guns, and our small force of Europeans was dreadfully cut up; the 1st B.E. Fusiliers being almost annihilated. General Nicholson fell grievously wounded, while trying to infuse the necessary amount of courage into his men to induce them to proceed to the attack of the Lahore Bastion. He at first would not allow himself to be removed off the field—saying that no soldier ought to retreat—but a sergeant's party carried him off, and he was only just alive when he reached camp; he has however since rallied, and is doing as well as can be expected. **Major Reid's column.** **Cashmeree troops.** **1st B. E. Fusiliers.** **General Nicholson wounded.**

"While the Infantry was taking the walls, the Lancers and other Cavalry marched down outside, offering themselves as a target to the enemy to draw off their fire from the Infantry, and suffered grievously in consequence, between 40 and 50 being wounded, and 8 officers' chargers hit.

"Poor Wilson is done up for the nonce; he can hardly stand —overcome as he is by nervous debility. **General Wilson.**

"We are going to strike our Camp to the Delhi side of the ridge. Mrs. Tytler, the only lady in Camp, is making herself most useful in nursing the sick.

"In *two* days we expect to have the City. The Engineers suffered much. Out of the party of three that applied the powder bags to the Cashmere Gate, the officer only escaped, badly wounded. The enemy had loop-holed the door, and the sergeant had only time to fix the bag and say '*I have lighted it*' when he was shot dead. **Cashmere Gate blown in.**

"You cannot imagine the hot burning grievous toil our troops have endured during the last week. Officers and men return from the batteries quite shrivelled up, and as brown as berries." **Hard work by troops.**

He adds: "I have been on duty for the last 50 hours."

Cocks, writing from Hattrass, sends the deposition of a man who had been in Delhi on Friday and who appeared trustworthy. "The whole of Delhi," this man assured Cocks, "seems to have been in our hands excepting the Fort; batteries having been erected at the Jumma Musjid, the dak bungalow, and the Chandnee Chouk." The man seems to be depended on, and had brought a letter to a respectable Sahookar here. **A. H. Cocks.**

Cocks adds with great truth: "It is strange how difficult it is to get the οἱ πολλοι to believe anything favourable to our cause; and how they swallow such ridiculous reports as are spread by the rebels. *In fact this Mutiny has been spread by a clever system of unlimited lying* and working upon the timidity of the people."

Mutiny spread by false reports.

Gwalior troops.

Troops at Gwalior seem again to be, after much altercation, subservient for the time to Scindia, and may not march till after the Dasserah. The Indore men still at Dholepore. We shall see the effect of the Delhi news on them.

Indore troops.

I send a brief message for the telegraph, this letter to be forwarded as usual by post to the Governor-General.

W. MUIR.

J. W. SHERER, ESQ.

## LXVIII.

AGRA, 22 *Sept.* Morning.

MY DEAR SHERER,—

. . . . . . .

As illustrating the "system of unlimited lying" practised by our opponents, I may mention that two days ago Cocks intercepted a proclamation sent for publication throughout the country by Ghous Mahomed, stating that on the 14th and 15th we had been completely routed, that the King's Forces were now in complete possession of our Camp on the heights, and that the "Infidels" were exterminated. It is by such deliberate and prodigious falsehoods that the simple population have been misled. More, I hope, during the course of the day.

A. H. Cocks.

Ghous Mahomed.

False rumours spread by natives.

W. MUIR.

## LXIX.

AGRA, 22 *Sept.* 1857. 4 p.m.

MY DEAR SHERER,—No letter has yet come in from Delhi, so I send another copy of yesterday's, in case any mischance has occurred to those already sent.

There is little to add from here, excepting as to the Gwalior and Indore troops; of the former we hear continued favourable accounts. They appear to be all for the present amenable to Scindia's influence, and therefore are not likely to move before the Dasserah. The Fifth Regiment and the Cavalry are said to have declared even that they would fight for the Maharajah against the others. Meanwhile they are collecting bullocks, etc., to be ready for a start. But the news of Delhi will interfere no doubt with their plans. The Indore men, though they have

Gwalior troops.

Indore troops.

no idea yet of the state of things at Delhi (at least, they had not up to a day or two ago), yet begin to shake. They seized our Tehsildar and Thannadhar in Kheyragurh down in their direction. They got away and have come in. They describe their condition as very wretched. Many of the Sowars finding no provisions or means of feeding their horses at Dholepore, are going back to Gwalior.

The party that passed lately through to Gwalior from Delhi as an escort to Captain Jehangeer and a Shahzada excited an uneasy apprehension amongst them, that all was not going on prosperously at Delhi. They begin to repent their position, and evinced an ill-concealed desire for restoration to the favour of Europeans.

Captain Jehangeer.

If any such overtures do come they will of course be met by Mr. Reade in the spirit of the Governor-General's resolution. As yet they have not assumed any tangible shape of any sort.

After writing the above, a letter from the Rajah of Bullubgurh was received, praying for orders to spare his buildings in the City. The King, he says, and his servants are alone in the Fort. The Army outside. The City in great distress.

Rajah of Bullubgurh.

Major Macpherson's news-writer's report has also come in, and I give an outline of it in the absence of our official record. (Translation):—

"On the 17th the King held a Durbar, and a great many officers of the Army were presented. They urged that numbers of their Force were running away; and begged that H.M. would make arrangements for the security of the Fort. H.M. replied: 'Attend you to the protection of the people, the security of the Fort will be my care.' The officers retired in wrath.

Position of the King at Delhi, 17th May 1857.

"100 Cavalry and 500 sepoys were observed flying across the bridge. H.M. ordered them to be brought back. When they had come into the Royal presence H.M. thus addressed them: 'You have introduced confusion into this City, and turned the whole country upside down, and now you are running off! This shall not be. Fight it out as best you can with the European soldiers;' so they were obliged to encamp under the walls of the Fort.

"The European Force holds half the City—the environs of the Canal, the Lahore Gate, and *the Chandnee Chauk*. The Rebel Force holds the quarter of the Hauz Cazee; the Khass Bazar,[1] the space outside the Palace, and Duryao Gunge; the English

Position of European force inside Delhi.

Khass Bazar.

[1] Khass Bazar was the main street which led from the Delhi Gate of the Fort to the Jumma Musjid. After the Mutiny it was entirely cleared away to make the esplanade.—W. C.

camp is as before, on the ridge. The ryots are fleeing in all directions. Those that remain conceal themselves in their houses—having provided themselves with a week's supplies—and do not venture out. Doors of the Fort and City shut. H.M. is in the Fort. The confusion in the City is beyond description. The entrenchments of the English extend from near the Fort to the Lahore Gate. The general belief is that in 2 or 3 days—or a week at most—the City and the Fort will be entirely carried.

Dissensions between Hindoos and Mahommedans.

"There is great contention between the Hindoos and Mahommedans. The latter accuse the former of not assisting them in the battles with the English.

Rajah of Patiala.

"It is reported that the English will put the King to death, and give the throne and the country to the Raja of Pattiala. This rumour is a cause of grief to the King; and the Shahzadas, hearing it, are flying from the Fort.

Bankers in Delhi.

"The Europeans have occupied 2 or 3 of the large Bankers' houses and made excellent arrangements for the protection of the people, so that no Sepoy or King's servant can molest them. Two or three of the great Bankers are still in confinement in the Palace, but it is said they will be soon released. The Sepoys are committing great excesses among the inhabitants.

"The European Army is in great strength, and advances with fearful force.

Gwalior and Indore troops.

"Three regiments of Sepoys and 1000 Cavalry have gone off towards Mewat and Bullubgurh, in the direction of Agra. Day and night they desert. The Gwalior and Indore troops have not yet made their appearance. When they arrive, we shall see *what* they can effect."

King of Delhi.

Is not this a vivid picture of confusion and distress? The wretched King! If he had only thought of it before.

W. Muir.

## LXX.

### Telegraphic Message—W. Muir to Foreign Secretary.

No letters received to-day.

A khureeta from Raja of Bullubgurh and the Gwalior news-writer's report have come in, both dated 17th. They concur in showing that our position advances, and that of the enemy becomes weaker. Rebels continue to fly in great numbers. Intense confusion in Palace and City.

W. Muir.

## LXXI.

AGRA, 23 *September* 1857. 3 p.m.

MY DEAR SHERER,—Our Delhi letters of the 17th did not come in till this afternoon. They confirm my account of yesterday, excepting that the Lahore Gate was still held on that date by the enemy. It was likely to be taken the next day. We were advancing steadily: our front pickets were in occupation of the Bank and the Begum's garden, and the communications between the right and the left are firmly established.

**Progress of operations at Delhi in occupying the city.**

"Kishengunge and all the suburbs," Mr. Greathed writes, "were evacuated yesterday. The enemy left their heavy guns in battery, and they have been brought in. This movement has improved our position very much; for the Camp—comprising all the sick and wounded, the treasure chest, provisions, and ammunition—was for two days exposed to great danger. We found in Kishengunge the bodies of two officers and many soldiers (plusieurs soldats) killed and left on the field on the 14th." The two last sentences are in French, and have been omitted in publication. I conclude he refers to *European* soldiers.

**Kishengunj.**

"Our batteries," he continues, "in the College Garden and the Magazine are firing shot and shell at Selimgurh and the Palace; 10 mortars play on the latter. No communication from the Palace.

**Artillery fire.**

"The Bareilly Brigade has sent off its baggage under charge of some picked men with light guns, and intend to join it by a forced march. They have taken the Muthra road, and are said to be making for Gwalior. A Cossid, just arrived from Rewarree, says he met about 500 Sepoys yesterday marching towards Jyepore. The numbers of Sepoys found dead in all directions are considerably more than was anticipated. Many must be men who crept into out-of-the-way places and died miserably of their wounds. The King has his own troops and one regiment in the Palace. They keep up a fire of musketry.

**Bareilly Brigade.**

**King's position at Palace.**

"The Lahore Gate and Bastion are still occupied in force by the enemy. An advance will be made on that side to-morrow perhaps. Our entire force in the city to-day—British and Native—is a little under 3000. You will understand that it is very necessary to spare our men. There are not too many of them. At the present moment it is not possible to send troops in pursuit. We bear you in mind. But complete success must first be secured here. The Palace in our hands and Selimgurh fallen, all will be well.

**Lahore Gate.**

**Estimate of British force in the city.**

General Chamberlain. Colonel Seaton. "Genl. Chamberlain is able to return to his duty, though he cannot ride; this is a great assistance. Col. Seaton is chief of the Staff; Genl. Nicholson is a shade better."

General Nicholson. Colonel Becher. There is a letter from Col. Becher, also of the 17th. Its details will be printed, and if in time a proof will be sent with this. He says 150 guns were taken in the Magazine; the small arms had been removed. He confirms the prospect of a forward movement next day. He states the loss on the 14th at above 800 killed and wounded, of whom 50 were officers. Since that date our loss has been trifling.

British loss.

Van Cortlandt. Greathed mentions that Van Cortlandt has routed the Hissar rebels.

Buroti. Shamlee. He mentions a report from Kurnal that the Buroti insurgents (in the Meerut District) had risen on Shamlee (a large town on the Canal between Meerut and Kurnal) "and killed a Sahib and a Tehseeldar —." Since writing the above, a letter has come in from Williams at Meerut. He confirms the attack on Shamlee and murder of the Tehseeldar by a body of some 2000 fanatics from Thannah Bhowan in the Moozuffurnuggur District. Williams has reinforced the Magistrate of Moozuffurnuggur, but he is hardly equal to cope with such a party.

Williams, C.S.

The Detachment at Haupper is all right, and guards Meerut on that side. The Meerut dak *via* Kurnal having been closed by the Shamlee disturbance, they endeavoured to open out a direct line to Delhi via Moradnuggur. Our party employed in this business, consisting chiefly of Pathan horse, killed 40 or 50 of the rebels. They had a hand-to-hand fight in the town. We had one officer—Armstrong—wounded, 1 man killed and 6 wounded. The effect will be good. I enclose for Lord Canning a slip from the papers, giving an account of proceedings at Gwalior. It is not official, but may be relied on, I think, as in the main correct.

Armstrong.

Macpherson (Major C.). Macpherson has news of a satisfactory character up to the 17th. After describing the altercation between the M. Rajah and the Contingent—the guns being drawn out on both sides with port-fires lighted for three days, and the M.R. having brought them to terms by stopping their supplies—the writer states that an arrangement was come to between them. Accordingly the Durbar sent them 1000 bullocks, 200 carts, 6 elephants, and 50 camels, and desired them to march at once. On the 15th instant the 1st and 2nd Regiments and the Artillery sent to say that they had not killed any of their

News from Gwalior.

officers, and entreated H.H. to forgive them; if he would allow them to stay, that they would obey his orders, and go where he desired them. Besides, all the Sepoys—inhabitants of the Gwalior Territory—declared that they would not join the Poorbeeas; that they were the M. Rajah's subjects, and if he would take them into his service they would depart to their homes. The Mutineers are also at variance among themselves, both as to the Magazine and the route which they should take.

Gwalior insurgents entreat Scindia's forgiveness.

Please send on as usual to the Governor-General; on the reverse is a telegraph message.

W. MUIR.

J. W. SHERER, ESQ., Cawnpore.

I send it on separate sheet.

## LXXIII.

*AGRA, 24th September* 1857.

MY DEAR SHERER,—This morning the despatches of the 18th and 19th came in nearly together. The letter of the 18th is from Greathed; that of the 19th from Colonel Becher, who I regret states that Greathed was labouring under a severe attack of Cholera, and "in a very precarious state." We shall greatly miss his clear and comprehensive reports for a time at least. His illness is also embarrassing, as there is no one else on the spot of qualification and standing sufficient to be invested with the office of Agent.

Greathed, B.C.S., seized with cholera.

Before I proceed to particulars, I mention in brief that the news is all good. We had moved forward to the "Burn" Bastion, which is as good as taking the Lahore Gate, and were clearly in possession up to the Chouk.

Burn Bastion.

The following is from Greathed's letter of the 18th: "An attempt was made this morning to advance our post on the right, and to occupy the Lahore Gate; but there were unexpected obstacles in the way, and it did not succeed. The troops withdrew with trifling loss, and brought away their wounded. Another plan will now be tried.

"The fire of Selimgurh is subdued and the Palace is continuously shelled. The enemy have at present no means of annoyance, excepting by means of musketry from the neighbourhood of the Bank. They continue to occupy the Lahore and Ajmere Bastions and Duryao Gunge.

Enemy's position in city.

"The population have abandoned the houses within our lines. A great number of women, old men, and children have been

Civil population.

passed out in safety. General Wilson has given orders for all men without arms, or who lay down their arms, to be allowed to pass into the country (I conclude the order applies to Citizens only, and not to Sepoys). But few adult males venture near the pickets, and as two instances have occurred of stray soldiers being cut down by citizens it would be difficult to carry out the order. Our troops are a good deal fatigued. It happens, un-

Drunkenness among the British troops.

fortunately, that there is much beer and brandy in the shops, and in spite of all precautions drunkenness cannot be repressed. Our position is well sustained. But it is to be regretted that the number of our troops is very small for the capture of such a City, and that we cannot proceed very rapidly."

Hence we cannot rely upon the advance of a moveable column at the present moment. This is vexatious. But our losses prove the undertaking to have been a most arduous one.

Estimate of killed and wounded.

They reckon 59 officers killed and wounded, and nearly 1000 men. (The last five sentences were in French.)

Captured ordance.

Greathed encloses a list of captured Ordnance; this will go in a printed form. Remarking on it he says: "You will perceive the Bastions were heavily armed. The shot and shell are in such vast quantities that the consumption by the enemy appears to have made no impression on the stock."

Pogson's death.

He mentions Pogson's death.

I have printed almost the whole of Becher's letter. We

Progress of operations in the city.

made good progress on the 19th. We have moved forward our left posts, *i.e.* those in the direction of the Palace, so as to embrace the dense buildings intervening between our former front and the Chandnee Chouk. On our right we have taken the Burn Bastion, which commands the Lahore Gate. We have thus uncontested possession of the Northern half of the city to the Chouk.

General Nicholson.

"Poor General Nicholson," Becher writes, "is very ill, and the greatest fears are entertained of his recovery. I fear there is little hope." This is a grievous misfortune.

We have consentaneous accounts from all directions that an

Fugitives from the city.

immense body of the fugitive force is moving down the right bank of the Jumna. Other parties are moving off eastwards to Rohilkhund in a broken state. But this force would seem to be in a formed and somewhat orderly condition.

Bareilly Brigade.

You will remember that Greathed said the Bareilly Brigade had sent on its baggage with light guns under picked men, with the view of hastily joining it when their position in Delhi was no longer tenable—rushing forth as it were from the edifice about to fall upon them. The advanced guard at any rate was at

Kosee yesterday, and it is probable that the main body are not far behind them. They may thus have evacuated Delhi on the 21st or 22nd. The body that is behind no doubt consists of the remains of the Bareilly Brigade, which Greathed said was preparing to take this direction, and probably also of the Neemuch and Nusseerabad Brigades. We are anxiously watching what course they will take. The most general report is that after passing through Muthra (which is already in a great panic) they will, if possible, form a junction with the Gwalior people; whether they will be inclined to join them in their present state is not at all certain. The party that went there from Delhi 8 or 10 days ago, under "Captain Jehangeer," may have been sent to sound them. Another report is that they will take a circuit and go by Etawah to Oudh. If that had been their object, I should have thought they would have crossed higher up.

At Hattrass the native report is that before the Palace was evacuated the King poisoned himself—likely enough. I add as usual a telegraphic message.

W. Muir.

To J. W. Sherer, Esq.

## LXXV.

Agra, 25 *September*. Morning.

My Dear Sherer,[1]—No fresh news in yet from Delhi. Cocks, from the statement of a man who professed to have been there, believes that up to the 20th we had not obtained occupation of the Palace. The King, the popular rumour went, had diamond poison ready to swallow at the last moment. King of Delhi.

We are however receiving intelligence this morning of the movements of the fugitive Mutineers down the right bank. They appear either to be breaking up to some extent, or to be about to take the line *via* Khoorja to Bareilly.

Salamut Ray, Deputy Collector in the North-western extremity of Allygurh, has collected a body of evidence from eye-witnesses to the following effect. At a ghat (Belochpore)—somewhere between Pulwal on the right bank, and Tuppul and Jewur on the left bank, of the Jumna—a body of 2000 men, Cavalry, Infantry, and camp followers, were effecting a passage. Half had crossed on the 23rd, the remaining half were to cross that night and next morning. Their intention, they said, was to go *via* Jewur and Khoorja to Bareilly. Movements of fugitive Mutineers.

[1] Copied by Lady Muir.—W. C.

Another body of 500 Cavalry and Foot were crossing at a ghat—Gurwaolie,—I believe a little higher up,—and they were to take the same route.

On the other hand, messengers are coming in from Muthra to say that a party of the advanced fugitive Cavalry had actually arrived there yesterday; that an immense mass of troops was behind; and that after staying a short time in Muthra, they were coming on towards Agra.

One can only speculate doubtfully as to probabilities in this case.

If Salamut Ray's account is correct—as it would seem to be—one would expect that the whole force yet retaining any form and organisation, with their guns, would unite in moving, by various ghats for the sake of rapidity—towards Rohilkhund—and there, perhaps in conjunction with Khan Buhadar of Bareilly and the Oudh Mutineers, form themselves into a last rallying-point. If this be the case, then the Mutineers moving on Muthra are likely to cross the Jumna there, and join the rest *via* Allygurh and the Anoopshuhur or Rānighat ferries.

On the other hand, if the force have no one common plan, but is breaking up into parts each with its own object, then the force expected at Muthra may have an eye to Dholepore and Gwalior. They have no doubt already sounded them as to a desire for combination. For the unprovided fugitive force the abundant Magazine at Gwalior would be a treasure beyond all value, and would at once set them up again for offensive operations.

But an amalgamation of this nature must of course depend entirely on the views and wishes of the Contingent itself.

Scindia's Contingent at Gwalior.

The Contingent is still subservient to Scindia. It is said that the common talk among them now is to go to Cawnpore—whither they have had pressing invitations from the Nana to proceed. The Contingent has compromised itself less than any other body of mutinous troops in the country. If a fraction of its least offending members could be brought under the merciful clauses of the Governor-General's Resolution, the whole force might be paralysed, and the Magazine saved from going over to the enemy. The Artillery, in whose charge I imagine the Magazine specially to be, are very submissive to the Maharaja. However, this is a digression.

The fugitive Mutineers from Delhi might join the Dholepore force—but that alone would form but a miserable auxiliary without ammunition.

It might, marching *via* Dholepore, proceed onwards to Etawah, and thence across the Doab to Furruckabad or Oudh.

Yours of the 19th just come in. Many thanks for it. God grant our gallant force a triumphant march on Lucknow, and a joyful day for that heroic band at the Bailey Guard.—Yours very sincerely,

W. MUIR.

## LXXVI.

AGRA, 25 *September* 1857.

MY DEAR SHERER,—No Delhi letter in to-day, but continued reports of the progress of the wave of mutinous forces surging down this bank of the Jumna. A considerable number have reached Muthra. They have given directions for a bridge of boats being constructed across the Jumna. One hundred of their number have crossed in boats already. This looks extremely as if that hypothesis were the right one, which makes them all to design a march towards Bareilly and a stand in that direction. More news will probably come in before I despatch this letter. Movements of Mutineers.

A native messenger who left Delhi on Monday 21st declares that the King has evacuated the Palace and taken refuge in the tomb of Hoomayun. King of Delhi.

From his account the whole place would appear to be in our hands.

By the way, when I mentioned that there was no one at Delhi qualified to take charge of the Office of Agent to Lieut.-Governor, I was under the impression that C. B. Saunders had not been able to proceed as he had been directed to Delhi. He is, I find, on the spot, and is a man of high character and good ability. His standing and experience would not of course entitle him to the permanent post, but he is well fitted to take temporary charge of the Office. C. B. Saunders.

26*th September*, 8 a.m.—Nothing in yet from Delhi. Native letters and reports received *via* Khoorja and Hattrass, as well as the stream downwards of mutinous Sepoys, prove that Delhi must have fallen completely into our hands some days ago. This at least is a fair inference.

From Muthra we have frequent reports by the panic-stricken population. On the afternoon of the 24th, a considerable number, say 4 or 500 Cavalry and Infantry, entered. They bear in their troubled downcast looks the marks of defeat, but as usual they are lawless and oppressive. They expelled our officials. Imdad Ally has wisely concealed himself. They burnt the Cotwalee records and have seized all the boats. They intend to have a Imdad Ally.

bridge thrown across, it is said. The rumour is that they are going to Lucknow. By way of bravado, they say half of their number proceed to Agra and half to Hatrass. It is not likely that they will go near European troops and guns willingly again. But Mr. Reade and Colonel Cotton have wisely determined to make the European detachment fall back to Khundowlee, about 10 or 12 miles from this, and to strengthen them, if we remain unthreatened on this side, by a further detachment and guns.

Gobind Singh, Talookdar.

This is the more necessary as Cocks has sent in news during the night that Gobind Singh, the Talookdar who was holding Allyghur for us, has been surprised there by a body of the fanatics of the district, and obliged to fly—leaving his guns (they must have been some native ones of his own) behind him. It is to be hoped that Gobind Singh will be able to protect Hatrass, which, by our movement in that direction, has hitherto been completely saved from plunder and violence.

Movements of Mutineers.

9 a.m.—The latest intelligence is, some 500 men crossed over at Muthra yesterday evening. A party has also come in this way towards Furra, it is said *en route* to Gwalior—but it may more likely be as a reconnoitring body to see that none of the dreaded European soldiery are upon them.

Send on this.

Moorteza Bakhsh.

I enclose a brief message in continuation. Moorteza Baksh Tehseeldar, in Zilah Futtehpore, has sent a representation through the Commissioner Meerut to say he is clear of any of the rebellious proceedings at Futtehpore, and left with his family for Meerut, where he now is.

Kindly give us a statement of what you know of his conduct in the proceedings. Do you wish him back? The case is before me at the Board—and I have intimated to Government that I would consult you about it.

W. Muir.

## LXXVIII.

**Agra, *26th September* 1857. Evening.**

My Dear Sherer,[1]—Still no letters from Delhi: it is now a week since the date of our last. It is probable that Greathed's illness, who had the business of arranging for the despatch of Cossids in his hands, and the multitude of other concerns to be attended to by all our people on the complete capture of Delhi, may have interfered with the regularity of the correspondence.

[1] Copied by W. Lowe.—W. M.

As regards ourselves, there is nothing fresh to say. Our accounts from Muthra are little more than corroborative of what we had before. A great multitude of the fugitives had arrived, and more were arriving, in Muthra; they were crossing at various ghats, and one party as low down as a ghat which would take them *via* Saidabad or Khundowlee and Mynpoory towards Oudh. Notwithstanding their big words, the people had begun to perceive that they were a defeated force, wounded and ill off for arms, etc. Two guns, dragged by bullocks, had arrived, and more were behind.

Movements of fugitive Mutineers.

We have had pretty certain intimation to-day that the Indore force at Dholepore are collecting carriage and contemplate a very early move. They *speak* of coming this way, but it is supposed that they will move *via* Futtehpore Sikri towards Muthra, to join the great body of the Mutineers, and with them proceed towards Oudh. The Maharaja at Gwalior has, we are assured, destroyed all the boats on the Chumbul, so that the Indore troops were in a very awkward position; and their only alternative was to go off *via* Etawah or Muthra; or to stand the chance of being attacked with the Chumbul in their rear. There is a talk by some that a move is projected on Bhurtpore, into the Fort of which the Mutineers are supposed to desire to throw themselves. But I cannot find any confirmation of the idea.

Indore force coming towards Agra or Muthra.

Upon the whole, so far as I can see at present, the universal intention of the Mutineers is to mass themselves either in Bareilly or farther to the eastward, in Oudh.

We have had letters from General Lawrence from Chiliawas dated the 20th. He had had an engagement for three hours with the Joudhpore Legion, without any successful result; but both in this and in an affair at Neembhera, the Bombay troops had shown themselves stable and trustworthy—and this is a matter of sincere congratulation.

General Lawrence.

I give Lawrence's account of his affair: "I left with a force of 5 H.A. guns, and 2 squadrons 1st Bombay Lancers, 200 H.M.'s 83rd, and 250 Mhairwarra Battalion, for Awah, a walled town and fort about 3½ miles from this (Chiliawas). I left Beawr on Monday 14th, marched the first day to Burr—(finding the road through the pass very much cut up by the bad weather we had during this month, which detained me at Beawr for upwards of a week). On Tuesday we moved to Peeplia, Wednesday to Bugree, Thursday to Chaputtia, about 6 miles from Awah. On Friday morning I moved the Force on the direct route to Awah, and pushed forward to about ½ a mile from the town. The

Battle of Awah.

approach was through thickish jungle, in which a few of the enemy's horsemen showed themselves, but speedily retreated before a few of the Lancers.

"Their guns opened fire upon us at about 800 yards and soon got our range pretty accurately. They were placed on the bank of a tank just outside the town, and their fire was kept up for some time. We returned it and forced them to quit their position, and silenced their fire for a time. Their horsemen tried to turn our right flank and threatened our baggage. By a change of position I placed my force between the enemy and our baggage again; and finally retired on this village.

"The whole affair lasted about three hours. As we were weak in Infantry, and I felt that I could not afford to lose any of my Europeans, and the force was inadequate to carry the place by a coup-de-main, I did not bring the Infantry or Cavalry where they could be actively engaged.

"You will be glad to hear *that the Lancers behaved very well,* and I have every reason to be satisfied with them, for they have had a great deal of hard work and irritation, more than half their numbers being daily on picket duties. I am very well pleased with the whole force, officers and men.

"The casualties were trifling, only one artilleryman killed, and 5 or 6 Europeans wounded, with about like number of natives; 2 guns disabled. But I am concerned to state that that excellent political officer, Monck Mason, was killed close to Lawrence's force in attempting to join it. He had pushed in from Pallee, and on reaching the jungle, which his camel could not penetrate, had dismounted, and was making on foot for our force, when some of the Joudhpore Sowars came across his path, and he was killed by 2 shots from them."

Monck Mason killed.

"I was not even aware," says Lawrence, "of his being anywhere in the neighbourhood; he must have been scarcely 300 yards from me at the time. The body has not yet been recovered, but I am endeavouring to get it."

Lawrence feared he would be obliged to return to Beawr, as the European provisions were nearly expended.

Captain Showers' attack on Neembhera.

Showers gives the following account of his attack on Nembhera. "We commenced operations yesterday (19th) about half-past one, but could not enter; the gate attacked found afterwards to have been bricked up—night stopped our operations. A column of assault against another gate was formed before day-break this morning (20th). On moving to the attack we found that the place had been evacuated during the night. The British troops were moved through the town and the British flag hoisted on the public Government Hall. *All the troops behaved admirably.* This affair has pleased them mightily. They crowd round the guns parked in the garden, and say they wish to be taken against Mundessore or anywhere. Our loss: one corporal H.M. 83rd killed in carrying the powder bag, and some 15 or 16 native troops killed and wounded."

Captain (?) Rose, in forwarding this to Nixon, writes: "Success is the usual criterion in such matters, and so far it is all right; but what the effect will be in this part of the country remains to be seen. *The 2nd Bombay Cavalry and 12th Sepoys behaved splendidly*, and I am especially glad of this. The fellows on the wall called out '*deen, deen*,' and tried to make them waver as they advanced to attack, but all they got in return was a shower of musketry." Three of the Cavalry and 9 of the 12th are wounded. Captain Rose adds: "I expect now since the 2nd and 12th have proved they are to be trusted, a force will be sent out from here against them." Bombay troops behave well.

These facts, as evidence of a good and loyal feeling on the part of the Bombay troops in these parts, are of unspeakable value. And we may well presume that troops which *then* proved faithful will, after they know of the actual fall of Dehli, be still more beyond the shadow of a doubt.

Tuesday morning, 27th September, 6.30 a.m. Nothing as yet from Dehli, so I despatch this at once. In all probability we shall be having news during the day.

Our Hatrass force safely retired on Khundowlee, 10 miles off, where it is now encamped.

W. Muir.

J. H. Sherer, Esq.

## LXXX.

Agra, *27th September* 1857.

My Dear Sherer,—At last the joyful news! On the 22nd inst. the British flag waved over the Palace of the Kings of Dehli. Send this and the telegraphic message on quick to the Governor-General. His Lordship is greatly to be congratulated on this grand event. Announces capture of the Palace of the Kings of Delhi.

I give Becher's letter to Nixon verbatim:—

"22nd. All is going on wonderfully well here. The King, the Begum, Zeenut Muhal, are close prisoners, and to-day the Princes Mirza Moghul, Aboo Bucker, and Khizzur Sultan were King and chief Queen prisoners. Three Princes shot by Hodson.

brought in by Hodson from Humaioon's Tomb, and shot at the Dehli Gate. Their bodies are now lying exposed at the Kotwalie, where so many of our poor countrymen were murdered and exposed. A pursuing column under Colonel Greathed of H.M. 8th leaves this to-morrow morning to go in your direction. It consists of 1600 Infantry, 18 guns in 3 troops, and 600 Cavalry. They will soon join you, I trust, and render complete the effects of the fall of this City. The City is a perfect picture of desolation, completely abandoned.

Loot.

"A vast amount of property left behind, which our Native troops are possessing themselves of with great gusto, but with demoralising effect.

"There are a great number of city Budmashes[1] and others collected near Humaioon's Tomb,[2] but it is to be hoped our column will meet them.

Banquet in Diwān-i-Kháss.

"Last night 'Her Majesty the Queen,' proposed by the Conqueror of Dehli, was drunk with all honour in the Deewan Khass by the Headquarter Staff. Never has the old building re-echoed with any sound half so fine. The cheer was taken up by the gallant Goorkhas of the Sirmoor Battalion, who form the General's personal guard."

Sirmoor Battalion.

"All is well in the Punjaub and elsewhere."

God be praised for this glorious termination of this arduous struggle.

W. Muir.

## LXXXI.

## TELEGRAPHIC MESSAGE.

### From W. Muir, Esq., to G. F. Edmonstone, Esq.

Agra, *27th September* 1857. 2 p.m.

An Extra just issued to this effect—

Fall of Delhi Palace announced to Governor-General.

Telegraphic summary of foregoing.

"On the 22nd inst. the Palace of the Kings of Dehli was occupied by British troops, and the capture of the City was complete. *God save the Queen!* A Royal salute is about to be fired from the ramparts of the Fort." A pursuing column about to start this way. King and chief Queen close prisoners. Three of principal Princes shot.

W. Muir.

[1] Bad characters.—W. C.

[2] Some 5 or 6 miles S.E. of Delhi.—W. C.

## LXXXII.

AGRA, *27th September* 1857.

MY DEAR SHERER,—I enclose copy of a letter I sent off an hour or two ago; I now add a few particulars regarding ourselves, or rather the mutinous force that surround us.

From Muthra we have Cossid intelligence, and have caught one camp follower, who gives a complete account of the Mutineers—the following is an outline of the story.

He left Delhi on Tuesday the 22nd at 4 p.m. in company with men of the 44th and 67th Regiments, and the débris of mutinous corps, in all 20 in number, beside Cavalry from Meerut, Neemuch, Bareilly, Nusseerabad, and Oudh. He reckons from 100 to 500 in a regiment, so that there may be some 5000 or 6000 men of the Mutineer army at Muthra. The Cavalry men have their horses, but they are in a wretched condition, and obliged to feed on churru or chopped stubble—2000 are sick and wounded and conveyed in carts. There are 20 H.A. guns, each drawn by six horses; 20 tumbrils with ammunition; and three carts containing barrels of gunpowder. They have 20 of the elephants that left this on the evening of the battle.

**Movements of mutinous troops.**

**Their condition.**

The Sikhs crossed from Delhi in boats for their home in the Punjaub. The force at Muthra intend leaving for Lucknow in 2 or 3 days. They have only one of the old golundazes: all the rest are newly employed on the guns. They have no reserve of cartridges. The above may be of use to Outram and Havelock if these fellows escape the avenging column, which ought, by this time even, to be at their heels.

**Sikhs leave for their homes.**

The Cossid who brought the Delhi news said the bridge was being constructed, but they had a gap of 15 boats, which they could not supply. It is fervently to be hoped that they may not escape Oudhwards with their guns.

**Bridge at Muthra.**

Up to the 25th all was quiet at Gwalior. The Maharaja has certainly taken all the boats away from the ghat to a creek several miles off, where they are guarded by a party with guns. There are now no boats at the ghat. It is said he has also posted a small party of horse and guns at Cheounda, between Gwalior and the Chumbul, to deter the Murar troops from coming this way. The 5th Contingent Regiment has gone over to him, with all the Cavalry. There are about 3000 men in the 4 remaining regiments.

**Affairs at Gwalior.**

The Muthra Mutineers have sent messengers to them to see if there be any chance of a combination with them.

Macpherson has a letter saying that they want to make money of their Magazine. Tantia Sahib, uncle of the Peishwa, had arrived with a purwanah summoning the Murar Force and Captain Jehangeer Khan to go to his aid. All the Poorbeas want to go in that direction.

Tantia Sahib invites Contingent to Cawnpore. Jehangeer Khan.

There is not likely to be any movement there till after the Dussehra. The fall of Delhi will have a further sedative effect. The Dholepore troops are said to have squeezed about a lakh of rupees from the Rana,[1] and to have paid themselves with it. Send this on, please, with the message.

W. MUIR.

## LXXXIII.

TO G. F. EDMONSTONE, ESQ.

FORT AGRA, 27*th September* 1857.

(Supplementary Message)—Some letters from Delhi of 19th to 22nd evidently miscarried. Details of occupation of Palace wanting. It was taken possession of on 21st. On that night Her Majesty's health drank in Dewan Khass with grand effect. Cheers taken up by Goorkhas outside.

Banquet in Diwān-i-Khāss. Goorkhas.

Princes brought in and shot are Mirza Moghul, Abu Bakr, and Khizr Sultan. Zeenut Muhal in confinement with the King.

Prince Mirza Moghul, Prince Abu Bakr, Prince Khizr Sultan, shot.

Pursuing column is under Col. Greathed, 1600 Infantry, 600 Cavalry, and 18 guns. City strange spectacle of desolation. All well in Punjaub.

Pursuing column.

Débris of 20 Rebel regiments besides Cavalry congregated at Muthra with 20 guns, preparing bridge to go to Oudh.

Movements of rebel regiments.

Scindia has taken away all boats on Chumbal from Dholepore ghats. Indore force still at Dholepore.

Scindia. Indore force.

Morar regiments quiet at Gwalior; 5th and Cavalry are with Scindia, who is for the present successfully keeping all back.

W. MUIR.

## LXXXIV.

AGRA, 28*th September* 1857.

MY DEAR SHERER,—You will have observed that we were a little confused yesterday by getting Colonel Becher's letter of the 22nd without the intervening despatches of the 21st and 20th.

[1] *i.e.*, of Dholepore.—W. M.

In the enclosed printed paper you will find the progress of affairs now distinctly described.

A despatch from Mr. Saunders of the 20th has just come in; he says: "Mr. Greathed was attacked with cholera yesterday morning, and expired at about midnight.

Greathed's death.

"In the afternoon he told me that as his Principal Assistant, the Senior Assistant present with the Force, he wished me to take up his duties, and I have accordingly, with the concurrence of the General Commanding, this day assumed charge of the appointment. I shall of course act entirely in concert with the Military authorities, and be guided by what I have ascertained to be Mr. Greathed's views and general line of policy, and also by the written instructions received by him from time to time from the late Lieutenant-Governor, and from Sir John Lawrence."

Mr. C. Saunders takes civil charge at Delhi.

As to general matters, his letter does not add much to what is contained already in the printed Extra. The Mutineers would seem to have hung about to the last moment, and then to have blown up their surplus ammunition and set out on their march, or rather flight, this way. They left, Saunders says, with 8 guns, but evidently had sent others ahead with their baggage. The general belief is that they will ere long scatter and disperse to their homes, being perfectly disorganised and dispirited.

Mutineers leave Delhi.

In his message of the 14th, Barnes says: "Out of our Force we have scarcely fifteen hundred European Infantry fit for duty." But probably the number of disabled men was increased by those temporarily unfitted by fatigue or the effects of drunkenness for immediate duty. If so, the numbers of effective men would soon increase. Colonel Becher reports a satisfactory thing, that in the final operations our men sustained little or no loss. Our medical authorities here have been written to from Delhi for the purpose of ascertaining whether the sick and wounded could be properly accommodated and attended to here. There would, I conceive, be no difficulty in this arrangement, which would have many advantages. For many of the duties in the Fort, invalids in certain stages of convalescence would, I believe, be suited, which might set at liberty some of the 3d Europeans now here.

Weakness of European force.

Young Wigram, writing from Meerut on the 22nd, states that early on that morning a force of Sikhs, Rifles, Carabineers, with 4 guns and mortars and a party of the volunteer horse, had started for Mozuffernuggur. They will no doubt give a good account of that body of wretched fanatics from Thanah Bhowun which has been committing such excesses throughout the Mozuffernuggur District. "The Magistrate's people," Wigram

Thanah Bhowun excesses in Mozuffernug-ger District.

says, "attacked them a few days ago. They got in, captured the enemy's guns, but the Sikhs and Goorkhas failing to follow the first party, they were forced to retreat, leaving the guns they had taken, and losing 12 men killed and several more wounded." Now that Delhi has fallen, peace and tranquillity will soon be restored to that quarter of the country.

At Muthra the bridge of boats was not completed yesterday. The Mutineers expected it would be ready to-day, when they would cross over. But before that I trust Colonel Greathed will be upon them with his column.

There was heavy firing heard last night from 8 to 10 in the direction of Muthra or Bhurtpore, but it may have been (as the people about think) only the celebration of the Dussehra.

Nothing new from Dholepore.

Scindia and Gwalior troops.

To-day is the great Dussehra festival at Gwalior. The Contingent *talk* of marching to-morrow; we shall see what Dinka Rao and his master can do. Some half of the 5th are still with the Maharajah and 2 guns. Five days ago the news of our successes at Delhi had not reached Gwalior. Scindia's hands will of course be greatly strengthened when he gets the news.

Our little force is still at Khundowlie.

W. MUIR.

To J. W. SHERER, ESQ., Cawnpore.

## LXXXV.

### SERVICE MESSAGE.

FROM AGRA—W. MUIR, ESQ.,

TO CALCUTTA—G. F. EDMONSTONE, ESQ.

AGRA, 28*th September* 1857.

Mr. Greathed's death.

DESPATCHES from Delhi of 20th received. Mr. H. H. Greathed died on night of 19th. Mr. C. B. Saunders assumed charge of his office.

King's flight, Palace seized, and whole of Delhi occupied.

On the 20th, Mutineers evacuated Delhi, and, leaving camp standing outside Delhi Gate, fled towards Muthra. King and his family took refuge in Humaioon's tomb. We blew open gate of Palace, and took possession of Palace and Selimgurh. That day we occupied the whole City. Detachment ordered to Hindun bridge to meet party from Meerut; they would clear communication between Delhi and Meerut.

Little or no loss in final operations. Rest of news and subsequent proceeding given in yesterday's message.

. . . . . . . .

W. MUIR.

## LXXXVI.

AGRA, *29th September* 1857.

MY DEAR EDMONSTONE,—I write regularly giving the daily news to Sherer (the Intelligence Department having been for the present assigned to me). But as the present letter will give cover to the despatch of General Wilson reporting the capture of Delhi, I address it direct to yourself. It was enclosed in a letter from C. B. Saunders, which, though of date the 22nd, was received only this day. The results reported by Saunders are old, but some of the particulars are fresh, and I therefore give the following extract from his letter. "I am glad to be able to report that the King of Delhi, through the exertions of Captain Hodson and of Moulvie Rujjab Alli, was induced to yield himself prisoner to the British *on the sole condition that his own life and that of the Beegum Zeenut-oon-nissa should be spared.* He is now a prisoner under my charge, and is placed in the house of the above Beegum, under a European guard, and is well guarded, and treated with the consideration his present position, rather than his former circumstances and conduct, entitled him to expect.

King's surrender.

"Captain Hodson also went out again this morning with a strong party of Cavalry and surrounded the tomb of Humaioon, and took prisoners Mirza Moghul, Mirza Khizr Sultan, the King's sons, and Mirza Abu Bucr, his grandson (all of whom had been prominent in the insurrection), and, after having made them prisoners, shot them on the spot.

Execution of Royal Princes.

"A moveable column has been formed which marches to-morrow morning to the Kootub, and from thence in the direction of Agra, with a view to relieve your force and to prevent the possibility of the defeated Mutineers from this part of the world forming a junction with the Indore and Gwalior troops and besieging Agra.

Moveable column starts towards Agra.

"The troops have been greatly demoralised by the severity of the duties they have so long had to perform, their heavy losses, and the immense amount of plunder and liquor which fell into their hands on their obtaining possession of the City; and it has been found impracticable to organise a column earlier to pursue the enemy. A Brigade now hardly consists of as many men as formerly were comprised in the strength of a whole Regiment. From deux to trois cents soldats is now the average of most of our European Regiments. The force proceeding in pursuit will

Demoralisation of troops.

consist of European and Sikh Infantry and Cavalry, and will be accompanied by 18 Lt.-Fd. Guns.

"General Wilson and Brigadier Chamberlain wrote to Sir J. Lawrence begging that the Chief Commissioner of the Punjaub would assume charge of the administration of the Delhi Territory. Sir John, in reply, said by telegraph that if General Wilson considered that he could be of use in the present emergency he was willing to carry on the administration of the Delhi Territory through you (Mr. Saunders) as Commissioner, subject to the wishes of Mr. Reade and the Supreme Government, adding that he would be ready at any moment to resign the duty." So long as our communications with Delhi are so tardy and uncertain, while instant correspondence can be had at Delhi with Lahore, no doubt the arrangement is a good one. But our dak will now, I trust, in a few days be re-established, when I hope things will revert to their old footing. Mr. Reade will, I think, be sending a message on the subject to his Lordship to-day, intimating his concurrence in the arrangement that Mr Saunders should for the present follow the instructions of the Chief Commissioner.

Sir John Lawrence agrees to assume charge of Delhi territory.

Desolation and ruin of Delhi.

Saunders describes the City as a fearful picture of desolation; the retribution has indeed been awful, but it is a meet return for a city which has for so many months nursed this brood of monsters.

"Everything," Saunders says, "is perfectly quiet in the vicinity of Delhi, but the place is deserted by all but our own troops, who have plundered and ransacked it from one end to the other. The Chandnee Chouk, and in fact every street in the place, presents a most mournful spectacle of ruin and desolation. Our enemy, since the commencement of the siege, must have lost an almost incredible number of men, and the destruction of house property by our Artillery fire from the time when we opened our advanced batteries is very remarkable."

Young Wigram Clifford comes along with Colonel Greathed's column.

Metcalfe attacked by cholera.

Greathed's death.

Metcalfe had a severe attack of cholera, but was said to be recovering rapidly. I need not say how greatly we have deplored Greathed's death. How very strange that it should have pleased Providence to take him just in the very hour of the complete triumph which he had so long been watching for. But how many of her best Sons has not our country lost in this great struggle.

Anson to Mrs. Muir.

The following particulars regarding the Palace and City, in a letter from Anson of the Lancers to Mrs. Muir, may be interesting. It is dated 21st: "Delhi is wholly and completely ours. Not a shot has been fired to-day, and the Prize Agents are busy at work. I was in the Palace this morning and picked up a few playthings for the children. Wilson is going to make it his Headquarters.

**Picture of state of Delhi.**

"When the Palace was stormed and gates blown in there were not more than 10 men in it. They were all killed, and the first comers served themselves to some nice loot in the shape of English guns and rifles and native curiosities from the Zenana. There are really some rare copies of Persian books found. The streets are strewn with literature of all sorts. 250 lbs. of powder in bags blew the ponderous doors off their hinges. Delhi is being well sacked. The Chandney Chouk presents a miserable, forlorn aspect, and everything looks dirty. The Bank is a frightful ruin. The Jumma Musjid has not suffered much from our fire. None but Englishmen *could* have worked and toiled as our people have done for the last 12 days. I am sorry to say the Mutineers did desecrate the Cantonment burial-ground. We are too weak to pursue; more than trois mille in Hospital. Taking Delhi cost us 61 officers and 1300 men killed and wounded. Our regiment (9th Lancers) had 40 wounded. The regiment has been very useful during the siege, working the guns in the batteries as well as Artillerymen."

**Plunder in Delhi.**

**Loss of officers and troops in taking Delhi.**

**9th Lancers.**

As to Agra and its vicinity, the only fresh intelligence is that the Mutineers at Muthra find difficulty in planking and completing the bridge so rapidly as they expected. It is said that they have received intelligence that pursuing column is at hand, and that they have accordingly commenced preparations for entrenching themselves.

**Bridge at Muthra.**

This is the day the Contingent used to say they would move upon Agra. But we trust that the Maharajah, who has with Dinka Rao's assistance kept them in hand so wonderfully hitherto, may still be able to play with them. He must know by this time of the fall of Delhi, which will vastly strengthen his hands. The restless part of the Contingent were, it is said, looking towards Cawnpore. The Nana has been busy with money and emissaries among them.

In yesterday's letter I said our medical officer had been consulted from Delhi about receiving the sick here. I find that they had only been speaking on the subject themselves, and had not received any communication from Delhi about it. Our advantage here would be water-carriage for the sick, who could in many cases with difficulty stand a long land-carriage to Umballah. Shall we not be obliged largely to increase our sanatoria in the Hills? Lord Dalhousie favourably entertained a proposal for establishing one in the vicinity of Naini Tal, which would be conveniently near troops in these parts. It might be well to bring forward the papers about this again.

Hill sanatoria.

We are all getting on famously here, excepting for a short time soon after we came into the Fort, when cholera and sickness prevailed. The Fort has *been wonderfully healthy.* During September it was *greatly more healthy* inside than outside the Fort, and the doctors actually ordered families back into the Fort who had gone out for change. It is now discovered that years ago the Fort was medically recommended as the healthiest place in Agra at the close of the rains. Captain Nicolls, of the Engineers, is busy as possible in the Fort. He says it should be greatly strengthened, and that while we are about it the place should be made really secure, and advantage taken of the additions, otherwise indispensable for safety, to provide suites of rooms for public offices, etc.

Healthiness of Agra Fort.

W. MUIR.

G. F. EDMONSTONE, ESQ.,
For. Secy., Calcutta.

## LXXXIX.

## SPECIAL GOVERNMENT MESSAGE.

### E. A. READE TO GOVERNOR-GENERAL.

*29th (?) September* 1857.

Reade, acting Lt.-Governor, reports appointment of Saunders as Commissioner of Delhi.

IN place of Mr. Greathed, Mr. C. B. Saunders directed to officiate as Commissioner of Delhi and Agent-Lt.-Govr. In matters of special importance, relating to districts in that Division and Native States under that Agency, directed to refer to Chief Commissioner, Punjaub, for instructions.

This arrangement made at the suggestion of Sir J. Lawrence and General Wilson until regular communication re-opened with Agra.

W. MUIR.

*Colonel Fraser appointed Chief Commissioner.*—W. M.

## XC.

### URGENT.

To Colonel Greathed, Commdg. Column Marching down the Doab.

Agra, *30th September* 1857.

My Dear Sir,—Mr. Clifford's letter of the 25th inst. from your camp at Ghazeeoodeen-nugger gave us the first intimation that you are marching down the left bank of the Jumna, and not, as we understood from Mr. Saunders' letter, *via* the Koottub down the right bank on Muthra. Col. Cotton commanding at Agra had been looking for communications from you to enable him to regulate the movements of his troops here. Colonel Fraser (who has just been appointed Chief Commissioner here, with supreme Military and Civil command over these provinces) has requested me to write to you, and desire that you will hurry down to the river opposite Muthra and attack the mutinous force now congregated there. You will use your discretion in destroying the bridge of boats at Muthra. It is uncertain whether the force may not possibly have crossed over into the Doab before you reach the vicinity of the river; if so you will of course attack them whenever they are found. The rebels are now encamped at Muthra in force, about 5 or 6000 fighting men, of whom perhaps 1000 or 1500 are disabled. They have, by various accounts, from 17 to 28 guns, probably nearer the former figure, and they are said to be horsed. They have been pressing forward the completion of the bridge of boats there. It is nearly complete so far as the boats are concerned, but by our last accounts there was delay expected in flooring it sufficiently to admit of the guns being passed over. In this delay, then, consists the hope of our being able to crush the mutinous force and seize their guns. But in order to any successful results, it is of the utmost consequence that your march should be urged forward with the greatest despatch.

Urges speedy advance of Greathed's column.

These instructions are issued in ignorance of the orders which you may have received from General Wilson, and on the supposition that the force is destined for immediate march this way *via* Allygurh.

W. Muir.

*P.S.*—Our last news is that the Gwalior force is likely to move on Cawnpore.

Kindly send this on to Mr. Saunders at Delhi, to be shown to General Wilson. W. M.

Advance to Lucknow.

Good news from Cawnpore; our force was within 14 miles of Lucknow, the enemy flying before them, and we had fired a Royal salute to intimate our early approach to the gallant garrison of the Bailey Guard. W. M.

## XCI.

AGRA, *September 30th*, 1857.

MY DEAR SHERER,—Thanks for yours of the 24th. Colonel Fraser has received the message appointing him Chief Commissr., and has desired me to acknowledge its receipt. The Copy enclosed in your letter to me arrived first.

. . . . . . . . .

To our surprise I received a letter this morning from young Clifford *from Gazeeoodeennugger*, saying that the pursuing column under Colonel Greathed was taking that route this way. We cannot make out whether they intend to cleanse out the Malagurh nest on their way—it lies only a short distance to the right of their next stage, Dadree. But if not,—if they were to march straight on,—then, as they were at Dadree on the 26th, they ought to have reached Allygurh by this time; yet we have no intelligence of their advent.

I give extracts from Clifford's letter. B. Sapte, who has now joined as Civil Officer with the force, is a man of judgment and fair ability.

Clifford, C.S.

Clifford writes: "A column composed of about 2800 men, of whom 800 (500 Infantry and 300 Cavalry and Artillery) are Europeans, reached this (Ghazeeoodeen-nugger) yesterday morning, *en route* down the Doab. I was sent with it as Civil Officer to accompany it till Sapte joins. He arrived here from Meerut this morning, so I return to Delhi. We were to have marched on towards Dadree this morning, but have to halt to-day to force the camp followers to disgorge their Delhi loot, with which they have encumbered themselves to such an extent as to render the camp equipage, etc., a large store of merchandise" (one is apt to think this might have been accomplished by a flying column without a day's halt).

Sapte, C.S., Civil Officer with Greathed's column.

Loot at Delhi.

"All accounts seem to agree in saying that the fugitive army, or rather rabble, of Pandies are crossing the river and making for Oudh. We find hardly any in villages. Wullee Dad Khan has, I am afraid, bolted, or will do so as soon as he hears of our reaching Dadree. A drum-major of the 29th N.I.[1] who came in to us declares that the Pandies had determined to cross the river at Muthra and join the Lucknow rebels;—not having any notion of forming a junction with the Gwalior men or of attacking Agra."

Nicholson's death.

I grieve to add that Clifford mentions the death of that great soldier Nicholson on the 23rd. It is felt to be a serious loss to the army at large, but his end was well in unison with his life and reputation, a glorious one. Clifford mentions a rather unhappy occurrence which took place the day before: "Our Army was looting the wretched Bunnias of Ghazeeoodeen-nugger, a very harmless set of men, so Colonel Greathed at my request put a guard on the gate of the town. A Sikh, one of Green's (?) splendid corps, forced his way past the sentry with loot in his possession, and was shot by him. A very bad feeling on the part of Green's (?) men is the consequence, as this is the second similar occurrence in a week."

Collection of Revenue.

"The villagers along our route all express their readiness to pay up the revenue, as soon as it is called for. Saunders, however, ordered me not to collect it just now. Several of the Goojur villages have already paid it to the late King;—what should be done in this case? I think as the Jat villages resisted the King's demand for revenue, that the Goojurs should suffer for their ready compliance by having to pay it over again. If they desert their villages it will be a good riddance!!" Most certainly I would in such a case take the full revenue, at the least, from men who have been feeding the rebellious Treasury. Where collections have been forcibly taken from otherwise loyal subjects the case would deserve consideration, but none can be shown to these aiders and abettors of the rebel cause.

Goojurs paid revenue to the King. Jats refused.

In another private letter Clifford complains of the slowness of the advance of the Column, and of the vacillation which destined it first for the one bank, and then for the other. Of course no judgment can be formed on passing remarks of this nature, but the sudden change of the route of the pursuing Column requires explanation, which our Delhi despatches will in all probability shortly bring to us.

I enclose the copy of a letter I have, at Col. Fraser's instance, addressed to Col. Greathed in command of the pursuing Column, urging a speedy advance this way. The letter will explain itself.

[1] *i.e.*, Native Infantry.

There *would seem* to have been a want of communication with us as to intended movements, but the Cossid correspondence is so irregular and uncertain that we must not be precipitate in judgment.

Bridge completed at Muthra.

From a spy just come in it would seem that the bridge was completed at Muthra last night, when men and horses had begun to cross, and the whole force would *probably* move over to-day, unless they have any ulterior design which we have not heard of. The Dholepore (Indore) Mutineers are said to be moving towards Futtehpore Sikri, and report is that they contemplate a visit to Bhurtpore; but the object of such a step is not very apparent, and it is likeliest that they will go the same way as the Muthra band *quam celerrime.* Our intelligence as to their intentions is not, however, clear and good.

The Muthra men, it is said, have had a discouraging reply from Gwalior to say that they could not possibly expose their Magazine by joining them at Muthra, and I conclude they have given them no encouragement to join their own party at Gwalior.

But the Gwalior people seem to be certainly contemplating an early movement in your direction. Major Macpherson's message to the Governor-General will I hope be ready to accompany this despatch. He has heard most satisfactorily from Scindiah himself, who has been forced to supply the Mutineers with carriage. They openly talk of going to Cawnpore. The Nana's agent has been tampering with them, and promising them great largesse. Scindiah says the 5th and remnant of the 6th (2 Companies) with the Cavalry, some 400 or 500 Sowars, are subservient to his wishes, and have come to his lines, and he seems to expect that they will not go off. If he could divide, and thus break up, the Force, and detain as much of the Magazine as possible, it would be a great point gained. Scindiah mentions that Durand has sent 400 Cavalry to Mehidpore, and that they will likely assist in an attack on the insurgent Mussulmans of Mundasore.

Scindia's loyalty. Gwalior Contingent

Lucknow.

I do trust that Lucknow will not be abandoned. Things are beginning to brighten so much in all quarters, and the Empire is so unspeakably relieved by its deliverance from that monster incubus at Delhi, the head, heart, front of the rebellion, that it would be surely not too great an abstraction of force to leave a garrison at Lucknow, especially after the Mutineers there have been defeated. The abandonment of Lucknow would be felt as a loss of prestige in all the Native courts, and would be viewed as a retrograde step. If things had been as they were a month or six weeks ago, it might have been a necessary step. I earnestly hope it may not be thought so now. We eagerly look for the relief of our gallant countrymen who have so gloriously defended the Bailey Guard.

W. MUIR.

J. W. SHERER, ESQ.

## XCII.

### SERVICE MESSAGE.

FROM AGRA—FROM W. MUIR,
TO CALCUTTA—TO G. F. EDMONSTONE.

AGRA, 30*th September* 1857.

PURSUING Column is moving down Doab, not down right bank of Jumna; was at Ghazeeooddeen-nugger on 25th.

Bridge at Muthra said to have been finished last night.

Mutineers there may be now crossing.

Gwalior Mutineers likely to march towards Cawnpore.

No despatch yet come in from Delhi to-day.

W. MUIR.

## XCIII.

FROM AGRA—FROM COLONEL FRASER, C.B.
TO CALCUTTA—TO GOVERNOR-GENERAL.

I HAVE the honour to express my gratification at having been appointed by the Governor-General to the temporary post of Chief Commissioner of these Provinces: and I beg to assure his Lordship that it will be my care to conduct the duties of this office with all the attention and vigour which my abilities admit.

I have this day assumed charge of the appointment.

H. FRASER.

30*th September* 1857.

## XCIV.

AGRA, 1*st October* 1857.

MY DEAR SHERER,—Lucknow has taken the place of Delhi in the mind of the Fort (here). We wait in eager expectation for the news of the relief of the noble band which has so long withstood like a rock the waves of mutiny surging all around.

No letter from you received since those acknowledged yesterday.

Now for ourselves. The Muthra bridge is I think certainly finished, but the force has not yet moved. It *may* be moving to-day into the Doab. Or it may be waiting the Indore force, which was invited to march and form a junction with them.

Dholpore force moving on Agra.

The Indore Mutineers intended to move last night from Dholepore, and are probably encamped to-day at Jajon on the Ootangun, some 18 or 20 miles from this, thence *via* Khyragurh to Futtehpore Sicri and Muthra. If the Delhi fugitives wait for them they will be detained 3 or 4 days, and may yet fall into the hands of Greathed's Column. One of my messengers says that the Indore people had seized four of the Dholepore Rana's large guns—described as 24 prs., and were arranging to have them dragged by elephants. The report will be communicated to Colonel Greathed, with whom, or with the Civilian marching with him, I propose to hold daily correspondence.

Movements of pursuing Column.

Regarding the pursuing Column, we have had no further direct letters, but the statement of an eye-witness confirmed by native letters renders the following account highly probable. The Column left Ghazeeoodeen-nugger on the morning of Saturday the 26th, and halted at Dadree; next day, 27th, at Secunderabad, which is only a short step northwards by a metalled road to Boolundshuhur. Early on Monday morning the Column turned towards Boolundshuhur by this road, and came up with the enemy a mile or so from Boolundshuhur, where the Meerut and Delhi roads separate. I conclude it was the Jhansi Brigade with Wulee Dad Khan's levies. The enemy opened on us with three guns, and afterwards two more in Boolundshuhur. The loss to the enemy is described as very great. An expedition was then started off for Malagurh, which is some 6 or 7 miles N.E. of Boolundshuhur, a little off the Gd. T. Road on the right. It was taken. Wuleedad Khan said to have fled. It must not be forgotten that this is entirely from native sources, and that, though substantially correct, it may not be accurate in its details.

Action at Boolundshuhur.

Malagurh captured.

The force might be detained a day or so arranging matters at Boolundshuhur, which is 3 stages from Allygurh. It can hardly, therefore, reach that place for a day or two yet. But if the Mutineers hold on at Muthra, they may yet be entrapped.

The accounts from Gwalior though vague seem all to point towards a movement your way—one man says the Contingent had a fresh quarrel with the Maharajah and burnt their lines.

There were reports that 2 Regiments had actually gone off towards Cawnpore. When *Dholepore* is cleared of these Indore Mutineers, we shall no doubt get more speedy and accurate information as to Gwalior. They have studiously intercepted all our communications.

Colonel Fraser has desired me to say, for communication to General Outram, that he concurs in the views I stated yesterday as to the inexpediency of relinquishing Lucknow, adding: "provided Cawnpore is strong enough to take care of itself," and suggesting at the very least that "Lucknow should be held till the fate or destruction of the Mutineers in this quarter, which should certainly be settled within the next 6 or 8 days, is known."

Chief Commsr. advises against abandoning Lucknow.

One important consideration is that Lucknow, once evacuated, would be reoccupied as the head of the Mahomedan rebellion. They would again have a Capital, a King, to rally around—the material vantage-ground which they have now lost in the fall of Delhi. There would be some difficulty, no doubt, in having an orthodox King on the throne of Lucknow; for a Sheea one would find little sympathy from the great mass of Hindoostanee Moslems. But that difficulty might perhaps be got over, and we are allowing the risk of the re-establishment of a new Head of the rebellion—to be again destroyed, but not without loss to ourselves—if we allow the reoccupation of the Capital of Oudh by the Mutineers.

Arguments against it.

I don't think I mentioned to you that the Gwalior news-writer at Delhi continued his reports up to the 22nd or 23rd, and will, I suppose, now write reports of the doings of the new Dynasty. The decorum of Majesty was preserved to the last. It reads like the "Arabian Nights," and there is a strange mingling of burlesque with tragedy in the later scenes.

Native reports of the King of Delhi.

The "Captain Sahib" is introduced with joined hands as come to convey the General's representation that His Majesty must give himself up, whereupon His Majesty delivers himself of reflections on the strange upshot of the rebellion—50,000 Sepoys having been discomfited by a few thousand English. I shall try to get the whole series of these reports,—they would be a real curiosity. Macpherson thinks he may be able to get them.

In a message from George Barnes, dated the 21st inst., there is mention of "a local disturbance in the wild country between Mooltan and Lahore, against which a force has been sent." This is the first I have heard of it. A letter from Meerut encloses one from Mr. Saunders dated 23rd, which is our latest from him.

Local disturbance in Punjab.

He simply mentions in it that "a Column would march the next day to Dadree, thence to Secunderabad, and then it will turn off to Malagurh to polish off Wulleedad Khan, if the blackguard is still holding out."

In addition to this Column, says Mr. Saunders, "the Beeloch Battalion, about 300 strong, march to-morrow morning for Meerut, and will greatly add to your strength. It is a good regiment, and the men are armed with rifles."

Saunders complains of the difficulty of getting good men at present in that part of the country as Tehseeldars and Thannahdars.

Williams also writes to us for College lads. When the country has settled down a bit, and they begin to see that there is *no fear of another inroad of insurgents*, good men will come forward willingly enough. At present they are afraid.

Williams, Commr. of Meerut.

Williams from Meerut writes: "We rode out the storm with nearly 5 lacs in the Treasury, and lots more coming."

The latest accounts from Muthra are that parties are crossing and proceeding *via* Hathrass, but not yet, so far as we can yet hear, any important part of the army.

Dissensions among Mutineers.

The Bareilly and other Brigades are not on good terms. The former has money which the latter wants to be shared with them, and there is hence a want of unanimity as to the object of their march.

W. Muir.

## XCV.

## TELEGRAPHIC MESSAGE.[1]

From W. Muir.—To Calcutta, to G. F. Edmonstone.

Agra, 10*th October* 1857.

Telegram to Government of India as to relieving column from Delhi.

Good native report that Colonel Greathed's Column defeated the enemy at Bolundshuhur on the 28th, inflicting great loss and taking guns. Malagurh captured and Wulee Dad Khan said to have fled into Rohilkhund. Column shortly expected at Allygurh; Indore Mutineers believed to have left Dholepore and to be to-day about 18 miles from this on road to Muthra *via* Futtehpore Sicri.

Delhi fugitives crossing in small parties and going *via* Hatrass; no information yet as to moving of main body.

Part of Gwalior Contingent said to be leaving for Cawnpore.

W. Muir.

[1] Copied by Lady Muir.—W. M.

# INTELLIGENCE DEPARTMENT, AGRA.

MSS. VOL. I.

*SECOND SERIES.*

# LETTERS

ADDRESSED TO

# DELHI AND MEERUT,

**From 10th August to 1st October 1857.**

(*See Sir William Muir's Prefatory Note, page* 60.)

# INTELLIGENCE DEPARTMENT, AGRA.

## MSS. VOL. I.

## *SECOND SERIES.*

# LETTERS

ADDRESSED TO

# DELHI AND MEERUT,

### From 10th August to 1st October 1857.

## XCVI.

AGRA FORT, *August* 11*th*, 1857.

MY DEAR WILLIAMS,—I told Thornhill to acknowledge your last letter to me. Nothing specially new has happened since, but I write that I may hear from you again. There have been unfounded reports, which will have reached you, of the early advance of General Havelock's Brigade. It has gained great victories, and captured 42 guns. But it has still Lucknow to relieve, and bring away women and children down to Calcutta. Our latest date from him, the 3rd; Cossids overdue. A 2nd Brigade with the 5th and 90th Queen's, the latter armed with Enfield rifles, will soon proceed upward from Allahabad. The rifles of the 78th Highlanders did great execution in General Havelock's actions. General H. proceeds very cautiously, and I daresay wisely; but more rapid dash and advance would be all the better. I have urged in the strongest terms that both Brigades should move onwards into the Upper Doab "*quam celerrime.*" I trust this will be sanctioned. Nothing new here or from Gwalior. We must patiently await events. Pray write to me often, avoiding the direct Allygurh route, which is now dangerous; try not to cross your letters here. Tell Mrs. J. S. Campbell that all well at home by mail of 26th June. Our latest Delhi date 6th, and *Lahore Chronicle* Extra of 3rd July, with mention of the Mutiny of 26th N.I. disarmed at Meean Meer. Latest Calcutta date July 29th; all well. The *Roorkee Gazette*, July 23rd, under head of Meerut, July the 22nd, speaks of 2 Regiments Infantry, one

Havelock's Brigade.

Cavalry, and 4 guns having left Delhi by the Bridge. Possibly for Boolundshuhur. Has there been any such permanent move?

*Note.*—By Mr. Colvin's desire I added a statement regarding the Proclamation for apprehension of Mutineers, and requested Williams to direct all his officers to act on it, and show to the officers commanding.

W. MUIR.

## XCVII.

FORT AGRA, 13*th August* 1857.

MY DEAR GREATHED,—I enclose copy of a letter received from Brigadier-General Havelock;. it is without date, but must have been written about the fifth. Please show it to Brigadier Wilson. Nothing new here to-day. Native reports of your having an action during the day of the eighth. The *Γυαλιορ νευς-ριτερ σενδς* the intelligence *ανδ κολουρς ιτ αλωαις ιν φαυουρ οφ θε πανδεις.*

H. H. GREATHED, ESQ.

W. Edwards. W. Edwards is safe in a village opposite Furruckabad. Wm. Blake is in the Fort.

## XCVIII.

FORT AGRA, *August* 13*th*, 1857.

MY DEAR ALEXANDER,—Your letter of the 24th ult. only arrived to-day.[1] I send it on to Calcutta. The principal events of Rohilkhund must have been known there before. You will have received a letter from me through Meerut. Mr. Williams has acknowledged its having reached him. I trust that before very long something will have been added to your stock of funds. We are not very well off in that way ourselves, but can carry on. Much depends upon the course of events at Delhi. You will hear of that later than I can tell you. Our news thence to August

Havelock's force. 8th is good. General Havelock's force, after fighting 6 battles and capturing 63 guns, marched on to Lucknow about the 5th, and in a few days we expect to hear of its having relieved the garrison, and brought away the ladies and children there. I feel

Nawab of Rampore. with you confidence in the Nawab of Rampore, and I would give him encouragement in all ways you can. We are living in the Fort. Bungalows all burnt and wasted. But we have no immediate threat of attack. The messenger has taken a long

[1] Letter of 24th July received at Agra, August 13th; *i.e.*, in 20 days from Mussoorie or Nainee Tal.—W. M.

time to bring your letter. It came only this morning. I should add that European regiments will assemble at Bombay and Calcutta in great numbers: 25,000 men at least. Before long a vast change will be seen in the state of affairs. The messenger says there was another messenger with him carrying a letter from my son Bazett. The man got frightened and tore it up. Pray mention this to Bazett, and say that we have all sorts of reports about him, and that Elliot and I are fairly well.

J. R. COLVIN.

R. ALEXANDER, ESQ.[1]

## XCIX

FORT AGRA, *16th August* 1857.[2]

MY DEAR GREATHED,—Various letters received from Cawnpore and General Havelock's force to the 10th instant. The general result is *that*[3] *an immediate advance of that force in this quarter is not to be expected. He has quite enough to do where he is, and had not immediately continued his march towards Lucknow;* though he had again advanced, gained another victory, and *again fallen back. Cawnpore was threatened by the Mutineers from Futtehgurh, and he had to look to its protection,* as well as to the *relief of the post at Lucknow.* I quote from various letters. Sherer writes, Cawnpore 9th. Police stations from Futtehpore to Allahabad, with Cotwallee at Futtehpore. *The 42nd Regiment from Saugur interfere with the Thannahs around Cawnpore.* Steamer doing useful service on the river at Cawnpore. The Soobahdars *active in our cause.* Captain Bruce says that a Brigade of Madras troops with Cavalry is expected in Calcutta. Lucknow holds out well, and the last accounts are cheerfully written. *Detachment at Hazareebagh gone. Fears entertained for Chota Nagpore.* Chester, August 4th and 7th, writes that *the outbreak of the 3 Regiments at Dinapore was delaying the arrival of more European Regiments at Allahabad.* These mutinous corps had been severely punished and driven back to Sasseram from Arrah; *though there had been some loss also in a partial affair on our side; a good deal of cholera in General H.'s camp.* Sir J. Outram and Mr. J. P. Grant expected at Allahabad soon, for what purpose not mentioned. Captain Olphert's half-battery had reached Cawnpore, where also a heavy elephant battery was being equipped.

**Havelock cannot advance towards Agra.**

**Cawnpore threatened.**

**Lucknow, Hazareebagh, Dinapore.**

J. R. COLVIN.

H. H. GREATHED, ESQ.

[1] Mussoorie, or Nainee Tal (?).

[2] August 7th: from Allahabad, reached 16th; *i.e.*, 9 days.—W. M.

[3] Italicised words in Greek characters.

## C.

FORT AGRA, 19*th August* 1857.

MY DEAR GREATHED,—I have received yours of the 14th.[1] We are glad to hear of the arrival, in such excellent order, of the reinforcements from the Punjaub. There is nothing fresh here to communicate. Our Cossids from Cawnpore are again overdue. Hindun bridge. About the Hindun bridge, I have myself thought it desirable that it should be broken, if possible, in order to save the Meerut troops acting against Malagurh from the risk of a flank move of the Pandies. This still seems to me the most important present consideration, under all the information we possess. The march of troops *υπυαρδς* is not, you have been told, *likely to be quite immediate.* The matter is, of course, one for the decision of the Brigadier commanding, but I would beg you to state these views on my part.

J. R. COLVIN.

H. H. GREATHED, ESQ.

## CI.

FORT AGRA, 20*th August* 1857.

MY DEAR GREATHED,—Letters from Cawnpore to the 12th,[2] and from Allahabad to the 11th, have been received. General Havelock, after having made all his arrangements for recrossing, suddenly turned, attacked the enemy again, and defeated him, with what precise amount of loss is not known. His retreat may have been a ruse. I have nothing further direct from himself. Our account is from General Neill. It is mentioned in the letter that Lieutenant Thomson, 53 N.I., in addition to Lieutenant Delafosse of the same corps (whose account of his escape has gone on to General Chamberlain), a private of Artillery, and a private of H.M. 84th, are the only survivors of Gen. H. Wheeler's force. The Allahabad letter of August 11th states that the Telegraph and Dak communication *to Calcutta* had been for the time *stopped*, probably from the *Dinapore Mutineers*[3] being on the Trunk road near *Sasseram.* General Lloyd has been suspended in his command in consequence of his conduct *in the matter.* He is greatly *blamed for not disarming the Dinapore Regiment* before. The 5th and 90th, 37th and 10th

Havelock's movements.

Thomson, Delafosse, and survivors of Cawnpore Massacre.

Dinapore.

[1] In 5 days from Dehli.—W. M.

[2] 12th: Cawnpore, to 20th; Agra = 8 days: Allahabad, 11th; 9 days coming.—W. M.

[3] Italics in Greek.

Queen's are all *kept for the present in Behar.* The Cawnpore letters mention that *the 12th Irregular Cavalry at Segolee had gone, and was believed to be somewhere in Jaunpore, wishing to effect a junction with the Dinapore Regiments. They had been prevented by those corps being driven back eastwards.* The same letter mentions that 3 Royal Regiments are expected from Malta by the first steamer. I wrote to you yesterday regarding the *Hindun bridge* as follows:—"I have myself thought it desirable that it should be broken, if possible, in order to save the *Meerut* troops marching against *Malagurh* from the risk of a flank movement of the *Pandays.* This still seems to me the most important consideration, under all the information we possess. The march of troops *upwards is not (you have been told) likely to be quite immediate.* The matter is, of course, one for the decision of the Brigadier commanding, but I would beg you to state these views on my part." A demonstration will be made by an advance from this upon Hattrass: so as to keep [sentence unfinished]. Tell your brother, the Engineer, with my regards, that his servants have behaved well, and saved his plate and horses at Allahabad. Furniture destroyed, as elsewhere.

**Segowlie.**

**Hindun bridge.**

J. R. COLVIN.

I trust Baird Smith keeps well; my very kind regards to him.

## CII.

*20th August* 1857.

LETTER to F. Williams about the demand from Delhi for the rifles. He is to state his views to the Officer Commanding at Delhi, "but not to fight against their decision. Discretion given as to sending Shakespear to Bijnour District."[1]

## CIII.

AGRA, *22nd August* 1857.

MY DEAR GREATHED,—Our latest date from Cawnpore is the 17th.[2] It was mentioned that General Havelock had marched on Bithour, where he had again defeated the Nana and taken 2 of his guns. No actual letter had been received from the

**Havelock's movements.**

[1] The words within inverted commas added to the draft by Mr. Colvin in his own handwriting.—W. M.

[2] 17th-22nd, 5 days from Cawnpore.—W. M.

entrenchment at Lucknow since the 22nd July. Native reports stated that General Havelock's advance had led to the raising of the siege, which had enabled the garrison to get in provisions for another month. A reinforcement of about 700 European infantry expected soon at Allahabad, which would come up to Cawnpore. Dinapore Mutineers had left the road, and, in consequence, daily dak with Calcutta open. We have but to wait a short time, and the reinforcements will be overwhelming. I strongly advocate the Bombay, Kurrachee, and Punjaub line, as the direct one of reinforcement to Delhi. The route is through a quiet and friendly country. Mayne said to have gone back to Banda, and MacNaghten going down to Futtehpore immediately. Outram to command the Dinapore Division. Lord Elgin, with the greater part of the China force, arrived in the Hooghly on the 8th. I heartily hope you can so aid Meerut as to enable the force there to act with some vigour towards Malagurh. We have sent a demonstration to Hatrass, which will show that we are not quite shut up here. Floating rumours of the 23rd N.I. intending to march from Gwalior with miscellaneous Cavalry and some guns towards Delhi. You shall hear more of this if it should come to anything. I fear that a letter of mine of the 4th never reached you. It contained only expressions, which could not be too strongly stated, of admiration of the noble gallantry of the force before Delhi. Our force at Cawnpore relieves you in some degree by detaining Saugor and other Regiments. My latest date from you the 16th. Your report of the health of the troops very satisfactory.

Reinforcements expected.

Outram.

Lord Elgin arrives in Hoogly with China force.

Agra sends out a force.

J. R. COLVIN.

Central Provinces.

I have said that J. P. Grant comes up as L. G., C. Provinces, Benares, Allahabad, and Saugor Divisions—cut off from this.

## CIV.

FORT AGRA, *August 23rd*, 1857.

MY DEAR WILLIAMS,—Thanks for yours of the 16th. I have told you that, in matters of reinforcement, bridge-breaking, etc., you can state your views fully and respectfully to the Brigadier-General at Delhi, but that beyond this there is a point in his decision which none of us can resist.

The great thing now is to screw up his determination to the point of attacking Delhi when the siege train arrives, and any attempt to interfere with his own plans might indispose him to this crowning effort. I have before given you *carte blanche* about sending Shakespear and Palmer to Bijnore, if you see any solid good from it.

Tell G. Campbell that I am in receipt of his letters of the 12th and 17th, but that we must wait a while before we can have the country in such order as to admit of commencing the work of civil reorganisation. I really cannot think of anything for him to do, unless you can find work for him at Meerut. **G. Campbell.**

Our last news from the Eastward is Cawnpore, 17th.[1] General Havelock had reoccupied Bithoor, but had not been able to relieve Lucknow, which must be his first object. Advance here or upwards within any time that can be named must be regarded as postponed. Things as before with us. Write often. **Havelock.**

. . . . . . . .

J. R. COLVIN.

## CV.

FORT AGRA, 23 *August* 1857.

MY DEAR GREATHED,—Yours of the 18th received this forenoon. We have, along with your letter, a batch of others from Cawnpore and Allahabad. I quote the passages from Court's at Allahabad, which most nearly affect you. The date is 15th.[2] It mentions that a telegraph came on the 14th from Benares to say that Colonel Gordon at Benares had, by orders of the Commander-in-Chief, stopped there all detachments of the new corps that were on their way up. Reason not stated. General Outram's arrival, armed with supreme military authority in Benares and Dinapore, may accelerate matters. But General Havelock has evidently enough to do at and about Cawnpore. You cannot look for him soon. Pray mention this to the Brigadier-General. It postpones quite indefinitely the march of troops upwards. The arrival of your siege train with additional materials may thus be of most important consequence. Your views on the Chain Bridge and Bridge of Boats, which are those doubtless of Brigadier-Gen[l] Wilson, you will have communicated to Williams. I also shall enforce, on my own part, his deference to General Wilson's decided judgment. You are right not to embarrass yourself in correspondence with Shazadahs. I have told you que, la ville prise, le Governor-General attache beaucoup de prix à ramasser soigneusement tous les papiers qu'on puisse trouver en Palais et à les garder pour remise à Calcutta. Pas **Outram.** **Shazadahs.** **Direction to preserve documents found in Palace.**

[1] 17th–23rd = 5 or 6 days.—W. M.

[2] 15th–23rd = 8 from Allahabad.—W. M.

Direction as to imprisonment of members of the Royal Family.

aussi de conditions avec la Famille Royale. Tous les personages principales doivent être gardés en Prisonniers.

. . . . . . . . .

J. R. Colvin.

*P.S.*—Every effort will be made, of course, to strengthen Meerut that can be. It is of vast importance, and every means used that engineering skill and daring can suggest to break up the bridge of boats. The state of the Upper Doab is a great evil. You should allow General Wilson to see Williams' memo[a] and he will decide on them, but he should see them in full.

## CVI.

Fort Agra, 25 *August* 1857.

My Dear Sir,—I have received such strong representations from the Commissioner at Meerut and other intelligent officers there, regarding the danger of allowing the rebel power to consolidate itself in the Doab, that I cannot be doing wrong in bringing them to your notice. The evil certainly is of the gravest consequences, as we have full experience in our own neighbourhood. If there be a good prospect, on the receipt of the Ferozepore train, etc., of a final blow at the great aim, then to that everything must yield. If, however, the question, for some indefinite time, should be only of strictly maintaining our ground, then I would request you deliberately to consider whether additional aid cannot for a time be sent to Meerut. The point is one on which I can only state my great sense of the value of acting from Meerut on Malagurh and other places. It might even perhaps save the troops some unhealthiness in a stationary camp at this season near Delhi. The mischief done by the country being from week to week organised against us, and the affair being thus one not only of a mutinous Army, but of a generally hostile *population, is of a very serious character.*[1] It is right to state this; while the military decision is, of course, one with which it would be out of my place to interfere further than by what I have now said. The English Mail of the 10th July[2] is in, and does not promise any early arrival of troops. Neither is there a move upwards of troops from the Eastward. These are the facts of our position, and I would be obliged by your

Aid to Meerut.

Action against Malagurh.

[1] The words in italics are a correction in pencil written by Mr. Colvin himself.—W. M.

[2] English Mail, 10th July, a month and a half old.—W. M.

telling me the result of your best reflection on them. I will ask you to show this letter to Mr. Greathed.

J. R. COLVIN.

BRIGADIER-GENERAL WILSON,
Delhi.

*P.S.*—Extract of letter from Brigadier-General Neill, dated 19th inst., from Cawnpore.

## CVII.

FORT AGRA, *25th August* 1857.

MY DEAR WILLIAMS,—I have received yours of the (?)th regarding the expediency of reinforcing Meerut and taking more vigorous steps against the insurgents in the Doab. I can only in reply send you the enclosed copy of a letter which I have this day written to General Wilson, from which you will see that I have pressed the point as far as I can. There must be some mistake in the reports about Sir Patrick Grant, as he has not yet left Calcutta. But a note of your views and a copy of your letter shall be sent on to Calcutta.

J. R. COLVIN.

## CVIII.

FORT AGRA, *August 29th*, 1857.

MY DEAR GREATHED,—An E. T. message has been received from G. F. Edmonstone, Calcutta, of 20th August, to the following effect:—"Rumours have more than once reached this Govt: that overtures have been made by the King of Delhi to the Officer commanding the Troops there, and that the overtures may possibly be renewed upon the basis of the restoration of the King to the position which he held before the Mutiny at Meerut and Delhi; the Governor-General wishes it to be understood that any concession to the King, of which the King's restoration to his former position would be the basis, is one to which the Government (as at present advised) cannot for a moment give its assent. **Government orders as to overtures by King of Delhi.**

"Should any negotiation of the sort be continued, a full report of all the circumstances must be submitted to the Governor-General in Council before the Govt: is committed to anything."

I telegraphed at once in reply how the matter stands, having before written on it by post, on the 23rd July, to the Governor-General. You will have the goodness to show this extract to

Brigadier-General Wilson. I also mentioned to the Governor-General in my answer the allusion to a Palace message in yours of the 22nd. Tell your brother that I had great pleasure in receiving his yesterday of the 23rd.[1] It came alone, and not with any official letter from yourself, as its purport seemed to imply.

We have some renewed talk of the Gwalior Regiments moving this way; in a month or five weeks hence I think it will be probable enough, should it not be possible before then to reinforce us.

Our small expedition to Hattrass and Alyghur has been so far very successful. They have had information sent to them of the move of the Jhansi men from Delhi to Alyghur.

J. R. COLVIN.

## CIX.

FORT AGRA, *4th September* 1857.

MY DEAR GREATHED,

. . . . . . . . . . .

Proposed pardon for Ranghurs of Rohtak.

*P.S.*—I have brought to the notice of the Governor-General the circumstance you mention of the petition for pardon of the 2000 Ranghurs of the Rhotuck District. The Supreme Government may give directions for such cases of quieting a whole revolted population. You could not, I think, do wrong, meanwhile, in promising the strongest recommendation to the Governor-General on arms being laid down, with exception of such persons as have been guilty of heinous crimes, especially against Christians.

J. R. COLVIN.

To H. H. GREATHED, ESQ.

[*Note in Sir W. Muir's hand:* "Mr. Colvin's last letter to Dehli."]

(6th September, I gave Greathed our latest news of the movements of the Indore force.—W. M.)

## CX.

FORT AGRA, *September 8th*, 1857.

Mr. Colvin's last illness.

MY DEAR WILLIAMS,—I received your two notes of the 3rd yesterday evening. I am sorry to tell you that Mr. Colvin

[1] 5 days from Delhi.—W. M.

has been getting rapidly worse during the night, and we fear the worst.

Reade has undertaken the duties, and by his desire I write now to tell you that it was not intended to give any authority regarding the Sikh Horse police to Spankic independently of your control.

. . . . . . . .

C. B. THORNHILL.

[*Note by Sir W. Muir*: "C. B. Thornhill (Secy. to Govt.) wrote above by Reade's directions."]

## CXI.

AGRA, 10 *September* 1857.

MY DEAR HAVELOCK,—Mr. Colvin's remains were buried this morning, seventeen minute guns were fired, and every respect shown by the Military. Mr. Reade has assumed, as before intimated, charge of the Government.

**Mr. Colvin's burial.**

**Mr. Reade assumes charge of the Government.**

We have just received very satisfactory accounts from Dehli up to the 5th inst. The siege train arrived safely on the 4th. "The supply of shot and shell," Greathed writes, "seems inexhaustible. It was escorted by 230 of the 8th Queen's and a wing of a Beloch Battalion." The Detachment of Rifles and Foot Artillery from Meerut was to come on on the 5th. Each of the siege guns was drawn by two elephants. Lt.-Col. Hogge had arrived from Meerut as Commissary-General of Ordnance, and, Greathed adds, "is admirably suited for the post." Wild's Punjaub Infantry was at Paneeput on the 4th. Goolab Sing's force *was not to be waited for*. They were marching leisurely, and probably had no great inclination to be on the front of the action. "My brother's Regiment, the 8th," writes Greathed, "claim the post of honour, being the Senior Regiment in camp. Our troops are animated by the best feeling." He writes in warm admiration of the noble bearing of the Sirmoor Battalion. "Too much cannot be said in their favour. They have served as the main picket at Hindoo Rao's ever since we arrived, and have lost half their number in action. They insist on having their sick and wounded on the upper storey of Hindoo Rao's house. Traverses have had to be erected opposite the windows to keep out round shot, and only yesterday a 10-inch shell carried away a corner of the roof. Major Reid has never been in camp. He is our watchman. The Corps should bear the motto of 'Vigil et tenax.'"

**Arrival of siege train at Delhi.**

**Lieut.-Col. Hogge, R.A.**

**8th Queen's.**

**Sirmoor Battalion.**

**Major Reid of the Goorkhas.**

*Disorder in Delhi.*

*Pay of King's troops.*

*Patiala receives present of guns from Sir J. Lawrence.*

The disorder in the City continues to increase. The troops are dissatisfied at not receiving their pay. The King has made them an advance of one Rupee to each Sepoy, 2 to each Cavalry, and 4 to each Officer. "The four Hindoostanee guns taken by Genl. Nicholson have been given to the Putiala Raja by Sir J. Lawrence, who purchased them at a valuation, as they were prize of war."

*General Bukht Khan.*

The zemindars of Paniput and Sonput reported to the King, on the 3rd, the approach of the siege train, and offered to help in capturing it. The project was referred to General Bukht Khan.

*Patiala army.*

Greathed had a letter from Mr. Ford, dated the 1st instant, stating that a conspiracy had been discovered among the Mussulmans of the Puteeala army. No harm has been done, but the discovery justifies Van Cortland's caution.

*Lumsden at Candahar.*

*Evacuation of Herat by the Persians.*

A letter from Major Lumsden at Candahar intimating the evacuation of Heerat by the Persians on the 27th July.

All was quiet in the Punjaub. Writing on the 5th, Greathed says: "It is confidently expected that the ball will open on the 7th, Monday."

*Sickness in Delhi camp.*

The Artillery force is mentioned as the healthiest in camp. Fever prevalent among the Infantry. Admission to hospital of Europeans about 100 a day. Cholera had appeared among the 61st (?).

*Offers of service by Delhi princes.*

*Palace overtures.*

The offers of service on the part of some of the princes, which were rejected by Mr. Greathed, were made again to the General in a somewhat altered form. There was a distinct offer to destroy the Bridge and to enlist the services of the Cavalry, and with their aid to put an end to the Infantry, on condition of favour being shown to the Royal Family. General Wilson refused positively to entertain any communications from the Palace. Greathed says he wrote full accounts to Mr. Edmonstone *via* Bombay of all that was passing on these occasions between the end of June and middle of August; and explained all the particulars regarding the Palace overtures. It is not known whether the communications have reached.

*Gwalior.*

*Indore troops.*

There is nothing fresh from Gwalior side. As far as we can make out, the *Ινδωρ* troops have all *κροσσεδ* the *Χυμβυλ*, but whether they mean to *μουε θις ναι*, or to go to Dehli, or to stay for a time at *Δώλπωρ*, so far as we can make out the *κοντινγεντ*, they have none of them moved or intend to do so till after the *Δυσσεχρα*.

The above intelligence should all be communicated to the Governor-General.

I have now at Mr. Reade's desire taken a more exclusive charge of the "Intelligence Department," and will endeavour to send daily news for Calcutta either in MSS. or printed. **Intelligence Department.**

As you will be away shortly, I shall address in future to Sherer, that they may be surer of immediate despatch.

Our last from your camp is dated the 4th from General Neill. We are all in high spirits at hearing that so large a force is on its way up, and that you will be able to go on now to Lucknow. God preserve them till you reach, and give you a final glorious victory over the enemy there—is the prayer of many hearts.—Ever yours,

W. MUIR.

GENERAL H. HAVELOCK, C.B.

*Note.*—In future addressed through Sherer.

Dehli gets Calcutta news through Bombay.—W. M.

## CXII.

AGRA, 11 *September* 1857.

MY DEAR GREATHED,—The Indore people remain *in statu quo*. It is not indeed certain whether all have got across the Chumbul. We have a native account from Dehli up to the 7th, stating that the King had issued an urgent perwanah to the Indore and Gwalior troops to come to his aid, and sent it by Gholum Hyder and Jehangeer Khan—the latter an old deserter from Scindia. You will know better the particulars of the summons, and whether it is likely to have any other effect than showing in what straits the unfortunate monarch must be. The City and Country near have been in some alarm in consequence of these Mutineers. We look anxiously for the grand denouement of the Dehli play and for the march of Columns downwards. We hope they will come on both banks of the Jumna; but, as you observe in one of your letters, the movements of our Army (depend) on the course taken by the fugitive Mutineers. Hattrass doing well; accounts of Lucknow confirmed; they have plenty of corn, and millstones to grind it with. **King calls on Indore and Gwalior troops to aid him. Jehangeer Khan.**

We should be glad to entertain Sikhs or Punjabis here, either mounted or foot, for our police. We hear you (have) hangers-on of this class in camp. Would they come down, if given to understand that they should have employment here? See, please, if anything could be done in this respect. **Sikhs, Punjabis.**

You might send down a few as Cossids to be kept here. One of your letters by the Customs men reached. The other you mention I do not recollect. I have distributed the 3 letters sent with yours of the 5th.

W. MUIR.

H. H. GREATHED, ESQ.,
Agent Lt.-Govr.

## CXIII.

AGRA, 12th *September* 1857.

MY DEAR GREATHED,—Macpherson has received information of a serious character from Dinka Rao this morning. It is probable that the Contingent regiments have been unsettled by the departure of the Indore Rebels. They appear to have raised the green flag, and demanded carriage of Scindia. He remonstrated with them, and succeeded in detaching the 5th and what remains of the 6th, with the 2 Mahidpore guns, and the whole Cavalry, say 600, from the main body—so that they are for the present amenable to Scindia's commands.

**Gwalior Contingent Regiments and Scindia's loyal attitude.**

The remainder, say quatre (?) full Regiments et cinque batteries, are in opposition to Scindia. They demand carriage, and the messenger who brought the letter says that they had their guns out on the roads leading to Scindia's Lushkar. It seems almost certain that he will not be able to detain them any longer. You may imagine, consequently, how anxiously we look for the movement of a column from your force this way. If the Contingent unites with the Indore troops, we are exposed to all the chances and risks of a siege. Please God, however, by that time General Wilson will be set at liberty from his present position, and able to succour us. Kindly let General Wilson see this, and give us as early intimation as you can of what movement may be made hither. We know well that his movements will depend in great measure on the course the fugitives from Dehli may take, but our necessities should also be borne in mind.

Our last from you is the 5th. Durbar native news we have up to the 8th. It is here stated that 4 Companies, 200 Sowars, and 2 guns have been despatched to Dholepore. Coupled with yesterday's notice regarding the perwanah to the Indore and Gwalior troops, it looks like an escort to the two men Golam Hyder and Jehangeer, who were directed to take the perwanah.

**Movements of mutinous bodies.**

The news-writer also says that 4 Companies of Sappers and Miners were ordered to go off for the purpose of driving a mine under the Fort of Akbarabad.

Cawnpore letters up to the 6th. Reinforcement would be there by the 10th. Lucknow expected to be relieved before the 20th.

W. MUIR.

## CXIV.

AGRA, *12th September* 1857.

MY DEAR GREATHED,—The following is the copy of a Message received from the Government of India in reply to a letter from Mr. Colvin and Colonel Cotton to the Governor-General, suggesting an advance from the East in order to crush the rebels in the Doab.

"The letter of the 11th instant addressed by the Lieutenant-Governor and Lieut.-Col. Cotton to the Governor-General in Council has been received.

"I am directed to acquaint you, for the information of the Lieutenant-Governor and of Lieut.-Col. Cotton, that it is impossible to name the time at which a column from the south will be able to advance beyond Cawnpore. The force under General Havelock, when joined by that under General Outram, will still be too weak for the work which lies before them at Lucknow and Cawnpore. Parts of Behar are in insurrection, and the means of protecting Bengal are altogether inadequate. You must not build upon the prospect of (?) an early advance to Agra. Several Regiments must arrive before this advance can be made in force, and their time of arrival is very uncertain. As to Cavalry, it does not exist in this Presidency, and the 14th Dragoons cannot be spared from the Bombay Moveable Columns in Central India, where there is plenty for them to do.

Views of the Governor-General in Council as to position at Agra.

"The organisation of the rebel power in the Doab is greatly to be deplored, but there is no force to direct against it from here at present, and the Gov.-General in Council desires me to say that he trusts to the Lieutenant-Governor being able to maintain his position in the midst of his difficulties with the same success as hitherto has attended his efforts, and with his own resources and defences. Not a day will be lost in pushing on relief to Agra when the means of doing this are at the disposal of the Government.

"You are requested to send a copy of this letter in a safe form to Brigadier Wilson, and to inform him that the expectation expressed by the Governor-General in a private letter to Major-General Bernard, that a force might be detached from Dehli southward, was founded upon the reports from General Bernard that an assault was about to be made. The Governor-General in Council does not doubt that Brigadier Wilson has used a sound judgment in not attempting an assault hitherto, but he reckons confidently that at least the intention to retire from Delhi will have been abandoned now that the Army has been largely reinforced, if indeed no opening for a decisive blow can be found.—I have the honour to be,

"B. H. L. BIRCH, Col.
"Secretary to the Government of India, Military Department.

"COUNCIL CHAMBER, FORT WILLIAM,
*the* 31*st August* 1857."

. . . . . . . .

W. M.

CXVI.

AGRA, 12*th September* 1857.

MY DEAR GREATHED,—Enclosed the translation of two letters intercepted on their road from Gwalior to Dehli. They tally with our other information that the Contingent are determined to move on the twenty-fourth Mohurrum, that is, on the dix-huitieme of this month.

Gwalior Contingent.

All our Authorities here are very urgent that this circumstance should be pressed upon the notice of General Wilson. If all has gone well, Dehli has by this time fallen, and if so a Column could be spared to at the least protect our frontier, if not to attack and punish these mutinous bodies. With a small body of additional Europeans and some horse we would be able to repel anything that came near us; for we have a superabundance of heavy artillery. Our field battery, however, is not strongly horsed, and we need more Artillerymen.

Agra applies to Delhi for troops.

I think I sent a list of our Ordnance and Ammunition. I am going to send, at Colonel Collins' instance, a duplicate of it. . . .

We have Colonel Becher's letters up to the 9th.[1] Yours to the 8th.[1] We eagerly look out for more tidings. Of the final result we can hardly hope to hear for a couple of days. When it does, we shall look out anxiously for the appearance of a Column to protect this frontier and scatter the threatening bodies of troops.

. . . . . . . .

W. MUIR.

[1] 3 or 4 days to Dehli.—W. M.

Letters just come in from Havelock. He speaks of an early advance on Lucknow, and says, I regret to say, that it is but too certain that Mr. Ommaney, Civil Service, was killed during the siege. Mr. Ommaney, C.S., Oudh Commissioner, killed.

## CXVII.

Agra, *15th September* 1857.

My Dear Greathed,—Yours of the 10th come in this morning, with a copy of General Wilson's to Sir J. Lawrence. Also a letter from Anson, for which kindly thank him, and one to Captain Chalmers from Captain Dickens. They have all been taken advantage of for the "Memo. of Intelligence," as you will see in to-morrow's budget at any rate. The eagerness with which intelligence from Dehli is sought after is naturally very great. Added to the general considerations which turn the eyes of all India at present to Dehli, we are at this moment more than ever dependent on its speedy fall. On Saturday the 12th I wrote at length regarding the position of affairs at Gwalior, and every day confirms the intelligence that the Contingent are resolute on moving sur le dix-huitieme de ce mois ci. They will join the Indore Troops, and intend moving on Agra. But long before that we trust that the "flying Columns" will be striking terror not only into the fugitive rebels of Dehli, but into those of the Gwalior Contingent. Captain Anson, Captain Chalmers, Captain Dickens. Gwalior troops to move, 18th September.

It is the wish of Mr. Reade and Col. Cotton that these circumstances, as I before wrote, should be prominently brought under Gen[l] Wilson's consideration, in order that his plans, however they may be affected by the direction taken by the fleeing "Pandies," may, under any circumstances, make provision for the security of our frontier towárds Gwalior and for the community of this Fort.

. . . . . . . .

W. Muir.

## CXVIII.

Agra, *16th September* 1857.

My Dear Greathed,—Colonel Becher's and your letters of the 11th came in last night, and have given high satisfaction and confidence to all here. The position held by you during these stirring events has been a very enviable one, as you have seen so closely all the proceedings and known the causes which influenced them.

. . . . . . . .

W. MUIR.

H. H. GREATHED, ESQ.

## CXX.

AGRA, *September 18th*, 1857.

Mr. H. H. Greathed thanked.

MY DEAR GREATHED,[1]—Late last evening your most satisfactory despatch of the 12th reached. I believe I only express the general opinion here, when I say that we have reason to be deeply indebted to you for the full, clear, and comprehensive manner in which you communicate to us the details of these momentous proceedings. You will see from the printed precis the reports which Cocks has sent us. We do not build upon them, but must wait patiently one or two days.

We have had a letter from Beadon, dated 4th Sept. He says: "I begin to think that succour will reach you (at Agra) first from the direction of Dehli, and I trust it may be speedy and effectual." So they are beginning to perceive the real position of affairs.

Our reports from Gwalior are that the Contingent intended to march last night, but it has continued to rain heavily, and that may detain them.

We wait to see the effect of the news of the state of things at Dehli upon them. Anyhow, we look to General Wilson to furnish us with a Column sufficient to ward off and disperse these mutinous bodies, for they still talk of this Fort as the object of their attack.

Enclosed is a statement of Ordnance and Ammunition; Colonel Cotton is desirous that it should be submitted to General Wilson, in order that he may know what heavy Artillery is mounted and in readiness here, and not send down with the coming Column what we can ourselves supply.

W. MUIR.

H. H. GREATHED, ESQ.,
Agent and Commissioner, Dehli.

[1] This letter, and the subsequent ones up to CXXIV. of 26th September, never reached Mr. Greathed. He died on the 19th September.—W. C.

## CXXI.

AGRA, *September 22nd*, 1857.

MY DEAR GREATHED,—My last to you was on the 18th, Friday. Saturday and Sunday we had not a line from Dehli, and began to get anxious. Native reports, however, from various quarters, and especially the budget of the Gwalior news-writer at the Dehli Court, assured us (notwithstanding Ghous Mahomed's ishtehar that the Royal troops had taken the Puharee) that all was going on well.

Yesterday forenoon your welcome letters of the 15th and 16th arrived. Thank Anson also for his of the 16th. What noble fellows English soldiers are! What do we not, under God's providence and blessing, owe to them for the noble daring, intrepidity, and endurance they have displayed in this great struggle! **News of the assault on Delhi reaches Agra.**

I send the sheets of printed intelligence. I may add that the Ramgurh battalion with the freebooter Kooer Singh are reported to have made their way to Rewah, so that Osborne has been obliged to fall back on Dumoh (it is said, but more probably Nagode if that continues firm).

After all, the Gwalior Contingent did not march on the 18th, as far as we know. They had a quarrel with the Maharajah, demanding of him treasure and carriage. On his refusing, both parties had out their guns, but after a time the Contingent came to terms. The 5th and the Cavalry are entirely subservient to him; the rest wait till he gives them carriage, so it seems probable there will be no move until after the Dussehra. The Indore men are still at Dholepore. Some Sowars with one Lall Khan are said to have reached Gwalior on the 16th with a perwanah from the King asking why they did not come to Dehli. There are symptoms of shakiness in the Indore men already, I imagine occasioned by the reports from Dehli. They are feeling if there be room for pardon. We are now looking out for your despatch of the 17th. **Gwalior troops.**

W. MUIR.

H. H. GREATHED, ESQ.

I do trust to hear that General Wilson has recovered from his fatigues. How prudent and admirable all his arrangements have been!

## CXXIV.

AGRA, *26th September* 1857.

MY DEAR GREATHED,—Nothing has come in from Dehli since the 19th. Our native reports and the flight of the mutinous soldiery give us a tolerably firm assurance that Dehli must have completely fallen some days ago. Still, we crave for details. We are also anxious about yourself.

C. B. Saunders, C.S.

By the way, it was not till I had written my yesterday's letter that I was aware Mr. Saunders was at Dehli. I fancied he had not been able to join. So long as you are disabled from writing, kindly ask him to give a daily bulletin of proceedings so long as there is anything of great public interest to chronicle. Some account of the state of the buildings in and about Dehli would be interesting. Have they been much injured by the protracted cannonade and final bombardment? The Church, the Palace, the Jumma Musjid? Have the burial-grounds been respected? What is the state of the little one outside the Cashmere Gate?[1]

By this time we doubt not that, with God's assistance, our troops have effectually relieved the heroic band in Lucknow.

Movements of mutinous bodies.

We continue to get panic-stricken accounts of the rebel forces from Muthra, etc. A considerable number crossed, as I before wrote, by ghats higher up. Say 2 or 3000 men, some 4 or 500 reaching Muthra on the afternoon of the 24th. An immense body is reported to have arrived yesterday. A number are said to have already crossed, and to be taking a north-easterly route. A body of horse is also said to have come on in this direction as far as Furruckabad, people say with the view of going to Gwalior. It *may*, however, be only a reconnoitring party to see that no attack is intended from this side. There is a report, but as yet unconfirmed, of a move by the Gwalior Contingent this way. We long to hear some tidings of the pursuing column.

Allygurh attacked.

Allygurh was attacked yesterday by the fanatics of the district, and Gobind Singh, our chief there, obliged to flee.

Detachment from Agra.

We are withdrawing our European detachment from Hathrass to Khundoulie, 10 miles off. We very much need, in all these quarters, the support of the pursuing column. And it will be a

[1] Where our little Maggie was buried in 1855.—W. M. Grave seen in good order in 1894.—W. C.

grand object when Allygurh can be occupied by a force that will be able to retain it against all comers.

W. MUIR.

H. H. GREATHED, ESQ.

*P.S.*—This morning's news from the south is that the Indore troops at Dholepore are collecting carriage. They are in an awkward predicament at present, as Sindia is said to have destroyed the boats at the Dholepore ghats. They talk of coming this way; but it can be only bravado: they will probably join the Dehli fugitives.

## CXXV.

AGRA, 27 *September* 1857.

MY DEAR COLONEL GREATHED,[1]—The last I had from your brother was the 18th. Colonel Becher's letter of the 19th mentioned that your brother was very ill of cholera. The despatches of the 19th, 20th, and 21st have apparently miscarried. And we knew only by native report of our success at Dehli till this afternoon, when Colonel Becher's letter of the 22nd arrived. He mentions that you are coming down in command of the pursuing column. We shall be very glad to have copious details from you of all the proceedings from the 19th. We were then in occupation of the northern half of the city down to the Chouk. What were the operations which led to the occupation of the Palace?

**Agra hears on 27th September of the complete fall of Delhi.**

You will no doubt now be near Muthra. We hear that the debris of some 20 Infantry Regiments, besides Cavalry, is congregated there. Say 5 or 6000 men, of whom 2000 are sick and wounded; some 20 H.A. guns. They are making a bridge; but I hope you will get to them before they have finished it.

**Position of rebel forces at Muthra.**

They are corresponding with the Gwalior Contingent, who have a siege train and well-furnished magazine. But it is expected that the Maharaja will be able to hold them back. The Dholepore men have no ammunition, but some 10 or 12 guns. The Contingent are about 4000 men; the Dholepore people about 2000 or under. The troops at Muthra have not much ammunition.

**Gwalior Contingent.**

**Dholpore troops.**

. . . . . . . . .

W. MUIR.

TO COLONEL GREATHED.

[1] Supposed to be marching down by Muthra. (He came by the Doab.)—W. M.

## CXXVI.

AGRA, 28 *September* 1857.

MY DEAR SIR,[1]—I was very glad to receive yours of the 20th. It was very long on the road, having come in only to-day. Your letter to Mr. Williams had already acquainted us with the melancholy tidings of Mr. Greathed's death; and Colonel Becher's of the 22nd, which reached yesterday, had communicated the news of the complete capture of Dehli.[2] I enclose our printed budget, which contains some other information.

Mr. Greathed's death.

It is a cause of great satisfaction that there was on the spot one so well fitted as yourself for taking up the important and delicate duties of the Agent's office.

Besides the ordinary news of the day, we shall be much interested by any political intelligence you may communicate regarding the Chiefs and Princes in and about Dehli. Evidence regarding their complicity in the late proceedings will be best obtained by immediate investigations. I am very anxious to hear whether the Jhujjur Chieftain has compromised himself. The acts of his *subordinates* were certainly hostile to us.

Jhujjur Chief.

The Cawnpore news in this extra is not official. Cossids are overdue from that place.

W. MUIR.

C. B. SAUNDERS, ESQ.

*P.S.*—Pray offer very hearty congratulations to General Wilson for the glorious conclusion he has achieved to the long struggle.

## CXXVII.

AGRA, 29*th September* 1857.

MY DEAR SIR,—We have good accounts from Cawnpore, which I hope to be able to send you in a printed form. In case the proofs should not come, I may mention in brief that on our first march on Monday morning, the 21st, Havelock drove the enemy before him with great loss to them, and the capture of 6 or 7 guns; and with the loss of only one or two killed on our side. No further opposition had been experienced that day, or on the march on the next, and all were in high spirits.

Havelock defeats the enemy near Cawnpore.

[1] Copied by W. Lowe, C.S.—W. M.

[2] The garrison of Agra heard on 27th of the complete capture of Dehli by letter of Dehli, 22nd.—W. C.

I was delighted to hear from one of our native Christians here that my excellent friend, Professor Ram Chunder, was safe. He tells me he is with Captain Tytler of the Pay Office. Pray tell him that I have mourned deeply over the fate of Chimman Lal, and trust that he himself has been spared to be a blessing to his countrymen.

Professor Ram Chunder. Captain Tytler. Chimman Lal.

It was on my mind several times to write and ask Greathed to save as many rare MSS. as he could, but I forgot. In Captain Anson's note I observe that some *valuable books have been taken possession of.* They should be carefully arranged and catalogued. . . . . . . . . . . . has a fine library. Especially a good copy of the *Seerut Hishamee*, which should, if possible, be saved. Ram Chunder will know about it.[1]

Copy of the *Seerut Hishámi.*

In which burying-ground was Mr. Greathed interred? Kindly mention about the state of the new burying-ground outside the Cashmere Gate. Are any of the former gravestones standing, and were any of the graves desecrated?

We have not had a word from Colonel Greathed, but there is a warm report in the bazar that the pursuing column has come upon the Muthra men and dispersed them, etc. But this is, I fear, rather what the people desire than what has been obtained from carefully checked evidence.

W. MUIR.

C. B. SAUNDERS, C.S.

## CXXVIII.

AGRA, *30th September* 1857.

MY DEAR SIR,—Your last letter is dated the 22nd. It surprised us rather to get a despatch from W. Clifford from Ghazeeooddeen-nugger, as your last communication led us to expect that the column would march *via* the Kootub down the right bank of the Jumna. Colonel Greathed has been written to, to hasten down as rapidly as he can, otherwise the Muthra Mutineers will elude pursuit, as they have got their bridge ready, and will be able to carry off their guns to annoy us hereafter in Rohilkhund or Oudh.

Greathed urged to rapid advance, as against Gwalior and Neemuch advance.

It is now probable the Gwalior Mutineers will go towards Cawnpore. The Nana has been tampering with them. A message from Calcutta has come in to-day appointing temporarily Colonel H. Fraser, C.B., to be Chief Commissioner in these Pro-

Nana tampers with Gwalior Mutineers.

[1] We got this, and I gave it over to the India Office Library.—W. M.

Col. H. Fraser, C.B., appointed Chief Commissioner, N.W.P.

vinces, with supreme Military and Civil command, but not affecting the Dehli force, or other forces in the field;—in Revenue and Judicial matters to have the advice of the Board and Court.

Other news you will get from the enclosed printed slip.

W. MUIR.

C. B. SAUNDERS, ESQ.,
Delhi.

## CXXIX.

AGRA, *October 1st*, 1857.

MY DEAR SIR,—

. . . . . . . .

Disposal of documents found in Palace,

What has been accomplished in the matter of seizing correspondence and papers in the Palace at Dehli? The Governor-General desired that all documents of the kind should be taken into custody and carefully preserved, with the view of examination as to whether they incriminated the Royal Family. We shall be glad to hear from you how your political investigations go on, and what proofs you find of any previous plot. Subsequent participation will be more easily susceptible of proof.

and Arabic and Persian MSS. *Seerut-Hishámi.*

In a previous letter I asked about the preservation of rare Arabic and Persian MSS., particularly a copy of the *Seerut-Hishami* belonging to the Principal Sudder Ameen.

Hoping soon to hear from you again, and begging that you will still favour us with a daily report.

W. MUIR.

C. B. SAUNDERS, ESQ.,
Off. Agent and Commissr., Dehli.

INTELLIGENCE DEPARTMENT, AGRA.

MSS. VOL. II.

*THIRD SERIES.*

# LETTERS DOWN COUNTRY

TO

# CAWNPORE, CALCUTTA, ETC.

From 2nd October 1857 to 19th November 1857.

## INTELLIGENCE DEPARTMENT, AGRA.

### MSS. VOL. II.

### *THIRD SERIES.*

# LETTERS DOWN COUNTRY

TO

# CAWNPORE, CALCUTTA, ETC.

**From 2nd October 1857 to 19th November 1857.**

## CXXX.

AGRA, *2nd October* 1857.

MY DEAR SHERER,—Letters from Col. Greathed's Camp confirm the news I gave you yesterday on native authority.

Mr. B. Sapte, writing from Boolundshuhur on the 29th, states that on the 28th they marched on Boolundshuhur and came upon the enemy at daybreak—our Force consisted of 2 European Regiments, the 8th and 75th, 2 Punjab Infantry Regiments, 3 Punjab Cavalry Regiments, the 9th Lancers, 18 guns and 2 mortars. Wulleedad Khan had besides his Malagurh levies the whole Jhansi Brigade. They had entrenched themselves outside the town on the road leading through the Civil Station. "They fired as we advanced, and after two hours' pounding or more we drove them from their position, *killing* some 150 of them, and losing ourselves some 50 killed and wounded, among the latter six officers. We took one 9-pounder gun and one 3-pounder, two 9-pounder ammunition waggons, a quantity of small-bore ammunition, and 25 barrels of gunpowder." Wulleedad Khan, as I feared, escaped from his fort during the action and fled to Rohilkhund. "The Nana Sahib was said to be with him," but I conclude it is the Nana's wounded brother, regarding whom I had information about a fortnight ago that he had passed up with a retinue of sowars through Anoopshuhur to Malagurh.

**Fight in Boolundshuhur (Malagurh).**

**The Nana.**

Malagurh taken.

On the morning of the 29th we took possession of Malagurh, and operations were in progress for mining and blowing up the Fort. The detachment would then march *via* Anoopshuhur and Debhaee to Allygurh, which they might reach on the 4th or 5th.

Mr. Sapte says he has applied to Meerut for a force to settle his district, which is naturally, after Wulleedad's long reign, in a disturbed state,—Greathed of course cannot spare any men from his column.

Country settling down.

Notwithstanding this, things are already beginning to tranquillise, for "he is establishing his Police, and hopes the Mail Carts will be running in a very short time, *the road between this and Meerut will be quite safe in a few days.*" After that, who can say *the country* is against us? It has only to be rid of a few of these heads and fomenters of rebellion to quiet down again into peace and order.

Country not against the Government.

Movements of Mutineers.

The Jhansi Brigade still retains 3 of its guns, but can have but little ammunition. The fugitive Sepoys almost all have taken the road to Rohilkhund.

Sapte says: "It is uncertain what road this column will take after Allygurh—but possibly Futtehgurh."

"*There is another column out on the other side under Showers.*" This is the first intimation we have had, and that in a passing remark, as to any column being out on the right bank of the Jumna.

We have not had any letters from Delhi later than the 22nd, and cannot make out what has stopped our communications.

Meanwhile we have authentic information that the Bareilly portion of the fugitive troops at Muthra have crossed the bridge, and are now encamped within a few miles of the bank.

The policy of the remaining portion we cannot exactly make out. There have been violent altercations between the Bareilly and the other Brigades; the latter are hungry and ill furnished, the former have their purses well stocked with silver and gold. There was a strong party against the Bareilly troops being allowed to cross with their arms and treasure and go off to Bareilly. It talked loudly (after the repose of a few days had recruited their strength and again raised their spirits) of the necessity of striking some blow nearer at hand, and of improving their impoverished resources.

The Bareilly Brigade,[1] however, has evidently the advantage in every way, both in resources and *mind*,—and having actually led the way, its authority is not unlikely to draw all the rest of the

[1] Dr. Farquhar's handwriting. -W. M.

force over. A recent report, in fact, states that a portion of the Neemuch Brigade has actually crossed the river.

Of the Dholepore Mutineers we cannot learn that the main body has even yet moved. They have been detailing bodies of cavalry to reconnoitre, and perhaps collect supplies. They have also been looking at the road to Bhurtpore. What all this may portend one cannot say, but I still incline to thinking that, unless scared away by the *Flying* Brigade—(people begin to smile when it is called by that name), they will pass over into the Doab by Muthra.

Nothing new from Gwalior.

Col. Fraser has recalled the detachment from Saidabad, and ordered it to fall back on Agra. He does not wish it to risk the chance of an encounter with a body of mutinous troops on their flight across the Doab.

The Hatrass expedition has nevertheless done great service. **Hatrass detachment.** It prevented the "Naib Soobah" establishing himself at Allyghur, raising levies, and collecting the revenue, at a very critical period. It also protected a large quarter of the country. I do trust Hatrass may yet escape being plundered by the Mutineers as they pass.

A letter from Meerut of the 23rd ulto. gives the following **Engagement at Mozuffernugger.** particulars of the Mozuffurnuggur business. "All our available force has gone out northwards, to punish a very large collection of Mussulmans at a place called Thana Bhowun to the north-west of Mozuffurnuggur. It is the breeding place of all those Irregular Cavalry. Brigadier Smith's brother with a small force went at them last week, but failed in polishing them off altogether, owing to the Seikhs and Goorkhas having held back in a most shameful manner. The former are young soldiers and the latter mongrel Goorkhas,—both requiring Europeans to show them what to do. Smith Johnson of the 18th, and Low, C.S., were wounded. Of course this has made the faithful very cocky, but it will soon be taken out of them by the Rifles, Dragoons, H. Artillery Mortars," etc. The same writer adds a few interesting details regarding Delhi.

"The breaches were found impracticable, and scaling-ladders **Assault of Delhi.** had to be used. You recollect how little of the walls could be seen at the distance of 200 yards. Salkeld with 5 Sergeants went to blow in the gates; but one escaped unhurt. Salkeld has **Salkeld.** lost an arm; they hope to be able to save his leg. Of 14 engineers told off for duty, ten were knocked over. The casualties **Engineers' casualties.** amount to 65 officers and 1160 men—many but slightly wounded." I give the figures, as the writer, an engineer, is likely to be well informed. He adds that loads of caps were found in the city, and indeed that nothing but powder seemed to be scarce. They had begun a field work near the church; the dome of the latter building is well perforated. The health of the troops is better since they came into the city. "The town people are asking to come back, but the General will not allow them at present." I fancy there must be some mistake about this latter statement.

Church at Delhi.

Nothing yet about Lucknow. We have had nothing from you later than the 24th.

W. M.

Sick from Delhi said to be going to Agra.

J. W. SHERER, ESQ., Cawnpore.

## CXXXII.

AGRA, *3rd October* 1857.

MY DEAR SHERER,—Still no letter from you,—your last is now 9 or 10 days old.

After a silence of nearly a week, a Delhi letter came in yesterday to Capt. Nixon from Col. Becher. Mr. Saunders' despatches of previous dates may have miscarried. But he has officially been reminded that the Government of India wishes a *daily* Cossid communication between this and Delhi to be regularly maintained. I have given the scanty intelligence of Becher's letter in the extra sent herewith. Col. Brown is Military Governor of Delhi, and Col. Jones Commandant of Palace. From the manner in which the expedition under Brigadier Showers is mentioned, it would appear to be a mere local business—not to imply a march down the right bank of the Jumna to Muthra. The words are—"a small Force under Brigadier Showers is at Humaiyoon's tomb. A number of city badmashes had assembled there and at the Kootub, where the Force will go afterwards."

Administrative arrangements at Delhi.

Colonel Brown, Governor. Colonel Jones, Commandant of Palace.

Two more sons of the King had been sent in by Brigadier Showers,—Mirza Mundoo (Mehdi ?) and Bukhtawar Shah. I do not remember to have heard their names prominently mentioned in any of the rebel proceedings. They are to be tried by a Military Commission.

Delhi Princes.

General Cortlandt had arrived at Rohtuck on the 26th.

Van Cortlandt.

The quotation given from General Penny's letter is gratifying; the fall of Delhi has had, as we expected, "a marked effect on the Meerut District, revenue being brought in rapidly."

Payment of revenue in Meerut.

From Muthra our intelligence is that the entire Bareilly Brigade had crossed the bridge by the evening of the 2nd. They are still encamped on the opposite bank, but may have moved towards Hattrass to-day. From Saidabad an El. Tel. Message came in this morning (for the *wire has been set up so far*) to say that heavy firing had been heard in the direction of Moorsaun (between Muthra and Hattrass). Mr. Cocks had heard that the troops which crossed had been recalled to Muthra, and attributed the cannonade and recall to the approach of the Flying Brigade down the right bank. But we havé no reason to expect this Brigade at Muthra. The fact of the recall is not corroborated by any reports we have yet received direct from Muthra, and no very certain conclusion can be drawn from the mere cannonade. Col. Greathed and Mr. Saunders will, I trust, have got my letters urging on their column towards Muthra; and these Mutineers may yet be crushed. **Bareilly Brigade.**

Our last account direct from Muthra was that numbers from the other brigades had crossed after the Bareilly Brigade and were following them. A detachment which the Neemuch men had sent to Bindraban had returned on the night of the 1st with some money realised there. They had also collected some at Mahabun. **Movements of Mutineers.**

The Indore Mutineers had not moved from Dholepore up to yesterday forenoon, but they were preparing to start, and were likely to march yesterday evening or this morning. A later messenger says that they had not moved last night: that they daily made preparations to start, and daily deferred them. It will take them three or four days to get to Muthra, and their course may yet be altered by the advent of Greathed's column. At present none of the Indore troops seem to have any other idea than to go to Muthra. **Indore troops.**

The Contingent are said to have invited them back to Gwalior, as they stood in need of their Cavalry; but Scindia's arrangement in carrying off all the boats effectually prevented this. **Scindia's arrangements.**

There are at Dholepore 25 sowars deputed by the Delhi fugitives at Muthra; and a daily correspondence is kept up between the Mutineers at both places.

From Gwalior we have news to the 30th ultimo, both by messenger, and by letter received by Macpherson from the Gwalior Durbar. **Gwalior news.**

The messenger's account, which is consistent and intelligent, is to the effect that the fifth Regiment and 50 or 60 men of the

4th, with the Cavalry, had gone over entirely to Scindia. The remaining four Regiments with 250 Cavalry remain at Morar. They have forty guns, of which 3 or 4 are 24-pounder, the rest light. They have laden a part of the Magazine on 1200 bullocks, 1000 camels, and 800 carts (the figures as given by a mere spy must be taken with reserve), and they want more carriage still.

Scindia's arrangements.

The Maharajah has entrenched himself on one side the stream, the Mutineers on the other. He has given them no pay for last month. They have not yet decisively fixed where they are going to. The Poorbeahs are resolute in demanding to be led to Cawnpore. The men from the upper Doab talk of advancing on Agra. The two parties are about equal in numbers perhaps; but the Poorbeahs are the most influential, and likely to carry the day.

The Maharajah has told the Contingent he will not allow them to march towards Agra; they may, he says, if they choose, go in the direction of Cawnpore.

The Contingent endeavour to stop desertion by severe punishment. They made an example of one man who tried to run away, by cutting off his nose and parading him about the camp on a jackass.

Major Macpherson's letter also contains particulars which make me hope that no *immediate* attempt will be made on Cawnpore.

Movements of Mutineers.

The following is an extract from the letter he got: "The Morar Mutineers have changed their mind. Now they want to go first to Duttiah, Jhansi, and Jaloun, to ask them to join; if not, then to take from their Rajahs certain sums; then they will go by Calpee: this is what they are talking about.

"The guns and army which were put out for (*i.e.*, to check) the Morar Mutineers are still at the same place, and will remain there till the Mutineers start from Morar."

Colonel Durand disarms troops.

The following is about some troops disarmed by Durand, the particulars of which we have not yet had. "The four Companies 6th Contingent Regiment who were in Aseergarh, and one Company 5th Regiment who were at Boorhampore, were disarmed by Colonel H. M. Durand; they first came to the Lushkur and asked for service; H. H. refused them, on account of Colonel Durand's order. Now they are with the Morar Mutineers."

The scene described in this sentence is one of the most ridiculous that can well be imagined.

"Yesterday (29th September) the Mutineers were all in full dress, and gave a salute to the Nana's Vakeel, who is still with them. In return, the Vakeel granted the rank of Brigadier-Major, Brigade-Major, Captain, and ensign to some Subahdars and Jemadars, and has promised that when they will arrive at Cawnpore they will then get pay and batta and Enám (gifts)." Nana's Vakil grants military titles.

A letter has been received from Mr. Donald, 2nd Assistant at Sirsa, giving, on the whole, an encouraging account of the state of Bhuttiana. He is, however, anxious lest the disturbances in the Punjaub towards Gogaira should spread to his district. The only previous intelligence we have had of these is in the notice on the 21st ultimo by Barnes of a "local disturbance in the wild country between Mooltan and Lahore, against which a force has been sent." This I quoted in a previous letter. Mr. Donald, on the 24th idem, speaks of it thus: "I regret to say that on the opposite bank of the Sutledge towards Gogaira the country is up. Mr. Davis, the patrol, writes that the people have attacked the jail and Tehseel. A plundering party came over to Fazilka and plundered one of the small villages there. Mr. Oliver has therefore moved up there with a gun and some troops to awe the Wuttoo tribes at Fazilka. The Natives have a report that the troops at Mooltan have mutinied, and have possession of the fort; this latter part of the story appears to me improbable. All about Sirsa is quite quiet. The Buhawulpore troops stationed here appear at present well disposed. I am all alone at Sirsa, and on the 'qui vive.' It is generally supposed that the Minister of Bahawul Khan is at the bottom of the rise of the Beloch tribes on the Ravee." Mr. Donald's account of Sirsa and Bhuttiana. Sirsa news. Gogaira revolt. Mr. Oliver proceeds to overawe the Wuttoos at Fazilka. Bahawul Khan.

Of his own district he gives otherwise a fair account. The town of Sirsa is gradually becoming reinhabited. All the revenue had been paid in, plundered and deserted villages being reoccupied and cultivated. The crops as forward as could be expected from the season. Crime rare. All heinous cases being taken up; restitution of property insisted on, camels, cattle, etc., being recovered. It is very remarkable that here, as in very many other places, "next to the troops, the Customs establishment took the most active part in the rebellion" and outrages. He speaks of a vast number of claims for restoration to property. If it be so in this thinly populated tract, what will it be in the crowded districts of these provinces? How have you found this in Cawnpore, or has your authority not yet become so generally re-established as to bring you to this stage? Sirsa District. Customs establishment disloyal.

Notwithstanding the present tranquillity of his district, Mr. Donald is very anxious as to the effect of the Gogaira rising on the connected tribes of Bhutties and Wuttoos.

As Col. Becher on the 28th makes no mention of any Mooltan mutiny, or any disturbance at all in the Punjaub, we may hope that the local rising has been quelled.

Wahid-uz-Zamán, Dy.-Collector. Waheed-ooz-Zamán, Dy.-Collr. of Humeerpore, has written an exculpatory address to Government. He says he obeyed the Nana for a week as a "put off"; that he has now been proclaimed as a rebel by the Rajah of Chirkaree, whom he accuses of being himself guilty of traitorous correspondence with the Mutineers, and in proof thereof sends a letter written by the Rajah in reply to the invitations of a Soubadar.

Rajah of Chirkári.

What has been done about Waheed-ooz-Zamán? I grieve over the defection of so many of our old settlement Dy.-Collectors.

W. MUIR.

J. W. SHERER, ESQ.

*P.S.*—A Telegraphic Message has just come in from Saidabad dated midday: "Intelligence has just been received of a portion of the rebels having reached Moorsaun, taken possession of the Rajah's fort, and burnt Mr. Saunders' factory at Chutoa. It is said they have two guns."

Outbreak at Moorsaun.

I enclose a copy of my Revenue Administration Memorandum. I will send one occasionally, and you can supply the Commr. with copies. One copy you can send on to the Gov.-General, to show that we are doing our best to commence a restoration of Government at the earliest possible moment.

## CXXXIV.

AGRA, 4 *Oct.* Sunday.

Movements of Mutineers.

MY DEAR SHERER,—The train of events at Muthra has had a denouement, in one respect unexpected. The Nusserabad and Delhi troops followed the Bareilly Brigade as we expected. The Neemuch Brigade alone remained on this side. And instead of the Indore troops marching from Dholepore to join the fugitives at Muthra, the Neemuch men, under Heera Singh (an old friend —he was Brigade-Major of the force that attacked us on the 5th July), are marching to join the force at Dholepore.

Neemuch Brigade.

Indore troops.

They are now nearly half-way. The Indore troops are still at Dholepore. They talked yesterday of coming on a stage this way and attacking Agra. They will probably form a junction with the Neemuch Brigade a couple of days hence. We must wait to see what their course will be then. The Nawab who was with them from Bhopal has gone over, it is said, to Gwalior to see whether no combination can be made with the Contingent force. The Neemuch and Indore troops might perhaps go eastward *via* Etawah, or they might, as they threaten, ravage this district. Col. Fraser has written to Gen. Wilson, begging that if Gen. Showers' or any other column can come down the left bank, the demonstration would have the happiest effect. **Nawab from Bhopal.**

Poor Hatrass has at last suffered the fate of most of our towns. It was plundered yesterday by the Bareilly and other troops, who have gone off towards Secundra Rao, and will either go on northward by the Kuchla Ghat and Budaon to Bareilly, or by the Trunk Road to Mynporee, and Furruckabad or Canouge. You shall hear more of their movements the moment we have intelligence. Nothing further from Greathed's column or from Delhi, and no news of Lucknow! **Hatrass plundered.**

Yours of the 25th to Capt. Nixon, and the 27th to Col. Fraser, came in yesterday. The latter conveying the letter of appointment of Col. Fraser—the receipt of the *Message* I have before acknowledged.

W. MUIR.

## CXXXVI.

AGRA, 5 *Oct.* 1857.

MY DEAR SHERER,—It is not often we have two Royal salutes fired within eight days. The ramparts of the old Fort gave proudly forth to the country far and wide the booming of 100 guns yesterday, to testify our joy and thankfulness at the rescue of the gallant Lucknow band. But after the first burst of joy is over, anxiety again overclouds us till we know who have fallen and who survived the hardships of those terrible three months. We trust that you will give us the earliest information of all casualties. **Relief of Lucknow. Agra Fort fires salutes.**

Yesterday more letters came in from Delhi, but of no later date than the 28th. Mr. Saunders has given the reasons for the change in the intention to send a Column down the right bank of the Jumna. The Army was too greatly reduced from the grievous losses and other disabling effects of the siege to admit of 2 efficient Columns being detached.

"The preponderance of evidence went to show that they—the fugitive Mutineers—would certainly avoid Agra, and in all probability cross at Muthra, or even higher up." It was expedient therefore to endeavour to intercept them as they crossed the Doab, so it was determined to take that line. **Movements of the pursuing column.**

Their long stay at Muthra would no doubt have enabled Col. Greathed to effect this, if he could have come down promptly after his victory of the 28th. But he was delayed two days at Boolundshuhur, and I much fear the fugitive troops will have by this time clean eluded his grasp. But more of that below.

The other Column is, as we apprehended, a smaller one, and destined for comparatively local objects. Mr. Sapte says "it is now marching about the neighbourhood of Humaiyoon's Tomb, and will from thence go towards Rohtuck or Goorgaon to reorganise our Police and Revenue Establishments in those districts."

W. Ford, C.S.

General Van Cortlandt's force in Rohtuk.

J. S. Campbell, C.S.

Sir T. Metcalfe, C.S.

A letter had just been received from Mr. Ford announcing his arrival at Rohtuck with a portion of Van Cortlandt's force, and "had re-established our rule in that district." Mr. Ford is to be relieved at Rohtuck by Mr. J. S. Campbell, when the former will proceed to Goorgaon again. Sir T. Metcalfe had so much recovered as to be able to assume charge of the Delhi district. Guthrie was expected from the hills, and would go probably to his old charge at Hissar. So things are shaking into order throughout the Division. Everything is quiet. Mirza

Mirza Jewan Bukht.

Jewan Bukht is mentioned, in addition to the other princes, as in confinement, and about to be tried. Nothing has been said as to the discovery of documents, etc., in the Palace. Saunders has been reminded of the Governor-General's wishes on this point.

Instructions to Colonel Greathed's relieving column.

Saunders mentions the instructions given to Col. Greathed as follows: "He was directed to place himself in communication with Agra as soon as practicable, but to use his own discretion with reference to following up and cutting off any detachments which might be crossing the Doab to get into Rohilkhund or Oudh in the direction of Anoopshuhur and the other ghats in the neighbourhood, and he was directed to march promptly to the relief of Agra, if necessity required the presence of the Column in your neighbourhood."

Movements of Colonel Greathed's column.

A message just received from our Detachment at Khundowlie states that Mr. Cocks had received a letter from Colonel Greathed, dated Khoorjah the 3rd. He had been "unavoidably detained 2 days at Boolundshuhur." He was to be at Somna on the 4th, and to-day would certainly reach Allygurh. But to-day the fugitive force with all their guns and elephants are at Secundra Rao, some five and twenty miles in advance of Allygurh, and I fear can march faster than our flying column, so they may be regarded as *gone*. Unless Col. Greathed sees any near and certain prospect of overtaking them (which he might possibly do if he heard they were entangled at the Kuchla or Kadur Gunge ghats), he has been requested to move without loss of time this way, with a view to attack Dholepore and crush the combined forces of Heera Singh and the Indore men. From the nature of the messages sent to Col. Greathed, and from the great probability of the Doab fugitives being beyond his reach, it is not at all unlikely that the Column may be here in 3 or 4 days, and that a movement may be made towards Dholepore.

**Neemuch Brigade.**

Heera Singh, with the debris of the Neemuch Brigade, is now on his way to Dholepore, which he may reach to-morrow or the next day. I cannot ascertain with any closeness his numbers: some say a portion of the Neemuch Brigade followed the rest with all their guns into the Doab; others, that all have come this way with 6 guns. The fighting men are likely not above a thousand, half cavalry and half infantry—they are wretchedly off for everything. The latest intelligence gives number of the whole as under 1000, including camp-followers, and without guns. It is not unlikely they may disperse of themselves, unless taken by the hand by some better-equipped force.

**Scindia's loyalty.**

Macpherson continues to hear good accounts from Scindia—who says he fired a salute in honour of the fall of Delhi.

**The Gwalior Contingent.**

There are three parties bidding for the Contingent: 1st, "Capt. Jehangeer of Delhi," who has now lost the small chance he ever had; 2nd, the Nana's Vakeel, who promised money, but gave only titles; 3rd, the Jhansi Vakeels have been urging the Contingent to proceed there and support the Ranee in her possessions. They have promised a payment of 2 lacs to them on their reaching Jhansi—which is supposed to include 1½ lacs as payment for the Magazine.

All their talk is now to go *via* Jhansi levying contributions as they march, from Duttiah, Jaloun, etc.; eventually they might go by Calpee to join the Nana. It would be rash to venture an opinion as to the movements of the Contingent, but I agree with Macpherson in thinking that on the present information their likeliest course is *via* Jhansi. The Nana's present inducements are hardly substantial enough to make them espouse his cause.

**Bareilly Brigade, movements of.**

It is doubtful what course the Bareilly and other Brigades will take. If they continue in the same direction their line of march from Secundra Rao, it would take them across the Ganges *via* Budaon to Bareilly. They may, however, dread the ghats with a force behind them. They may go on towards Furruckabad if their relations with the Nawab are friendly; they may go on to Canouge and cross into Oudh there; or, which seems highly improbable, they may move your way towards Bithour.

Bareilly Brigade, equipment of. The latter step they would hardly take unless joined by some other body of Mutineers. They have 17 or 18 guns (light), and from 50 to 80 elephants.

Thannah Bhowun. A letter from Meerut of the 25th states "that the force that went to Thannah Bhowun found it empty. The rebels were said to have gone towards Shamlee and Baroti,"—*i.e.* down the E. I. Canal. "Our force is after them, and we are making arrangements to secure the individuals. The body will evaporate, I fear, and not fight." Williams says that the people are urgent in petitions for our return to Rohilkhund, which he advocates our doing at once in force. (Rohilkhund, loyalty of people.) But we had better first secure the Doab. "All well here," says Williams, "and loyalty the order of the day. The city to be illuminated to-night." He adds the following particulars about Delhi. "The Muzhubi Seikhs came across a party of Mahomedans in Duryao Gunge who had English property on them and boasted of their maltreatment of our people. (Muzhubi Sikhs at Delhi.) They killed one or two of the Muzhubees, who set to work and polished off 300 of them, and among them one of the head Moulvees of the Jumma Musjid."

Fleet post-runner. Yours of the 28th just in. I mentioned in a P.S. in yesterday's letter that the news of the relief of Lucknow had been brought in by Nixon's wonderful runner in 2¾ days.

W. Muir.

J. W. Sherer, Esq.

*P.S.*—The country is now all quite clear from this to Delhi. A dak is immediately to be run, and indeed is already organised, if not running, to Delhi; so the days of Cossids in that direction are numbered. My last letter to Saunders I hope, *by Cossid*, goes to-day.

W. M.

## CXXXVIII.

Agra, *6th October* 1857.

My Dear Sherer,—Yours of the 30th reached yesterday to Nixon's address. To-day we have letters from Col. Greathed's camp, which reached Allygurh yesterday morning, the 5th. You will remember that a week or ten days ago the Mahomedan fanatics of this district, joined by some of the bad characters, ejected our adherent, Rajah Gobind Singh, who with Doorgah Pershad, Dy.-Collr., and a few others, were holding Allygurh for us. Since that time they have been strengthening themselves there, and they were bold enough to offer opposition to our pursuing column. They took up a position on the Meerut road with 2 5-pounder guns, and as Campbell rode up towards the gate "the Jehádees saluted us with a round shot which," he says, "sent my sowars flying, and we were obliged to wait for Artillery; then they were quickly smashed." We took their two guns and several of the little ordnance they have attempted to construct out of the El. Tel. screws. "The Cavalry," writes Col. Greathed, "did most excellent service, and cut up fully 400 men with arms in their hands." They rode round the outskirts of the town and cut up the fugitive rebels. A few hours after our first appearance, Campbell "marched in with some Sahibs and took possession of the town unopposed."

**Affairs at Allygurh.**

**Town of Allygurh occupied.**

The Column was to move on this morning to Akrabad, half-way to Secundra Rao, to inflict chastisement on that town, which is the nest of fanaticism and disaffection. After that, Col. Greathed says "his movements must be regulated by circumstances, and he is unable to say whether he will go to Khassgunge or Hatrass." "I am in great hopes," he continues, "of intercepting some part of the rebel force, who appear to think of nothing but escape with their plunder." But the fugitives must have been at Secundra Rao on Sunday night, and have therefore a clear start of 2 or 3 days in advance of Col. Greathed, who cannot reach it till to-morrow morning. Under these circumstances I have written, at Col. Fraser's instance, to say that, as the chance of overtaking the flying force appears to be gone, "the Chief Commissioner still desires Col. G. to march direct on Agra. He may now come *via* Secundra Rao." When he approaches we can then send out a small force for the permanent reoccupation of Allygurh, and Col. G.'s Column can operate first on the Dholepore and other rebels to the south, and then upon Mynpoorie, perhaps on Furruckabad on the N.E. The Doab and the left bank of the Jumna will thus be gradually swept clean of these rebel bands.

**Movements of pursuing column.**

**Colonel Fraser's communication to Colonel Greathed's column.**

In a previous letter, dated the 3rd inst., from Khoorjah, Col. G. mentions an unfortunate accident at Malagurh, terminating in the death of a valuable officer. The Column was detained, he says, at Boolundshuhur "by the necessity of providing for the safety of my wounded men and blowing up the Fort of Malagurh —in doing which, I regret to say, a most excellent officer, Lt. Home, Engineers, lost his life by the explosion of a mine which was fired too quick." He complains of the small number of his

**Lieutenant Home, R.E., killed at Malagurh.**

effective European force. "If you can give me any European Infantry it will be a great boon—I have not 400 with me fit for duty." We shall be able to help him for any near duty with 200 or 300 at least.

Movements of Delhi Mutineers.

From all I can hear, the Delhi fugitives are making straight for Bareilly *via* Khassgunge and Budaon. We have no actual information of their movements after Secundra Rao, but the sepoys generally talked of taking that course.

Greathed's force will not, however, be the worse of a little rest. George Campbell (now the Civilian with the column) writes: "At that point (Agra) I think it *most* desirable that some of your fresh Europeans should join the Column, for there is no mincing the fact (their officers say) that the European Infantry from Delhi, besides being so small in numbers, are quite done up in pluck as well as in everything else, and unfit for hard work and hard fighting." Greathed left a small detachment at Allygurh. "In spite of the fighting," says Campbell, "I think I have managed to save the wretched people of the town from further looting. It is rather empty, but they will soon return." Poor Allygurh has fared, excepting Delhi, worse than any other town, having changed masters so often.

Condition of Greathed's column.

Allygurh in the Mutiny.

The Terai.

Ramsay[1] gives a capital account of the discomfiture of Khan Bahadoor's army sent against Nynee Tal. It occupied Huldwanee on the 17th, and in the evening advanced to Burokhuree, whence they were driven back by Ramsay's people on Huldwanee. At night Ramsay sent down a force of "150 Goorkhas, 80 levies, with sowars and Volunteer cavalry to the amount of 60." In the morning they went against the Bareilly army, which was drawn up in array outside the little town. They stood till our army got within 400 yards of them, when the Goorkhas gave a cheer which put all to flight. "The bag" (such is Ramsay's sporting phrase) "was 114 killed and *counted*. On our side one Naib Ressr. was killed, and one Goorkha wounded." Two Flags and an immense amount of cooking utensils were captured. Huldwanee was uninjured.

Major Ramsay.

Action at Huldwanee.

Heera Singh must by this time have reached Dholepore, but it is a miserable band he has with him—the mere wreck of the proud force which measured its strength with us on the 5th July. What the Dholepore people mean to do we cannot divine. Some say they are already beginning to cross over on the single ferry boat left by Scindia to the other bank; some, that they think of levying contributions from Bhurtpore, as they have done from

[1] Afterwards General Sir H. Ramsay, K.C.B.

Dholepore. One of their Nawabs is said to have gone off to Muthra with 300 or 400 followers, horse and foot,—the other two Mohammedan Chiefs (a Bhopal man and a Shazada) are said to have quarrelled, and some believe that the whole force is breaking up. They still *talk* of Agra, and have been trying to mount an immense gun, but the moment they began to have it dragged by 20 bullocks and propelled from behind by elephants the carriage broke down. In fact, all we can say is that we must *wait* to gather their intentions—meanwhile I trust they will hold on till Greathed's Column comes up to give them a lesson.

Dholpore and Neemuch Mutineers talk of Agra.

At Gwalior the troops still hold on at Morar. Macpherson has received tidings from some outposts of vague rumours that the Maharaja has gathered his troops around the Contingent, and was pouring grape into them. The account even mentions that H. H. got wounded in the shoulder, but we have been so often misled by rumours that we must suspend credence till further evidence is received.

Gwalior.

At Muthra all is quiet. Imdad Ally, the Deputy Magistrate and Collector, resumed his office as soon as the Mutineers were fairly away—on the 4th inst. The town is quite loyal and quiet.

Muthra quiet.

The following from a young officer at Dharwar, dated 6th September, may be interesting. After referring to a few incipient and suppressed mutinies in the Bombay army, he says: "There is no doubt that the Collector of Belgaum, a Mr. Seton Karr, has saved the whole of this country, and both Belgaum and Dharwar in particular. The native Regiments were to have led off the ball, and were to have been joined by all the scum found in large places. About the 1st August this pretty business would have come off had not Seton Karr found out, little by little, what was intended. We here were in some anxiety till we got in about 120 men of our two European Regiments. The Fort, being the place where the Treasury and all the arms and ammunition are kept, would have been the first place they touched. It was no too desirable thing living in the Fort a month ago, but now that we have two guns and 120 Europeans inside, we who live in the Fort are objects of envy. I think all danger in this part of the Presidency is now over."

Dharwar

Seton Karr.

I enclose a letter for Lord Canning, which please send on with this, and specially acknowledge its receipt at Cawnpore.

You mentioned delays in the Post Office affecting despatches to Calcutta—were they of any material extent, and affecting our despatches from Agra?

Find out about *the woman* who brought in one of my despatches to you—it was that of the 23rd, I think—what was her story?

W. MUIR.

J. W. SHERER, ESQ.

## CXL.

AGRA, 7*th Oct.* 1857.

MY DEAR SHERER,—Last evening information came in both to Macpherson and myself (though of a conflicting character and directly opposed to some other tolerably good evidence) that the entire Indore Force had moved with its Artillery from Dholepore to Munnia, a stage ten miles this side, where it was joined by the Neemuch remains. The force, it was said, menaced Agra. This morning the Dholepore Vakeel confirmed the intelligence, but we have had no messengers in to-day, and the information is open to some doubt,—if true, it will no doubt very soon be corroborated.

Advance of Dholpore Mutineers.

It is possible that a *detachment* may have been mistaken for the whole force. Detachments have been out frequently in various directions plundering the country, and this may be one of them.

Call to Greathed.

Meanwhile, to be prepared for any advance on Agra and to prevent the possibility of our enemy gaining time to entrench himself in any near vantage-ground, Col. Fraser has ordered Col. Greathed's Column to march this way with all practicable despatch. And in case anything delays him he has been desired to detach 500 Cavalry and one troop H.A., and send them in advance to our relief by forced marches. Reinforced thus, we shall be able to maintain our position outside the Fort, and can wait quietly for the rest of the Column.

Akrabad occupied by Greathed's Column.

A tel. message came in from our detachment at Khundowlie this morning to say that "information had been received of the occupation of Akrabad by Col. Greathed, and the destruction of a great number of rebels together with the capture of the leaders Mungal Singh and Metab Singh." This, however, seems to be a native report; no direct communication from the Column seems to have reached Mr. Cocks. Our little detachment is to return to Agra this evening in consequence of the news from Dholepore.

Agra detachment recalled to head-quarters.

Reported aid from Nepaul.

A letter received here from Nynee Tal, dated the 22nd ult., states that Jung Buhadoor had sent two Goorkha Regiments and 1500 recruits to Almorah, and that Major Ramsay proposed at once coming down and occupying Rohilkhund. This is the first we have heard of it.

Boolundshuhur still much disturbed.

Sapte has just sent me a brief receipt for a letter I addressed to him on the 3rd: it is dated Boolundshuhur, 5th. He says: "No news here; Boolundshuhur district still very much disturbed." Nothing further from Gwalior. If the Indore men are really contemplating an attack on Agra, they must merely be calculating on the assistance of the Gwalior Contingent.

To-morrow's letter will no doubt contain some more certain intelligence.

W. MUIR.

J. W. SHERER, ESQ.

## CXLI.

AGRA, *8th October* 1857.

Intimates near approach of Indore Mutineers and Neemuch Brigade.

MY DEAR SHERER,—It is now certain that the Indore Force, joined by the débris of the Neemuch Brigade, is advancing this way. A considerable portion of the troops were 2 days ago at Munnia. To-day they are probably pitched in some numbers at Jajow, some 18 miles off. Some camp equipage was sent on yesterday to a spot on the other side the Kharee, 4 or 5 miles this side of Jajow, and the Zemindars have been seized and ordered to furnish supplies at Kakooba on this side the Kharee, and only 8 or 9 miles off. Bodies of sowars are also moving to our Tehseelee and Police posts on both sides the river.

Orders to Greathed's Column.

We are directly *threatened* by this enemy whatever course they may eventually take. The orders issued to Col. Greathed have accordingly been a peremptory reiteration of yesterday's ultimatum, that Col. Fraser wished him to march promptly to Agra.

I enclose a copy of my letter to him of this forenoon, which please forward with this to the Governor-General.

Operations at Akrabad—Mungal Singh and Muhtab Singh, Rajputs, killed.

This morning has brought us letters from Col. Greathed's Camp—dated the 6th inst., Akrabad—confirming the statement which I gave yesterday on native reports of the operations at Akrabad. Greathed's account is "that the Cavalry caught and cut up the 2 brothers Mungal Singh and Mühtab Singh, and about 100 of their Rajpoot followers. A great number of armed rascals have been since destroyed; and as I have just set the place on fire, and sent the whole Cavalry out to cut up any fugitives who may be found in the fields, I hope we shall make an example which will ring through this District. Mungal Singh's house has been blown up with his own powder. We found 4 guns primed and loaded at the entrances."

The village was no doubt a *very* bad one, and a severe example was required, but I fear, from what Campbell says, that our troops are too ready to execute indiscriminate vengeance on the innocent and guilty alike. Campbell's statement is, that as he was afraid the Column at its ordinary pace "was not likely to catch any one here, I got the Commander of the Cavalry to give me the Irregulars in advance, and we made a *very* successful *Chapao* (surprise); killed the notorious town Thakoors, and took several native guns and powder, grape, plunder, etc. I think we polished off almost all the Thakoors' followers, and the refugee Mahommedans from Coel, etc. But I fear when the camp came up they killed a great many more besides, whom we had spared, as they went out native shooting in the fields, besides getting a good many in the town." In fact, he says in another place that "we have established such a terror, that it is impossible to get any one to come in."

Indiscriminate slaughter.

The thing may be overdone; it will require a very careful and judicious officer to restore confidence to the District, and this we have in Cocks, who will, I conclude, go out in due course.

A. Cocks, C.S.

Greathed left 100 Sikhs in Allygurh "as a temporary measure, but must withdraw them in a few days." In fact, our paramount object now is to be relieved of these Indore Mutineers, and until that is done we cannot detach any of the troops here to hold Allygurh. If, therefore, Greathed withdraws (as I conclude he will) his Punjabees from Allygurh, its reoccupation must be delayed for a little.

Allygurh.

Greathed was to march yesterday morning "a short distance towards Hattrass: my men and cattle," he says, "are both weary. I shall make my way on towards Agra." He expects a reinforcement of 240 fresh Europeans, 50 natives, and 20 gunners from Delhi shortly. They will join him, I suppose, here.

Route of Greathed's Column.

Campbell's information as to the route taken by the Muthra fugitives was uncertain and imperfect, as he could get nobody to come near him. So far as he could hear, only the 8th Irregular Cavalry had taken the direct road to Bareilly, the rest having gone on towards Etah on the Grand Trunk Road. This information, at any rate, decided Col. Greathed to give up the pursuit even before (I conclude) he received our summons to Agra.

Campbell adds: "Now that Lucknow is relieved, I trust that soon Havelock's Infantry, being joined to our Cavalry and Artillery (after clearing the country about Agra), there may be formed about Mynpooree, or Etah, a force fit for anything, which will quite clear the Doab, etc., and do a great deal more besides." There will be no great difficulty in clearing the Doab, I fancy, Furruckabad being the only tough work, as they will try to entrench themselves. But the great battle will be, I apprehend, on the borders of Rohilkhund and Oudh, and for that the Cavalry, etc., of Greathed's force will be of essential service. The Dholepore and Gwalior people must, however, be first disposed of, and then the country south of the Ganges cleared of rebel bodies. Once thrown north of the Ganges, the enemy can be operated upon in strength by a combined force.

At Gwalior things are as before—the Maharajah has now every inducement to bind him to our cause, and he seems to make no secret of his attachment to us. Macpherson's letter conveying the news of the fall of Delhi was taken first to Dinka Rao, who read it and sent it at once to Scindia. H. H. was at the time on the ramparts; he read the letter aloud with exultation, ordered a Royal salute, and had it fired before him. The Contingent still talks of going to Jhansi, and thence to Cawnpore. It would almost seem that Scindia has it commanded by his own forces and guns, and if so he may prevent them taking away their Magazine. But one requires to be on one's guard against the "couleur de rose" reports which we too often get, so some grains may be taken from the conclusion that the M. R. has the Contingent at his feet. A letter has been received from Delhi, dated the 2nd Oct., from Capt. Halsted, who says: "We are now working hard to get matters settled here and in the District." Showers' force had returned from the Kootub. "He found great numbers of Delhi people at Hamaiyoon's tomb and at the Kootub, and drove them away. They are scattered all over the surrounding country, and in the greatest misery." I do not quite understand this policy; if persevered in indiscriminately it must drive these exiles into lawless habits. The guilty should be punished —sufficient example made, and the remainder, if peaceably inclined to return to their homes, allowed to do so.

**Gwalior.** **Scindia's loyalty.** **Gwalior Contingent.** **Captain Halsted.** **Policy at Delhi.**

"Another force," the same writer says, "under Brigadier Showers, will march to-morrow towards Goorgaon, and will visit Rewaree and other places." The Delhi news-writer, who still flourishes under the new regime, mentions, in his entry of the 2nd Oct., this force as ordered *in consequence of the receipt of a letter from Agra*; so until we got Capt. Halsted's letter we thought it possible it might be coming on here, but that seems more than doubtful now. It is odd to find the news-writer

**General Showers.**

News-writer's amusing reports from Delhi.

chronicling the acts of the "Sahib Kulan," his retiring to sleep, rising in the morning, taking exercise, holding durbars, etc., just as he before did, the acts of the old King. He states the force coming down in this direction at 400 Europeans, 2 Sikh and Guide Regiments, 8 guns, and 20 elephants.

Hoping that we may soon be able to give you a better account of our Indore invaders.

W. MUIR.

J. W. SHERER, ESQ.

## CXLII.

### MESSAGE.

W. MUIR TO G. F. EDMONSTONE.

Telegraphic summary of foregoing.

INDORE Force has made two marches this way from Dholepore, joined by the Neemuch Brigade. They threaten to attack this Fort. Reiterated summons to Col. Greathed to advance rapidly.

Akrabad chastised by Col. Greathed on the 6th. On 7th he made first march this way. He may be here by 10th or 11th. Ordered to send on some Cavalry and H.A. to us by forced march.

## CXLIII.

AGRA, *9th October* 1857.

Advance of the Indore force.

MY DEAR SHERER,—The Indore Force is moving steadily this way. It is to-day at Tehra, and is making preparations for bringing its guns across the Kharee river, about 10 miles distant. Some hundreds of Sowars have already crossed, and are prowling about the country and obstructing the road. A reconnoitring party of our Militia Cavalry went out this morning. It was fired on at the river, and followed—though at a respectful distance—by the enemy's Cavalry to within a few miles of Agra.

Meanwhile succour is at hand, providentially, in Greathed's Column. Urgent summonses have gone out to hurry him on. I give copies of some of these as an enclosure to this letter.

Agra cut off for more than three months.

It is now more than three months since we have been cut off from the rest of the world, and have not seen a new face excepting 2 or 3 officers, who joined us from Ajmere. We look forward therefore with special pleasure to receiving the Column here to-morrow.

A letter has been received from Delhi, dated 5th October, from Captain Shute. General Wilson left on the 4th for

Meerut and the Hills, on Medical Certificate for 2 months. General Penny had arrived to take the command. Colonel Becher had left some days previously for Simlah. He speaks thus of the Column now out on this bank. "Another strong Column is out in this District under Brigadier Showers, having for its object the visiting of Goorgaon, Fureebabad, Bullubgurh, Rewaree, etc., and to look up any Mutineers in these parts." They were supposed to be at Goorgaon on the 5th.

**General Penny succeeds Gen. Wilson at Delhi.**

**General Showers' Column.**

The reinforcements for Greathed's Column were to leave Delhi on the 6th. They would be here in a week. The 52nd (H.M.) had returned to the Punjab at Lawrence's summons. There remained at Delhi the 60th, 61st H.M., and 1st European Regiment—4th Sikhs, Guide Infantry, and Sirmoor Battalion, "all weak," and 2 troops H.A., so that the garrison of Delhi is regarded as not more than is necessary for holding it.

**Reinforcements for Greathed's Column.**

**Details of Delhi garrison.**

A letter, dated the 30th ultimo, has been received from Mr. Ford at Rohtuck. General Van Cortlandt had arrived there, as I think I before stated, on the 26th ultimo. They had visited Bhewani, which was illuminated on the occasion. Tehseels, Thannas, and Daks are being re-established. The large villages have tendered their submission, and the land revenue collections are coming in well. The roads are opening again for travellers; the Customs Line is being set up. Ford is detained till Mr. Ricketts joins from the Punjab, whose place is to be supplied by Colonel Clarke, who is on his way from Kurrachee. Although the country is pretty quiet, Ford thinks the presence of a Military Force will be required for some time, as the Mahommedan population there "have been particularly opposed to us." Our Cavalry is, a good deal of it, from that quarter.

**W. Ford, C.S.**

**General Van Cortlandt.**

**Re-establishment of Civil Government.**

**Land revenue coming in.**

**Geo. Ricketts, C.S.**

**Opposition of Mahommedan population in Rohtuk.**

Rao Toola Ram of Rewarie, in Goorgaon, will need to be proceeded against. He was frequent in protestation that he was holding the Pergunnah for us, and complained to us of the invasion on his domain by some of the Delhi Nawabs; but from Ford's present statement he would seem to be still in arms, and that of course against us.

**Rao Toola Ram.**

This morning we received letters from Greathed's camp, dated the 7th June, Akrabad. The Column was to have marched that morning towards Hathrass, but the night before Colonel Greathed had countermanded the order, and "announced a halt and a return to Allygurh"—so Campbell writes. On receipt, however, of Colonel Fraser's orders to march on Agra, he issued orders to move forward next morning—and this

**Movements of Greathed's Column.**

morning he would be encamped at Hathrass. "The reason for changing his mind yesterday," says Campbell, "was that his Quartermaster said the road was very bad; but it turns out the Quartermaster looked at the wrong road." The Sikh Guard will probably be left at Allygurh till the European reinforcements arrive from Delhi, when a portion of them will probably be stopped there.

**Colonel Greathed advocates disarming population.**

Colonel Greathed strongly advocates the disarming of the population. "The villages appear all to be in arms against each other, and till they are deprived of the means of warfare there will be a great difficulty in telling friend from foe." Is this question being discussed below?

**Bareilly Brigade gone to Etah.**

Regarding the main body of the rebels, Greathed says: "The Mutineers' force which goes by the designation of the Bareilly Brigade has certainly gone down to Etah. The messenger who was sent round from Allygurh to Khasgunge and Secundra Rao came in this morning and reported that not a Mutineer is to be seen on the Khasgunge Road."

**Captain the Hon. A. Anson.**

**Rapid advance of Greathed's Column.**

3 p.m. The Hon. A. Anson has just ridden in from the advance Cavalry and Artillery camp. It consists of 500 sabres in all, including 200 H.M. Lancers and 2 troops H.A., and was just 17 miles off at 11 a.m. to-day. They marched 25 miles last night, and are to come in to Khundowlie in the afternoon, and if necessary into Agra this evening. It is commanded by Major Ouvry, and is in excellent order. He thinks that Col. Greathed with the main body cannot be here till the day after to-morrow, the 11th, as "the hot weather before Delhi and the fatigues of the siege have seriously affected the health of the men." We shall help them in with waggons, and bring them in to-morrow morning.

**Movements of Mutineers.**

Regarding the general body of the rebels, a letter just received from George Campbell, dated yesterday, half-way between Akrabad and Hathrass, says: "I finally ascertained from Secundra Rao that only the Mahommedans and the residents of Rohilkhund among the Mutineers took the direct road to Bareilly. All the rest, with *all* the guns (22 I believe), took the Etah route to Cawnpore and Lucknow, they said,—but no doubt Futtehgurh must now be their point, where they will either join the Nawab or cross.

**Mutineers' force disorganised.**

All accounts agree that they are very much disorganised, and marching like a rabble, not by regiments. But it is also clear that there are a great many of them. Our move has certainly had a good effect in making them go off in a more fugitive style.

The Bareilly Brigade were to go to Bareilly, and a division of guns had taken place; but when he heard of our being at Coel, Bukht Khan discovered that the cutcha Road would not do for his guns. Bukht Khan.

All this is of importance to you.

By the way, Colonel Cotton was talking the other day about the investigations into the Palace traitorous proceedings in 1845 (?) (he formed a member of the Court of Inquiry) as being in their incipient stage very analogous in many points to what may be supposed to have been the first stage of the present Mutiny. It would be a good thing—if indeed it has not already been done—that these papers should be had out and gone over again at Calcutta. They might help to elucidate the *modus operandi* of the Mutineers. Traitorous proceedings at Delhi Palace, 1845 A.D.

I have been writing to-day under more than usual interruptions, so the disconnected style of the letter must be excused. What with messengers every half-hour, or oftener, from the Mutineers' vicinity, and communications with Greathed's camp, and our first reinforcements after three months' expectation coming in to-day, the mind becomes rather unsettled.

W. M.

A letter from Baroti, in Meerut, dated 30th ult.,—the Rebels had been dispersed. "Every one is humble and submissive, and the Revenue for the Rubbee of 1857 is coming in fast." Meerut district quieting down.

## CXLIV.

## MESSAGE.

FROM W. MUIR TO G. F. EDMONSTONE.

*9th October* 1857.

REINFORCEMENT of Cavalry and Artillery expected this evening. Capt. the Hon. A. Anson just ridden in from camp. Rest of moveable column probably to-morrow. Telegraphic summary of foregoing.

Indore Mutineers are crossing the Kharee, and insolently menace us. They will be attacked to-morrow or next day, unless news of our reinforcement makes them fly before.

Meerut quiet and Revenue coming in; same at Rhotuck.

## CXLV.

AGRA, *10th Oct.* 1857.

MY DEAR EDMONSTONE,—I write this to you direct, as it contains some important intimations regarding the political correspondence captured at Delhi. But first for the stirring intelligence of the moment. We have had a fight,—I trust a signally decisive one.

The Governor-General is already aware, from my letter of yesterday and its enclosures, that the Indore Force has been threatening us most insolently. Our information last night was that they were crossing the Kharee some ten miles off. Urgent despatches were sent off to Col. Greathed by reiterated messengers during the last two days, directing him to march on with all practicable speed to Agra. Copies of some of these have been sent through Sherer. This morning the entire Column marched in—first the Cavalry, then the two troops H.A., which had been marching in advance at our first urgent call; then all the Infantry, and the remaining troop H.A., the two latter greatly fatigued by a march of some 30 or 40 miles within the last 24 hours.

*Arrival at Agra of Greathed's Column.*

They were encamped on the Parade-ground, opposite the Metcalfe testimonial, our Militia picket, and near the burying-ground; and the baggage being mostly behind, they were endeavouring to have a little refreshment as best they could. They were all about in this miscellaneous way about 9 o'clock when I drove over the camp.

*Sudden attack by the Indore troops.*

About 11 we were all startled in the Fort by hearing a heavy cannonade in the direction of the camp, and, hurrying to the ramparts, found the whole front of our Column was engaged by the enemy. It had come suddenly upon our camp, concealed by the fields. And the first notice they had was a round shot bowling in upon the tents.

How they brought these guns over in this quiet way no one can yet tell; however, more of this hereafter.

*French killed. Jones severely wounded.*

Some of their sowars got in upon our camp, and cut up some of the Lancers and others—one officer, French, is killed, and Jones badly wounded, a third slightly.

But we were not long before we were ready for them; in fact, although we were surprised in one way, they, I suspect, were greatly more surprised, and to their cost, in another. They could have no idea that they had ventured into the vicinity of a well-equipped force of above 3000 men and 4 troops H.A., with 3 or 4 eighteen-pounders.

I believe they had not fired five shots before our Artillery replied. Col. Cotton hastened from the Fort to the scene of action (some one or two miles off), and sent back for the 3rd Europeans.

This corps was soon in full march under the inspiriting cheers of the Fort; meanwhile the Artillery was loud and fast, but it gradually became more and more distant, and it was evident that we were rapidly dislodging them from their position. By midday they might have been three miles off—a tumbril blew up at that time; we don't yet know on whose side. By one o'clock the firing had become very distant, with frequent long interruptions, indicative of successful pursuits and unlimbering. A Sikh horseman has come in to say that 6 guns have been already taken. As theirs is bullock-drawn Artillery, and ours all horsed, I confidently trust that we shall have all their ordnance; we must come up with it at any rate at the Kharee. There is evidently just now a full pursuit. I trust I shall have more to communicate before I close this letter.

**Attack beaten off.**

I could get no information in this morning, and what the Magistrate and other parties brought was to the effect that, alarmed by our reinforcements, the enemy was running away. Two days ago I reported that the enemy was about to cross the Kharee, and recommended a reconnoitring party and mile pickets. The reconnoitring party was sent out yesterday morning, and was fired upon. I do not know what Military arrangement of the kind was made this morning to prevent surprise.

At any rate, as I said before, the surprise has in reality been on their side. They expected to beard us and break our bridge, I believe, before our reinforcements came in; but the wise urgency of Col. Fraser in hurrying on the Column prevented this.

Now for the Delhi news. Saunders, in reply to my inquiries, reports on the 4th inst. that the whole of the correspondence of the King and the Mutineer chiefs was carefully collected on our taking possession of the Palace. He is having all the papers of any importance "carefully arranged and docketed, with an abstract in English of their contents. The information thus acquired," he says, "is of the most important character, and affords ample proof of the wide extent of the insurrection. Hardly a native State in Upper or Central India escaped the contagion; and against some of the more nearly situated States, like Jhujjur and Bullubgurh, the correspondence discovered is of a character

**Delhi Palace correspondence seized.**

**Native States implicated in the rebellion.**

**Jhujjur.**

**Bullubgurh.**

to implicate their Rulers most thoroughly." "No papers have yet been discovered which prove that the King or his family were engaged in a treasonable correspondence with other foreign States, or with the Leaders of the Mutiny in our Army at a time antecedent to the Meerut outbreak."

Rare and valuable MSS.

I had asked him also about rare and valuable manuscripts. He says great numbers have been wantonly destroyed by our own uncontrollable soldiery; but he is endeavouring now to save such as are yet available, and have them arranged and catalogued. Ram Chunder, the Christian Professor of Mathematics there, is assisting the Prize Agents in this task.

Professor Ram Chunder.

Lucknow.

Captain Bruce's letter about the urgency of reinforcements for Lucknow will be at once communicated to Delhi, both by Dak and by Cossid. After all, the effect of leaving a garrison in Lucknow thus strengthened in position will be infinitely less unfavourable to our prestige in public opinion throughout India, than a clean withdrawal would have been.

Sir John Lawrence administers Delhi.

Employment of military civilians in Delhi Division.

I have another letter from Delhi, dated the 5th inst. Sir J. Lawrence is arranging the disposition of the officers there. Saunders enquires whether the Chief Commissioner has any objection to the employment of military officers in the charge of Districts in that Division. It will be as well for the Government of India to express an opinion on this point. I suppose, in the absence of a sufficient number of civilians, no objection would be raised.

Brigadier Showers' Column.

Rao Toola Ram.

Sir T. Metcalfe, C.S.

He gives the following additional particulars regarding Brigadier Showers' Column. It was at Goorgaon on the 5th, and is on its way to Rewaree "to coerce Rao Toola Ram, and to disperse a small force of Ramgurh Irregular Cavalry and others whom he had collected in that neighbourhood." Metcalfe is out with it.

Wullee Dad Khan.

A Bareilly letter,[1] dated last Wednesday, states that Wullee Dad Khan[2] had arrived there two days before—*i.e.*, on the 5th—with about 1500 troops and 2 guns; it adds: "Nana Sahib's troops, said to be about 4000, are reported to have left Budaon yesterday for Lucknow." .

All the Hindoos almost are believed to be well disposed to us in that direction. I had been keeping this open for more news about our fight; but the Column has evidently pursued on to the Kharee, and will no doubt cut up all they meet. The enemy had made one or two stands at villages, which were immediately carried and the pursuit continued. It is *said* we have taken 7 or 8 guns; one messenger returned who saw *three.*

Six or seven guns taken.

[1] William Lowe's writing.—W. M.

[2] Mahommedan leader of Malagurh.

I hope to have full details for you to-morrow. What strange infatuation in these people holding back till the very hour when we were prepared for them! Is there not cause to recognise the hand of a protecting Providence?

W. MUIR.

G. F. EDMONSTONE, Esq.,
Foreign Secretary.

*P.S.*—Col. Fraser (to whom I have read the first sheets of this) has just come in to say that there is good reason to believe 8 guns have been captured, one an immense brass one, about 24 pounds, and an elephant.

## CXLVII.

AGRA, 11*th October* 1857. Sunday.

MY DEAR SHERER,—Enclosed is Col. Fraser's Report of the brilliant affair of yesterday. My letter to Mr. Edmonstone, sent open through you yesterday, contained a generally correct view of the action, to which I can add little without descending to details, which I have not leisure and hardly yet materials for; the only point of difficulty was the first surprise, and, considering the suddenness of the attack and the number of pieces brought into a converging position against our Camp within a few hundred yards, the loss is astonishingly small—only 3 or 4 killed, and some wounded. Their Cavalry got into the Camp and created a momentary panic and confusion. The charge of our noble Lancers soon drove back the foolhardy enemy. Our guns returned the fire of the enemy after their guns had fired only a few rounds—the whole front of the enemy fell back, and the retreat soon became converted into a flight. Our 20 to 24 guns steadily pursued, flanking the Gwalior Road on both sides, and pouring continuous discharges into their enemy—and the Cavalry cutting them up as they sought to steal along behind the high crops. As our advance was rapid, their cannon, drawn by bullocks, soon fell into our hands; the heavier ones—immense unwieldy affairs, between 18 and 24-pounders, were seized at the opening struggle, and the rest one by one along the road. Some of them they had dragged off to near the Kharee, but were abandoned before we reached its banks. We took all their guns. Col. Fraser, I see, says 13. I think the number was stated as I heard it in Greathed's camp at 11.

Description of action of 10th October 1857.

Col. Fraser has desired me to ask if you can ascertain any

information regarding Major A. Robertson of Futtehgurh. He was there when the affair broke out. Fraser is interested in the family, as trustee or something of the sort.

W. MUIR.

J. W. SHERER ESQ., Cawnpore.

## CXLIX.

AGRA, 12*th October* 1857.

MY DEAR EDMONSTONE,—After all, as you will see from my printed slip of intelligence, we took 13 guns. They are all drawn up in two rows in the Armoury Square, excepting the big brass one, which is so unwieldy that some difficulty is experienced in bringing it up. So the Mutineers must have got 6 guns from the Rana of Dholepore.

Thirteen guns taken.

Rana of Dholpore thought to have supplied guns.

Guns in Native States.

It is worthy of serious consideration whether these petty States should be permitted to possess any heavy guns or even ordinary field-pieces. They cannot retain them in the face of an enemy. The only real use they make of them is to surrender them to the first strong enemy who comes into their neighbourhood. Two or three pounder guns would be quite sufficient for all their administrative wants, and for salutes, etc.

Reoccupation of Delhi.

Regarding the question of the reoccupation of Dehli by its inhabitants, Saunders writes, on the 6th inst.: "The City is still all but deserted—the Military authorities being very averse to allow the residents to return to their homes. I have been anxious to induce them, at any rate, to permit the respectable Hindoo merchant families, bunyas, and trades people generally, to return to their occupations, but hitherto with but little success. I conceive that there is really no good ground for excluding the above, as no danger need be anticipated from allowing them to re-enter the town and return to their avocations. The case is different with a very large proportion of the Mahommedan population who have taken so prominent and violent a part against us."

Mr. Saunders advocates permission to the Hindoos to return to their homes.

In a later letter of the 8th inst. he says on the same subject: "With reference to the means at our command, the Military authorities have considered it absolutely necessary to insist upon the inhabitants of the city, who deserted the place from the day of the assault, being kept out of the place. The greater number of the gates have been closed and blockaded up with stones. The Cashmere Gate is kept for ingress, and the Lahore Gate for egress; all the others, with the exception of the Calcutta Gate leading to the bridge of boats, are scrupulously barricaded, with the view of reducing the number of guards required to defend them."

I have already referred to the Brigade under Showers now out in the direction of Goorgaon. Col. Fraser has been desirous that the Column should move on to Muthra, and, in that position, protect the whole of the country between this and Delhi. Rewaree, he suggested, might be advantageously occupied for the present by Jyepore troops. Saunders, on the 8th (but before the suggestion about Jyepore troops had been received), has replied, on the part of General Penny, that the Column cannot be spared from Delhi. After doing what is required at Goorgaon, the Column is to return to Delhi. "It is urgently required," Saunders writes, "to restore peace and tranquillity in the neighbourhood of Delhi, and to prevent the possibility of the mutinous Irregular Cavalry and the numerous defeated but not yet entirely disbanded adherents of the King once more gaining head in this part of the world." I suppose we cannot help this; but as they keep the Column, it is a pity they cannot allow the well-affected portion of the community to return to Delhi. It sounds a monstrous barbarity, unless really called for by imperative military necessity, to exile 150,000 inhabitants indiscriminately, and without reference to their political crimes and feelings; and I fear we shall drive them into lawless courses. It should have been better to have demolished the gateways and the wall in their vicinity, and have withdrawn the Military posts to some strong position where they might have concentrated, and to have permitted all except the disaffected to return.

Brigadier Showers.

His column cannot be spared from Delhi.

Exclusion of inhabitants from Delhi.

But I am stepping out of my province.

I give the following extracts from the Chief Commissioner of Lahore's memo. of intelligence, dated 4th October. "The plunderers who have lately infested the Mooltan Road have disappeared, and are reported to have betaken themselves to the high grass jungles on the right of the Ravee, where, notwithstanding the very difficult nature of the country, they will speedily be coerced. Four Detachments are now employed in hunting them down, under command of Lieut.-Col. Patten, Majors Jackson and Chamberlain, and Capt. Cureton."

Colonel Patten, Major Jackson, Major Chamberlain, Captain Cureton.

A letter from Seharunpore gives the following encouraging account of the state of feeling there. "The popular tide is now running fast in favour of government; all the large towns in this district were illuminated in honour of the fall of Delhi."

Returning loyalty in Seharunpore.

A letter from Secundra Rao (between Allygurh and Etah) says that a small portion of the retreating force went, as before

Movements of Mutineers. stated, direct to Bareilly, taking three guns with them; and that the remaining 26 (the number is, I believe, magnified) went on towards Etah.

We cannot learn to-day that the Indore Force has recovered and re-formed elsewhere. But there are rumours of the Gwalior Contingent having moved, some say towards Jhansi, others Cawnpore, others this way. On the other hand, there is tolerably good evidence that up to the 7th or 8th things were there *in statu quo.*

W. Muir.

G. F. Edmonstone, Esq.

## CL.

Agra, 13*th October* 1857.

My Dear Sherer,—Yours of the 7th has been received. We long for more Lucknow news, but must exercise patience.

Greathed's Column is still here. To-morrow it crosses the river and encamps near the river on the Mynpoorie road. It will probably march towards Mynpoorie on the following morning, the 15th. George Campbell goes on with the force, but Cocks, who has great experience and local knowledge at Mynpoorie, will go as special Commissioner to adjust the difficult local questions that may arise there and in the vicinity. The Rajah will, I suppose, be hung. But Rao Bhowaney Singh, who so long protected Power, will afford difficulty in determining what course should be pursued in regard to him. He says he has got our treasure, near 2½ lacs, all safe and ready to deliver up to us, —and in that case, though, since our withdrawal, he has been guilty of joining the Rajah in some of his unauthorised raids, yet his conduct on the whole may be found such as can be pardoned.

George Campbell, C.S. A. Cocks, C.S.

Rao Bhowani Singh.

We cannot afford a garrison for Mynpoorie, and in that case the Rao might be left in charge. However, these will be all points for Cocks' careful judgment. After the Column passes on, Cocks will return to his post at Allygurh. Greathed will then either march on to Furruckabad or to join Havelock's Column, as circumstances may then show to be most expedient. You had better have despatches for his camp sent up the Trunk Road by Cossid.

Indore fugitives. The Indore fugitives have not re-formed anywhere. The Bhurtpore Durbar has reported that parties sought refuge in their territories near Bhurtpore. The Durbar troops were ordered out, the fugitives resisted the attempt to disarm them, and were attacked—some flying and some being killed. There is a party of them, consisting of several hundreds, at Roopbar not yet dispersed, but they are not likely, I think, to form the nucleus of any new opposing body. The Dholepore people also tell us that they have been cutting up some of the fugitives, but this needs confirmation.

At Gwalior our last news does not signify any change, notwithstanding the rumours which I mentioned in my letter of yesterday to Mr. Edmonstone. **Gwalior.**

From Delhi I have a letter dated the 9th inst. Saunders says that all is quiet, and everything going on satisfactorily in the neighbourhood. He had heard from Metcalfe, who was with Showers' Column. When our troops reached Putowdee, Rao Toola Ram "sent messengers with petitions expressing his great attachment to our Government, and the preparations which he had made for the reception of our troops. It would appear, however, that these latter had been entirely of a hostile character." He fled at our approach. Rewaree was found almost deserted. Rampoorah, Toola Ram's Fort, was in a complete state of defence, —12 loaded guns and mortars on the walls. "He had a gun foundry, in which two new brass guns just made and very neatly turned out were found. He had several muskets in store, and also a capital *mistree-khana* in which several were being made, and he had a large supply of iron bars, round shot, and other ordnance stores." It is just as well he ran away. **Delhi.** **Patowdee.** **Rao Toola Ram.** **Rewaree.** **Toola Ram's fort.** **His ordnance stores.**

The Column next proceeds to Jatoosana to disperse a body of Irregular Cavalry said to be in that vicinity. It will then move on Jhujjur, in which chiefship Van Cortlandt's Column from Hansi and the Cashmere troops under Captain R. Lawrence will also concentrate, by Sir J. Lawrence's instructions. The Nawab of Jhujjur will then be called on to surrender himself, a fair trial being guaranteed. "He will also be called upon to give up his father-in-law, Sarmund Khan, who commanded the troops which he sent to Delhi." Saunders says he has ample evidence against him, and is confident he will not be able to clear himself of the charge of "aiding and abetting the King in rebelling and waging war against the E. I. Company." **Jatoosana.** **Jhujjur.** **Captain R. Lawrence.** **Evidence against the Nawab of Jhujjur.**

W. Muir.

J. W. Sherer, Esq., Cawnpore.

## CLI.

## TELEGRAPHIC MESSAGE.

### W. MUIR, AGRA—TO G. F. EDMONSTONE, CALCUTTA.

*13th October* 1857.

Telegram to Governor-General.

INDORE Force believed to have in most part dispersed. Some cut up by Bhurtpore troops.

Summary of foregoing.

Greathed's Column will cross Jumna to-morrow, and on 15th probably march towards Mynpoorie. Toola Ram fled from Rewaree; his evacuated fort found to have been strongly armed for defence. Military stores seized.

There will shortly be a concentration of Showers' Brigade, Van Cortlandt's force, and the Cashmere troops—on Jhujjur. The Nawab will be called on to surrender himself and father-in-law for trial.

W. MUIR.

## CLII.

AGRA, *14th October* 1857.

MY DEAR SHERER,—Thanks for yours of the 9th. I agree with you that the effect of the continuance of the whole force at Lucknow will be good, so far as regards the impression on the native mind and the native States. I wish, however, it had been the result of choice and not of such unhappy necessity.

Colonel Greathed's force starts for Cawnpore.

Colonel Greathed has seen all the urgent summonses, and as *we* are now happily relieved from the *immediate* apprehension of danger, he has got orders which I have just put into shape to start at once for Cawnpore, and not to diverge towards Furruckabad unless directly menaced or attacked from that quarter.

As good as one march has already been made this morning in the crossing of the river, which, with so large a force through narrow streets and over the pontoon bridge, is a matter of some little time, for the breaking down of a single cart stops for the time all behind.

Gwalior Contingent still at Morar.

You must duly appreciate our magnanimity in so soon parting with our reinforcements. For the Gwalior Contingent still hangs in suspense within 80 miles.

But truly there is a concentration of forces in your direction, or that of Lucknow, which demands that every effort be made for re-enforcing the army which will have to face it.

The main body of the Delhi fugitives with their guns seems

to have passed Bhougaon about the 7th inst. A man who passed Chebramhow four or five days ago says, on the 9th or 10th he saw them at Chebramhow. They then declared they were bound for Lucknow. **Delhi Mutineers.**

The force of Indore Mutineers which we dispersed on the 10th has not gathered again anywhere. A body of some 500 horse and 500 foot has been traced in its flight *via* Furrah across the Jumna, half-way to Hathrass. It too may be destined for Oudh or for Furruckabad. It is said the Dholepore Rana has slain seven of the fugitive Cavalry. The services of the Bhurtpore Durbar, stimulated by Captain Nixon's advice, were mentioned yesterday; 35 that were caught and resisted being disarmed, nine were killed by the four guns turned on them, and the remainder were pursued. **Indore Mutineers scattered.** **Services of Dholpore Rana: of Bhurtpore Durbar.**

Another party of twelve are said to have been taken up in the villages and sent on to Bhurtpore. We have not heard yet what has become of the large section, 600 or 700 they say, which fled to Roopbar.

Another considerable body attacked Muthra, but the citizens and the Delhi people resisted and drove them out. This is a good symptom, when our own people begin actively to oppose the fugitives. The force may be held, I hope, to have been irretrievably broken. **Muthra attacked.**

Macpherson has a letter from the M. Rajah saying that he does not expect to be able to hold back the Contingent after the 15th (to-morrow): that they will then probably march *via* Jhansi towards Cawnpore. Thus the wave is passing downwards, and I fear will be heavily felt in Oudh and the Lower Doab. If the Contingent takes the course it purposes, then the whole Upper Doab and the upper portion of the provinces generally, with exception of Rohilkhund, will be quite free from any local enemy in force. **Scindia and the Contingent.**

No doubt we shall have abundance of stray marauding parties, and we have little to meet them with.

Our Jat horse at Allygurh will, I hope, turn out a really valuable assistance. They are under a capital officer, Captain Murray. We are detaching 150 Europeans of our little garrison to hold Allygurh, and Greathed leaves 50 Sikh horse there, as well as 200 here. That is all we take from him. Bramley goes as Magistrate to Allygurh; Cocks, as before, is Special Commissioner with full Revenue and Judicial powers. But Cocks will have to accompany Greathed first to Mynpoorie, as some delicate questions may arise there as to the Rao Bhowany **Captain Murray commanding Jat horse.** **Allygurh.** **Bramley, C.S.** **Cocks, C.S.** **Rao Bhowani Singh.**

Singh, who says he is keeping the treasure, above 2 lacs, there safely for us. The Rajah, if caught, will probably be hung. But the Chowhan influential men will require careful treatment. Cocks has excellent judgment and good local knowledge, and will do this well.

I have a Delhi letter dated the 10th inst. He says he has "no news of any description to communicate." What a change from this time last month!

**Trial of King of Delhi by Military Commission.** A Military Commission is to try the King, "in order to place on record the evidence against him." This is being prepared by Saunders, and he hopes to be ready to open the proceedings to-day or to-morrow. The Commission will be empowered to find the King guilty; but as his life was guaranteed to him by Hodson, "under General Wilson's sanction," no sentence will be passed.

**Arrangements for Police.** Saunders is very anxious "to introduce a Military Police on the model of that in force in the Punjaub"; and wishes Capt. Stewart of the 9th to be appointed Commandant. Is anything being settled about these Battalions in Calcutta? I briefly expressed in a letter to Beadon, I think, my own opinion on the subject. Instructions on the matter are much wanted.

**King's sons shot.** The old Gwalior news-writer at Delhi says that the King's two sons, who were under trial, have been shot, and their bodies hung up at the Kotwalie, and that the third is under trial.

The following extract from Greathed's report of our affair on the 10th shows the wonderful exertions of the troops before they reached their camp.

**Extraordinary march of Greathed's Column to Agra.** "The Cavalry and Artillery marched over at least *64* miles, and the Infantry *54* miles of road, in less than 36 hours. Capt. Bourchier's 9-pounder Battery had marched in during the night from Hathrass, 30 miles without a halt." And all that chase down to the Kharee and back, a couple of hours after they reached the camp, *i.e.* some 18 miles more, fighting all the way. What noble fellows these Europeans and Sikhs are, truly!

W. MUIR.

J. W. SHERER, ESQ.

**Governor-General's order on the fall of Delhi. Tribute to Sir John Lawrence.** *P.S.*—The Governor-General's admirable order on the fall of Delhi was received with your last letter. It is being republished in the *Gazette*, and the original I will forward to Sir J. Lawrence. The tribute to his exertions is well merited, and expresses the sense of all India.

Col. Greathed has just seen your letter of the 8th, and begs me to say that "nothing shall be wanting on his part to make the best of his way down the river."

## CLIV.

AGRA, 15*th Oct.* 1857.

MY DEAR SHERER,—Thanks for yours of the 10th. Harington has determined to leave with the Column. But he has wisely resolved to leave Mrs. H. here. I feel his departure much. I know no man on whose judgment and discrimination I place so great reliance; and we have long been on terms of intimate friendship. May God go with him, and carry him safely to you. H. Harington, C.S.

The Column marched in to-day to Etmadpore. Col. Greathed is fully alive to the necessity of the speediest movement towards Cawnpore. It is a noble Column, and described as moveable in the best sense of the word, viz., handy and easily and promptly worked. We had, indeed, the fullest evidence of that on the 10th inst. Greathed's Column eulogised.

Some 2000 or 3000 camels are going out at once from our Contingent for carriage eastwards; and more camels and as many carts as can be got together by the time will be sent five days hence with an escort to catch up the Column. Tell this to the authorities at Allahabad and Benares. Provision for carriage.

The Cavalry and H.A. will be invaluable to Havelock. It is a splendid sight to see the guns galloping along, turning corners, and making all sorts of evolutions, as if they were carriages.

Letters to-day have been received from Delhi of the 11th and 12th, the latter by Dak, the former by Cossid, so that the Cossid is now westward entirely out of date. Regular post to Delhi opened.

Saunders again says: "I have positively no news of any kind to communicate."

Colonel Burn, Governor of the city, says that "Delhi is still under the influence of the plunderers. He has no police, and is only allowed 50 Europeans and 50 sowars for the whole duties of the place." Colonel Burn, Governor of Delhi. Delhi being plundered.

Our troops are recovering their health. "Our sick list was a fearful one. The day we attacked we had about 3000 sick, and the assault added at least 1000 wounded to the number." Sick list on day of assault.

Nawab Hamid Ali Khan (you may remember him as an aspirant to be on the College Committee) is mentioned as the Nawab Hamid Ali Khan arrested.

only man of rank and influence who has, besides the Royal Family, been apprehended.

**Break-up of force of Indore Mutineers.**

We continue to receive accounts of the Indore Force breaking up. It has chiefly gone towards Bhurtpore westward and northward. The body repulsed from Muthra passed farther up the right bank, and will probably cross over towards Rohilkhund. Large parties of 400 and 500 have crossed opposite Furrah, and, avoiding our posts at Hathrass, etc., crossed by Sassnee to Secundra Rao, on the Grand Trunk Road: may either go to Furrackabad or Rohilkhund. They are all broken and only partially armed. Great numbers of the force will no doubt go off to their homes.

**Returning loyalty of the people.**

As showing the returning loyalty of the people, I may mention that the Zemindars, on receiving encouragement from Mr. Cocks to do so, rose on the Furrackabad Nawab's Tuhseeldar and Thannahdar at Khassgunge (between Allygurh and Furrackabad), and made them fly for their lives.

A considerable party of the Indore Mutineers were also pursued by the Tuhseeldar of Hathrass, but got off.

At Hathrass they received intelligence from Khassgunge "that 2000 Cavalry, Muthra men, have gone into Rohilkhund, and the Infantry into Futtehgurh." The circumstantial account I gave yesterday of the progress of the main body past Chebramhow appears more likely. However, a portion may not improbably have turned off to Furrackabad.

**Gwalior Contingent about to move.**

Nothing further from Gwalior. Macpherson thinks it likely the Contingent may be moving now for Jhansi and Cawnpore, but also adds wisely, that "no one can possibly be responsible for their holding to that or to any other plan."

The number of momentous and stirring events in these parts is fortunately diminishing daily, and I trust I may soon find the office of chronicler a sinecure; but, in proportion, the plot thickens and becomes of intenser interest below.

If you can give us a daily letter, if even to say that there is no news, and to enclose duplicates of the previous day's despatch, it is satisfactory to Her Majesty's lieges in these parts.

W. Muir.

J. W. Sherer, Esq.

*Note.*—I think there is hardly matter for a telegraph message Yes; say Greathed's Column marched this day to Etmadpore, which is five regular marches from Mynporee.

CLV.

AGRA, 16th Oct. 1857.

My DEAR SHERER,—First for your own matter. The Gwalior Contingent, we have good reason for believing, has started. Several days ago it left the Morar Cantonments and moved into camp. On the 13th its advance guard was sent to Sonee Puchoulee, on the S.E. Road, and on the night of the 14th the main body was to follow. Move of Gwalior Contingent.

The road, Macpherson tells me, leads either towards Jhansi or towards Calpee, so that we cannot yet say whether their course will be direct or not. The road, I believe, goes by the Antree Pass. They will have two rivers to cross, the Sind and the Jumna; the former, I believe, presents no great obstacles.

Greathed marched 13 miles to-day, so he will be close at hand, at any rate, with his noble Column before you can be subjected to much inconvenience. I hope it may have it in store to beat off from Cawnpore the Gwalior Contingent in the same brilliant manner in which it destroyed the Indore army. "Destroyed," I may say in the fullest sense, for it has been so broken in pieces and scattered as to be now contemptible. There is a wonderful change in the feelings of the people since that victory. They refuse supplies, and even oppose the defeated bands as they pass by. To-day's reports add new instances of this to the ones I gave yesterday. Some of our Zemindars in the Muthra district were wounded in an encounter with a party of the horse, who were injuring their fields by the wayside. They would not have dared to do this a month ago, perhaps not ten days ago. Progress of Greathed's Column. Returning loyalty of the people.

Of other news there is little to give.

Saunders, writing on the 12th, says that the two princes, Mirzas Bukhtawar Shah and Mehndoo, whom I before reported as under trial by a Military Commission, have been sentenced to be shot, and the execution was to be carried out on the 13th. Mirza Bukhtawar Shah and Mirza Mehndoo to be shot.

The trial of the King would not take place until some day after the 19th. They are waiting for the arrival of Major Harriott, Deputy Judge Advocate General, who will conduct the prosecution.

He adds "that some of the chief rebels amongst the Mahommedan gentry of Delhi are being gradually arrested (this does not exactly agree with what I quoted yesterday from Colonel Burn, that Hamid Ali Khan was the only one yet apprehended), and will be brought to trial when sufficient evidence to convict Rebels among the Mahommedan gentry of Delhi.

them has been collected. In the present deserted state of the town it is, however, difficult to produce any but documentary proof against offenders. We have recovered an immense number of papers which will afford convincing proof of the complicity in the present insurrection of many who have been hitherto considered well-wishers of the British Government."

W. Ford, C.S. Sir J. Metcalfe, C.S.

On Ford's joining the Column at Rewaree, Sir T. Metcalfe would return to Delhi, where Saunders much desired his presence. His local knowledge must be very useful.

D. M'Leod, C.S., gives opinion of Sir John Lawrence on the disarming question.

I have a letter from M'Leod at Lahore. He writes for Sir J. Lawrence, whom the sudden opening of the Daks, after being for some time closed (probably by the Mozuffurnugger disturbances) had overwhelmed with work. He gives Sir John's opinion on the disarming question, on which I had solicited his views, as follows: "Sir John begs me to say that he considers our safety in a great measure depends on the population being disarmed. But for this it would assuredly have been impossible to preserve the peace in the Punjaub thus far; and he is most decidedly of opinion that it should be carried out with you likewise so soon as you have the power.[1] Our frontier districts have not been disarmed in the north-west and west, but then the countries beyond us in that quarter are turbulent to a degree unknown in your confines; and along the Jummoo, Bhawulpoor, and other more peaceable frontiers, the work of disarming has been fully carried out here, in like manner as in the interior. He thinks you will find but little or no difficulty in doing so likewise, and that no evil or danger will result; at all events, he thinks the rule for disarming should be relaxed only in very exceptive cases."

I mentioned the subject in a letter to Beadon some time ago. It would be very desirable to have an expression of the opinion of the Supreme Government upon it—if favourable, the measure could be introduced as we found ourselves strong enough to do so. M'Leod adds, "the atmosphere is at length, thanks be to God, clearing on almost every side in a very decided manner, now that He has allowed us to regain complete possession of Delhi." Further on, "the rising between this and Multan has not yet been put down thoroughly; but I earnestly hope it is now drawing to a close. It has shown us clearly that had the fall of Delhi been longer delayed, the whole country would have been in a flame." Thus, in labouring for others so nobly, Sir John was really doing the best that could have been done for the Punjaub itself.

Position of affairs in Punjab.

Insurrection between Lahore and Multan.

Sir John Lawrence's action eulogised.

Macpherson hears that the Gwalior troops will march in two divisions, but the details we do not know,—the road *via* Kunch and Orai is good and may probably tempt them. Men of the fourth Cavalry and some of the Contingent Horse were found on the battlefield on the 10th.

Scindia had received the news of our victory of the 10th, and Macpherson's correspondent says "that Scindia's happiness was wholly beyond expression." He is going to send his Vakeel to Macpherson as soon as possible, and thus openly renew the political link which has been so long ostensibly broken, though privately maintained intact. **Scindia's loyalty.**

W. MUIR.

A message accompanies.

*P.S.*—Amanut Ally, Soobahdar Major of the 1st Grdrs. (said to have been Commander-in-Chief of the Contingent), and Muhadeo Singh, Adjutant-General, had gone over to the Maharaja. It is not mentioned whether they brought over any men with them, or anything about the Magazine. Our informers say they had 1000 bullocks and 1000 carts to carry it.

## CLVII.

AGRA, 17*th Oct.* 1857.

MY DEAR SHERER,—Thanks for yours of the 10th. Your receipt of the 11th also received.

We are delighted at the mention you make of two or three bodies of troops marching up between Allahabad and Cawnpore. You do not state their numbers,—remember our avidity for details.

Our Column will give you abundance of Cavalry; so, with the blessing of God, you will, I trust, be quite independent and able to crush the Contingent. We have more correct intelligence to-day of the movements of the Contingent. It marched by Bejoulee, which on a good map you will find due east of Gwalior. **Move of Gwalior Contingent.**

The first division, consisting of three Regiments (1st, 2nd, and 5th) with three Batteries (1st, 2nd, and 4th Co.'s Artillery), marched on the night of the 14th or morning of the 15th inst. The remainder would follow the next day. The Cossid who brought the despatch saw two regiments and two batteries marching as he left.

They have carried with them as much of their Magazine as they could get conveyance for. I presume they have taken their siege train with them. If so, it will prevent them from marching very rapidly.

They burn lines and bungalows.

After the 1st Division started, the remaining one began to burn down the lines and all the bungalows they could lay hands upon. Everything that had been left was destroyed.

The road through Bijoulee leads direct to Jaloun and Calpee—but what their destination is it would be hazardous decisively to say.

The Nana's movements.

Your letter of to-day announces the attempt of the Nana to cross the Ganges *en route* to Gwalior. I conclude that he was aware of the intended movement of the Contingent, and that his object is to join it on its march, not to go to Gwalior where he would have met with cold reception.

The Contingent may now be regarded as retained by the Nana. At the head of this force he may attack Cawnpore, or he may return to Bithoor, or he might try to recross the Ganges. It is of vital importance that the Contingent should not cross the Ganges, for they are richly stored with all sorts of ammunition, while the Delhi fugitives at least are very badly off for ammunition. To intercept the Contingent, seize their guns, and capture their Magazine, is therefore an object of paramount weight. Brigadier Grant quite understands this.

The 5th Regiment, it is believed, adheres to Scindia: and the two remaining Companies of the 6th with the two Mehidpore guns. In place of the old 5th and 6th, two new corps of these numbers have been organised by the Mutineers.

Returning loyalty of the people.

Every day gives fresh proofs of the returning loyalty of the people, and the quietness of the country the moment military parties are out of the way. With only a handful of soldiers at Allygurh, and the same at Boolundshuhur, the Horse Dak runs now all the way from Meerut to this. Brigadier Grant left Meerut at 5 last evening, and reached this (above 130 miles) by 10 this forenoon. With Rohilkhund yet unreclaimed, it is astonishing to find the Upper Doab so rapidly settling down.

Horse Dak open to Meerut.

General Hope Grant.

Arrest of Mutineers by police and people :

At Areeng (?), in the Muthra District, nine or ten Sepoys have been captured by the police, aided by the villagers. They have several thousand rupees worth of gold and gold mohurs upon them. The money has been relinquished to the captors as an inducement to make similar captures.

by Bhurtpore Durbar.

This morning some 15 of the fugitive Indore Force, attacked and captured by the Bhurtpore Durbar, have been *brought in*, and are now under trial by a military court. The escort of Bhurtpore sowars which brought them in takes back Captain Nixon to his post of Political Agent at Bhurtpore. A satis-

Captain Nixon returning to Bhurtpore.

factory mark of the returning confidence of the country in us—the Durbar applied for him.

The Dholepore Durbar are also said to have captured some Mutineers for us.

By the way, when I wrote yesterday I believed Gwalior to be nearer Cawnpore than I find it actually is—it is between 150 and 160 miles, so that, after all, Grant's Column, if not delayed at Mynpoorie, or by the Furruckabad troops, will anticipate its approach.

Williams, Commissioner of Meerut, writing on the 14th, says that the collections are coming in wonderfully—already $1\frac{1}{4}$ lacs from Boolundshuhur. He expects to have cleared off the *whole balances* of May and June for the Division (excepting Allygurh, of course, where Cocks is going on well also) before the first instalment for the autumn crops is due. **Land Revenue freely paid in Meerut Division.**

Williams mentions the surprising number of guns that are being recovered throughout the several districts; altogether, in the Division, there must, he says, have been 50 pieces of various sizes. **Recovery of guns in Meerut Division.**

He adds: "The country is settling down. Our Revenue and Police officers are reinstated everywhere, and the Doab to the Allygurh District is all right." **Civil government re-established.**

Williams hears that Nynee Tal has again been threatened by Khan Bahadoor, who has sent 5000 men and some guns. They have taken possession of Haldwanee and Bhunowree. **Naini Tal threatened.**

Ramsay intends to leave them alone below, and only hopes that they will venture a little up the hills, as he would then be able to inflict a signal chastisement.

I have been talking[1] with Hope Grant about the exile of all the inhabitants from Delhi. I have not quite made out what is the state of the argument against the return of the well-disposed. Besides the difficulty of guarding the City, he speaks of the impossibility of distinguishing the guilty from the innocent, requiring that all should be involved in punishment until they have proved (as I understand) their active loyalty in our behalf throughout the struggle. And again he says that the inhabitants have yet to pay the ransom of the City, and seemed to imply that if this were arranged for, permission to reoccupy might be obtained. **Question of reoccupation of Delhi by the inhabitants.**

I am not satisfied that against the unoffending portion of the community, especially the middle classes of the Hindoos, a harsh if not unjust procedure is not being adopted; but I have not

[1] W. Lowe's hand.

time to follow out the subject. I can understand the argument of the military necessity, and I fancy that that is the true reason.

W. MUIR.

J. W. SHERER, ESQ., Cawnpore.

## CLVIII.

## SERVICE MESSAGE.

FROM AGRA—W. MUIR,

TO CALCUTTA—G. F. EDMONSTONE.

To Governor-General.

INTELLIGENCE confirmed of departure of Contingent from Gwalior on night of 14th or morning of 15th. First march, Bejowlee on Calpee Road.

Greathed's Column at Shekhobad to-day.

Brigadier Grant arrived here to-day, and goes on to take command of Column. Has been urged to proceed with speed.

W. MUIR.

## CLX.

AGRA, 19*th Oct.* 1857.

Gwalior Contingent.

MY DEAR SHERER,—Yesterday news came in from Gwalior dated 16th. Above half the Contingent force moved on the 15th. The second half was delayed by the desertion of 130 pairs of bullocks provided for them, and could not march as intended on the 16th. Scindia, however, is anxious to be rid of them, and the carriage will not be long wanting.

Col. Fraser still thinks it possible that when they hear of Grant's Column having left, and that it will anticipate them in the advance on Cawnpore, they are not unlikely to return upon us here. I am inclined to regard that as highly improbable. They have apparently cast in their lot with the Nana, and the Nana's antecedents will rather keep him in your direction.

Position in Punjab.

We have letters from Lahore dated 10th Oct. Sir J. Lawrence, on that date, says: "We are all well in the Punjaub, thank God; but Delhi did not fall a day too soon." I conclude from this that the Googaira rising is now passing off.

Showers.

From Delhi I have a letter from Saunders dated Oct. 13th. All quiet there. Brigadier Showers' force was at Jatoosana. Several of the Jhujjur sowars whom they came across delivered up their arms without resistance. "We are gradually appre-

Nawab of Jhujjur.

hending some of the chief offenders. The Nawab of Jhujjur and others being anxious now to testify their loyalty and affection for the British Government by apprehending for us some of their not less guilty but not so powerful co-partners in rebellion."

The two princes had been shot that morning by the banks of the Jumna. Princes shot.

. . . . . . . . .

Here we are all free; the only remnant of our enemy is a body of some 400 or 500 Sowars and a couple of hundred Sepoys, who have taken refuge at Futtehpore Sikri. They are described as not knowing whither to turn, having been repulsed from Bhurtpore, and they say they are resolved to die where they are. A force will go out to attack them, and Bhurtpore will be invited to assist, if not to anticipate our attack by themselves, dislodging the refugees. Futtehpore Sikri, you know, is only 12 miles or so from Bhurtpore. Remnant of Indore troops.

Nine of the Mutineers whom I mentioned in my letter of the 17th as having been captured at Areeng with quantities of gold on their persons, were brought in by the Police to Muthra, and are now in the Cotwalee there. Is not Muthra a marvellous instance of loyalty to us? Not a soldier of ours has it seen since the Mutiny broke out, excepting the 2 Cos. of the 44th and 67th, which mutinied and went off to Delhi; yet, whenever the actual pressure of Mutineer forces has passed away, immediately our Cotwalee has been reoccupied and our Deputy Magistrate and Deputy Collector, Imdad Ally, again recognised as the ruler of the submissive city. Much is, of course, due to the good feeling of the Seth; but even with all this, the absence of lawlessness and opposition to the authorities appointed by our Government is very remarkable, when there were such opportunities for their display. Police capture Mutineers. Muthra's loyalty. Imdad Ally. The Seth.

The country north of Muthra, on the confines of the Goorgaon District, is yet disturbed by the unruly Jats and Mewatties, who need chastisement, but we have not the means of chastising them. Jats and Mewattis disturb the country north of Muthra.

Mrs. Drummond has gone with Grant's Column, much against the advice of all here. Drummond speaks well of the crops. (See quotation in the printed slip.) Mrs. Drummond. Harvest promising.

Our latest regarding Nynee Tal is in a letter from H. S. Reid, from which I quote the following; it is dated Mussooree, October 14th:— H. S. Reid.

"I have just heard from Maxwell; they are besieged at Nynee Tal by 5000 Pathans, but are all jolly. Ramsay has more men than arms; a supply went off from this some days back. A note in from Beckett, dated 9th (he ordinarily lives at Naini Tal besieged. Beckett.

Ramsay. Peoree). He writes that Ramsay has written to say that they are besieged by 5000 men, and will go at them on a favourable opportunity; there is no alarm on their account." I do not think there is much cause of anxiety about Nynee Tal.

Major Eld. Major Eld, who is commanding at Allygurh, has caught a man of his old regiment, the 9th, who was left behind sick by the Delhi fugitives. He is getting much information out of him as to the manner in which the regiment went; whether anything more general as to the causes of the Mutiny is doubtful. A remarkable fact is *that the men on leave* generally joined their regiments at Delhi, which were all greatly stronger than we calculated. Eld says: "Rampershaud, the man who commenced our mutiny and seized my horse on parade, I am happy to say was shot in the leg by our grape-shot, and had his foot and ankle carried away by another, but was accompanying the Mutineers on a tattoo." Eld wishes to spare the man. The regiment killed none of its officers.

Men on leave rejoined their regiments at Delhi.

Gwalior troops. Since commencing this letter, communications from Gwalior to the 17th have been received. The 2nd Division on that day marched from Gwalior. They have taken with them the whole of the Magazine and guns, excepting the Station gun. "Their declared intention is still to go by the Indoorkee Road to Calpee. They may make, say the Durbar, a few halts in Zillah Kuchwahagurh, one of Scindiah's assigned districts." Grant will, I hope, get hold of all their magazine.

Cossids killed. I fear the 2 Cossids despatched from this on the 9th have been killed on the road; one of our return men says he saw their *heads* lying in the road, and the waxcloth covering of the despatch they were carrying. I think a duplicate of my letter went on the 10th, but not copies of my letters to Colonel Greathed urging his speedy march this way, which I should have liked the Governor-General to have seen. It cannot be helped now. I think I have now given you all the news.

W. MUIR.

J. W. SHERER, ESQ., Cawnpore.

*P.S.*—I have just read a letter from Saunders, dated 14th. He says the Sappers and Miners were to start the next day *via* Ghaziuddeen-nugger for Agra. This is the first we have heard of it.

He says they had not heard that day from Showers' Camp, but that there was a Native report that he "had taken a couple of guns belonging to the Doojana Nawab at Nahur without resistance."

## CLXII.

AGRA, *20th October* 1857.

MY DEAR SHERER,—There is little of news to-day. Everything here is quiet. Urgent orders are being issued to Grant to hurry on towards you. 2600 camels accompany his force for use below. In another week we shall have collected 2000 more, and say 500 carts. If you can send an escort, say to Mynpoorie or Etawah, we could undertake to convoy them so far to meet you.

General Grant ordered to hurry on.

I have news from Delhi to the 15th. In sending on Greathed's Column we at the same time wrote to Delhi that, as we were still threatened by the Contingent, it was necessary that we should be re-enforced here. General Penny on this parted with his Muzbee Sikhs, 500 strong, under the command of that admirable officer, Captain Taylor, to whom so much in the later operations against Delhi is due. They marched on the 16th by way of Ghaziuddeen-nuggur, and should be here in some 5 days. We shall then be able to reoccupy Muthra and Etawa. We have asked for some field Artillery, if they can spare it, from Meerut, and if we get that we shall then be completely set up, so far as we can be without Cavalry. Saunders says that Showers' Column was to be at Dadree on the 16th, where they were to be re-enforced by a portion of Van Cortlandt's force, and R. Lawrence's Cashmere Auxiliaries. "From Dadree they march on Jhujjur, and will then call on the Nawab to surrender himself a prisoner to the British Government, and our troops will then take charge of his fort and guns. Capt. Lawrence is to remain in charge of the Jhujjur territory, which will be occupied by the Cashmere force, to enable Showers' force to march back towards Delhi."

Captain Alec Taylor, R.E., brings 500 Muzbee Sikhs to Agra.

Showers. Van Cortlandt. Captain R. Lawrence. Dadree. Jhujjur.

Captain Lawrence in charge of Jhujjur.

"Our force in the City is inadequate to hold the defences of the place when occupied once more by its inhabitants, unless supported by a small force like Showers' Column marching within call."

The movement against Jhujjur and Dadree was directed by Sir J. Lawrence's orders, and was no doubt imperatively called for, "to prevent these 2 independent States, which have during the campaign taken a prominent part against the British Government, becoming Alsatias for our disbanded mutinous troops."

Jhujjur and Dadree disloyal.

Everything was quiet at Delhi and elsewhere to the N.W.

W. MUIR.

*P.S.*—A letter from Mussooree, dated 16th (our post, you see, has reached nearly its normal rapidity again), states that the force which had attacked Huldwanee and Nynee Tal had retreated.

## CLXIV.

AGRA, 21*st October* 1857.

MY DEAR BEADON,—Many thanks for your letter of the 5th. I shall be glad to get your promised communication giving the views entertained by the Supreme Government on some of the more pressing topics advanced in my former letters. Some of them press very urgently.

**Policy regarding reoccupation of Delhi by inhabitants.** I take the liberty of enclosing a letter which I wrote yesterday to Mr. Saunders, the Agent Lieut.-Governor at Delhi, regarding the policy maintained towards the City. It is right that the Governor-General should be at once in possession of this —although you will see that several of the points alluded to are not established facts, but rest merely on the tenor of the conversation of the officers of the Column as they passed through Agra. The language held was however general, and was used by high officers as well as low. The subject of the reoccupation of the City has been repeatedly touched on in my letters to Sherer, and once, more at length, in my letter to Edmonstone, dated the 12th inst. I will not fail promptly to communicate the reply I may receive from Saunders.

**Sikh soldiers laden with plunder.** Already the Sikh soldiers are laden with plunder, and some sensible men who have been long in the Punjaub express some apprehension lest when they return to their homes their friends **The danger of this.** among the mountain tribes may have their cupidity excited by the sight of so much silver and gold, and long for the opportunity of acquiring for themselves, by means less friendly to us, a similar booty in this land of gold and silver.

The apprehension may be futile, but having been expressed, as I say, by some persons of judgment, I have thought it not improper to allude to it.

Col. Fraser, you will see from his remarks in a memorandum **Sikh element in the army.** by your friend Brown on Bundelkhund, is afraid lest we should introduce too large a Sikh element into our soldiery in these provinces. But so long as we judiciously mingle other troops with them, I believe that there is at present no practical cause **Their great services.** for alarm in this respect. They are now doing us most admirable service. In fact, our forward and advancing position could never have been so soon gained and so triumphantly maintained without them.

Now that Delhi is down and the Mutineers fled, the feeling of the country is decidedly favourable to us; and supposing that no ground is lost in our progressive reconquest of Oudh and Rohilkhund, we may now rely on the Hindoo population generally, and on all that portion of the Mahomedan population which has not compromised itself. What the effect would be of any serious check or reverse in these quarters one cannot say. The population is so timid, and stands in such awe of the possible return of the Mutineers, that any even momentary advantage gained by them would probably unsettle our hold on the people again. The rebels lie so outrageously and in so specious a manner, that the simple people are quite carried away by them.

**Feeling of the country favourable.**

**Misrepresentation by rebels.**

In Rohilkhund, *e.g.*, even although multitudes of retreating troops have passed, the fall of Delhi is, it is said, not yet believed in some quarters.

But, *Deo juvante*, we will not anticipate the possibility of a reverse. Grant's Column is pushing rapidly on—flushed with victory—and will carry all before it.

I enclose a copy of Brown's memo. alluded to above. Fraser has sent it with his opinion, leaning to Europeans over Sikhs for the duty. No doubt Europeans will be needed, but I see no reason why large bodies of Sikhs should not also be employed. It is the best place to send them to—a wild hilly country, half-savage like their own, and with less temptation to pillage than in the richer provinces; besides, it appears to me a good policy to scatter the Sikhs.

**Sikhs should be sent to Rohilkhund.**

We are getting up Jat and other horse here, and if things go on smoothly below I think we may now calculate on their loyal services.

**Jat Horse raised.**

I am more glad than I can tell you that Lucknow was not evacuated—the Mahomedans would have felt that they had still a head and rallying-point if that Capital had been abandoned to them. As it now stands we have (excepting Bareilly) the main towns. It is only the *Mofussil*, and not the *Suddur* (as they will think), that we have to contend against. The effect of abandonment, as regards Native States, would, I think, have been bad.

**Lucknow.**

I have been talking with Macpherson about the return to the proprietary status as it existed anterior to the Rebellion. He says he has discussed the subject often with Dinkur Rao, and is very much opposed to our system of Civil Decree sales, which

**Proprietary status in land.**

Sale of land by Civil Court.

he believes unsuited to the state of society and violently disliked by the people. At last he admitted that we had so compromised the Government to what had been done that all transfers enforced prior to the Mutiny must be upheld. But he strongly urges that for the future the sale process should not issue as against land for simple debts. He says Dinkur's system works admirably. It admits, as I understand, suits to enforce sales or transfers by private act, or the sale of land if pledged for repayment of a debt; but for simple debt, transfer for a limited period only is allowed; and that, I believe, to some party already connected with the village. The subject attracted my attention last year, and in submitting (while alone in the R. Board) the Rohilkhund report to Government I ventured to suggest the plan of temporary transfer for realisation of decrees. Mr. Colvin referred the proposal to the court: they did not entertain it favourably, and it was shelved. I have thought it worth while to get the entry in our abstract of the passage referred to, and enclose a copy. It is in an abridged form; the original has been lost with our records.

Dinkur Rao's system.

Plan of temporary transfer by Civil Court proposed.

The subject may be worth discussing now, as we have a *carte blanche* for future action. It is worth while considering whether the absolute sale of real property might not be restricted to cases in which it was hypothecated for the debt, and temporary transfers allowed for simple debts.

European barracks: Sir Herbert Edwardes' opinion.

Edwardes at Peshawur is greatly in favour of the square block of building for European Barracks, and our Doctors here seem to be in favour also of a plan of that description with double storeys, the upper tier being more healthy than the ground storey.

Pucca quarters on this plan would certainly have afforded greater security during the late outbreak than our thatched lines. The ventilation, one would think, would be impeded by the quadrangular form, but it certainly has many advantages.

Nicolls here of the Engineers has written a good paper on our Fort. To be at all defensible against any scientific or regular attack, it will require very material alterations and additions. While we are all cooped up here, some of our engineers would be well employed, if they had a commission to do so, in reporting on the subject.

Rao of Mynpoorie.

The ordinary news I will give in my letter to Sherer. I trust that the Rao at Mynpoorie, who has given up the 2½ lacs of treasure he had in his keeping, may be found by Cocks sufficiently free of guilt to be left in charge of the Station. In that case our horse dak may continue to run between that and this.

All to the N.W. quiet, and rapidly settling. Mutineers being brought in both by Native States and our Police. Revenue coming in and all looking cheerful. There is a serious concentration of forces in the Cawnpore direction now that the Contingent is marching there; but our reinforcements are concentrating there also.

Mutineers being brought in by Native States and Police.

Concentration of forces in Cawnpore.

We look anxiously for news of Lucknow. Grant's Column will, no doubt, anticipate the Contingent. The wave has fairly left us behind.

W. MUIR.

C. BEADON, ESQ.

## CLXV.

AGRA, *20th October* 1857.

MY DEAR SHERER,—Grant's Column will reach you, I hope, as soon almost as this letter. I need not therefore give you what will not be news to you regarding its movements. Grant pushed on the troops 23 or 24 miles on the 19th: the Rajah Tej Singh fled. Rao Bhowany Singh came out to meet the Column, and Mynpoorie was taken quiet possession of. We got back, what we had long looked on as lost, the 2,30,000 Rs. left there by Power in June; took one 6-pounder, and two or three small guns, and 80 to 100 maunds of powder.

Sir Hope Grant's Column.

Mynpoorie taken.

All this you probably will have heard of before this reaches you, and also that the body of troops which had taken up a position at Bewar on the part of the Nawab Raees with guns, had retreated—at least the report in camp was such. One camp letter says they expect to be in Cawnpore by the 27th, which I hope will prove true.

Cocks, we hope, will be back to-day or to-morrow. I trust he may be able to leave Rao Bhowany Singh in charge of the Station, and that our mail carts may continue to run to that as a terminus, until our entire line to you is re-established.

All is well here and to the N.W.

A body of some 500 Cavalry and Foot was reported to be at Tuppuhl, some 20 or 30 miles from Allygurh. It is probably exaggerated in numbers, and an offshoot of the Indore fugitive Cavalry, which were wonderfully numerous.

Indore fugitive cavalry.

There is a small body of the same Force at Futtehpore Sicri, probably under 200; and another said to be at Behra beyond Furrah. A Force from here is going in a day or two, to make a circuit in that direction, onwards to Muthra, and thence perhaps to Allygurh.

Captain Gowan.

A letter has been received from Capt. Gowan from his hiding-place, Khera Bughaim, beyond Shajehanpore. He says there are many other refugees in his vicinity—ladies and children—and thinks that if a reward were offered to the Hindoos they would bring them in safely.

Reward promised for refugees.

Replies have gone promising a reward of 10,000 Rupees if a Hindoo escort shall bring them safely to this bank of the Ganges. You should also make this known. So long as Furruckabad remains in the Mutineers' hands their position is precarious. This is an additional reason for early operations against Furruckabad, so soon as they can be undertaken with reference to the more imperious calls upon the troops farther to the East. The following is Bramley's account of his examination of Gowan's Cossid yesterday:—"Talking to the Cossid, I find there are in all 7 persons in Khera Bughaim. Besides Gowan, one man, one boy, three girls, and one woman. He names 14 persons more in villages, 8 to 10 coss some N.E. some W. of Khera."

Seven persons in Khera Baghem. Fourteen in villages near.

The Thakoors will hardly venture to escort to the Ganges more than Gowan's party—at least, so I gather from the Cossid.

Kuchla Ghat, you may know; it is on the direct road between Khasgunj and Budaon—the direct Agra and Bareilly road was to cross there.

This Ghat, they say, is about 30 coss from Khera, which again is 7 or 8 coss W. of Tilhun on the Ramgunga.

If Futtehgurh could be quickly relieved, the Thakoors would then find little difficulty in conveying the Europeans there. The Kunhal have been licking the Jelalabad Sowars, the Cossid says. There is no difficulty that I know of between this and Kuchla —the Sikh Infantry and Gobind's Sowars would be sufficient escort from Kuchla.

Captain Nixon's return to Bhurtpore.

Captain Munbee writes very cheerfully from Bhurtpore; he accompanied Nixon. He says: "Our arrival here has been hailed with satisfaction by all parties, and is calculated to do much good." He speaks well of the behaviour of the Durbar authorities. He says their troops, being now better paid, look more respectable than before, and that all the vacancies have been filled up by other than Poorbeeas. The cultivation is "splendid," and every prospect, he says, of an excellent harvest. The salt is all stored, waiting for the quieting down of the country eastward, and the opening of our line. "The catching of mutineers," says Munbee, "is the chief 'shikar,' and the Kamowlee Rao Rajah has taken up the game. They will soon be

"Catching" of Mutineers.

Rao Rajah of Kamowlee.

extirpated from Rajpootana, I hope." There is a letter from Alexander, Nynee Tal *via* Mussorie, dated Oct. 6th. He says the Bijnore Nawab had written to him, saying that the charge of the district had given him much trouble, but still he hoped to be able to "make over the district in peace, and with satisfaction to the Government. This is one effect," says A., "of our arms at Delhi." He thinks the Nawab of Rampore to be our "consistent and staunch friend," but he distrusts his troops, and fears that Moradabad will not be reoccupied by us, in consequence of the strongholds of Mahomedans at Sumbul, Amroha, and Moradabad itself, without resistance.

**Nawab of Bijnore.**

**Nawab of Rampore loyal.**

George Campbell, whom I asked for a statement of the condition of the crops from Seharunpore downwards, believes that, excepting in a few localities especially exposed to the influence of enemies, the crops are well spread over the land. Perhaps a tenth below the average. The Khureef happens, from the favourable rains, to be an abundant one, and the preparations for the Rubbee are promising.

**Condition of crops.**

You will be probably hearing more of the movements of the Gwalior troops shortly than we. We have news from Scindia up to the 19th. The Contingent was proceeding onwards. His Vakeel started for Agra on the 18th.

W. Muir.

J. W. Sherer, Esq., Cawnpore.

## CLXVI.

Agra, 22 *Oct.* 1857.

My Dear Sherer,—Thanks for yours of the 16th. Yes, it is hardly fair in the Military Authorities at Cawnpore touching my messages; they should have been all forwarded intact to Calcutta, unless obviously out of date, and containing no new information. They have been in effect messages from me on the part of the Government N.W.P. to the Foreign Secretary on the part of the Gov.-Gen. I trust that the grand emergency in this part of the country has passed over, and that our Tel. Messages will in future be of only secondary interest, or I should have been inclined to make a fuss about it. As it is, I enclose a note for Captain Bruce, which please to give to him.

Central India begins to look a little uneasy just at present, but I do trust it will blow over. One can hardly think that now any serious opposition will be offered to us from that quarter, when for many months they had us greatly in their power, and every day is at present rendering us stronger and more independent of

**Uneasiness in Central India.**

the course taken by native States. But these are the natural heavings of the surface following the hurricane in the N.W. First, I have to report the murder of Major Burton, P.A., at Kotah. Captain Macdonald, "on special duty at Deoli," reports in a letter without date, but marked "Express" and received yesterday, that "two Rajpultans, calling themselves *Narain* and *Bhowaney*, went with guns against the bungalow of the political agent. They surprised and murdered both him and his two sons (the rest of the family is believed to be at Neemuch), also Mr. Solder, a subordinate officer of the Medical Department, and a native doctor. This happened in the forenoon of the 15th inst. And the remains of Major Burton and his sons were lying on the floor of the house till 6 a.m. of the following day." Major Burton, with his sons, it seems, had arrived at Kotah on the 13th, and "had the usual visits with the Rajah on the 14th." The intelligence was conveyed to Captain Macdonald by a Bengalee Baboo; and he adds that it cannot be doubted.

Murder of Major Burton at Kotah.

Nothing is said of the feeling of the Durbar itself, or whether the troops are in rebellion against it. We must patiently wait for further information.

In a letter from Bhurtpore of the 20th, Capt. Nixon gives a somewhat less encouraging account of affairs than I quoted yesterday from Capt. Munbee. He says, "I am afraid the political horizon is going to be overcast. Jyepore is not getting on so well as it ought to do, and the great Feudatory of the State, the Rawul, has very unfortunately allied himself with the Mahommedans, and is inclined to kick up a row. The Rajah is a first-rate fellow and our friend." There was a rumour received from Khoorja and Meerut to-day that some mischief was brewing at Jyepore; but Eden, I hope, will be able to keep all straight.

Uneasiness at Jyepore.

Loyalty of Rajah of Jyepore.

"Bhurtpore," Nixon adds, "is not so happy as it might be, but with temper and discretion I hope to be able to drive the coach, please God. It is, however, not to be wondered at that men's minds are unsettled when the whole world has been turned upside down." He anticipates some trouble in putting down the Mewattees of the District, who have been the cause of much mischief.

Bhurtpore.

Turbulent Mewattis.

In another letter Nixon says that the Joudpore Mutineers have left Awah and gone to Mertu, a town to the west of the Sambhur Lake. He thinks from this that they intend "to cross the Jumna somewhere between Agra and Delhi."

Joudhpore Mutineers.

In our own jurisdiction matters continue to look well.

Williams, the Comr., writing from Meerut on the 20th, says,

"The Doab is quite quiet hereabouts, and we are all watching the Ganges. I have a little army on the other side—Bijnore Chowdries, Goojurs, Juts, etc.—about to attack Mahmood Khan (the Nawab) at Bijnore on their own account." Doab quiet.

Williams has been very anxious to move on Rohilkhund, but this has been discouraged, as we have enough, and far more than enough, on our hands already, and it can wait. But there are many favourable elements there. When we can afford to move into the Division, "thousands and thousands of Hindoos would join any advancing column. The whole Hindoo population are praying for our advance." Rohilkhund. Loyalty of Hindoos.

From Boolundshuhur Sapte writes cheerfully. He is busy seeing all the boats on this side the Ganges. He crossed at Anoopshuhur, and walked a little way on the Rohilkhund bank. They talk of an invasion of the Doab, but it seems unlikely. Walidad of Malagurh has been appointed Chuckladar of Islamnuggur in the Budaon District; and it would not be surprising if, to prop up his ruined fortunes, he were to league himself with the Joudpore Mutineers; and it is possible that he may have had a hand in the unsettlement I have already alluded to in Rajpootana. So the sooner you can send up troops to overawe our neighbours, both East and West, the better. Simultaneously with, or very shortly succeeding, your offensive and expanding measures in Oudh, it would be of great importance also to threaten Rohilkhund, whither some of the Lucknow fugitives will probably retreat. There will also be a rush eastward, or rather there has (as I gather from F. Gubbin's letter to you) already been such a rush. But very shortly our welcome and ample succour from England should enable the Commr.-in-Chief to provide for both objects. Boolundshuhur. Wullee Dad Khan.

We have Gwalior letters up to the 20th. The Contingent, with its 40 guns, had reached Gohesur on the 19th. By this time it will have crossed the Sind and be about Indoorkee. Gwalior Contingent.

I have letters from Delhi up to the 15th, with reports of Brigadier Showers' proceedings before Dadree and Jhujjur. Brigadier Showers at Dadree and Jhujjur.

On approaching Dadree the Nawab came out to meet the Brigadier, and received the Column "with the utmost respect." He expressed his readiness to submit to any inquiry the Government might institute into his conduct, and promised to "afford his assistance in arresting any Mutineers and insurgents who might take refuge within his jurisdiction." Nawab of Dadree.

Two brass guns, two iron ones, and two Amaselles were taken; the four latter were destroyed. Ordnance seized.

On the 17th the Column proceeded to Chuchukwas, the Shikargah or sporting residence of the Nawab of Jhujjur. It lies midway between Dadree and Jhujjur. The Nawab of Jhujjur came out to this spot to meet Brigadier Showers. He sent forward a deputation to say that he was there, and awaited instructions to come into the camp. When he arrived, Showers communicated to him the instructions of the Government, and after the delivery of the Perwaneh from the Commr. he was arrested. He has since been under the charge of Capt. R. Lawrence, who, with his Cashmere troops, joined the Column on the 16th, and will occupy Jhujjur.

Nawab of Jhujjur.

Arrested.

"The Nawab," Showers writes, "was frank in his communications regarding the state of his troops, and of the objection he suspected his father-in-law, Abdool Summud Khan, would make to give himself up." Preparations were accordingly made for opposition; but during the night the whole troops at Jhujjur, both Cavalry and Infantry, fled, and the Cantonment was found deserted, all that remained being the Nawab's own horses in the Cavalry stables. The few men who remained gave up their arms without opposition. The Fort was afterwards taken possession of, with about 21 guns and extensive munitions of war, including a large quantity of powder.

Abdool Summud Khan:

Jhujjur troops flee.

Ordnance and stores of powder seized at Jhujjur.

A detachment of the Guide Cavalry and Punjaub mounted Police had been posted at Nahar to cut off the Nawab's retreat, in case he should attempt (to escape ?), to cut up all the troops of the chiefship whom they could overtake.

It was believed that the fugitive soldiery were making for the Fort of Kunound. A mounted Detachment was accordingly despatched, which expected to reach Kunound on the 19th, and anticipate any hostile occupation of the Fort. The main column was to reach it on the 20th. Treasure was understood to be collected in the Fort.

It was likely that the Column would visit the chiefships of Bahadurgurh and Furrookhnuggur before returning to Delhi. The southern portion of Goorgaon is again in flames, from these wild Mewattees. Twenty thousand were reported to Mr. Saunders to have gathered there, and attacked and plundered Sohna, and killed some 50 men. The disturbance will no doubt be quelled by Mr. Ford, or by a movement from Delhi. I trust it is not connected with matters at Jyepore.

Turbulence of Mewattis.

All is quiet at Muthra.

Four of the Mutineers, caught at Areeng, were yesterday blown away from guns.

Sapte has seized two Havildars and 5 Sepoys of the 23rd (our friends of the 10th inst.), a Duffadar, and two troopers of the 14th, and some other trooper. He has taken in all 47 guns, some of them of large calibre. He is very anxious for the issue of the disarming order. **Large quantity of ordnance seized at Boolundshuhur.**

News has just come in that the Mutineers who had established themselves at Futtehpore Sicri have gone off towards Biana, and those at Behri seem inclined to take the same course. There is some mischief brewing in that quarter, I fear. **Indore Mutineers.**

W. MUIR.

## CLXVIII.

AGRA, 23 *Oct.* 1857.

MY DEAR SHERER,—I have very little to report to-day. The Mutineers are still at Futtehpore Sicri, and the party that was at Behree is joining them. Those that had left for Biana are said on hearing this to have come back to Futtehpore Sicri. I hope our troops will soon move out to dislodge them. Col. Fraser is waiting for the Muzbees, who I trust will be in to-morrow. But Capt. Inglis speaks of them as raw, ill-drilled recruits. Still we hope to find them sufficiently organised to fight; and in that case our expedition will start probably to-morrow or the next day.

I have a reliable native letter from Bareilly; it gives the following information:—

Wallee Dad, with 500 followers, reached Bareilly on the 5th, and waited on Khan Bahadoor; the latter gave him 4 pultuns, 1100 Cavalry (the numbers you know in these accounts are not worth much), and two guns, for the reconquest of Malagurh. The troops refuse to go without pay; and the Nawab himself displays no great anxiety to expose his person to danger, but he was arranging for a nephew to go in command, and the troops were expected to start on the 16th. Whether they will get the reach of the Ganges is doubtful; but my letter of yesterday will have shown that both the Meerut and Boolundshuhur authorities are on the alert. **Wallee Dad.**

The Malagurh man's "Naib" spoke of going to Furrahabad to get more troops there.

Wallee Dad remains at Bareilly.

Bukht Khan, with the Nana's brother (who is followed by a personal guard of 400 persons), has gone *via* Budaon to Furrahabad. Khan Buhadoor is trying to collect one and **Bukht Khan.**

a half anna of the Revenue balance, but he meets with an absolute resistance from the Hindoos. The Thakoors of a village in Shahjehanpore (I rather think it is J. Barnes' famous Khundur) attacked and killed above 100 of his troops when they demanded payment, and the Aheers of Gonour in Budaon showed so determined a front that the Bareilly Sepoys slunk away without attempting to enforce their demands.

Hindoos loyal.

Attack on Naini Tal.

The force sent against Nynee Tal had been defeated with loss. On its return to Bareilly the Khan was much displeased, and ordered them at once back again. They clamoured for their pay, but did not get it. A large force, however, has set out with four guns for Nynee Tal. There is not much danger of our friends there. The news of Nepal troops being expected at Nynee Tal had reached Bareilly. Intelligence of the occupation of Lucknow by Havelock was also known there. Both Hindoos and Mahomedans are deserting Bareilly by thousands and living in the villages. . . .

Khan Buhadoor at Bareilly.

Khan Buhadoor retains 10 pultans, some cavalry, and two guns at Bareilly. He has in all 30 pultans (you may calculate as you please) and 21 guns. But his troops are ill-armed: some have muskets, some swords, some clubs; many cannot use a gun. The Artillerymen are also unskilful. So much for the native account contained in the letter.

The up-country dak has just come in; it brings a letter from Saunders, dated the 21st. He sends a copy of the message of the Governor-General, dated the 10th, regarding the City and King of Delhi. I rejoice to see the Gov.-General's order to destroy the fortifications and defensive portions of the walls and gates of the City. In regard to the King, Mr. Saunders says that as his life "was guaranteed by Hodson, under the authority of General Wilson, it will, of course, be necessary to send him down to Allahabad when the country is sufficiently tranquillised to admit of his travelling down country. His eventual destination ought certainly to be kept secret, to prevent a chance of a rescue being attempted on his way down country."

Governor-General's orders as to walls and gates of Delhi.

King's life guaranteed by General Wilson.

Trial of the King deemed desirable.

Saunders adds: "I regret that he is not to be tried, with a view, not to his being sentenced, but to the evidence being recorded against him, and his guilt or innocence asserted. The documentary evidence forthcoming against him is of a character the most convincing, and there certainly ought to be some means of making it public for the information of Europe and in justification of our conduct."

A trial, however, may not be necessary for the arrangement

and elucidation of the evidence against the King. It can all be placed on record and published by the Government in a form suitable for transmission to Europe. The evidence is all documentary. The printed Gazettes of the Palace are sufficient alone to prove the open part taken by the King with the rebels; and there will be other documentary evidence of his secret machinations.

Strong evidence against him.

The Nawab of Jhujjur was safely conducted into Delhi on the 20th. He is now in the Palace under a European guard, and in the custody of Lieut. Ommaney. He will be brought to trial in a few days under instructions from Sir J. Lawrence. No news had been received of the operations at Kanound.

Nawab of Jhujjur a prisoner.

The post brings a letter of yesterday's date from Williams, at Meerut, and of the 14th inst. from Ramsay, at Nynee Tal. The latter says that the second body that attacked them consisted of 5000 and 500 good horse. Col. Story was against any attack, but Ramsay, with difficulty, got 300 men and went down. He had a trap to catch the Cavalry, by decoying them across the Gola Canal, and then taking possession of the bridge. "But they escaped by galloping up when I expected," says Ramsay, "they would have walked. We killed a horse and wounded four men; but they thought we might do them more injury, and they bolted that night."

Attack on Naini Tal.

Defeated by Major Ramsay.

The Kemaonees, the people of the district, have behaved admirably. When Ramsay sent for men to defend the passes, "they came in thousands without any pay and without a grumble." Williams thinks Ramsay's chief difficulty will be money, and he has sent him up, *via* Mussoree, 2000 gold Mohurs. At Meerut they have above 6 lacs in the Treasury; here we have little more than four, and Reade is very irate at Grant for carrying off the 2¼ lacs from Mynporie, which he had set his heart upon getting! You must send us up treasure with the first detachment that moves this way.

Kumaonis loyal.

W. Muir.

## CLXIX.

Agra, *24th Oct.* 1857.

My Dear Sherer,—The Delhi post has just brought this letter, with a message for Capt. Bruce to forward to Calcutta, from General Penny. Please make it over to Capt. Bruce.

In forwarding the above, Saunders gives the following explanation regarding the guarantee for the King's life:—"It was

History of guarantee for King's life.

King of Delhi. certainly guaranteed to him by Capt. Hodson, by permission of the General commanding. I was absent at poor Greathed's funeral on the 20th Sept., when Hodson went to the General and asked his permission to endeavour to secure the King's person through Mirza Elahie Buksh, one of the family who had come to Hodson and promised to induce him to come in, if his personal security was promised to him. At that time it was not known where the King and his family were; and I very much doubt whether we should have suceeeded in obtaining his person, had it not been for the authority granted to Hodson to treat with Mirza Elahie Buksh for the surrender of the King upon the guarantee of his life being secured to him.

"Hodson, after having got the permission, rode off to the Cantonment, and met me leaving the funeral-ground, where we had just interred poor Greathed. He called out to me as he passed, that Gen. Wilson had given him authority to promise the King his life. I was not surprised at the General having done so, as poor Greathed told me a few hours before his death that Mr. Colvin had authorised him to treat with the King, on the understanding that his life might, or rather would, be granted to him. I had not been able to look at a single document at that time, having only just assumed charge a few hours previously, during which we had all the excitement of attacking and taking possession of the palace and remainder of the City; and I, moreover, had been engaged in attending to the funeral arrangements, etc., of my predecessor. Mr. Greathed had never shown me the instructions which he had from time to time received from either Agra, Lahore, or Calcutta; and I was perfectly ignorant of the views of Government, with the exception of having heard Greathed once before say that he had been empowered to offer the King's life." I have copied this out *in extenso*, as it is important that it should be known to the Gov.-Gen.

Walls of Delhi. I trust that, as proposed by Sir J. Lawrence, so much of the City wall will be spared as will serve for a protection against the marauding attacks of the plundering population of the vicinity, without being allowed to retain any military aspect or character. Even the very summary line of walls and gates which have been run up here at Agra have given confidence, and would, I believe, serve as protection against predatory attacks. I believe that this, in respect to Delhi, is perfectly compatible with both the words and spirit of the Governor-General's order, as I conclude that in desiring the walls to be so far destroyed as to make them "useless for defences," *military* defences were intended. But I am travelling a little out of my line.

Saunders reports that Showers had taken possession of the Fort of Kanound, and that our troops had cut up about 400 of the Nawab's people. With the Fort, we secured 5 lacs of rupees. Showers seizes Kanound, and five lacs. Four hundred killed.

From Brigadier Lawrence's official report of the tragedy at Kotah, it is satisfactory to learn that he believes the Maharajah to have been unconcerned in it, and "greatly grieved" by it. Dreading that the unruly troops would proceed to plunder the city, he had closed the gates, and called to his aid the Thakoors with their Rajpoot followers. Rajah of Kotah and murder of Major Burton.

Greathed's news you will have from himself. I hope you will be able to maintain a runner dak to Mynpoorie. If the Rao is able to hold his position there, we shall keep up the mail carts so far.

The Gwalior Contingent was supposed to be yesterday at Ameen, 36 miles on the Jalown and Calpee road. The 2 Divisions of the force were expected to unite there. They seem to be taking their time. Gwalior Contingent.

You will see from the printed slip that I have ventured upon native report to announce a victory gained by your troops, as I suppose, over the Nana's followers on the 18th or 19th. We have not a syllable from you later than the 16th, excepting a receipt. Your letter has probably been intercepted.

Cocks believes the Rao Bhowaney Singh of Mynpoorie to be innocent of rebellion against the Government, and to be "deserving of the kindest consideration from Government." I am glad he has found sufficient evidence for coming to so satisfactorily a conclusion. It admitted of the only arrangement which for a short time to come it seemed feasible to make, viz. to leave the Rao as Nazim in charge of the Station and District. Rao Bhowani Singh of Mynpoorie.

As soon as troops can be spared, General Outram will, I doubt not, send an expedition against Furrackabad, and then we shall have the Doab clear; but some troops will need to be left there, and a body of considerable strength should be posted somewhere between that and Meerut, so long as Rohilkhund maintains its present hostile attitude.

Allygurh is probably the proper post. Our communications with the up-country depend upon its being free.

W. MUIR.

J. W. SHERER, ESQ.

Scindia's Vakeel, as stated in my message, arrived here yesterday, and is very friendly.

## CLXXI.

AGRA, *25th Oct.* 1857.

Muzbees under Captain Alec Taylor, R.E., arrive at Agra.

MY DEAR SHERER,—I have not much to tell you to-day. No local news except that the Muzbees, under Capt. Taylor, have arrived, and that our expedition against the small body of Mutineers, who still hold on at Futtehpore Sicri, starts on Tuesday the 27th.

General Hope Grant's Column hastened.

Yours of the 20th, with message to hasten Grant's Column, just received. The Governor-General's wish has been anticipated, and I congratulate myself on having been one of the strong advocates of the policy which hurried the Column towards Cawnpore. I doubt not Lucknow will very soon be free, and the enemy flying in all directions. In your letter of the 20th you do not allude to the progress of events broached in your "confidential" note of the 18th. With the Column, however, Havelock ought to be independent of Man Singh.

Allygurh and Boolundshuhur threatened.

Reiterated reports are received at Allygurh and upwards, of an immense gathering in the direction of Budaon, whence an armed force with guns is said to threaten Allygurh; and Boolundshuhur is also similarly menaced. It would be very sad, not only for the people who would be again abandoned to the Mahomedan tyrants if this occurred, but also for our communications, which, now re-established on their old footing, would in that case be again closed.

Troops required in Upper Doab.

The Telegraph, too, which is advancing towards Allygurh and will be steadily pushed forward, would also be again destroyed. Wherefore I cease not to urge the claims of the Upper Doab so soon as the first necessities of Lucknow have been met.

Jyepore and Dholpore seize fugitives.

Nothing fresh from Rajpootana. What we have is good. Nixon at Bhurtpore "hears that several fugitives have been seized by the Jyepore authorities at Hardoun." Dholepore is also sending in some.

Gwalior Contingent.

Nothing new of the Contingent. By the last report, half were at Amaen and half at Munowur.

Your letter of the 18th, enclosing Beadon's of 13th, did not reach till this morning, the Cossid having taken it out to Nixon at Bhurtpore.

Major Williams appointed Superintendent of Police Battalions, N.W.P.

Major Williams has come down from Meerut, and is appointed Superintendent of Police Battalions in the N.-W. Provinces, an appointment I hope the Gov.-Gen. will approve. He is just the man for the post. Col. Steel has also come.

W. MUIR.

## CLXXIII.

AGRA, *26th October* 1857.

MY DEAR SHERER,—Grant's Column is, I trust, this morning entering Cawnpore, and Lucknow ought speedily to be relieved.

Will you oblige us all by a numerical statement of the troops in Cawnpore, distinguishing those left by Havelock when he last advanced on Lucknow, and each subsequent re-enforcement, stating the strength of each; also enumerating the troops stationed and in transit in the country below you, and not forgetting Artillery? We all greatly desiderate such a statement, and Col. Cotton has asked me to obtain detailed information on the subject.

Urgent requisitions for the presence of more troops in Rajpootanah are being received from General Lawrence, Capt. Eden, etc. General Lawrence has applied for Punjaub Irregular Cavalry and European Artillery I fear it may not be possible to meet the requisition. They are much in need of troops. I trust the re-enforcements from England will soon be making their appearance on the Bombay and Kurachee side. **Requisitions for troops.**

"The condition of the Meywar," Eden writes, "requires prompt and active measures. Jodhpore is in trouble, and the 'Legion' moving about with impunity." **Meywar.** **Joudhpore.**

As regards Jyepore itself, Eden says, "We are quiet and well-behaved here, but one or two 'pultans' in the district are mutinous, and in one instance set free some 30 or 40 of our Mutineers whom the Civil Authorities had contrived to disarm and capture. Lastly, this ruthless murder of Major Burton, his two sons, and others, has made us all not a little anxious." **Jyepore.**

Eden has written to General Penny for help, and thinks Showers' Brigade might assist him. Poor Penny must be perplexed by all these calls! for we have been impressing on him the necessity of watching our Ganges frontier and the gatherings beyond it.

You see thus that whenever the successful progress of events towards Lucknow or the arrival of re-enforcements from below admits of it, European troops should be, without the loss of a day, pressed upwards.

The orders to the Commissariat for the procuring of Establishment, carriage, etc., were duly received with your letter of the 20th, and I have made them over to Capt. Chalmers for transmission to the proper authorities at Meerut and Delhi. **Calls for carriage, etc.**

By the way, you will of course send all our despatches *via* Mynpoorie. Clark will arrange for their being then taken up by the mail cart, which I hope we shall be able to keep running, notwithstanding the withdrawal of all our own officials from Mynpoorie. It is hoped that the Rao will be able to hold his position there, unless directly attacked by the Rajah Tej Singh, who may possibly appeal to the Nawab Raes, or some other of the floating Mutineer forces for aid.

**Rao of Mynpoorie.**

**Rajah Tej Singh.**

The telegraph line is completed to within two miles of Allygurh. To-morrow it will be run on to our camp. It has been resolved to occupy the old Fort at Allygurh. It is, as you know, very strong, and constructed on the European principles of fortification.

**Allygurh.**

Letters from Delhi of the 23rd have just come in. I quote the following extract of a letter from Sir J. Lawrence to Saunders: —"I see by a message from Norman that the moveable Column was at Shekoabad on the 17th. *I hope it will not go below Futtehgurh.* If we leave the Upper Doab without troops, we may have another insurrection, and the Gwalior troops may cross the Chumbul and move on Agra." No doubt Sir John, had he fully known the straits of Lucknow, would have approved the forced march of the Column on Cawnpore. Still his views as to the necessity of having more troops in the Upper Doab are valuable, as confirming all I have ventured to write on the subject. Will you kindly communicate what has been said about it to General Outram?

**Sir J. Lawrence deprecates Upper Doab being left without troops.**

I see by a private letter to Mr. Parsons that Man Singh being in Treaty with us was known beyond official circles. I have therefore given a notice of it in the extra.

**Man Singh.**

A despatch from Brigadier Showers is enclosed by Saunders, dated Kunound, 20th October. The Cavalry Force which, when advancing from Dadree on Jhujjur, he sent forward to cut off fugitives from Jhujjur towards Kunound, was eminently successful. From 300 to 400 were destroyed, and the Jhujjur forces are believed to have been irretrievably dispersed.

**Dispersion of Jhujjur force.**

In continuation of this movement, Showers sent on another Cavalry Detachment, consisting of a wing of the 6th Dragoon Guards and Hodson's Horse, to proceed by forced marches to Kunound, under command of Colonel Custance of the 6th Dragoons. The movement was executed with ability and marked success.

**Kunound taken.**

The Cavalry Detachment reached Kunound on the morning of the 19th. Colonel Custance finding the gates closed, called upon the place to surrender, on which the gates were opened, and the Fort taken possession of, with 18 guns, 8 of which were mounted on the bastions, a quantity of military stores, and nearly 5 lakhs of treasure. Only about 60 men were found in the Fort, who laid down their arms. About 500, said to be Poorbeeas, had fled during the night and morning. Some of them were cut up by Hodson. None of the fugitives from Jhujjur had succeeded in reaching Kunound.

With treasure.

Hodson.

Showers with the rest of the Column reached on the 20th. He proposed to remain at Kunound for two days to rest the Artillery horses, and then to return to Jhujjur by Dadree.

I fear my bulletin will not be ready; but it doesn't much signify, as I think I have given all the news above.

W. Muir.

J. W. Sherer, Esq.

My love to Harington. Mrs. Harington and her party all well.

An expedition to Futtehpore Sicri starts to-morrow.

## CLXXIV.

Agra, *27th October* 1857.

My Dear Beadon,—Thanks for yours of the 13th. It is quite delightful again to get into such rapid correspondence with the rest of the world! The dismal feelings occasioned by being cut off from all communication for so long with any other station were at one period very oppressive. But things are fast brightening now; and if success attends our arms at Lucknow, and a force can soon be spared for Furrackabad and the Upper Doab, the Mail-Cart and the Telegraph will soon again connect Calcutta with Peshawar. There is a little uneasy feeling in Rajpootanah; and the hordes over the Ganges menace our now peaceful districts on the Upper Doab. But I trust things will keep quiet till Cawnpore can afford a portion of its daily increasing forces. We need them much to overawe Rajpootanah on the one hand, and Rohilkhund on the other—not to say that we cannot look upon ourselves as secure until Rohilkhund be reconquered. That, however, will not be a difficult or tedious operation the moment a respectable body of troops is available for the purpose.

Communications opening.

Rajputana.

Rohilkhund.

I was very glad to hear your opinion on the topics touched on in your letter. It is satisfactory that Agra will be retained as the

Agra.

seat of Government, but we ought to have a Military Post on the Chumbul in Dholepore to guard the approach to Agra. We are very bare and vulnerable on that side.

Saugor and Nerbudda territories.

By the way, would it not be a good arrangement to transfer permanently the Saugor and Nerbudda Province to the Chief Commissioner of Nagpoor? It is very inconveniently situated for supervision from Agra. In the rains the Daks in ordinary times are 10 or 15 days; for the Betwa and a difficult and wild country intervene. Jalaon, and Jhansie to the Betwa, would of course remain with us. Bhuttianah and Hissar might similarly be transferred to the Punjaub, and half of Paneeput. Thus lightened, Oudh might be annexed to the Govt. of the N.W.P. Surely it must eventually come to this; and now, when a new series of administration is to be commenced, would it not be well that the whole should be consolidated together?

Suggestions as to rearrangement of administration, including the inclusion of Oudh in N.W.P.

As a further compensation, it would be not amiss if Bengal took a slice of Benares. Permanently assessed districts do not unite kindly with temporarily assessed ones.

Is there any chance of such a scheme being carried out, or is Oudh always to remain a severed preserve in the midst of these provinces? Anyhow, I trust the Lieut.-Governorship will be maintained on its former footing. The labour of Government must be facilitated by the superior authority and influence it confers. Appointments and important administrative orders all emanating from the Supreme Government must diminish the influence of a Chief Commissioner; such at least is the impression I formed from Temple's statements regarding the Punjaub.

Lieutenant-Governorship, N.W.P.

With reference to what I before wrote about Delhi, I think it worth while to enclose a letter I have just received from Ramchunder, who was Professor of Mathematics in the College at Delhi. You may remember him and the Sub-Assist. Surgeon, Chimmun Lall, being baptized some 5 or 6 years ago at Delhi. Both have maintained a very high character both as Christians and as officers of the Government. Ramchunder wrote a work on some abstruse problems which was commended by some of our best mathematicians at home. Chimmun Lall had a considerable native practice, and the old King whenever he felt himself unusually ill constantly sent for him.

Professor Ramchunder.

Chimmun Lall.

You will see what Ramchunder says of Chimmun Lall's widow. I trust the Government will assign her a liberal pension; considering her husband's salary and private practice, 50 rupees a month would certainly not be too much.

Pension for Chimmun Lall's widow.

The simple tale of Ramchunder's well illustrates the miseries which innocent people, delicate females, and tender children must have suffered in their temporary exile.

You do not touch on two of our most pressing subjects—Police Battalions, and disarming the people. So soon as any determination is come to regarding the former, let us know. We are aware that it hinges greatly on the course which may be decided upon as to the reorganisation of the Native Army. But something needs to be done at once in the way of rebuilding the Police, which has crumbled away everywhere, and it would be well to begin on the footing which is intended to be pursued. Our difficulty is as to the relative position of the Commandant of the Battalion and the District Officer. Raikes says he found his inability to interfere as Commr., affected the usefulness of the Military Police. But I apprehend that if the Battalions are to perform the duties generally which were required of the Sepoys, so far as regards internal administration, they must have a certain considerable degree of military form and character—and in that case the discipline must be, I should think, exclusively in the hands of the Military Commandant. The Detective Police would of course be exclusively under the Magistrate.

**Reorganisation of Police.**

There is one portion of your letter which I don't think correct. You say we must depend entirely upon the inferior Castes. I believe at the time our army went, that the feeling was so strong that we had clean fallen, that any body of Natives, high caste or low caste, were ready to leave us. Now that the tide has turned, all, both high and low, Hindoo and Mohammedan (the latter, though, only so far as they have not already compromised themselves by taking up the cause of their religion), are beginning to be trustworthy; and will remain so unless we meet again with any serious check.

**Caste in the Army.**

It would be a grave misfortune if we were compelled to exclude any class from any employment in our administration; and I believe that (if things continue to go on well) it will not be necessary to do so. We must judiciously intermix all classes in our Native Army. The Sikh mania may go a little too far. As one of the elements for our future army, they are admirable. They ought to have had their own officers when introduced into the Sepoy Regiments. Corps of mixed Castes are what we need, both for military and police purposes.

**The Sikh element in regiments.**

Saugor seems to be closely threatened by the Banpore Rajah. I have suggested to Macpherson whether he could not create a diversion through Scindia, by a movement on the Banpore man. It would relieve Saugor at once.

**Saugor.**

Scindia. Scindia's difficulty is the 5th Contingent. But Dinkur Rao is a great Statesman, and I hope we shall soon see that he has resources equal to the occasion.

The Contingent are now fairly over the Sindh, which is a great relief to Scindia.

W. Muir.

C. Beadon, Esq., Calcutta.

Sir J. Lawrence's opinion on disarming the population in N.W.P. *P.S.*—In a letter of the 7th October, just received from Sir J. Lawrence, he says: "I certainly think that it" (*i.e.* disarming the population) "should be a general measure in the North-Western Provinces."

## CLXXV.

Agra, 27*th October* 1857.

My Dear Sherer,—Captain Bruce's of the 22nd has just been received. His enclosure from Mr. Edmonstone for Sir John Lawrence will be forwarded at once.

Rohilkhund. The reports from Rohilkhund are perhaps less threatening to-day. The Rohilkhund troops have, they say, constructed an entrenchment opposite Kassgunge; which looks as if they were going to settle for a short time at least where they are. You will, however, readily understand that such neighbours, and the possibility of a visit from them, keep up the irritation on this side — give the disaffected Mussulmans a fulcrum for their machinations, and make the Hindoos in a ferment of trepidation, fearing that their enemies may return and redouble their persecutions from their ready submission to us.

Mynpoorie. News has just come in that Mynpoorie is threatened by an attack from the Rajah on the 26th; also, the Dy.-Postmaster at Mynpoorie (a Baboo), writes that no Dak has come in from Bhowgaon, but that the Dy.-Postmaster there (also a native) has addressed an Urzie to the Rao, "intimating that two Regiments of Sepoys and a few Sowars from Futtehgurh have arrived at Muddumpoor, 6 miles beyond Bewur, and that they intend to plunder the mail and kill the Hurcarras." There is evidently no reliance to be placed upon our hold of Mynpoorie until either Furrackabad is in our hands or we can occupy the place in force.

Gwalior Contingent. From Gwalior the news continues good. The Contingent, finding the water of the Sind deeper at Indoorki than they expected, have crossed somewhat higher up at Seonda. Letters dated yesterday from Gwalior report that a large portion of the force had actually crossed. Now that they are clear out of the

Gwalior country, and on their road towards Calpee, Scindia is still more relieved, and will, I hope, take steps against the 5th now with him. He has given orders for salutes being fired at every Fort in his territory at our successes. The Bundelkhund Wakeels presented Khurreetahs, and the Maharajah vouchsafed replies to those only who have remained faithful to us. Scindia's loyalty.

Nothing fresh from Rajpootana. Our expedition started this morning for Futtehpore Sicri. Expedition to Futtehpore Sikri.

W. MUIR.

W. SHERER, ESQ.

It will be as well to send duplicates of your letters *via* Etawah, if the Mynpoorie Road continues dangerous.

## CLXXVI.

AGRA, 28*th Oct.* 1857.

MY DEAR SHERER,—Brigadier-General Lawrence has written very urgently to Brigadier Showers, requesting him, if he possibly can, as "the aspect of affairs in Rajpootana is so threatening, to march his Column through Sheikhawattee towards Jyepore with all possible expedition." It is necessary, he says, to "show the people that we have troops at command. You will hardly deem it credible," he continues, "yet many in this quarter do *not* believe in the fall of Delhi; and, on this disbelief, on the 15th inst. two regiments of Hindoostanees, belonging to the Raj troops of Kotah, mutinied, seized 8 guns, attacked the Agency, and murdered the Political Agent, Major Burton, his two sons, a Sub-Assistant Surgeon and native Doctor. After this they gave out that they intend taking Ajmere, and then marching to the King at Delhi. The Political Agent, at my desire, will already have informed you of the mutinous state of the Jyepore troops at Hindown, and of their having insisted on the release of several (35) of our fugitive Mutineers from Delhi. Tank, too, is supposed to be filled with them. The Marwar and Meywar chiefs are all more or less disaffected. Of the former the Ahwas chief and others opposed the British troops at Awah on the 18th ulto., and we were not in sufficient strength to punish them. Re-enforcements are expected from Deesa, but they will be small, and much mischief may in the meantime ensue." Unrest in Rajputana. Fall of Delhi not credited. Murder of Major Burton at Kotah. Some Jyepore troops mutinous. Disaffection in Meywar and Marwar.

The whole force available for Rajpootana is stated as follows:— Available force.

500 European Infantry, of whom 100 sick.

70, a weak troop, European Horse Artillery; 20 sick.

1st Bombay light Cavalry Lancers.
Two Squadrons of the second ditto ditto.
12th Regiment B.N., about 300 strong; also Bheel corps at Khairwara and Mhairwara Battalion at Beawur, which has to protect the whole surrounding country, including Ajmere, Neemuch, and Nusseerabad.

You see from the urgency of Lawrence's call that there is really cause for anxiety in Rajpootana. Not a day should be lost in pressing forward European troops in this direction the moment you have any to spare. I enclose for Mr. Grant a letter from Sir J. Lawrence. He enclosed it as a copy to be sent on to him, the original being sent to Williams at Meerut, and he left it open for me to read. It was in heavy paper and bulky, so I had it copied small.

Requisitions for troops cannot be met.

I have just received a letter from Saunders dated the 26th, Delhi, stating on the part of Gen. Penny, in reply to an application from us, that no troops are available at Meerut for location in the direction of Allygurh. He says that General Penny has had applications for Showers' Column, and for re-enforcements generally, from "Agra, Boolundshuhur, Meerut, Jyepore, and Ajmere. It is impossible that they can all be complied with." But General Penny has so far responded to the wants of the Doab, as to promise that if the insurgent population of Rohilkhund should cross into the Doab, the Column will be directed, on the requisition of the authorities, "at once to cross the Jumna and clear it." General Penny admits that "Brigadier Grant's Column having gone down all the way to Cawnpore, has, there is no doubt, left the middle of the Gangetic Valley very much exposed to attack, and afforded the rebels a great temptation to commit excesses in the Doab."

Everything is quiet about Delhi.

Showers' Column left Kunound on the evening of the 22nd for the Mewattee country, *via* Rewaree, Taoroo, and Sona. The

Rising of Mewattis.

rising of the Mewattees there has begun to assume a threatening aspect, and it was necessary to put them down promptly.

Showers' Column.

The Column was expected to be at Sona on the 26th. This will rapidly open out the communications between Delhi and Muthra, which have been closed on account of the turbulence of these Mewattees.

Agra Column.

Our Column will probably move from Futtehpore Sicri, round by Muthra, and the demonstration by both forces ought not only to have a good local effect, but also an effect on the adjacent parts of Rajpootana.

W. Ford, C.S. Kanound.

Mr. Ford, writing from Kunound, says they have secured 7 lacs and 2563 rupees which they were sending in to Delhi. This is good, and with the $2\frac{2}{3}$ lacs at Mynpoorie is a little set-off to our former treasury losses.

Williams is sending us down 150 mounted police from Meerut.

J. Cracroft Wilson, C.S.

J. C. Wilson has made a "dour" down upon Allygurh, and has some mysterious plans in connection with some information he has of refugees over the Ganges. He is in communication with Capt. Gowan. It is most earnestly to be hoped that he will be successful.

He has got the depositions of a sowar of the 8th Irregular to the effect that he went by Wilson's orders as a spy to Furrackabad, and in disguise got admittance into the female apartments of the Nawab, where he saw a young English girl of 11 or 12 years. She said privately to him that there were other European ladies in confinement at Furrackabad. Wilson seems to believe the statement fully; it appears to me to be doubtful.

Stories of English ladies in confinement at Furrackabad.

Miss Emily Goldie.

Wilson had at first heard that Miss Emily Goldie was alive at Furrackabad, but he afterwards ascertained that she had been killed by a grape-shot opposite Singrampoor. By the way, Eden, writing from Jyepore, says that the attack on Nimbhera "was a mistake altogether, and I am much surprised Tank has not got on its hind-legs in consequence. The Nawab is quite ready; he wrote to me for advice. I told him if he moved a man out of his territory I would set the Nagas at him. Jyepore is quite ready to try its luck on Tank itself. He is wonderfully quiet now!"

Tank.

Rajah of Keraolee's loyal service.

The Keraolee Rajah, aided by our old friend Saifoollah (you remember his Keraolee levies who did us good service prior to the 5th July), has intercepted a band of some 50 or 60 fugitives of the Indore Force who were endeavouring to cross the Chumbul into his territory. They were caught in the midst of a hilly tract; some were cut up, others fled, but were afterwards apprehended wandering about the devious paths; some tried to cross the Chumbul and were drowned, their horses being caught. Seven, I believe, are to be sent in for trial here.

The Gwalior troops have, we hear, passed Indoorkee, and still talk of attacking Cawnpore.

W. Muir.

J. W. Sherer, Esq.

## CLXXVII.

AGRA, *29th October* 1857.

MY DEAR BAKER,—I was very sorry to learn that you contemplate an early departure from the country. Every Department will, after this universal bouleversement, require to some extent reorganisation and reconsideration, and the D.P. Works among the rest. In this work your experience will be much missed.

**Encloses Note on East Jumna Canal.** I intended, before these disturbances broke out, to have sent you a copy of the enclosed note on the East Jumna Canal. I happened in my tour last year, as Member of the Revenue Board, to march along the whole length of this canal, and prepared this memo. for Mr. Colvin. Mr. Colvin, you will see, was prepared to have the question discussed as to the best mode of adjusting the cost and repairs of Rajbuhas, but the rebellion intervened.

**Assessment of Rajbuha charges.** I am very anxious that the mode of assessing Rajbuha charges should have a fair reconsideration. The abuses and the dissatisfaction on the East Jumna Canal are, as I have shown, and as I believe is generally admitted, great. There is no check either on the laying out the Rajbuha lines, or the realisation of the disbursements for their construction and repair. The arrears of collection for the large sums advanced by Government on this account are assessed arbitrarily. The people were much dissatisfied.

**System on Ganges Canal.** On the Ganges Canal the system is, I know, free from some of these faults. The lines of Rajbuhas are laid out systematically, and after careful survey. But the mode of charging the zamindars with the cost of construction and repair appears to me equally open, as on the E. J. Canal, to objection. The account of each Rajbuha is to be kept separate, and the expenditure charged as the zamindars take the water. But the immediate realisation has been postponed, and some years hence we shall be having similar discontent on the arrear being claimed, as we find on the E. J. Canal. Besides, the rate falls, or appears to fall, arbitrarily. We fix a water-rate with reference to the value of the water to the zamindar. The Government lays out the Canal and the Rajbuha on the calculation that at such reasonable rate it will repay the cost with interest. Why complicate the assessment and account by making a separate Rajbuha charge? You do not charge a higher rate at the tail of a canal because it has cost more to bring the water there than you charge at the canal-head, if the water be at both places equally valuable to the cultivator. Similarly, why should you be obliged to charge higher on one Rajbuha which happens to require expensive works than on another which can be cheaply constructed? It would seem to be a far simpler course to charge one consolidated water-rate, so adjusted as to include a fair return for all original expenditure, both on the Main Canal, and its Rajbuhas, and for the repairs on both accounts.

**Baird Smith's views.**

Excepting the tremendous authority of Baird Smith, who clings to the existing system, I have not found any single Canal Officer who did not decidedly prefer the consolidated rate as above. I trust that you will see cause to concur, and lay the subject before the Govr.-Genl.

**Raising Police Battalions.**

I enclose copy of a note I prepared for Col. Fraser, on a proposal for the raising of Police Battalions. If the subject is under discussion, it may be of advantage to see what is said regarding it up here.

**Castes and races in Native Regiments.**

**One cause of loyalty of Punjab.**

I also enclose a copy of an admirable letter of Sir J. Lawrence to Mr. Grant, on Punjabee and other levies. There is no doubt that the principle of separate corps only for aboriginal races, and mixed corps for all others, is the right one. In some other letters Sir John expresses his astonishment at the Punjabees standing as they did. One great reason, however, was that they had European regiments in the Punjab; the Punjabees *saw* them. Here we had practically none. The Sikhs who came down this way asked in a half-surprised mood, "where the *Goras* were?" And it was no doubt the universal knowledge of the absence of all European forces of any arm, excepting here and there, at widely scattered intervals, hundreds of miles apart—and even there, generally, in very small numbers—which shook the national confidence in our power of recovery, and led to the universal defection. The presence of a large European force throughout the Punjab forced on the Punjabees a more adequate conception of our independent power, and (though there were no doubt other important causes) aided in holding the Sikhs and Punjabees to their allegiance.

**Rajputana uneasy.**

**Movements of Contingent.**

Excepting the rising in Googaira, which does not seem yet to be extinguished, all is quiet S.W. of the Ganges, to our North-West. Rajputana is a little uneasy. The presence of a few thousand European troops would at once restore confidence to our friends, and crush the disaffected. The Contingent seems to be moving heavily with its siege train. It will, I hope, not come near enough to trouble Cawnpore till Cawnpore is strong enough to discomfit it easily. Grant's Column ought, by this time, to be at Lucknow.

W. Muir.

Col. W. E. Baker,
Secy. to Govt. of India.

*P.S.*—Some important papers on the W. J. Canal have, I fear, been lost in the late disturbances. There was a very able and comprehensive report on the Canal, as affecting the resources of the neighbouring estates, by Mr. W. J. Sherer, who visited the country along its whole line; a paper by Baird Smith, and memoranda both by Reade and myself. I am not sure whether these had reached the Government or not when our troubles broke out. The subject would have specially interested you.

**W. J. Sherer's Report on the West Jumna Canal.**

## CLXXVIII.

Agra, *29th October* 1857.

My Dear Sherer,—Yours of the 23rd, with the Governor-General's message to Colonel Fraser, a message for Macpherson, and sundry commissariat communications, was received this morning. All the enclosures will be duly attended to.

**European reliefs.**

I am glad to hear what you say about European troops. You will evidently soon have a supply more than sufficient for your local wants, and be able to push some upwards. I conclude that both Rohilkhund and Bundelkhund will be attacked as soon as two strong brigades are available. I suppose Rohilkhund will be the first object,—so that all north of the Jumna may be secure.

I am sending on the requisition for all spare Artillery and Cavalry Horses, but they will need some sort of escort, for it would not do to let the Furruckabad Rebel on the one hand, or the Contingent on the other, catch them. The same difficulty attends compliance with the very urgent requisition of the Commissariat Officer at Allahabad. We can get carriage to some extent, but we have not the means of securely forwarding it. A considerable aid must have been experienced from the 2600 camels which Captain Chalmers, our excellent Commissariat Officer here, forwarded with the Column. We have some 600 hackeries and a considerable number of camels ready for despatch now. Calculating on the sluggish movements of the Contingent, we are going to try to send 500 camels *ριγ́τ ακροσς θε* country to *Καυνπωρ, προβαβλι βι θε Ραιλωαι λινε.* Joteepershaud himself will supply his own escort of sowars, charging an additional rate of 2 Rs. a head, which is reasonable

**Supply of carriage.**

**Joteepershad, contractor.**

enough. The proper way to secure carriage would be for you to send out as far as Mynpoorie for it, and we could convey it with our own troops from here that distance.

**Success of Agra Column at Futtehpore Sikri.**

You will see from my printed bulletin the success of our expedition at Futtehpore Sicri yesterday, so I need not recapitulate details here. It is to-day at Achneyra, half-way to Furrah, and will probably go on to Muttra.

**Rohilkhund: attitude of Hindoos.**

The reports from Rohilkhund are less threatening as respects the chances of an irruption of the insurgents into the Doab. Large forces had come in the direction of the Ganges, but were fully occupied for the present in making the refractory Hindoo zemindars pay revenue. They are generally resisted by them, and large gatherings are again spoken of against Khan Bahadoor; but they will not accomplish anything till we can take the lead.

**Hurdeo Bux, Talookdar.**

We have a report from the Dy.-P. Master at Mynpoorie, dated yesterday. He had received no Dak from your direction for two days, and fears something has gone wrong from the interference of the Furrackabad people. You had better therefore not trust exclusively to that line, but send duplicates *via* Etawah. The accounts of Furrackabad itself were, however, less threatening as regarded Mynpoorie. Some troops which the Raees had advanced were withdrawn,—through fear, it was thought, of an attack from Hurdeo Bux. The latter Talookdar had also, it was reported, cut up some of the Furrackabad troops who had fled towards Bareilly on fear of Grant's Column. He has been exhorted from here to do all he can to harass the Nawab and disperse his troops.

**Rajah of Mynpoorie.**

The Rajah of Mynpoorie has deposited his family in a place of security, and gone, people think, to join common cause with the Raees.

**Gogaira rising.**

**Lieutenant Horne attacked on Yoosufzaie border.**

From a message of the 22nd instant, sent by Sir J. Lawrence to Peshawur—copy of which was sent here for information—it would seem that the Googaira rising had not yet been extinguished. Sir John writes to say that he had detained the 21st P. Infantry, which was on its route to Huzara, and sent it to Googaira, "where the insurrection is becoming somewhat serious." Colonel Edwardes replies: "Pray keep the 21st. Huzara is quiet, and we can manage for the present very well;" he adds, however, that Lieutenant Horne, encamped on the border of Yoosufzaie with insufficient escort, was surprised last night (21st) by a party of Punjtar men, and only escaped with his life."

W. MUIR.

J. W. SHERER, ESQ.

## CLXXIX.

### SERVICE MESSAGE.

FROM AGRA, W. MUIR—TO CALCUTTA, G. F. EDMONSTONE.

AGRA, *29th October* 1857.

Affair at Futtehpore Sikri.

OUR expedition successful at Futtehpore Sicri. Most of the rebels fled; but some occupied the buildings on the height and fought desperately. Some 17 killed; a few wounded on our side, including Lieutenant Glubb, wounded through both legs.

Lieutenant Glubb.

Showers' Column punishes Mewattis.

Showers' Column, after punishing Mewattees at Sonah, will proceed towards Bullubgurh.

All quiet towards the North-West, excepting at the Googaira district, where the rising seems not yet quelled.

W. MUIR.

## CLXXX.

AGRA, *30th October* 1857.

MY DEAR SHERER,—Thanks for yours dated one o'clock morning of 25th; we are all very happy to hear that Grant had by that time got almost within sight of Cawnpore.

Despatch of 500 camels from Agra.

Of our friends of the Contingent you will be now getting far earlier news than any we can give you. We are despatching *το* you cinq cents chameaux *vià ετανα* and probably the *λινε οφ Ραιλ*. They will *λεανε*, I hope, on the 1st, and will make *καυνπωρ* in *σιξ δαις*. You will hear further on the subject. If the vicinity of Cawnpore be at all unsafe at that time, you would do well to send out a small escort 2 or 3 stages to meet them.

With your letter was one from Beadon dated 19th, for which, if you are writing, pray thank him.

Nothing locally new here; all the news is in my bulletin, but in case it be not ready in time for the post I give a brief outline.

Casualties in the Futtehpore Sikri affair.

More execution was done at Futtehpoor Sicri than at first reported. Forty of the enemy were killed, among whom two recognised as Sepoys; rest supposed to be Ghazies. The wounded on our side nearly *20*; but most of them slight.

All the strong buildings at Futtehpoor Sicri will probably be blown up when we can spare men to send out for that duty. They are capable of a strong resistance by a small body of occupants, as you may remember. But the Durgáh will be spared.

Affair at Jeerun.

There has been a sharp affair at Jeerun, 10 miles from Neemuch. The Mundessore rebels having had the insolence to advance thus far, a reconnoitring party under Captain Tucker, 2nd B. Cavalry, was sent out on the 23rd. He was fired on, and imprudently followed the enemy to within a short distance of Jeerun, where he was killed by a shot from a matchlock; a trooper also was killed, and others wounded. The party retired. **Captain Tucker killed.**

Meanwhile a detachment of 50 Europeans, 100 Bombay Infantry, and 200 Bombay Cavalry, with 2 9-pounders and a mortar, had been sent out early on the 23rd from Neemuch. It met the reconnoitring party half-way, and all marched on to Jeerun. The guns and mortar were put in position and opened fire on the village, outside which the Mutineers were drawn up under 6 or 7 standards. They were subsequently ascertained to comprise *all* the real fighting men of the Mundessore insurgents. Our little force of horse and foot attacked them, but were driven back after being close in the town. The Cavalry retired so fast that the mortar was left in the enemy's hands. Our guns only limbered as the banner of the enemy was seen over the crest of the eminence on which they were planted! The Cavalry were, however, soon rallied on a height a little way off and rushed into the intervening valley. The enemy fled, our Infantry advanced, and retook the mortar, which had, however, in the meantime, been rendered useless for the day. The insurgents took refuge from our fire in the Fort, and we remained in possession of the field and the eminences close by the town, where they ate their dinner. The place was too strong to be stormed by our little party; and there being also a report current that Neemuch was threatened, the detachment returned to Neemuch, which it reached by sunset. Captain Tucker's body was recovered. Another officer, Captain Read, H.M. 83rd, was killed, and 5 wounded: 10 men (including 2 Europeans) were wounded. **Captain Read killed.**

The effect was admirable. The enemy evacuated the place next day: and it was occupied by the Civil authority. Dissensions are said to prevail at Mundessore, where this virtual repulse will be felt.

We still get no post from the Camp or Cawnpore *via* Mynpoorie. An officer, Mousum Ally, with 500 men, is said to have been posted at Chibramow to stop our communications with Cawnpore. But the travellers from Furrackabad give a miserable account of the Nawab. He has fallen sick out of terror at our troops and the fate awaiting him. He has told his followers that they can be of no eventual avail to him, and that he will take poison, and advised his people to fly, which they are doing. **Mousum Ally.** **Nawab of Furruckabad.**

The Raja of Mynpoorie had repaired to him, and he had said **Rajah of Mynpoorie.**

the same to him. Such is the tale told by the passers-by at Mynpoorie.

No news yet from the N.W. to-day.

W. Muir.

J. W. Sherer, Esq.

*P.S.*—The up-country dak has just come in. No news. Things look quieter over the Ganges, *i.e.* so far as an attack this way is concerned. The Hindoos are sending over letters full of anxiety for our approach on account of the oppressions of the "Affghans." Wilson has passed Eastwards towards Kassgunge. I do not know what his exact plan is, but hope he will be able to rescue somebody. He is just the man for a roving life of the kind, and the commission of hunting down Mutineers will be admirably performed by him. I hope the appointment will be approved by the Governor-General.

Cracroft Wilson, C.S.

A. Cocks, C.S.

Changing attitude of people.

Cocks writes on his return to Allygurh: "There is a great change in the manners of the Zemindars and others since I was last here, and I am getting several letters daily from the Thakoors and others over the Ganges."

Jats coming forward to enlist.

"The Jats are now coming in with a will," *i.e.* to be enlisted.

Gwalior Contingent.

We hear that the advanced guard of the Contingent reached Calpee on the 27th, but the main body was, we understand, still about Indoorke on the 27th. They may have sent their advanced guard to Calpee to secure the bridge, etc.

Rajah of Mynpoorie.

The Mynpoorie Raja is prowling about in the Etawah district with 500 men.

## CLXXXII.

Agra, 31st *October* 1857.

My Dear Sherer,—Yesterday the Cossid brought no letter from you, but one to Mrs. Harington giving a satisfactory account of your welfare. We cannot make out from yours of the 25th whether the Column would go direct to Lucknow or make any stay in the Doab; we always understood it was to hasten to Lucknow, but the tenor of one of your letters rather threw doubt on this.

Colonel Fraser makes a good suggestion that the equipage, etc., of Grant's Column might be with great advantage curtailed, and the carriage so saved used for the troops on their upward march. The Column would thus be lightened and enabled to march long stages with less difficulty. Its *tail* would be less obnoxious to attack, and require fewer guards to attend to it.

Greathed, I think, or Grant, described the Column when on march as *10 miles* in length!

We have letters from Sir John Lawrence up to 27th inst. He writes very cheerfully, and as he does not allude at all to Googaira, we may conclude that things are settling there, or at least are not of serious moment.

**Sir John Lawrence's account of the Delhi Division.**

Of the Delhi Division he writes: "The main point was to get off the moveable Columns, the one down country, and the small one to clear the division of Moofsids. These two things accomplished, all has gone well, as I anticipated. The country has settled down. Guns tumbled in; 'Khair Khwahs' have started up; 'Moofsids' have obsquatulated, as the Yankees call it; and, but for those who are dead and gone, and a little loss of property, public and private, all would seem like a dream."

**His views on the treatment of Delhi.**

My letter to Saunders of the 20th would seem to have miscarried: the one about the treatment of Delhi. For Saunders has not alluded to it, and Sir John, who was to have had a copy of it from Saunders, says he has heard nothing of it. But Sir John's views seem to have much coincided with those urged in my letter. He says: "As regards the city and fort of Delhi, I wrote until I was tired; and, as in such cases, both parties probably adhered to their own views. I would have taken all the guns from the ramparts of the town; mounted as many as I could on the Palace, so as to command the town, and let back all the peaceable folks. I should be happy, in case of necessity, to do all that was necessary with 1000 men at my back at Delhi."

**Wretched condition of Delhi people.**

**Almost incredible plunder.**

The following extract gives the impressions of a young intelligent Assistant-Surgeon who has gone up to Delhi from here, in a letter to another doctor here. "Delhi is still standing in all its magnificence. There is scarcely a trace of shot and shell from one end to the other, but the houses are desolate and plundered. The wretched inhabitants have been driven out to starve; and I cannot help thinking they have been rather cruelly treated. You used to blame me for my sentiments of death without mercy to every Sepoy: but I think this Government is behaving too sternly to the poor Bunniahs and Kayeths. The plunder daily being found in the city is more than enormous; it is almost incredible. I fancy every officer present at the siege might be able to retire at once."[1]

All this is very illustrative of what I before wrote. I am

[1] This is given as it stands. No doubt the plunder in a rich and deserted capital must have been vast; but the statement about Officers is absurd,—a mere figment of imagination.—W. M.

sending a duplicate of my letter to Saunders in case the first may have miscarried. I do think the views in it were sound.

Details of Artillery with Gwalior Contingent.

The following statement of the Artillery believed to be with the Contingent may be of use. It is by Meade, the late Major of Brigade at Gwalior:—

"6 18-pounders, of which 4 were equipped for service,
3 heavy howitzers,
4 or 5 mortars, with full supply of ammunition,
20 9-pounders,
4 24-pounder howitzers;

with five companies of golundazes, fully equipped, with the exception of the draught bullocks, which averaged about 20 short in each battery.

"There were about 500 barrels of powder in store: and close on 4 lacs of musket ammunition, besides the regulation proportion with the regiments. There were also 1000 stand of muskets complete, spare in the magazine, together with a large number of swords, pistols, etc. Two of the 18-pounders were equipped for elephant draught for field service—4 elephants having been trained for this purpose."

Machell, our Commissary of Ordnance, gives the following approximate statement of the ammunition with the heavy Artillery, viz.:—

"4 18-pounders,
4 8-inch howitzers,
4 8-inch mortars,
4 5½-inch mortars,

| | |
|---|---|
| shells spl. filled 8-inch howitzers . . | 374 |
| " common . . . . . . | 5844 |
| " 5½ common. . . . . . | 476 |
| shot case, fixed bottom, 8-inch howitzers . | 429 |
| " round, 18-pounders. . . . . | 12,850 |
| shells spl. 18-pounders . . . . . | 552 |
| shot case, 18-pounders . . . . . | 274 |
| pounder ordnance lbs. . . . . . | 273,000 |

and other material in proportion.

Light pieces . . . 20 9-pounders, brass guns.
4 24-pounders, howitzers.

—

24"

A goodly array, certainly. If possible, I trust they will be caught in the field and not allowed to entrench themselves. Col.

Fraser says: "Tell Sherer that his only chance with the Gwalior fellows is, if possible, to attack them *in the field*; for, as they have heavy guns and mortars, they would prove very troublesome if they attacked any entrenchments of ours."

W. MUIR.

J. W. SHERER, ESQ.

*P.S.*—Captain Bruce's of the 26th to Colonel Fraser just received. The Governor-General's message will go on to Delhi. But I doubt their being able to spare a Carabineer. In reply to an urgent application for some to reinforce Allygurh and the Middle Doab, General Penny, on the 26th, wrote: "At Meerut there are not more than 180 Carabineers mounted—and certainly with the rebels in force in Rohilkhund it would be madness to part with them. There is 2 years' supply of tea, rum, etc., for Europeans at Meerut, besides estimated property of Government amounting to 33 lacs of rupees; and if this went, double that sum would not supply the loss. The few remaining men of the Carabineers mounted are recruits, and probably do not exceed 60 men."

**Details of Carabineers.**

Apart altogether from the stores, the Military position could not of course be left without a sufficient force. Any reverse in the Upper Doab would throw us all into a flame again.

The sending of the remount horses, etc., will be again urged on the Meerut and Delhi authorities. But the country between this and you is—what with the Nawab Raees on the one hand and the Contingent on the other, for the present insecure; and unless you sent up a Detachment more than half-way, Colonel Fraser could not guarantee the safety of the horses. I am glad to see that Captain Bruce is aware of the Furruckabad parties at Bewar and Goorsuhaegunge.

**Insecurity of country between Agra and Cawnpore.**

W. MUIR.

## CLXXXIV.

AGRA, 2nd *November* 1857.

MY DEAR SHERER,—Yours of the 28th received. We mourn over the detention of the Column at Cawnpore. But by this time I trust it is at Lucknow. Had we been able to keep the Column back 2 or 3 days here, instead of at Cawnpore, we should have given you a large additional amount of camels, and *hackeries* also.

Gwalior Contingent.

The Contingent must have already shown you what its plans are. They were no doubt terribly burdened with their Magazine, etc.; we hear contemplated leaving it at Jalaun or Calpee, and then going on to fight. The news from Gwalior of the 31st was that the Contingent has moved on from Indoorkee to Jalaun. If the Column had been active they might have relieved Lucknow and been back in time probably to beat the Contingent.

Our local news will be sufficiently in detail in my printed bulletin, which I hope will be in time to send to you as an enclosure.

Muthra loyal.

Some describe the reception of the Column (Cotton's) at Muttra as gratifying. It has certainly been a very loyal city throughout.

Captain Gowan, Sergeant-Major Belcham and family brought in by Cracroft Wilson.

A message has just come in from Allygurh to say that Mr. Wilson had returned, bringing with him Cap. and Adjt. Gowan, 18th N.I.; also Sergt.-Major Belcham of the same corps, Mrs. Belcham and 4 children. Particulars will follow by letter. Wilson has evidently done good service.

Tell Mr. Tucker, please, that his letter of the 4th October has just come to hand. When he has anything important to write he should ask you to send it by Cossid. We none of us know who the "Mundi Raja" is, but I will ask Sir John Lawrence. Thank Tucker, but ask him to write oftener.

Allygurh. Talookdars loyal. Murray's Jat Horse.

Cocks writes very cheerfully about the aspect of things at Allygurh. All the Talookdars coming in to pay their respects. They are all delighted with Murray's Jat horse. They performed their part in the surprise of Adhoura (in bulletin) in a manner that satisfied everybody.

Khan Buhadoor.

Wilson reports that Khan Buhadoor is not prospering. His grandson and nephew are said to have been shot in a village in the Bareilly district, where they were committing acts of oppression.

At the Kuchla Ghat, where I fancy Gowan crossed, and where Wilson went to meet him (it is, you know, north of Eta), Wilson secured on our side all the boats in the vicinity.

Gogaira rising.

In a letter dated 29th October, Sir J. Lawrence says that he had prepared for us a Sikh Cavalry regiment, but had been obliged to retain it in consequence of the insurrection in Googaira. He adds: "I anticipate being able to send them off in another week," whence I conclude the Googaira business is going down.

Sir John writes to me in considerable anxiety as to the disastrous results that would ensue if the Contingent were allowed to attack and ravage these parts in their unprotected state. "You would have," he says, "another insurrection." He had not known fully at the time that the Contingent had gone your way. It is still, however, a possibility that, avoiding Cawnpore, they may cross higher up—at the Sheregurh Ghat, for instance—though even then their probable course would lie towards Oudh, the Eldorado, as you well know, of the rebels now. There is a report to-day that they have sold their Magazine and siege train, which would be not unlikely if they had that design.

. . . . . . . .

W. MUIR.

J. W. SHERER, Cawnpore.

*P.S.*—The up-country Dak has just come in bringing letters from Delhi of yesterday's date. Showers' Column is still engaged with the Mewattees in the Goorgaon district. A portion of the Force attacked a body of the insurgents who had taken up a position on the hill. They were dislodged and driven away; 60 to 100, including several Sepoys, being killed. The only casualty was a very lamentable one, poor Wigram Clifford—the same whose sister was one of the first victims in the surprise of Delhi. He was killed by a shot from a Mutineer Sepoy; he died almost immediately on being wounded, as the ball passed through his head. He had apparently ridden in advance of the party.

Mewattis.

Wigram Clifford killed.

Brigadier Showers has written to Delhi to say that he considers it necessary that the Column should march in force against the Mewattees. "They are," he says, "in numbers on the hills and in the villages near Sonah. Some Pandies and horsemen are associated with them, and if I were to leave this part of the country without going in among them they would come forward again and give a great deal of trouble. I have therefore decided on going to Sonah *via* Kasun and Taoroo." Saunders does not say where he writes from. It may be from Goorgaon. Yes, it must have been. For in a letter of the 31st, Saunders says that Brigadier Showers rode into Delhi on the 30th from Goorgaon, and rejoined his Column there in the morning. He reported that his men "were greatly knocked up, and many completely ineffective from sickness and fatigue, and required rest." The horses of Scott's Battery hardly able to drag

Showers determines to punish the Mewattis.

His Column requires rest.

the guns. The Infantry portion musters not more than between
Kamaonies. 500 and 600. "One regiment, the Kemaonies, have only 90 effective men out in camp." "It will be necessary," Saunders adds, "for the whole Column to march into Delhi to refit, or to have other regiments substituted for those that are unable to march." This was apparently determined on Showers' visit to Delhi. But on his return to Goorgaon he found that the Mewattees were too strongly posted without having a regular expedition in force against them. A considerable reorganisation of the Column was evidently intended, for Saunders adds in a *P.S.* to his letter of the 31st, "the moveable Column will be sent across into the Doab I believe in a very few days, when the force has been reconstituted."

Joudhpore "Legion." He also states that "the Joudpoor Legion is believed to have crossed the Jumna." But this is not confirmed by any information we have.

. . . . . . . .

W. MUIR

## CLXXXV.

### SERVICE MESSAGE.

FROM AGRA—W. MUIR,

TO CALCUTTA—G. F. EDMONSTONE.

AGRA, *2nd November* 1857.

To Governor-General. IN a message to Mr. Saunders, dated Lahore, 31st October, Sir John Lawrence requests that the following message may be telegraphed to the Supreme Government, viz.:—

Candahar Mission. May I recall the Mission from Candahar? Major Lumsden desires it, and seems to think that Sirdar Hyder Khan desires it. Lumsden says that if he delays much longer the snow will prevent his returning until spring. All well in the Punjaub. Two squadrons of Sikh Horse march for Delhi on the 3rd. The rest will follow quickly. Sir John's message ends. The Mewattees are still in force south of Goorgaon. In an affair on the 31st a detachment from the Column cut up 60 to 100, including some Sepoys. Young Clifford killed in this affair. The only casualty. The Column is to go in force, *via* Kasun and Taoroo, to Sonah, effectually to put down these insurgents.

All quiet here and to N.W.

W. MUIR.

## CLXXXVI.

AGRA, 3rd *November* 1857.

. . . . . . . .

*P.S.*—Macpherson hears that the Maharajah is breaking up the 5th Contingent. Some agree to lay down their arms; others who refuse to do so will be sent to Morar. We shall see how he will manage his difficult business.

## CLXXXVII.

AGRA, 4th *November* 1857.

MY DEAR SHERER,—

. . . . . . . .

On the other hand, we have evident proofs of the alarm of the Nawab Raees, in a letter forwarded by him to the Government in an exculpatory strain. Of course, no notice will be taken of it. It is in a lady's hand. But we know that there were one or more females of English extraction in his household. The Nawab Raees.

In a letter from Eden, dated Jyepoor, 1st instant, reporting all well there, he says: "I am glad to hear that the Mhow Column is acting at last most successfully to the westward; they attacked Dhar, and cut up a lot of Wilayaties; the report I got says 700. Angherra will be the next; and the force moves up *via* Rutton and Jowreh (?) towards Mundessore." The rebels are said to be in confusion already in this latter place.

A letter has come in of the 26th ultimo from Major Ramsay, Nynee Tal. He writes very cheerfully, and says the Rohilkhund force is a perfect rabble without any discipline whatever. He begins to think of reclaiming the Bhabur with his Goorkhas.

We are all delighted to hear that the Column marched in such strength on the 30th for Lucknow.

W. MUIR.

J. W. SHERER, ESQ.

*P.S.*—A letter just received by Macpherson from Gwalior, dated the 3rd, says that on the 2nd the Contingent were moving towards Jalaon, from which they were still 8 coss off at Gopalpoora. His information has hitherto been accurate as to their movements.

## CLXXXVIII.

AGRA, *5th November* 1857.

MY DEAR HARINGTON,—I was much gratified by the receipt of your long and interesting letter from Cawnpoor.

I look to you to carry out your promise of writing, not only by giving us the news in the lower sense of the word, but also by letting me know (confidentially where necessary) the future plans and schemes of the Government, and any legislative movements in prospect.

. . . . . . . .

Proposal for Commissioner on Revenue Settlements.

In some districts it may be expedient to appoint a separate Commissioner for the work, including the reconstitution of the Settlement record. Ordinarily, where we have a good man at the head of the district, it may be the more advisable course to place the work in his hands, or at least under him. I think Mr. Colvin carried somewhat too far the commitment of Settlement duty to the hands of the district officer. It has answered well in some places, as in Seharunpoor, where an able man, Spankie, had an unlimited staff. But in some other districts, as Jalaon, and some quarters in the Saugor and Nerbudda Territories, the effect was utterly to *swamp* the district officer. Freeling, a capital officer, was so overpowered that he declared he could not have held on upon the same footing for 5000 Rupees a month. The proposed operations will be to some extent analogous with resettlement proceedings.

Question of District Officers performing Settlement duties.

A few days ago I sent to Colonel Baker a paper on the establishment of Police Battalions. I should like you to see it. I am going to send to Beadon a detailed memorandum by the Supd[t]-General of Police Battalions (an appointment I earnestly trust the Supreme Government will confirm) on the subject. Major G. W. Williams is, as you know, admirably fitted by experience and other qualifications for it, and the system, if approved, will be excellently consolidated and set in operation by him. The appointment should be united to that of Supd[t] of Cantt. and Grand Trunk Road Police. At present the Supd[t] is expected to control all Police Establishments from Peshawur to Dinapoor. No one man can efficiently superintend establishments scattered over so vast an extent of country. One Supd[t] can take up the duty for the N.W.P., including Oudh. Saugor should be attached to Nagpoor, excepting Jalaon, Jhansie, and perhaps Chundeyree.

Superintendent-General of Police Battalions.

Major G. W. Williams.

Has the question of a fine upon the country, in compensation, for losses inflicted on property in the late disturbances, been entertained at all in Calcutta? It is favourably spoken of here; the only plan that I can see at all feasible would be by a general assessment all over the country, partly on houses. A discriminatory assessment, according to local guilt, could hardly, I think, be carried out. Of course, all would be excepted, as Gobind Sing and Teekum Sing, who had shown themselves actually in our favour.

**Question of country being fined to compensate losses.**

Has anything been said as to the plan that was being introduced in these Provinces of large central Jails? The opportunity would be a good one of getting rid of our monster Jail here. Would the Railway Engineers like it for a terminus? Longden suggests that a portion might be made over for his Press, which must in future be a Government one, as all seem agreed. The proper place for our Jail, as he suggests, would be opposite the Taj and Fort; it would be under the guns of the latter.

**Large Central Jails.**

Tell Beadon that a Committee of Engineers has been appointed to consider the best mode of improving our Fort with reference to a paper on the subject by Nicholl which I mentioned in a former letter. I don't see well how our Public offices could be removed with advantage, though they might have a defensible entrenchment run round them, and have a Guard from the Police Battalions over them. But portions of the propósed outworks of the Fort would be available as receptacles for the security of the more valuable records and documents.

**Improvement of defences of Agra Fort.**

I see something is doing already below for providing accommodation for the large increase of European troops against next hot weather. It is time the matter were being taken up here.

Major Pole writes from Meerut on 31st ultimo: "Ought we not to be doing something in the way of providing shelter for the additional European troops that may be expected to remain in these parts during the next hot season? At Meerut I could easily carry out what the Commander-in-Chief recommended to Government in Decr. last, viz., to build additional accommodation for the Artillery, and so allow of the European Infantry Barracks being occupied by *two* Regiments. They were originally intended for that number, and it would be much better for the Artillery to be away altogether by themselves. I have lots of bricks at Meerut, but not a stick of wood. The latter will take some time to procure." Here we have few bricks and no wood. But the old and new barracks could be speedily re-thatched.

**Shelter for the additional European troops.**

We have moved out again into a bungalow; this time I

trust permanently. I am going to have my double-storeyed house re-thatched. Mrs. Harington and the Phillipses looking well.

W. MUIR.

H. B. HARINGTON, ESQ.

## CLXXXIX.

AGRA, *5th November* 1857.

MY DEAR SHERER,—There is not much to write about to-day. Cotton's party is still out towards Cosee; but it has been written for to come rapidly back in order to cross over to Allygurh. There is, Cocks says, certain information of a large gathering at Kuchla Ghat. The Infantry and Cavalry are few in numbers, but the Ghazies form a large multitude. They have a few guns. It is probable that the main object of the party is to collect the Budaon Revenue, and that the detachment at the Ghat is intended to guard against surprise, but at the same time they give out that Allygurh is their object. They have hardly any boats, however. A demonstration in that direction will be of great service.

**Cotton's party.**

**Gathering at Kuchla Ghat.**

In a day or two we shall be again looking out earnestly for Lucknow intelligence. We look to you to give us early information as to the course to be probably taken with Furruckabad. So soon as an effective and conclusive blow is struck at Lucknow, we conclude that a rapid movement will be made on the craven traitor there.

A letter from Deolee dated 31st instant. All right there just now. "Rajpootana continues," the writer says, "wonderfully quiet: the secret is, the people and Thakoors have no desire to come again under Mahomedan powers and to send their daughters to the Zenanehs of Delhi."

**Feeling in Rajputana.**

I enclose a letter from Harington, and leave it open for you to read.

W. MUIR.

J. W. SHERER, ESQ..

I have just received a letter from Umballa, dated 2nd October, from Browne of Jalaon; he says: "The road from Agra is so clear and safe that a lady might travel alone. The Googaira affair is still going on; and as the rebels have taken to the thick jungle, there is no prospect, I hear, of the disturbance being put down until they burn them out next month." But excepting the local unsettlement and insecurity (travelling by

**Gogaira rising.**

the river is no longer safe) the affair is, I conclude, not of serious moment.

*P.S.*—A letter just received from Alexander, dated Nynee Tal, 28th ultimo, states that "they are fully aware at Bareilly that the game is up. Mahomed Shufee and Wuleedad are there, but inactive. Bukht Khan has been written for from Furruckabad. Waleedad's nephew with a force was last heard of at Aoulah, *en route* for the Ganges." This is the party that has appeared at the Kuchla Ghat. The Nawab of Rampoor continues to behave well. He is a trump. **Bareilly.** **Loyalty of Nawab of Rampore.**

"Noubut Ram of Bareilly," Alexander says, "has sent me replies from most of the Thakoors, saying they will rise the moment a force enters Rohilkhund. The Powain man, who has the most money and the largest following, is, however, playing a doubtful game,—while he responds verbally to my call, he sends a large sum of money to Khan Buhadoor Khan." **Noubut Ram.** **Powain.** **Khan Buhadoor Khan.**

## CXC.

AGRA, *6th November* 1857.

MY DEAR SHERER,—There is nothing of special importance going on.

The Kuchla Ghat and the tract on this side is still threatened by a large body of Rohilkhund insurgents, who have raised up some of the boats which Mr. Wilson sunk when there. Mr. Churcher is now firmly established as Joint-Magistrate of Etah; so that good information of any approach from that direction will be obtained. I think the people over the river will hardly be bold enough to come anywhere near Allygurh. **Rohilkhund Insurgents.**

Macpherson's account of the Contingent is that by the latest intelligence received at Gwalior up to the 3rd, it was still at Jaloun. Of the 5th Contingent, which you know stayed with Scindia, 150 Sepoys with the two Mehidpoor guns have gone off from Gwalior with the view of joining the rebels at Jaloun. **Gwalior Contingent.**

The report at Gwalior was that Durand's Column, besides cutting up many insurgents at Dhar, had taken three guns. We, it is said, were shelling the Fort into which the rebels had retired. The Rajah of Dhar is reported to be co-operating with us. **Colonel Durand's success at Dhar.** **Dhar Rajah reported loyal.**

Colonel Macpherson from Lahore has telegraphed to Mr. Saunders to have it communicated to Captain Green, commanding 2nd Punjaub Infantry, "that it is proposed to make over all **Captain Green, 2nd Punjab Infantry.**

the recruits with his depôt here to the 4th Regiment and to recruit afresh for him." Will you kindly communicate this message?

Alexander, C.S., Naini Tal. I have a letter from Alexander, dated Nynee Tal, the 2nd instant; the dak direct is now re-established. All is well. The Loyalty of Nawab of Rampore. Nawab of Rampoor behaving to the satisfaction of all. Alexander has entertained a small body of sowars at the foot of the Hills to protect Huldwanee, the elephants, etc. They were Feeling of the country changing. raised about Moradabad. This shows the change in the feeling of the country even over there: for two months ago the thing would have been impossible. The only untoward event reported is that Ramsay had met with an accident, his rifle accidentally going off, and the ball passing through his left hand. Only one bone is broken, and the wound is doing well.

Gwalior, 5th Contingent breaks away from Scindia. Since writing the first part of this letter Macpherson has further news from Gwalior to the 4th instant. The whole 5th Contingent appears to have gone to Jaloun.

It is also reported that of the Mutineers' Corps at Jaloun one Regiment and a Battery have gone on the summons of the Nana Sahib. Nana Sahib to Calpee.

Baird Smith. Baird Smith, who went up to Mussoorie, laid up with all manner of ailments, and a bad ankle from a bit of a shell, writes now in capital spirits, and seems to be all right and up to any Roorkee. kind of work. At Roorkee, he says, "we go on with our work very much as usual. You would see no sign of revolt except the business-looking muzzles of a few big guns that look daggers down each main road," etc.

W. MUIR.

J. W. SHERER, ESQ.

*P.S.*—Dunlop, writing from Meerut on the 5th, says that Hoshiarpoor. news had been received from Hoshiarpoor (though, as he hoped it might turn out to be untrue, it cannot be regarded as unquestionable) "that the remainder of the 9th Irr. Cavalry had mutinied, Outbreak of 9th Irregular Cavalry. and murdered poor Campbell of the 52nd." No further particulars given.

He says there is still an unpleasant feeling abroad that we are giving out that reinforcements are coming while none are actually on the way; and he suggests that it would be an expedient mode of destroying the idea to send up 100 or so of the Sikhs who had seen our new Europeans. When escorts, etc., are being sent up this can be kept in mind.

Revenue paid at Meerut. His revenue is coming in well. The Khurreef collections beginning.

## CXCI.

AGRA, *7th November* 1857.

MY DEAR SHERER,—No special local news. We begin to get anxious for Lucknow news. The last from you and from Captain Bruce is the 31st.

There are still gatherings on the left bank of the Ganges, and rumours of invasions from Roorkee and Etah. But the insurgents have not, I apprehend, the stuff in them for that. Baird Smith writes cheerfully from Mussorie on the 4th, and laughs at the alarmist views of the officer commanding at Seharunpoor. Our nearer neighbours over the river are not, I suspect, really more likely to carry their threats into execution. Indeed, one spy declares that they were busy sinking the boats on their side, in an alarm lest *we* should cross.

**Gatherings in the Doab.**

We have letters from Jyepoor of the 5th; Eden writes in good spirits. He has $1\frac{1}{4}$ lac of tribute money ready to send, which greatly rejoices Reade's heart (by the way, I enclose in this letter an abstract from Reade of his Financial Memorandum for last month). Eden takes advantage of the passing of the Nusserabad officers, expected to reach Jyepoor about the middle of the month, to send the treasure, and also some rebels caught by the Durbar. By the way, Bhurtpoor sent us in seven-and-twenty rebels a day or two ago. At Allygurh some are also being caught, and Eld blew from guns two of the Mutineers belonging to an Irregular Cavalry regiment.

**Arrest of Mutineers by Native States, etc.**

Regarding the Kotah tragedy, Eden writes that the feeling is against the Rajah: "The apathy and culpable indifference he displayed on the occasion are a common topic of conversation amongst the higher classes of the people. The ruffians would seem to have been some four or five hours in completing their bloody work. The Chief was shut up in his Palace within a mile, and neither stirred himself nor sent a single follower to rescue the poor fellows."

**The Kotah Rajah: his apathy.**

If all this be correct—and Eden should know—the Kotah Raj does not deserve to survive.

The passage to which I referred yesterday in the *P.S.* of my letter regarding the impression abroad about our reinforcements has attracted Colonel Fraser's attention, and he wishes it to be prominently noticed again: he wishes that the subject may have attention from the Commander-in-Chief. I had better quote Dunlop's remarks in full on the matter: "Lastly, there is an unpleasant feeling abroad, not only among the Hindoostanees but also among our friends the Sikhs, as to our ability to get any reinforcements. We have so completely stultified ourselves by promising arrivals which never appeared, that it is now getting generally believed that our chances are desperate and our reinforcements a humbug. It would be well worth while to send down a number of Sikhs from this, and get up a hundred or two, if no more can be spared, of the late arrivals, just to quiet the public mind."

Need of reinforcements. Sikhs.

We have letters from Neemuch up to the 2nd November. They are uneasy about the movements of the Mundessore rebels, who are said to be moving in that direction. They cannot hear any tidings of the movements of the Mhow Column; and if it does not come in that direction, and if the rebels, who are very numerous, do attack Neemuch, they may have to retire into their Fort. "They have some guns," says the writer, "and are thousands in number. Our available force barely more than 400," and the greater part of these Natives. Their field-pieces, too, are not fully effective, being worked by volunteers partly, and not very well equipped. The writer, who is an intelligent young officer, adds: "If we could only get a troop of Dragoons to lead the 2nd Cavalry, one hundred more European Infantry, and field-guns *properly* manned (if only half a troop Horse Artillery), I think we could polish off the Mundessore fellows pretty well."

Mundessore Rebels.

Weak position of Neemuch garrison.

Rajpootanah certainly deserves the very earliest consideration. It has stood most wonderfully; but we cannot even now afford the chance of having a check, or allowing our garrison at Neemuch to be besieged. The effect would be very bad throughout Rajpootanah.

Rajputana.

I have not heard anything lately of the Joudpoor Mutineers.

W. MUIR.

J. W. SHERER, ESQ., Cawnpore.

## CXCII.

AGRA, *7th November* 1857.

MY DEAR BEADON,—I sent as an enclosure of a letter I was writing to Colonel Baker the other day, a Memorandum of mine about Police Battalions. In continuation of that I now enclose a copy of a letter from Sir J. Lawrence on the same subject, and a Memorandum by Major Williams, who has been appointed Superintendent Police Battalions pending sanction of the Governor-General.

Police Battalions.

You will see that Sir John does not think a Superintendent required, and would substitute a Military Secretary.

When the whole thing is organised and in satisfactory play, the Military Secretary would probably suffice. But to set up the system and introduce it effectually upon a uniform system in these difficult times, when great care must be taken in raising and recruiting parties for our Corps, it seems to me that the Superintendent will be invaluable. Sir John Lawrence too was not aware that it was proposed to amalgamate the post with that of Superintendent of Cantonment Police and of the Grand Trunk Road. It seems out of the question to expect that any effectual supervision can be exercised over places so far separated as Peshawur and Patna; and in fact I believe much supervision and control was needed to make the system effective. The Superintendent would have the selection of the Cantonment Joint Magistrates from amongst the best of the passed Battalion Officers, and the Preventive portion of the police both in Cantonment and on the Grand Trunk Road would be drawn from the Battalions. I trust, at any rate, till the machine has been put together and set in motion, that the General Superintendentship will be allowed.

. . . . . . . .

We are again on the strain looking out for news from Lucknow. When things are a little easier there we greatly need a portion of the European force, now rapidly gathering at Cawnpoor, for the North-West. Rajpootanah holds on, but the Mundessore insurrection needs to be crushed with a high hand. It would be a sad calamity if those rebels gained any advantage from our Neemuch Garrison, which hardly numbers 400 of all arms, and ⅔rds of these natives.

W. Muir.

C. Beadon, Esq.

## CXCIII.

Agra, *8th November*. Sunday.

My Dear Sherer,—The aspect of affairs maintains still pretty much the same complexion as it has been doing for some days. All quiet on this side the Ganges, but rumours of gatherings beyond it.

The Bareilly troops had a fight with the Budaon Aheers on 5th, and discomfited them. Sapte says the cannonade was distinctly audible from his camp at the Ramghat below Anoopshuhur on the Ganges. Some firing was also heard on the **Affair with Budaon Aheers.**

morning of the 6th. The battle was fought at Tiktu Ghat, between Islamnuggur and Suheswan. The Hindoos fled almost as soon as the fight began, so it is supposed there was not much loss of life. "At Islamnuggar," Sapte writes, "there are said to be 6000 rebels with 5 guns, and they are reported to be about to move to Gunour, 4 coss only on the other side. Another body are said to be at Gambhul."

The Mussalmans, inflated by their triumph over the Hindoos, may be unwise enough to venture over the river. This is not likely; but the state of things on the left bank is certainly a strong argument for no longer delay than is absolutely indispensable being allowed in the pushing up of troops from Cawnpoor.

I gave you yesterday a strong appeal on behalf of Rajpootana tending to the same conclusion.

Yours of the 3rd came in yesterday. We begin again to thirst for Lucknow news.

W. MUIR.

**Gwalior Contingent.**

*P.S.*—The news just received from Gwalior is that the Contingent *have* at last moved forward from Jaloun towards Calpee. You will no doubt have later intelligence.

**Murder of Lieutenant Tomkinson.**

Macpherson hears that a L$^{t}$ Tomkinson of the 53$^{d}$ Reg$^{t}$, who brought treasure from Orai to Gwalior, remained concealed at Amaen till the Contingent marched that way, when a Poorbea there betrayed him for 50 R$^{s}$. He was arrested in his hiding-place a few miles off, and killed. Macpherson fears the news is too certain.

W. M.

## CXCIV.

AGRA, 9*th November* 1857.

MY DEAR SHERER,—Thanks for yours of the 4th received yesterday. The defeat of the insurgents at Khujwa will have an important moral effect over and above the actual loss to the enemy.

On the 7th they had a report all over Mynpoorie that the rebels had been dispersed at Lucknow and were flying in all directions. I do trust it may turn out to be founded on fact.

**Movement against Etah.**

We have a telegraphic message this morning from Allygurh, intimating that 1200 Infantry and 600 Cavalry are said to have marched from Furruckabad with two guns towards Etah, with the intention of dislodging Mr. Churcher and our post there. Their men were reported to have already reached within 20 or

30 miles of Etah, but I question whether they will dare advance farther.

There are the usual vapouring reports from Rohilkhund, but a station occupied on the Trunk Road—as at Etah—by rebel troops would be the likeliest thing to embolden them to cross.

One hundred and fifty Sikh Cavalry have just arrived from Meerut at Allygurh for use in these parts. Commissariat stores from Meerut on 140 carts are at Khoorja to-day, on their way down. Mr. Sapte with the Belochees is there also. **Sikh Cavalry.**

Saunders has just sent us a copy of a message by him to Sir J. Lawrence (but without date), from which it would seem that the Joudhpoor Legion is somewhere south of the Jhujjur Territory, and is supposed to be moving up the western border of Sheikhawattec, "with the intention of going into Hurriana through a portion of Bikaneer." General Lawrence had heard that they were in the neighbourhood of Khetrec, some 30 miles S.E. of Kunound. All are on the alert, and Showers' Column had been ordered to *Rewaree.* This takes it a bit farther to the west, and so much farther from the Doab. **The Joudhpore Legion.** **Showers' Column.**

You will not fail to notice all these things to the Commander-in-Chief through the proper channel, in order that His Excellency may be aware of the need of succour as soon as it can be sent up the Doab.

Colonel Fraser is to-day sending an interesting paper by Colonel Troup to the Commander-in-Chief regarding the force necessary to reoccupy Rohilkhund. He says 6 Regiments and 2 Batteries will be required with Cavalry. He wants an advance on Bareilly, both by Moradabad and Shahjahanpoor, to prevent escape. The main point from which the attack should be made, Sir J. Lawrence rightly thinks to be Furruckabad. If a second Column can simultaneously move on Bareilly from the Meerut side, so much the better. **Colonel Troup's proposals for reoccupation of Rohilkhund.**

Furruckabad is a great thorn in our sides. I hope it will be attacked at the earliest possible moment. We shall then have the Mail Cart all the way, and a letter may reach Calcutta from Lahore in 8 or 9 days, and a message in 2 or 3. The electric wire would soon follow. **Furruckabad.**

Spankie, writing from Seharunpoor on the 6th, says that he is beginning his Khurreef collections—the May and June instalments are nearly all in. His settlement field-measurements are going on, and will be all concluded by the end of the year! But it will be advisable to postpone the final settlement and assessment till the disturbances entirely blow over, and especially till **Revenue collections in Seharanpore, and Settlement operations.**

those are known who have acted a traitorous part among the landholders.

Bijnore insurgents.

"The Bijnour people," he says, "are afraid of our crossing, and we are afraid of their crossing, playing at Bo-peep along the Ghats. They have a rabble, and we have a few hundred good troops, but still I would rather they would not come, as it only distracts the district to have raids made upon it, or rebels passing through."

Gwalior Contingent attacks Rampoora.

The Contingent have taken a new turn, as I suppose you must have heard. They have attacked Rampoora, the Fort of a considerable Jaloun Talookdar, some 10 or 12 miles south of the junction of the Sind with the Jumna. They demanded a month's pay, and on the Chief's refusing opened fire on his Fort, which he was replying to with 14 guns. This was on the 4th. Unless it be a mere erratic excursion beating up for money, this looks as if they were likely to cross by the Sheregurh Ghat. I think it likelier, however, that they will keep to Bundelkhund for the present.

I have a letter from Sapte of the 7th. News as before. "The rebels (in Rohilkhund) constantly give out that they are coming across the river, but I have secured all the boats to Ramghat." From Ramghat downwards, Cocks is on the look-out.

W. MUIR.

J. W. SHERER, ESQ., Cawnpoor.

## CXCV.

AGRA, *10th November* 1857.

Fort of Rampoora taken by Gwalior Contingent.

MY DEAR SHERER,—Intelligence has come in from Gwalior of date the 9th inst., to the effect that the Contingent had taken the Fort of Rampoora and had carried off the petty chieftain of the place to Jaloun. This looks as if Jaloun were considered and treated by them as their Headquarters, and I trust they will retain it as such till we are more at liberty to go after them.

Prinsep has a letter from Becher, who has returned to Delhi, and speaks of a Column starting about the middle of the month *for Cawnpore* after the return of Showers' Brigade. The latter, however, as you will know from a previous letter, is likely to be delayed a little by its westward movement on Rewarree. We have no further mention than this yet of any Column intended for Cawnpoor. It may probably be a convoy for the horses,

Cavalry, and Artillery, the Governor-General has ordered, if possible, to be sent down.

All well at Allygurh. Mr. Churcher at Etah does not believe that the Furruckabad troops will come near him. But the latest intelligence certainly is that they have occupied Allygunge with above 1000 foot, 500 Horse, and two Guns. Allygunge is 20 or 30 miles from Kassgunge and Etah. The force is throwing out its Thannahs here and there in reoccupation of the country. It is likely enough that this is a preliminary to attempting a collection of the Khurreef instalments of Revenue. But its effect is of course bad on Allygurh. It fans the embers of fanaticism still smouldering in the district; and strikes terror into the loyal subjects who have so often already experienced the horrors of a revolution. Until this nest of insurgents—Furruckabad—be put down, there will be no permanent security for the middle Doab.

Furruckabad troops occupy Allygunge.

The following from Allygurh is additional evidence of the slowness of native belief as to our reinforcements. "It is a great pity that carriage is so scarce, as natives never will believe there are any more troops in the country until they see them, and their being at Cawnpoor is without its effect on this part of the country."

Hume is keeping up the administration in Etawah through influential men in a manner which, considering the difficulties and successive bands of marauders that district has had to contend against, is quite surprising. A new Cotwalie is going on being built, crime punished, a Customs tax levied, and Abkari Settlement made, etc. etc. There are of course abundance of bad characters, Mewattees, etc., who raise their heads whenever they think there is nobody to chastise them; and they have gained in insolence since our troops, they say, passed by the Nawab of Furruckabad without chastising him. But with all this the comparative quiet and subordination which has prevailed is very remarkable, and decisively indicates that the country is at the least not against us. You heard, I conclude, of Juswunt Rao having defeated Rampershaud and a party of our ill-wishers near the Shere Ghat, killing 17 and wounding a considerable number.

Hume's successful administration of Etawah.

Country not against us. Juswant Rao defeats Rampershad.

I enclose a note for the Commander-in-Chief from Colonel Fraser. It is a reiteration of our call for fresh European troops as soon as you can spare them.

Chief Commissioner calls for European troops.

Colonel Fraser wishes to know who has charge of Sir Hugh Wheeler's Estate—this to enable a Mr. John here, to return some

Property of the Misses Wheeler.

jewellery he has, that belonged to the Miss Wheelers. Better inquire of friends in Calcutta.

Gwalior Contingent. Just as I am closing my letter, a despatch is received from Gwalior of yesterday's date, intimating that the Contingent has actually moved from Jalonn towards Calpee.

W. MUIR.

J. W. SHERER, ESQ., Cawnpoor.

## CXCVI.

AGRA, 11*th November* 1857.

Arrest of the Rajah of Bullubgurh. Bullubgurh annexed to Goorgaon by Mr. Ford. MY DEAR SHERER,—Showers in a letter of the 6th mentions that he had arrested the Rajah of Bullubgurh that morning, and taken possession of his Fort, in which he was leaving a force. He states that Mr. Ford had annexed the Pergunnah to Goorgaon.

. . . . . . . . . . .

Naini Tal. A letter from Nynee Tal, dated 7th November, reports all well there. The Nawab giving satisfaction to all at that station. Alexander corresponds daily with him. But "he is as weak to act *openly* for us as ever, and tied to *Maslahat* or expediency in all his ways." But we must not judge either him or Scindia by too rigid a standard of morality. They have both had difficult parts to play.

Bhurtpore. Nixon writes to say that he has resumed the direct management of affairs at Bhurtpoor to the exclusion of the Minister who had been making himself strong with his Goojur brethren inside the Fort. All was quiet; but he was uneasy at reinforcements not coming up, and deprecates our little detachment here moving far from Agra. He is anxious for Colonel Fraser "to press upon the Supreme Government the necessity of troops being sent up here. Agra full of troops would be a Tower of Strength to the officers isolated in Rajpootanah; but denuded of them it is of but little use, so we have *pro tem.* to rely on ourselves."

Rajputana.

Colonel Durand. Colonel Durand, writing from Mhow on the 18th October, tells me of his intention then of attacking Dhar. He says, "We have hot water all round." In expressing his hope that he would be able soon to strike down the Mundessore insurrection, he adds: "However, there is no foreseeing what may turn up in these parts from day to day. And our successes in the North, turning many rebels to the South, promise to give Central India a critical time of it before reinforcements from Bombay and Madras can come up to strengthen us."

Central India.

The report of our postmaster at Mynpoorie on the 9th is,

that Rao Bhowany Sing had gone to Pertabner to see his family said to be sick; but that his absence was attributed by the people to the fear of the Nawab Raees' force, which it was said had crossed the Kalee Nuddee. Nawab of Furruckabad.

The same writer adds the probable reason of the movement of the Furruckabad troops westward, viz. that finding himself unequal to restrain the mutinous soldiery about him, and without money to bribe them to remain quiet, he encouraged them to spread themselves abroad for the purpose of plunder and the collection of outstanding revenue. But, anyhow, the effect is the same in keeping our adjacent stations in trepidation. It will be a cause of deep regret if they again ravage Mynpoorie, Etah, and Kassgunge. Furruckabad.

A message received to-day from Allygurh reports that the Meerut stores (I reported before that they were coming down in 140 hackeries) had arrived safely, and were to start for Agra this afternoon with above half a lac of surplus treasure for us. The heavy guns we sent out for the Allygurh Fort had reached safely. We sent them from this under the sole charge of native troops, without even an English officer! so you see how the tide of feeling is turning here. Allygurh. Change of feeling in the country.

The message states that a letter had been this morning received at Allygurh, mentioning that Colonel Gerrard had gone with a force to attack the Jodhpoor Legion, which had ventured into the Jhujjur Territory. Colonel Gerrard. Joudhpore Legion.

Our little party at the Kuchla Ghat had caught a Duffadar of a Bareilly Irregular Cavalry Regiment, who, not knowing of their presence, had crossed over the Ganges the night before. He was captured with his horse and arms. The message states the Futtehgurh people to be still advancing on Etah. Bareilly.

We have letters from Neemuch of the 6th instant, written in better spirits than the last. They had heard the report of Dhar being taken by the Mhow column, and believed that it had come in their direction already 4 or 5 marches. The native report was that it had marched from Dhar on the 2nd. The Neemuch troops were accordingly hoping that they might soon be able to co-operate with it against the Mundessore insurgents. We may look for some early good tidings from that direction.

W. MUIR.

J. W. SHERER, ESQ., Cawnpoor.

*P.S.*—A Gwalior letter, dated yesterday, reports that 2 Regts. and 2 Batteries had gone forward to Calpee, and the remainder Gwalior Contingent.

were still at Jaloun depositing their spare ammunition in the Fort.

Banda Mutineers.

They had heard of the Banda Mutineers joining the Contingent at Calpee, and having broken the bridge of boats on the report "that British force of 4000 men with 2 batteries and an elephant battery were posted on the other side the river 7 coss from Calpee!"

## CXCVII.

AGRA, *12th November* 1857.

MY DEAR SHERER,—J. Power's of the 5th to Mrs. Muir came in yesterday.

We cannot understand the delay in the advance on Lucknow. Every day's postponement is not only a tempting of new outbreaks in the upper Doab and Rajpootanah, but a throwing backward of the general campaign farther and farther into the hot weather. We have enough before us this cold weather, what with Rohilkhund and Bundelkhund. People here judge hardly of the delay. We are, however, always in danger of judging hastily on imperfect data. So the more you can tell us in explanation of the delay in advancing, the better.

A. Cocks, C.S.

Cocks moves out to-day in the direction of Etah, to check the advance of the Futtehgurh rebels in that direction.

The Agra Column.

Our column is now here. I hope Colonel Fraser will send it out again soon. It wonderfully inspires our friends with confidence and our enemies with awe, to know that we can move about in force in this manner. It is most needed in the direction of Mynpoorie, to repress the Furruckabad invaders in that direction and towards Etah.

Rajah Tej Singh.

From the Postmaster at Mynpoorie it appears that Rao Bhowany Sing returned early that morning with the report that the Rajah Tej Sing intended to attack Mynpoorie that day, on which the Deputy Magistrate and Cotwal with their people fell back on Shekoabad. It may probably be a groundless alarm, but it keeps all that tract in a ferment.

Showers' Column returns to Delhi.

Since writing the above I have received a letter from Saunders dated the 10th instant. He says that Showers' column returned to Delhi on the 8th instant. It has been broken up, as both men and cattle were greatly fatigued after the laborious campaign they have gone through.

New Column organised.

A new column was organised, and the intention was to have despatched it at once down the country with the carriage and supplies which have been collected at Delhi and Meerut, for the reinforcement coming up country.

Joudhpore Legion with Rao Toola Ram invades Jhujjur Territory.

Intelligence, however, was meanwhile received that the Jodhpoor Legion, having formed a junction with the force of Rao Toola Ram (of Rewaree), the Jhujjur Irregular Cavalry and our own mutineer Ranghur horse, had actually invaded the Jhujjur Territory. They were encamped at Nurnoul on the 8th and 9th, and were threatening the Fort of Kunound. In that Fort we had one of the newly raised Sikh Corps, and it is believed to be strong enough to hold out in security till succour arrived from Delhi.

Sikh Corps in Fort of Kunound.

Joudhpore Legion. The Mewattis: their strength.

The Jodhpoor Legion are said to contemplate a junction with the Mewattees, whom Showers has been engaged in chastising. He burnt 50 of their villages, and otherwise severely punished them. But you will find by a reference to the Goorgaon Statistical Report, what a large and influential body they are (see page 15); they number 110,000 in this district, and own 409 villages with an area of 300,000 acres.

It is to be hoped that the Jodhpoor Army, which has got from 9 to 12 guns, may be intercepted before it gets down into that region.

Column sta under Colonel Gerrard for Goorgaon.

The moveable column having this object, started from Delhi on the night of the 9th under Colonel Gerrard for Goorgaon. It would then move on Rewaree, and there follow the rebels whatever direction they may have taken. This duty performed, they will be at liberty for service in the Doab.

Wullee Dad.

Saunders had just received an express from Sapte from the banks of the Ganges in the Boolundshuhur district, "that Wullee Dad had made his appearance at Ram Ghat with a large force of rebels and 8 guns."

General Penny has accordingly ordered as large an available force as can be spared, to proceed from Meerut in support of Sapte's party. Saunders hopes that a respectable body of troops may be got up at Meerut, as Hodson's Horse, a wing of Coke's corps, Tombs' troop, and Scott's battery, have all been sent over there lately to refit.

General Penny, writing himself, says, "My earnest wish is to send this column" (the one that has gone towards Rewaree) "to Cawnpore to escort a large convoy for the European troops coming up." He says that the Headquarters people are collecting at Delhi in the hope of proceeding down with this column. He adds that Sir John Lawrence is collecting some Cavalry, which will also be pushed on.

I am writing to Saunders to suggest that measures should be concerted for sending down their carriage, etc., and ours, with one and the same convoy. Nothing has ever been replied to Col. Fraser's proposal that you should send out as far as Mynpoorie; and that we would escort the carriage so far?

W. MUIR.

J. W. SHERER, ESQ.

*P.S.*—The news about Wullee Dad in the last sheet has made Col. Fraser determined on stopping the Allygurh expedition to Etah. But our Column will move out towards Allygurh, and having joined Cocks' party, may then make a demonstration on the Etah Road.

## CXCIX.

TO HIS EXCELLENCY SIR C. CAMPBELL, G.C.B., COMMANDER-IN-CHIEF.

AGRA, 12 *November* 1857.

Colonel Fraser's proposals for military operations.

YOUR EXCELLENCY,—In ignorance of the course you mean to adopt after your success at Lucknow, which may be looked upon as certain, I venture, though well aware that I may be deemed presumptuous in doing so, to bring the following scheme to your Excellency's notice, premising from all we know here that the want of carriage is likely to cramp you to such a degree that its supply is at present a consideration paramount to all others.[1]

. . . . . . . . . . . . . . . . . . . . . . . . . . . . . . . . . . . . . . . . . . . . . . . . . . . . . . . . .

H. FRASER, Col., Chief Commr., N.W.P.

[1] NOTE.—*The rest of the letter contains Colonel Fraser's proposals as to what Sir C. Campbell's operations in the Doab might be.*

## CC.

AGRA, 13*th November* 1857.

MY DEAR SHERER,—We have nothing from you later than J. Power's of the 5th. Nothing further from the North-West.

Mynpoorie affairs.

Things at Mynpoorie are, however, again falling into confusion. The Rajah of Mynpoorie has been in the Jaloun District with the Contingent, and has succeeded in getting some body of followers from amongst them. He has recrossed the Jumna, and a portion of the Contingent was said to be following him—some say 5 Companies, some one "pultun," some two. The Rajah has picked up guns somewhere; but as none are mentioned to be with the Contingent auxiliaries, it is probable that none of the *regular* Contingent regiments are coming with the Rajah. He has probably succeeded in making some of the loose hangers-on about the Contingent espouse his cause; or, not improbably, they may be the new levies which the Contingent, if you remember, formed into a new 5th, and a new 6th regiment, when they stayed behind them at Gwalior.

**Movements of Rajah Tej Singh of Mynpoorie.**

Whatever the real succours coming with Rajah Tej Singh, the effect of his reappearance on the left bank of the Jumna, and with expected reinforcements, has completely unsettled both Etawah and Mynpoorie.

In respect to Mynpoorie, it seems that the Rajah has been writing to all his brother Chowhans, and, being still their *Rajah*, they have been unable to resist the appeal. They have forsaken the Rao Bhowany Sing, our representative at Mynpoorie, and some of them even assumed a threatening attitude towards our people there. This, coupled with the report that the Rajah would shortly attack the town, so alarmed our people that the Tehseeldar and Cotwal, with the Rao himself, evacuated the place, and have fallen back towards Agra.

**Chowhans of Mynpoorie.**

The Rajah, further, is supposed to be in league with the Nawab of Furruckabad; and as the troops of the latter are extending their ravages in this direction, having occupied Puttialee, and being said to have crossed the Kalee Nuddee, in the direction of Mynpoorie, it is highly probable that the Rajah will shortly reoccupy his Fort, and co-operate with the Furruckabad rebels.

**Troops of the Nawab of Furruckabad.**

**Rajah of Mynpoorie.**

Thus you see our politics are becoming complicated; and the good effect caused by the passage of Grant's Column, and our occupation of Mynpoorie, is likely to be entirely lost.

Unless the Rajah of Mynpoorie should threaten us at all from the side of Etawah, which is in the last degree improbable, our Column, which marches for Allygurh to-morrow morning, will proceed round by Secundra Rao as far as Etah. This will check the Furruckabad troops from any further advance. It will also shake the Rajah of Mynpoorie if he has ventured to reoccupy the town. I do not think Colonel Fraser will allow the Column to go beyond Etah; otherwise, if there were no great force with the Rajah, our Column might have marched round *via* Mynpoorie.

This is a long story about our own affairs. But it shows how much we stand in need of reinforcements; for it is vain to expect the country to continue quiet while threatened by the Furruckabad troops on the one hand, and the rebel Rajah on the other.

It may be advisable for you to give the Commander-in-Chief a copy of this, that he may be fully aware of the state of things here; and make such arrangements as the progress of events in Oudh may admit of, for the destruction of the Nawab of Furruckabad and the reoccupation of Mynpoorie.

W. MUIR.

J. W. SHERER, ESQ., Cawnpore.

## CCI.

AGRA, 14*th November* 1857.

MY DEAR SHERER,—Yours of the 8th arrived last night.

. . . . . . . . . . .

Communication with Cawnpore difficult.

The Cossids seem to have encountered great difficulties on the road, and passed large bodies both of the Furruckabad and Nana's troops. But this is to be expected, and, indeed, in the present state of Mynpoorie and Etawah, owing to the Rajah of Mynpoorie's return, I anticipate great risk to our messengers. It will be well if our communications with you are not cut off.

The Rajah of Mynpoorie.

The Rajah of Mynpoorie has reoccupied his Fort there with a small Force. He has some guns. Our officials have retired to Shekoabad. Our well-wishers will suffer for their ready subordination to us; and anarchy will prevail till the Rajah is again put to flight.

From your letter of the 8th there appears no early prospect of any reinforcements coming this way. But when Lucknow falls we hope that no time will be lost in pushing them up.

Neemuch threatened.

Neemuch is again in peril. We have news up till the 8th. "The Mundessore rebels have been advancing upon us in force for the last two or three days, and a report has just come in that they are at Jumooneya, a village about 5 miles off." A reconnoitring party of the Bombay Cavalry had gone out to see. They have heavy guns with them, which have delayed their march. If they come on, as was expected, the intention seems to have been to remain inside the Fort, as with their very small force there was a risk of being cut off.

Their hope lay in the Mhow Column. But they were very much in the dark as to its position, the only direct information being through the Bombay newspapers. "However, it is rumoured that it is only two days' march or so on the other side of Mundessore."

"If we be not soon reinforced," says the writer, "by *Europeans*, we may form another example of the cases of Cawnpore and Lucknow."

He adds: "I believe the condition of Nusseerabad itself is not very cheerful." **Condition of Nusseerabad**

Nixon, writing from Bhurtpoor on the 13th, says that "information has reached him that Neemuch has been besieged by the Mundessore people." **and Neemuch.**

All this must, of course, affect the temper and spirit of Rajpootanah generally, if a commanding force does not at an early period appear either from the Bombay side or this. Our news regarding the Contingent is that a portion of it is still encamped near Calpee. A Detachment from Jalaon had been deputed to Bhandere to occupy it in the name of the Nana. A messenger, who has just come in, says that on the 10th the remainder of the Contingent moved on to Calpec, and that it still talks of attacking Cawnpore. **Rajputana.** **Gwalior Contingent.** **The Nana.**

W. MUIR.

J. W. SHERER, ESQ., Cawnpore.

## CCII.

AGRA, *November 15th*. Sunday.

MY DEAR SHERER,—There is not much that needs to be communicated to-day.

Sir J. Lawrence, writing on the 11th from Gujranwala, 40 miles from Lahore, tells me that the disturbance in Googaira is coming to an end.

Sapte is still detained with his Force at Ramghat, below Anoopshuhur, watching the movements of Wullee Dad, who is ravaging the country opposite with a large force. His threats of an incursion have the effect of unsettling the district and keeping Sapte away from portions of Boolundshuhur greatly requiring his attention. He has got in 3 lakhs of the rubbee balances. **Movements of Wullee Dad.** **Revenue being collected.**

Etah is still menaced by the Furruckabad rebels. But we hope the troops marching that way from Allygurh and this will arrive in time to prevent Mr. Churcher being dislodged. **Etah menaced.**

I am not without hopes that if the rebels cross the Kalee Nuddee, then they may be cut off and cut to pieces by our people.

The last from you is dated 8th, received on the 13th.

W. MUIR.

J. W. SHERER, ESQ.

## CCIII.

AGRA, 16*th November* 1857. Monday.

MY DEAR SHERER,—Yours of the 11th just received, with enclosure from Brigadier Grant up to 10th inst. We are greatly encouraged by the account he gives of his force, and at the prospect held out of the early entire discomfiture of the enemy at Lucknow.

Brigadier Hope Grant.

I do trust it may be possible at an early date to occupy Mynpoorie in force. That done, the Doab would be clear, and carriage could move down without risk, and almost without guards.

We have been for some time paying ruinous sums on account of carriage detained here to be sent on with the first convoy. There is also a good deal at Delhi. Captain Simson writes: "I have got heaps of carriage and Establishments for five Regiments, and expect to make up a sixth before the Column is ready to leave this. I have got 142 Doolies with bearers, about 150 tents, and all other appliances for the Europeans. About 500 Carts are collected, besides those you got with the stores."

Carriage collected at Delhi.

Colonel Gerrard's Column marched on the 12th from Delhi. "It will return," says Captain Simson, writing on the 14th inst., "in about four days if they catch the enemy" (at Kunound or Rewari); "if not, it will be longer. After its arrival it will be joined by the Headquarters Camp, and will proceed all together:—lots of Cavalry and Guns, so there will be no fear for our long train of carriage. I believe the Column will march to Allygurh, and be joined by my Carts, etc., at Khoorja; and yours must catch it up somewhere near Mynpoorie, and then all will go to Cawnpoor."

Colonel Gerrard's Column.

We must manage to arrange this so that full advantage may be taken of the opportunity; but you will see that if we were only able to hold Mynpoorie, all transactions in the way of furnishing carriage, establishments, supplies, etc., would be vastly facilitated. But Mynpoorie cannot be occupied until the Comdr.-in-Chief is able to spare some infantry for us.

Mynpoorie.

The prize sales are going on at Delhi at prices vastly satisfactory to the army. "Some few jewels, the crown jewels as they are called, are to be sent to Calcutta, but they are nothing very grand."

Prize sales at Delhi.

Nothing further as to Neemuch.

I learn from a letter Lord Elphinstone desired his Private Secretary to write to me, that the remainder of H.M. 95th arrived on the 31st ultimo, and now forms part of the Bombay garrison. Not having been originally intended for India, it is weak, and numbers only 750 men.

Bombay is to have three regiments Cavalry, 4 of infantry with detachments, and a troop Horse Artillery. One Cavalry and one Infantry Regiment are expected "very shortly."

The Mhow Force was to be strengthened by the Head-quarters 14th Dragoons, a Native Infantry Regiment, and 250 3rd Europeans. These were expected to reach Mhow about the 12th or 14th. It will be a seasonable though small relief. **Garrison of Mhow.**

Henry Stewart Reid has been to Delhi. He says, "I saw the ex-King yesterday. He is looking very ill, and certainly not residing in that state that the newspaper writers would make out." **The ex-King.**

W. MUIR.

J. W. SHERER, ESQ., Cawnpore.

. . . . . . . . .

*P.S.*—Capt. Bruce has been writing to Zalim Singh that troops will "soon" be sent in his direction. Z. Singh is our Nazim of Etawah. "Soon" is, I suppose, very indefinite. We shall, of course, have early intimation from you of any move in that direction, as Hume must be present with any troops passing through Etawah. The 500 camels we were sending *via* Etawah are in great peril. What with the Contingent, Furruckabad rebels, and the rebel Rajah of Mynpoorie, the whole country is in trouble between Etawah and Sheolie, and from Calpee to Etah. If possible, we are trying to get the camels returned here. **Zalim Singh.** **Disturbed state of the country.**

## CCIV.

AGRA, 17 *November* 1857. Tuesday.

MY DEAR SHERER,—Yesterday's post brought us intelligence of Neemuch being actually besieged by the Mundessore insurgents. **Neemuch besieged.**

General Lawrence writes from Ajmere on the 11th inst., enclosing the copy of a letter he had received from Capt. Lloyd, dated Neemuch, the evening of the 9th inst.

Lloyd says they had been besieged all day. The enemy had only one large gun—supposed to be a 9-pounder—the rest small ones; but others were said to be coming up. But their practice was bad, and there had been hardly any casualties. The Cavalry was outside, hanging on the enemy; but there is not much of it. They were well off for musket ammunition, but wanted artillery ammunition, having only 120 round shots for the 9-pounders. **Lloyd.**

The rebels burned the few remaining bungalows. Neither at Neemuch nor Ajmere was there any certain information as to the approach of the Mhow Column; but it was believed to be approaching. Lloyd writes in good spirits, and Lawrence expresses his belief that "the enemy will not be able to make any impression on the fortified square, or materially injure the troops."

A small detachment, under Baumgarten of the 83rd, was on its way from Nusseerabad to Neemuch escorting ammunition. It had been ordered to fall into the strong fortress of Chittore.

**Naini Tal.** I have a letter from Alexander from Nynee Tal, dated the 13th inst. He says all is well there. He had been down to the foot of the hills to see his new levies. There were 160 horse —pronounced "very fair"—and more coming. He says "there is a good deal of intrigue going on between the bad men of Moradabad, Sumbhul, and Muroha, with those in Bareilly; and they wish to incite Khan Buhadoor Khan to go against Rampoor and Moradabad, promising success through their aid and combination. But I do trust Lucknow will fall, and the game be over before Khan Buhadoor Khan can act on the offensive."

**Khan Buhadoor Khan.**

Ramsay is doing well.

**Baird Smith.** Baird Smith writes from Mussoorie on the 13th instant. He returns immediately to Roorkee, greatly reinvigorated by his stay on the Hills, and goes out into camp as soon as he can. Dunlop and Sapte had proposed to close the Canal in order to increase the water in the Ganges and diminish the facilities for the enemy crossing. The Government were unwilling to take any step of the kind, as the inducements offered to irrigate must have the best effect upon the people. Baird Smith tells me that "the people not only continue to take water, as before, where they can get it, but to extend their consumption of it; and in the Northern Division there have been applications received for 30 additional Pymanas since the current Rubbee commenced. It is the same in the Jumna Canals, and there the cry for water is greater than I am able to meet in consequence of the want of officers in the Department—a want I don't see my way to rectify just yet. The blanks in my ranks are sickening to think of, and I half shrink from looking the extent of the evil fairly in the face, though this must be done as soon as possible."

**Canal administration.**

**Bhurtpore.** Nixon reports all to be going on quietly at Bhurtpoor. He is in a more secure position now that he has taken the administration into his own hands.

He is helping with levies of Jat horse. **Jat Horse.**

Cocks finds that with the menacing aspect of affairs in the direction of Furruckabad and Mynpoorie, the station of Etah cannot be maintained; so he has withdrawn Mr. Churcher. He is making a demonstration up by the Kuchla Ghat, which will do good, though Colonel Fraser thinks it is going too far away. **Churcher, C.S., withdrawn from Etah.**

W. MUIR.

J. W. SHERER, ESQ., Cawnpoor.

We have heard nothing later of Colonel Gerrard's Brigade. The Postmaster at Muttra says that his runners have brought intelligence of its being at Hodul; but it is not likely to have come down so far, excepting it be in pursuit of the Joudpoor Legion.

The following force is believed to be at Meerut:— **Force at Meerut detailed.**

Hodson's Horse.
Coke's Rifles.
Stafford's—a wing.
Carabineers, excepting one squadron.
3 troops Horse Artillery.
300 Rifles.

Besides large levies of drilled Police, horse and foot.

## CCVI.

AGRA, 18 *November* 1857. Wednesday.

MY DEAR SHERER,—I have heard from Saunders, dated 16th inst. His last from Colonel Gerrard's Camp was a letter from Mr. Ford, dated the 13th. The Column was then at Rewaree. On the 14th they were to march half-way to Kunound. The enemy was still at Narnoul, but it was feared that they were meditating a retreat, which will give trouble to our Column. They are said to have but a small body of Infantry; their Cavalry is very numerous; and they are, of course, the most difficult to come up with. But if our Column can only manage to take their guns it will be so far satisfactory. **Gerrard's Column.**

At Kanound our Column will have been joined by Captain Stafford with the 23rd Punjab Infantry, some Puttiala Infantry, 4 Seikh guns, and the Mooltanee Horse, 300 strong, under Captain Lind. **Captain Stafford.** **Captain Lind.**

Captain Pearse, with 200 horse, was out reconnoitring the enemy. **Captain Pearse.**

Captain Macdonald. Oudeypore District. Neemuch.

We have nothing more from Ajmere about Neemuch. But Captain Macdonald, who is at Deolee, has sent an extract of a Native letter from an official in the Oudeypoor district, giving the purport of a communication from the Prime Minister now with the Rana's force near Neemuch. It consisted of 1000 horse, and ought to give some assistance. The letter states the rebels at 4000 or 5000; and says that they had erected two batteries—one at General Lawrence's house, the other at a village called Yagana. The Garrison was said to have got the enemy within grape distance, and to have killed two hundred of them from their entrenchments.

The Rebels were said to threaten an assault; but Captain Macdonald, who was recently there, thinks that "there need be no fear for the safety of the Garrison; the *Loochas* of Mundessore have not the means of breaching the walls, nor sufficient dash to escalade." He adds that in June a good supply of grain and firewood was laid in, and that water is abundant within the entrenchment.

Kotah.

Everything, he says, is quiet at Kotah. The Rajah pretends that his troops have been brought round by an increase of 8 annas per man. Macdonald suspects that he secretly connived at the tragedy; at all events, entirely neglects any endeavour to protect our people.

Etah.

Coming nearer home, Mr. Churcher has been relieved at Etah, where his life was in danger. No further attempt will be made to hold that station. He gives a bad account of the Country in that direction: "Unless a force is sent very soon from Cawnpoor to Futtehgurh, this part of the Country will be overrun by Futtehgurh troops, with whom are collecting thousands far and near. Our arrival will delay their plunder for a few days, but for very few." There are, he says, gatherings all around.

Futtehgurh troops.

Rajah of Mynpoorie.

The Rajah of Mynpoorie is said to have gone to Furruckabad to seek for reinforcements from the Nawab.

Condition of the country.

The *Country* generally, Colonel Riddell (who had reached Secundra Rao with his Column) says, "is looking well, and cultivators apparently going on as if nothing had happened—the only perceptible difference being the absence of all traffic on the Grand Trunk Road," and that will continue, of course, till we occupy Mynpoorie.

W. Muir.

J. W. Sherer, Esq., Cawnpoor.

## CCVII.

AGRA, *November 18th*, 1857. Wednesday.

MY DEAR BEADON,—On the 20th October I had the pleasure of sending you the copy of a letter I wrote to Mr. Saunders about the reoccupation of Delhi; and I promised to let you know of his reply. I have only now received it, and lose no time in sending you a copy. Saunders places the case in a very fair light. I am delighted to see the broad and sound views Sir John Lawrence has proposed in his despatch of the 20th ultimo. The policy of the Military Authorities has, it is too evident, occasioned a vast amount of misery and distress indiscriminately among the innocent; even among those who suffered bitterly from the Mutineer reign at Delhi. But that cannot be helped now, and I trust every day will help forward a juster and more generous policy. But I find from applications made *here* for certificates, etc., of being well affected, by persons who have been steady servants of Government throughout our troubles at Agra, and whose families are still in extreme misery, crowded in hovels in the villages about Delhi, without change of clothes, shelter, or any of the conveniences of life, that the practical working of the rule throwing the *onus probandi* on the person desiring to return, presses very hardly. No doubt the authorities have had great difficulties to contend with, and much allowance is to be made for the circumstances detailed by Mr. Saunders.

**Reoccupation of Delhi.**

**Distress at Delhi.**

We are in hourly expectation of some decisive news from Lucknow, where our forces ought to command early and complete success. Locally our position is not so good as it was. Mynpoorie and Etah have been abandoned, and the boundary of anarchy is expanding. The Upper Doab keeps quiet. Money comes in from *all* the tracts that we have occupied, freely—including Muthra. The submissiveness and comparative security of the reoccupied districts is wonderful, considering the smallness of our forces, and the manner in which they are threatened on many sides.

**Mynpoorie and Etah abandoned.**

**Security of the reoccupied districts.**

I trust Neemuch will soon be relieved. The effect of the siege will be unfavourable in Rajpootana.

The sooner you can have Mynpoorie reoccupied, the more readily and freely will you get carriage for your reinforcements. We have plenty both here and at Delhi, but it cannot be sent down without a large force. I hope that a signal success at Lucknow will soon enable the Commander-in-Chief to send up some of the new troops in this direction.

W. MUIR.

C. BEADON, ESQ., Calcutta.

## CCVIII.

AGRA, *19th November* 1857.

MY DEAR SHERER,—Nothing from you later than the 11th. The regular Cawnpore dak of the 12th to 14th came in to-day. You might with advantage have duplicates of your letters sent by the dak. It is more liable to stoppage than the Cossids, but now and then comes in quickly.

Nothing further from Neemuch.

Gerrard's Column defeats Joudhpore and other troops—

Intelligence, I am glad to say, has come in of a most complete victory gained by Gerrard's Column over the Joudpoor and other rebel troops near Kunound on the 15th. The letters (Saunders has not written) give the date as the 16th, but as Sunday is mentioned it must have been the 15th.

At Kunound.

I mentioned before that the Column had reached Rewaree on the 15th, and heard of the enemy being then still at Narnoul. On the 14th they marched half-way to Kunound, and I suppose on the 15th to Kunound itself. (One letter says the battle was at Narnoul, but I conclude the others are right in stating Kunound.)

The rebels seem also most simultaneously to have marched on Kunound.

Our Column had hardly reached its encamping-ground at 11 a.m. on Sunday morning, when the rebels came boldly out to meet us. The action began a little before 12 o'clock; the firing on both sides was heavy and sharp. The cavalry made one splendid charge. The enemy had 5000 to our 1300, but they had only 5 or 6 guns, and we had a troop of H.A. and 2 18-pounders. The rebels' horse fought bravely, and as the enemy was entrenched in a Serai the fight was a hardly contested one, and was maintained for several hours. At last we completely dislodged him, took all his guns, and put the whole body to flight. The rout, however, did not commence till sunset, so that I fear darkness would speedily cover the enemy's retreat. They fled southwards.

The Carabineers (the Crimean squadron) and Guide horse made a noble charge. All the troops are said to have behaved well—the Fusiliers splendidly.

Casualties at Kunound.

Col. Gerrard mortally wounded.

Our officer, writing from Kunound, mentions the number of officers killed and wounded at 24, but this is generally thought to be a mistake. It is certain, however, that Col. Gerrard was mortally wounded, and died shortly after. The only other names given are the following as wounded:—Lieut. Craigie, Guides, badly; Lieut. Kennedy, ditto, slightly; Captain Pearse, Lieut. Humphreys, Sappers; the two last doing well.

Our force consists of 1st Fusiliers, squadron Carabineers, Guides, 400 Mooltan Horse, 200 Puthan Horse, and Artillery as before.

Rao Toola Ram of Rewaree is supposed to have been with the enemy. Rao Toola Ram.

I do not know when the Column is likely to proceed downwards. But it will require a little time to refit.

I have given the particulars in a bulletin, but have also detailed them in this letter as the extra may not be ready in time to send.

Twenty-four of the Shahzadas, or rather the Sulatin, were hanged at Delhi yesterday morning. Two were brothers-in-law, two sons-in-law of the King, the remainder nephews, etc. Execution of Sulatin at Delhi.

The Allygurh Force was yesterday at Kass Gunge, marching round by the Kutchla Ghat. Colonel Riddell's Column still on the Trunk Road; he has "upwards of 800 fighting men of sorts, of whom 375 are Europeans." Colonel Riddell's Column.

W. MUIR.

J. W. SHERER, ESQ.

*P.S.*—Two of the four Cossids despatched by you on the 14th (Saturday) have just come in. They describe the road as in a most dangerous state. They with difficulty escaped the Nana's force on the Canal at Sheolie, and were captured somewhere about Tiroo by horsemen and foot. Two of the four men had letters which were discovered on them,—they were found and carried off; two had none, and with difficulty got off. These are the men who have come in, so your despatches of the 14th are lost. If there was anything especially important, pray repeat it. I anticipated that our communications would soon become difficult and uncertain. Cossids intercepted.

I fancy the Contingent are moving on, and find you are well prepared to receive them, and then to move up and clear out the Doab, occupying Mynpoorie and Furruckabad.

Our intelligence from Mynpoorie is that the Raja has gone to Furruckabad to seek assistance, and that entrenchments are being thrown up. Rajah of Mynpoorie.

Wullee Dad is expected at Furruckabad. The Nawab Khan Bahadoor is busy casting more guns. He has 150 men working at the Foundry. Wullee Dad. Khan Buhadoor.

W. MUIR.

INTELLIGENCE DEPARTMENT, AGRA.

MSS. VOL. III.

*FOURTH SERIES.*

# LETTERS DOWN COUNTRY

TO

# CAWNPORE, CALCUTTA, ETC.

**From 20th November 1857 to the end of January 1858.**

# INTELLIGENCE DEPARTMENT, AGRA.

## MSS. VOL. III.

### *FOURTH SERIES.*

# LETTERS DOWN COUNTRY

TO

# CAWNPORE, CALCUTTA, ETC.

**From 20th November 1857 to the end of January 1858.**

## CCX.

AGRA, *November 20th*, 1857. Friday.

MY DEAR SHERER,—To-day's post has brought in Saunders' account, which corrects in some few points the statement I yesterday drew up from private letters. The action was at Narnoul, so that the Legion must have held on to their own Encampment, which was reached just before the enemy advanced, and which was about 2 miles from Narnoul. The only additional name given is *Wallace* wounded (a private letter received to-day mentions him as killed; but I trust this is a mistake). Captain Money had a horse killed under him. I will enclose copy of Saunders' message to Sir John Lawrence, but it gives nothing new. The date is still mentioned as 16th, so that the action must have been on Monday, not, as stated in the private letters, Sunday.

**Action at Narnoul.**

**Captain Money.**

Captain Macdonald writes from Deolee that he has intelligence, through Nusseerabad, of Neemuch, date not given, but supposed to be 12th instant. The enemy had up to that time produced no impression by their fire on the entrenched square. They had one siege gun in position, but ammunition supposed to be short, as its firing had almost ceased.

**Captain Macdonald.**

**Affairs at Neemuch.**

Captain Wallace of the Commissariat (21st Bombay Native Infantry) was the only person injured, and he only slightly grazed.

**Captain Wallace injured.**

Durand's Column—of which we heard as being at Dhar on

**Durand's Column.**

the 24th October—had advanced northwards. He appears to have been at Anjera from the last intelligence, and was to march on Mundessore "as soon as he had settled matters" there, which Mr. Stedman, an Opium Agent, reported would be on the 5th. If Durand made haste he ought to have been at Neemuch before the 15th. Besides, his attack on Mundessore (28 miles distant from Neemuch) would probably produce a diversion, as it is the Head Quarters of the Insurgents.

Captain Macdonald says that the movement on Neemuch by the rebels had not apparently affected his position at Deolee.

Allygurh. The impression produced by our Columns in the Allygurh district is excellent. The enemy had retired from Puttialee.

A Cossid had been traced to this bank of the Ganges in the
Wullee Dad. vicinity of the Kutchla Ghat, sent by Wullee Dad towards Kotah to communicate, it was supposed, with the Joudpoor rebels at Narnoul. It is not unlikely that if not encountered by Gerrard's Column they would have gone over to Rohilkhund to join him.

W. Muir.

J W. Sherer, Esq., Cawnpoor.

## CCXI.

## TELEGRAPHIC MESSAGE.

### From W. Muir to G. F. Edmonstone.

Agra, *20th November* 1857.

Saunders' report has just come in. The action was at Narnoul, not Kanound. Wallace also mentioned as wounded.

Neemuch said to be safe up to 12th. Mhow Column expected to leave Anjhera on 5th for Mundessore; early relief of Neemuch by it expected.

W. Muir.

*P.S.*—Two men have just come in who left Cawnpoor on Monday the 16th. They bring only one letter for Mr. Matthew of the Bank. They say that the two others who had letters from you lost them *in Cawnpoor*.

## CCXII.

*21st November* 1857. Saturday.

Defection of the Mehidpore or United Malwa Contingent. My Dear Sherer,—I am sorry to have to communicate intelligence of the defection of the Mehidpoor or United Malwa Contingent. Macpherson has received, through Gwalior, news of its having mutinied and killed its officers. No other particulars are given, excepting that Major Timins, the Commandant, escaped with his wife from Mehidpoor to Oujein, and was conducted by Scindia's local authorities there to Durand's Camp, then at Jeerun. Major Timins escaped.

I reported yesterday that Durand's Column was expected to march northwards from Anjera about the 5th instant. This would take our troops through Kuchroud. That place was full of Mewattee rebels of the Mundessore party. Macpherson thinks it probable that the approach of Durand caused Kuchroud to be evacuated by the insurgents, who then went over to Mehidpoor. This would have been a quite sufficient cause for the Malwa Contingent (which, from its proximity to the long-existing insurrection in the Mundessore Province, must have had its loyalty shaken) to revolt. Mewatti rebels.

However this may be, it is fervently to be hoped that Durand's march towards Mundessore and Neemuch will not be delayed by this unfortunate occurrence.

The Mehidpoor Cavalry all deserted before with the Neemuch Brigade. Two of the Mehidpoor guns also, which Hamilton sent to Augur (when Neemuch was reinforced by Gwalior troops), followed the Augur Mutineers to Gwalior, and are now with the Gwalior Contingent. It is supposed that there was also some Mehidpoor Artillery with the Neemuch Brigade. This I am not sure about. The Mehidpoor Contingent had two 24-pounders, two 12-pounders, and four 9-pounders originally.

The Infantry is only 640 strong. I conclude they will join the Mundessore rebels.

I mentioned yesterday that a spy of Wulleedad's had been traced on this side the Ganges, *bound for Kota.* You will find Kotah to be in close proximity to Mehidpoor and Mundessore. It is not at all improbable that intercommunications have been maintained by Wulleedad with the disaffected inhabitants of those parts. Wullee Dad communicates with Kotah.

It is also to be considered what connection the Kotah Durbar forces may have had, or may now assume, with this spreading revolt.

Of Neemuch we have nothing further to-day.

A letter from Delhi, dated the 19th, confirms the former account of the Narnoul action. We took 9 guns; three were not mounted, but carriages were being prepared for them. The enemy was reinforced the day before the action by three thousand men. No other names of the wounded are given. The total loss was *60*; viz. 15 killed and 45 wounded. Summund Khan, Narnoul action. Summund Khan of Jhujjur.

father-in-law of the Jhujjur Nawab (who commanded the Cavalry of that State in Delhi), and his son, are said to have been among the killed in the Serai.

Captain Stafford.

The enemy is reported by Captain Stafford to have fled in the direction of Bamul. A party was out following them up; and if they were found in force in that quarter, the Column was to march on the 18th to Kantee. This, you will see, is due *east* of Narnoul; not south, as was first reported. They may be making for Rohilkhund, or seeking for refuge among the Mewattee villages.

General Penny had not received any official despatch, and it was not even known who had succeeded to the command of the Column.

Execution of twenty-four members of the Royal Family, and of Hukeem Abdool Huk.

"There is no news," says Saunders, "at this place. Twenty-four of the inferior members of the Royal Family of Delhi were yesterday executed by order of a Military Commission before which they were tried. Hukeem Abdool Huk, who is one of the most influential of the rebels, and foremost in his hostility to our Government, was executed this morning."

On the 18th Cocks wrote from Kasgunge: "The people who have not seen a white face here for six months came out of their villages by troops; and here the Hindoos are really happy to have us even for a day. To-morrow we just look at the Ganges, bring over some boats and then return."

Hindoos welcome British officers.

Action near Khass Gunj.

The "look at the Ganges" ended in a distant cannonade from both sides. The rebels had three guns, one a 12-pounder. No one on our side was touched, though the 12-pounder shot fell close to us. A spy, who came over after the cannonade, said that the rebels had lost 28 (including 3 Sepoys) killed; and some 30 wounded. They are said to have been about 1200 strong, with about the same number of rabble. 200 of them were Irregular Cavalry, 300 Sepoys. They all ran away, and removed their camp to a distance.

Muthra pays in revenue.

Muttra has brought us in nearly three lacs.

Baird Smith.

Baird Smith, writing from Roorkee, "hopes that no long time will pass before effective military provision will be made for the protection of the Doab. *Till then its position must be precarious*; and we can only hope that the Trans-Gangetic Mutineers will find other work to do than coming over to us."

Wullee Dad Khan.

Wulleedad Khan has retired from the Boolundshuhur frontier and gone to Suheswan in Budaon.

W. Muir.

J. W. Sherer, Esq., Cawnpoor.

## CCXV.

AGRA, 23*rd Nov.* 1857. Monday.

MY DEAR SHERER,—Still nothing from you. Your last is dated the 11th inst.

Our last news through Gwalior is that Durand had moved on Mehidpoor from Kuchroud. This takes him due east, and so far out of his way to Neemuch. Two officers of the Contingent are said to have been killed. **Durand's Column had moved.**

We suppose that the Contingent must have by this time marched on Cawnpoor, if it is going to do so at all. We hear that it has taken all its Artillery across; but that 150 of the Gunners and 700 of the Infantry, residents of Gwalior, refused to cross, and are believed to have returned to their homes. If this be the case it will materially weaken their Artillery. **Gwalior Contingent.**

Some of their Ammunition, considered useless for their present trip, they are said to have left at Calpee. Two companies of new levies have been posted in Jalaon, and two at Madhogurh. The party sent to take possession of Bhundere is reported to have been driven out by the zemindars who were raised by one of Scindia's officers. **Companies posted in Jalaon and Madhogurh. Affair at Bhunder.**

Cocks' force took down their guns again to the Kutchla Ghat.

A letter received by Dr. Clark from Lahore, dated the 19th inst., states that all is quiet in the Punjaub, "but there is a rumour that Dost Mahomed has been assassinated by his brother."

W. MUIR.

J. W. SHERER, ESQ., Cawnpore.

*P.S.*—J. Power's of the 18th just received. We shall look out eagerly for news of the expected grand attack of the 17th.

We must have lost your account of the taking of Jelalabad, Dilkhoosha Park, and the Martiniere. Your recapitulation of the events there was the first we heard of it. A little recapitulation comes of use sometimes.

## CCXVI.

24 *November* 1857. Tuesday.

MY DEAR SHERER,—I have a letter from Saunders of yesterday's date. He says "the Column will not be removed from the neighbourhood of Rewaree for some little time, in the present **Showers' Column.**

unsettled state of our Frontier relations with some of the Rajpootana States."

Sir J. Lawrence advises force to be sent to Rajputana.

In consequence of the unquietness of some parts of Rajpootana, Sir J. Lawrence "is very anxious that a force should if possible be organised for employment in Rajpootana."

W. Ford, C.S.

Ford, writing of the action of the 16th, says it must have been productive of the most beneficial effect on the neighbouring States, as "it was fought close to the Joudpore and Jeypore forces, who, mustering, it is said, some 15,000 men with 28 guns, were afraid to attack the rebels." He adds that some Jeypore troops came up just as we had finished the battle, and caused anxiety on our right flank. Ford is suspicious that they meant to play false with us. He says: "Had the Jeypore Force advanced beyond the place where they had taken up their position on our right flank, I told Caulfield to attack them. These rascals are a serious obstacle to our movements. A zemindar, whom we found on the road, told me it had been proclaimed in the rebel Camp that Raouljee would join them immediately with 5000 men. The gunners of the Joudpore and Jeypore Force were, I hear, in a state of mutiny."

Joudhpore and Jyepore forces.

Fears for Rajputana.

He adds, which I trust and believe is overstating the case: "Government must keep a sharp look-out on this frontier,—all Rajpootana will, I fancy, break out." But there is abundance to support the earnest wishes of Sir J. Lawrence and Colonel Fraser for the presence of our troops in force in that direction.

Ulwar Sepoys, suspicious behaviour of.

Some Ulwar Sepoys had threatened to fire on Ford if he came close to them, and the Vakeel would not agree to Ford's sending a party into the Ulwar territory to apprehend some wounded fugitives.

Loyalty of Ulwar troops.

On the other hand, it has been ascertained that the Ulwar troops had a brush with the fugitive Cavalry, and lost seven or eight men killed, sixteen wounded, and 20 horses. The loss of the Rebels is not known; but the fact of the engagement proves that at any rate, after the insurgents were routed, the Ulwar army had no sympathy with them.

The fugitives took the road towards the Jumna, the Foot going *via* Toojara, the Horse *via* Tapookrah.

Affairs at Allygurh.

About midday we received telegraphic intelligence from Allygurh and Hatrass that two large bodies of fugitive troops had appeared in the Allygurh district. One at Tuppuhl, to the North-West of Allygurh, and opposite the Goorgaon district; the other, some 2500 strong, in the direction of Hatrass or Sydabad. They were burning Chowkies and committing ravages. I conclude they are making for the Ganges, Rohilkhund, Furruckabad, or Oudh.

Riddell's Column, 800 strong, is at Sasnee, and was to be to-morrow at Hatrass. He will no doubt push forward and inflict chastisement on the fugitives if he can catch them up. **Riddell's Column.**

On the 19th a small detachment went from Sona towards Hutteen, which had been attacked by the Mewattees. Our troops burnt 12 villages with their stacks at Roopraka; the Mewattees, in a force of 3500, opened a matchlock fire on our little body of troops (only two Native Companies and about 100 horse). Our men reserved their fire till within one hundred yards, then gave them a volley and closed with the bayonet. About fifty were killed in the village, and 400 were cut up by the Cavalry outside it. **Mewattis attacked.**

Colonel Seaton takes the command *vice* Gerrard. **Colonel Seaton succeeds Gerrard.**

Captain Macdonald writes from Deolie that all was well up to the 16th at Neemuch. The enemy had almost ceased firing. It is to be hoped they are short of ammunition. **Captain Macdonald.**

He says Captain Eden writes to him "to be prepared for an attack on my post (Deolie) by the Budmashes of Tank. He has received information that such a move is contemplated." Captain Macdonald "has taken measures against a surprise, and for the rest will trust to the God of Battle." **Deoli likely to be attacked by the Budmashes of Tank.**

All this points to the necessity of aid being speedily sent to Rajpootana.

Yours of the 19th just received,[1] or rather Power's, with the good news of the successful advance on the 17th. The lithographing is bad, and some of the names very indistinct. However, I trust I have made out all correctly.

W. MUIR.

J. W. SHERER, ESQ., Cawnpoor.

*P.S.*—Our 600 camels are returned back safe from Etawah.

## CCXVII.

*25th November* 1857. Wednesday.

MY DEAR SHERER,—The Cossids we despatched on the 17th and 18th have all returned, saying that they were plundered of all their letters. One party went by Ooreya, the other by the Canal. **Cossids sent from Agra plundered.**

On the 17th I despatched 2 packets for you; and on the 18th, 3 for you, 1 for Beadon, and 1 for Colonel Baker. On

[1] 19th–24th = 5 days—from Cawnpore to Agra.—W. M.

the 17th there was one for the Commander-in-Chief and one for Strachey. I will try and supply the loss as far as I can. The letters of the 17th are lost, as well as the duplicates I sent on the 18th. The item of chief importance in these was the siege of Neemuch.

To-day I have nothing of much consequence.

Movement of the Joudhpore rebels.

The Joudpoor rebels, it seems, must have crossed the Jumna somewhere opposite Hodul; they then held a south-easterly course, passing by Noh and Moorsam, and came upon the Allygurh Road a few miles this side of Hatrass. They are flying in the greatest possible haste and confusion, without baggage, guns, or anything; and are avoiding all the large villages. The Tehseeldar of Hatrass caught one of the Joudpoor Sepoys last night; this man says there are some 1300 fugitives, horse and foot—that they are all taking the same route, that they have no particular destination in view, but are making for the Ganges as rapidly as they can.

Riddell's Column.

Riddell marched from Sasnee to Hatrass last night. He had heard of another detachment of 400 fugitives being behind. It is to be hoped he may be able to overtake some of them.

Rampershad Subahdar leads fugitives.

The Sepoy said the fugitives were led by Rampershaud Subahdar.

Our last news was that they were pushing on, and would probably reach the Grand Trunk Road, somewhere east of Eta, during the day.

State of Rohilkhund.

The rebels in the Rohilkhund side seem to have had a fresh fit of activity. Baird Smith says that there are menaces of a descent there, though he does not think they will venture over.

Dunlop, C.S.

Dunlop, from Gurhmuktesur, says that they are "collecting in very large numbers, and are now threatening many points on the river." He is watching with a very inadequate force the banks from Pooth to Hustnapoor. He has only 100 Police Cavalry and 50 of Coke's Rifles; but there is a considerable body of Rao Golab Sing's (of Kochesur) men with 4 small guns;—of these, 200 horsemen are good, but the foot very inadequately armed.

Rao Golab Singh of Kochesur.

On the 20th heavy firing was heard in the direction of Amroha in the Moradabad district. It was an engagement between the troops of the Nawab of Rampoor, and 1000 Mussulman insurgents headed by a noted enemy of ours, Goolzar Ally, who was a leader of "Jehadies" at Delhi. The rebel was defeated and driven out of Amroha, and his house destroyed.

Nawab of Rampore. Goolzar Ally.

General Penny writes to say that under the threatening

aspect of our relations, from the various forces against us in the road between this and Cawnpoor, he has postponed, till further advised from there, the despatch of the convoy he had intended sending down the country, "as he does not deem it at all judicious to risk the loss of the stores and carriage which I have been collecting for the European troops, and on which they are so entirely dependent."

. . . . . . . . . . .

Nothing further from Neemuch.

W. MUIR.

J. W. SHERER, ESQ., Cawnpoor.

*P.S.*—Information has just come in from Allygurh that Wullee Dad has joined the Futtehgurh rebels, who have advanced towards the Allygurh district, and are now at Puttialee. They have ordered supplies on the road to Kassgunge towards Allygurh, and the district in that direction is panic-struck. If they come on and are not repelled, the Mussulman population of the Allygurh district will again be in a flame. Riddell has therefore been ordered to hold on at Hatrass. It would be a sad pity if anything occurred to unsettle the arrangements at Allygurh, on which our communications with the N.W. entirely hang. **Wullee Dad joins the Futtehgurh rebels, and threatens Allygurh.**

W. M.

## CCXVIII.

*26th November* 1857. Thursday.

MY DEAR SHERER,—The messengers of the 19th have been equally unfortunate as those of the 17th and 18th. One was seized, and one got off, after losing his letters, and returned here. I am endeavouring to supply the loss. Yesterday I sent duplicates of the 17th and 18th. To-day I send those of the 16th, 19th, and 20th. **Cossids again seized.**

. . . . . . . . . . .

The Joudpoor fugitives have passed over towards the Ganges or Mynpoorie—that is to say, the first body of them. A second detachment, said to be 1500 in number (with 5 guns, which I much doubt), are reported to have crossed some way above Muthra—near Nohjheel—and to be on the same route as the others. **Joudhpore fugitives.**

Riddell continues to halt at Hatrass. There are still threatening reports of Wulleedad at Puttialee. **Riddell's Column.**

More Sikh Police coming down *via* Meerut for us. **Sikh Police coming.**

The Puttialee Rajah is sending a force of 2000 horse and

Rajah of Patiala sends aid to Dholpore.

H. S. Reid, C.S.

foot, with 4 guns, for his relative the Dholpore Rajah, to maintain order. Sir John Lawrence asked if there was any objection to this, and the Government here replied, none. H. S. Reid is going up to escort the Force this way. It will have a good effect if it marches through the Meewattee country *via* Goorgaon and Muthra. Located in Dholpore itself, this body will have an excellent effect upon our frontier, which, in that direction, is in a very unsettled state.

Nawab of Rampore defeats Goolzar Ally at Umroha.

Mr. Alexander reports publicly in a letter, dated the 22nd instant, Nyneetal, that the Nawab of Rampoor has written to say that his troops defeated Goolzar Ally and his rebel adherents at Umroha, "killing many and dispersing the rest." This is the engagement reported yesterday on Dunlop's authority. Alexander justly dwells on the significance of the fact that the Rampoor troops should have attacked and routed fanatics of the Mussulman faith headed by Syuds. It is really cause of satisfaction.

Nawab of Rampore's loyalty.

The Christian women and children, whom the Nawab sent off from Moradabad, after having had them maintained so long there hospitably, have safely reached Meerut; another material proof of his good wishes.

Subscriptions for relief of the sufferers in the Mutiny.

Captain Eden has just sent us Rs. 2011 subscriptions for relief of the sufferers in the Mutiny. Of this, 1000 Rs. are from the Maharaja, and the remainder chiefly from natives of the Court and City. This is gratifying.

We are looking anxiously for your bulletin of the proceedings of the 18th at Lucknow.

W. MUIR.

J. W. SHERER, ESQ., Cawnpoor.

## CCXIX.

AGRA, *November 27th*, 1857. Friday.

Neemuch relieved.

MY DEAR SHERER,—This Cossid will, I. hope, get through with the happy intelligence of Neemuch being relieved. I have given almost all the particulars in the printed bulletin. The information is contained in letters from Captain Lloyd and Captain Simpson, dated 22nd inst. They were forwarded by General Lawrence from Ajmere, where all was well on the 23rd. The fresh proofs now afforded of the faithful and gallant conduct of the Bombay troops is peculiarly satisfactory.

Faithful conduct of Bombay troops.

In the attempt to escalade, when the enemy lost some couple of hundred men, we had only *two* Sepoys slightly wounded.

Lloyd says it was generally reported that a heavy cannonade was heard on the 21st from the direction of Mundessore. This is highly probable. Durand's Column would have heavy fighting there. And it was that which, no doubt, caused the besieging force to withdraw so unexpectedly to the little garrison.

"We are hard at work," says Lloyd, "clearing away the houses and trees which have been so damaging to us; and if possible will destroy the trenches. Parties are out in search of supplies, etc., in case we may yet have to hold our own."

Captain Simpson promoted two men of the Bombay 12th N.I. on the spot for signal gallantry, and recommended a third to General Lawrence. He says, "The guns of the enemy made little impression, but their matchlockmen annoyed us greatly from the entrenchments; . . . we want ammunition and an officer for Europeans; . . . we require a larger force here." It is to be hoped that the party which was escorting ammunition under Baumgarten, and which was obliged to take refuge in the Chittore Fort, will now be able to reach Neemuch. A young Cavalry Officer, Brett, was dying—but not of wounds.

Bombay Sepoys promoted for gallantry.

An Electric Telegraph message from Allygurh reports that six more refugees from Rohilkhund have reached this bank of the Ganges at the Kutchla Ghat, and are under the care of the blind Tehseeldar—the Choubey. What a courageous old man that Choubey is!—holding out there with a small band of Sowars and people of the surrounding villages. He has been all along the most valuable support to us, and an able adviser while we were shut up in Agra. He will, I trust, receive by and by substantial tokens of our favour.[1]

Refugees from Rohilkhund.

Choubey Gunsham Dass: loyal services.

Cocks expects the refugees at Allygurh to-morrow or the next day. Their names are not mentioned.

The reports from Puttialee continue more and more threatening;—the force there is exaggerated into 4000 and 12 guns.

Your despatches of the 21st came in this morning. I conclude that the "enigmatical" character of the Lucknow despatches you complain of was caused by the anxiety to conceal the intention of evacuating Lucknow, which, of course, it was important should not be known at Cawnpore beforehand, as the knowledge would no doubt have encouraged the enemy to making preparations for annoying our rear.

I continue to regret the determination, for the reasons I formerly stated. But it will have the important advantage

Evacuation of Lucknow, comments on.

[1] He was killed (see p. 358, *post*), and his brother, Raja Jey Kishen Doss, made C.S.I.—W. M.

(besides setting free the troops otherwise required for the Garrison) of affording a secure field, for the present, to the disaffected; who will no doubt draw thither from all quarters, and stay there till we are at leisure to dispose of them. They will also have a dearly bought lesson of the miseries of anarchy when left to themselves. The Province deserves it for the almost universal enmity it has displayed. A month or two ago the abandonment of Lucknow and Oudh might have had an untoward effect on Central India and Rajpootana; I trust that we are now too far advanced in our recovery of power for that. I trust that Power's news of a Column for Furrackabad is well founded.

W. MUIR.

J. W. SHERER, ESQ., Cawnpore.

## CCXX.

AGRA, 28*th November* 1857.[1] Saturday.

MY DEAR SHERER,—We have nothing of news to-day.

Nothing later from Neemuch. A letter from Lloyd says that "he has every reason to believe that there will be little difficulty in restoring order in the Neemuch district when once the rebel invaders are expelled." The people themselves in that vicinity seem well affected.

**People in vicinity of Neemuch well affected.**

**Ghulam Moheiood-deen.**

He says that "the principal leader in the late inroad has been the late Bukshee of Neembhera, by name Ghulam Moheiood-deen, who has openly proclaimed his object to be revenge for his expulsion from Neembhera."

**Gwalior Contingent.**

Two of our scouts have come in who were at Calpee three days ago. They say that our troops with guns were there, and that the Contingent had fallen back seven or eight coss on the Jalaon side. We think this possible; but I do not like to enter it in my bulletin till I hear from you. I conclude the first steps now will be to reoccupy Mynpoorie, and attack Furrackabad, which will at once open our communications again.

Our last from you is of the 21st.

**Riddell's Column.**

Riddell's force will make an advance towards Shekoabad, and will be in a good position there to co-operate with any parties you may send up the Doab.

W. MUIR.

J. W. SHERER, ESQ., Cawnpoor.

[1] Received by Sherer, Decr. 10th = 12 days.—W. M.

## CCXXI.

Agra, 29*th November* 1857. Sunday.

My Dear Sherer,—I have no news of consequence to-day. The despatch from Calcutta for Saunders has reached safely, and been forwarded by express.

The King is, after all, to be brought to trial by a Military Commission, which is also to try the Nawabs of Jhujjur, Furrukhnugger, and Dadree, and the Rajah of Bullubgurh.

**The King to be tried by Military Commission, also the Nawabs of Jhujjur, Furrukhnugger, and Dadree, and Rajah of Bullubgurh.**

Eden writes from Jyepoor, dated the 27th. All going on quietly and well there.

**All well at Jyepore.**

Buldeo Singh, the Gwalior Thakoor, who did us good service when our refugees fled from Gwalior, has brought safe away from Narwar two persons belonging to the Telegraph Department, one lady and three children. They were to be at Dholpore yesterday. That man deserves well of us.

**Buldeo Singh, Thakoor, brings in European refugees.**

At the Kutchla Ghat there were five or six persons brought over from Rohilkhund, the only names given being Wilkinson (who has a brother clerk in the Ch. Engineer's Office here) and Maclean.

**Wilkinson and Maclean, refugees from Rohilkhund.**

The Furruckabad people, with Wullee Dad, continue to creep onwards to Etah. But nothing can be done under present circumstances effectually to counteract them.

**Wullee Dad.**

W. Muir.

## CCXXII.

Agra, 30*th November* 1857. Monday.

My Dear Sherer,—I have no special news to communicate.

Macdonald writes from Deolee, dated the 26th; all well there. He gives news from Nusseerabad of the 25th. Neemuch continued quiet. Mewattee prisoners, "several without noses," were being brought in by the villagers to the fortified Square. The mutilation of these captured rebels is rightly concluded to "show that the country people do little sympathise with the Mewattee movement." Macdonald is satisfied that there is no fear now for Rajpootana, "if all goes well elsewhere." But he looks out anxiously for news from Lucknow. In order to counteract the evil effect which our withdrawal from Lucknow, distorted as it will be into a reverse and expulsion, it is essential that there be an immediate show of strength upwards. You should press this so far as you can do so with propriety. The

**Macdonald reports all well at Deoli. Neemuch quiet. The country people not in sympathy with the Mewatti movement.**

first step will, of course, be against the Contingent and your other more immediate enemies; but after that I hope the earliest possible movement will be made to crush the rebellion at Furruckabad, and occupy it and Mynpoorie. At Gwalior the disaffected section still maintain (I am assured by Macpherson) that the cause, the *Deen*,[1] is in the ascendant even at Lucknow. It is easy to see what use these, and other similarly minded people throughout the country, will make of our withdrawal, unless it be followed by a prompt demonstration of power.

Sergeants Carrol and Jervis of the Seepree Regiment.

Two Sergeants, with the wife of one of them, brought in yesterday from the Gwalior territory, turn out to belong not to the Telegraph Department but to the Sepree Regiment[2] (the third). When it mutinied, the Officers went towards Indore, while these poor people came northwards; and after infinite hardships, and living for months in the Jungle (kindly treated, however, by the people), they were now, in the improved state of our name, enabled to be brought in. They were, however, still brought *concealed* in native conveyances, followed by music and drums to simulate a wedding procession.

J. Cracroft Wilson, C.S. Wullee Dad Khan. Christian refugees.

Wilson is bearding Wulleedad Khan by passing up to the Kutchla Ghat within 10 or 12 miles of the enemy, in order to bring in *another* party of six Christians who are said to be on the North bank of the Ganges. It is to be hoped that the rebels will not stop him on his benevolent mission. He is a man of rare activity and daring. A few days would enable, it would seem, many to be brought over. "Our presence at Soron," Wilson writes, "if we can only hold our position, will enable the Rajpoots to bring all the Christians who have arrived in safety within a reasonable distance of the Ganges, across to us. But if we are compelled " to retreat, then there is great risk of their being murdered by Wullee Dad's people."

Wullee Dad, with the Furruckabad rebels, continues to advance, and will not improbably embarrass the Allygurh demonstration.

But before that leads to any ill result, we will trust that the Commander-in-Chief will have threatened the rebels from the opposite direction.

W. MUIR.

J. W. SHERER, ESQ., Cawnpoor.

The Nana.

*P.S.*—Macpherson's Gwalior news makes the Nana and Ballajee to have been at Lucknow on the 17th and to have

[1] Religion.

[2] Sergeants Carrol (with family) and Jervis. They have been almost entirely in the jungles ever since the 7th June!

escaped to Futtehpore, where they were not received. Ballajee then went "to arrange" with the Contingent; and moving some of his other adherents to Akberpoor, emboldened the Contingent to go forward. This is from a correspondent with the Contingent. Ballajee.

W. M.

## CCXXIII.

AGRA, 1st *December* 1857. Tuesday.

MY DEAR SHERER,—My Cossids of the 23rd and 24th have both returned, saying that they were robbed of their letters near Akberpoor. It is a good thing that my letters of late have not been of any great importance; the only news of much significance being the siege, and the raising of the siege, of Neemuch. However, I have had prepared copies of the letters supposed to have miscarried, and send them to you to supply the gap. Cossids robbed.

General Penny is sending down a convoy with stores and carriage for the use of the troops coming up country. His letter to the Headquarters Staff goes by this Cossid. There are 1500 carts of grain, 80 elephants, 600 camels, 3000 camp-followers. The escort is a troop Horse Artillery; 336, First Bombay Fusiliers; 400, 7th Punjaub Infantry; one Company Sikhs, Pioneers; one squadron Carabineers; and Hodson's Horse. The convoy starts on the 10th, but halts at Allygurh till you can send up an escort to convey it down. General Penny is quite right in this, for he justly says "the force under my command is βαρελι συφισιεντ to enable me to garrison this city and to keep the district in order." General Penny sending convoy with stores and carriage.

No news from the North-West. That from Gwalior is good. Scindia is getting under control his rebellious vassals. We are arranging for laying horses, etc., on the road to Gwalior, so as at the earliest possible date to reopen the Bombay dak that way. Scindia recovering his position.

W. MUIR.

J. W. SHERER, ESQ., Cawnpoor.

*P.S.*—Edmonstone's message to the Chief Commissioner regarding the treatment of the Royal family and others at Delhi has been duly received, and will be communicated at once to Saunders, who has been acting exclusively under Sir J. Lawrence. I have alluded to the subject of the message by anticipation in my letter to Harington forwarded yesterday.

## CCXXIV.

AGRA, *2nd December* 1857. Wednesday.

MY DEAR SHERER,—No news to-day, except growing alarm in the Allygurh District from the approach of Wullee Dad. I am writing to Delhi to urge that the escorting Column I reported yesterday as to leave on the 10th may be despatched as early as possible. That, once at Allygurh, will repress the insurgents; and, if necessary, we could send out reinforcements if it were advisable to offer battle.

Wullee Dad approaches Allygurh.

Captain Macdonald writes from Deolie that the native report is that the Mhow Column reached Mundessore on the 20th ultimo. We have no direct intelligence regarding it.

The force that was going from Nusseerabad to raise the siege of Neemuch does not now march; but ammunition, stores, etc., are being escorted thither.

Reinforcements at Deesa.

Her Majesty's 95th with Enfields, a European Battery, and a Company of Royal Engineers, are expected on the 10th prox. at Deesa. This will prove seasonable relief for Rajpootanah.

The Headquarters of Her Majesty's 83rd were to be at Nusseerabad on the 29th.

Pray say that I have received Mr. Talbot's letter of the 17th, and am taking measures for securing as early and complete a reply as possible.

W. MUIR.

J. W. SHERER, ESQ., Cawnpore.

## CCXXV.

AGRA, *3rd December* 1857. Thursday.

MY DEAR SHERER,—We have nothing from you later than the 25th ultimo.

I have letters from Delhi of yesterday's date. Goorgaon appears to be quieting down. "The Mewattees," Mr. Saunders says, "are all tendering their submission, and praying to be allowed to return to their villages and resume their peaceful occupations. They, moreover, promise to pay their revenue for both crops." The Putiala Force coming to the aid of the Rana of Dholpore will march down the right bank of the Jumna, and will have a good effect in the Goorgaon and Muttra districts.

Mewattis tendering submission.

Patiala force.

Our Deputy Postmaster (a Baboo) has resumed charge of his office at Gwalior. Dinkur Rao is prepared to give every assistance in his power to open out the road onwards to Indore

Dinkur Rao's loyal aid.

the moment the country about Sipree becomes quiet, and this may be expected immediately, as the Nurwar Chief has tendered his submission.

At Gwalior the Durbar believes that arrangements are being made from Indore to Goona for replacing the horses on the road, so that we may hope at no distant date again to have our postal communication open direct with Bombay. Letters now take 12 days.

A despatch has just been received from Durand, dated Mundessore, the 28th November. His operations have been entirely successful. The insurgents have been dispersed. They are nowhere in any force. The strongest body is believed to have fled *via* Chendwasa, towards Jalra Puttun and the Kotah country.

**Durand's operations.**

I need not detail what he says regarding his operations against Dhar, where he first encountered the Shahzadah's forces. Particulars have no doubt been received *via* Bombay of this, as well as of the escape of the garrison northwards, their attack on Mehidpoor, and the fraternization with them of the United Malwa Contingent.

**Operations against Dhar.**

Our Cavalry (Hyderabad Contingent) came up with the enemy carrying off the Mehidpoor guns, ammunition, etc., towards Mundessore, at Ravul, "dashed at them at once, cut up a great number, took many prisoners, and not only recovered all the Malwa Contingent guns, stores, ammunition, etc., but took two guns of the enemy's own in addition."

**Performances of Hyderabad Cavalry.**

On the 21st the Shahzadah, reinforced by a portion of the troops who were besieging Neemuch, attacked our Column four miles south of Mundessore. They were driven back with loss; and on the 22nd we crossed the Sonwa river without opposition, and encamped near Mundessore.

**Shahzadah attacks our Column.**

Our Cavalry pursued the enemy's horse to some difficult country, 10 or 12 miles north of Mundessore, on the Neemuch road, but withdrew on approaching the main body.

On the 23rd we moved 4 or 5 miles in the same direction, "and had just taken our point when standards were seen coming over a ridge in our front. They occupied a strong village as their centre, placed their six guns on a mound on their left centre, and deployed right and left, overlapping both our flanks. A nullah and low ground with palm-trees covered their front. On the whole the ground they took was as well as could be, for we had caught them as I wished, *i.e.* on the move."

"The battle commenced with a cannonade, in which our

superior Artillery had the best of it. We advanced by échelon from the right, refusing the left; and at last, as our Artillery fire had driven the enemy from the mound and guns, Martin charged with a small party of Dragoons and took the mound top and guns, but could not hold it, as the enemy behind the mound opened a heavy fire, wounded Martin, and made the place too hot for the party of Dragoons, who had to retire from the guns and mound, which were again occupied by the enemy. This lasted but a short time, for we brought up our right, reopened fire, and doubled them back on their centre and right: the Dragoons again charging and recapturing the Rebel Artillery. A strong body threw themselves into the village, and fought desperately all the 23rd and 24th; but the mass was routed, pursued, and many cut up by our Cavalry. The débris of the Shahzadah's forces are now scattered in small parties, making their way through the jungles, and avoiding towns and villages, for the people have turned upon them, and destroy them. The only body of any size has gone across the Chumbul towards Chendwassa, probably making for the Jalra Puttun and Kotah Country."

Fight with the Shahzadah.

Keatinge appointed Political Agent of Western Malwa.

Durand had appointed Keatinge Political Agent of Western Malwa, as he finds an officer urgently needed there. Lieutenant Cumming is acting for him at Nimar.

Bheels giving trouble.

The Bheels are giving trouble on the Candeish frontier, and infesting the Bombay road about Sindwa. But the grass can now soon be burnt, when operations can be commenced against them.

83rd Regiment.

The Headquarters 83rd reached Nusseerabad on the 28th ultimo from Dessa.

Kassgunge invested.

Telegraphic information has just been received from Allygurh that Kassgunge was invested yesterday; and it is feared our old and staunch friend, Choubey Gunsham Dass, has been taken prisoner. This we feel much. Our messengers despatched from here on the 23rd have returned, and say that on the 27th the Contingent, having brought up the heavy guns, forced back our troops to near Cawnpoor: that Saturday was quiet, but a tremendous cannonade on Sunday. We look anxiously for tidings of these proceedings.

W. Muir.

J. W. Sherer, Esq., Cawnpoor.

Neemuch.

*P.S.*—We have letters also from Neemuch of the 28th. On the 26th a party of Cavalry went in chase of some Mussulman fanatics who had been engaged in a fanatic insurrection at

Jamud. They were pursued 16 miles, and 30 brought in as prisoners. Thirteen were shot, and one hanged.

It was very fortunate that Durand appeared when he did, as there had been three desertions from the 12th Native Infantry, and "the men were beginning to disbelieve in the existence of a Mhow or Nusseerabad force at all; so often had they heard of their approach without seeing them."

It will be a good day when a few thousand Europeans can show themselves in Central India.

All the Nusseerabad officers (some 28, with ladies, etc.) have arrived, having had a safe and pleasant journey across Rajpootanah. **Nusseerabad officers arrive at Agra.**

The organised Police are making excellent progress. Fancy 12 Sowars escorting a lac and a quarter of rupees from Baroti and Bhagput to Meerut. It would have required 12 hundred to have done it 3 months ago. **New Police.**

W. Muir.

## CCXXVI.

Agra, *4th December* 1857. Friday.

My Dear Sherer,—The roads so far as Cawnpore is concerned seem to be impervious to our Cossids. Until you drive away the Contingent and other bodies hanging about, I fear things will not improve. But we look for tidings of decided success against the parties who have been menacing Cawnpore shortly. **Communications interrupted.**

Wullee Dad and the Furruckabad rebels continue to αδυανς, and our noble friend the blind old Choubey has been σειζεδ and σ'οτ by them. All honour to his memory. It will, I doubt not, be the care of the Government to mark their appreciation of his services by the highest rewards to his family. Harington will be able to tell at Calcutta how much we owed to this man in the times of our difficulty. He was the originator of the first Allygurh expedition, and his counsel to us throughout was invaluable. Only conceive the daring of this man, who was *blind* and hardly able to walk from paralysis, maintaining so long his position in the very front and almost within sight of the enemy. **Advance of Wullee Dad and the Furruckabad rebels. Choubey Gunsham Dass shot. His valuable services.**

The following particulars, given in a letter from Neemuch, regarding the battle gained by the Mhow Column will be found interesting. "Colonel Durand got word of the Insurgents' movements, and met them three coss this side of Mundessore, and had a desperate engagement with them. They fought from 11 a.m. to 6 p.m. and renewed the engagement at sunrise next day, and **Proceedings of Mhow Column at Mundessore.**

fought till the evening. By that time the Velaities were nearly all killed. The rest bolted. Twelve hundred dead bodies have been counted. A couple of hundred have since been blown away from guns, and 150 are being sent in here (Neemuch) for trial."

"The 2nd Cavalry it is believed will join the Mhow Column, and proceed to attack Rampoor, where the remnant of the rebels have fled."

The attack by the Cavalry on the Insurgents while endeavouring to carry off the Mehidpoor guns to Mundessore is said to have resulted in 300 of the Velaities being killed, and about 100 of the Contingent blown away from guns.

Mr. Saunders has sent a full report in reply to the letter calling for an explanation regarding the allegations of the *Friend of India* on the proceedings at Delhi. I have sent it by Bombay, as I dare not entrust it to the uncertainties of our present Cossid transit. The report is manly and satisfactory. The only point on which the vindication is not entire and complete is the carrying out of young Jewan Bukht on an elephant by Colonel Hogge.

. . . . . . . .

I send a message. If you have telegraphed already about the Mundessore fight you had better omit that part of the message.

W. Muir.

J. W. Sherer, Esq.

## CCXXVIII.

Agra, *5th December* 1857. Saturday.

My Dear Sherer,—Still nothing from you. The Gwalior news, however, of your proceedings is good. They explain the retreat of our troops on the 27th into a feint which succeeded in killing 1300 of the enemy—though to accomplish it they say we abandoned at the Canal ten tents, ten elephants, and two guns. The truth of all this and the final result we are anxiously looking for.

Hurdeo Bux of Dhurmpoor. On the other hand, we learn from a plaintive address of Hurdeo Bux of Dhurmpoor that the "Shah Oudh" had been issuing orders as if he had δριυεν us ουτ with λοσς on the 22nd ultimo, and regained possession of Lucknow; was sending out armies to settle the country and to arrest Hurdeo Bux. This will be the turn which the disaffected will endeavour to give to the proceedings. The speedy advance of the Commander-in-Chief against Furruckabad will alone tend to disabuse the people of the idea; and the sooner it is made the better. My messenger from Hurdeo Bux seemed quite to understand the real posture of affairs; and it is probable that the well affected in Oudh do so, though I fear they are few in number. Our man said that we had withdrawn all our guns, ammunition, stores, etc., successfully; and, about the 26th, were at Begumgunge, on the way to Cawnpore; and that we had given Man Sing's people a salutary round of grape which killed 4000 of his followers. I tell you all this, as it is important that the impression produced by the proceeding of withdrawal should be known. The people here evidently do not yet know of the intention.

**Unrest in Boolundshuhur.** **Rohilkhund affects Doab.** **Goojurs join Joudhpore Legion.**

Meanwhile the Insurgents are *πρεσσινγ υπον υς*. Sapte from Boolundshuhur writes that the "rebels are getting very 'cocky,' and *κροσσ* the *Γανγες*, and are even showing themselves in *μασσες* near the *βανκς*; so our presence is required there urgently." He feels that the presence of the Insurgents at *Κασσγυνγ* has a very *πρεϳουδισιαλ* effect all along towards his district, and that immediate measures must be taken against them. The last remnant of the Joudpore Legion has also taken up a *ποσιτιον* in *'ιζ διστρικτ*, and being *ϳοινεδ* by the *Γοοϳυρς*. He is obliged to send a strong party against them.

A letter received from Delhi this morning (which I have not, however, seen) states that a petition was thrown into Mr. Egerton's carriage, saying that *Γαζιες* were gaining admittance into the City by making use of other people's *πασσες*. This may be a mere idle rumour, but it may also tend to make them *υνυιλλινγ* to send the convoy on to Allygurh. If there had been anything serious in the report, Saunders would no doubt have written to me about it.

**Mundessore affair. Captain Redmayne.**

A letter mentions the loss in the Mundessore affair of a Captain Redmayne, 14th Dragoons, killed, 7 officers wounded, and 68 men killed and wounded. One would have expected more in such a hard-fought battle. The Velaities seem to have been desperate, coming on with cries of "Deen deen," "Ya Husein," "Ya Mahomed."

**Mehidpore affair.** **Lieutenant Mills, Dr. Carey, and two sergeants killed.** **Mrs. Timins.**

From the further accounts we are now getting of the Mehidpore affair, it would appear that some of the Contingent did continue to fight against the Insurgents who attacked the Cantonments. Lt. Mills and Dr. Carey and two Serjeants were killed. But you will have all this by Bombay. Poor Mrs. Mills was at Neemuch, and was confined shortly after hearing of her husband's death. She is doing well. Mrs. Timins had a wonderful escape, her horse being wounded.

W. MUIR.

J. W. SHERER, ESQ., Cawnpore.

## CCXXIX.

AGRA, *6th December* 1857. Sunday.

Dinkur Rao arrives at Agra.

MY DEAR SHERER,—We have nothing further from you. Our last is now 12 days ago. Nothing new. Except that Dinkur Rao has come in here on a visit. He had been meditating this for some time; but did not know exactly what effect it would have on the Maharajah's troops. We have a day or two ago given him 4 light guns (a part only of a number due to him by treaty), and this mark of confidence has no doubt enabled the Dewan to come over. The proof of the unity existing between the Government of Scindia and our own given by Dinkur's visit will have a good effect, and pave the way for our return by and by. Our messengers sent for tidings come back, but with no precise intelligence, excepting that after our first success there was very heavy fighting, the result of which they cannot ascertain.

Desolation at Delhi.

There was nothing whatever in the story of the Ghazis at Delhi. Travellers who left a day or two ago report everything as quiet, and (excepting for the awful desolation stamped upon the wretched city) as peaceful as if nothing had happened.

General Penny, in consequence of our solicitations, has altered the date for the convoy to leave, from the 10th to the 7th. We shall therefore soon be able to organise a force, if necessary, for the chastisement of the Furruckabad rebels who have been advancing westward.

W. MUIR.

J. W. SHERER, ESQ., Cawnpore.

## CCXXX.

*7th December* 1857. Monday.

Communications interrupted.

MY DEAR SHERER,—All our efforts to get letters from you by the ordinary road having proved fruitless, this goes *via* Furruckabad. We were *σορρι* to hear that about a week ago you had been *συρρουνδεδ* by the *νανα Σαχιβς* forces. We earnestly trust that long ere this the Commander-in-Chief has reached *καντπωρ* and *ρελιευεδ ιου*, dispersing the *ενεμι*. All well to the North-West. Three European Regiments and one of Dragoons, with Artillery, expected at Kurrachee a week ago. They will be soon in the field. Sir John Lawrence has written down to say that when the Commander-in-Chief can *σενδ* up

Nana Sahib's forces.

Troops from England expected at Kurrachee.

*τωο ευροπεαν ρεγιμεντς* an immediate advance can be made into *Ροχιλκυνδ*. In the uncertain state of the communications, I do not send the communication on the subject for Commander-in-Chief. But pray mention this to His Excellency. I will send copy *via αλλαχαβαδ*.

W. Muir.

J. W. Sherer, Esq., Cawnpore.

## CCXXXI.

Agra, *7th December* 1857. Monday.

My Dear Chester,—Please send the above to the Commander-in-Chief, and also a copy for the information of the Governor-General.

We cannot get our Cossids through the hordes of barbarians which have settled around Cawnpore. **Communications interrupted.**

The *ναυαβ οφ φυρρακαβαδ* is also *πρεσσινγ* southwards, and has *οκκυπιεδ ετανα*. We hope to have a strong force by Friday at *αλλιγυρχ* to chastise the same chief's troops which have *βεεν υεντυρινγ* in the direction of *ετα*. **Nawab of Furruckabad occupies Etawah.**

I do not write more, as I am not very certain of this reaching you soon. All well in the North-West. Three regiments, Europeans, one of Dragoons, and Artillery expected at *κυρραχεε* the beginning of this month, to move immediately on *Λαχωρ*, as you will see from Sir John's letter;—so that our hands will shortly, *Deo volente*, be strengthened from the North-West, even if the Commander-in-Chief's hands are occupied in the Middle Doab. But we look forward with confident expectation to his being able to burst through all opposition, and triumphantly sweep up the Doab.

W. Muir.

C. Chester, Esq., Allahabad.

## CCXXXII.

Agra, *8th December* 1857.

My Dear Chester,—I send a duplicate of yesterday's letter. I have nothing particular to add to-day. A strong Column will reach *αλλιγυρχ* on Friday the 11th; and, joined by the troops there and also by some *φρομ 'ερε*, will proceed towards *φυρυκαβαδ*;—this will check the enemy in his quarters. All well to the north-west.

Dinkur Rao's visit to Agra.

*Δινκυρ* Rao is paying us a very satisfactory visit. A good proof of the friendly feeling at *Γυαλιορ*.

The Rajah of Patiala loyally aids Dholpore.

The *Πυττιαλα* force of 2000 horse and foot, with guns, will soon reach *Δώλπωρ*. The object is to assist the *Ρανα* (a relative of the *Ραγα'ς*) to settle his country; and as *Δώλπωρ* borders on *Αγρα*, the effect *ἡρε* will be excellent.

W. MUIR.

## CCXXXIII.

AGRA, *10th December* 1857. Thursday.

Furruckabad still threatens.

MY DEAR SIR,—I enclose for your Excellency's information the copy of a correspondence of which I have already sent two or three copies by Cossid *via* Allahabad. I trust that the operations at Cawnpore, undertaken after your Excellency's return from Lucknow, will permit of the present despatch reaching the Headquarters camp. We have had no letter from Cawnpore of later date than the 25th. But we have heard by messengers of the proceedings there, in a general way, up to about a week later. A Column under Colonel Seaton, of nearly deux mille, will reach *αλλιγυρχ* demain. It will chastise the *ρεβελς*, who have *αδυανσεδ* from *φυρρυκαβαδ* half-way to *αλλιγυρχ*.

Etawah and Mynpoorie occupied by Furruckabad insurgents. Mozuffernugger threatened.

*Ινσυργεντς* from the same quarter have occupied *μινπωριε* and *ετανα* with both *τρωπς* and *γυνς*. The right bank of the *Γανγες* in *μοζυφερνυγερ* has been *θρεατενεδ* by an *ινκυρσιον* of *Ρεβελς* from *Ροχιλκυνδ*, and a force has gone from *μεερυτ* to *ρεπελ* them. But it does not seem that the movement is one of much importance. All is well here, and generally to the N.W. European troops are arriving at Kurrachee. The Mhow Column has completely routed and dispersed the Mundessore rebels, and Neemuch is again *φορ θε πρεσεντ* quite safe. There is a large collection of carriage and supplies from *Δελι* and *μεερυτ*, brought down with Colonel Seaton's Column. This will for the present be left at *Αλλιγυρχ*, under the guns of the fort there. We have also a large gathering of carriage, etc., *ἑρε*, waiting the first opportunity to be sent down to *Καυπωρ*; also establishments of servants, etc.

Neemuch.

I remain, Your Excellency's obedient servant,

W. MUIR.

TO HIS EXCELLENCY
SIR COLIN CAMPBELL, Cawnpore.

## CCXXXIV.

AGRA, 11*th December* 1857. Friday.

Communication with Cawnpore still very difficult.

MY DEAR SIR,—We have been trying in a variety of ways to get letters through to Cawnpore, but for some time unsuccessfully. I trust that long ere this Cawnpore has been relieved by the return of your Excellency from Lucknow, and the hordes surrounding it dispersed. All well to the North-West. A Column, deux mille strong, has this day reached *αλλιγυρχ*, and proceeds towards *ετα*, etc., to chastise the rebels who have advanced in that direction from *φυρρυκαβαδ*. This force would be in a good position to join any body of troops which your Excellency may be *σενδινγ υπ θε Δωαβ*. There is a great deal of carriage, supplies, establishments, etc., at *Αλλιγυρχ* and *Αγρα*, ready to send down the country the moment the road is open, or a sufficiently strong escort available.

Carriage at Allygurh and Agra ready for use.

General Penny, under instructions from Lahore, is prepared to organise an immediate advance into Ροχιλκυνδ the moment your Excellency can *σπαρε τωο* European *ρεγιμεντς*.

European troops are arriving at *Κυρραχεε* to be pushed to *Λαχωρ*.

We have had no letters from Cawnpore since the 25th.

I remain, Your Excellency's obedient servant,

W. MUIR.

TO HIS EXCELLENCY
SIR COLIN CAMPBELL, Cawnpore.

## CCXXXV.

AGRA, 12*th December* 1857. Saturday.[1]

MY DEAR SHERER,—All that has come in since your letter of the 25th ultimo is General Mansfield's of the 3rd instant, in which he refers to the women, sick, etc., as on their way to Allahabad; and expects a decisive action after they are well out of the way. Through Calpee, Jalaon, and Gwalior we have heard of what we believe has proved the utter discomfiture of the Contingent and all the Nana's forces on the 5th, 6th, and 7th inst., and we are hourly looking out for despatches from you regarding it.

Discomfiture of Contingent and Nana's forces.

Colonel Seaton's force reached Allygurh yesterday, bringing with it a large convoy of carriage, supplies, establishments, etc.

[1] Received by Sherer, 19th Dec. = 7 days.—W. M.

These remain at Allygurh for the present, and, as I have repeatedly before said, we have considerable store of carriage and establishments here, only waiting for the road to open. Colonel Seaton will go against the rebels at Kassgunge, and probably on to Mynpoorie, and will there be in a good position to form a junction with any force the Commander-in-Chief may be sending upwards. He has some 650 Sikh Horse, and about 140 European Horse, Carabineers, etc., which would be of inestimable service to His Excellency. Moozuffernugger was threatened some days ago by an inroad of some of the Bijnore rebel dacoits, etc., and a force went from Meerut thither. The thing seems to have died out; and, indeed, never to have been very important. Baird Smith is said to have the military command in Seharunpoor and Moozuffernugger.

Details of Seaton's Column.

Baird Smith.

Kotah.

There appears to have been an emeute at Kotah. Captain Macdonald writes from Deolee that the troops intercepted a letter from the Raja to General Lawrence, inviting him to send a force to Kotah, and promising to detach his own regiments in small parties on duty elsewhere. On this they attacked the Palace and demanded the Raja's adviser to be given up. This was refused, when they assaulted the Palace and apprehended the Minister. Firing was still going on at the Palace when Macdonald's messenger left. If all this be true it speaks well for the Raja. Dinkur Rao (who has just been with me) has a good opinion of the Raja, and says he was helpless in his troops' hands.

Rajah reported loyal.

Dinkur Rao.

Dinkur Rao's visit has had an excellent effect, and is only the prelude, I believe, to a visit from the Maharajah Scindia himself, who will probably be over in a few days. Dinkur's views are very satisfactory, and openly given. Though he does not conceal some of the defects of our administration, he asserts that the *people* were not discontented, that the revolt is *not* a popular one, and that the idea of interference with their religion did not extend beyond the soldiery.

His opinion of the revolt.

Macdonald says that the rebels have entirely abandoned the country towards Neemuch, and that Lloyd is now making his collections.

W. Muir.

J. W. Sherer, Esq., Cawnpoor.

Ladies leave Agra.

*P.S.*—Mrs. Harington and a great number of ladies left to-day to go *via* the Punjab to Bombay.

## CCXXXVI.

*13th December* 1857. Sunday.

On the reverse is the copy of my letter of yesterday's date. The messenger who carries this will be directed to take it if possible to the Commander-in-Chief, or to the Commanding officer of any force between this and Cawnpore, or to Mr. Sherer.

Colonel Seaton's Column halted yesterday at Allygurh, and to-day made a double march as far as Secundra Rao. To-morrow it will move on Kassgunj—if the enemy stand there, which it is not likely they will do, I fear. Mr. Sapte, with the Boolundshuhur force under Colonel Farquhar, is at Churra, half-way (15 miles) between Atrowlie and Kassgunj—with the view of co-operating with Colonel Seaton, but that force belongs to Boolundshuhur, and must return thither. **Colonel Seaton's Column advances on Lower Doab. B. Sapte, C.S.**

Colonel Seaton will, I hope, move on eastwards so as to be at Mynpoorie in 3 or 4 days. *Βυτ ἡ νιλλ νοτ* go beyond that. He will be in an admirable position to form a junction with any force the Commander-in-Chief may be sending towards the N.W. or Furruckabad. The Cavalry of his force are noted in yesterday's letter; but of these, 50 Seikhs belong to the Allygurh garrison. **Seaton's advance on Lower Doab.**

Major Williams has been very busy organising Police Battalion Sowars. If His Excellency urgently desires it, a body of 300 of these mounted police—Seikhs, Vilayatees, Mahommedans, etc.—could be placed at his disposal. It would cripple during the time of their absence the district police, but that is a small matter compared to the imperial exigency His Excellency has to deal with. They are tolerably drilled, and could do the work of Irregular Cavalry. **Major Williams organising Police Battalion.**

Seaton's Column is deux mille et deux cents strong, with neuf guns. **Details of Seaton's Column.**

W. Muir.

## CCXXXVII.

*14th December* 1857. Monday.

My Dear Sherer,—Still no letters from Cawnpore. But we have abundant proofs by messengers, and native letters from various sources, of the complete defeat of the Contingent; it is supposed on the 6th inst. All is well to the North-West. The Allygurh Column will be at Gungeree to-day, some 10 or 12 miles from Kassgunge, and it is to be hoped will have an opportunity of discomfiting the insurgents. The Boolundshuhur Column, some 600 or 700 strong with 2 guns, would form a **News of the defeat of the Gwalior Contingent.**

Colonel Becher. junction at Gungeree. Colonel Becher with the Headquarters Staff are at the Allygurh Fort.

Emeute at Kotah. The emeute at Kotah took place on the 5th instant. The opposition offered to them must have been trifling, as no lives were lost. The mutinous troops are in possession of the city and Palace. The City Gates were kept closed for two days. It is to be hoped that a force may soon be available to satisfy justice against the murderers of Burton.

Major Williams will have the 300 horse brought together here in 8 or 9 days, so that they may be able to work in a combined body.

W. MUIR.

J. W. SHERER, ESQ.

## CCXXXVIII.

*15th December* 1857. Tuesday.

MY DEAR SHERER,—The enclosed slip will give you an account of our victory at Gungeree, 30 miles east of Allygurh. The officers killed are Captain Wardlaw and Lt. Hudson, Carabineers. Lts. Vyse and Head were severely wounded—one since dead, but not stated which. The enemy got off, it is supposed, with two horse artillery guns. Our force is to-day at Kassgunge, but it is not likely the enemy would wait to receive us again. They are, however, in great strength, as they were estimated at about 5000, of whom only about 150 were left dead on the field. Seaton's Column will be in an admirable position to co-operate with any force that may be sent in the direction of Mynpoorie or Furruckabad.

Victory at Gungeree. Captain Wardlaw and Lieutenant Hudson killed.

. . . . . . . .

W. MUIR.

J. W. SHERER, ESQ., Cawnpore.

## CCXXXIX.

*16th December* 1857. Wednesday.

Action of Gungeree. MY DEAR SHERER,—Our loss at the action of Gungeree was heavier than at first supposed: 56 killed and wounded—14 killed. The Carabineers suffered severely, besides the officers (3 killed and 1 wounded), having 6 killed and 22 wounded, and this out of 140! There was no loss among the Artillery or Infantry. So it would appear that the Cavalry had made their dash too soon. The force moved on to Kassgunge yesterday, and found it entirely evacuated by the enemy.

We have still nothing later than your letter of the 4th: and the latest prior to that was of the 25th ultimo. I conclude you have been equally unfortunate in receiving our despatches. Communications with Cawnpore almost cut off.

The moment the Doab between us and you is quite clear and safe, we shall have a speedy income of above 20 lacs, it is hoped, on account of duty on salt, which is ready to be brought over our Customs line so soon as a passage eastward is opened out. This is a financial consideration of some consequence, which should be known to the Commander-in-Chief. Accumulation of Customs income.

All well to the North-West. The Puttiala force will soon be marching down the right bank of the Jumna, *via* Goorgaon and Muthra to Dholpore, and will be of use indirectly in its effect on our districts. Putiala force.

W. MUIR.

J. W. SHERER, ESQ., Cawnpore.

*P.S.*—E. A. Reade has mislaid the bill I proposed for restoring property to the status existing prior to the disturbances, with my memo. on the subject. The Chief Commissioner had ordered it to be sent down to the Supreme Government with his concurrence. Will you kindly ask Harington to send me up a copy of the memo. and of the draft bill? Proposals for restoring property.

W. M.

## CCXL.

*17th December* 1857. Thursday.

MY DEAR SHERER,—We are grievously disappointed at still hearing nothing from you, although private Cossids and Commissariat messengers, and our other spies sent without letters, now come from Cawnpore without difficulty. We cannot make out what is the cause of our getting no letters. . . .

Our spies and the Gwalior reporter tell us of some chastisement inflicted by our troops on the fugitives at Sheorajpoor.[1] But I conclude it was merely a scouring party, and not a regular move westwards.

Will you oblige us by bringing to the Commander-in-Chief's notice, that the Government of India have long destined a large amount of treasure for Agra; and that opportunity should be taken for sending up with the first available force as much of the treasure as possible? The drain on the North-West Treasuries, Suggestions as to sending up treasure.

[1] Town on Cawnpore road.

especially when troops move up from the east, and into Rajpootanah and the Punjab from the south, will be very serious, and without aid from Bengal very embarrassing.

Everything quite quiet to the North-West. I have heard nothing further from Colonel Seaton's Column. Rajpootanah seems to be settling down since the discomfiture of the Mundessore rebels by Durand's Column.

I trust the Commander-in-Chief received General Penny's communication. Troops are quite ready, under Sir J. Lawrence's instructions (by order of the Supreme Government), to advance on Rohilkhund the moment His Excellency can spare a couple of European Regiments.

W. Muir.

J. W. Sherer, Esq., Cawnpore.

*P.S.*—Colonel Becher is here; we expect Scindia over immediately. It will be a new era in our fast reviving prestige.

## CCXLI.

*18th December* 1857. Friday.

My Dear Sherer,—Yesterday evening I was rejoiced by again receiving one of your despatches, dated the 10th instant. We are all very glad that Outram maintains his position at Alum Bagh, and hope that the idea of temporarily abandoning Oudh altogether has been relinquished. I mentioned in one of my letters, which perhaps you may not have received, that we heard of the intended evacuation by a letter Lady Outram received from Sir James.

**Allygurh Column.** Everything continues quiet to the westward. The Allygurh Column was on the 16th at Suhawur, 12 miles east of Kassgunge; yesterday it was to advance on Putteealee, where the enemy are said to have been assembling. I conclude that there was prolonged fighting in that vicinity, as reports have come in from various quarters that heavy firing was heard in the direction of Kassgunge from 5 a.m. till 10 a.m. yesterday. The result must soon be known.

**Fighting in Central Doab. Action at Gungeree.** The following particulars regarding the action at Gungeeree may be of interest as explaining the unusual proportion of loss amongst the Carabineers and Hodson's Horse. It is from a letter of Sapte, who, with Colonel Farquhar and the little Boolundshuhur Column, had reached Gungeeree the day before.

On Monday morning Seaton's Column arrived at that place,

and encamped 2 miles in advance of Farquhar's. "About two hours after his arrival a large body of Cavalry suddenly appeared on some rising ground in front of his camp. The Carabineers, Hodson's Horse, and some Horse Artillery, got ready sharp and went at them and away they bolted, but a heavy fire was opened on our advancing troops from two 6-pounders and one 9-pounder, which the gallant Carabineers charged and took, but not without heavy loss. Three charges of grape were poured into them at about 150 yards, which told fearfully. Wardlaw, Hudson, and Wyse of Carabineers were all shot by musket shots. Head of 9th Lancers wounded by a shell, said to be mortally (no; he is doing well). Doyley, who charged with them, had a very narrow escape from being cut down, but his English hunting-cap saved him. Our total loss was about 12 killed and 50 wounded. The Carabineers lost about 25 horses killed and wounded out of 70! Hodson's Horse suffered too. The enemy lost between 400 and 500 killed—and their three guns which the Carabineers took. The two 6-pounders are the post guns of Shahjehanpoor, and the 9-pounder the last of the Bareilly Battery. As it has turned out, *our* move on Gungeeree was a good one, for it brought the rebels into the open, which they would not have done had they known of the proximity of Colonel Seaton's Army. Kassgunj was evacuated during the night, the rebels having fled towards Puttialee. We were ordered to halt here to-day, and to-morrow we retrace our steps towards Boolundshuhur. I have now recovered 60 guns in all, and hope I shall pick up some more in my wanderings. My own district, Boolundshuhur, has been perfectly quiet in my absence."

Furruckabad rebels discomfited.

Wardlaw, Hudson, and Wyse shot. Head, of 9th Lancers, wounded.

Kassgunge evacuated.

Sapte reports he has recovered sixty guns. Boolundshuhur quiet.

A letter, dated the 14th inst. from Deolee, reports all right in that direction. Neemuch is quite quiet; but the "Shahzada," with a party of the Mundessore fugitives, is supposed to have gone *via* Jalra Puttun in the Kotah territory. This, however, is uncertain.

Neemuch quiet.

The Deesa Column is expected to proceed towards Rajpootanah about Christmas.

Colonel Fraser has asked that the following statement, furnished by a native, of the supposed forces of Khan Buhadoor be made known to the Commander-in-Chief. He has 35 guns, of which 12 are 12-pounders, a few sixes and nines, and a great number very small ones of native make. His Infantry are estimated at 18,000; but by far the greater part are an undrilled rabble. Of 5000 Cavalry, 2000 are said to be fit for service; the remainder new levies. Of this force, 10,000 men and 8 guns are at Budaon, 5000 and 4 guns at Buheree, between

Detail of Khan Buhadoor's forces.

Bareilly and Nyneetal, 2000 and one gun at Meergunj, 5000 and 10 guns at Bareilly:—the rest scattered in detachments. But this must be received merely as a very loose estimate.

The dak with Nyneetal has been somewhat irregular of late. Kaladoongee attacked. Alexander, writing on the 7th, says that his post at Kaladoongee had been attacked by some mounted Insurgents, supposed to have been some of Ramsay's sowars who deserted in June last, and who had a spite against the Thanadar. They "killed the Thanadar and 3 others, and an advance vidette of my new Hindoo Cavalry," Alexander writes. "They have bolted without going against my Cavalry, who were unarmed on parade, about a mile from the Thannah. 200 of the Goorkhas are ordered down, but too late, I fear, to do any good." From a person Nawab of Rampore. who has lately come from Rampoor, Alexander learns "that the Nawab is still the object of the vilest abuse among the Pathans. So he cannot use them for us; and only keeps them, by gratifying their mercenary propensities, from going against us. The relief to him from an advance into Rohilkhund will be as great as to us. Judged with a due regard to the difficulties with which he has had constantly to contend, he should indeed deserve well of us, if he come out successful at the last, which indeed I hope he will." This is the concurrent opinion of all who are acquainted with the state of things in Rohilkhund.

I have a letter from Sir John Lawrence, dated the 15th. He says he has marched that day for Mooltan, where he hopes to be early next month to see Lady Lawrence off. He then returns to Lahore.

W. Muir.

J. W. Sherer, Esq., Cawnpore.

## CCXLII.

*19th December* 1857. Saturday.

My Dear Sherer,—The enclosed bulletin will give you the result of the firing referred to in my letter of yesterday. The Defeat of Furruckabad force at Putiala. discomfiture of the Furruckabad rebels at Puttialee, though strongly posted and protected by an entrenchment with 11 guns, has been most complete—600 killed.

The effect will be immense. Mynporie will probably be evacuated; at any rate the Column, if it (as we understand it will) advances there, will meet no serious opposition. And the rebels at Etawah will also be shaken. They form a detachment, you know, of the Furruckabad troops—two regiments, it is said, of Infantry, and a rissala of Cavalry, with 6 guns. From Mynporie the Column will be able to communicate with any force the Commander-in-Chief sends westward.

. . . . . . . .

W. MUIR.

J. W. SHERER, ESQ., Cawnpore.

. . . . . . . .

*P.S.*—The following is a copy of Reade's epitome of our financial operations for November.

"Cash balance for October, Rs. 4,29,590; for November, 9,73,180. Military expenditure larger than usual, owing to purchase of grain and stores for Cawnpore, and demurrage. Principal receipts, land revenue collections of Allygurh, Muttra, and Agra; one lac of rupees from Jyepoor received; no more will be required from that quarter." **Financial position of Agra.**

## CCXLIII.

*19th December* 1857. Saturday.

MY DEAR BEADON,—This is now about a month old, and rather out of date; but as my copyist had made a transcript of it along with other letters supposed to have miscarried, I think it is well to let it go.

The ransacking of unransomed houses by the Prize Agency has at length been stopped, I believe. With two months' license to dig and hunt for valuables, little can have been spared. **Prize Agency at Delhi.**

Sir John Lawrence is as much disinclined as any to involving the innocent indiscriminately with the guilty in punishment. But his tenure of Delhi is so very peculiar that he complains of a want of power to give effect to his wishes. It will be well when things there return to a more normal state. But it cannot be doubted that a large Military authority must be permitted in the City for some time to come; and a stringency of administration allowed,—especially in reference to the Mahomedan population,—in order to secure perfect security. A good idea has been started by Fraser of forming the space from the Palace (inclusive) to the Cashmere gate into the cantonment, clearing away the City to a little distance inland. This would give a healthy locality, and maintain the City well under command. You may like to see the enclosed from Ramchunder. The appeal has been attended to by Sir J. Lawrence. I merely send it to show the feeling at Delhi. As to the pension to Chimmun Lall's widow, this Government has moved Sir John to make an **Sir John Lawrence's views on Delhi.** **The pension to Chimmun Lall's widow.**

application; and I trust a liberal annuity will be allowed. It is a peculiar case. Chimmun Lall was held in great estimation by the people, and had a city practice. The King, when ill, used to send for him. The Government should mark its sense of the value it places upon a Christian servant, massacred as he was.

Charles Saunders, C.S.

Saunders' reply to the allegations of the *Friend of India* was forwarded early in the month by Bombay, and will soon, I trust, be in your hands. I am getting a copy prepared to send by Cossid. It is a complete vindication of himself in all respects, except perhaps in that of allowing Colonel Hogge to take the King's son out for a ride on his elephant. I think it is a matter of congratulation having at Delhi a man of so sound a judgment as Saunders; for it is not every man who could have resisted the popular cry for indiscriminate vengeance which rings through Delhi, and is re-echoed by the *Lahore Chronicle.*

Will you mention to Lord Canning that I have obtained four or five of the returns I called for before venturing to record my opinion on the point of violation being a frequent concomitant of the massacre of European females?[1] All the evidence that can be got is directly and strongly opposed to the tales that have been so industriously circulated on this head. Native opinion, which ought to be a good test, is universally and conclusively against them. I hope soon to put together the various opinions I have collected, and submit them with a memorandum for his Lordship.

I hope my letters to Sherer are again beginning to reach regularly. The siege and relief of Neemuch, and the rout of the Mundessore rebels, must have been events narrated at the time of the break in my correspondence. Rajpootana, excepting Kotah, is now quiet; and our late signal successes at Allygurh will be of great effect in the central Doab. Mynpoorie, I expect, will be immediately occupied without opposition by Seaton's Column.

Rajputana, excepting Kotah, now quiet.

There are still some two or three thousand Insurgents at Etawah, with 6 guns. But they are dependent on Furruckabad, and will hardly survive its fall. They will probably move off betimes, either into Bundelkhund, or more likely over the Ganges.

Furruckabad rebels still at Etawah.

Proposals for reinstatement of proprietors.

I trust a bill will soon be passed giving summary power to reinstate proprietors with compensation in possession. I sent a copy to Harington of a bill of this kind which I proposed, and which Fraser approved. But Reade has kept it by him so long

[1] See separate Report, *post.*—W. M.

that he has mislaid it. I have asked Harington to give me a copy—or I may submit to Fraser a new draft.

I should much like to see the disarming process universally carried out in the wake of restored peace. **Disarming.**

W. MUIR.

C. BEADON, ESQ., Calcutta.

## CCXLIV.[1]

*December 20th*, 1857. Sunday.

MY DEAR SIR,—I forward copy of two letters received for you from Sir J. Lawrence and Major Macpherson of the 16th inst. I will send the originals by another Cossid.

All is going on well to the North-West. The affair at Puttialee was most complete. The Insurgents lost 14 guns, and made off in such haste and confusion that they probably did not stop till they reached Furruckabad. **Putiala affair. Defeat of Furruckabad rebels.**

Yesterday Seaton's Column was to fall back on Kassgunj, with the view of taking the road to Mynpoorie, where it will, I trust, be able to open up communications with any troops the Commander-in-Chief may be despatching towards Furruckabad. I do not think there will be much, if any, opposition at Mynpoorie. At Etawah there are some 2000 troops, including a rissala of Cavalry; but the Infantry, at any rate, are new levies, and not worth much. They have 6 guns. At Furruckabad there will no doubt be some fighting. Bukht Khan commands the troops there. But I conclude Mr. Sherer is able to supply you with later information regarding Furruckabad than we could give you.

Will you oblige me by showing this letter to Mr. Sherer, for whom I have no further news of importance to-day, and also by giving him the enclosed copy of my letter to him of yesterday's date?

At Puttialee there was only one man on our side killed, and 2 or 3 wounded. This, coupled with the fact that the rebels had their guns playing on us for a length of time, is evidence that their Artillery was very badly served, and indeed we may hope that skilful artillerymen are now getting scarce on the Insurgents' side—a want they will not readily be able to supply.

W. MUIR.

GENERAL MANSFIELD,
Headquarters, Cawnpore.

[1] Handwriting of W. Lowe, C.S.

## CCXLV.

*21st December* 1857. Monday.

MY DEAR SHERER,—There is nothing new to-day. But the following particulars which Cocks gives regarding the affair at Puttialee will be of interest. The slaughter, he says, exceeds the estimate officially given. "I followed the enemy," he writes, "for upwards of two miles from Puttialee, and the bodies lay in heaps. We have had no loss to speak of—one of Hodson's men killed, and a few slightly wounded. Colonel Kinleside, Horse Artillery, won the victory, and the Cavalry followed it up right well. You can scarcely conceive such a complete affair. The Enemy's shoes, puggrees, and kummerbunds strewed the road for miles. Every gun-carriage and tent left. An elephant with silver howdah, and Hukeemjee (one of the Furruckabad chiefs), captured; the latter shot. I can hardly fancy their stopping until they reached Futtehgurh."

Putiala victory complete.

Colonel Kinleside, H.A.

Hukeemjee.

Colonel Seaton was to halt another day (19th) in consequence of a rumour, which, however, Cocks did not believe, that the Enemy intended to cross over from Rohilkhund. It is in the last degree improbable that the Insurgents would venture over while our Column is anywhere in the vicinity. Besides, Cocks understands that Khan Buhadoor's orders to the troops on the bank are that they should only watch, and if attacked fall back on Bareilly.

Khan Buhadoor.

From Puttialee the Column marches back to Kassgunge, as there is no bridge over the Kalee Nuddee lower down, and thence probably in 4 or 5 days to Mynpoorie, where I trust it will be able to communicate with the Commander-in-Chief's advanced force. Chalmers is having his Commissariat stores all ready. And there is a vast supply of carriage awaiting the first convoy both here and at Allygurh. The Column is looking forward to co-operate in the proceedings against Furruckabad.

Colonel Seaton's Column.

Ramsay writes from Nynee Tal on the 10th of December that the Bareilly troops are occupying the Terai and cutting off their supplies. A letter had, however, been received from the Resident at Nepaul, says Ramsay, "telling me that Jung Buhadoor has ordered his general, now encamped at Burmdeo, to give me assistance if we were in need. I immediately wrote off asking for a thousand Goorkhas, though I don't expect to get more than 600. We can muster as many Sepoys of our own, and 300 Cavalry, with 4 guns; and as soon as the Goorkhas come, we'll go at these scoundrels that have reduced us to such diffi-

The Terai.

Nepaul offers assistance.

culties, and soon open up our communications, and get in lots of provision." This clearing out of the Terai, which they will no doubt do easily, will be a great point; as otherwise they might take up strong positions, and attract the fugitive troops of Bareilly there also for shelter.

They are busy at Nynee Tal, or below it, getting ready the limbers, etc., for their 6-pounders, and will soon, they hope, be able to take the offensive again. But Ramsay's hand, I fear, will hardly allow him to join personally in the attack. The direct dak with us is cut off, and sent round by Mussoorie.

W. MUIR.

J. W. SHERER, ESQ., Cawnpore.

*P.S.*—J. C. Wilson's account of the Puttialee affair is interesting. It is as follows, dated the 18th: "We marched yesterday at 5 o'clock a.m. from Suhawar, and we were told on the road that the rebel force would be found at this place. About three miles short of Puttialee we halted, and grog was served out. The line was formed. Horse Artillery on both flanks—on the right the 1st Fusiliers, then the 3rd Europeans—Seikhs Muzhubees. The Cavalry, except a strong body in the front on the right, was kept in the rear to act as circumstances might require. The rebel force was commanded by Ahmud Yar Khan, the Governor of the Western part of the Futtehgurh district, and Mohsin Allee, the Governor of the Eastern part of the Futtehgurh district, both Governors being in the service of the Nawab Raees of Futtehgurh. Their Artillery consisted of 12 guns, and the heavy 9 and 6-pounder iron guns opened upon us at a great distance. Our Artillery proceeded to the front, and when they got into range they opened upon the enemy's guns. The Infantry gradually drew on, and by the time our 3 eighteen-pounders were placed in position the Staff and the Horse Artillery gave a cheer and galloped into the enemy's camp, which was left standing. Then began the chase, and the result was that the 12 guns were captured, tents, ammunition, etc., and some 700 or 800 men were killed. Four elephants were a portion of the plunder."

**Wilson's description of the Putiala affair.**

**Ahmud Yar Khan and Mohsin Ally command the enemy.**

**700 or 800 men killed.**

## CCXLVI.

*22nd December* 1857. Tuesday.

MY DEAR SHERER,—

. . . . . . . . .

General Mansfield's of the 14th came in to-day,[1] with one from Jackson (of whose accident I am sorry to hear) to

[1] Dak from Cawnpore = 8 days.—W. M.

Raikes, C.S.

Raikes, saying that he had nominated him to the Commander-in-Chief to accompany His Excellency. Raikes, however, has left for England. The Commander-in-Chief could not get a better man for the purpose than A. H. Cocks. I may be able to tell you whom Fraser has fixed on before closing this letter. We were glad to learn from General Mansfield's letter that an early movement is contemplated on Furruckabad, and that a smaller Column simultaneously sweeps round by the Jumna to Mynpoorie. This will effectually clear out Etawah, so that when Furruckabad falls the entire Doab will be free of insurgents. I enclose copy of a note sent in reply to General Mansfield by a separate Cossid, who has been directed to proceed direct to Headquarters.

A. H. Cocks, C.S.

Measures against Furruckabad and Etawah.

Slaughter at Putiala.

The slaughter at Puttialee was very great. Colonel Seaton says, to be moderate he has put it at 700, though he thinks it must have been nearer 900.

From Kassgunge they send the captured guns, sick and wounded, on to Allygurh. The Column will probably reach Eta to-morrow, and be there joined by the convoy from Allygurh. It will then proceed to Mynpoorie, and there await news or instructions from the Headquarters.

Effect of Putiala victory.

The effect of this signal chastisement has been most decisive. The fugitives did not stop anywhere till they got close to Furruckabad. Allygurh, Mhow, Shumshabad, Kaimgunj, all evacuated by the rebels; and our people sending for orders to re-establish Thannahs.

A combined movement from the Rohilkhund side had evidently been determined on, as the insurgents and rabble actually crossed over on the 18th to this bank, in ignorance evidently of the discomfiture of their confederates, for on the 19th they hastily retreated to the other side.

Mackenzie (8th L.C.), Gowan, and Daniell, C.S., have been posted on the Ganges to facilitate the escape of some more refugees believed to be in Rohilkhund.

Cracroft Wilson collects documents.

The two Governors of the East and West Furruckabad (Mohsin Ally Khan and Ahmud Yar Khan) were in the engagement at Puttialee, and all their records have been seized. Wilson says these papers will be invaluable to him, as they implicate hundreds in the rebellion. He is getting lists made out. He has made a good suggestion to the Chief of the Staff, that all documents, English or vernacular, found upon rebels, or taken in their camps or houses, should be carefully preserved. This should be mentioned to General Mansfield in case Wilson's letter may have miscarried.

The Postmaster of Moradabad (a Baboo) writes from that place to say that our troops attacked the rebels near Kaladoongee, below Nynee Tal, on the 10th inst.; killed 70, and dispersed the rest, with the loss of only two on the British side. This of course needs confirmation. But Wilson says he knows from independent sources that an attack was intended about that date; and, as I mentioned yesterday, Ramsay intended to take the offensive soon. **Rebels beaten near Kaladoongee.**

I was glad to see by an incidental remark on one of John Power's letters that the telegraph as well as the dak was open from Cawnpore to Calcutta. We were afraid that it had been injured by the Gwalior rebels. **Telegraph open from Cawnpore to Calcutta.**

W. MUIR.

J. W. SHERER, ESQ., Cawnpore.

Poor Mrs. Kirk (widow of Dr. Kirk, killed at Gwalior) is anxious to have the following message communicated to Calcutta for her sister, Mrs. Ommaney. Will you help her? "From Agra, Mrs. Innes—To Calcutta, Dr. Macpherson. Tell Mrs. Ommaney from Lucknow to write to Mrs. Kirk at Agra." **Widow of Dr. Kirk.**

I have written, by Fraser's desire, to General Mansfield that the services of Harvey can be placed at his disposal; that Wilson, as Commissioner for hunting down the Mutineers, might accompany the Camp; or that, if H. E. prefers it, A. H. Cocks could be deputed with the Army. **Harvey, C.S. Cracroft Wilson, C.S. A. H. Cocks, C.S.**

## CCXLVII.

*22nd December* 1857. Tuesday.

MY DEAR SIR,—Your letter of the 14th to the Chief Commr. has been duly received. I send this brief acknowledgment, as I am forwarding a Cossid to Captain Bruce. **Recounts general position in N.W.P.**

Colonel Seaton's Column was still at Puttialee on the 20th, and was likely to remain there another day; it would then fall back on Kassgunge, and move to Eta, sending the captured guns, sick and wounded, to Allygurh—and being joined at Eta by the carriage, stores, etc., now at Allygurh. He would then move on direct on Mynpoorie, which he may reach probably from the 26th to the 28th. He has been directed by Colonel Fraser to halt at Mynpoorie till he hears from the Commander-in-Chief.

The carriage and stores which are ready here will wait for further news of His Excellency's movements and wishes. The Chief Commissioner thinks it better not to risk their passage direct to Mynpoorie while their flank might be threatened by the Mutineers at Etawah. But if His Excellency desired he could send the carriage by a détour *via* Hatrass and Secundra Rao, round by Eta to Mynpoorie.

It is, however, almost certain that Etawah will shortly be evacuated by the insurgents, on their hearing of the discomfiture of their comrades at Puttialee and the advance of Seaton upon Mynpoorie—certainly on the onward movement of the Column, which, we learn from your letter under acknowledgment, His Excellency is sending *via* Akberpoor and the left bank of the Jumna. In that case, of course, the direct road to Mynpoorie will be quite free for the passage of carriage and stores.

**Repair of telegraph line.** I wish we had wire to begin the telegraph. But every inch has been expended in endeavouring to complete the line to Delhi, and yet there is a gap of 10 miles.

**Kotah.** All is well Westwards. In Rajpootana, the only place where active measures are at present required is Kotah, where the Durbar troops will need chastisement for their atrocious proceedings in the murder of Major Burton.

We expect Scindia over in a day or two to pay a visit.

W. Muir.

To General Mansfield, Cawnpore.

**Mr. Raikes.** *P.S.*—Mr. Raikes has left Agra to proceed to England on medical certificate. But Colonel Fraser says "that the services of Mr. Harvey, Commr., can be put at the disposal of His Excellency; that Mr. J. C. Wilson has been appointed Commr. for the detection and punishment of rebels and Mutineers, which duty he could carry on very well in Camp; and that it is believed that he would also be found most useful from his knowledge of native character and of the country; and finally, that should His Excellency prefer, Cocks, an officer of high character and attainments, can (if preferred) be put at his disposal."

## CCXLVIII.

*23rd December* 1857. **Wednesday.**

My Dear Sherer,—I enclose a copy of a letter to General Mansfield.

There is nothing new. But there is a rumour of some unpleasant anticipations in Rohilkhund. What the exact nature of the apprehension is I do not exactly make out. But it would seem as if some attack from Bareilly were expected on

Moradabad, and other proceedings which imperil the Nawab of Rampoor. His whole soldiery, you know, are composed of very inflammable matter, and any movement of the kind would place him in a position of great delicacy and probably of peril. On the other hand, our Nynee Tal force is becoming stronger, and would probably repel any attack which approached the Terai; and Colonel Seaton's successes should have a good moral influence. **Moradabad in danger.**

It cannot, however, be doubted that the establishment of any hostile body at Moradabad would render our reacquisition of Rohilkhund a more difficult task than it otherwise would have been. And it is an object to expedite as much as possible the proceedings which may be in contemplation for its reoccupation.

W. MUIR.

J. W. SHERER, ESQ., Cawnpore.

*P.S.*—A telegraphic message has just been received from Mr. Cocks, at Kassgunge, of yesterday's date. They were to remain over on the 23rd in order to mature some police arrangements, and then move on to Eta. Cocks' information was that Mynpoorie was evacuated. I think, however, if it had been we should have heard of it here.

Mr. Wilson expected to have over by the 22nd 20 more Christians from Rohilkhund, 7 of them Europeans. **Rescue of Christian refugees.**

There must have been some Gwalior Contingent men in the affair of the 14th at Gungeree, as Major Eld picked up the Dak Bungalow book of Bhudwas, the last entry of which was that some officers left without payment, as they were fleeing for their lives, and carried off some spoons, etc., or more probably it might have been brought by some of the Mhow force after the battle of the 10th of October.

## CCXLIX.

AGRA, *23rd December* 1857. Wednesday.

MY DEAR SIR,—I send herewith the copy of a letter which I despatched to you yesterday. I have no fresh intelligence to communicate. But the Chief Commissioner has made a slight alteration in the orders to the Allygurh Column. He thinks it safer that the carriage should not join it at Eta, but should wait at Allygurh until Mynpoorie has actually been taken possession of by Colonel Seaton. This will be a delay in the arrival of the convoy at Mynpoorie of some four or five days;—but it will in all probability be there as soon as the road onwards is sufficiently clear for it to be escorted to Cawnpore. W. MUIR.

TO GENERAL MANSFIELD,
Chief of the Staff, Headquarters.

Mr. F. Williams, C.S.

*P.S.*—Colonel Fraser desires me to say that for the Army which will proceed into *Rohilkhund*, Mr. F. Williams is the Civil Officer who will accompany. He has been nominated to the Commissionership of that Province.

Sir John Lawrence desired to arrange for operations in Rohilkhund.

I subjoin extract of a letter from myself to Mr. Sherer, which His Excellency the Commander-in-Chief may like to see. It is quite possible that the apprehensions referred to may be unfounded. His Excellency has, I conclude, received a communication which I forwarded by various opportunities from Sir J. Lawrence, saying that, with the addition of two European regiments, a force could be organised from Delhi to proceed against Rohilkhund. Sir John had been desired to arrange for that object by the Governor-General. W. M.

## CCL.

*24th December* 1857. Thursday.

MY DEAR SHERER,—Nothing from you of date later than the 10th. No Cossid has returned from Cawnpore these two days.

. . . . . . .

B. Sapte, C.S.

Boolundshuhur quiet.

Sapte writes from Ramghat; he had been absent from his district (Boolundshuhur) with Colonel Farquhar's force for above a fortnight. They found all perfectly quiet on their return. This says a great deal for the disposition of the people. While at Gungeree, there were no troops whatever in the large section of the Doab lying between Allygurh and Meerut.

Sapte was sinking or bringing to this bank the boats at the several ghats. At one place they were fired on by matchlockmen from the opposite bank, and had to bring their guns to bear on the rebels. A party, under cover of our fire, went over the river to secure the boats, and at this demonstration the whole of the insurgents, who had before been loudly challenging us to cross, ran off.

Nawab of Furruckabad.

Cocks writes to say that the report of the Rajah of Mynpoorie having fled is not corroborated; but our messengers state that the Nawab of Furruckabad has withdrawn the Regiment which he lent him. This he did immediately on hearing of the defeat at Putteealee. He has also sent, we hear, four Regiments with guns to guard the passage of the Kalee Nuddee at the suspension bridge on the Cawnpore road. They are the fugitive Delhi Corps. The Seetapoor Regiments and horse are retained in Furruckabad, and all the city gates are guarded by Artillery. **Furruckabad.**

A correspondent of the *Delhi Gazette* states that sentence of death has been passed on the Nawab of Jhujjur, and that he was to be hanged yesterday afternoon. **Nawab of Jhujjur.**

W. MUIR.

J. W. SHERER, ESQ., Cawnpore.

*P.S.*—Can you in any way get us lists of the *Uncovenanted* portion of the Lucknow garrison? The greatest anxiety prevails here regarding the fate of many; and Mr. Montgomery has written to me also from Lahore to do all I can to get him information. We should have complete lists both of the Covenanted and the Uncovenanted. A letter from Deolee reports all continuing quiet there. The news of our success at Cawnpore was received by the natives there with pleasure, but without the old feelings of the Delhi days, that anything affecting themselves depended on the result. **Deoli quiet.**

Sir R. Hamilton and Sir H. Rose were expected at Mhow on the 15th. **Sir R. Hamilton. Sir H. Rose.**

A portion of the Hyderabad Contingent is located at Mundessore.

Everything is so tranquil that Captain Macdonald was about to ride into Nusseerabad, 60 miles, for Xmas, with a single attendant to point out the road.

## CCLI.

AGRA, *25th December* 1857. Friday.

MY DEAR SHERER,—Letters came in last night up to the 19th, but still none from you.

I have a letter from Durand dated the 15th inst. It says his return to Mhow had enabled Holkar to disarm his regular Cavalry (chiefly Rampore Mussulmans) and Infantry. By Durand's arrangement, Holkar did this himself, though our Column was at hand ready to have gone to his assistance had coercion been necessary. **Durand. Holkar disarms his troops.**

Sir R. Hamilton was expected with Sir H. Rose on the 16th. Major Rickards has returned to Sehore. **Major Rickards.**

Seaton's Column will reach Mynpoory on Sunday, or, if able to make a forced march, to-morrow. **Seaton's Column.**

Wale's Horse have reached Allygurh. I do not know the strength. It is to take on the immense convoy of carriage, establishments, and supplies at once towards Mynpoory. One of **Wale's Horse.**

the private letters of the 19th mentioned that the Column for Etawah had marched from Cawnpore that morning. This will open up the way for our carriage, etc., being sent towards you.

. . . . . . . . .

Christian refugees from Rohilkhund.

The 20 Christians from Rohilkhund reached this side all safe; and another, a Mr. Erith, is expected.

Scindia comes in this afternoon.

W. MUIR.

Maharajah Scindia visits Agra.

*P.S.*—Scindia has just come in. The salute is firing.

## CCLII.

### TEL. MESSAGE.

FROM W. MUIR, AGRA,

TO G. F. EDMONSTONE, FOR. SECY., CALCUTTA.

HOLKAR successfully disarmed his soldiery, Horse and Foot, on 15th. Sir R. Hamilton expected next day. Scindia has arrived here on a visit.

## CCLIII.

### EXTRACT OF ABOVE LETTER TO GENERAL MANSFIELD,

Temper of Scindia's troops.

Adding:—"Your letter to the Chief Commr., dated the 18th inst., has just been received. Major Macpherson, the Governor-General's Agent, will be consulted about the Mahratta Horse from Scindia, but Scindia is as badly off as ourselves. I should say, far worse off for reliable troops. There must be a great disarming at Gwalior, so soon as a British force can be brought into the vicinity."

W. M.

## CCLIV.

*26th December* 1857. Saturday.

Scindia received in Durbar at Agra.

MY DEAR SHERER,—No news of any kind to-day. The Government is beginning to resume its functions, for the Chief Commissioner received Scindia to-day in Durbar style. Scindia was near an hour beyond his time, but the excuse given by Macpherson was so fine a compliment that it disarmed criticism. The Maharajah, during the past six months, has not had a single night of quiet sleep. Last night, for the first time, he slept soundly in the security of the British Capital—so soundly that nobody dared awake him, and Macpherson found him asleep when he went to fetch him to the Durbar!

Everything quiet to the north-west, and also to the south-west;—excepting Kotah, where the disaffected Mussulman troops and refugees, etc., are said to be collecting revenue preparatory, it is supposed, to their flight northward. They may possibly make for Rohilkhund or Oudh. Unrest in Kotah.

W. MUIR.

J. W. SHERER, ESQ., Cawnpore.

*P.S.*—Scindia says he feels so comfortable and happy here that he is inclined to stay on and send Dinkur back to manage Gwalior! Maharajah Scindia.

## CCLV.

*26th December* 1857. Saturday.

MY DEAR SIR,—

. . . . . . .

Will you kindly inform General Grant, if he is near you, that his horses and servants, with Capt. Hamilton's horses, are all safe here? They had a narrow escape from Etawah, where they were taken by mistake of the servants.

Colonel Seaton's Column is believed to have been at Eta on Thursday the 23rd; it will be at Mynpoorie, if all has gone well, to-morrow, I believe. Colonel Seaton's Column.

I have consulted with Major Macpherson about the Mahratta Horse for Cawnpore; he fears Scindia is quite unable at present to help in this respect. He has two rebellious vassals on his hands, and his troops at Gwalior are a considerable portion of them not trustworthy, and will have to be disarmed. Temper of Scindia's troops.

W. MUIR.

To GENERAL MANSFIELD, Headquarters.

## CCLVIII.

*28th December* 1857. Monday.

MY DEAR SHERER,—Yesterday I acknowledged the receipt of your letter of the 19th, but had no news for you.

To-day a letter has been received from Capt. Macdonald at Nusseerabad saying that the "Raj Troops" at Oudeypoor have mutinied. A private letter from Neemuch, dated the 22nd inst., contained the information. Macdonald says there are Mutiny of Oudeypore troops.

three thousand of these men at Neembhera, and a considerable number at Jahazpoor near Deolie, who are likely to follow the example of their brethren. As yet we have had no further corroboration of this news. If the Mutiny has been an open and decisive one, the rebels will probably act in co-operation with the Kotah insurgents. Poorbeas are believed to be numerous in the Oudeypore service.

There is stated to have been no British officer at Oudeypoor.

We are in hourly expectation of news of the occupation of Mynpoorie. The post cart runs to Shekoabad—40 miles, and the horses are all ready at villages near the Chowkies to run all the way to Mynpoorie the moment the road is clear. We have heard of Colonel Walpole's Column only as far as Bhagneypoor.

Colonel Walpole's Column.

The insurgents still hold Etawah.

Roorkee.

Baird Smith, writing from Roorkee on the 26th, says that, "excepting an occasional dacoitee raid from across the water on police chokies, we are quiet enough here. Though I have accepted, as a *possible* event, a passage of the rascals to this side in force, and made such arrangements as I can to provide against it, yet it has always seemed to me, and seems to me now, an extremely improbable one—at the same time, there can be no doubt that Moozuffernugger is thoroughly disorganised and ready to kick up a row on no great amount of temptation, so I will be very glad when inaction ceases to be considered expedient, and we can have our posts on the left instead of the right bank of the Ganges. As we drive rascaldom back, its influence on our own people disappears, but till we do so I am quite prepared to hear of night surprises and the like, as the natural price we pay for our temporary weakness. It won't last long now, however, I hope."

Mozuffernugger thoroughly disorganised.

Colonel Seaton's Column.

A message has just come in from Colonel Seaton, dated Mynpoorie, yesterday afternoon; it came round by Allygurh and thence by telegraph.

Affair at Mynpoorie.

On their approach to Mynpoorie, about a mile to the west, the enemy was found posted behind some high trees. As we advanced he opened with 4 guns. Colonel Seaton on this sent the Horse Artillery and Cavalry by a flank movement to the right, following with the Infantry and heavy guns. The insurgents, seeing their way back to the City intercepted, soon began to retreat. We took all their guns, 6 in number, and cut up 250. None reported killed on our side.

Our mail carts will now forthwith begin to run to Mynpoorie. They run all the way from Allygurh to Mynpoorie, and we have material for setting them up immediately in the rear of any advancing column;—this with reference to a request to have a horse (saddle) post established—we are far ahead of that. Mynpoorie road opened.

W. MUIR.

J. W. SHERER, ESQ., Cawnpoor.

## CCLX.

*29th December* 1857. Tuesday.

MY DEAR SHERER,—Your letter of the 23rd reached last night. Many thanks. It is pleasant returning to the normal state of getting a reply within a fortnight. In another fortnight I hope the post will only take a day. Communications improving.

We have had letters from Mynpoorie of yesterday's date. The Rajah had escaped, no one knew exactly where; some said towards Etawah, but more likely towards Furruckabad, unless (which perhaps is the most probable) he contemplated a flight into Bundelkhund, where his family is. Col. Seaton had given orders for the town not to be plundered, but it was found impossible to enforce their observance. He proposed moving on towards Bhowgaon on the 31st—with what object is not stated. But as Colonel Fraser is anxious to cover the convoy, he has directed the Column to remain at Mynpoorie till further orders, unless Col. Seaton should have other instructions from the Commander-in-Chief. The Rajah of Mynpoorie escaped. Mynpoorie plundered.

A further letter from Nusseerabad, dated the 26th inst., states that communications from Deesa corroborate the mutiny at Oudeypoor. The troops at Jehazpoor had not up to that time displayed any mutinous symptoms.

Regarding Kotah, Capt. Macdonald gives the following as the result of inquiries instituted at Deolee. "It appears that at Kotah there are now about 7000 men, collected from different parts; amongst them 1500 Mundessore rebels; they are said to have 32 guns outside of their cantonments—4 or 6 on a Boorj, in which they keep their magazine, and 2 before one of the gates of the City. The Rajah is in his palace guarded by his Nujeebs, who do not number more than 200. The rebels are pressing the Seths and wealthy men for money." Affairs at Kotah.

W. MUIR.

J. W. SHERER, ESQ., Cawnpore.

## CCLXII.

*31st December* 1857. Thursday.

My Dear Sir,—We have private letters from your Camp up to the 27th at Arroul, and are hopeful that by this time the Insurgents, who seem to have contemplated some opposition at the bridge over the Kalee Nuddee, have met with a severe chastisement from His Excellency.

Chief Commissioner asks that Mynpoorie be occupied in strength.

The Chief Commissioner is desirous that the Commander-in-Chief should be aware of his anxiety that Mynpoorie should be occupied in strength, so as to be able to put a detachment at Etawah. Furruckabad will, no doubt, immediately fall into His Excellency's hands, and be garrisoned. With the three points held,—Etawah, Mynpoorie, and Furruckabad,—our Exchequer will soon be replenished. An area yielding a land revenue of between 50 and 60 lacs will be secured. The greater part of the instalments which fell due in May and June, as well as the Revenue payable from the autumn harvest, will be at once demandable, and (as experience has proved elsewhere) be speedily realised on the restoration of quiet and security. Facilities for the transit of salt, from which, as I had occasion to mention before, a very large revenue will be collected, will also be partially provided, although not fully until the passage of the Jumna is rendered secure by the reduction of Bundelkhund. I need not refer to the importance of these financial questions, considering the immense drain there will shortly be on our western treasuries from the advance of European Regiments.

Large revenue expected.

Chief Commissioner issues instructions for preventing plundering.

The Chief Commissioner has felt it his duty to issue instructions in the Gazette holding the Commanding officers of detachments responsible for preventing, as far as lies in their power, the plundering and destruction of villages where that course may not have been justified and directed in consequence of opposition or rebellious proceedings. Apart from all other considerations, the plunder and destruction of villages will affect our future sources of revenue. Col. Fraser has desired me to mention the subject, feeling confident that His Excellency will promote his views on this important point by every means in his power.

W. Muir.

General Mansfield,
Chief of the Staff of
H.E. the Commander-in-Chief.

*P.S.*—Colonel Fraser having just heard, from what he considers reliable native information, that Etawah was occupied two days ago by Brigadier Walpole, and believing the Mynpoorie road to be now perfectly safe, has determined on starting our immense convoy to Mynpoorie on the 2nd. He expects that it will reach its destination about the 8th proximo.

W. M.

## CCLXIII.

31*st December* 1857. Thursday.

MY DEAR SHERER,—No further news from Rajpootana. From Muthra we hear that a small body of Horse and Foot, 200 or 300 in number, have been committing some depredations in the southern parts of Goorgaon. They may be a remnant of the Joudpoor rebels. They are said to find shelter in some Ulwar villages. We must be prepared to find light bands of marauders in various parts of the country. Our organised police horse will be of service in their suppression. **Marauders in Goorgaon.**

Besides this, all is quiet to the north-west.

. . . . . . .

Mynpoorie news you will get, no doubt, more full and earlier from Mynpoorie itself. The Chowhans are in great alarm throughout the district, feeling that they have compromised themselves by the support of Rajah Tej Singh. Cocks' measures are judicious, and will no doubt prove successful. He is issuing a proclamation for all to return, or to consider themselves offenders against the State. Tej Singh is to be proclaimed a traitor, and Rao Bhowanee Singh installed in the dignity of Rajah. This will, I think, bring them round. **Chowhans in alarm.** **Tej Singh proclaimed traitor.** **Rao Bhowani Singh created Rajah.**

You will hear, of course, of Hodson's deputation yesterday with a hundred horse from Mynpoorie, to open communications with the Commander-in-Chief's force. Colonel Seaton has also sent back a detachment to guard the convoy, which must by this time be nearing Mynpoorie under charge of Wale's Horse. Seaton himself has marched to-day to Bhowgaon, and sent on a party of Horse to watch the bridge at Mudunpoor over the Kalee Nudee. **Hodson.** **Seaton's Column.**

In reply to the Financial Secretary's letter, pray telegraph to Mr. Lushington that "the accountant promises to have the accounts completed by the 15th of next month, and despatched about the 20th (January), by which time it is hoped the post will be able to carry the mass of papers. The abstracts kept open to the last moment in hope of receiving some accounts yet missing." **Accounts.**

Normal condition of Mynpoorie district.

Cocks, after a ride of 24 miles, says that the country about Mynpoorie is looking as of old, excepting the Chowkies and Electric Telegraph Posts. The harvest, he says, promises to be abundant; and the villagers came out in crowds to welcome him. "They had not seen a white face for eight months."

Sufferings of those who sided with Government.

I trust you are getting rapidly on in the establishment of order. The people should now be able to see that they will not be again abandoned to Insurgent forces, and ought therefore to co-operate willingly. They had an excuse before, for nothing has exceeded the horrors of those wretched localities where we have been obliged to come and go over and again. Our partisans, of course, paid dearly for their signs of friendship towards us. But all that, so far as the Doab is concerned, is, God be praised, fairly over now.

W. Muir.

J. W. Sherer, Esq., Cawnpoor.

## CCLXIV.

Agra, 1st *January* 1858. Friday.

My Dear Sir,—

. . . . . . . .

Agra garrison cannot afford detachments.

If, as Mr. Cocks tells us, Captain Hodson led His Excellency to understand that the Agra garrison could detach parties to hold Mynpoorie or Etawah, he must have acted on wrong information. From the weak force here it is all that the Chief Commissioner is able to do to hold Allygurh.

W. Muir.

General Mansfield,
Chief of the Staff of H.E. the C.-in-C.

## CCLXV.

1st *January* 1858. Friday.

Hodson's ride.

My Dear Sherer,—Nothing new from the North-West. We have letters from Cocks at Bewar of yesterday's date, mentioning Hodson's brave ride with 100 horse to the Commander-in-Chief's camp, of which you have of course heard. He came across the fugitive Etawah force and had a narrow escape, losing one of his Sowars. He was charmed with the imposing appearance of the Force and the look of the Highlanders; but he told the Commander-in-Chief what was a stretch of imagination, viz.,—that we could garrison Mynpoorie, and I suppose Etawah, ourselves;—this, considering that we hold Allygurh from our weak garrison, was rather overstepping the mark. The tendency of the separate Brigade (as they cannot at present cut out any independent work for themselves) is *towards* the Commander-in-Chief, as at the Headquarters there will be, for some time to come, prospect of distinction. I fear, accordingly, that both Mynpoorie and Etawah will be again denuded of troops, and unsafe for our officers. At neither place have the troops been long enough to probe the nests of fanatics and rebels hatched during the long prevalence of the Insurgent rule; and unless our officers are supported by some military display, such persons might reappear and have their revenge.

**Civil officers require support.**

Dunlop says of things in Meerut, that "we have never collected a *kist* so fully, promptly, and easily as the last one (*i.e.* the Khurreef instalments). We have already six lacs of it, and the whole will come in during January, excepting that of a few bad villages by Dusna and the places destroyed by Goojurs in Mouana." I hope you will soon (I don't see why you should not) be able to tell the same story. The fact is, that wherever our authority is re-established, it is so in an incomparably stronger form than before.

**Prompt collection of revenue in Meerut.**

Dunlop does not anticipate any attack from Bijnour, excepting small predatory bands, which will not cease till we cross the Ganges.

W. MUIR.

J. W. SHERER, ESQ., Cawnpoor.

## CCLXVI.

*2nd January* 1858. Saturday.

MY DEAR SHERER,—As the dak of the 30th has come in from Cawnpoor, of the 29th from Allahabad, and the 26th from Calcutta, I shall for the present suspend our expensive Cossid system, and hope that we may wash our hands of it for ever.

**Cossid system suspended.**

Sir R. Hamilton is now endeavouring to reopen direct dak communication with us, and I have a letter from him dated the 23rd ultimo. I trust very soon the Horse dak, etc., will be running in that direction too.

**Sir R. Hamilton.**

I wish you were in the Commander-in-Chief's camp; we can get nobody to write to us from it. Colonel Becher, who left Allygurh with the Convoy for Mynpoorie, etc., had heard of the Commander-in-Chief having halted to depute Windham to blow up the Futtia Raja's "Palace." It is a pity he halts for so petty an object; our great want now is the reduction of Furruckabad, and a speedy advance into Rohilkhund.

Raikes. Raikes is anxious to throw up his leave and join the Commander-in-Chief's camp.

W. MUIR.

Convoy started. Our convoy started this morning,—the lines of hackeries seemed endless: from early morning till 10 or 11 o'clock they were moving along in double line.

J. W. SHERER, Cawnpore.

## CCLXVII.

*4th January* 1858. Monday.

MY DEAR SIR,—

. . . . . . . .

All is well to the west.

Allan Hume, C.S. Mr. Hume is on his way to occupy Etawah, but without any military force but 50 Sikhs. He will not be able to do much in the way of authority and retribution.

Establishment of Police. As to the establishment of a Police, as urged in your letter, we are doing what we can,—but it is little more than 2½ months since the Delhi column, by beating the Mhow Mutineers, enabled us to move freely about outside. Since then a good deal has been done in getting up horse and foot police; and notwithstanding local necessities, Colonel Fraser offered the Commander-in-Chief 300 horse—part of our Police. But since the Native army has clean swept away everything, it will take some time to work up something to take its place, and I do not see how officers in Mr. Hume's place, for example, can get on for a time without the detachment of some of His Excellency's troops to places like Etawah, which were formerly held by Sepoy detachments.

Troops required to support Civil officers.

W. MUIR.

CAPTAIN BRUCE.

## CCLXVIII.

4 *January* 1858. Monday.

MY DEAR SHERER,—

. . . . . . . .

Etawah. Hume has gone to Etawah, but he has only 50 Sikhs with him; and Walpole has gone, as you know, to Mynpoorie. It is a pity some detachment was not left at Etawah. But Hume will, I expect, be well supported by loyal Talookdars; and if, as he expects, he finds things (not) unfavourable, will go on to occupy the City. Our officers, however, should return to their stations with more prestige than that; and though Hume may be able to hold his own, and get in some revenue, he will not be able to do much in the way of authority and retribution. Civil officers should have military support.

Cocks is all right at Mynpoorie, as Walpole has left a European Regiment there. Cocks finds it somewhat difficult to get supplies for the immense convoy from Allygurh, and he will find it more so when ours reaches him. I said, I think, in a former letter, that it took from early morning to 10 or 11 to cross, but the fact is, the carts, etc., were crossing in a continuous line over the bridge of boats till near 4 p.m.! Cocks says, "between the plunder which has been carried on by the enemy and ourselves, it is very difficult to quiet the apprehensions of the people." But things will soon settle if the Mutineers keep, as I have no doubt they will, north of the Ganges. Cocks at Mynpoorie. Large convoy down country.

All perfectly quiet and tranquil to the west.

W. MUIR.

J. W. SHERER, ESQ.

## CCLXIX.

6 *January* 1858. Wednesday.

MY DEAR SIR,—Colonel Fraser has, I think, already reported the attempted descent upon Boolundshuhur by the Rohilkhund rebels, on receiving telegraphic information of the same. We have now received Mr. Sapte's letter. It is dated the 4th. He says that on the previous day the rebels attempted to cross at Anoopshahur, but were driven back. "We move out towards Anoopshahur to-night. I hear they are also collecting opposite Ramghat," which is some miles farther down the river. Mr. Sapte accordingly requested Major Eld if possible to move out from Allygurh towards Atroulee, in order to check the rebels at the latter ghat. He adds that the enemy had brought down guns to the ghat and were firing across. Attack on Boolundshuhur from Rohilkhund. B. Sapte, C.S. Major Eld.

Major Eld, writing from his camp in the interior of the Allygurh district, in a letter dated yesterday, expresses his intention of starting for Allygurh this day, and of being at Atroulee to-morrow.

I do not know exactly how many men either Colonel Farquhar (commanding in the Boolundshuhur district) or Major Eld can bring into the field—not more, however, I think, than 500 or 600 at the outside. The march eastward of the two

Columns (Grant's and Seaton's) has of course greatly weakened the available forces in the Meerut Division, and any incursion from the opposite bank would have a most agitating effect upon the Doab. It is in the last degree improbable that the pusillanimous and ill-furnished troops of Rohilkhund could effect a lodgment on this bank; but their attempts, and their reported intentions, have a very harassing effect.

In addition to the military reasons for the early occupation of the western portion of Rohilkhund, which must be under the consideration of the Commander-in-Chief, there is one to which Lt.-Col. Baird Smith has just called my attention in a letter dated Roorkee the 4th inst. He says that unless something is soon done for the reoccupation of western Rohilkhund he believes our capacity to give cover to the troops will be seriously affected, for it "essentially depends on the reopening of the Patlee Doon forest," to the north of Bijnore. "We can get no timber fit for barracks anywhere else." Colonel B. Smith, as Director of the Ganges Canal and Controller of the Roorkee workshops, has the charge of the forest in these parts, and is the highest authority on the subject.

*Baird Smith anxious to secure timber for new barracks.*

*Patlee Doon.*

*Major Ramsay's force.*

Major Ramsay, Commissioner of Kumaon, is ready to commence operations for clearing the Terai, which would otherwise no doubt afford dangerous shelter to the fugitive troops. He has 1000 foot—viz., 600 of the 66th, 250 Nepaul Goorkhas, and 150 of his own levies. He speaks well of the whole. He is badly off for cavalry. There are 300 newly raised horse, but as yet only 50 are fit for use. He has a few 6-pounders and some mountain guns. Two of the mountain howitzers are on elephants.

*Naini Tal.*

Captain Ramsay is about to commence barracks for a Regiment at or near Nynee Tal.

I believe that I need not apologise for writing at such length, as I am expected to keep the Headquarters informed of any general intelligence which is received at Agra bearing upon His Excellency's operations.

*Affair at Khodagunga Bridge.*

It afforded us great satisfaction to hear of His Excellency's success at the Khodagunge Bridge, preliminary, as we do not doubt, to the entire dislodgment long before this of the rebels from Furruckabad.

*Mr. Raikes.*

Mr. Raikes writes from Umballa that he intended to start on the 4th, and hoped soon to join the Commander-in-Chief.

W. MUIR.

GENERAL MANSFIELD,
Chief of the Staff, Headquarters.

## CCLXX.

*6th January* 1858. Wednesday.

MY DEAR BEADON,—The enclosed copy of a letter I have just written to General Mansfield will give the greater part of our news.

H. S. Reid reached here this morning, having marched down from Delhi through the Goorgaon and Muthra districts with the Putiala force, which is on its way to Dholpore. He found the country quite quiet. The small marauding body which I mentioned some days ago as disturbing the southern part of Goorgaon seems to have been dispersed. Reid rode along the road without any escort.

H. S. Reid.

Putiala Contingent goes to Dholpore.

The Putiala troops are about 2000 in number, with 2 guns: —they are Sikhs and Punjaubees; rude-looking people, but useful probably as light skirmishing soldiers. There was a considerable number, a hundred or more perhaps, mounted on camels, with formidable-looking Jezails.

Composition of above.

I do not know what is intended to be done at Dholpore. The Dewan, Deo Kuns, a Goojur, has a faction in favour of a Goojur Rana. The Rana has not much strength of purpose, I fancy, but is understood to favour the Jat party. Deo Kuns should be tried for his alleged junction with the Mhow Mutineers against us. It would have been a convenience if during the late events Dholpore had been under this Government, or under Macpherson. It lies between us and Gwalior.

Goojur Diwan at Dholpore.

Baird Smith, in answer to an enquiry about the workshops, says that for months to come they will be fully occupied in preparing wood and iron-work for barracks and canal works. "I have now received," he says, "reports from all the canals in the Doab; and the destruction of everything that was destructible or plunderable has been sweeping and complete, except in our own neighbourhood, where vigorous measures of repression were used from the beginning."

Baird Smith preparing to erect barracks.

Destruction of canal property.

You will see from my letter to General Mansfield the argument he uses for the reoccupation of western Rohilkhund. "We can get no timber fit for barracks anywhere else; and if we fail to get it, and the men die, as die they certainly will, the Crimean cry will be re-echoed about India, and there will be a pretty mess."

Timber required for barracks.

Ramsay, I am glad to say, is getting over his wound, and will be fit to take an active part in the proceedings in the Terai. His presence will double the force, and more than that.

Major Ramsay.

Writing on the 30th ultimo, he says that he had been with Maxwell to look for a site for barracks near Nynee Tal. At Koorpa Tal, the position of which Harington and Campbell will be able to explain, there is abundance of room, and the elevation above 5000 feet. They were going to look at Shamkhet, where there is also ground, and the point would be immediately settled, so far as Ramsay is concerned. He is a gloriously energetic fellow, and will have everything ready, no doubt.

Force at Huldwanee.

You will see from General Mansfield's letter the force which Ramsay has collected at Huldwanee. He strongly urges that the Terai be taken into consideration in the military movements now projected. "If the forests," he says, "are neglected, all the villains who found the plains too hot for them will take refuge on the edge of the forest, and I shall have a huge population of dacoits to blacken my name;" and it will be exceedingly difficult to remedy the evil.

The Terai.

He says the roads are still close, there being some 2000 men at Rooderpoor and Buheree, but he expects to turn them out soon;—"I had fortunately stored up a couple of months' supplies, so we are not in want. The Nepaul Sepoys are good men. I have put Baugh in command of them, and got five Officers from Mr. Causland; for the little fellows require a lot of brushing up, and on service 'holding in.'"

Nepaul Sepoys. Major Baugh.

I wrote you on the spur of the moment, and I fear very hurriedly and imperfectly, about the territorial changes you mentioned in your letter of the 26th as in contemplation. The more I reflect on the dismemberment of the Doab, the more confirmed am I in believing that it would be a highly inexpedient measure, and that the Jumna should be maintained as the boundary; the entire Doab remaining an integral part of the N.W.P.

Territorial changes.

Entire Doab should remain in N.W.P.

Regarding the changes at Headquarters, although Allahabad certainly was not cut off from Calcutta as we were,—an admitted inestimable advantage,—yet had the seat of Government been there, the Lieut.-Governor would have been cut off from more than three-fourths of his Province;—while at Agra, from its more centrical position, communications have been more or less kept up all round. Efforts were made for restoration of government and order, which, to a great extent, would have been impossible at Allahabad, and an influence exercised in Rajpootana which cannot be overrated.

Agra *versus* Allahabad as seat of Government.

But the decision of the question will not, I imagine, depend upon argument derived from the position of affairs on so entirely exceptional an occasion as the insurrection. For the purposes of ordinary government, the most central point must be the most advantageous. And that Allahabad surely is far from being.

. . . . . . . . . . .

W. MUIR.

C. BEADON, ESQ.,
Home Secretary, Calcutta

*P.S.*—The Commander-in-Chief has a prodigious concentration of force at Furruckabad. We do not understand why he does not depute, as requested by Sir J. Lawrence, some portion of it towards Meerut, to make a descent on the west of Rohilkhund, and clear it eastwards. It will complicate matters if an opening be left for the escape of the insurgents in any force westwards from Bareilly. An advance from Bijnore or Moradabad would probably meet with little opposition, and prove a barrier in that direction. The Commander-in-Chief might, at any rate, have sent back Seaton's Column. Delhi and Meerut are left weak by both Grant's and Seaton's Column being retained by him. **Commander-in-Chief's force at Furruckabad.**

## CCLXXI.

*7th January* 1857. Thursday.

MY DEAR BEADON,—

. . . . . . . . . . .

Even at Mynpoorie (some 40 miles only from Furruckabad) not a hint had reached them on the 5th of what had occurred.

At Mynpoorie all is going on well. Cocks is delighted with the discipline of H.M.'s 38th under Sparkes; this begins to restore confidence. "And the wretched plundered Bunnias, etc., are gradually returning to their business." Colonel Seaton's Column was not so well held in hand. **Cocks at Mynpoorie. H.M.'s 38th under Sparkes.**

Things seem settling down, but there will be some work yet to do. "There is one Achhar Singh, the late Raja Tej Singh's right-hand man,—he is holding out in his village and 'gurbee,' about 10 miles from Mynpoorie, with 100 matchlockmen, and swears he will die." A party was being organised to dislodge him. **Achhar Singh to be dislodged.**

General Mansfield writes to Cocks that the stationing of a Detachment at Mynpoorie is only a temporary measure, and the Commander-in-Chief declines leaving any troops at Etawah. "He conceives that your own Jat horsemen, to support the future arrangement lately made by Capt. Bradford in combination with the Mynpoorie and Cawnpore arrangement, should be sufficient for revenue business for the present, while the few troops at his **Etawah cannot be garrisoned.**

command are so much required to carry out the views of the Governor-General in Council."

Of course, if the troops at His Excellency's disposal are no more than suffice for field operations, that settles the question. Hume, I doubt not, will be able to maintain his hold on the district, which has been in general wonderfully amenable to our influence, even when it was at its lowest ebb. But one would like to see our British officers reinstated in their posts with a greater show of authority, and more power to vindicate our honour by bringing the rebellious forthwith to condign justice.

Allan Hume, C.S., at Etawah.

Civil officers require military support.

Rohilkhund hostility.

Meanwhile the Rohilkhund rebels continue to keep the country about Ram Ghat and Anoopshahur in an uneasy state. Attempts made to cross have been repelled, but there the Insurgents remain massed on the opposite shore and fire away with their guns. This is more serious just at this season, when the river is low and fords easily found. We have a report to-day that rebels have again appeared at Saron, which is north of Kassgunge. We do not yet know how they got there; but it shows that the Commander-in-Chief would need to be sending some part of his army to replace the strength he has been draining downwards from the Meerut Division.

Harvey, C.S.

Harvey, who has accompanied the convoy to Mynpoorie, writes on the 5th from Shekoabad that the presence of the convoy is having a good effect. The passage of the long line of carriage and troops induces the belief "that a larger army than any since the days of Xerxes is proceeding through the country." The preceding day a notorious rebel near Shekoabad endeavoured to get off with a gun given him by the rebel Rajah of Mynpoorie. The Tehseeldar with his people captured the gun, but the rebel eluded their pursuit. "The respectable people of Shekoabad," he adds, "are rejoiced at the restoration of order. The whole population turned out to welcome us, and I rode on with two or three Sowars an hour before the troops. All will come rapidly right here if we are firm and uncompromising with rebels and their aiders and abettors, and conciliatory with the agricultural community, who have in some instances paid off old scores without the least intention of embarking in the rebellion, but driven into excess by the absence of order and the license of turbulent neighbours." It is of the most essential consequence to our future success in the administration of the country that this latter class—a prodigiously numerous one—should be carefully discriminated in treatment from those who acted treasonably against the Government.

Skekoabad.

Attitude of the agricultural community during the rebellion.

Nothing new to the west; but the following statement presents an interesting feature of the injury done to the morale of even the well-disposed peasantry by the long prevalence of anarchy. Imdad Alee, our excellent Deputy Collector of Muthra, was deputed to Kosee to collect some telegraph posts that had been left there. There had been a fight among the people the day before,—seven wounded, eight killed: and the Deputy Collector arrived just in time to stop another fight. "It was reported to the Deputy Collector by the Kosee people that some thousands of fellows were collecting to loot Kosee itself. They are composed of many castes,—originally banded together for mutual protection; now, led away by long license and disorder, are prepared to loot on their own account."

**Influence of disorder on the well-disposed peasantry.**

**Kosee.**

The following abstract may be interesting, of the orders for execution of mutineers and rebels by court-martial and special commission, at the station of Agra, from July to November inclusive.

**Abstract of orders for execution of mutineers and rebels at Agra.**

78 persons were sentenced; of these, capital sentences were commuted in two cases,—62 were condemned by court-martial; 16 by Special Commissioner.

17 were Mutineers: viz., 10 Mussulmans and 7 Hindoos; 4 were blown away from guns.

The remainder were for the most part sentenced on account of general rebellious proceedings, murder, plunder, arson, etc.,—viz., 61, of whom 32 were Mussulmans and 29 Hindoos.

Directly concerned in the riot here succeeding the 5th July are 13 persons, of whom 6 are Mussulmans and 7 Hindoos.

The charge in one court-martial case is remarkable:—"For having attempted to excite a spirit of opposition among the prisoners in the Fort of Agra, by taunting the sick prisoners about loss of caste from receiving medicine from the hands of their European medical attendant." I mentioned this to Harington, who will recognise the case as that of Ameer Khan.

**Remarkable charge.**

W. MUIR.

C. BEADON, ESQ., Calcutta.

Raja Bhowanee Singh, who is to succeed Tej Singh at Mynpoorie, and who, you will remember, was our Nazim after Grant's Column passed down, has returned to Mynpoorie with Cocks, who is much pleased with him. "He is acting," he says, "most sensibly, moderately, and well,—he has no personal spite against the Chowhans who acted against him, but at the same time gives me every assistance in unferreting ringleaders."

**Rajah Bhowani Singh.**

W. M.

## CCLXXII.

*8th January* 1858. Friday.

Rohilkhund hostility.

MY DEAR BEADON,—The Rohilkhund insurgents still threaten the Doab at various points, and as the Commander-in-Chief has not yet sent back any part of either Seaton's or Grant's brigade the Upper Doab is rather vulnerable.

At Meerut they had a report that the Bijnore rebels had crossed into the Moozuffernugger district and reached the town of Meeranpoor. This, however, has not yet been corroborated; but the report (received from Edwards, Magistrate of Moozuffernugger) was sufficiently serious to make Williams, the Commissioner, keep back two troops of mounted police he was sending down to us.

The rebels are still in considerable numbers opposite Anoopshahur, and other ghats farther down. When attacked in Shahjehanpoor and Bareilly, the fugitives may partly take that direction, though their more natural, because at present safer, course is eastward.

Huldwanee (Kumaon) attacked by Bareilly rebels.

Huldwanee (Kumaon) was again, for the last time I fancy, attacked by the Bareilly rebels. Fortunately the Goorkhas were at hand, or the supplies might have been destroyed a second time.

Baugh and his Goorkhas.

They were about a thousand strong, with two little guns, which they fired when about 250 yards off. But the moment Baugh let loose his Goorkhas at them they fled in such haste that there was no getting up with them. They lost 20 killed;—we, only one man.

Major Ramsay's force ready.

Ramsay expected all his commissariat arrangements to be completed by the 4th, and on the 6th "the Huldwanee force," he says, "will be ready to start anywhere and to do anything."

Kala Khan, near Naini Tal, fixed on for barracks.

He has fixed on a place called Kala Khan for the barracks, near to Nynee Tal, on the Bheem Tal side. "The water will run round and round the hill, so that the children may wash their faces in the running stream." The water-course for this charming arrangement is commenced, and the energetic Commissioner is already busy in laying in materials for the building. He wants sheet-iron for roofing. I have mentioned this to General Mansfield, as they may be able to pick up some at Furruckabad.

He will need money, but I trust he will be able to get a couple of lacs soon from Bareilly; without this I fear there will be a lack.

He says: "Don't be uneasy about us. The appearance of Khan Buhadoor's army at the foot of the hills causes no alarm whatever. In ten days you shall, I hope, hear of the whole of the Terai armies being destroyed or dispersed for the time; but they will grow again when all the budmashes are driven out of Bareilly."

Khan Buhadoor.

Hume has made a triumphal entry into Etawah, notwithstanding the departure of the British bayonets. "The whole population of the town and its environs, and almost every Zemindar of importance in the district, came out to meet us. There could be no doubt that the people were glad to see us. Illuminations were prepared, guns were firing, music playing, and the rich were throwing alms before us in handfuls."

Hume makes a triumphal entry into Etawah.

Nevertheless, it cannot be concealed that in the present unsettled state of the country one would like to see the Collector supported by more than his handful of Sowars. The district is quite quiet, excepting near Oreya, where the rebel, Roop Singh, has collected from all quarters an immense body of desperate characters, matchlockmen, etc. They are encouraged by the Calpee Mutineers, who have a guard of 100 Cavalry and 150 Foot at the Sheregurh Ghat. Oreya is, you know, in the Cawnpore border, and should be amenable to the Cawnpore moveable column; but so long as Calpee is held, the banks of the Jumna in that direction will be in an insecure state.

Supported by only a handful of Sowars.

The rebel Roop Singh at Oreya.

Calpee.

Hume gives the Calpee rebels at 2000 men with 8 guns. Macpherson has intelligence that they are 5000 strong with 15 guns (2 eighteen-pounders, 4 nine-pounders, and other little ones for which they are making carriages); and they are doing as much damage to Gwalior as to us, for "they are corrupting Scindia's neighbouring districts" and drawing men from them.

Hume can command some three thousand matchlocks, he says, but untrained they would be useless against any regular attack. He is organising a hundred District Horse and 250 Foot, which will be of use as auxiliaries to the Sikhs. "They are chiefly Thakoors, and for every man a written guarantee is given by some loyal and influential Zemindar."

Hume organising District Horse and Foot.

Hume's conviction that "the people as a body are most unmistakably and cordially with us," is quite in accordance with what the officers of Seaton's Brigade said. One of them, writing in a letter not meant for any official eye, says "the people of the country (speaking of the Etawah district) hail our approach with delight."

Loyal attitude of people.

The precedent of Futtehgurh having escaped plunder because

Futtehgurh escaped plunder.

the rebels had evacuated it, will, I trust, be of great use as showing that we do discriminate; and as encouraging the people on the approach of our troops to get rid of the insurgents, though I fear they will seldom have the power to effect much that way.

W. MUIR.

C. BEADON, ESQ., Calcutta.

Major Williams' investigations as to the origin of the Mutiny.

*P.S.*—Major Williams is getting on marvellously with his Meerut police investigation, and will have a mass of evidence as to the origin of the Mutiny which will not fit in easily with the popular notion of a long preconceived plot.

## CCLXXIII.

*8th January* 1858. Friday.

Rebel force at Calpee.

MY DEAR SHERER,—This is a memorandum by Macpherson. You no doubt have better and earlier information than we can have regarding the Calpee assemblage.

Hume believes it to be 2000, with 8 or 10 guns.

I hope Hume is in correspondence with you. He is threatened from Oreya, where Roop Singh has a great congregation of dacoits, etc., in correspondence with the Calpee rebels. The latter have a post at the Sheregurh Ghat.

Your moveable column should suffice for Oreya.

The ordinary news I now send on direct to Beadon.[1]

Keep us informed as to what you hear of the Calpee and Jalaon people.

W. MUIR.

J. W. SHERER, ESQ., Cawnpoor.

## CCLXXIV.

*8th January* 1858. Friday.

MY DEAR SIR,—At the risk of giving you over again what you may have already heard from Mr. Thornhill, I mention that Major Ramsay is anxious to have collected and sent up to him as much sheet-iron as possible; it will be required for roofing the Nynee Tal barracks. Perhaps you will kindly give instructions to some officer at Furruckabad, where there used to be great stores of sheet-iron, to secure what he can.

Naini Tal barracks.

A charming site has been selected near to Nynee Tal. "The water will run round and round the hill, so that the children may wash their faces in the running stream."

[1] Beadon communicated with direct, since road open.—W. M.

Huldwanee (at the foot of the Nynee Tal Hills) had been attacked on the 1st; but the Goorkhas put the rebels to an ignominious flight. By the 6th, Major Ramsay says, he would be ready to operate actively against the Teraie Insurgents. **Huldwanee attacked.**

Mr. Hume has been well received at Etawah, and things are generally quiet there, excepting towards Oreya, where the rebel, Roopsing, has gathered an immense band of dacoits and matchlockmen, and is in communication with the Calpee rebels, who have a post at the Sheregurh Ghat. The Calpee men are variously estimated at from 2000 to 5000, with from 10 to 15 guns. Their presence unsettles the Eastern districts of Gwalior equally with our own; and, so long as Calpee stands, the Jumna bank cannot of course be secure. But the Oreya insurgents being close on the Cawnpore border, will no doubt be attacked by the moveable column of that district. **Mr. Hume well received at Etawah.**

W. MUIR.

TO GENERAL MANSFIELD.

## CCLXXV.

*9th January* 1858. Saturday.

MY DEAR BEADON,—All still quiet at Etawah. But Hume has been told from Mynpoorie that no reinforcements could be sent to him even if he were besieged! Luckily, he says, the Mutineers do not know this, or they would be paying him a visit. As yet they have made no move beyond sending a small detachment to Roopsing at Ayana, near Ajeetmull.

He is having an entrenchment prepared, which will be in order by the middle of the month. This is necessary, for Etawah will, for some time to come, be our weak point from the distance of troops. **Etawah a weak point.**

The rejoicings in the city continue unabated, he says, notwithstanding that they have been rather discouraged. The Sikhs also are popular, and becoming friends of the city people. **Sikh soldiery popular.**

Hume praises in high terms the discipline of Walpole's Column. It passed through without any plunder or injury to the town. Two Europeans were punished for attempting to rob a shopkeeper. "Several equally judicious and decisive measures are related by the people of the officers of our force—which I am sure have contributed no little to restore confidence and inspire goodwill." It is quite refreshing to read this after the interminable complaints of oppression and plunder by the Columns from Delhi. **Walpole's Column.** **Complaints of oppression by the Columns.**

The news from the Upper Doab is much as before. The

parties on the opposite bank are in no great force, but being at many points they distract and harass our people.

I was glad to hear that Major Weller found the Grand Trunk Road in good order. He has examined it from here to Allygurh, and thence downwards. His last report was from Goorsuhaegunge.

All reports say that the Futtehgurh rebels had made up their minds to hold out in the city—which would have occasioned great loss to us probably, but for their thorough defeat and flight on the 2nd.

**Execution of the Dewan at Futtehgurh.**

The execution of the Dewan seems to have been bungled . . . It is also a pity the soldiers were allowed (as is said) to stuff pork into the wretch's mouth. The *English* ought to be above such proceedings.

All Furruckabad news you of course get fresh and prompt from the Headquarters camp. They come to us by driblets, and uncertainly. The move on Mhow Shumsabad is good. The

**Bungash Pathans.**

Bungish Pathans, who supported the Nawab, deserve no quarter and must be rooted out.

W. MUIR.

C. BEADON, ESQ., Calcutta.

## CCLXXVI.

*10th January* 1858. Sunday.

MY DEAR SIR,—

. . . . . . . .

Etawah continues in the same satisfactory state excepting towards Oreyah. Mr. Hume has, I believe, addressed you direct as to what he believes to be the menacing position of the Calpee Mutineers in reference to Cawnpore.

I should not think they would have much heart left for an

**Letter from Nana to the Rajah of Mynpoorie intercepted.**

attack again on that place. But a letter from the Nana to the Raja of Mynpoorie has been intercepted, in which, after adverting to his misfortune in the rout and dispersion of the Gwalior troops, he informs him that he looks to a fresh assemblage at Calpee with the view to another attack on Cawnpoor.

I give the following quotation from a letter of yesterday's

**Proceedings of rebels near Boolundshuhur.**

date, received from Mr. B. Sapte, Magistrate of Boolundshuhur: "The rebels opposite Anoopshahur are very cheeky; they fire at us every day, but as yet have not done any harm. But it is almost impossible to hit them, as they hide like jackals in the sugar canes, and blaze away at us. They are all up and down the river. But I hope we shall nobble them if they attempt to cross. We want a couple of heavy guns sadly, and I hope General Penny will send them to us if he can spare them."

From native accounts I gather that they are almost all new levies. Their object is probably not more than to watch the ghats, though they keep us in a ferment. Opposite Seharunpoor and Moozuffernugger they appear to be more lively, and plan a descent on our side every now and then.

W. MUIR.

GENERAL MANSFIELD,
Chief of the Staff, Headquarters.

## CCLXXVII.

*11th January* 1858. Monday.

MY DEAR BEADON,—I enclose copy of a letter I sent yesterday to General Mansfield.

On the 8th, 8 of the 8th Irregulars were traced near Mynpoorie. Four of them were killed on resisting apprehension; the remaining 4 were captured by the Thakoor's zemindars, and sent in with the 8 horses, trappings, etc. The Sowars were in uniform, and had a perwana in their possession from Khan Buhadoor.

**Men of the 8th Irregulars killed and captured.**

**Khan Buhadoor.**

Harvey, the Commissioner, writes from Mynpoorie: "I find many of the old Amlah, against whom there is nothing, but who, having been hiding in villages till the late tyranny be over past, have come in, and all will go smoothly here." "The Raja," he adds, "fled slipperless and coatless, and got a 'rezai' from a compassionate traveller near Bhowgaon."

**Court Amlah.**

**Flight of the Rajah of Mynpoorie.**

Unwin, late Magistrate and Judge of Mynpoorie, and well acquainted with the people, writes also from Mynpoorie (he is on his way down the country on medical certificate):—

"You will have heard from Cocks how serene all is here. The Chowhans terribly ashamed of themselves, and anxious to show loyalty by paying up revenue. Very few of my old Chowhan friends have had the imprudence to present themselves yet. A few examples must be made; but large allowance should be made for a clan which followed its chief, and was foolish enough to suppose us done for."

**Chowhans at Mynpoorie terribly ashamed.**

**Allowance to be made for them.**

A requisition has just come from the Commander-in-Chief to despatch from this Magazine a large addition to his siege train, with ammunition, etc. Every effort will be made here to despatch it with all celerity. I conclude that this portends a movement *via* Shahjehanpoor on Lucknow. We are keeping the thing as quiet as can be; but I fear it is getting wind, though the eventual destination of the train is of course not public.

**Requisition from the Commander-in-Chief.**

Christian woman brought in.

Mr. Wilson, from Meerut, says that some Brahmins have brought over from Cader Chouk, in the Budaon District, a Christian woman named Susan, the daughter of a drummer of some regiment near Calcutta.

Women and children desirous of going home.

Mr. Poynder writes to me from Nynee Tal, that there are a great number of women and children desirous of going home, both at Nynee Tal and Almorah. Including both places, he says, they are "not far short of a hundred."

I fear it will be some little time before active operations in Oudh (if that, as we suppose, be the first scene of operations) will permit of an escort being furnished for them. I have sent his letter to General Mansfield.

W. Muir.

C. Beadon, Esq., Calcutta.

Affairs at Oudeypore.

*P.S.*— . . . No actual outbreak, he says, has taken place at Oudeypoor, though the troops, especially the Mahommedans, are "ripe for mutiny." The Rana's warning to Captain Brooke and others, that he could not guarantee their safety in passing through Oudeypoor, originated (Macdonald thinks) the report on an actual Mutiny.

Tonk.

Macdonald gives a cheering account of the state of things at Tonk since the fall of Delhi; and especially since the execution of the Nawab,[1] the Nawab of Tonk has become wonderfully anxious to prove his loyalty to us. "On the 3rd he ordered his brethren, who in July and August last threatened to attack me (Macdonald) in this place, together with his maternal uncle" (Meer Alum Khan) and other disaffected persons, "to be seized. The uncle resisted, and was killed with others."

The brother, Moneer Khan, with others, including fugitives from Delhi, put in chains.

W. M.

## CCLXXVIII.

*12th January* 1858. Tuesday.

My Dear Beadon,—The state of things along the Ganges seems to remain pretty much as before. There are still numerous bodies of insurgents, who fire guns and set afloat vapouring reports, but it appears probable that their sole object is to watch the ghats.

The eight Sowars whom I mentioned yesterday were

[1] Probably refers to the Nawab of Jhujjur.

apprehended on the other bank near the Kutchla Ghat by Thakoor Dara Sing of Piproul, in Zillah Budaon. He has, I believe, been handsomely rewarded, as he deserves. Thakoor Dara Singh.

Cocks is "getting on famously" in recruiting for local Cavalry. The Thakoors, he says, come in much more willingly than the Jats. Cocks recruiting local Cavalry. Thakoors and Jats.

His collections too are beginning to come in well. Revenue collections.

There are still refractory Zemindars, both Thakoor and Aheer, in some quarters of the district—which is not to be wondered at. But Cocks will soon put them straight, and visit the rebellious with due punishment.

I have got a Memorandum from Major Williams, who has been investigating the conduct of the Meerut Police, on the result so far of his enquiries. It is an interesting paper—the precursor, I trust, of a still more interesting one. I will send a copy. Meanwhile I may state the purport briefly. Though a latent discontent had been smouldering, no premeditated plan of revolt can be traced. The first overt act was an oath taken by two of the 3rd Light Cavalry not to receive the cartridges till the whole army had taken them. The confinement of 85 men of that Regiment led to the belief that the Government intended to force the cartridges upon the army. Rumours that chains were being prepared at once for all the recusants, and that the Rifles were to march upon them, confirmed that belief and precipitated the general Mutiny. The most would have returned to their allegiance had they not been compromised by the few wretches who fired at their officers. From the evidence of persons who met them on their way, "it appears that the Mutineers went to Delhi, accompanied by a large body of convicts and rabble as a disorganised mob, with no express object in view, excepting that the Cavalry, principally composed of Mahommedans, taking the lead, naturally resorted to the acknowledged head of their sect (the king); and hence the insurrection took at once a Mahommedan complexion." Major Williams' Memorandum on the conduct of the Meerut Police. Revolt not premeditated. The Cartridges. Mutineers' progress to Delhi. How the insurrection took at once a Mahommedan complexion.

The rumours above referred to were circulated by the cook-boys of the European regiments and bad characters of the Sudder Bazaar, which he describes as having been in a corrupt and dangerous state. The liberated prisoners, with electric rapidity, spread the news of the revolt, and that very night hordes of robbers joined the vagabonds of the Bazaar in the savage riot. "The respectable portion of the community, as the evidence negatively proves, did not join in the riot." Rumours. Respectable portion of the Meerut community did not join the riot.

The police may in parts have remained neutral; but in some

quarters at least they have been identified as having taken part in the outrages.

Williams does not pledge himself to these opinions until he shall have completed and compared the evidence.

W. MUIR.

C. BEADON, ESQ., Calcutta.

## CCLXXIX.

*13th January* 1858. Wednesday.

MY DEAR BEADON,—Thanks for yours of the 7th. The daks are now getting very regular.

Governor-General proposes to disarm the population.

I am very glad to hear that the Governor-General proposes eventually to disarm the population.

Seat of Government for N.W.P.

As to the change of the seat of Government, I have already fully said my say in my former letters to you and Harington.

Saugor and Nerbudda territories.

The new point you mention now as to our retention of the Saugor and Nerbudda territories does not appear to me to improve the case. However much the communications with Jubbulpoor and the near parts of the province may be facilitated, the tract itself is, and will always be, alien from us in manners, laws, institutions;—it far more assimilates in these respects with the South, and could be better managed from Nagpore.

Raising of Police Battalions.

I am glad to see what you say about Police Battalions. Men are being raised everywhere. Cocks is getting on with foot and horse. Landholders, like the Zemindar of Peproul, who caught the Irregular Cavalry men, are desired to bring in 50 good men or so:—in a week Cocks will have one troop at least—"every man's character is well sifted before enlistment."

71st Native Infantry.

A mutineer of the 71st Native Infantry was caught and hanged at Mynpoorie. He, as well as the Irregular Cavalry men, were "brought in by the people of the country."

A. Cocks, C.S., describes attitude of the people.

Writing yesterday, Cocks says: "I took a ride this morning perfectly alone, making a circuit of 16 miles and entering 9 different villages. I was recognised in all, and heartily welcomed. The people are thoroughly ashamed of what has occurred, and are contrite and humble to an extent I should not have imagined possible."

Unrest in Meerut Division. Raids on Meeranpore and Kunkul.

Meanwhile the aspect of affairs is a little uneasy in the Meerut Division. The raid on Meeranpoor in Moozuffernugger has been followed by another at Kunkul near Hurdwar, where the Telegraph assistant (of the Canal Telegraph) was seized and his bungalow burned. All this tends to keep our population in a state of excitement. I send a "private" letter from Mr. Dunlop on the subject. You will see that other causes have added to the uneasy feeling:—the treatment of Meeranpoor; draining of troops eastward, and non-fulfilment of long-promised new re-enforcement from England. The apprehension of Janfishan's Moulvee for seditious language (see para. 4 of the public letter) is not insignificant, especially as it is the act of a Walaitee. The retention of both the Delhi Columns, Grant's and Seaton's, by the Commander-in-Chief, has undoubtedly left the N.W. districts weak, and tempts the development of disaffection and revolt. **Janfishan's Moulvee.**

Williams, the Commissioner, has submitted Dunlop's public letter officially. Re-enforcements are going from Meerut towards Moozuffernugger, etc.; but Meerut and Delhi can ill spare anything more.

Meanwhile the Commander-in-Chief remains at Furruckabad, with the accumulated force of his own and the Delhi Column. The siege train won't be with His Excellency for a fortnight probably. It is to be hoped that he will be doing something in the interim. **Commander-in-Chief at Furruckabad.**

At last we have seen the face of new re-enforcements here. A detachment of the 38th has come over as a convoy. **First new troops.**

. . . . . . . . . . . .

You will have received the scheme for Police Battalions officially—also the memo. on the subject which Sir John Lawrence sent me: though drawn up by Arnold, it embodies Sir John's sentiments, as you will see from the note which I enclose. **Scheme for Police Battalions. Sir John Lawrence's sentiments.**

There is a great amount of valuable matter and argument in it — though he has not correctly apprehended what Major Williams' scheme is. I agree with Sir John about having better paid native officers.

. . . . . . . . . . . .

You have not said a word about the proposal of the Chief Commissioner to transfer Jackson to the Court. I am still holding on in the Board, pending the Governor-General's answer to that appointment.

W. Muir.

C. Beadon, Esq., Calcutta.

## CCLXXX.

*14th January* 1858. Thursday.

My Dear Beadon,—The enclosed extra gives account of a brilliant affair on a small scale at the head of the Ganges Canal.

It will do much good in restoring confidence and repressing disaffection in the Upper Doab.

Oreya and Etawah threatened by Calpee force.

Hume, from Etawah, writes rather bad accounts of the advance of the Calpee force on Akberpore, and of its threatening Oreya and Etawah. I trust the moveable column of Cawnpoor will prevent such a contingency. If the district is liable to raids and plunder, we shall get no revenue. It would be a good plan to place the Mynpoorie force at Etawah,—this would keep the Doab intervening between Etawah and Furruckabad, including Mynpoorie, quiet. Captain Bruce is over here, having been sent over by the Commander-in-Chief to communicate direct with Colonel Fraser (he came over by the dak cart), and I hope this may be arranged with him.

Rohilkhund.

The last accounts from Rohilkhund are that the rebels opposite Anoopshahur have been refused aid from Bareilly. There are said to be 40 guns at Bareilly, of which 3 are very large—but most are of country manufacture. There are some 8000 foot and 2000 horse at Bareilly; 2500 foot and 300 horse at Shahjehanpoor; about half that number at Budaon. The Infantry are generally new levies and raw;—the Cavalry better. They have lately had re-enforcements from Oudh. Wullee Dad Khan and a son of the King of Delhi are said to be at Bareilly.

Details of rebel force at Bareilly.

Wullee Dad Khan and Delhi prince.

Deesa force takes Rawal Fort.

Captain Macdonald, from Deolee, on the 10th instant, says that the Deesa force has begun well. You will perhaps have heard by telegraph, but I may mention that the fort of Rawal in the Serowie district was taken after two hours' fighting. It is in the vicinity of Aboo, and was "gallantly carried in a rush:—the Thakoor and a part of the garrison escaping to the hills. Three officers of the 10th Bombay Native Infantry, one of H.M.'s 95th, are wounded;—further casualties do not exceed a dozen—one of the 95th alone being killed."

Kotah Rajah.

The Kota Raja, Macdonald says, is strengthening himself against his rebellious soldiery, and he may be able to dispose of them himself yet. "Should he not succeed unaided, we shall soon be strong enough for anything in Rajpootana." This is cheerful language from a solitary European officer in a place like Deolee.

Macdonald alone at Deoli, but cheerful.

The Jowra Nawab had recently been at Neemuch.

. . . . . . . . . . .

W. MUIR.

C. BEADON, ESQ., Calcutta.

## CCLXXXI.

*15th January* 1858. Friday.

MY DEAR BEADON,—I have no news to-day.

Harvey (Commissioner of Agra) has reached, and been cordially received by the Commander-in-Chief at Furruckabad. But you will have all the news from that quarter earlier than I get it. Harvey joins Commander-in-Chief.

He says the 64th go to Allygurh. This is a good move, showing to the people up the Doab new Europeans. It will produce an excellent effect, both locally and throughout the Upper Doab. 64th Regiment.

The 23rd are out making a bridge over the Ramgunga, some 7 or 8 miles on the Shahjehanpoor road, so that I trust there will be an early move in that direction. 23rd Native Infantry.

W. MUIR.

C. BEADON, ESQ., Calcutta.

## CCLXXXII.

*16th January* 1858. Saturday.

MY DEAR BEADON,—Boldero, the new Magistrate of Mynpoorie, has joined. He has an unusually intimate acquaintance with native character, so his opinion concurring with that of Cocks and Harvey may be of interest. "The people in this district," he says, "in general seem quite delighted to see Europeans coming back amongst them, and their civility beats the famed civility of the Delhi folks" (Boldero had lately been there),—"theirs being in a great measure forced, and here entirely of their own accord. They seem tired of all the anarchy that has been going on, and seem inclined to settle down very quietly. Of course there are some few choice spirits who object to the old style of things, as they will not be able to loot *ad libitum* as they have been doing." Boldero reports loyalty and returning order in Mynpoorie District.

The revenue is coming in fairly, and the Sowar levies "getting on very briskly." Boldero very properly looks to these local levies for the settlement of the district. Revenue coming in.

From Etawah, Hume writes cheerfully; Oreya has hitherto escaped. A party of Sepoys, who came to reconnoitre it, got fired on from several quarters and fled. Still, there are parties of rebels about in various places between Secundra and Ajeetmull. Hume is getting on with his entrenchment, which will be a very respectable one, with a ditch 10 feet deep and 18 wide. Hume, C.S., and Etawah. Fortifies Etawah.

He is also running a line of defence round the city, at which the people work cheerfully. The low Mewattee and other disaffected Mahommedans all took themselves off before the advent of Walpole's Column.

General Lawrence reports on Kotah Rajah.

General Lawrence, writing from Ajmere on the 12th, has enclosed a letter for Edmonstone, in which he gives, I conclude, his own views. The Rajah of Kotah, he says, is strengthening himself in the citadel there by calling on the Rajpoots; and the mutinous soldiery are daily quitting in dread of our approach. Lawrence insists rightly on his delivering up the ringleaders in the murder of Burton.

We have heard of a success at the Ramgunga, and that Peel is constructing the Bridge—but no further particulars yet.

Commander-in-Chief praised. Sikhs' propensity to plunder.

The Commander-in-Chief is greatly praised for combined caution and activity, and for "doing his best to maintain discipline," but the truth is the Sikhs are unrestrainable when plunder is before them.

W. Muir.

C. Beadon, Esq., Calcutta.

## CCLXXXIII.

*18th January* 1858. Monday.

My Dear Beadon,—Yours of the 6th was received by me yesterday through Sherer, simultaneously with one from Harington of the 12th.

Nothing is stirring to the West.

Affair at Myapore.

Baird Smith has officially reported the affair at Myapoor under Captain Boisragon and some of the Canal officers. It was most complete and decisive; what with killed and drowned, the loss is estimated at 400.

Mr. Debrass. Unrest in Rohilkhund.

The damage by the invaders was not great, but the capture by them of Mr. Debrass, the signaller, is much to be lamented. They also seized a number of the Canal people.

Inroad at Meeranpore.

Baird Smith says "the general agitation along the Ganges front has materially increased of late. While the incursions above referred to were taking place near Hurdwar, an almost simultaneous inroad had been made at Meeranpoor in the Moozuffernugger district, and for some time before petty raids on Choukies or outposts had been occurring. The cause I believe to be that fugitive Mutineers from the southward are finding their way in larger numbers than before into the Bijnour District. Both at Kunkul and Meeranpoor, the extremities of the line under my charge, the invading parties were clearly seen to have both Regular Infantry and Cavalry among them. The sole permanent remedy for such a state of things seems to me to be the occupation of the left bank of the river, and until this can be done I am prepared to find these isolated incursions persisted in by the Insurgents, whose general object seems to be to avoid any collision with the troops, but to create feelings of alarm, want of confidence in the local administration, and insecurity of life and property among the population of the Districts."

Baird Smith advises occupation of the left bank.

Mr. Spankie, too, writing from Seharunpoor on the 14th, anticipates that when there is a pressure felt to the East, the safety of the Western districts will need to be looked to and re-enforcements provided. "In my opinion, Bijnour should be reoccupied simultaneously with any movement from Meerut or Agra or elsewhere on Rohilkhund." He says, however, he understands from Barnes that there is a column preparing at Lahore for Rohilkhund service. We have had no later intimation on the subject than Sir John's letter, which I sent on to the Commander-in-Chief last month.

Mr. Spankie advises re-occupation of Bijnore.

Column preparing at Lahore for Rohilkhund.

The end of the Irregulars who did Spankie such good service has been unfortunate. They "were sent," he says, "by me to Baird Smith, and by him to join a force at Meeranpoor. They went very unwillingly, and evidently the cause of their unwillingness was the fear of the Afghans and Sikhs in the 1st Punjab Cavalry, who they thought would do all they could to ruin them. The result has been unfortunate: 25 of their 33 have been tried for misbehaving themselves before the enemy, and have been transported for life—7 went boldly over to the enemy. I am very sorry for all this, and think there will be strong feeling on the subject, as their friends are numerous in this district. They collected a great deal of revenue for me here, and did very good service against the insurgents in May and June and subsequently."

Sad defection of Irregulars who had done good service.

Young Daniell has gone out to take charge of Eta, and finds everything quiet, though "there are constant reports of the Mutineers on the Budaon side of the river; and yesterday (15th) they appeared in great force at the Kutchla Ghat." The collections are getting fairly on.

Daniell, C.S., reports on Eta.

I have a memo. from Reid regarding the attendance in the schools in the Meerut, Moozuffernugger, Delhi, and Boolundshuhur districts—the only ones for which he had materials at hand. I will send you a copy of it. In 18 Tehseelee Schools the attendance in November was 593—being 33 per school. "The

H. S. Reid, C.S., reports on attendance in the schools.

schools are gaining ground again. The Haupper Sehool showed an attendance in Deeember of upwards of 80 boys."

At Kosee, Reid found on his way down from Delhi 100 boys, and at Muthra 90, at the Tehseelee Schools. He attributes great importance, and I think rightly, to keeping these institutions at work. They are Government Institutions, which should always be to the fore.

His next memo. will cover a larger area.

W. MUIR.

C. BEADON, ESQ., Calcutta.

Agra Colleges well attended.

The Agra College was hardly closed for a few days, and it, as well as the Chureh Missionary College here, have been for months well attended.

## CCLXXXIV.

*19th January* 1858. Tuesday.

MY DEAR BEADON,—

. . . . . . . .

Rebel activity in Western Rohilkhund.

I fear that the pressure is already beginning to tell in Western Rohilkhund. Sapte writes to me in a letter of yesterday's date from Boolundshuhur, that the Insurgent army opposite Anoopshahur has been re-enforced, and that on the 17th they brought down to the river six guns—two of them 9-pounders, the others smaller. Their fire killed one of Sapte's Jats and wounded two. Our guns silenced theirs after two hours' firing.

Colonel Farquhar (commanding the Boolundshuhur foree) is very anxious for some more Europeans and heavy guns, but General Penny cannot assist him. Perhaps something will now be done for him from this side. The European Regiment (64th), destined by the Commander-in-Chief for Allygurh, is going on towards Meerut. Perhaps a portion of it may be diverted to Boolundshuhur. Sapte also needs something more than 6-pounders. The boats must be guarded, and the force on our side should be strong enough to repel all attempts at a descent upon this bank.

64th Regiment (Europeans).

Sinee writing the above I have seen Fraser, who thinks that the 64th might be with advantage posted at Boolundshuhur, and this will probably be suggested to General Penny.

The Deputy Postmaster of Moradabad (a Baboo) writes from that plaee, under date the 14th, that about 150 horse and foot, said to be fugitives from Furruckabad and Bareilly, arrived at Moradabad on the 13th—stayed there that night, and went on next morning to Amroha, which is a town full of disaffected Mahommedans, long nurtured by Jageers in the Moradabad district; some also went on to Seoharȧ, a town in Bijnour. As Shahjehanpoor, etc., are occupied by us, I fear that, if we do not soon break ground on the Bijnour and Moradabad side, they will get strong, and our advance (which could probably be easily made now) be eventually contested.

**Fugitives from Furruckabad and Bareilly to Amroha.**

The Furruckabad Nawab is said to have fled to Bareilly, and to have been sent back with troops and guns by Khan Buhadoor to fight with us. I suspect the wretched Nawab has not much fight in him left of any kind.

**Furruckabad Nawab. Khan Buhadoor.**

Dunlop (writing from Meerut on the 16th) confirms the good effect of the affair at Mayapore. Ahmedoolla, the Nawab present at the engagement, was brought back to Nujeebabad in Bijnour "on an elephant, wounded on the shoulder, and Shuffeeoolla was killed. The rebels are greatly disgusted at the ease with which our handful of men thrashed them, and the affair will have a very wholesome effect throughout the district."

**Ahmedoolla Nawab wounded, and Shuffeeoolla killed.**

The labours of peace are being resumed in Meerut. Dunlop says they are getting on fast there with the revision of the Settlement papers. "Haupper and Mooradnugger are the only two Tehseelees not occupied, and we have 66 *jureebs*[1] going in the others. We shall be able to act as the depôt for supplying detachments of Surveyors, as well as Police, to other districts."

**Settlement work proceeding in Meerut under Dunlop.**

The records were generally saved, but some of the measurements, papers, and maps completed before the Mutiny were destroyed. After the outbreak all the records were packed off in hackeries to the entrenchment; and have since been sent back:—a heap of confusion, but mostly in good condition. For two or three days the Goojurs had access to the office, and the gaudy colours of the bustahs (the papers of each pergumah are wrapped in cloth of one colour) attracted the fancy of the Goojur women, who tore off every scrap.

**Records generally saved at Meerut.**

**Bustah cloths torn off by the Goojur women.**

We have not heard of Raikes from Furruckabad, but Harvey seems to be getting on well with the Commander-in-Chief. They are getting the Fort into order and supplying it. The Treasure to be kept there. A regiment will garrison it when the Head-quarters leave. The Thannah has been replaced at Bewur, and a Tehseeldar sent to Chibramow on the 16th.

Hume writes in distress from Etawah that the Calpee

[1] Measuring chains.—W. C.

Action of the Calpee Mutineers.

Mutineers, having made havoc of the Jumna side of Cawnpoor, are supposed to be making for him. But a private letter from Colonel Inglis mentions active movements against the insurgents in the direction of Calpee, so that it may be hoped the rebels will have enough to occupy them at home without thinking of Etawah.

Captain Bruce objects to the fortification of Allygurh.

Captain Bruce has run over to Allygurh. The Magistrate there has been strengthening the defences of the City, to which Bruce advances serious objections, as in case of its occupation by the enemy at any time it would be very strong:—not that that contingency is at all likely—but it is a contingency, and walls with bastions, etc., are not necessary for Police purposes. Fraser will attend to this.

Active operations of Dr. Clark, Postmaster-General, at Allygurh.

Bruce is astonished at the busy scene Dr. Clark has already set in operation with his Postal Department, constructing waggons, etc.; only, he thinks it should be closer to the Fort, which I fear Clark would not find convenient. Clark told me, I think, he was turning out two waggons a day.

Bruce says the Fort is very strong, and could be amply held by 300 to 350 men.

W. Muir.

C. Beadon, Esq., Calcutta.

King and Delhi.

Private letters from Delhi speak of the King as dying. It is a wonder he has lived so long. How often poor Mr. Thomason and old Metcalfe thought he was going! It is most satisfactory to find from your letter that a discriminating justice is intended. The Andaman Islands will be a most suitable place of banishment for the less guilty mutineers and rebels.

Delhi Field Force broken up.
Civil Government reverted to at Delhi.

Saunders writes on the 13th: "Colonel Burn has been ordered down to Futtehgurh to rearrange the Clothing Agency; and the Delhi Field Force having been broken up, and the Military Government abolished, the City has reverted to the Civil Authorities. The Gates and Defences of the place, however, remain as before under Military charge."

## CCLXXXV.

*20th January* 1858. Wednesday.

My Dear Beadon,—Everything seems quiet at present in the Upper Doab.

I have a letter from Sir John Lawrence of the 15th instant. He does not allude to the preparation of any force for Rohilkhund.

But he says: "I have sent, or am sending, the Commander-in-Chief 32 rissalas of Horse, equal to more than 5 Regiments—besides three and a half corps of Punjaub Infantry. All these I hope will be in his vicinity by the 15th of next month—some, long before." The Commander-in-Chief has been written to, to know what His Excellency wishes the destination of these troops to be.

Sir J. Lawrence sends down more than five Regiments of Horse, and three and a half Regiments of Punjab Infantry,

Sir John adds: "I have sent a good Police Battalion of 800 strong to Delhi, and another of 1100 men has just started for Benares; I do hope that no more troops will be required of me. If so, I must raise them, and this is not politic." The number of Sikhs that have already been sent down is immense, and the feeling is becoming strong on all sides that it is time to stop.

And Police Battalion to Delhi and Benares.

Large number of Sikhs sent down.

I have a letter from Captain Macdonald, dated the 15th instant. The Tank Nawab seems to be making violent plunges to regain his name for loyalty;—he proposes, it is said, to despatch his brother and other disaffected characters to Lawrence by Ajmere, bound hand and foot.

Nawab of Tank.

The agitation continues at Kota. On the 12th there appears to have been a fight there between the Rajah's adherents and those opposed to him, including the murderers of Burton; firing had been heard throughout the night. The result was not yet known.

Agitation at Kotah.

There were rumours at Deolee that a number of the insurgents having crossed the Chumbul were moving on Deolee, but Macdonald did not credit them.

The whole available Nusserabad force was understood to be on the 15th before Awah.

Nusseerabad force before Awah.

One hundred and fifty of the 2nd B. Cavalry had been sent from Neemuch to Deesa to make over their horses to the 8th Hussars.

8th Hussars.

Both Neemuch and Nusserabad are therefore for the moment weak; but it will not last long—and it is for the last time, I trust, they will ever be left so exposed.

Macdonald thinks that the two parties at Kotah are pretty nearly balanced; but the reports he receives are so contradictory that it is difficult to make out the precise state of affairs.

Alexander, Commissioner of Rohilkhund, writing from Nynee Tal on the 15th, says: "We have still enemies in and about the Bhabur, between Rooderpoor, Wilson Gunge, and Huldwanee"—places lying between Moradabad and the foot of Nynee Tal Hills. He says: "Now is the time to strike at Bareilly. If it be left behind, and a move be made on Oudh, Khan Buhadoor Khan will wax bolder, if not stronger; and

Enemies in the Terai.

Khan Buhadoor Khan.

the suffering of those left in the town and district will be proportionately augmented, and hope of getting a stiver of revenue will go."

W. MUIR.

C. BEADON, ESQ., Calcutta.

## CCLXXXVI.

*20th January* 1858. Wednesday.

MY DEAR HARINGTON,—Here is my first instalment for you in the matter of the three bills. It contains nothing which I have not already urged in private letters; but it is put in official form, and will probably go up to Government. I have not spoken with Reade on the subject, and do not know his views regarding it.

Inexpediency of alienating Meerut from N.W.P.

I have not, however, as yet heard any dissentient opinion as to the inexpediency of alienating Meerut.

Concurred in by Sir J. Lawrence.

I sent Sir John Lawrence the copy of a letter which I wrote, entering fully into the question both of the change of the seat of Government and the transfer of Meerut. He says: "I was much obliged to you for your last letter and its enclosure. I think with you that it is not a good plan dividing the Gangetic Doab under two different administrations. The annexation of the Delhi Division to the Punjaub would not matter." Kindly let this opinion be known to Lord Canning; and you might also show His Lordship the Memorandum—though I fear there is nothing new in it.

I have not, of course, touched on the question of the change in the seat of Government.

W. MUIR.

H. B. HARINGTON, ESQ., Calcutta.

## CCLXXXVII.

*21st January* 1858. Thursday.

Fighting at Kotah.

MY DEAR BEADON,—Fighting seems to have been kept up at Kotah for several days, and was still going on on the 14th. Communication with Deolee was cut off, and Captain Macdonald was still ignorant of the result. He has been told that the Oudeypoor, Keraolee, and other neighbouring chiefs have been sending Contingents to the aid of the Kotah Rajah—who is anxious to chastise the mutinous forces before our arrival.

In the forenoon of the 16th Capt. Macdonald and others at Deolee heard a report like a distant salvo of ordnance. It could hardly, he says, be ordinary firing at Kotah—the sound of which would not reach Deolee, as hills intervene. He hopes it may have been the explosion of a grand Magazine the Mutineers had got together. But it is premature to speculate.

Rebellion in Rohilkhund.

The rebels maintain their position opposite Boolundshuhur; but Sapte has ascertained that they lost, by our cannonade of Sunday the 17th, fourteen killed, and some 40 or 50 more wounded.

The shutting of the Canal at the Mayapoor Dam raised the water in the river at Anoopshuhur 2 feet, but I doubt whether such a rise would be permanent if the Canal were shut. I am, however, sending Sapte's letter to Baird Smith, who formerly assigned what appeared good reason for not closing the Canal.

There is a strong body of the rebels at Ram Ghat about 18 miles below Anoopshuhur with 3 guns—and the water is very shallow there.

The posting of the 64th, or a part of it, at Boolundshuhur will, however, protect this side.

Etawah.

Hume, writing from Etawah on the 19th, says he is entirely relieved from the apprehension of attack; the insurgents had hastily retreated to the southern side of the Jumna. The cause he did not know; but it was evidently the presence of the Cawnpoor moveable column near Secundra, or the Etawah frontier. This column was magnified by native report into 10,000 Europeans! Meanwhile, however, much damage has been done. Ajeetmul and 13 other towns or villages between Sukna and Oreya have been burned or plundered; and Hume fears that some portion of the Oreya revenue will be lost. If the Cawnpoor force had been out 10 days earlier, this misfortune, he says, would have been averted.

Damage done by insurgents

What the Commander-in-Chief is doing with his vast concentration of forces we cannot make out. The siege train will leave this to-morrow. But in the interim between his occupation of Furruckabad and its reaching, something might surely have been done either south of the Jumna or north of the Ganges. Every expedition in which a single gun is taken has an important bearing on the final struggle, as it emphatically draws the teeth of the insurgents.

W. MUIR.

C. BEADON, ESQ.

## CCLXXXVIII.

*22nd January* 1858. Friday.

My Dear Beadon,—Up to the 17th instant Capt. Macdonald had received no authentic intelligence of the result of the fighting at Kotah; but he had a native letter from Jahazpoor (the reports of which place had ordinarily turned out correct) saying that the Rajah of Kotah had subdued the insurgents, killing 600 and taking all their Artillery—with a loss of 200 on his side.

The Lahore Government have intimated the march from Dera Ismail Khan towards Ferozepoor of the 1st Sikh Infantry and Moultan Horse, and expected arrival at Lahore of the 2nd Punjaub Cavalry and 5th Punjaub Infantry. But all such movements are probably reported direct to Calcutta.

**Khan Buhadoor raises the Crusading flag in Rohilkhund.**

I have a letter from the Postmaster at Moradabad stating the prevalent report that 5000 of Khan Buhadoor's troops had deserted from him, and that he had in alarm raised the Crusading flag, but with little success.

A proclamation has been affixed by some rebels on the Jumma Musjid at Moradabad calling upon the faithful to rally round Khan Buhadoor and proceed to Bareilly, but it had not met with any response in that city.

**Furruckabad Nawab.**

Numbers of the respectable people of Bareilly were flocking to Rampoor and Moradabad for shelter. They stated that the Furruckabad Nawab was at Bareilly with some of his attendants.

**Disturbance at Oojhanee.**

There is a little disturbance in a village about 20 miles north of Muthra. A Fakeer there (the village is called Oojhanee) during the disturbances took possession of some Government timber—railway posts, I think—and on our resumption of authority refused to give them up. Imdad Ally, the Deputy Collector, expected to persuade him to do so amicably: as there are no available troops whatever at Muthra, Colonel Fraser forbade the attempt of forcible measures. But Imdad Ally attacked the place, and found it defended by a wall from which he was obliged to retire. Imdad Ally holds his place in an adjoining village surrounded by numerous matchlockmen of the loyal neighbouring Zemindars. The Goorgaon troops will probably be able to detach a small body to put the Fakeer down; and indeed the thing is so unimportant but that for the general tranquillity of the country westward it would not have deserved mention.

Our contribution to the Commander-in-Chief's siege train is starting to-day. The string of hackeries seems endless. Seven 24-pounders, six 10-inch mortars, among other pieces, have gone; —above 30, I believe, in all; which will give His Excellency, with what he already has, some 68 pieces of siege ordnance.

**Agra contribution to Commander-in-Chief's siege train. His Excellency has 68 pieces siege ordnance.**

W. MUIR.

C. BEADON, ESQ., Calcutta.

## CCLXXXIX.

*23rd January* 1858. Saturday.

MY DEAR BEADON,—Captain Macdonald's favourable anticipations have not been realised. The Hakim of Jehazpoor has informed him that "the day has gone against the Rajah of Kota, who has been forced to make terms with the budmashes."

**Rajah of Kotah forced to make terms.**

I have no other intelligence from the West.

But I have a message from Lahore of yesterday's date, in reply to my question as to whether a force might be soon expected from the Punjaub for service in Rohilkhund; it is to this effect: "The following troops are now *en route*. A portion will reach the Meerut district early in February; the remainder by the middle of the month. One troop of Horse Artillery; one light Field Battery; one Regiment of Punjaub Cavalry. Two Infantry Regiments, and a wing of Punjaub Infantry." Aided by some Europeans, this force should be fit for anything at present in Western Rohilkhund.

**Troops *en route* from the Punjab.**

We have a letter from Mr. Daniell at Etah of yesterday's date. He is getting on well, but somewhat alarmed at the reported inroads of the insurgents from the opposite side of the Ganges. "Fifteen hundred rebels and five guns are reported to have occupied Kaimgunge, and killed the Thannahdar and some Chuprasees. The enemy held every ghat opposite those in this district."

**Daniell, C.S., at Etah.**

Kaimgunge is not more than 20 miles from Furruckabad, and, as our letters from the latter place dated the 21st instant make no mention of the inroads, we hope Mr. Daniell's information may be at fault. What he says as to the ghats being all in possession of the rebels is not satisfactory. One does not see why, in this pause, expeditions should not have been planned some little distance up the river. Dinkur Rao is over here again. The Narwar Rajah, he says, has run away. He hopes the Bombay road may be open all the way in another week.

**Kaimgunge. Dinkur Rao. Narwar Rajah.**

I trust Sir R. Hamilton will be able to move towards Bundelkhund from Saugor. It would be a great relief.

W. MUIR.

C. BEADON, ESQ., Calcutta.

Baird Smith is in distress about the bursting of the Canal above the Daboulee escape, and anxious for the assistance of more officers in this Department.

. . . . . . . .

## CCXC.

*23rd January* 1858. Saturday.

Cocks, C.S.

Chowbey's family. Dilsookh Rai.

MY DEAR HARINGTON,—Cocks has run in for a day or two from Mynpoorie, and I have had a talk with him about Chowbey's family and Dilsookh Rai. I had a long conversation with Dilsookh Rai himself. He gave me a deeply interesting account of the noble Chowbey's last days. Wilson was wrong in sending the Tehseeldar, the Chowbey, and Dilsookh Rai back to Kassgunge with the enemy so close at hand. From what Cocks wrote at the time, I believe Wilson was sensible of this afterwards, and felt it deeply. They seemed to have behaved with the greatest gallantry. At the time of the inroad of the enemy's horse, Dilsookh Rai was not with the Chowbey, who was overtaken; his head was cut off and then stuck up at the Tehseelee. Dilsookh Rai himself, with a small body of his own horse, effected his escape with the utmost risk. They killed some of the enemy and lost one or two of their own men.

Dilsookh Rai recommended for title of Rajah.

I send Dilsookh Rai's testimonials. He is a fine, brave, open fellow—and will bear his honours well. Cocks agrees with Phillips that the title of Rajah is not too much, and I quite agree. Dilsookh Rai is anxious to succeed the Rajah of Eta, who has died without heirs—his family having no claims (but the reverse) to our favour. Cocks thinks this would be appropriate. But the disposal of the confiscated estates and conferment of suitable ones, both in this and the Chowbey's families' case, might be left for future consideration by the local authorities. Both should have suitable landed property to support their titles, and that can be easily arranged.

Also Jaykishen Dass.

Cocks thinks that Jaykishen Dass, the Chowbey's eldest brother, might suitably be made a Rajah also; and, with reference to our deceased friend's signal services, I think it would be warranted. Jaykishen Dass himself rendered important service as Tehseeldar of Hatrass.

Our friend, Chowbey Mohun Lall, the nephew or cousin who used to attend the old Chowbey, might be made a Rao. Chowbey Mohun Lall.

W. MUIR.

H. B. HARINGTON, ESQ.,
Legis[te] Council, Calcutta.

## CCXCI.

*25th January* 1858. Monday.

MY DEAR BEADON,—No fresh incident at Kota; but the facts of the disturbance are now better understood. Jey Dial, one of the worst of the traitors, was passing through the City with some of his followers when they seized a number of horses belonging to one of the citizens. The latter resisted, when a general fight ensued. Jey Dial brought up guns and destroyed the house where he was attacked. He then turned the guns against the Fort and Palace. The insurgents appear first to have been repelled and driven out of the City with considerable slaughter and loss of 6 guns, as before reported. But they attacked the Fort again, and, bringing guns and ladders close up to it, alarmed the Rajah, who abandoned one of his advisers to them, and agreed to confer a Khillut, Jageer, etc., etc., upon Jey Dial. On this the insurgents retired, and peace was restored. Facts of the disturbance at Kotah. Jey Dial.

. . . . . . . .

All is right at Muthra. The rebellious Fakeer evacuated Oojhanee, and the telegraph posts are in our hands. Muthra.

Hume writes in good spirits from Etawah. He has been re-enforced by a couple of hundred Sowars by the Commander-in-Chief. Hume at Etawah.

I have a letter of the 23rd from Dr. Farquhar, our Civil Surgeon, who ran over the previous day to Furruckabad. He met waggons laden with the telegraph wire at Shekoabad (40 miles off from this), so that it will shortly be here. The line has now reached Mynpoorie, but you probably know this already. Dr. Farquhar.

Some of the Mynpoorie Sowars accompanied Farquhar as orderlies. They are quite village men; "they are very greatly interested in the crops, which are rather backward for want of rain, which the clouds promise to-day" (we have had heavy showers since). The opinion of such men is worth recording. "They spoke freely of the rebellion of the Sepoys—lots of whom they describe as hiding in holes and corners, begging to be Feeling of Sepoys who had mutinied.

screened from detection. They said they (*i.e.* the Sepoys) have no further desire to fight; but from fear of the gallows, as the only alternative to death on the field, continue to resist."

Trade reviving. "In riding from Mynpoorie to this (Furruckabad) we met several carts with good potatoes and cloth of sorts from Futtehgurh bound for Agra. No guards or fear of molestation seemed to be near them."

Naval Brigade. "The praise of the sailors," he says, "is loud in every one's mouth" in camp.

Hanging of rebels. Feeling in camp. "Three hundred men have been hung here already. The feeling is not so bitter in camp as you would expect, though a recklessness of life prevails in the conversation." Farquhar noted the feeling closely at Delhi, and this statement, coming from him, is satisfactory.

W. MUIR.

C. BEADON, ESQ., Calcutta.

Call of Mr. Muir to Allahabad. *P.S.*—Since commencing this letter I have received the message, dated the 23rd, directing me to proceed to Allahabad with part of the Secretariat establishment. The first convoy proceed on the 7th proximo, when I propose starting.

In a letter of the 19th instant Captain Macdonald writes: "Awah will be invested on the 21st: it is now said to have a garrison of 700, but will possibly be found empty."

"I have heard nothing of Tank for some time." The attack of the insurgents on Kaimgunge and the murder of the Thannadar is, I fear, confirmed.

[I was simply acting member of the Revenue Board at the time; Thornhill being Acting Secretary to Government. My "Intelligence" correspondence may have suggested the call to Allahabad, possibly.—W. M.]

## CCXCIII.

*26th January* 1858. Tuesday.

Lieutenant Keatinge marches into Goona. MY DEAR BEADON,—You have probably telegraphic intelligence regarding Lt. Keatinge's movements. But in case you have not, I give the following particulars from a letter of his, dated the 22nd instant. He marched into Goona on that day with 600 Hyderabad Cavalry. Major Orr's instructions are to return again to Bioura; but Keatinge is anxious to arrange for the force remaining at Goona.

Sir R. Hamilton. On the 18th Sir R. Hamilton with the 2nd Brigade were on march from Bhopal on the way to Saugor.

The 1st Brigade was to march from Mhow on the 26th or 28th; on the arrival of the siege train from Ahmednugger, Keatinge expects the brigade to march in his direction by the Bombay road.

In coming up to Goona, he says, "we have met no sort of opposition on the road; and it is evident that the petty Rajahs about here, though willing enough to fight with one another and with Scindia, do not wish to try the chances of war with our Government. There is nothing, I hope, to hinder the post going regularly between Agra and Bombay now."

Feeling of chiefs in Central India.

The enclosed letter received from Mr. M'Leod states in detail the force moving down from the Punjaub; but from Sir J. Lawrence's letter you will see that he has made no arrangement in regard to "Rohilkhund in particular." He is mistaken in thinking that the Agra authorities have any voice in the matter; and Colonel Fraser does not now like to send any communications to the Commander-in-Chief.

One does not see why the direct route suggested by M'Leod should not be adopted if His Excellency destines these troops for the reoccupation of Rohilkhund from the West. The Governor-General would be in time to direct such a movement by telegraph if it is deemed advisable.

I enclose a letter from Charles Raikes, as you may care to see what he says about the protection of this bank.

One does not readily understand why in this pause the Commander-in-Chief should not have been scouring the country by miscellaneous detachments, without separating them from Headquarters for more than a week or ten days. One can understand why he is determined not to break up his force; but such a course would not have done so. However, such speculations are of little use now, for I conclude the period of inaction is close at an end. One grand point is that the whole force has the most thorough confidence in its leader, and implicitly believes in him. Dr. Farquhar, who has just come back from Furruckabad, describes the feeling as unanimous and enthusiastic. This is good.

Confidence in the Commander-in-Chief.

The officers justify this month's inaction by saying that "if he put out his hand" (to anything but the object in view) "he might not be able to draw it back again" at the moment required.

I send also a letter from R. Alexander, which will be interesting as showing his views as to the facility with which Rohilkhund could be reoccupied.

What appears good intelligence has come in that the

Principal Sudder Ameen of Agra and Mahomed Hussu Khan killed.

Principal Sudder Ameen of Agra and Mahomed Hussun Khan have been killed by Khan Buhadur's people. We knew that they had long been held under surveillance and exposed to indignities for their rumoured loyalty to us. The Principal Sudder Ameen has been spoken against for not coming to Agra when invited back; but it is impossible to overestimate the difficulties a man with a family of helpless women and children would encounter in attempting flight. Whether the unfortunate old man has been guilty of any disloyalty since he left this will be decided by Major Williams' investigation. He certainly induced his brother Hamid Hussan Khan to withdraw from Khan Buhadur's service when he (the Principal Sudder Ameen) returned home.

Difficulties of a loyal Mahommedan official.

Kindly mention all this to Harington;—it will interest him, though perhaps hardly you.

General Lawrence, writing on the 22nd January from Ajmere, says: "Awa is being attacked;—this time, I hope, effectually."

Awa attacked.

Nothing from Kotah to-day.

W. MUIR.

C. BEADON, ESQ.

## CCXCIV.

*27th January* 1858. Wednesday.

MY DEAR RAIKES,—

. . . . . . . . . . . .

M'Leod mistakes in thinking that the Government of Agra has anything to say in the direction of the troops; but his suggestion about a direct inroad upon Bijnour without taking the détour to Meerut may be worth His Excellency's consideration, unless opposed to arrangement already determined on.

W. MUIR.

Mr. Muir leaving for Allahabad.

I leave for Allahabad, *D.V.*, on the 7th with part of the Secretariat establishment.

B. Sapte, C.S.

Rohilkhund.

Sapte, writing on the 25th, says that at Anoopshahur "all has been quiet since 17th, though there is still a considerable force there with guns. The Infantry consists of 18th Regiment N.I. and a lot of good Irregular Cavalry. There is a gathering at Kutchla Ghat under Ismail Khan. He has now 2000 men and five guns there. It is said he means to cross. This party should be watched carefully."

Ismail Khan.

C. RAIKES, ESQ., Furruckabad.

## CCXCV.

*27th January* 1858. Wednesday.

My Dear Beadon,—Sapte, writing on the 25th, says everything has been quiet at Anoopshahur since the 17th. But there is still a considerable force on the opposite bank with guns. It consists of the 18th Native Infantry and a good number of Irregular Cavalry,—the latter efficient.

He adds: "There is a gathering at Kutchla Ghat under Ismail Khan. He has now 2000 men and five guns there. It is said he intends to cross. This party should be watched carefully."

I have communicated this to Raikes for the Commander-in-Chief. Our latest accounts from the Kutchla stated that the force had disappeared there, which may be connected with the inroad in Kaimgunge, or with a retrogressive movement to cover Budaon.

I have also sent a copy of D. M'Leod's letter (of which you had a copy yesterday) to Raikes for His Excellency.

Daniell, writing from Etah on the 24th, hears that the rebels were still in force at Kaimgunge with three guns, and that another body with three guns were ready to follow them. You will no doubt have later accounts on the subject from Furruckabad. **Rebels in force at Kaimgunge.**

W. Muir.

C. Beadon, Esq.

## CCXCVI.

*28th January* 1858. Thursday.

My Dear Beadon,—An assault on Awah was intended on the 24th; but on the night of the 23rd, under cover of a dark and stormy night, the garrison evacuated the place and got off. **Garrison evacuates Awah.**

Besides the Nusseerabad and Deesa forces, there was present a regiment of Scind Horse,—so there ought to be no difficulty in following the insurgents up. The Enfield seems to have told severely on the besieged.

Things at Kotah remain much as before, according to Macdonald's last letter of the 22nd. The rebels had applied to the Jalra Patun Chief, who declined to aid them. **Kotah affairs.**

The enemy again crowd the Kutchla Ghat; they have guns, and are said to threaten Kassgunge. Daniell has a report that *Ulleegunge* is occupied by the same rebels who attacked Kaim- **Rohilkhund.**

gunge. One can scarcely credit it. But if the Chief allows his immediate vicinity on this side to be invaded with impunity, such advances cannot be wondered at.

Intended Mutiny known to a few before outbreak of 10th May.

Major Williams, writing from Meerut on the 26th, says that he has evidence of the intended Mutiny being known to a few at 2 p.m. of Sunday the 10th (May). A woman of the Suddur Bazaar sent word to a Kasmiri female living with a Dr. Smith (who was murdered), "that a trooper had told her the Europeans would all be murdered that night." Williams has traced the girl, and will probably get something more out of her.

Fakeer said to be prince in disguise at Umballa.

You may remember a Fakeer, said to have been a prince in disguise, having been about Meerut. This man, Williams has traced at Umballa with the Sepoys at the Enfield Rifle Depôt. "Here, after being ordered to leave the Sooruj Koond, he took up his quarters in the lines of the 20th, the worst Regiment here, and then is said to have gone to Agra and Gwalior."

Sir J. Lawrence says the Commander-in-Chief does not require the light field battery, and that it remains at Umballa, where there was no European Artillery. From Umballa he expects that the other troops will receive orders from the Commander-in-Chief as to their destination. I conclude His Excellency has issued instructions. Sir John quite agrees as to the advisability of an early advance on Rohilkhund.

W. MUIR.

C. BEADON, ESQ., Calcutta.

The dak of the 24th has been delayed below Benares by the rain, I conclude.

## CCXCVII.

*29th January* 1858. Friday.

MY DEAR BEADON,—I have no news of importance to-day. At Kotah the native letters imply that the compromise continues.

You will, I conclude, have intelligence from Furruckabad regarding the force that started on the 26th for Shumsabad, etc.

Kassgunge threatened and Allygunge occupied.

It was high time, as Kassgunge was actually threatened and Allygunge occupied. Hodson's Horse will, I hope, teach them a lesson.

The dak of the 23rd came in afterwards all right yesterday; that of the 24th arriving in the evening;—but I have still nothing from you in expansion of the message of the 23rd. I have, however, made a selection of clerks to go down, about one half of the office or something less. I hope, however, to have something more specific from you by to-morrow's dak.

The coils of wire are, I see, beginning to come in on hackeries.

W. MUIR.

C. BEADON, ESQ., Calcutta.

## CCXCVIII.

### Memorandum, drawn up at the Request of the Governor-General, of Enquiries into the Alleged Dishonour of European Females at the Time of the Mutinies.—Submitted 30th December 1857.

(*This Memorandum is written at other end of MSS. Vol. III. from that which contains foregoing* (*Fourth*) *Series.*)

Agra, *30th December* 1857.

My Lord,—I have now the honour to submit the result of the enquiries I have instituted in compliance with your Lordship's wishes, expressed in the Private Secretary's letter dated the 17th December last.

I might have replied sooner, but I deemed that your Lordship would be desirous that the area of investigation should be as wide as possible, and to secure this object involved some little delay.

I propose despatching this by Cossid to-day, and a duplicate similarly to-morrow. I also propose sending a copy of my Memorandum, with the original enclosures for your Lordship's satisfaction, by Bombay, unless (as I have reason to hope) a regular and safe post be immediately opened between this and Cawnpore.

I venture to believe that your Lordship will view the result, substantiated generally by the opinions now submitted, as satisfactory. A melancholy satisfaction indeed it is;—but yet such as may be calculated to lighten many a heart bowed down with a grief which the thought of simple death even in its cruellest form would not occasion.—I remain, Your Lordship's faithful servant,

W. Muir.

To The Right Honble. Lord Canning,
Governor-General.

## Memorandum containing the Result of Enquiries made by Desire of the Governor-General into the Rumours of European Females having been Dishonoured during the late Mutinies.

On receipt of His Lordship's instructions to submit any evidence I might be able to obtain as to the credibility of the statements current regarding the dishonour of English women during the late disturbances, I immediately addressed such officers as appeared to me likely to possess the widest and most accurate information on the subject.

Attached to this Memorandum is a copy of the opinions which I have collected. I might have waited for others, but these are quite sufficient.

1. E. A. Reade, Esq., Member S.B.R., N.W.P.
2. F. Williams, Esq., Commr., Meerut.
3. Major G. W. Williams, Supt. Cant. Police.
4. Rev. T. C. Smyth, Chaplain, Meerut.
5. C. B. Saunders, Esq., Commr., Delhi.
6. C. B. Thornhill, Esq., Offg. Secy. to Govt. N.W.P.
7. R. Alexander, Esq., Commr., Rohilkhund.
8. A. H. Cocks, Esq., Special Commr., Allygurh.

I proceed to notice the several statements in detail.

I.—The long service and great experience of Mr. E. A. Reade will add peculiar weight with His Lordship to his opinion. Mr. Reade has been in constant communication with the best informed natives of this city; he has also been in correspondence with people of other quarters, and has had ample opportunity for enquiring into the evidence which has from time to time been received from the scenes of the various tragedies. His deliberate opinion is that the stories of dishonour done to European females are generally false.

This conclusion he founds on the unvarying statement of eye-witnesses of the massacres. He adds as a supplementary reason, that the colour of European females is repugnant to the Oriental taste, and that crimes of the nature alluded to never have been perpetrated, even when there was full opportunity for their perpetration. I do not myself allow the natives of this country credit for dislike or insensibility towards the European complexion, and, even if admitted, it might not prove a conclusive argument in the present question; because it is apparently one of the current theories that dishonour was done, not to gratify passion, but to inflict shame and degradation upon the English name.

But the object of the Mutineers was, I believe, not so much to disgrace our name as to wipe out all trace of Europeans, and of everything connected with foreign rule.

In the massacres perpetrated with this object the demon of cruelty was let loose, and barbarity in every inhuman shape indulged. The set of passions, however, called into play was, I conceive, distinct from those which would have tempted to the commission of the suspected practices. There was cold and heartless bloodthirstiness, at the farthest remove from the lust of desire.

As there was, therefore, no dishonour committed on principle, with the view of inflicting disgrace, so likewise, as it appears to me, there was no dishonour done from passion.

Mr. Reade has mentioned the singular absence of this kind of crime in past times. But it has, I believe, been greatly owing to the awe with which Europeans have always been regarded by the natives of India. This awe, it is true, was rudely violated when the rebels ventured on their work of wholesale murder. But I apprehend that it still, at the very moment of the massacres, operated to chill and repress the idea of any familiar approach. I speak of the general native feeling, without venturing to assert that there may not *possibly* have been exceptions.

I have thought it right to add so much on my own part, because the remarks of Mr. Reade appeared open to some variety of opinion on the two points I have alluded to.

II.—The second letter is from Mr. F. Williams, Commr. of Meerut. He was present as Judge at the outbreak there, and has had the best possible means, both then and afterwards, for reaching the truth. His evidence is decisively against the commission of any act of female dishonour.

The case of horrid mutilation, after death, of a pregnant lady, noticed by Mr. Williams, may serve, perhaps, to explain the manner in which the painful rumours of violation gained currency. Such diabolical outrage to the human frame hardly bears to be narrated. Words fail to express the shocking nature of the barbarity. But the very veiling of the transaction by the remark (a likely one in ordinary correspondence), that it is too horrible to be mentioned, would naturally lead the reader to the conclusion that the dishonour was of the worst character, and that the poor victims had been abandoned to the brutalities of lust as well as to the last cruelties of a fiendish rage.

I believe that the most of the stories—those which are not wanton fabrications—must have grown up in this manner. The instance of the half-caste girl referred to in Mr. Williams' postscript is not one of the kind contemplated in the investigation directed by His Lordship.

III.—Major G. W. Williams, Superintendent of Police Battalions, from his long connection with the Cantonment Police, his residence of some months at Meerut after the outbreak, and his employment in that district with the Volunteer Horse, is peculiarly qualified to give an opinion which may be relied on. His testimony, founded as well on the evidence of competent witnesses, as on the universal impression amongst the natives, is that there was no dishonour done to our females at the breaking out of disturbances anywhere.

It will be remarked that Major Williams' evidence extends to the massacres at Futtehgurh and Cawnpore. The enquiries which he has been prosecuting at the request of Government into the conduct of the native officials here have brought him into contact with numerous persons able to give evidence on the subject.

IV.—I requested Major Williams to procure a written statement from the Rev. T. C. Smyth, M.A., as he was said to know of some cases of the kind. But the deliberate opinion of Mr. Smyth, who has been in the most favourable position for sifting the evidence, is that no females were violated at Meerut.

V.—The report of Mr. Saunders, Offg. Commr. and Agent to the Lt.-Governor at Delhi, is most complete and decisive, that neither at Meerut nor Delhi was murder preceded by dishonour. Like Mr. Williams, it will be observed he thinks it possible that some women of colour may have been forced to sacrifice their honour to save their lives; but this is mentioned only as a possible case.

The evidence of Ramchunder is valuable. He is one of the Christians baptized a few years ago at Delhi by Mr. Jennings, is an accomplished mathematician, and was Professor in the Delhi College. He was present in the City during the massacre, and is therefore in every respect a most competent witness as to the nature of the proceedings.

VI.—Although Mr. C. B. Thornhill's views are already known to His Lordship, I thought that it would be satisfactory to have a further recorded expression of them. Mr. Thornhill's position, officiating as the Secretary to Government, and the numerous enquiries which he has personally directed with the purpose of ascertaining the fate of near relatives, render his authority second to no other. He states truly that Hindoos, except of the lowest grades, would have become outcasts had they perpetrated this offence. Neither would Mahomedans have done so in the unconcealed manner which has been supposed at home. Such procedure would have been repugnant to the feelings and habits of the country, and would have required strong and direct evidence to have secured any credence:—while Mr. Thornhill shows that there is absolutely none. It must, however, be admitted that there is nothing in the habits or tenets of the Musulman population which would prevent them from taking females seized at the general outbreak to their homes with sinister designs. By the Mahomedan law, captives taken in war are not lawful to the captors till the expiry of at least a month and a half. But since the Mahomedans have set their laws, human and divine, at nought throughout the rebellion, it is not to be expected that those laws would have checked them even to the observance of that period.

While, however, there is nothing to have prevented the Mahomedans from carrying off women, whom they intended to preserve alive, to their harems, all the evidence yet obtained is entirely opposed to the supposition that ladies of English blood were anywhere reserved for that disgrace. There may have been instances in which females of colour have been forcibly subjected, or, to save their lives, have consented to such treatment.

Mr. Alexander's communication, numbered VII., refers to one or two cases supposed of this nature. But it must be remembered that, as regards Rohilkhund, the evidence cannot be complete or satisfactory till our reoccupation of the Province.

There is one point, however, on which His Lordship may rest assured, viz., that wherever females, whether English or Eurasian, have been taken into the Mehals of natives, the fact cannot remain concealed. All such cases will, as soon as we re-enter the locality in power, be susceptible of full enquiry and proof.

VIII.—The note of Mr. A. H. Cocks (I have extracted from it all that relates to the subject) contains no direct evidence excepting his belief that at Futtehgurh and Hissar no licentious insult was offered, and a statement of the general opinion that at Delhi the ladies and children were simply massacred. No stress need be laid on the boast of the Mutineers; even if correctly stated, it may have been an impudent and idle defiance, and anyhow, until closely enquired into, it can carry no weight. Mere hearsay has so often turned out unfounded, or founded upon something bearing quite another construction, that it cannot be received in this paper at any value.

In respect of Jhansi, there is evidence, direct and indirect, that there was there no dishonour done to the women. The same is the case with Cawnpoor,—the solitary exception being the story regarding Miss Wheeler, the truth of which can be best sifted by Mr. Sherer on the spot.

My own views have been, perhaps, sufficiently stated in the foregoing remarks. But His Lordship may desire a more distinct expression of them.

My connection with the Intelligence Department at the Headquarters of the Govt. of Agra has brought me, during the past six months, into contact with messengers and spies from all parts of the country. I gladly add my testimony that nothing has come to my knowledge which would in the smallest degree support any of the tales of dishonour current in our public prints. Direct evidence, wherever procurable, has been steadily and consistently against them. The people—those who must know had there been cases of outraged honour, and would have told us—uniformly deny that such things were ever perpetrated or thought of. The understanding of the people on this point (if, as I believe, we have correctly apprehended it) cannot be wrong.

That there may not have possibly been exceptional instances it would be hazardous to assert, until the occupation of the whole country, and complete re-establishment of our power, shall have given us the entire command of all available evidence. Judging, however, from the great accumulation of negative evidence, supported as it also is in many important points by direct and positive proof, it may safely be asserted that there are fair grounds for believing that violation before murder was in no case committed; and that, if women of colour have anywhere been carried off and dishonoured, such cases must be rare and peculiar, and have occurred under circumstances which in all likelihood will hereafter be explained.

It is necessary, in conclusion, to remark that this Memorandum applies specially to the N.W.P., including Bundelkhund and Oudh: to those tracts, namely, where the mutinies were the most fatal, and the ensuing anarchy the most widespread and disastrous. They apply indirectly to the mutinies in all other quarters, so far as intelligence regarding them has reached us.

For the stations from Cawnpoor downwards, His Lordship will probably be able to collect evidence, more complete and circumstantial than we can obtain, from the Officers on the spot.

W. Muir.

Agra, *30th Decr.* 1857.

## I. Memorandum by Mr. E. A. Reade, Senior Member, Sudder Board of Revenue, N.W.P.

I am of opinion that the stories of violation, by the Mutineers and their associates in crime, of English females at Cawnpoor and elsewhere are generally false, and that this aggravation of horror has existed only in exceptional cases.

I formed this opinion on these grounds:—

1. That the native informants who have come to the Fort of Agra have fully detailed the sanguinary atrocities as they saw them or heard them described by others, but have not mentioned violation, and their negative answers to the question have rather indicated surprise at the question being put.

2. The first written account received here was from an East Indian who had escaped before the entrenchments at Cawnpoor were attacked, who was not an eye-witness of subsequent scenes, and wrote from hearsay. This class is apt to indulge in a prurient imagination.

3. The natives of India, both Hindoos and Mahomedans (and the latter are much Hindooised in their habits and notions), have a repugnance to sexual connection with European females. During thirty years of Indian experience the only instances that have come to my knowledge have been a few cases of voluptuaries sated with Oriental beauty seeking for variety. If it were otherwise, would not Indian gold easily procure from England and France any number of fallen creatures?

4. Let any one reflect how many young girls without any escort or protection have travelled alone in palankeens from Calcutta to Delhi; or, again, call to mind cases where such travellers on boats have been attacked and plundered in former days, and yet I cannot recollect any instance of violation of European females, either by their attendants or by robbers. Fanaticism and idolatry are equally cruel, but Indian lust is almost always the lust of bloodshed and plunder only.

E. A. Reade.

Agra, *2nd December* 1857.

## II. From Mr. Fleetwood Williams, Commissioner, Meerut, to Mr. Muir.

Meerut, *December 3rd*, 1857.

I never heard any sort of mention of European females having been violated here, at Meerut.

The horrid work here was executed in such a hurry, and in such a bloodthirsty spirit, that I believe the taking of life at once was all that was thought of. There was most frightful mutilation here. One poor lady who was advanced in pregnancy was ripped open, the child taken out, and was found put round the poor lady's neck. But, as far as I can ascertain, violation was not added to the other atrocities here as regards Europeans.

At Secundrabad, in the Boolundshahur District, the poor native women suffered the utmost wickedness of savages in this respect. According to all accounts, except the few killed here on the 10th of May, Europeans have been most mercifully preserved from all evil in this Division, with the exception of two officers killed by their men. But don't forget Cawnpoor.

F. WILLIAMS.

MEERUT, *Dec.* 3, 1857.

*P.S.*—There was one Eurasian girl found in the Boolundshahur District coming with a native, but there was no finding out who she was, and she objected to being rescued from her situation.

## III. MEMORANDUM BY MAJOR G. W. WILLIAMS, SUPERINTENDENT OF POLICE BATTALIONS.

MEERUT, 23*rd Dec.* 1857.

MY DEAR MUIR,—You must have already heard from Mr. Saunders, as he told me he had written to you, and that he knew of no proved cases at Delhi or elsewhere to justify the prevalent opinion of our poor helpless ladies having been dishonoured.

To every one from whom I thought it likely I could procure information on this painful subject, especially to witnesses from Futtehgurh and Cawnpoor, I have put the question, and have been invariably answered in the negative, and most decidedly. I believe the native idea is as strongly against the opinion as, strange to say, the papers are positive in asserting it. Mr. Smyth's letter is conclusive as regards Meerut, where dishonour is supposed to have been offered. But the dead, it would seem, were only grossly insulted. The enquiry I am now making will, I trust, clear up the whole of the Meerut affair of the 10th May.

G. W. WILLIAMS.

IV. FROM THE REVEREND T. C. SMYTH, TO MAJOR G. W. WILLIAMS.

MEERUT, *December* 16, 1857.

MY DEAR MAJOR WILLIAMS,—Since receiving your letter of the 11th instant I have made enquiries in several quarters as to the painful subject upon which you write. I have learned from several unquestionable sources that the bodies of females murdered at Meerut on the 10th May were brutally insulted *after death*; but I cannot discover a single case in which it is clearly proved that violation was actually perpetrated. I am now of opinion that no females were violated at Meerut.

The statements which appear in the English newspapers regarding the atrocities perpetrated by the rebels here and elsewhere are, in many instances, grossly exaggerated, as in the case of Riding-master Langdale's child of the 3rd Cavalry, who was actually killed with one blow of a tulwar while sleeping on the charpoy; whereas she is stated to have been cut in pieces by little and little, with every refinement of gradual torture.

The Sirdhanah Nuns were also mentioned in an English paper as having escaped to "a valley in Thibet," instead of which they were housed from June till early in September within the walls of the Rifle Hospital.

THOMAS SMYTH.

V. FROM MR. C. B. SAUNDERS, OFFG. COMMISSIONER AND AGENT LIEUTT.-GOVERNOR, TO MR. MUIR.

DELHI, *Decr.* 17, 1857.

MY DEAR MUIR,—With reference to the enquiry which Lord Canning's Private Secretary has desired you to make, I would beg to state that I believe there is no reason whatsoever to suppose that the European ladies and girls massacred either at Meerut or Delhi were violated or outraged before death put an end to their sufferings. I have taken considerable pains to ascertain whether there is any foundation for the tales which have obtained publication in the public prints regarding violence having been offered to poor Miss Jennings and Miss Clifford, and am perfectly satisfied that there is no ground whatever for the supposition that they were in any way ill-treated before death. Every account which I have received confirms the fact that they were at once killed by the Palace rabble and others, who rushed up into the quarters of the Commandant of the Palace Guards and there and then massacred the whole party assembled. Articles like that which I return, and which appeared in a

Bombay paper purporting to have been communicated from Umritsur, are in my opinion most dastardly and unwarrantable. I much wonder at an editor having allowed such a statement to have found room in his paper, calculated, as it was, to harrow the feelings of relatives and to do no earthly good, but, on the contrary, much evil by hounding on our troops and officials to what I cannot but term an unholy and unchristian thirst for vengeance.

I have before written to Sir John Lawrence on the subject of the atrocious tales which obtained currency in the papers regarding poor Miss Jennings and her companion, and was glad to find in the last *Lahore Chronicle* an authoritative contradiction to the rumours. The atrocities which have been committed during the rebellion have been quite sufficiently appalling without the need of any exaggeration, which the papers of the "blood and scalp" school have deemed necessary to introduce, with a view to inflame the feelings of our countrymen and turn them into fiends. Poor Wigram Clifford, who was killed at Sonah, was very much distressed by hearing from England tales of his sister having been for days saved and kept in the King's harem, and for which there was no possible foundation.

As you say, there may have been rare and exceptional cases in which ladies at other stations have been ill-treated, and possibly some half-caste women may yet be alive who have been obliged to sacrifice their honour, but I doubt much if there have been many such.

I have spoken to Ramchunder on the subject, and he tells me that the only instance which came to his knowledge of any women having been ill-treated in any way at Delhi was when one of the 3rd Cavalry troopers insultingly patted the cheeks of some poor creature at Durayogunge, on which her husband shot the man, and both husband and wife were immediately killed by the bystanders.

C. B. Saunders.

*Decr.* 1857.

## VI. Mr. C. B. Thornhill, Offg. Secretary to Government, N.W.P., to Mr. Muir.

Agra, *December* 26, 1857.

My Dear Muir,—I am very glad that my note to Dr. Kay has caused an enquiry into the foundation upon which the numerous reports of violation of English women are based.

My own attention was first drawn to the question in consequence of a letter referring to the barbarous murder of a lady in Meerut having been amplified, by the persons to whom it was addressed, into a case of violation previous to murder.

The writer had no intention of conveying such an impression, and I thought it probable that many other letters, similarly worded in general and equally comprehensive terms, might have produced a like result, and I have therefore endeavoured to trace the reports to their source whenever I had an opportunity, and I have invariably found that no sort of evidence existed which in any way substantiated them.

We all know that Hindoos would regard connection with a Christian as involving loss of caste, and that the feelings of Mahomedans would lead them to veil such act with the closest secrecy. It is also contrary to human nature to believe that promiscuous intercourse could have occurred in the public manner which is supposed.

Again, who have described these occurrences? All the European sufferers were massacred, and the natives most positively deny their existence in fact. I feel, therefore, little doubt that the more this painful subject is brought under close enquiry, the more satisfactory will be the evidence that our country-women have not suffered that last insult which would have rendered their awful death, if possible, more horrible, and have caused additional anguish to their relatives and to their country.

C. B. THORNHILL.

## VII. FROM MR. R. ALEXANDER, COMMISSIONER, ROHILKHUND, TO MR. MUIR.

NYNEE TAL, *Decr.* 21, 1857.

MY DEAR MUIR,—It is not possible to give a complete or satisfactory answer to the question put in your letter of the 5th Decr. (which I have only just received, the dak having been interrupted) until I go down to the plains.

I have heard only of two cases which I look on as *credible.* In the one, a son of Mujeedooddeen Ahmed Khan (a Mujjoo) of Moradabad, who is stated to have violated a child of one of the Moradabad victims, and afterwards to have caused her death, was the guilty actor. In the other, Meerun, one of the Naumuhallea Syuds of Bareilly, has detained and, it is supposed, has defiled, a child of one of the clerks (Mr. Fanthome, a Eurasian). When we go down, the truth and particulars of other cases will come out, I believe. But in those cases I think it not (?) unlikely that the victims may also be produced. With the exception of that one case at Moradabad, I have not heard of any such horrible case as that of violation preceding murder; but I am inclined to believe that women or girls have been taken to Zenanahs.

The Hindoos have suffered in this way wherever the Mahomedan rabble soldiery have had their sway.

R. ALEXANDER.

VIII. EXTRACT OF A LETTER FROM MR. A. H. COCKS, SPECIAL COMMISSIONER OF ALLYGURH, TO MR. MUIR, DATED MYNPOORIE, 29 DECR. 1857.

ABOUT the alleged violation of our country-women, I wrote that I had felt a distaste to make enquiries on the subject from natives, especially as at Allygurh nothing of the kind had occurred. I had, however, heard officers who had been at Delhi express their opinion that in most instances the poor ladies and children had been killed at once; although one Mutineer had at his execution boasted of his guilt in this particular. At Cawnpoor we can hardly hope that the captives escaped violation. At Futtehgurh I believe the rule to have been instantaneous death. I have never heard particulars of Jhansi, but at Hissar there was also no brutality committed in addition to murder.

AGRA, *5th January* 1858.

MY LORD,—In reference to my letter of the 30th ultimo, I beg to submit the following additional statement.

I requested Major Macpherson to ascertain for me freely what the views of Dinkur Rao upon the subject of my memorandum were.

In respect to all other places but Cawnpoor, there was no doubt but that my memorandum distinctly indicated the sense prevalent at Gwalior. The case of the Gwalior ladies is a good sample of the general feeling. They were as much in the power of the soldiery as the ladies anywhere else, and were far from escaping insult and cruel treatment, insomuch that swords were presented at their throats to extract even their wedding rings. Yet the shadow of an attempt at their honour there was not.

But regarding Cawnpoor, a man who came to the Durbar from that place certainly led Scindia and Dinkur Rao to the conclusion that during their confinement some of our women were taken by the Sowars to their houses; and the impression left upon the mind of Scindia and his able and discerning Minister is that at Cawnpoor licentious insult was offered. It becomes now a matter of greater consequence even than before to probe the truth of these suspicions. It may be that they are unfounded, for other evidence is opposed to them.

If otherwise, the Nana's name will, if possible, be rendered still blacker and more vile by the stigma of encouraging an atrocity elsewhere unknown.

Should your Lordship make any use of my memorandum as already submitted, I would beg the addition of the following postscript.

*Postscript, 5th January* 1858.—There are points connected with the long detention of the Nana's victims which render Cawnpoor a peculiar case, and may cast a suspicion on the treatment of the prisoners there;—certainly (so far as present evidence goes) attaching to no other quarter. I would recommend further particular enquiry there.

I remain, your Lordship's faithful servant,

W. MUIR.

TO THE RIGHT HONBLE. LORD CANNING,
Governor-General.

# INTELLIGENCE DEPARTMENT, AGRA.

## VOLUME IV.

*FIFTH SERIES.*

# CORRESPONDENCE WITH COLONEL GREATHED'S MOVEABLE COLUMN,

**1st October to 20th October 1857.**

## BEFORE AND AFTER THE ENGAGEMENT OF THE 10TH OCTOBER 1857.

[N.B.—*The opposite side of the Volume* (*MSS. No. IV.*) *contains Memoranda, etc., of Intelligence.*—(*Sixth Series.*)]

# CORRESPONDENCE WITH COL. GREATHED'S COLUMN.

## Before and after the Engagement of the 10th October 1857.

### CCXCIX.

AGRA, 1st *October* 1857.

MY DEAR SAPTE,—

. . . . . . . . .

Indore Mutineers from Dholpore.

From Dholpore we hear that the Indore Mutineers intended to break ground last night, and they are probably at Jajou on the Ootangan, some 18 or 20 miles from this, to-day. They are said to be moving *via* Khyragurh and Futtehpore Sikri on Muthra.

Dholpore guns.

Our messenger states that they have succeeded in carrying off four of the Dholpore Rana's big guns (24-pounders), tackling them to elephants. Colonel Fraser said he wished this point to be specially mentioned to Colonel Greathed, who will of course see this letter.

Lucknow.

No news in yet from Lucknow; we are waiting for it with great anxiety. The last was all favourable up to the 22nd, when we were within 14 miles of our beleaguered garrison.

Gwalior Contingent.

The Gwalior Contingent are said to be breaking off from Gwalior with the view of moving on Cawnpore. Congratulate Colonel Greathed on his successes (if our reports be, as I trust they are, true) at Boolundshuhur. Hoping soon to hear from you.

W. MUIR.

B. SAPTE, ESQ.,
With Colonel Greathed's Pursuing Column.

### CCC.

AGRA, 2nd *October* 1857.

Calls for frequent reports of Column. Bareilly Brigade.

MY DEAR SAPTE,—Still we get no letters from your camp. But we have great hopes that you must be at Somna, if not nearer. In case my previous letters should not have reached, I may repeat what I said before, that Colonel Fraser is desirous that full and frequent reports should be sent in to me of the proceedings of the Column. The last we hear of the Muthra people is that the Bareilly Brigade had crossed over the Bridge, but was yet encamped on the opposite bank.

After writing the above, yours of the 29th to Mr. Reade was

received here. The news is very good, but I fear the delay may allow of the Muthra Mutineers escaping with their guns. They seem to have heard of the Column on the right bank, and talk of moving across to Allygurh. Some of the Neemuch Brigade are also reported to have crossed over. I do trust you may be able to catch them up.

**Neemuch Brigade.**

Colonel Fraser has ordered the Hatrass detachment to fall back on Agra, while the Mutineers are crossing the Doab, as he does not think it strong enough to risk the chances of an encounter with them. Hoping to hear from you soon.

**Hatrass Detachment.**

W. MUIR.

B. SAPTE, ESQ.,
With Colonel Greathed's Column.

## CCCI.

AGRA, *3rd October* 1857.

MY DEAR SAPTE,—Yesterday we received a letter from Delhi, from which we gather that Brigadier Showers' Column is only a local force, not intended to proceed farther than the Kootub; and there is nothing else which leads to the idea of its being destined to move down to Muthra, except the expression in your letter, which was too readily construed here according to our wishes, rather than according to its strict meaning. The Bareilly Brigade is, we hear, to-day at Moorsan, and to-morrow probably will be at Hatrass, but that may be only the advanced portion of it. I am sanguine that Col. Greathed will yet be in time to intercept and chastise these Mutineers, especially as the rest of the force is still at Muthra. A portion of the other brigades is said to have already followed the Bareilly Brigade, and all will likely go the same way. It will be a point of consideration which line to take at the Allygurh bifurcation. The Mynpoorie road will probably afford the best chance of cutting off the retreat of the Bareilly Column.

**Showers Column.**

**Bareilly Brigade.**

The Indore Mutineers were still at Dholpore yesterday. They give orders for a march every day, but have not as yet carried them out. It is still highly probable that they will go *via* Muthra, unless their plans are altered by hearing of your approach. The Gwalior people by the last accounts had not yet marched; it was not unlikely that they might go *via* Dhuttia, Jhansi, Jaloun, etc.

**Indore Mutineers.**

Let us hear often and fully from you.

W. MUIR.

B. SAPTE, ESQ.

## CCCII.

*4th October* 1857. Sunday morning.

Warning Greathed's Column of the possible approach of the Indore rebels from Dholpore. Sends Memorandum for Colonel Greathed.

MY DEAR SAPTE, or CAMPBELL,—Herewith a memo. which I sent to the Chief Commr. and Colonel Cotton last night. Colonel Fraser is very anxious that news of the actual state of things should go on at once to Colonel Greathed, so I send this as it is. I much fear that you are too late to catch these fugitives across the Doab.

You see how things stand on this side. If the Neemuch and Indore forces form a junction and are so foolhardy as to attack us, you shall hear. If they move *via* Etawah, your Column might catch them up.

Pray lay this before Colonel Greathed.

W. MUIR.

## CCCIII.

### TELEGRAPHIC MESSAGE.

FROM COL. FRASER, CHIEF COMMR., TO MR. A. H. COCKS, C.S., ALLYGURH (?)

*5th October* 1857. 8.30 a.m.

Greathed to follow the Mutineers if reasonable chance of overtaking them, or

REQUEST Colonel Greathed to follow the Mutineers sharp, if there is any reasonable chance of overtaking them at the Kuchla or Kadir Chouk Ghats.

March at once on Agra.

But if his information leads him to suppose that they are making for Furruckabad or towards Cawnpore, and that from their rapid flight there is little chance of overtaking them in that direction, then beg him to march at once on Agra, with the view of dislodging the Mutineer force from Dholpore.

## CCCIV.

### TELEGRAPHIC MESSAGE.

FROM THE SAME TO THE SAME.

*5th October* 1857. 11.30 a.m.

Colonel Greathed instructed to move directly to Agra.

INFORMATION just received from Dholpore renders it still more probable than before that a combination may be forming there against this place. The Mutineers there must consequently be crushed.

Unless there be the near and certain prospect of overtaking the Bareilly and other fugitives now at Secundra Rao, I would wish Colonel Greathed to move directly and without loss of time to Agra, in order that immediate measures may be taken to attack Dholpore.

## CCCV.

AGRA, *5th October* 1857.

MY DEAR SAPTE, or CAMPBELL,—I trust you will before this have received the purport of the two messages despatched by the Telegraph through Mr. Cocks.

Our information is that the fugitive forces are to-day at Secundra Rao, above 25 miles from Allygurh. The only chance of catching them up would be at the Budaon ghats, if they take that course. You will have better information probably than we could give you of their movements after Secundra Rao. But unless Colonel Greathed has an early and certain prospect of being able to attack the retiring force, Colonel Fraser is desirous that he should move direct on Agra, with the view of making an immediate advance on Dholpore. **Fugitive forces at Secundra Rao.**

I hope, therefore, we may soon see the whole force over here.

Heera Singh, with the wretched remains of the Neemuch Brigade, will be at Dholpore to-morrow. **Neemuch brigade.**

As I was writing, Colonel Greathed's letter to me of the 6th instant reached me. Pray thank him for it. I have shown it to Colonel Fraser, who replies: "Order Greathed over here at once; he cannot do anything with 400 Europeans only. We can shelter and accommodate his sick here, and give him strength enough to smash the Dholpore force. **Greathed instructed to come to Agra at once.**

It is late, and I have no time to add more.

W. MUIR.

C. B. SAPTE, ESQ.
G. CAMPBELL, ESQ.

## CCCVI.

### TEL. MESSAGE.

FROM COL. FRASER, CHIEF COMMR., TO A. H. COCKS, C.S., ALLYGURH.

*5th* (?) *October* 1857.

ARE you prepared to hold Allygurh with 150 Europeans, 4 guns, and the Militia you now have? **Inquires if Cocks can hold Allygurh.**

## CCCVII.

### TEL. MESSAGE.

FROM SAME TO SAME.

*October 6th*, 1857.

Colonel Greathed instructed to march direct on Agra.

MAJOR MONTGOMERY'S message of to-day received. The fugitive force has got the start of Colonel Greathed by 2 or 3 days. There seems little use in pursuing them. The chance of overtaking them is gone. The Chief Commissioner still desires Colonel Greathed to march direct on Agra. He may now come *via* Secundra Rao. Until he approaches, we cannot arrange for occupation of Allygurh. When he reaches Hatrass, orders will be given for a part of the Khundowlee force to advance and hold Allygurh.

## CCCVIII.

### TEL. MESSAGE.

FROM SAME TO SAME.

*October 6th.* 5 p.m.

Suggests route for Column.

THE Chowbey says that the road from Akrabad is better and shorter than that *via* Secundra Rao to Hatrass. The road by Sassna may therefore be taken if not too late. Send information to Colonel Greathed accordingly.

## CCCIX.

### TEL. MESSAGE.

FROM W. MUIR, SUDDER BOARD, AGRA, TO A. H. COCKS, C.S., ALLYGURH.

*7th October.* 10.15 a.m.

Dholpore troops move on Agra.

INTELLIGENCE come in of movements by Dholpore troops this way. Chief Commr. desires that your detachment should come in at once. In connection with Col. Cotton, I have orders to request that Major Montgomery should fall back without delay on Agra.

Colonel Greathed to come on quickly.

Send on express messenger to Col. Greathed to come on as quickly as he can without unnecessary fatigue to his troops. Repeat by two or three successive messengers at intervals of one hour.

It is possible that the Indore troops may be in communication with the Gwalior Contingent, who may be coming to join them.

## CCCX.

### TEL. MESSAGE.

From Same to Same, Allygurh.

1 p.m.

If Colonel Greathed is unable from any cause to push on very rapidly, the Chief Commr. desires that he will detach 500 Cavalry and one troop H.A., and despatch them by forced marches to Agra.

**Advance detachment to come by forced marches.**

Send on this message by express messengers as before.

W. M.

## CCCXI.

Agra, *7th October* 1857.

My Dear Sir,—I trust you will have received before this the instructions I sent you out by Telegraph yesterday to Mr. Cocks, under the Chief Commr.'s orders, for you to march this way with all practicable speed, but without unnecessarily fatiguing your force.

The reason of this urgent order is as follows:—

Intelligence has come in that the Indore Mutineers marched yesterday from Dholpore, a stage 10 miles this way, where they were joined by the Neemuch Mutineers. They have 7 or 8 small guns, 6 or 9-pounders, and have got 3 or 4 heavy ones, 24-pounders or 18-pounders, from the Dholpore Rana. They threaten now to put in execution their long expressed intention of attacking Agra. It may possibly be bravado, to cover a movement eastward, but is certainly the common talk of the Sepoys, etc., and if it is their real intention it is not unlikely that they have engaged the Gwalior Contingent to follow them. We know that there have been communications between them of late; under any circumstances, it is of the first importance that these troops should be dislodged from their present advanced position and driven from the Doab of the Chumbal and Jumna. They cannot be allowed to threaten the Fort and City of Agra.

**Indore Mutineers marching towards Agra joined by the Neemuch Mutineers.**

If immediate measures are not taken against them, they may possibly entrench themselves in some advantageous position near Agra, from which it may not be possible to dislodge them without loss.

The moment you arrive a movement will be made against them—400 or 500 Europeans can be added to your force.

Necessity for Colonel Greathed's rapidly advancing.

You will see from the above statement the urgent necessity of your marching on Agra with the greatest rapidity.

W. MUIR.

To COL. GREATHED,
Commanding the Moveable Column.

## CCCXII.

*P.S.*—1½ p.m. 7 *Oct.* 1857.

Urgent call.

Reiterates instructions for rapid advance of Column.

MY DEAR SIR,—The above is the duplicate of a letter which I sent about two hours ago by Mr. Cocks. Since then I have, by Colonel Fraser's desire, sent a Telegraphic Message to ask you to send on by forced marches 500 Cavalry and troop of H.A., if you find yourself unable from any cause to march *very* rapidly this way. We should be much set up by that reinforcement, at any rate until you could come up—but pray come on as quickly as you can.

W. MUIR.

To COL. GREATHED,
Commanding the Moveable Column.

## CCCXIII.

### TEL. MESSAGE.

FROM W. MUIR, SUDDER BOARD, AGRA, TO A. H. COCKS, C.S., ALLYGURH.

3.30 p.m. 7 *Oct.* 1857.

Jat Horse.

THE Jat horse should go on to Hatrass under a native officer. Our officers should come in here. This is in reply to Captain Murray's message.

## CCCXIV.

AGRA, *October 8th*, 1857. 11 a.m.

MY DEAR SIR,—Your letter to Mr. Cocks of the 6th instant, and Mr. Campbell's to me of the same date (for which please thank him), have just been received. I am glad to find that you have turned your face this way. A movement against the Indore troops becomes daily of more urgent consequence. A portion, if not the whole, have quitted Dholpore, so there is no fear of their standing a siege, as you apprehend, at that place. They are

A movement against Indore troops of urgent consequence.

certainly advancing a portion of their troops this way, with the intention, as they give out, of attacking us here; but not unlikely with the view of covering a movement either to the east or to the west. But *in either case* it is equally important that they should be promptly attacked and destroyed. The Chief Commr. is therefore decisive in his instructions that you should march without delay this way. And I trust you have received the intimation of his desire, despatched yesterday, that in event of any delay on the road you should send on 500 Cavalry and a troop of Horse Artillery in advance by forced marches to us. Hoping soon to have the pleasure of shaking you again by the hand, and personally congratulating you on your success.

Chief Commissioner's instructions decisive

W. MUIR.

COL. GREATHED,
Commanding Moveable Column, Hatrass.

*P.S.*—I believe you are aware that the Commission conferred on Col. Fraser invests him with authority over all forces in the field not commanded by a General Officer.

Explains Chief Commissioner's military authority.

*N.B.*—A portion of the Dholpore force is now within a long march of Agra. No time is therefore to be lost.

Dholpore force nearing Agra.

## CCCXV.

MIDDAY.—The above is the duplicate of a letter I despatched half an hour ago by a Cossid. I propose sending this by a Sowar if I can get one.

The Indore troops' camp is believed to be—at least the camp of a portion of their force—at Jajou, some 18 miles off; and they have, it is said, ordered supplies at Kukowa, distant some 8 or 10 miles. There is therefore every reason for rapid movement on your part.

Reiterates foregoing instructions describing near position of Indore troops.

W. MUIR.

TO COL. GREATHED.

## CCCXVI.

AGRA, *8th October* 1857. 2.30 p.m.

MY DEAR SIR,—I enclose an original memo. of local intelligence laid before the Chief Commr. He has desired me to send you "the news of the day," and I cannot do so more fully than by sending this memo. The Chief Commr. bids me "again urge on you the necessity of sending 500 Cavalry and a troop of H.A. on at once, so that they may, if possible, reach this on the

Reiterates instructions for advance detachment.

morrow; for, if not, we may be compelled to fight the Dholpore Mutineers alone, and under great disadvantages."

We are looking anxiously for you.

W. MUIR.

COL. GREATHED,
Commanding Moveable Column.

## CCCXVII.

## EXPRESS.

AGRA, *October 8th*, 1857.

Indore troops 18 miles off.

MY DEAR SIR,—The enemy are encamped to-day at Jajou, some 18 miles from this. They have made preparations for crossing the Kharee to-morrow, and will then be within an easy march of Agra. The whole force declares its intention of attacking the Fort, and we must be at once prepared to repel and chastise them. Colonel Fraser has therefore desired me to send out an *express* to you urging upon you the speediest movement to Agra in your power; and desiring that you will send forward the 500 Cavalry and troop of H.A. with all despatch as before in advance of you.

Urges Colonel Greathed to move rapidly to Agra, and to send advance detachment.

W. MUIR.

COL. GREATHED,
Commanding Moveable Column.

## CCCXVIII.

## EXPRESS.

AGRA, *9th October*. 8 a.m.

MY DEAR GREATHED,—Many thanks for yours of the 7th. Colonel Fraser is writing a few lines to you himself.

Position of enemy.

The enemy is encamped on the other side of the Kharee, and professes to intend a passage of that river to-day. They will probably find it a more difficult matter than they fancy to transport their heavy guns (of which they have got 3 or 4 from Dholpore) across the stream, which is deep. But the main body of their force may, if they choose to risk the thing, cross over to-day, and to-morrow beard us in our Fort and plunder the City. Hence our urgent anxiety to be provided with Cavalry and another troop of H.A. We want this in advance of you, lest these desperadoes should cast themselves suddenly upon us.

Repeats request for advance detachment.

As far as we can see, our enemy is playing the part of a madman, and thrusting his head into the lion's jaws. But you must come on rapidly, in order yourself to play the lion's part. There are not wanting indications of some advisers in the enemy's camp who wish to carry the force either towards Bhurtpore or Etawah. Some detachments in these directions were expected, it is said by them, to return to-day. But it would be even more disastrous to allow their escape than to have to bear their menaces here for a day or two. You have therefore every inducement to hurry on.

Enemy should not be allowed to escape.

Arrangements can be made to assist your Infantry the last stage or more, by bullock train waggons, if you will give us details as to your period of reaching each.

This letter, enclosing Colonel Fraser's despatch, goes by mail cart, and the coachman will have instructions to bring back your reply in the same manner.

W. Muir.

*P.S.*—They have given out that they wish to fire their first 5 shots at the Fort on Sunday next, for luck's sake!

## CCCXIX.

### EXPRESS.

Agra, *9th October*. Afternoon.

My Dear Greathed,—I send a line in case it may catch up the mail cart before it starts.

Our reconnoitring party has come in. Numbers of the Cavalry have crossed the Kharee, and our party was fired on. 300 Infantry about had crossed.[1]

Informs Colonel Greathed the enemy have crossed the Kharee.

This all looks as if they meant to come on.

The Cavalry are spreading over the country, and will be committing all kinds of excesses and outrages.

Their cavalry spreading over the country.

Come on quickly.

W. Muir.

Colonel Greathed.

[*Note.*—Next day (*i.e.* on 10th October) Agra was attacked by the Indore troops just after Greathed's Column had arrived. An account of the engagement, and of the enemy's defeat and flight, is given elsewhere. (See CXLV., p. 186 *ante*.—W. M.)]

[1] On the day before, as the enemy were in force within a few miles of Agra, and it had become a case rather for military scouts than for the spies of the Intelligence Department, in sending the evidence of the enemy's close approach to Colonel Fraser and Colonel Cotton, I made the suggestion of sending out "a reconnoitring party and continuous mile pickets." See No. CCCLV. p. 429, *post*.—W. M.

## CCCXX.

AGRA, 14*th October* 1857.

Mutineers at Jowar.

MY DEAR GREATHED,—A party of 500 Horse and 500 Foot, probably fugitive from the force you routed on Saturday, was reported to be at Jowar, half-way between Muthra and Hatrass, yesterday afternoon. They spoke of coming on to Hatrass;—what course they will then take I cannot say, but be on the look out.

W. MUIR.

COLONEL GREATHED.

## CCCXXI.

The same to Major Eld, Allygurh.

THE same as above to Major Eld, Commanding Allygurh Detachment, with the following words................ "look out":

It was reported that last night, before they crossed (this side of Muthra), they were in a very sorry plight, some with and some without muskets, and as they are running away, try and have a slap at them.

I wrote the above by Muir's orders.

W. ALEXANDER.

No *guns* were seen—nor are they likely to have any.

## CCCXXII.

AGRA, 16*th October* 1857.

Gwalior Contingent said to be about to march.

MY DEAR GREATHED,[1]—The news to-day, received in various forms and by a reliable communication to Major Macpherson from the Gwalior Durbar, is that the Contingent was to march on the evening of the 14th. Their "line doree" had gone on on the night of the 13th. Their line lies by the Antree Pass, and may either take them *via* Jhansi or *via* Koonch and Orai. If the latter route is taken, then the distance to Cawnpore is under 130 miles. So they are considerably nearer than you; but you have the better road, and they have the Jumna and Sind to cross. The game will soon thicken at Cawnpore. I trust you will have the glory of repulsing the Contingent from Cawnpore in the same brilliant style as that in which the Column annihilated the Indore Army. It has broken up, as every day's report more fully proves, in the most signal manner, the townspeople and the Zemindars even rising on the fugitive parties.

Indore force broken up.

[1] Oldfield's hand.—W. M.

When you may not have time yourself to write, will you kindly charge one of your staff, or some other officer who may have the *Kakoëthes scribendi*, to give me occasional details of progress.

I hope to hear both from Campbell and Harington; but when communications are also received from a military Officer, a complete and more accurate picture of events is obtained. I trust the maps are what you wanted, and now may success and victory attend you.

W. MUIR.

## CCCXXIII.

AGRA, *16th October* 1857.

Regarding Brigadier Hope Grant coming to Agra.

MY DEAR GRANT,[1]—Colonel Fraser urged you to come in from Allygurh here on the impression that you were on your way down under orders to take the command of the Column. This was assumed, perhaps too hastily, on the report current in the camp of the Column, that you were coming down, with the recruits, for that purpose.

As this turns out not to be the case, and as the former letters were merely intended to make you hurry on to the end of a journey supposed to have been then more than half completed, Col. Fraser is anxious that you should be stopped if still possible. I send this, therefore, by express, and trust it will reach you in time to prevent your having set out.

W. MUIR.

BRIGADIER H. GRANT, C.B., Meerut.

## CCCXXIV.

AGRA, *October 20th*, 1857.

Brigadier Hope Grant to hurry to Cawnpore.

MY DEAR GRANT,[2]—Colonel Fraser is now pressing in his instructions for you to hurry on towards Cawnpore as rapidly as you can.

500 Muzbees are coming down to reinforce us here. So that we shall be quite set up.

Nothing else that is new.

W MUIR.

BRIGADIER H. GRANT, C.B.,
Commanding Column.

[1] W. Lowe's hand.—W. M. [2] Lady Muir's hand.—W. C.

# INTELLIGENCE DEPARTMENT, AGRA.

## MSS. VOL. IV.

*SIXTH SERIES.*

# DEPOSITIONS OF SPIES,

## NOTES OF INTELLIGENCE COLLECTED,

AND

## MEMORANDA OF THE RESULT, DRAWN UP ON IMPORTANT OCCASIONS FOR CHIEF COMMISSIONER, AND OFFICER COMMANDING, AGRA.

**31st August to 23rd October 1857.**

# NOTES OF INTELLIGENCE AND MEMORANDA FOR CHIEF COMMISSIONER AND OFFICER COMMANDING, AGRA.

**31st August to 23rd October 1857.**

## CCCXXV.

*From Lalla Joogul Kishore (apparently addressed from Gwalior to Major Charteris Macpherson, Political Agent with Scindia, then at Agra).*

31*st August* 1857.

SIR,—I beg to acknowledge the receipt of your two letters of the 15th and 24th August, and we are happy to learn that you are all well and happy.

The contents of the letters of the 24th of August gave every satisfaction to my Master. He begs to state that he is well aware of the British friendship and justice from the time they granted him the Guddee (or throne) of Gwalior, and begs to present his respects to His Honour the Lt.-Governor, yourself, and all others who know him.

**A Delhi Prince at Gwalior.** The Mutineers of Indore have lately brought a Mussulman who, they say, is the first Prince of the Delhi King. When this forge (false ?) Prince arrived into their camp they saluted him with 22 guns. A few days ago they wanted that my Master should pay the respect to Prince—the answer to my Master was that the Rajahs of Gwalior have been several times deceived by . . . . [Here ends.—W. C.].

## CCCXXVI.

*Translation of a vernacular Memo. received by Captain Nixon, from Dholpore. Gwalior news—Wednesday and Thursday.*—

**Proceedings of mutinous Regiment at Gwalior.** Yesterday early the . . : regiment marched to the Residency, the Bhopal Nawab, and the Shahzada and an assemblage of others accompanying and entering the Residency, took from it glass articles and other things whatever was worth taking, and took flowers and fruits from the gardens, and cut down the roadside trees. The Raees (Maharaja) got news of this, and was much annoyed, and sent a message to say that all the buildings there belonged to him: "Do not commit any excesses;" and he sent orders to the watchmen to beat any one who disobeyed, and drive him off. Narain Rao went there to arrange matters, and took back the house things from them, and made them remove their camp half-a-koss from the Residency. The messenger is official.

The fourth regiment stationed at Morar is on the move, and will go along with them.

The Magazine (ammunition) has been distributed. *Finis.*

## CCCXXVII.

### KHUREETA, OR OFFICIAL LETTER FROM THE RANA OF DHOLPORE TO THE LT.-GOVERNOR AT AGRA, DATED 3RD SEPTEMBER 1857.

[*The original is on native paper, sprinkled all over with gold leaf, and with gilt floral border and heading. It is written in the best style of Persian caligraphy.*]

NAWAB SAHIB,[1] of high dignity, appreciator of merit, affectionate and kind to me, your humble servant, may your dignity increase!

After paying such respects as a suppliant should offer, and expressing my desire for the honour of serving you (your service having the virtue of changing the base into the noble), which is the dearest wish of my heart, I beg to submit to your exalted mind of sunlight splendour the following information. To-day, the 3rd September 1857, news arrived, conveyed verbally by a trustworthy person, that yesterday, Wednesday the 2nd inst., the infantry of Indore with the troops of the Nawab of Bhopal, having marched from Morâr, have encamped at the Resident's house in Lashkar, Gwalior: and to-day, Thursday, they would halt there. The rumour is that on Friday they are marching in this direction. The troops of Morâr and Indore are united in purpose, "You go one stage ahead, and we will follow stage by stage." It is necessary that you should be informed of this, so I now send you this letter. Whatever you wish I am ready to do. I am but an old dependent and sincere well-wisher of the Government of the East India Company. Night and day do I cherish the desire that it may prosper, and be victorious. I trust that you will kindly continue to favor me by sending me letters with tidings of your health.

May the star of your dignity and glory shine brightly![2]

[1] The proper style in addressing the Lt.-Governor in Persian.—W. C.

[2] This letter bears no signature.—W. C.

## CCCXXVIII.

*5th of September.*—The Tehseeldar of Khyragurh reported that on Friday, the 4th, 70 Sowars, 300 Infantry, and 2 guns crossed at Dholpore; that the rest was at Choundee.

Tehseeldar of Khyragurh reported Gwalior troops to assemble at Dholpore.

The whole force—3 "pultuns," 3 troops, and 1200 Gwalior Sowars—would assemble at Dholpore on Wednesday, and on Thursday, having formed a camp, start for Agra.[1]

W. M.

## CCCXXIX.

*Major Macpherson's Memorandum of the 6th September* 1857. —On the 2nd of August the Indore and Mhow insurgents, under Shahzada Ferozeshah of Dehli, marched from Morar Cantonment to the Residency They consisted of:—

Indore and Mhow insurgent force.

| | |
|---|---|
| 23rd N.I. strength about | 800 |
| Irreg. 1st Cavalry | 120 |
| Holkar's Foot | 400 |
| "Gole" of Hindustanis, under Sirdar Waris Mahomed Khan of Bhopal, late prisoner at Indore | 300 |
| Ghazees | 700 |
| Golundaz | 100 |
| The 4th troop of the 2nd Contingent Cavalry, which requested the Maharajah's permission to depart because, from having killed English officers, it considered itself beyond pardon both by the Government and the Maharajah | 100 |
| About 10 men from each Contingent Regiment, excepting the 5th | 60 |
| From the 4th Contingent Infantry, in the same position as the 4th troop of 2nd Cavalry | 100 |
| | 2680 |

This force, on the 3rd, detached by forced marches to the Chumbul about 500 men, consisting of three companies of the 23rd N.I., 100 Horse in English uniforms, 100 Gole and Ghazees, and 2 guns. They reached the Chumbul on the 4th, and the Infantry and Cavalry crossed at the Katree Ghat that evening.

Part of force crossed the Chumbul on the 4th September.

The object in pushing on this detachment was said to be to secure against the supposed advance of an English force the

[1] More than a month before they advanced on Agra (Oct. 10th).—W. M.

river Ghats and the Fort at Dholpore on the river's bank, and especially, it is said, with a view to depositing in the Fort the contents of the Gwalior Magazine. The Fort was left open to this party. I have not yet heard of its entrance into it.

On the 4th the remainder of the Indore insurgent force moved from the Residency, and was to reach the Chumbul to-day, —it has 400 or 500 carts, with very many women and children; they will take at least to-morrow to cross. They had on the 3rd no share of the Gwalior Magazine, and only 40 maunds of powder brought from villages, and from 10 to 20 . . . (?) guns. **Indore force advancing on Dholpore.**

Their further movements depend mainly on the course which the rebels at Gwalior shall take.

Charteris Macpherson,
Political Agent.

## CCCXXIXA

*6th September. Statement of Huttee Singh Meena, employed by Mr. Phillipps, Magte. and Collector.*—Was with the Indore troops when they left, having had no pay for 5 months. I went with them to the Residency on the 2nd. There was no plunder or disturbance there. They halted on Thursday, and intended to remain there 2 or 3 days in hopes of getting the Contingent to go with them. While encamped there, about 10 or 11 a.m., a letter was received from some one at Dholpore by the Bhopal Nawab, saying that whoever came first, the British or the rebels, would take Dholpore—the Fort and Ghats—that there would be no local resistance. The Nawab immediately called the Havildar Major and Subadar Major (both Mussulmans) and ordered 2 companies, 2 guns, 2 troops, and 100 of the new levies to go forward and seize the Ghats and occupy Dholpore; so they set out about midday and pitched at Cheounda, and started in the morning.

[*Here follows detail of troops, about* 7000; *and of arrangements at ferry, etc.*]

. . . . . . .

No Contingent Regiments are with them. Only a few here and there from Contingent Regiments joined the Army on Thursday. They have no certain hopes now of the Contingent Regiments coming. They hope the 2nd and 5th will join. The 5th has gone to the Body Guard, but not yet got its pay.

The Magazine of the Contingent has not been opened or touched. The Indore people say they have plenty of ammunition, but little grape; they hope to get some heavy guns at Dholpore. I saw 2 big guns (say 18-pounders) and 5 or 6 smaller ones—these unmounted.

The Ootangun is fordable, but the Kharee is deep. I crossed on a platform on earthen pots: the boat is taken away. He adds that the main force is probably crossing to-day, but that it will probably not cross entirely before the third day—*i.e.* Tuesday. They will therefore not march probably till Wednesday.

## CCCXXX.

*7th Sept., Monday. Statement of Ghoolam Mahomed, as given by Major Macpherson.*—He left Dholepore at daylight on Sunday morning.

Report of insurgents at Dholpore.

250 Foot, 80 Regular and 20 Irregular Horse, with 25 or 30 camp-followers and 2 small guns, had crossed to this side. Mewattees of Sont kee Mundee and from Cóel and Hatrass were coming behind.

The Rana and Soobah were at Dholepore. But the Rana's son and his ladies were at Baree.

The advanced force above described demanded the Rana's guns, and took possession of them; but let them go on getting a present of 200 rupees and a meal for each.

They are pitched at the Dak Bungalow, which they spared on its being represented to be Dholepore and not British property.

An Irregular Sowar told this witness that they were going to Agra; he met him with 4 or 5 Sepoys at Munniah (4 or 5 coss this side Dholepore) ordering supplies.

A man of the Regular Cavalry, on the other hand, said the force was going to Dehli. He said the Contingent had given them neither guns, powder, nor shells. Scindia was angry with them. They were going to Dehli lest he should attack them from behind. "We are Poorbeas," they said, "and intend going Eastward; you are from the West, and had better go thither."

## CCCXXXA.

*7th Sept. Statement of Jemadar belonging to the Magistrate, as given by Mr. Harington.*—Came in from Jajou this morning. Yesterday fell in at that place with a party from Dholepore consisting of some of the Indore troops and men from Bhopal. They said they had come there for "russud." Their report was that they were going to Dehli.

## CCCXXXB.

*Midday. Statement of Mullour Singh, Kachee, Resident of the vicinity of Agra.*[1]

WAS at Dholepore yesterday, 11 a.m.; saw the advanced guard there. Could see nothing of the main body coming behind. The guard said it was following, and that they expected the Contingent would come too.

. . . . . . . .

## CCCXXXC.

*7th Sept. Afternoon. Statement of a man belonging to the Vakeel of Dholepore, communicated by Mr. Reade.*

STATED that the advanced guard, principally Horse, have crossed the Chumbul. The Infantry had not arrived, but were coming on with small guns. **Indore people at Dholpore.**

The 4th Contingent was certainly expected to accompany them.

Mahomed Waris Khan, said to be a Shahzada of Dehli, is in command of the force, but other names are also mentioned.

They give out decidedly that they are coming to Agra. They met with no opposition at the Chumbul.

The Kharee not fordable. Crossed on a platform on earthen pots.

## CCCXXXD.

*Sept. 7th. Midday. Reports recorded by Major Macpherson.*

MAHOMED ZALIM. Reached Residency on the 2nd; started on the 3rd with detachment, and went to Cheounda; 4th, across the Chumbul. There was but (?) 1 company of the 23rd, and 1 English Rissalah—150 Gole, Ghazees, and 2 guns; news that "Goras"[2] and a battery had come to Khetri. Intention, if they found "Goras" at Dholepore, to return back; so they did not take the guns across. Sent 6 or 8 Ghazees in advance two hours by Raj Ghat. Say mostly they are going to Dehli by Keraghur, but some say "we want to go to Agra." It is generally said, however, "our small guns will be of no use against Agra; we will **Insurgents moving to Dholpore.**

[1] Brought to me by Isree Pershad; gave 5r., and encouraged to go back for further intelligence.—W. M.

[2] *i.e.* Europeans.

go and see the state of Dehli, and return upon Agra." They do not hope that the Contingent will come after them. They say "we should have been at Dehli two months ago had not the Contingent deceived us, saying, 'We will go to-morrow and to-morrow.'" They came away hopeless of the Gwalior Contingent. The Contingent said, "We stand inseparable from the Magazine: let it go first and we follow. Where it remains, there we stand." So we came away. They wait two days at Dholepore to see if they can get together very many boats for a bridge, and tempt Regiments from Morar to come on with half the Magazine and big guns. Then they will go to Agra. If not, they will go to Dehli. The Indore and Mhow force have but 60 or 70 carts; would arrive at midday on the 6th. An immense mass of plunderers who want to plunder Agra.

Attitude of Gwalior Contingent.

## CCCXXXE.

*7th September.*, (*Major Macpherson writes.*)—Having no news from Dholepore since the 4th, received on the 5th, wrote to Rana. Vakeel Sunder Lal says 1 rebel Sowar and 5 men were seized on road and taken on to Munniah, and then let go. . . . a Chaubay Brahmin of Muthra said we go on to Agra. More Regiments are coming from Gwalior. Had the carriage provided for a Regiment to go to Nirwar. Ordered food to be prepared at Munniah. Shere Khan Subadar of the 23rd, which came to Dholepore, asked "russud." Ordered to buy. In Baree a 24-pounder, and 5 or 4 other smaller ones, not big; in Dholepore, 4 or 5 small, say 6-pounders; in the Fort, 4 or 5 small; 6 in old Chowni, 3 or 4 small.

Attitude of Dholpore.

Ordnance at Dholpore.

Mewattis.

*N.B.*—There are Agra Mewattees with this party who can guide the plunderers to every man's house. May make any rush when over the Kharee.

## CCCXXXF.

*7th September. Afternoon. Evidence of a Meena Informer employed by the Magistrate.*

Insurgent force.

LEFT Dholepore after 12 yesterday. The main army, it was said, consists of 13 companies and 300 Cavalry. Half had come over, and half remained still on the other side. Five guns crossed over about 9 or 10 on Sunday morning. Two are left on the other side. Expects that all the army will be over to-day (the 7th).

They have 10 or 20 hackeries, 15 to 20 camels; not much ammunition. What assistance from the Morar Regiments was to be obtained (*i.e.* occasional volunteers) has already joined. Scindia is keeping back the rest. **Scindia's attitude.**

Two-thirds of the men say they will go to Delhi. One-third say they are bound for Agra.

Believes that 30 or 40 have gone into the Fort.

The Dholepore Rana has three big and 10 small guns, all mounted. There are both rebel and Dholepore guards over them.

Met no Mutineers this side of Dholepore.

[Not very intelligent, but straightforward. His report differs from others in making the main body of the force reach the opposite bank of the Chumbul on Saturday (the 5th), on which day 2 guns, and on Sunday 3 more, crossed. They were afraid of the Maharaja's attacking the two left on the other side, and left a part of their body to guard them.]

## CCCXXXG.

*7th September. 7 p.m. Statement of Danee Kuhar, Servant of Chowbee Ghunsham Dass.* **Describes insurgents at Dholpore.**

. . . . . . . . .

No Contingent troops have come with them; nor are any expected. Scindia keeps them back. **Attitude of Scindia.**

. . . . . . . . .

## CCCXXXH.

*7th instant. 5 p.m. Extract from Major Macpherson's Book.*—*Dholpore Vakeel* brings letters of Saturday and Sunday, 5th and 6th.

On the 5th, 300 or 400 Cavalry and 2 guns of the Indore rebels, crossing by the Khetri Ghat, encamped near the Bungalow at Dholpore. Required that the Bungalow be vacated and burnt. The Soobah and the (?) with Chowdhry went to them. After a talk, to avoid a row, they took away their guns and halted in the Putialawallah's garden. The Rana removed the boats from the Raj Ghat. Told them to buy "russud" in the Bazaar. **Reception of Indore rebels at Dholpore.**

6*th.*—Rana sent word to rebels to march thence. Morar "pultuns" have not marched. They say there are 4000 of us. The dak is stopped. We have no power near Khetri Ghat, but we have told them distinctly they shall not have the Raj

Ghat boats. Had any Sahib come, the same arrangement might have been made for the Khetri Ghat. The Rana has gone to Purana Chouni (?), 2 coss from Dholpore.

. . . . . . . .

## CCCXXXI.

*Résumé* of foregoing intelligence.

8*th September, Tuesday.* 7 *a.m.*—The reports of yesterday, to which nothing has yet to be added for this morning, are to the following effect.

The advanced guard of the Indore force—say 200 or 300 Sepoys and 100 Cavalry with 2 guns—continue encamped at Dholpore. The main body appears to be on the opposite bank.

The Chumbul rose very high on Sunday the 6th, and prevented the remainder crossing. They certainly had not crossed up to yesterday morning.

The statements of the advanced guard as to future intentions are various. Most say they are going to Agra. Many that they are going to Delhi. It is also said that they will stay at Dholpore for a time.

No Contingent Regiment has joined the Indore rebels. A few men only from the several Regiments have deserted to them.

Their guns are said to be six and nine-pounders, drawn by bullocks. They are not well-off for ammunition.

The advanced guard have been trying to get some guns from the Rana of Dholpore. W. M.

## CCCXXXIa.

Describes position at Dholpore.

8*th September, Tuesday.* 9 *a.m.* (*Brought by the Chowbey.*) *Ram Chunder of Butesur,*

. . . . . . . .

The Sepoys spoke of crossing yesterday (the 7th).

They said the Contingent troops would not move till the *Dussehra.*[1] They abused them heartily for keeping them back; and abused the Maharaja also, who had become a "Christian."

. . . . . . . .

A Sowar, with 10 or 12 envelopes in his hand, was on the road between the Ootangun and the Kharee. He was stopping and searching everybody and seizing papers.

[1] 28th September.

## CCCXXXIc.

*Mohkum and Bisasee, Servants of Lt. Browne, state:*—We arrived at Gwalior from Orai on Friday last. On that day the following troops left for Agra, viz.:—one "pultun," one rissala of regulars, about 200 or 250 of the Maharaja's cavalry, who cut their names. Seven guns of sizes, and a large crowd of plunderers. Describes military position of affairs at Gwalior.

They have 100 or 150 carts containing their families. A Dehli Shahzada commands them. We left them at the Chumbul the day before yesterday (the 6th). A few had crossed, some 60 or 80 men, and two guns. The river was very full; the boats could hardly cross. Half the force say, "We will go to Agra," and the rest say, "We have no ammunition, and will go to Dehli" (by Muthra from Dholpore). Every day three, four, and five men desert from this force, and go off to their homes. The Gwalior troops are at Morar; they have received three months' pay, and talk of waiting until after the Dussehra for his orders. The "Top Khana"[1] is at Gwalior. We saw many guns on the parade, and in one of the bungalows there are guns and waggons in great numbers. The Gwalior force say they are ready to march upon Agra if the Maharaja will give them a Karindah to go with them. He refuses to do this. We saw no cavalry in Morar. The Maharaja discharged from his army all Musulmans, and these men are with the advancing force. The Gwalior Sepoys desert daily. We met on our road *via* Jalaon (?) 10 and 15 every day, going to their homes with their wives and families, without their arms. They all said they were going home, and all these men regret the Mutiny. Those at Gwalior declare they are ready to march upon Agra whenever the Maharaja orders them. The Dholpore Rana has run away somewhere. The coming force may be 1500 men; that at Morar is about equal to 4 regiments. The Kharee Nuddi is very full. We crossed it on a platform with ghurras.[2] There are 40 or 50 boats in the Chumbul. Each boat holds four Sowars and four horses. The guns are dragged by bullocks. A Delhi Shahzada. Scindia's loyal attitude. Desertions from Gwalior force.

## CCCXXXIe.

*Information given by Mr. Harington.*

*8th September. Afternoon.*—Kiddernath, Soukar, had a servant in yesterday evening from Dholpore, who left that place in the

[1] Artillery. [2] Earthen water-pots.

morning. His report agrees with what we had previously heard. A few of the Indore men would appear to be still on the Gwalior side of the Chumbul. Five or six hundred of the Gwalior Contingent are said to have taken their discharge from the Maharaja and to have joined the Mutineers. I think this is very likely to be the case.

Gwalior Contingent.

## CCCXXXIF.

Guns of the Dholpore Rana.

*Major Macpherson* notes the guns of the Dholpore Rana as follows:—

At Dholpore . 4 or 5 small ones, say 6-pounders.

At Sheregurh . 4 or 5 do. do.

At Poorani Chownee 3 or 4 do. do.

At Bara (10 coss from Dholpore) one 24-pounder, 4 or 5 smaller, but still big guns.

At Raj Ghat there are 12 boats.

At Khentra there are 17 boats (13 ?).

Stages from Agra to Dholpore.

| | | |
|---|---|---|
| Agra from the Kharee (Oosra Ghat) | 10 | miles. |
| Jajow . . | 9 | " |
| Moonia . . | 8 | " |
| Dholpore . . | 9 | " |
| | 36 | " |

## CCCXXXIG.

*8th September. Evening.*—On the evening of the 8th of September *Mr. Courtenay* wrote from the Kharee as follows:—

Mr. Courtenay.

The following is the intelligence received from Dholpore this day from good authority. All the Indore troops are at the other side of the Chumbul, as follows:—

Detail of Indore troops.

7 brass guns.
300 Cavalry from Mhow.
600 Bugrungie pultun.
507 Caraputkee pultun.
150 Horse belonging to Raja of Indore.
327 Ghazies.
1 prince from Delhi, with 70 followers.

. . . . . . . .

Their camp ground is near the staging bungalow at Dholpore. They have placed horsemen all along the road into Munniah.

R. Courtenay.

## CCCXXXII.

*9th September, Wednesday.*—

. . . . . . . . .

The Rana has not given up his Fort. They have asked the Rana for three months' pay.

The Chumbul is so high that they can neither go back nor get the rest of the force over; and are in considerable apprehension.

A hackery crossed over the Kharee yesterday.

## CCCXXXIIa.

*9th September, Wednesday.* 7 *a.m.* — During yesterday several men came in from Dholepore bringing information up to the forenoon of Monday the 7th. They add no items of importance to what was stated in yesterday's memorandum, and confirm its main points. **Official Memorandum for Colonel Cotton.**

Mr. Courtenay from the Kharee Nuddee (10 miles off) sent in a written report yesterday afternoon; and came in himself in the evening. From his letter and verbal statements, it appears that the advanced guard on this side the Chumbul consists of—

2 brass guns.
150 Horse.
200 Foot.
50 Ghazies.

They are encamped near the staging bungalow at Dholepore, and have horsemen on the road as far as Munniah.

He gives the entire force as follows:—

7 brass guns,
300 Mhow Cavalry,
507 23rd Native Infantry,
150 Holkar's Horse,
600 "Bugrungie," probably Holkar's Foot,
327 Ghazies,
70 followers of Shazadah,
or 1177 Foot, 450 Horse, and some 400 Ghazies, etc.

His information was that the Chumbul was so high that the main body could not cross, and that the advanced guard was consequently cut off and in great apprehension.

I have just, however, received the following note from Major Macpherson:—"I heard late last night, not from any man of my own, but from a fair second-hand source, that the water had fallen and the boats were hard at work crossing our enemies." If I receive any information during the day corroborating this report I will give immediate information to Col. Cotton.

An important point mentioned by Mr. Courtenay was that a hackery crossed the Kharee yesterday. It would be satisfactory to have an examination of the Ghat, and the nature of the bottom there, by a competent officer, and Mr. Courtenay can send in a gauge of the height of the water daily.

W. MUIR.

TO COL. COTTON, Commg. Agra.

## CCCXXXIIB.

Vakeel of Dholpore gives details of rebels crossing Chumbul.

*9th September. Midday.*—The Vakeel of Dholpore represented that he had news from Dholpore up to Monday evening, the 7th.

Besides the first party, which crossed on Saturday, and consisted of—

300 Sowars } Dholpore,
2 guns }

400 Bhopal men stationed at the Ghat,

there crossed on Monday (none crossed on Sunday)—

4 Companies foot,

2 guns,

1 Ghole of Vilayaties (50 to 100),

and some Sowars—number not known.

These crossed notwithstanding the river was very high.

Yesterday it is probable that more crossed.

*Additional from Major Macpherson.*

Two or three boats laden with carts went from Khentra Ghat to Raj Ghat, where, from there being no carriage road, they remain. The officers of the Indore army have come often to us for assistance to move their carts. We have answered, "Take them to Khentra Ghat. They cannot come this way." These officers say that whenever the other guns shall arrive here this advanced guard will move forward, and that the army manifests the intention of moving on Agra; and when we ask if they mean to go to Delhi, they are silent. For two days there has been no news from Gwalior, but we hear that the Morar troops have not yet marched. Much rain. Jajow Zemindars called upon to furnish supplies there.

## CCCXXXIIc.

*10th September. 9 a.m., Thursday. Major Macpherson's Note of the 9th.*

"The main body of the rebels must be on this side the Chumbul to-day. **Describes position at Gwalior, 6th and 7th September.**

"At Dholpore on the 7th their officers said that their intention was to march on Agra, and that when the main body arrived the advanced guard would move forward.

"On the 7th the Gwalior Contingent had not moved, and at Dholpore it was not expected.

"A cossid reports that on the 6th or the 7th he saw 4 bodies, each of from 300 to 500, of Scindia's Sowars, Poorbeas, at the principal villages on the road to the Chumbul."[1]

They have left Scindia's service to join the rebels, are at heart with them, and several parties already gone to Delhi. Report wants confirmation.

The cossid saw along the road many Wilayatees, Arabs, etc., who had left the Baiza Bhaee's service. Plundering immense.

Rebels have 10 Sowars at Jajow, besides party at Munniah.

W. M.

## CCCXXXIId.

*Statement taken before Major Macpherson on the 9th.*—Jundoo, Soukari Cossid, Aheer of Kalait, uncle Jemadar of Jail:— **Position at Gwalior and Dholpore.**

Left Agra at 12 midnight on the 6th, reached Dholpore at 8 a.m., and Gwalior before midnight of the 7th. On evening of the 7th went to Morar; returned to Phul Bagh, and thence to Dholpore at 10 p.m.; left Dholpore 3 a.m., and reached Agra 3 p.m. of 8th. Monday, saw near Dholpore Bungalow 2000 men and 2 guns, 300 Telingas, 400 Sowars, some Vilayatees of Bai's, Sikhs, grass-cutters, and plunderers. At Ketri Ghat saw 2000 or 3000 men and 5 guns; viz. a Rissala and a pultun and Vilayatees, 250 or 300.

*10th Sept.*—At the village of Jarra, 1½ coss from Chumbul, the Shazadah lay with 3000 men, Telingahs, 200 or 300; Sowars with red coats and black turbans; 300 or 400 plunderers. At Bunda, 400 Sowars, and foot, 100 or 150, all black turbans and carbines (H.H.'s men have none); Chounda, 300 Sowars; Nourabad, 400 or 500 Sowars. Went to Morar, and asked some **The Shahzada.**

[1] See Brown's servant's statement, CCCXXXIc. *ante.*—W. M.

Sepoys, and they said, "We don't go for a month, till after the Dusserah." I saw they were collecting bullocks and carts and camels in a compound. A Pool Bagh army (man) said, "If the Morar people will send a few bullets at the City we will join and loot it." Saw 7 flags of Regiments and Maharatta Sowars, but none of H.H.'s regular Sowars. These are all on the road. On return saw at the Residency 3000 or 4000 outside, men placed there by H.H. Saw the same men (the Sowars above specified) on the road, but came by Raj Ghat, and there Sowars were crossing as also at Piperi Ghat and Ketri Ghat. Courtenay not at Kharee, but 3 coss on this side of it. Kharee very deep, and *no fords.* Ootangun fordable.

**Scindia's attitude.**

At Jajow are 10 Sowars.

W. M.

## CCCXXXIII.

**Résumé for 10th September.**

10*th Sept.*—From to-day's information this appears—the main body of the rebels must be on this side of the Chumbul to-day. At Dholpore their officers said that when the main body arrived the advanced guard would move forward, and that the army said "upon Agra." The Gwalior Contingent have not moved.

A cossid who left Gwalior on the evening of the 7th reports that Scindia's regular Sowars, Poorbeahs, have left his service, and are upon the road to the Chumbul in several bodies; and also that many Wilyaties, Arabs, etc., of the Baiza Bai's service, have done the same, and that the number of plunderers of every kind who are following the rebels is immense. Scindia's Poorbeah Cavalry, about 3 Regiments, are at heart entirely with the rebels, and small bodies of them have been constantly moving off to Delhi ever since the commencement of the insurrection. And such bodies are probably moving now, but until further information I shall hope the main body may be restrained until after the Dusserah.

**Old Gooroo from Dholpore. Bir Singh Grunthee of Patiala.**

The old Gooroo from Dholpore says that Bir Singh Grunthee of Putealah wrote from Dholpore on the 8th that 2000 men had crossed. They had only 7 small guns—a boat had upset with a gun; that the Gwalior Contingent is not expected. The hundred Sikhs of the 23rd Native Infantry will meet the Grunthi at Dholpore, who will send news.

W. M.

## CCCXXXIIIA.

*Statement of Hunuman Singh Brahmin, Informer, taken at 8 p.m., 9th September.*

SENT by the Tehseeldar to Dholpore; arrived there night of the 8th; left it early this morning (9th), about 7 a.m. There were 300 Sepoys and 2 guns formerly crossed; and 400 Sepoys, 2 guns, and 125 Sowars crossed over yesterday (Tuesday). Saw 60 horses by which the guns are dragged. Stayed at night in the "pultun." The troops say they will stay at Dholpore till joined by the Morar troops after the Dusserah. Saw no camels, but 15 or 16 hackeries, and about 40 ponies. The Chumbul is very high to-day (the 9th), and no troops will have crossed. It rained heavily yesterday. Kharee deep.

## CCCXXXIIIB.

*Note of Intelligence between 2 and 3 p.m. 10th September, Thursday.*—I have had no very good fresh information to-day from Dholpore; nor has any report come in from Mr. Courtenay or Mr. Phillipp's men. **Résumé, 10th September.**

A spy came late last night who left Dholpore about 7 o'clock yesterday morning. He says that about half the army had crossed by Tuesday the 8th; but that when he left yesterday the river was too full for any more to cross that day, I am doubtful as to his statement, and inclined to think with Major Macpherson that the whole force is most probably now on this side the Chumbul. **Rebels at Dholpore.**

We have nothing decisive yet as to the course they will take. The Tehseeldar and Thanahdar of Khyragurh have received a perwana from "Soobah Shere Khan Sahib and Captain Mahommed Alec Khan Buhadur," appointing them servants of the king from that date, and ordering them to Jajow, where they will learn the king's pleasure. If they fail to come, the writers will go to them. **Perwana issued by rebel leaders to British officials.**

If this be addressed only to this Tehseeldar (as Khyragurh lies N.W.), it may be symptomatic of arrangements for going to Delhi.

W. MUIR.

COLONEL COTTON, Commg. Agra.

## CCCXXXIV.

*11th September* 1857. *4 p.m., Friday. Memo. regarding the Indore Force.*—Our information as to the actual state of the

Indore force remains doubtful. A respectable messenger sent by Major Raikes left Gwalior on Tuesday the 8th, and passed over the Kentree Ghat on Wednesday the 9th. He declares that only three companies and 4 guns and 100 Cavalry are on this side, and that some two thousand men, including rabble and plunderers, are yet to cross. He met nobody on the road from Dholpore to this.

Position at Gwalior.

The Contingent were quiet at Gwalior when he left on the 8th, and had no carriage. Some 100 or 200 of Scindia's own horse had deserted to the Indore Mutineers. The Indore Mutineers talk of going to Agra and thence to Delhi, according to this man.

Perwana sent by King to Indore and Gwalior troops.

Major Macpherson has authentic intelligence that a perwana was sent by the King of Delhi on the 7th or 8th, ordering up the Indore and Gwalior troops at once to his assistance. The order will probably be not without its effect on the movements of the Indore Mutineers.

W. MUIR.

COL. COTTON, Commanding Agra.

## CCCXXXV.

*Memo., etc.*, 14*th September.* 2.30 *p.m.*—The Indore force seems to intend remaining still at Dholpore, and awaiting the Contingent.

Position at Gwalior.

Major Macpherson's news of this morning from Gwalior is serious. The Contingent, excepting the 5th and 6th Regiments and a couple of Mehidpore guns and some cavalry, have broken with the Maharaja, and seem to be arrayed against him. It seems improbable that he will be able to detain them long.

If they march soon it will gravely complicate our position.

W. MUIR.

TO COL. COTTON.

## CCCXXXVA.

14*th.*—*Moolah* (*Caste Koorie*), *inhabitant of Alexandra cantonment at Gwalior*, sent by Manuel Smith to Mr. Horn. Left Gwalior on Friday the 11th at 9 a.m., and arrived here last night. States that two Contingent Regiments with 17 guns are in position on the Cantonment side of the Nullah near the Phool Bagh. The other Regiments and guns still at Morar demanding carriage, which the Maharaja declines to give; also money. The

Mutinous state of troops at Gwalior.

Maharaja says he will give 5 lakhs, but they demand 25 lakhs. The Maharaja has placed guns in position opposite to those of the Mutineers, as also 11 guns on the Fort bearing upon the Cantonment. Zemindari levies are collecting, and have arrived in large numbers to assist the Maharaja. Moolah further states that he reached Dholpore on Saturday evening. Some of Scindia's Cavalry had still to cross the river; the guns and Infantry are encamped on the Maidan. The Gwalior troops ask the Maharaja to lead them on: he refused: also the Nana Sahib, but he also declined. At Munniah saw 50 Sowars, who, I was told by a villager, had come on to mark out the camp. I saw no Sowars on this side of Munniah.

**Scindia's loyal attitude.**

**Zemindar levies collecting to assist the Maharajah.**

**The Nana.**

W. M.

CCCXXXVI.

15*th.—Asadas, Brahmin,* who was sent with a Sowkaree letter to Gwalior, left that place on Saturday morning, states: Some of the Contingent troops with 12 guns had taken up a position near the Phool Bagh. They demanded money from the Maharaja, which he refused to give them. The Maharaja was supplying them with carriage. They intend marching for Agra on the 18th, with all their guns, etc.

**Affairs at Gwalior.**

One Regiment of Infantry had gone over to the Maharaja, and it was not expected to join the others. He also states that he left Dholpore yesterday morning. The rebels were still there, and waiting for the Contingent troops to join them. Saw a few Cavalry at Munniah. Heard that the Dholpore Ranee had left Dholpore.

W. M.

CCCXXXVII.

*Letters seized—*

(1) *Letter addressed to Ameer Aly and Moneer Khan Risaldars by Aulad Aly and Azim Aly, Sowars, Troop V., Regiment 1st, from Hingowna.*

19*th Mohurrum.*—All well here. On 14th, 15th, Doonda Khan, Sowar, and nearly 80 Sowars Regiment I., Rissala, marched.

On the 6th Mohurrum they had an interview with the Shahzada, Feeroze Shah (daughter's son of Mirza Ilahi Buksh, who had been to Mecca). The Sowars and Rissaldars were present on the occasion.

**Shahzada Firoz Shah. Mirza Ilahi Buksh.**

The letter which you and Wazeer Ali and Mahmoud Ali sent to Morar has reached, and its details been comprehended.

Your buffalo has been sold for 12 rupees 12 ans.; the buchha died.

[The rest filled with private details. The writer's house evidently in Delhi.]

(2) *Letter addressed to Captain Jehangeerkhan, from Dost Mahomed, Soobadar, 2nd Top Khana. Gwalior, 17th Mohurrum.*

**Position of troops at Gwalior.**

All well. The state of things here is as follows. There are nearly 500 or 600 Sowars from the 2nd and 3rd Regiments. Of these, those Sowars who were in debt have taken their pay and discharge and gone to Delhi; and some of the Bargeer Sowars, having taken away their horses, have also deserted altogether. Accordingly, Roshun Ali Khan, Rissaldar Troop 5, Regiment III., and Amanat Khan, Rissaldar of the same, and very many Duffadars and Jemadars, and the Adjutant Mustakeem Khan Sahib, having taken their discharge, all arranged it among themselves and went off with the intention of going to Delhi on the 15th Mohurrum.

**Troopers gone to Delhi.**

These are now with the Crawford Regiment, which, with some regular and irregular cavalry and 7 guns, stayed here some time on its way from Indore—and 5 or 6 days ago went towards Akberabad. It will remain at the Fort of Dholpore till the Morar camp comes up. The Morar camp, it is said, will march on the 28th Mohurrum.

**Indore troops to remain at Dholpore.**

Then all the people with the 23rd, with the Cavalry and Foot, and Ghazees, in all 6000 or 7000, and all the Morar Force, have arranged first to conquer the Fort of Agra, and after that we shall see what way they will go.

**Intention to besiege Agra Fort.**

The carrier of this letter has come from Lucknow. He says, and it is also written in my brother's letter, that of the nearly 1000 Europeans and Feringhees that were in the Belee guard, only about 150 or 160 remain. They will shortly be sent into Hell. And Birjees Cadr, son of Wajid Ally, has been put on the Guddee; and nearly 14 pultuns with the English contingents are in Lucknow and new levies are being raised; and the carrier of this letter, who is called Mowla Mahomed, is one of my friends. He has come for a livelihood; he can get none here. I send him to you; get him employment as a Ghazee or servant. It will be a favour. If possible, attach him to your own person.

**Native account of defence of Lucknow, and its affairs.**

Yesterday, the 15th, Torab Khan Sahib and Gholam Mahomed Khan, with Sowars of the Maharaja, and the 2nd Morar Regiment, with the 23rd, arrived and remain at Dholpore. If all is well they will go to you at Delhi. All is well; nothing new.

When you were with Dinkur Rao you promised to send for me; but no opportunity has yet occurred for this. I look for that now. I look for employment chiefly as a Mohurrur or even as Sowar. I can't get on on this small pay. Although there is nothing but fighting at Delhi—I have not been able to come. It is not my fault. If I give my life in the service of some Chief, Raees, or the King, or for Islam, it would be proper.

Golab Khan and Muddeh Khan, Bargeers of Gholam Mahomed Khan, ran off for Delhi. Muddeh Khan lost his carriage at the Chumbal, so Golab Khan took service with Luchmee Chand at Muthra at one rupee a day.

## CCCXXXVIII.

15*th.—Gholam Mahomed, who was sent to Gwalior for information* and returned last night, states that he left Gwalior on Saturday evening, the 12th, saw 2 Regiments and 15 or 20 guns of the Contingent in position near the Phool Bagh, with the Maharajah's troops and guns opposite to them. The Maharajah was doing all in his power to prevent them going to Agra. They had seized the Kotwal and confined him till he furnished them with 150 carts, the Maharajah having refused to assist them in procuring carriage (2000 carts, etc.) till after the Dusserah.

**Troops at Gwalior.**

**Scindia's loyal action.**

They were seizing carriage wherever they could find it. They have asked the Maharajah to allow the Dewan and Kura Moolah Khan Rissaldar, 1st Gwalior Cavalry, and Ameen Khan Rissaldar (both of whom had gone over to the Maharajah), to accompany them to the Chumbul, but the Maharajah refused to do so. They afterwards moved up the guns and two Regiments near the Phool Bagh. Great numbers of Thakoors with their followers have assembled to assist the Maharajah. He also states that he left Dholpore yesterday morning, and heard that the Shazada had not crossed to this side of the Chumbul, but was encamped at Jugurdah with some Cavalry and a few foot-men. The Indore rebels were still at Dholpore.

**Indore rebels at Dholpore.**

W. M.

## CCCXXXVIIIA.

15*th.—Sheikh Wuzeer, inhabitant of Agra, who was sent to Dholpore for information* and returned last night, states:—He

Mutineers at Dholpore.

arrived at Dholpore on Thursday 10th, and was seized by the Indore rebels, who kept him in confinement till Friday the 11th. He remained at Dholpore till yesterday (the 14th) morning. The rebels have 6 guns and only 14 carts of ammunition. Scindia's Sowars and others who have lately joined them are badly off for money, and are anxiously waiting for the Shazada (who is on the other side of the river) to join them, in hopes that he will provide them with money, etc. He heard them say to one another that if the British troops were to attack them, their ammunition would be expended in an hour, and they knew not what would become of them. They have no intention of moving towards Agra till re-enforced by the Contingent Troops from Gwalior. He saw 1000 Sowars, 1500 Regulars (Infantry), and 1500 Ghazees, etc. etc., at Dholpore.

W. M.

## CCCXXXIX.

16*th.—Translation of a Letter from Meer Khan, late Chupprassie Gwalior Political Agency, dated Gwalior*, 13*th Sept.*

Account of Mutiny of Scindia's troops.

The following is the state of the Morar troops. All the officers, accompanied by a number of non-commissioned officers and men, in all 250, came to the Durbar, and, after conversing with the Maharajah, went away dissatisfied. They have placed some heavy guns on the Morar Bridge, and small guns on the road leading to the Phool Bagh. They have guns in these positions, and the Maharajah has placed guns opposite to them, and posted eight hundred or a thousand men between the Phool Bagh and the (?) . The Mutineers have demanded 22 lakhs of rupees remitted by the British Government. In the event of the Maharajah's refusing it, they threatened to open fire and plunder the Lushkur. The Maharajah told them to do what they pleased. The Maharajah's troops are night and day on the alert (?), and the Maharajah is constantly visiting the batteries and encouraging the men in every way. The Mutineers are all ready to start. They have given the Crawfurd Regiment a small supply of percussion caps, cartridges, and balls.

## CCCXL.

18*th September* 1857. 7 *a.m.—Memo. of Gwalior Intelligence.*

Gwalior troops.

*A Messenger*, who left Dholpore yesterday morning, says that the Gwalior troops were expected to march last night, and reach Dholpore in about three days. The Chumbul, however, is still very high, and the rain may probably have delayed them.

The Indore force has got three more guns, probably from the Dholpore people, and expected more. They have 16 elephants. Indore force.

On the Indore troops being joined by the Contingent, the intention was still to march on Agra. Intention to march on Agra.

W. MUIR.

To COLONEL COTTON.

## CCCXLA.

18*th.—Nujor Khan, inhabitant of Agra*, who was sent for information and has just returned, states :—I accompanied Gholam Mahomed (the Cossid whose deposition was taken on the 15th) to Gwalior, and returned with him to Dholpore, where I was obliged to remain, from sore feet, till 10 o'clock yesterday morning. About 8 o'clock a.m. yesterday, when I was in the Serai, I heard cannon and musketry firing, which lasted for an hour and a half, and was told that the Indore and Mhow Mutineers had attacked the Soobah Dewbuns, who was wounded and taken prisoner, and that about 250 on both sides had been killed and wounded. A number of men on both sides had run away. I heard that the Shahzadah had crossed to this side of the Chumbul. I was told that the rebels attacked the Dholpore troops because the Rana would not give them money. I don't know if the Dholpore men lost their guns. It was currently reported in the Bazar, on the evening of the 16th, that Delhi had fallen, and the Sowars who put up in the Serai with me said they would not now go near Agra, and appeared frightened and uncertain what to do. I saw a few Sowars at Munniah, but none at Jajow. I was told that the Rana was at the "Old Cantonment." Indore and Gwalior Mutineers attack Dholpore.

W. M.

## CCCXLI.

21*st September.—Major Macpherson hears from Dinkur Rao* that the Morar troops had intended to make disturbances. The Maharajah prepared to punish them by new levies of about 10,000 Thakoors. But the rebels did not fulfil their intention. Affairs at Gwalior.

The Morar men have now come to terms.

The 5th Pultun have marched from Morar and are separate, and more are now also coming in . . .

There is no "fasád." To-day the officers of the Pultuns will have an interview with the Maharajah.

W. M.

[*Here follows Memo. about Gwalior troops and their movements.*]

## CCCXLII.

22*nd September.*—14th. *An Armenian reports* that the Morar men have withdrawn the whole of their heavy guns; but their light guns are kept out as picket guns. The Maharaja's guns and troops are still out. He says he will not withdraw his guns and troops until such time as the whole of them march away. Fifth Regiment and 2 Cos. of 6th and 2 guns have taken service with Maharaja and move into his quarters, and are ready with the other troops to fight for Maharaja. At Morar, three Regiments and 5 Cos. Artillery—about 3000—promised to leave in six days. Maharaja has sent them carriage, but not enough.

Mutiny at Gwalior.

W. M.

## CCCXLIIA.

*Hur Narain, Zemindar of Kehri*, near Agra, who was sent to Dholpore for information on the 19th and returned last night, states:—I arrived at Dholpore on the evening of the 19th, and left it at 12 o'clock a.m. on the 20th, when only about 1200 Sepoys and 500 Sowars with 5 guns were encamped at Dholpore, in front of the new cantonment. Many had gone away, some across the Chumbul and others towards the ravines, and I was told they were daily deserting in consequence of the fall of Delhi—the news of which had reached Dholpore some days previously. There had been a fight 8 or 9 days ago between the rebels and the Soubah Deobuns, in which 100 Sepoys and 16 Goojurs were killed and wounded. The Soubah was taken prisoner, and is living in the Palace with a guard over him. The Goojurs declare that they will attack and plunder the rebels. I heard that Jehangeer Khan had passed through Dholpore on his way to Gwalior from Delhi. There are no Sowars or Sepoys on this side of Dholpore. But the villagers, who have been entertained by the rebels, allow no one to pass without a strict search for letters.

Affairs at Dholpore.

Effect of the fall of Delhi.

Fight at Dholpore.

Dholpore Subah a prisoner.

Jehangeer Khan.

W. M.

## CCCXLIIB.

22*nd.*—*Gunnoo, Rajpoot Thakoor*, servant of Buldeo Singh, Dundontea Thakoor of Jharra, and who was sent by his master to give Major Macpherson the following information, states:—

Four days ago, the 17th and 18th, the Gwalior Rebels withdrew all their guns and troops from the position they had taken up in front of the Maharaja's palace. The Maharaja had moved forward his guns and troops to the Cantonment side of his new garden, where he had taken up a position. The Mutineers were daily deserting for their homes. The 5th and half the 6th Regiment have gone over to the Maharaja, who has distributed them among his own Regiment; as also a portion of their Cavalry.

Scindia and his mutinous troops.

Jehangeer Khan has returned from Delhi and gone to Morar. The Thakoor has gone to the Lushkur, and will send further information.

Jehangeer Khan.

W. M.

## CCCXLIIc.[1]

22nd.—*Translation of a Letter from the Nazim of the Gwalior Suddur Adawlut*, dated the 17th inst. The last letter I sent you by Syce must have reached you. This is the state of things here. The Morar troops have become excited, burned five bungalows, and demanded that the Maharaja should make over to them the treasure belonging to the British deposited in the Gunga Jullee.

They have also requested him to furnish carriage for their Magazine to enable them to start.

The Maharaja replied, "Very good; repay me the three months' donation and pay I have given you, and you shall have the balance." To this arrangement they would not agree, but demanded the Residency treasure, and what came from Orai, and spoke in a very insolent manner in the Durbar; after which they placed their guns opposite the Phool Bagh, and the Maharaja, seeing that he could do nothing with them, moved out his troops and guns to oppose them.

Description of the mutiny of Scindia's troops at Gwalior.

For three days and nights they remained in position, with portfires lighted on both sides. At length the Mutineers' provisions having been stopped, they became frightened or dispirited. The 5th Regiment, which was encamped a short distance from them, refused to join them, and its officers said, "We are the Maharaja's servants, and will execute his orders." On the 4th day the Mutineers, having become disheartened, begged the Maharaja to supply them with carriage and give them the balance that would remain after deducting the donation and pay they had already received. Accordingly, the Durbar sent them 1000 Brinjáree bullocks, 200 carts, 6

[1] This letter contains interesting details about the attitude of the Maharajah of Gwalior to Contingent, etc.—W. M.

elephants, and 50 camels, and desired them to march at once. On the 15th inst. (the 25th Mohurrum) the 1st and 2nd Regiments and the Artillery sent a message to the effect that they had not killed any officers, and entreated His Highness to forgive them; and if he would allow them to remain they would obey any order he gave them. Besides all the Sepoys, residents of Scindiah's territories declared that they would not join the Poorbeahs, that they were the Maharaja's ryots, and if he would not take them into his service they would go to their homes and fields.

The Mutineers are also quarrelling about the Magazine, each regiment and battery wanting its share of the ammunition and stores. Some say they will go to Cawnpore, and others to Agra. Dissensions among them. In short, there is so much dissension among them that they will either kill each other or break up altogether. Any fear of their acting together is at an end. Fight at Dholpore. I have just heard that the Dholpore men and Indore Mutineers had a fight—200 killed and wounded on both sides.

W. M.

## CCCXLIII.

*24th September.—Assadoss* left Gwalior on the 22nd early; went to Morar, and in the Lushkur and city.

The Subahdar said the army was going to Cawnpore, not to Agra. The guns are all mounted in the cantonment. One Pultun has joined Maharajah. The other four he will not take.

Rajah of Jhansi calls the Gwalior troops. A perwanah has come from the Maharajah of Jhansi, on Monday, asking them to go there as the country was disturbed. The Indore men called the Contingent. They declined to go, Also the Nana. as the Nana had called them. The Indore men are watching those at Gwalior.

W. M.

## CCCXLIV.

*28th September. Afternoon.—Memorandum.* There is not much to add to the statement regarding Muthra, Dholpore, and Gwalior contained in the printed Memorandum of to-day.

At Muthra the bridge of boats was not completed yesterday. The Mutineers expected it to be completed to-day, and may probably have crossed over, unless our pursuing Column, or any message from the Gwalior troops (which is not likely), should have detained them. It still seems probable that the Indore force will join the Muthra fugitives. But I cannot ascertain that any actual move has been made.

At Gwalior, the Contingent remains at Morar. This is their great Dusserah day; to-morrow the day they were to have marched. But the Maharajah seems to have them in hand. And the boats at Dholpore have been all taken away. So that they will find it difficult to come this way. If they move, they too will probably go towards Oudh. They have had an invitation and money from the Nana.

**Maharajah Scindia restrains the Contingent.**

**Nana calls the Contingent.**

8 *p.m.*—Two men who left Muthra this morning have come in this evening. They say the bridge was not finished, but that the Mutineers were urging the Mulláhs to finish it. They beat and incite them by every means in their power to get the bridge finished.

The report in the bazaar at Muthra is that pursuing Column is near at hand, at Kossee or Hodul. But the Mutineers do not allow the report. It is possible they may have crossed to-day, or may cross to-morrow. They speak of going by Hatrass.

W. M.

## CCCXLV.

29*th of September* 1857.—*Memorandum.*

. . . . . . . . . . .

**Delhi fugitives at Muthra.**

**Ordnance with the Muthra horde.**

The guns (with Muthra people) are given as follows:—

| | |
|---|---|
| Bareilly Brigade . | 7 |
| Nusserabad . . | 3 |
| Neemuch . . . | 4 |
| Delhi . . . | 3 |
| | 17 |

There is the old account as to their intentions. They, no doubt, are looking with the utmost anxiety for the completion of the bridge, and would cross over at once if it were ready. The Bareilly Brigade are the leading party in the movement.

W. MUIR.

TO COL. COTTON.

## CCCXLVI.

**Delhi fugitives at Muthra.**

30*th of September.*—*Memorandum.* A messenger has just come in from Muthra, who says that the bridge was finished fit for traffic yesterday evening, and that passengers and horses had begun to cross. The army had not then moved over; but may have crossed to-day. The Force were fixed in their intention of going to Lucknow, but some say they will go to Bareilly. They are still in a state of alarm and disquiet. But they talk of plundering Hatrass on their way. The messenger says he saw 18 guns in one place and 3 in another. There are numerous desertions.

**Bhurtpore Rana refuses ammunition to rebels.**

Fifty Sowars went to Bhurtpore for ammunition. The Rana refused to give it, and they returned yesterday at midday.

. . . . . . . .

W. MUIR.

COLONEL COTTON.

CCCXLVII.

**Indore force called by the Muthra men.**

1*st October* 1857. *Morning.—Memorandum.* A messenger gives intelligence of Dholpore up to yesterday morning.

The Indore force had received a message from the Muthra men to say that they had fled from Delhi beaten, and inviting them to go along with them to Lucknow. The Indore people were accordingly preparing to march. If they kept to their intention, they would probably reach Jajow to-day, and Futtehpore Sicri to-morrow morning. They expected the Muthra men to await their arrival at Muthra. They had seized four more guns belonging to the Rana—said to be 24-pounders—and were making arrangements to drag them along by the help of elephants. The Gwalior people said to have had another altercation with the Maharajah and to have burned their lines, but to be still held in check by him.

**Seize Dholpore guns.**

**Scindia holds troops in check.**

. . . . . . . .

**Movements of Dholpore Mutineers.**

1*st Oct.*—Phillips writes to Colonel Fraser:—Dholpore Mutineers leave to-day, and arrive at Jajow to-day, where they cross Ootangun and march to Muthra, *via* Khyragurh, Futtehpore Sicri. Bridge at Muthra completed, but Mutineers show no present intention of moving.

W. M.

## CCCXLVIIA.

*1st October.* 9 *p.m.—Memorandum.* A note from the Dy.-Postmaster at Muthra, dated the 30th September, despatched this morning from Muthra, has just come in. It has a postscript dated this morning.

From it, and the statement of the messenger who left this morning, I gather the following particulars.

The Bareilly Brigade began to cross over yesterday evening; kept crossing all night, and had crossed, or nearly so, by the time the messenger left this morning. He is certain that he saw five guns cross over. He says all the other guns (the whole number of which he gives at 24) were still on this side, with all the other troops, when he left this morning. Troops were still crossing in crowds. The Sowars of the Bareilly Brigade and 34 elephants had crossed. Doesn't know if there were other elephants left. **Delhi fugitives, Bareilly brigade, etc., cross Jumna at Muthra.**

There had been a contention among the Force—the Bareilly troops, which are best off, wishing to go off to Bareilly; the others, who after 6 or 7 days' rest have got up their spirits, declaring they will not go, and telling the Bareilly men that if they wish to go they should leave their guns and arms behind them. The messenger is of opinion that in the end all will follow the Bareilly men. I think the conclusion of the messenger is very likely. It is evident that the ruling mind has belonged to the Bareilly Brigade. It has made the bridge, and it has led the way. All the rest will, I doubt not, follow. But it is to be hoped in so slow and straggling a manner as to give the Flying Column the opportunity of catching them up before they reach the Ganges.

The messenger says they are likely to be at Moorsam to-day, and unless they make a double march and go beyond it that they will be at Hatrass to-morrow. **Delhi fugitives crossing to Doab.**

W. M.

## CCCXLVIII.

*2nd October* 1857. *Midday.*—All accounts of this morning concur in confirming my Memorandum of last night as to the movements at Muthra. The Bareilly Brigade certainly crossed over on the night of the 30th September, with 30 or 40 elephants, and a great number of tattoos laden with the sick and wounded. Four or five guns had also been passed over, one man says, drawn by bullocks. The two or three remaining guns of the **Bareilly brigade crossed the Jumna.**

Bareilly Brigade appear to have been forcibly detained, or attempted to be detained, by the remainder of the fugitive force. What the remaining body will do it is impossible yet to say. The bridge was crowded with people pouring over up to the last moment before our spies left, and it is possible the rest may follow the Bareilly troops. But there has evidently been a violent dispute between the Bareilly Brigade and the rest of the force; the latter opposing the march of the former towards Bareilly, and even threatening to destroy the bridge.

The last spy who has come in says that by midday yesterday "one and a half Kumpo" had crossed. He could not explain what a Kumpo meant,—it was what the people told him. In its ordinary meaning, this would imply that more than the Bareilly Brigade had crossed.

One intelligent reporter says that $\frac{2}{5}$ths of the fugitive force had crossed. Another gives the number at 3000 Infantry, including disabled men; and 500 Cavalry. (Captain Nixon's statement, 1200 Cavalry have crossed, probably includes camp-followers, or the sick on tattoos.)

. . . . . . . . . .

Some portion of the Neemuch force is still at Bindrabun.

. . . . . . . . . .

Ordnance with the Muthra force.

The guns of the whole Muthra force are particularly described by one witness as 24,—16 largish, and 8 very small; only the large-sized ones have tumbrils, two to each.

One spy said that a body of men 1200 strong with two guns were near Rye (5 or 6 miles on the Hatrass Road); it might be an advance guard.

W. M.

## CCCXLIX.

*3rd October* 1857. *Saturday Morning.—Memorandum.* Intelligence came in late last night from Muthra confirming what has been said in previous Memoranda.

Fugitive brigades cross at Muthra.

The Bareilly Brigade had completely crossed by the evening of the 2nd. On the forenoon of the 2nd they were still encamped on the opposite bank. A considerable number from the other brigades have also gone over, and there are only 12 guns left at Muthra. It appeared most probable from the conversation of the Sepoys that they too would cross over. The

Sepoys before leaving have as usual let themselves loose on the people, and the shops were shut.

The force that had gone to Bindrabun returned on the night of the 1st. They got some money there; they also got some at Mahabun.

A respectable messenger left Dholpore yesterday about 7 o'clock. The Indore force had not then left. It had been talking of moving for two or three days. They have about 50 carts for their baggage, and 80 or 90 camels. Of the 7 guns they took from the Rana they have returned three small ones and kept 4 large ones; they are drawn by bullocks. The Rana has not, that the messenger knows of, given them ammunition. They had been preparing to start on the 1st, but gave up the intention that day; the cause not known. Twenty-five Sowars came from Muthra to invite them there. There is daily correspondence between the Muthra Mutineers and them. They will go to Muthra. Nobody speaks of any other direction. They have altogether some 12 or 13 guns now. Their route will be by Khyragurh. They have about 25 Cavalry at Munniah. They will reach Muthra in 3 or 4 days. It seems that the Morar Mutineers wanted the Indore men to come back to Gwalior; but Scindia prevented them by taking away all the boats.

**Dholpore.**

**Muthra rebels communicate with Indore force at Dholpore.**

**Scindia's loyal action.**

A messenger left Gwalior on the afternoon of the 30th, and came *via* Pinnahut. He says that the 5th Regiment and the Cavalry and 50 or 60 men of the 4th have joined the Maharajah.

The remaining four Regiments and 200 or 250 Cavalry are at Morar with 40 guns and a Magazine, which they have partly laden on 1200 bullocks, 1000 camels, and 800 carts. They want still more carriage. Of the guns three are said to be 24-pdrs., one an 18-pdr., and the rest 9 or 12-pdrs. The Maharajah has still an entrenchment at the Lushkur by the river; the Contingent men have an entrenchment opposite his.

**Strength of rebels at Morar.**

The Poorbeas say let us go to Cawnpore; the men of the Upper Doab talk of Agra: they are about equal in numbers, but the Poorbeas the most influential. The Maharajah has not given them this month's pay. The Contingent wanted to get the Indore troops for the sake of their Cavalry. The Maharajah has stopped their passage by taking away the boats. He tells the Contingent he won't let them go to Agra, but they may go to Cawnpore.

They cut off the nose of a deserter and paraded him about the camp on a jackass.

W. Muir.

## CCCXLIXA.

*3rd Oct. Saturday Evening.—Memorandum.* Three or four men have come in this evening from Muthra. The Bareilly Brigade, it seems, sent over the river, back to Muttra, yesterday morning, two Companies to plunder Seth L(uchmee) Chund's house. Heera Singh hearing of this, ordered two guns down to protect it. The split between the forces became now irreparable. The Nusseerabad and Dehli Regiments sided with the Bareilly Brigade, and have gone over after it; they have marched on rapidly, and will probably be in Hatrass to-night. Heera Singh, with his Neemuch Brigade, gave orders this morning to march towards Dholpore, and the whole force was in motion on the Agra road this forenoon. It probably halts at Furra to-night. It will go on *via* Uchneyra towards Dholpore.

Heera Singh's (Neemuch) brigade marches towards Dholpore.

Rebels march from Dholpore.

A messenger from Dholpore who left this morning has just come in. He says the troops there have sent on their "line doree" with 25 Sowars to Munnia, and that they talk of nothing but proceeding to fight against this fort. They will probably form a junction with the Neemuch Brigade at Munnia or Jajow, but whether they will then go eastward *via* Etawah or come this way, one cannot say. The project of attacking the Fort one must regard as bravado; and if so, it covers the other design of moving across the Doab *via* Etawah. There is a third course threatened, and that is to lay waste this district and replenish themselves with plunder. The Dholpore men have from 10 to 13 guns, of which three or four got from Dholpore are heavy ones. The Neemuch men may have from 6 to 8 guns. They are described as the smallest of the brigades, the Bareilly being the biggest, the Nd.[1] the next, and the Neemuch the least—very much cut up and reduced by their engagements at Delhi.

Ordnance with force from Dholpore.

Ordnance with Neemuch brigade.

Strength of the several brigades.

. . . . . . .

Heera Singh's force.

An account received by Mr. H. gives the force under H. S. at 1000 Horse and 1000 Foot, with 6 guns. I should think the horse over and the foot under estimated in this statement; 600 horse and 1500 foot might be nearer it.

W. M.

## CCCL.

*4th Oct. Sunday, 3m.—Memorandum.* Later messengers give the numbers of Heera Singh's force as less than before supposed,

[1] Probably "Nusseerabad."—W. C.

say five or six hundred horse. And it seems doubtful whether he has guns. He is said to talk of going to Gwalior.

W. MUIR.

## CCCLI.

*5th October* '57. *Monday.—Memo.* A spy came in this afternoon from Heera Singh's force. He was with them all last night at Jungaroo—a town on other side of the Kharer, halfway between Uchneyra and Jagow, about ten coss from Agra. They went on again this morning, and by a forced march may reach Dholpore, or near to it, by to-night. He describes the whole camp as a very wretched affair—under 1000 men, five or six hundred Sowars, with one or two hundred Sepoys, including wounded men. He saw no guns. It is the Neemuch Brigade, but greatly weakened by fighting and desertion, and in need of money and food. They will go anywhere they can find food or get pay; if they fail in that, they are likely to break up. They spoke of half their force being behind at Uchneyra, but he himself returned by Uchneyra, and saw nobody; and he believes that there was nobody besides the force he saw at Jungaroo.

**Its condition.**

. . . . . . . . . . .

I have heard nothing of any movements to-day on the part of the Dholpore men, besides what was reported to-day by the magistrate.

W. MUIR.

## CCCLII.

6 *October.* 8 *p.m.* *Memorandum.* A messenger has come in from Kyragurh who reports that the Neemuch force was at that place last night. It intended to remain there all night, and march to Dholpore to-day. During the night it received a message to say that the Dholpore force wanted to march on "the fifteenth" to Agra—it was an auspicious day.[1] Upon this they made immediate arrangements for starting from Kyragurh about midnight towards Dholpore. The messenger described the force as containing 500 or 600 horse and the same number foot, and 6 guns.

**Neemuch force moves towards Dholpore.**

As I was writing this Memo. a messenger has come in whom I sent out yesterday. He says he went as far as Munniah, where he found the whole Dholpore force, which, having marched one stage this way, had been joined by the Neemuch troops.

**Dholpore and Neemuch troops at Munniah.**

[1] The 15th both of the Mah$^{dn}$ and Hindoo months is past.—W. M.

There were six guns, 5 smaller ones dragged by horses, and one large gun drawn by bullocks. They said there were two or three more guns behind. The Neemuch brigade brought no guns, this man says, with it—only 5 or 600 Sowars. The whole force consists, as they said, of 3 Pultuns and 2 Rissalas—say 5 or 6000 men altogether. They all declare they are coming to attack the Fort. There are 25 to 30 Sowars at Jajow.

Neemuch brigade.

## CCCLIII.

*7th October. Evening.*—I send on Macpherson's letter. I confess that, notwithstanding the explicit statements of my own people and Capt. Nixon's, as well as Macpherson's of last night, I am not satisfied that the main force is at Munnia. Dr. Clark's men have consistently said that the main body of the Indore troops is still at Dholpore. One man who has come in to-night and left Munnia early this morning, says that only 200 horse and 200 foot, with a couple of small guns, have come on to Munnia; all the rest remain at Dholpore. On the 4th the "Bhopal Nawab" left for Mutthra with 50 Sowars. A report got abroad that he had written a letter to the English, and the Sepoys were angry; therefore he left. With the Munnia force is a Soobahdar called a Chowbey; he goes out on various occasions in different quarters to collect revenue. They talk of coming to Agra in five or ten days, or after the Dewalee. They have a great store of large wooden pegs at Jajow, where there is the big ladder with 32 steps. This is the statement of a man who was at Dholpore for two or three days, and stayed all the night of the 6th at Munnia. It renders it doubtful whether our messengers have not mistaken a detachment for the whole force. At the same time there are so many concurrent testimonies received both by others and myself of the whole force being at Munnia, that we ought to be prepared for that contingency.

Bhopal Nawab.

W. MUIR.

## CCCLIV.

*8th October. Midday.—Memorandum.* The state of things towards Dholpore appears to be as follows:—

The Indore force, on hearing of the arrival of their Neemuch allies at Khyragurgh on the 5th inst., prepared to move. A considerable body with guns set off that day and encamped at Munnia. They have kept moving from Dholpore this way since that day, though we cannot make out exactly in what parties and strength. The main body, with the artillery, is believed now to be at Munnia, and a portion was expected to be pitched at Jajow to-day. The Thanadar of Mulpoora, five or six miles from this, says that parties of Sowars have come in to Kagaroh, a village a little way on the other side of the Akhola Ghat, and that they talk of coming that way. On the other hand, some camp equipage is reported to have reached Tehra, a village a little way on the other side of the Oosra Ghat; and it is stated that they have caught the Zemindars of Koora and Shamsabad, and ordered them to have supplies ready at Kukowa, a village a short stage from this on the Jajow road. There is still talk of movements by Bhurtpore or Futtehabad; but the common story of the army is that their object is Agra.

**Main body of Indore force believed to be at Munnia.**

W. MUIR.

TO COL. COTTON.

I do not know whether it is worth while now to attempt to throw an additional volume of water into the Kharee by opening the Futtehpore Sicri sluices. It would have been advisable to do so had Col. Greathed's Column not been so close at hand.

The Kharee is fordable at many places above, but less so below Oosra. Even if the Mutineers are marching towards Etawah they might from this consideration think it necessary to cross higher up than Oosra, if they meant to go by Futtehabad.

W. M.

## CCCLV.

*Agra, Oct. 8th, '57.—Memo.* The evidence of Huttee Singh,[1] sent to Col. Fraser and Col. Cotton with a suggestion for a reconnoitring party and continuous mile pickets to the. . .

**Mile pickets suggested to Cols. Fraser and Cotton.**

COTTON.

[*The Indore rebel force attacked the British Camp at Agra on Saturday the 10th October, and were routed and driven off by Greathed's column, which had arrived after a forced march that morning.* See CXLV. *ante.*]

## CCCLVI.

11*th October. Sunday Night.—Memorandum.* A messenger went out last night, reached Jajow this morning, where he met a man who had left Gwalior on the 8th. He had met, about an

[1] See p. 65, vol. ii.

Fugitives. hour before daylight, a number of Sowars followed by many foot soldiers, running away on the Dholpore road. Saw many dead bodies by the road. It was said they were intending to flee by way of Butesur. On the 8th all the Contingent Regiments were as before at Gwalior. They were wishing to come this way, but the Maharaja was succeeding in keeping them back.

Scindia's loyal action.

W. MUIR.

## CCCLVIII.

Fugitive force at Futtehpore Sikri.

18*th October. Sunday Evening.—Memorandum.* A man who left Futtehpore Sicri this morning, reports that the refugees there congregated amount to some 700 or 800. They occupy the Mahul and other buildings. About 300 are Wilayatee Sowars (*i.e.* foreigners to these parts), 200 are miscellaneous Ghazee Sowars, and 200 or 300 foot soldiers. They have matchlocks, etc., but no artillery. They say they are attacked on all sides—Dholpore, Bhurtpore, and Agra, and having no place to go, must die there.

I think Nixon might be desired to encourage the Bhurtpore Durbar to prove its loyalty to our cause by dislodging them from our territory

They have only some 20 camels for carriage.

W. MUIR.

To COL. FRASER, C.B., Chief Commr.
COL. COTTON, Commanding Agra.

## CCCLIX.

20*th*, 9 *a.m.*—Sent Saligram's evidence to Cols. Fraser and Cotton.

20*th October* 1857. 9 *a.m.—Memorandum of Local Intelligence.* A chuprassy has just returned from Futtehpore Sicri, who left it yesterday morning. Was there the whole of the 18th. On the 17th the fugitives had been in occupation of the Tehseelee and neighbouring buildings; they left them on that night, and spread about the town—one party occupying Adheen Shah's "tukya"; another the Tehra Durwaza; a third the Serai. When he left, they were still there. In the daytime they go armed about the bazaar, at night they retire to their several rendezvous. The man, who is intelligent, describes them as only 150 to 200 in number. They have 5 or 6 big horses only; and some 20 tattoos for baggage. The Mewattees on the hill are in their interest—say some 40 men. The fugitives say that no road is left open for them, and that they will die where they are. Some 20 of them are like Sepoys, but none have uniform. They are variously armed—matchlocks, carbines, and flint muskets. Some have sold their arms. Hopelessness of the fugitives.

The above is, I believe, a tolerably reliable account.

A man came from Muthra yesterday. *Met nobody* on the road.

W. MUIR.

## CCCLXA.

*23rd October.—Memorandum.* Yesterday an Urzee came from the Naib Thannahdar of Futtehpore Sicri (who is obliged to stay at Mendhakoor), saying that a messenger had reported that the 150 to 200 Cavalry there had gone towards Biana, and that the fugitives at Behree were likely to come to Futtehpore Sicri. Futtehpore Sikri.

To-day a second Urzee of yesterday's date has come from the same official. He says that some 50 Cavalry and 200 Infantry came on the 21st from Behree, and said that the rest would come the next day, *i.e.* the 22nd. The messenger waited till midday: no more troops had come from Behree by that time, but he believed that they were coming. He added that the former fugitives who had left for Biana, hearing of the arrival of these men from Behree, had *come back*, and that they were all together now at Futtehpore Sicri. Fugitives at Futtehpore Sikri.

## CCCLXB.

I have received a letter from Bareilly dated the 16th October. It confirms the account of the defeat of the troops sent against Nynee Tal. But a force was going a *third* time in that direction. The troops, however, are clamorous for pay. Bareilly. Attack on Naini Tal.

Wullee Dad had reached Bareilly, and Khan Buhadur had given him 4 "pultuns," cavalry, and guns, to go against Malagurh. These troops, too, want their pay. The Nawab is disinclined to go on the expedition himself, but has sent his brother or nephew. Wullee Dad at Bareilly.

Bukht Khan, with the Nana's brother, has gone with some troops *via* Budaon to Furruckabad. Bukht Khan. The Nana's brother.

Khan Buhadur is endeavouring to collect revenue, but meets with great opposition from the Hindoos. The news of our successful occupation of Lucknow had reached Bareilly. At Khan Buhadoor.

Bareilly, Khan Buhadur has kept 10 "pultuns," some cavalry, and 2 guns. In all he is said to have 30 "pultuns" and 21 guns, but none are properly armed—some have muskets, some swords, some clubs. The Artillery men are also unskilful.

W. MUIR.

COL. FRASER, C.B.
COL. COTTON, Comdg.

CCCLXC.

23*rd*, 10 *a.m.*—Forwards Phillipp's note reporting evacuation of Behree—recommend reconnaissance *at the least;* but demonstration in force infinitely preferable.

W. M.

# INTELLIGENCE DEPARTMENT, AGRA.

MSS. VOL. V.

*SEVENTH SERIES.*

CONTAINING

# NOTES OF IMPORTANT INTELLIGENCE,

## QUOTED AS EXTRACTS OR EPITOMES

FROM

## LETTERS RECEIVED BY THE LIEUTENANT-GOVERNOR AND OTHERS

**In the Fort of Agra, during August and September 1857.**

*This volume was of a private nature, but may perhaps be kept with the other records of the Intelligence Department.*

ALLAHABAD, 17*th* *June* 1860.—W. MUIR.

# NOTES OF IMPORTANT INTELLIGENCE, QUOTED FROM LETTERS

## CCCLXI.

### LAHORE.—LETTER FROM SIR JOHN LAWRENCE TO SIR HENRY LAWRENCE.[1]

*21st July* 1857.

MY DEAR HENRY,—We are all well. The Sikhs behaving nobly. No rows nor risings. We have disarmed every Native Infantry Regiment in the Punjaub, but two at Peshawar, and they are powerless. We have also disarmed all the regular Cavalry and some of the Irregulars; but none of them are trustworthy. There is at present not a hope of taking Delhi. We lost our chance when we did not try to assault it on our first arrival. **Affairs in the Punjab.**

Chamberlain has been badly wounded, and Wilson has got the command. He, I am happy to say, will not retreat. Our troops are few, but if only properly handled can hold their own. The great danger lies in the chance of our communication being cut off. I am now sending down upwards of 1300 Europeans and at least as many of the Punjaubees; also 3000 Infantry, 250 Cavalry, and 6 guns from (?) Richard is to command the latter, and I hope to see them all at Julundhur by the 1st of August. **Affairs at Delhi. Chamberlain. Wilson. Colonel Richard Lawrence.**

I have proposed to the Governor-General that, in the event of necessity, I may give up Peshawar and Kohat; this would give us 3000 European Infantry, 3200 Punjaubee Infantry, some few Cavalry, and 30 odd guns. With such an addition we might take Delhi. **Proposal to abandon Peshawar and Kohat.**

I see by your note to Colvin of the 21st, that poor Wheeler

[1] This letter was written by Sir John Lawrence to his brother Sir Henry, nearly 3 weeks after the latter had been killed in the defence of the Residency at Lucknow.—W. C.

and his force had been destroyed, and that you were holding out bravely, but in three different places. But surely you would be stronger if you gave up some of them. Colonel Neill was to have left Allahabad with troops of European Infantry on the 30th of June. If he did that, he ought surely to have been at Cawnpore before this. George was all right on the 6th at Ajmere.

With our united love.—Believe me, affectionately yours,

JOHN LAWRENCE.

## CCCLXIA.

DELHI.—14*th July*. *Estimate of Strength.*

Force at Delhi.

| | Artillery. | Cavalry. | Infantry. | Total. |
|---|---|---|---|---|
| European . | 620 | 537 | 2400 | 3557 |
| Native . . | 440 (200 Sikhs) | 437 | 1563 | 2440 |
| Total . | 1060 | 974 | 3963 | 5997 |

EXCLUSIVE of 583 sick and 352 wounded, we have had 159 killed, 574 wounded, to date. Health good—but cholera. All Poorbeas disarmed and turned out of camp.

As yet acting on defensive, but our batteries reply to enemy's fire from the walls. Enemy come out and attack every 3rd or 4th day, but are always driven back with heavy loss.

Native Infantry in Punjab disarmed.

All (Poorbea) Native Infantry in Punjaub disarmed, except 21st and 39th, who retain arms.

Mutinous regiments.

14th destroyed. 46th still at large, but pursued.

Punjaub quiet.

Bombay Fus. wing at Lahore, and wing at Mooltan.

Mutineers 12,000. Guns and shot abundant, but running short of English gunpowder and caps.

12 siege guns, 28 field do.; not sufficient ammunition for siege. Well off for small-arm ammunition.

Holy War preached.

Holy War preached.

14*th July*, 11 *a.m.* Mutineers turning out.

## CCCLXII.

(*Rough Jottings.* 4*th July* (?)).

ALLAHABAD.—Fort saved by a very close shave. (Letter from Mr. Court.)

LUCKNOW.—A message from Sir H. L. No Europeans, so all moved in. Birch, Innes, Plunkett, Hawes, Stewart, Pringle,

Munro, 6 ensigns, and 30 other Europeans murdered. More than 18 lacs plundered. Kucherries and houses burnt. 1 Madr(as regt. ?), H.M.'s 84th and 78th coming in. 400 Europeans, 400 Sikhs, 3 guns went out on 30th June. Halted on hearing that Wheeler, etc., massacred. 12 Eur. and guns to go out on 6th. All out-stations gone and Treasure plundered.

FUTTEHPORE.—H.O.K. killed Tucker, and reigns.

BANDA.—Only Cockerell killed.

HUMEERPORE.—All gone.

CAWNPORE.—Wheeler, 300 Eur. (?), 400 or 500 ladies and children; from 6, 53rd, 56th, N.I.; 2 Cavy. (?); 24-, 18-, and 6-pdrs. joined by Oudh regt.

## CCCLXIII.

(*In Pencil.*)

FROM ABDOOLLAH KHAN, TEHSEELDAR EGLASS. *14th July.*

. . . . . . . .

Has gone with Sudder Sudoor towards Shahjehanpore. The Peshkar of Hatrass (?), Zahoor Ahmed, asks leave to go to his home in Bansa in Oudh. Jye Kishn Das allowed to give leave.

## CCCLXIV.

CAWNPORE.—FROM GENERAL NEILL. *27th August* 1857.[1]

GENERAL HAVELOCK'S Column consists of 1st Madras Fusiliers and H.M.'s 64th, 78th, 86th,[2] ½ Regiment Seikhs,[3] Squadron Vol. European Cavalry; nearly 2 batteries. Crossed and would march on afternoon of 27th (should march on 28th). Reinforcements coming up, but season and cholera against them. General Havelock's Column.

Accounts from below good; in Calcutta, 1600 Chinese troops had arrived and would be sent on. 5th Madras Fusiliers to be at Allahabad in 8 or 10 days. Saugor Mutineers 3 days before at Calpee. Going to Delhi or Lucknow. Chinese troops. Saugor Mutineers.

Hopes soon to have a powerful steamer with European crew.

Brigadier Sage at Saugor; all safe.

[1] This letter appears much out of place serially, and the date in MSS. is not very clear; but I think, seeing that the letter mentions the arrival of China troops, that the date as here given is correct.—W. C.

[2] Should probably be 84th.—W. C. [3] Brasyer's.

## CCCLXV.

### DELHI.—FROM H. H. GREATHED, C.S. *July 23rd.*

Affairs at Delhi.

WANT of money will no doubt be a great difficulty with the King and his people by and bye. He is trying to squeeze some out of Jhujjur, Bullubgurh. It already prevents strangers from flocking to D. The maxim clearly is *point de paie, point de Ghazee.* The population also suffers, but as long as there is food in the country, and there are stores, Sepoys will eat. The Neemuch men did not succeed in raising much money at Muthra. Last heard of at Hodul. In time the Mutineers must run out of gunpowder, caps, and shells. They are making powder, but I hope the supply of sulphur will be soon exhausted. Our camp is abundantly supplied with provisions; it is the only safe market, and the Commissariat buy daily all that is over. Barnes sends 5 lacs. 900 Europeans; and 3 Punjaub, Beloch, and Goorkhas are on their way. Attacks made daily, with exception of yesterday, since the 18th. We suffer little loss. Little heart in their attacks. Guns, Infantry, and Cavalry fly like the wind when turned upon. No hope of forcing our position. General Wilson's appointment is regarded with general satisfaction. Sent Ford to Hissar. As troops supplied from Punjaub, he will be under J. Lawrence. Jheend Rajah holding. Anxiety to eastward, but do not expect any rapid movement. Meanwhile not idle in keeping such a mass of troops, provided with all the munitions of war, at bay. When they cease to get reinforcements and ours begin to come in, the tide will turn.

Neemuch Mutineers.

General Wilson.

W. Ford, C.S.

## CCCLXVI.

### DELHI.—FROM H. H. GREATHED, C.S. *July 29th* (?).

Improved position at Delhi.

I FEEL convinced that the project which was glanced at on the 18th will not have to be carried into execution. Since then our means of defence have increased, and spirit of offence in enemy rapidly decreased. Occupy a highly improved position. Arrival of Neemuch force failed to reinvigorate the Pandees. No attack since 23rd. Were to have come out to-day. Two or three Regiments did accoutre themselves, but it came to nothing. Project of shelling from the opposite bank, Gabions, etc. Pass-

Neemuch force.

ing to rear. Sick and wounded numerous. King's terms extravagant, and thrown over. Revenue coming in in Meerut since Sah Mull and Sardana man killed; Richards got $1\frac{1}{2}$ lacs. Quiet in Punjaub. Wellby constantly in defence. Baird Smith well. **King's terms extravagant. Revenue coming in.**

## CCCLXVII.

### DELHI.—FROM CAPT. ANSON, 9TH LANCERS. *27th July.*

THE Pandees, we hear, are meditating some deep scheme of attacking us—front, flanks, and rear, at the same time. Sun exceptionally hot: Lambert disabled by it. Mutineers thinking of mounting a 68-pounder gun they have got. Busy supplying their batteries with new guns and putting aside the old ones. Enemy disposed to disturb us in the rear. Late heavy rain has made the country so swampy that we are safe there. **Position at Delhi.**

## CCCLXVIII.

### DELHI.—FROM H. H. GREATHED, C.S. *26th July.*

REPLY to letters of 20th and 21st. Neemuch force at Bullubgurh. King wants it to go to rear. They wish to come at once to Delhi. Communication with Meerut *via* Baghput; and coolies go safely. Ford started that day for Hissar, temporarily made over to Punjaub. Lawrence being relieved by the destruction of 14th and 46th, and 9th Cavalry, he sends down the Moveable Column. **Neemuch force. W. Ford, C.S.**

## CCCLXIX.

### DELHI.—FROM COLONEL BECHER TO CAPTAIN NIXON. *29th July* 1857. *Answer to 24th.*

ENEMY evidently disheartened by the Cawnpore news. No attack since the 23rd, when they moved out with some guns to Metcalfe's house, but were easily dislodged by a small Contingent. Our loss small. Lt. Law, 10th Native Infantry, killed; Lt.-Col. Drought, 60th Native Infantry, Money, Horse Artillery, Colonel Seaton (?), 33rd, severely wounded; Major Turner, slightly. **Affairs at Delhi. Casualties among officers.**

Dissension spreading; want of money, ammunition, and leader. Tonk Ghazees threaten to slaughter cows before Juma Musjid on Eed. Impending row between Hindoos and Mussulmans— **Affairs within City. Dissension between Hindoos and Mussulmans.**

not the slightest idea of a retrograde movement, but look anxiously for the arrival of good men from England to settle the work that is before us. Seeks earliest information of their leaving Cawnpore, as of course we must prearrange their route up to form the junction, which I do think will be effected without difficulty and probably without a struggle, as Pandee is not the man he was, and our very presence here is a check upon him.

Mutineers depressed.

Kamaon battalion.

(Goorka) Kemaun Battalion to join Delhi on 31st, with treasure and ammunition. By 10th, H.M. 52nd, wing of H.M. 61st, Green's Sikh Regiment, wing of Beloch Battn. and others, with 2 batteries. Daily communication with Meerut. Seh. (aranpore ?) tolerably quiet. Goorka Battn., 2 guns, and a police battn. to join them. Punjaub perfectly quiet. Accounts up to 27th. Sialkot Mutineers all polished off, and most of the property recovered. Medical Depôt safe. Up to 25th all perfectly quiet at Peshawur. Well off in our camp in all respects. Sickness unfortunately prevalent, but weather has been favourable. Hissar to 25th. Cortlandt's force tranquilising the country. Ranghurs giving trouble, stirred up by Delhi. Tents will be required for troops coming up; ours also getting old, and will require renewal. Anxious for news. Nicholson coming down with 52nd, etc.; Chamberlain and Seaton doing well. Becher himself getting on well. Hill stations all right.

Punjab.

Cortlandt's force.

Nicholson coming.

## CCCLXX.

DELHI.—FROM H. H. GREATHED, C.S. *July 30th*, 1857.

Affairs at Delhi.

Neemuch Mutineers.

REINFORCEMENTS from Punjaub exceed 4000. Lull in city; no attack since 23rd. Neemuch Mutineers applied at Delhi for 2 lacs, cartridges, etc.. ¼ was offered of indent; refused to take any. Bullubgurh Raja said to be brought prisoner to Delhi for not giving money. Jhujjur man sent letter to G. with Mr. Kitchen's family. No reply given, as he is gravely compromised by acts of his servants. Want of money checks the formation of new levies at D., and distresses all classes who cannot help themselves; labour not remunerated; markets badly furnished, but distress does not reach rebels. They had plunder from Treasuries. Jhansi rebels had 600 each (?).

Nawab of Jhujjur.

Within City.

Plunder of treasuries by Jhansi rebels.

Military transport from Loodianah to Delhi organised by Captain Briggs. Military and provision stores come continuously. Country free from crime. Budmashes destroyed by village feuds.

Country free from crime.

Advance on Lucknow heard of.

## CCCLXXII.

CAWNPORE.—FROM GENERAL NEILL THROUGH CAPT. BRUCE.
29*th July*. *Letter sent on to Chester.*

LUCKNOW is being relieved, and then your wishes will come next. General Havelock marched yesterday from the left bank. Made another march this morning, and at 7 o'clock we heard firing, which lasted more than half an hour, and was evidently receding, which shows that we have driven everything before us. Cholera has nearly ceased, and the soldiers are in the highest spirits. **Havelock's march.**

The Native Infantry have bolted from Dinapore with their arms, but were being pursued when the message left.

Reinforcements coming up rapidly.

The garrison at L. all well.

The Saugor people crossed to this side Jumna, and are moving your way. 400 Cavalry and 1 Regiment Infantry with 1 gun. **Saugor force.**

All well here, and no time will be lost.

A. BRUCE, Captain.

*P.S.*—Asks about pontoons.

Country tolerably quiet around this, and decidedly improving.

## CCCLXXIII.

ALLAHABAD.—FROM MR. COURT, C.S. 27*th July* 1857.

OUR authority hardly extends beyond the Grand Trunk Road, excepting over Jumna. Raja of Manda has behaved splendidly. **Affairs at Allahabad.**

Dya man, rebel. Bara man waited to see what Rewa would do, and seeing him on our side is now working with us. If troops withdrawn from the other side the Ganges they will be sent to Benares, in which case Jounpore should be strongly held. **Attitude of Chiefs.**

Talookdars collecting men, but whether to oppose us or fight among themselves, not known. Mayne with Court. Banda Nawab said to be inimical, but playing a double part. Narain Rao holding Rajapore, ostensibly for us, but doubtful. Rewa helps with carriage, and will remain firm if pressure of Central India not too great. "Himalaya" arrived with 1700 troops. All at Allahabad live in their own houses without guards, but hopes they are secure. Massacre horrible. Calcutta *timeo in periculo*; *item Patna*, but with care and European troops will be safe. **Europeans at Allahabad. Fears for Calcutta.**

Reinforcements rapidly coming. 12,000 men said to be coming overland.

Sherer and Willock at Cawnpore with Havelock.

Jubbulpore. Saugor and Jubbulpore quiet. 31st Native Infantry behaved well.

## CCCLXXIV.

MEERUT. *27th July.*

Meerut quiet. DUNLOP asking for information about upward troops. All quiet at Meerut; revenue coming in satisfactorily; our only source of annoyance is the free ingress and exit allowed to the Delhi people at Shahdera.

## CCCLXXV.

MEERUT. *25th July.*

Mutineers at Delhi feebler. Deaths of officers from cholera. MUTINEER attacks becoming feebler; using inferior powder. Cholera bad in camp. Dr. Stewart, Artillery; Lt. Rivers, 75th; Ellis, Carabineers; Ross, 9th Native Infantry, died of it.

## CCCLXXVI.

NEEMUCH.—FROM CAPTAIN W. ROSE TO CAPTAIN NIXON. *29th July* 1857.

Position at Neemuch. WE have 100 of the 83rd H.M.'s, 150 men of 12th N.I., squadron of 2nd Cavalry. The latter, I am sorry to say, are shaky; and if our army, or any portion of it, does unfortunately go, I fear the Neemuch branch will be the first to show the bad example, as it did in (?) ; the temptation is great, especially in this part of the world, where they are being tampered with right and left. Bombay Column expected at Mhow on the 1st proximo. Mundessore only disturbed place on Bombay line.

## CCCLXXVII.

ALLYGURH.—FROM PEAREE LALL, TEHSEELDAR, ALLYGURH, TO DR. S. CLARK, CIVIL SURGEON, AND L. W. OUTRAM, ESQ., C.S., AGRA. *1st August* 1857.

Ghous Mahomed Khan appointed Governor at Allygurh by authority of King of Delhi. I BEG to inform you that Ghous Mahomed Khan of Secundra Rao, Zilla Allygurh, has arrived here as a Sooba of Allygurh. He says he has been appointed here as a Governor by the Nawab of Malagurh, who has been authorised to do so by the King of

Delhi. He came here with no force, no guns, and no treasure; but is very busy in enlisting Sepoys to make up 3 Foot Regiments and one Cavalry. About 500 men have already been enlisted; besides, he has taken into his service all the Nujjeebs, Sowars of the Foujdaree Court, and about 40 or 50 Mutineers who were passing Allygurh. A man by the name of Hussan Khan has been appointed as a Kotwal of the City. We hear that Ghous Mahomed Khan has written to Mahomed Ally Khan, the Chief of Chuttaree, Zilla Allygurh, to assist him with guns and ammunition, but has received no answer as yet. None of us has presented himself to this impostor Governor, and we sincerely hope he shall soon be rewarded by the English with a bit of string on his neck.

**Enlisting Sepoys.**

Yesterday Moulvee Abdool Julleel (he is considered a highly respectable and religious man amongst the Mohammedans) came here from Chuttara, and preached in the City Mosque to the Mohammedan Public that whoever shall kill a European or Christian shall get his salvation at once, and he will become as sinless as an innocent child, and whoever shall be killed in the religious war against the Kaffirs shall directly go to Heaven!

**Moulvee Abdool Julleel preaches Jehád.**

Last evening a suspicion arose amongst the Mohammedans that some Christians were hidden amongst the sweepers at Seesseea Para Street; instantly hundreds of Mohammedans assembled with their naked swords, and threatened to kill all the sweepers in case they did not point out the Christians. All the huts of the sweepers were searched, but no European or Christian was found; still, they have kept some sweepers with their wives in custody.

**Search for Christians.**

Yesterday morning about 10 or 11 Sepoys passed the station; some say they were fugitives from Delhi, others that they were disarmed at Punjaub.

The happy news of the arrival of the British force at Allahabad and Cawnpore has given us a new life. It was a rumour here that lots of European force is expected at Agra on the 30th ultimo.

Our daily and hourly prayers are that you may soon return to Allygurh and deliver us from the hands of these infernal rebels; the lives of the well-wishers of the Company are in a greatest stake.

**Dangerous position at Allygurh.**

May I earnestly and humbly beg to know till what date we may expect to see you at Allygurh. With due respects.—I remain, your most obedient servant,

Peearey Loll,
Tehseeldar of Kheree, Chandous.

## CCCLXXVIII.

JEYPORE.—FROM CAPT. EDEN TO CAPT. NIXON. *2nd August.*

Affairs at Jyepore.

ABOUT three days ago the "pultuns" (that went with me) encamped at the Ghat, displayed manifestly a desire to follow the Pandeys of our army—but quiet, and have stated their grievances. Want arrears; they have the guns. Hopes to get over it; thinks it a get-up for a purpose, else got up by the one or two ruffians in the city.

## CCCLXXIX.

DELHI.—FROM H. H. GREATHED, C.S. *2nd August* 1857.

. . . . . . . . . . .

Palace overtures came to nothing, and will not be renewed. On the 31st the Pandees moved out in great strength for the purpose of restoring the bridges over the Nujjufgurh cut, crossing to our rear and attacking the camp, while the troops left in the city made a simultaneous attack in front. It rained heavily during the afternoon of the 31st and forenoon of 1st, and their bridges have been swept away and floated down to our camp. The force returned to the city, and it was then resolved to attack our right throughout the night. It commenced at 5 p.m., and the musketry and cannonade were kept up by the Pandees without interruption until 6 a.m., but they made no impression. Every advance was repelled, and our loss was very slight. They have recommenced an attack on Subzeemundee Picket; it has not assumed sufficient importance to call up the supports. The Jumna is high, but the bridge still stands. Communication with Meerut *via* Baghput open. Kemaon Battalion arrived with treasure, and ammunition, and stores, yesterday the 1st. All quiet in the Punjaub. Captain Stewart, 9th, employed in Adjutant-General's Department. Ford gone to Hissar.

Fighting at Delhi.

## CCCLXXX.

GWALIOR MUTINOUS FORCE (as given by) MAJOR MACPHERSON.
*5th August* 1857.

| CAVALRY. | | INFANTRY | |
|---|---|---|---|
| 1st Cavalry . . | 300 | 1st, 2nd, 3rd, 4th, | |
| 2nd „ . . . | 250 | 5th. . . | 3000 |
| 1st L.C. . . | 120 | 23rd N.I. . . | 700 |
| Holkar's . . | 200 | Holkar's . . | 400 |
| | 870 | | 4100 |

Ghazees . . 1000 (?).
Gwalior . . 24 guns, 4 Batteries.
Indore . 7 „ (but without artillerymen).

## CCCLXXXI.

MEERUT.—FROM F. WILLIAMS, C.S. COMMR. *August 2nd.*

FROM the 23rd to the 1st nothing had been done at Delhi. Our people were strengthening part of their position by breast-works. 600 Coolies at work without attempt to interrupt them even by a shot. The walls and gardens in Teleewara and Subzee Mundee much cleared and knocked down. "And a sortie no fun to Pandee now, for he does not like the open." Position at Delhi.

Other reinforcements on 10th, but I question whether they will go at Delhi even then. I believe that, till they get the European reinforcements from below, they will not. It is highly desirable to push them up and settle Delhi. The people everywhere are looking to that, and partly believe the utterly false accounts which issue from the Dehli rebels, and which are most industriously spread by those who have already committed themselves, to induce the people to side with them.

Hopes himself that they will wait for the reinforcements in order that the destruction may be complete, and not a single Pandee escape. "Do, if you can, urge them on."

Without the Hindun or Jumna bridge is broken, we cannot take Malagurh—urges importance of this. "The Hindun was supposed to be broken by an Engineer from W.'s force; and I had the Ganges Canal escapes turned into the Hindun long ago. But the rebels had it repaired for the Bareilly Brigade, so it could not have been properly done. When urged again, got for answer that it was likely to be of more use than harm to us. Has had a cask bridge made for our people: and only waiting permission from Camp to do it. Does not understand why they don't break the Jumna bridge of boats. As soon as Hindun bridge broken and reinforcements received to enable Sapte to hold Malagurh, will go at it. Folly to go and have to come back. Hindun Bridge. Malagurh.

50 Carabineers and 50 Rifles attacked Wullee Dad Khan, who had advanced to Guloutha, killed 92 of them, and sent them flying in such a fright and haste that it is said they even left Boolundshuhur. Two wonderful guns made of the cast-iron screw piles of the Electric Telegraph posts, with grape made of Wullee Dad Khan.

the wire, brought in as curiosities. As soon as the Sikh corps (arrive), D.V., W(ali) D(ad)'s short reign is over, and you will hear of us at Allygurh.

Two 6-pounders sent to (?), who will keep his district in order. He says all fear of attack has passed. The Goojurs, Rangurs, and Rajpoots had been assembling.

Mozuffernugger quiet.

31*st.*—Pandee seems to be attempting to come out, but apparently cannot make up his mind to it.

## CCCLXXXII.

FROM H. GREATHED. 31*st.*

**Affairs at Delhi.**

FUGITIVES from camp telling dismal story of defeat in City.

Enemy out and moving along distant hills to Nujjufgurh Jheel, where the blown-up bridges are—musketry, cannonade, and thunder—so nobody knows what.

## CCCLXXXIII.

FROM C. BEADON, C.S. *July* 19*th*, 1857 (*reply to* 28*th June*).

**Nagode. Jubbulpore. Saugor.**

50TH at Nagode firm. 52nd at Jubbulpore, though highly insubordinate, still profess obedience. At Saugor the 31st have performed the extraordinary feat of attacking (though deserted by their officers, acting apparently under the order of Brigadier Sage) the mutinous 42nd and 12th Irregular Cavalry, and driving them from the station and district. (At Mhow, 23rd and 1st Cavalry staunch ?).

Sir H. Lawrence wounded in a sortie[1]—unsuccessful, owing to desertion of Golundazes. Banks assumed charge.

**Fleet of gunboats organised.**

Doing what we can to organise a fleet of gunboats. "Jumna" armed with six 12-pounder Howitzers, and goes up immediately. Ditto, two ships' boats, each with 12-pounders.

Patna, Benares, Naag, and Nujoo ferry-boats to be armed and sent up as soon as possible; only draw 2 feet.

**Jung Buhadoor. Wynyard, C.S.**

Jung Buhadur sent his Goorkhas; doing good service already at Goruckpore, where Wynyard conducting administration of the district.

Main body will be at G. in a fortnight. They are to make a diversion at Fyzabad, and cross on H.'s taking Lucknow.

[1] This is apparently a mistake; Sir H. was killed by a shot which broke into his apartment in the Residency.—W. C.

Azimgurh managed by Venables; but force small and position not strong. Jaunpore managed by Sheogholam . . . (?) and Hajee Imam Buksh, but district disorganised, and will be so till a military force goes. Futtehpore could be reoccupied if force could be spared. Azimgurh. Venables, C.S. Jaunpore.

Bengal uneasy where Sepoy troops in arms. Tayler discovered plot at Patna and suppressed; at Calcutta panic passed away. "In addition to the China troops, which are daily expected, we shall have 25,000 from England by the cold weather—half at Bombay and half here. With these and the Sikh Regiments, and with some assistance possibly from the Madras and Bombay armies, our authority, which has been grievously shaken, will be re-established on a firmer basis than ever." W.Tayler, C.S., suppresses plot at Patna. Calcutta panic passed away. Prospects of re-establishing authority.

## CCCLXXXIV.

CAWNPORE.—FROM GENERAL NEILL. 1st *August*.

HAVELOCK, engaged throughout the 29th, defeated the enemy. Killed 1500, and took all his guns, 20; but made a retrograde movement to reinforce his artillery and some Europeans, which would be immediately supplied in a few hours. Saugor (?) force gone towards Furruckabad. Havelock's operations.

## CCCLXXXV.

UMBALLA.—FROM G. BARNES, C.S., TO G. F. EDMONSTONE, CALCUTTA. 30*th July*.

PUNJAUB quiet, and Cis-Sutlej States. A week since last attack by Mutineers, Delhi (?). Vigour diminished and dissensions increase. Kemaon Battalion at Paneeput to be at Delhi on the 2nd. Brigadier Nicholson with 52nd now crossing the Sutlej. Second Punjaub Rifles left Ferozepore for Delhi. Only 1700 Europeans in Punjaub (exclusive of Peshawur) to guard 18,000 disarmed men. All establishments put 3 months in arrears. Greatest economy observed. Weather showery. Punjab denuded of European troops. Economy.

## CCCLXXXVI.

CAWNPORE.—J. S. SHERER, C.S., TO MR. COLVIN, LT.-GOVR. 1*st August*.

CROSSING took so long that Havelock did not get over till the 28th. On 29th set fairly out, "and on the very first day fought 3 different battles; the enemy were in great force, and were Havelock's operations.

utterly defeated; and 20 guns fell into our hands. But, for some reason not yet explained, the General has come back, to every one's great disappointment, and is now going to wait for reinforcements. Our camp is getting on very nicely. The entrenchments are nearly completed. We have several 24-pounders, and lots of little guns, and are ready to blaze away at anybody. Yesterday the 42nd, from Saugor, came within 10 miles of us—killed a Thannadar and broke down a bridge, and then passed in the direction of Futtehgurh. Nana is still on the other bank. The steamer went yesterday about 15 miles up the river to bring away boats. No one was seen, and they returned to-day. The town has great confidence in us, but naturally is agitated by the accounts of wandering bands of reckless people, and it is very difficult to get trade to go on as before. Troops at Dinapore; Lloyd after them, and it is hoped will catch them at the Soane. Rumour of Gwalior Contingent going to east through Calpee.

Position at Cawnpore. Nana. Lloyd.

Reinforcements come up from time to time. But in very small numbers. I do not think we can expect the 5th Fusiliers under a fortnight. A little cholera, but troops generally well, and in good spirits.

Latest from Delhi, 17th.

## CCCLXXXVII.[1]

FROM GENERAL HAVELOCK TO MR. MUIR.

OUDE, MUNGURWAR, *6 miles from Cawnpore*, *1st August* 1857.

Havelock describes his operations.

MY DEAR MUIR,—I have received several letters from you, but can only write one. I have beaten the enemy in 6 successive fights, and captured 42 guns; 19 of them on the 29th July at Onow, on the road to Lucknow. I cannot at present come to you, under the instructions I have received. With kindest love to all, ever believe me, affectionately yours,. (H. HAVELOCK.)

## CCCLXXXVIII.

DITTO, DITTO. *3rd August.*

His orders.

THIS force of only one thousand European infantry, 300 natives, and 15 guns. My orders are to relieve Lucknow, then take up a position on the Grand Trunk Road. (H. HAVELOCK.)

[1] These letters, and the Cossid or messenger letters in general, were all written on very tiny pieces of thinnest paper, that they might be easily secreted about the person of the Cossid, who would surely have been killed by the enemy had they been found upon him.—W. M.

## CCCLXXXIX.

DELHI.—FROM COL. BECHER TO GENERAL HAVELOCK.
*2nd August* 1857.

. . . . . . . . .

26th Native Infantry deserted from Lahore without arms. Excepting this, all right in the Punjaub, and El. Tel. open from Lussoulee to Peshawur. 26th Native Infantry desert at Meean Meer. Wire unbroken through Punjab.

All well in Sinde to 19th inst.

The enemy made what must have been intended as a final attack last night, but was completely driven back. Their loss must have been great, and the City letters so describe it. We had only 10 killed and wounded, including officer killed—Captain Fraser. Till yesterday, no attack since 23rd. Captain Fraser killed.

## CCCXC.

ALLAHABAD.—FROM C. CHESTER, C.S. COMMR., TO CAPTAIN NIXON.
*Dated August 1st.*

THE reply to ours of the 24th. Desired to remain at Allahabad.

We have here about 600 Europeans of H.M. 78th, 84th, and 64th and 1st Madras Fusiliérs, also 120 Sikhs. Force at Allahabad.

Yesterday evening Capt. Olpherts marched upwards with ½ Field battery and 60. men of 78th Highlanders. When these reach Cawnpore the total British force with Generals Neill and Havelock will be nearly 2000 men, and 400 Sikhs. (Will) pick up 200 or 300 Europeans and Sikhs at Lucknow.

H.M. 90th are on the way on Mirzapore and other steamers. The 5th and 37th will also arrive ere long. The Dinapore outbreak may probably embarrass us lower down. Should have been disarmed before. Movements of British troops.

Steamer will be sent up the Jumna if possible.

## CCCXCI.

DELHI.—FROM H. H. GREATHED, C.S. *2nd August.*

(Account of victory of 31st.)—10,000 of all arms, with 19 guns, marched out on 31st with materials to reconstruct the bridges over the cut. There was to have been a combined attack Account of the victory of the 31st.

on signal in rear and front. Rain, and bridge floated down. Those who crossed returned by the Nujjufgurh bridge; the rest marched back by the right bank, and consoled themselves with the attack on the night of the 1st. "It lasted from 5 p.m. 1st to 6 a.m. this morning, and the roll of musketry and peal of guns was unintermittent, and we could hear from the camp the continued yells and bugle calls for the advance." Our troops confined themselves to firing when they came near, and defeated every attempt.

Kumaon Battalion.

8 *a.m.*—Main body defeated, but still skirmishing. Main project defeated, and rear proved to be safe, and no apprehension about our security. The cut is worth 2000 men to us. Kemaon battalion valuable addition. Eed passed off quietly in the city. The bulk of the troops were out of it. Lately 5 butchers were put to death by the Pandees for cow killing, and the Mahomedans did not venture to retaliate.

Cow killing.

## CCCXCII.

### Delhi.—From H. H. Greathed, C.S. *August 4th.*

Mutineers at Delhi dispirited. Neemuch Brigade.

(Reply to letter of 31st.)—"We were never in a better position than now in this camp. The failure of the Delhi force, with the addition of the Neemuch horde, the last of their notable reinforcements, to carry our position has really dispirited them. They give up all hope of driving us away, and with that hope all chance of success. Above 900 of the Neemuch Brigade alone never returned to the City after the attack of the night of the 1st. The Sepoys estimate their loss at 3000, but a considerable number of these must be missing men, or else they exaggerate the loss to grace their defeat. Dispersion may now really be looked for. They are asking for leave to go home to look after their families, who are menaced in Oudh."

(Asks after W. Edwardes and the Gwalior Blakes.)

## CCCXCIII.

### Delhi.—From Major O. H. St. G. Anson. *4th August* 1857.

Fighting at Delhi.

"We had another fight on Saturday. It began by the enemy attacking about 6 p.m., and lasted all night till 10 a.m. on Sunday. Our guns and infantry waited till they came pretty close, and then fired grape and volleys into them. Some 500 in all were killed and wounded, and only about 20 on our side—

amongst them one officer, Eaton Travers, a fine young fellow, shot through the head. Heavy rains, all in our favour, prevent the enemy from molesting our rear—about which we are naturally very sensitive. **Eaton Travers killed.**

## CCCXCIV.

### Meean Meer.—Memo.

On the 30th ult., 26th N.I. broke out at Meean Meer, and 30 cut up by Sikhs, and 7 hung. **26th Native Infantry mutiny at Meean Meer.**

## CCCXCV.

### Cawnpore.—From General Neill.

Nana fled, whither uncertain; flinging their muskets down wells; cavalry gone, mostly dismounted. Nana said to be 24 miles up river with several thousands; 200 who crossed went back again. The steamer brought up 100 men and 2 guns. **Nana fled.**

General Havelock, on the 29th ultimo, marched 3 miles; met 12,000 men and 3 guns: 2nd battle, 13,000 men and 12 guns; sent all flying in half an hour—1 killed on our side, 3 wounded, including Seaton, A.D.C. **General Havelock's operations.** **Captain Seaton wounded.**

5th Fusiliers will be at Cawnpore in 10 days; 90th left Calcutta; asks about caps and H.A. harness.

## CCCXCVI.

### Delhi.—From H. H. Greathed, C.S. *August 6th.*

"The Pandees are out to-day on the old tack, except that they do not advance so far, and it appears to be an Artillery skirmish. The supports have been withdrawn. They still talk of getting to our rear by Nujjufgurh, where there is a bridge; some experiments have been made with infernal machines floating down the river with the view of destroying the bridges, but they have not answered as yet. A large body of unarmed men crossed to-day,—probably Cawnpore fugitives. *Metcalfe received by post a letter from the King asking after his health.* The seal is quite genuine. No notice will be taken of it. Our reinforcements are progressing quite satisfactorily. The health of our camp is on the whole improved. Men who are not positively ill look better than they ever did in a hot season before. Old Jan Fishan Khan hopes his letter will be forwarded to General Havelock. He and his sons and relatives, and his **Affairs at Delhi.** **Letter from King.** **Jan Fishan Khan.**

nephew, Sirdar Buhadur, with his followers, have been with the Army since we left Meerut, and are always to the front.

## CCCXCVII.

### Delhi.—From Major O. H. St. G. Anson, 9th Lancers.

*6th August.*

Fighting at Delhi.

The enemy is stirring to-day. They are attacking us on the right, and have sent 2 Columns out, one in the direction of our rear, or rather, right flank, and another with guns over the river.

300 of their Sowars charged shouting up the road by Metcalfe's picket, who turned out and with one well-directed volley sent them to the right-about like a flock of sheep. We expect Nicholson here on the 11th and the Commander-in-Chief on the 20th.

I shall be very glad to see Muir up here. The smash will be worth seeing, if they do not all run away before and leave us to walk into the place.

General Showers.

Showers had a narrow escape on Saturday night; large bits of shells twice falling quite close to him and frightening his horse, so that he fell with him and gave him a nasty fall.

## CCCXCVIII.

### Cawnpore.—From Capt. (?) Raikes, of 3rd Eur., to his Cousin here. *3rd August.*

The party, a small one, started from Allahabad to relieve Wheeler. On the way, hearing of the Cawnpore disaster, they waited for Havelock. Six miles from Futtehpore the enemy, thinking they were still the same small party, came out. Clouds of Cavalry; 12 guns taken; carried Futtehpore.

Havelock's advance from Allahabad.

The whole day fighting, and skirmishes in paddy fields up to waist in water.

Renaud wounded.

Next day (Monday the 13th) had another action, when Renaud was wounded (died in Cawnpore after amputation of leg); bivouacked, and fighting again in afternoon, and carried a bridge (Pandoo ?).

On 16th started, bivouacked from 8 to 1, attacked a very strong position, and had a grand fight all the afternoon: licked them tremendously.

Enfield rifle.

The Enfield does great execution: the Nana said, "The blue caps kill before they fire."

## CCCXCIX.

DELHI.—FROM H. H. GREATHED, C.S. *7th August.*

(Reply to letter of 1st.)—Proposes 6 per cent. loan, but individuals have little cash. A strong force has gone from the city to Jhujjur to force 5 lacs out of the Nawab. Another force of 800 Infantry, 150 horse, and 2 guns has gone across the river to Dusneh or Malagurh to levy money. The Marwaries and others are called upon for a forced loan. The Ghazees are going home; they get nothing to eat. The attack yesterday died out at 2 a.m. An attempt was made on the Metcalfe picket, but given up on the first show of resistance. Nicholson has arrived. The reinforcements will be here from 13th to 15th. Lord Clarendon, on the 27th, telegraphed having received Indian news, and that reinforcements would be sent at once.

Jhujjur.

Rebels attempt to get money.

Nicholson arrived.

A report comes from the City that Havelock has entirely defeated the rebel army before Lucknow.

## CCCC.

DELHI.—FROM H. H. GREATHED, C.S. *8th August* 1857.

(Reply to letter of the 3rd.)—Two cossids just come in with despatches of the 17th; had been confined in guard of Nusseerabad Brigade.

Cossids seized.

"Yesterday great confusion arose on the powder manufactory exploding in the city, and they escaped; another cossid, a Sikh, who had been wounded by a bayonet, left behind, and his letters seized. His companion, a Brahmin, released.

Explosion of powder manufactory in city.

"It was a grand explosion, and I hear this morning that 500 artificers and the stock in hand of sulphur and saltpetre were blown into the air, and we could see that the place continued to burn. The Pandies, suspecting that Hakim Ahsunoollah Khan was at the bottom of it, plundered his house." Reports that Havelock completely defeated Man Singh's army, and City given up to plunder and massacre for three days.

"There has been no serious attack since the 2nd. They have sent a force out to levy contributions at Nujjufgurh, and also towards Dusneh or Malagurh. They have taken now to attacking our position with field-pieces concealed among the trees and buildings, and yesterday they brought a heavy gun in Teleewara to enfilade the ridge. The fire of the field-pieces is ineffectual. The heavy gun was silenced. To-day all is quiet;

Attacks on camp.

the health of the camp has improved. I no longer hear of cholera. All are looking forward to the day when the approaches will be made. General Nicholson is in camp." Sir J. Lawrence cautions against 6 per cent. in creating a panic, as in the conversion of 5s. to 4s. (but not now), (but Greathed says make local and limited, repayable in 1 year unless with consent).

Loan.

*P.S.*—The result of all questionings of Sepoys who have fallen into our hands regarding the cause of their mutiny is the same. They invariably cite the Cartouche as the origin. No other cause of complaint has been alluded to. His Majesty of Delhi has composed a couplet to the effect that the Mighty English, who boast of having vanquished "Russ" and Iran, have been overthrown in Hindoostan by a simple cartridge—

The cartridge the cause of mutiny.

*Na Irán ne kiya, na Shah Russ ne,—*
*Angrez ko tabâh kiya Kartoosh (Cartouche) ne.*

Couplet composed by the King.

A consciousness of power had grown up in the Army, which could only be exercised by mutiny.

The cry of the cartridge brought the latent spirit of revolt into action.

## CCCCI.

DELHI.—FROM H. H. GREATHED, C.S., TO (F. WILLIAMS, C.S. ?).
*1st August.*

"IF they had succeeded (in their attack on front and rear) the King was to hold Eed in our camp, and the termination of our Raj was to be proclaimed. But it is one thing to make projects and another to carry them out; and with the country so much under water, Pandee will find himself in a fix if he tries to work on our rear."

Projects of attack.

## CCCCII.

MEERUT.—FROM F. WILLIAMS, COMMR. *4th August.*

"THEY are, it is said, throwing up entrenchments on this side the bridge of boats. We cannot send out a party strong enough to defy even 2 Regiments with guns from Delhi, in addition to Wullee Dad Khan and his Goojurs. Wullee Dad Khan has since his defeat got 500 men.

Meerut garrison too weak to attack.

Rs. 31,435 got in from Mozuffernuggur, so about Rs. 1,80,000 in Treasury, but 50,000 going out to Cant[t].

Revenue collections.

12 *August.*—Spies caught in Meerut taking plans, etc. Two hung. Attack possible.

Spies hanged.

CCCCIII.

DELHI.—FROM CAPTAIN STEWART, DY. ASST. ADJT. GENL., TO MAJOR ELD. *Dated 4th August.*

"WE have only 2000 effective European Infantry, about 500 Cavalry, European (part of which, the Carabineers, are useless because they cannot ride), and 500 European Artillery, 200 Guide Infantry, 600 of Coke's men, Sirmoor Battalion 300, Kumaon Battalion 350, Punjaub Cavalry 200. **Details of Delhi force.**

"We could take (a portion of) Delhi any day, but to do so we should have to leave our camp empty; and the risk of failing in our ability to *keep* the town after the assault has, I suspect, deterred us from making the attempt till reinforcements arrive. Brigadier-General Nicholson with his moveable column is expected here about the 14th or 15th instant. He has 1100 European Infantry with him. After his arrival you may expect to hear of our walking into Delhi, for it is not likely that we shall wait for Havelock. The troops of all arms, except the European Cavalry, are worked to death; they are, however, in first-rate spirits, and, barring the 75th, none have suffered from sickness."

CCCCIV.

DELHI.—COL. (?) BECHER TO CAPTAIN NIXON.

BATTERY established on our right—10 guns—which give trouble.

CCCCV.

DELHI.—H. H. GREATHED, C.S., TO THE HONBLE. MR. COLVIN, LT.-GOVR. *August 10th.*

THE enemy has given up Infantry attacks, and seeks to annoy us with Artillery and rockets, but does not inflict any material damage, and they will be paid out when the time comes. Le Roi envoie sa famille au Kootub. Le pillage de la maison du Hakeem par les Pandies l'a alarmé. Tout est tranquille du côté du Punjab et d'ici à Kurnal. Richardes a ramassé deux cent soixante huit mille Rupees de rentes. Les affaires sont bien avec Spankie, on lui a envoyé 264 Cavaliers du premier Régiment du Punjaub sous les ordres de Captain Hughes. La poste de Meerut par Baghput est interrompue; elle est arrivée ce matin par voie de Kurnal, je ne sais pas encore la cause. L'attentat sur le pont par moyen de machine infernale a manqué. Elles ont ou sauté avant d'arriver au pont ou ont été attrappé par les bâteliers montés sur des *mussuks*. La santé du camp va bien. **The King.** **Attempt to destroy bridge prevented.**

## CCCCVI.

MEERUT. *August 8th.*

Reinforcements arriving.

SAPTE enquires about reinforcements. H.M. 52nd and wing of 61st to be at Delhi on 15th. Beloches going to Meerut; 3000 Dogra Sikhs coming from Cashmere, all good.

Mutineers deserting.

Mutineers deserting in great numbers, going by Rohilkhund in great numbers to avoid your force coming up the Grand Trunk Road.

## CCCCVII.

ALLAHABAD.—C. CHESTER, C.S., TO CAPT. NIXON. *4th August.*

Dinapore outbreak.

DINAPORE outbreak causes detention of troops down below that are overdue here, and ought to be on their way upwards to relieve you and Lucknow and to reinforce Delhi.

Electric communication to Calcutta is open again, and post as usual. No answer about Jumna steamer. 73rd Regiment at Julpeegoree and Irregulars at Sowree said to have mutinied.

## CCCCVIII.

Do., Do. *August 7th.*

Affairs at Dinapore cause detention of troops.

MR. C.'s letter of 29th sent on to Governor-General. No troops arrive from east: they seem to have detained three whole British Regiments to punish or keep in check the Dinapore Mutineers. In pursuing these, H.M. 32nd and 10th got into an ambuscade and lost 150 killed.

Another party, more successful, punished them severely, and drove them back to Sasseram from Arrah.

Boondelas threaten Saugor.

Jubbulpore, Nagode, Seonee, Nursingpore, and Rewah quiet. Saugor threatened by Boondelas. Electric communication below Benares still cut off. Daks all right.

## CCCCIX.

CAWNPORE.—LT. GORDON, A.D.C., TO GENERAL NEILL.
*9th August.*

Cossids hanged.

Two of our cossids caught a short way out, and hanged yesterday. General Neill wrote to Lt.-Govr. lately.

A heavy battery drawn by elephants is being equipped here.

Preparations are being made for General Havelock's recrossing the river here. General Neill not in his secrct as to cause. But it appears to him that an advance must be made immediately in the direction of Futtehgurh to destroy the troops which have been collected there, and are now supposed to be on their way here.

Futtehgurh itself must be visited. 42nd with some Irregular Cavalry and 1 or 2 guns are close to this now, having been encamped a little beyond Bithoor for the last week. Havelock a second time fallen back on his original position, 3 miles on the other side. There is no mention made of the Lucknow force, but there is a native report of its having been relieved by Goorkhas. Reasons for Havelock's retrograde movement unknown. He had gained a victory on the day preceding each retirement. Good deal of sickness in camp. Dinapore (7, 8, 40) near Arrah severely beaten by Major Eyre. Sir J. Outram and Mr. J. P. Grant expected at Allahabad. Delhi news to 29th. Capt. Olphert's ½ battery arrived three days ago. Alarm in city from Havelock's retrograde movement.

Havelock's movements.

Sir J. Outram.

## CCCCX.

### Cawnpore.—Captain Bruce to Brigadier Chamberlain.

General Havelock decided to recross the Ganges; reason not known. Dinapore business retarded troops, "but still we shall be very strong in a short time; for, besides all those Regiments now in Calcutta, a brigade of Madras troops with Cavalry must have arrived ere this," and a majority of 3 or 4 overland regiments will come by next mail; also a Regiment from Australia, and German Legion from Cape.

Havelock's movements.

42nd N.I. and 3rd Irregular Cavalry with remains of C(awnpore) Mutineers at Sheorajpore. Furruckabad man would join them, but city too unsettled to move out far. Those now at Sheorajpore—3000 of all arms with 1 gun. The Nana is across the river abreast of Sheorajpore with Jussur [*sic*] Singh—about 2500 with 4 or 5 guns. On Agra Road only a few marauders and bands of 100 or 200 men got together by Agra jailbirds.

Position of rebels.

The Nana.

Country quiet otherwise; road to Allahabad quite free. Daks regular.

Lucknow still holds out, and last accounts cheerfully written. Lucknow.

The detachment at Huzaree Bagh gone, and fears for Chota Nagpur.

Huzaree Bagh.

## CCCCXI.

CAWNPORE.—FROM J. W. SHERER, C.S. *9th August.*

Cossids hanged and blown from gun.

Two Cossids hung, and one blown from gun at Meerun Ki Serai.

Havelock's movements.

Havelock returned from his attack on Busheerat Gunge, which was quite successful, very few of our men being lost, and great slaughter of the enemy being effected with our heavy guns. But he does not consider himself strong enough to go on with the force he has at present at his disposal.

Rebels threaten Cawnpore.

We are expecting an attack on the City. The 42nd from Saugor has been in this neighbourhood for some time, and has now been reinforced by troops from Furruckabad with a few guns. Neill is quite ready for them, but it might be difficult to save the City. If these cleared off a rude kind of administration would be possible.

Police arrangements in the district, etc.

Rajah of Asothur.

At present we have police stations all through Futtehpore on the Grand Trunk Road; a Cotwallee at Futtehpore, and a Thannah at Ghazeepore, where the fidelity of the Raja of Asothur and his mother has kept matters straight.

In this district I have now only Sirsoul—where there is a strong Thannah with Chokies in the neighbourhood.

Two Thannahdars murdered, third captured.

I had three other Thannahs, but the 42nd prowling about have murdered 2 Thannahdars and captured a third. This has shaken confidence terribly.

The City police is under Captain Bruce, and very well managed by him. Captain Young appointed at Sherer's request to manage the transit of troops, prevent plunder, etc. This will strengthen police.

Willock and Macnaughten with me; Mayne at Allahabad.

Nawab of Banda.

Nawab of Banda has raised a good many troops, but not aggressive, only taking care of himself.

Steamer returned, having had an encounter yesterday with the 42nd at Bithoor; very little damage done us, and it is hoped many men killed on their side.

The Soobahdar's son is active in our cause, and was on board the steamer.[1]

Collecting a little revenue.

Sherer's District arrangements.

Appointed Umarnath (?) of Ghazipore, Suddur Tehseeldar of the whole Zillah here, on 300 Rs. with Commr.'s sanction.

As Pergunahs become safe he will move into them and collect. The records are safe in most of the Tehseelees.

[1] Steamer trying to ascend above Cawnpore.—W. M.

## CCCCXII.

CAWNPORE.—FROM CAPTAIN BRUCE. *11th August.*

LATEST date from Agra, 3rd inst., and through it from Delhi to 29th ultimo.

The 41st and 42nd, with some of the second Lt. Cavalry and stragglers from the other Cawnpore corps, are at Bithpoor and Sheorajpoor—perhaps 1500 and 4 guns. Broken down one or two bridges. Search and hang our messengers. Hopes they will soon be disposed of. General Havelock recrosses to-day; his force about 4 miles off. **Rebels at Bithpoor and Sheorajpoor.** **Havelock recrosses.**

We have heard nothing from Lucknow, but native report is that the rebel force turned so many of their guns on Havelock's advance that for several days the firing on the garrison almost ceased. They are surrounded by a perfect cordon, and every letter almost intercepted. The last accounts, however, were cheerful and good. The Civilians are said to have left Goruckpore with the 3000 Goorkhas *en route* to Allahabad. They could manage the district no longer. **Lucknow.** **Goruckpore.**

Reinforcements from all sides—Australia, the Cape, England both routes. The first instalment *via* Egypt is already in Calcutta and Bombay. **Reinforcements.**

It is said Sir J. Outram coming up to Allahabad to superintend the Military operations in the North-West Provinces, with Mr. J. P. Grant as Civil adviser. **Sir J. Outram.**

Major Eyre's battery reported to have thrashed the Dinapore Mutineers; afraid the Hazareebagh detachment going may temporarily intercept the communication and the dak. **Major Eyre.**

No post from Calcutta yesterday or to-day.

## CCCCXIII.

PUNJAB.—FROM SIR J. LAWRENCE TO W. MUIR. *5th August.*

I SAW a note from Mr. Colvin deprecating the retreat of our army from Delhi, and asking what reinforcements I was sending. I quite concur in Mr. Colvin's views. I consider that defeat and ruin would follow a retreat. I have sent, and shall send, every soldier we can spare. But though the country is friendly we have a long border to guard. The majority of these men are desperate. We have lately sent off large reinforcements. Between the date of Mr. Colvin's letter and the 15th of August **Sir J. Lawrence considers ruin would follow retreat from Delhi; and promises troops.**

Troops sent down to Delhi.

I trust that full 3000 troops will reach Delhi, and probably 1200 more shortly after. I am not sure, however, that these will suffice to enable our army to storm. It is possible that we shall have to wait until Havelock arrives. I am not sure that this officer will be able to get up to Delhi soon. It is possible that he may be detained by the state of Lucknow; or not have the force necessary for such an advance.

Sir J. Lawrence's opinion as to military advance, and attack on Delhi.

Unless it be necessary to go round by Agra and Muthra in consequence of the bridges over the Hindun being broken, or for any other good reason, I would say that Havelock would do well to march straight up the Doab and take up a position at Shahdera opposite the Palace, so as to make an attack from that side. His advance up the Doab would do much good.

Punjab quiet.

We are very quiet in the Punjaub, and have got the Poorbea and Hindoostanee troops well under our control. We have destroyed 4 Regiments of Native Infantry, and disarmed the greater part of the rest. But none of them are to be trusted. Asks after Lucknow. I am raising Cavalry for service down below. Good horsemen, however, are not to be made in a day.

Mutinous regiments destroyed and disarmed. Cavalry being raised.

## CCCCXIV.

JOUDPORE.—G. W. MURCHISON. 11*th August.*

Explosion of magazine at Joudhpore.

AT 2 p.m. on morning of 11th, in a thunder-storm, Fort was struck and magazine exploded. Loss of life fearful; estimated 1500 to 2000—a tremendous shock.

## CCCCXV.

DELHI.—H. H. GREATHED, C.S., TO HONBLE. J. R. COLVIN, LT.-GOVR. *Dated* 12*th August.*

Enemy's attacks.

THE enemy had been skirmishing on our front with field guns for the last 4 or 5 days; and though they did no material damage, they annoyed our pickets and kept up their own spirits.

General Wilson allowed them to gain confidence, and thus to offer some tangible point of attack, and his patience was rewarded this morning with a signal success. A Column organised over-night fell upon their post at Ludlow Castle at dawn, taking them completely by surprise. The result was that a number were shot and bayonetted, and 4 field guns were captured and brought into camp. The force returned by 6 in

Successful attack on them.

Four field guns captured.

high spirits. Coke's Regiment is in a great state of exultation at having captured two of them. There were no such prizes in the mountain warfare to which they had been accustomed. The returns not sent in; but loss probably 10 killed, and 20 or so wounded. Brigadier Showers commanded; wounded in chest and hand, but not dangerously. Major Coke shot through leg. Lt. Shirreff, 2nd Europeans, wounded mortally. G.'s brother took the command on Brigr. Showers being disabled. It is considered a very satisfactory affair, for their facilities for getting away their guns are very great, and they must see that their new tactics avail them nothing. General Nicholson's Column comes in to-morrow or next day. Heard from Williams that he intended to send force against Malagurh on 10th, tidings having been received of the Jumna Bridge being broken. All well at Seharunpore and Dehra. Burn recommends Keene to be suspended for indifference to danger. Greathed considers Dehra depends on Seharunpore, and discouraged expenditure on Dehra, and exonerates Keene. A lac of rupees was sent to Dehra from Umballa at my requisition. Relieved financial distress. Keene's paper currency exceptional.

Showers and Coke wounded. Lieutenant Shirreff mortally wounded.

All quiet in Punjaub, Hansee, and Hissar. Enemy has a detachment of all arms towards Jhujjur, levying contributions, and parties of Sowars in the E. pergunnah; some of whom have advanced to Moradnugger. Road *via* Baghput open.

Mutineers levying contributions.

Latest from Cawnpore, 31st; heard of Havelock's victory of 29th.

## CCCCXVI.

DELHI.—H. H. GREATHED, C.S., TO W. MUIR. *August 13th.*

(Reply to 7th and 8th.)—Colvin's of 8th. We are all in high admiration of General Havelock's successes. The native report is strong that he was in occupation of Lucknow, and that the city had been plundered for three days.

17*th August*.—Raja Golab Singh is really dead. No apprehension has been expressed of his death causing any complications, and tranquillity is maintained in the Punjaub. The rest of the disarmed Regiments at Lahore are encamped, and their lines have been demolished, and it is said that arms and ammunition were found concealed in them. I told Mr. Colvin yesterday of the successful surprise of the enemy at Ludlow Castle, and the capture of 4 field guns. And the enfilading battery they established at Teleewara is silenced by our guns. There were 2 attacks on the Metcalfe picket last night. The fusilade was sharp but

Rajah Golab Singh dead.

Disarmed regiments at Lahore.

Fighting at Delhi.

ineffective, as the enemy kept at a respectful distance. Nos pertes hier heavy enough. 19 killed, 90 wounded. Nevertheless the troops in high spirits.

. . . . . . . .

## CCCCXVII.

### DELHI.—H. H. GREATHED TO THE HONBLE. MR. COLVIN.
*August* 14*th*.

Nicholson's Column arrives in Delhi. Details of his force.

GENERAL NICHOLSON'S Column marched in this morning. It consisted of the 52nd Light Infantry, and wing of the 61st, two Punjaub Infantry Regiments, a horse battery and 200 Cavalry. These troops are in excellent order, and form an important reinforcement. The enemy were more quiet yesterday. They must see that their new system of tactics makes no impression. The Teleewara battery is not allowed to speak, being always shut up by our fire, and the skirmishing with light guns is of course ineffective against an entrenched position. The pickets on our left in advance of Metcalfe's house, which for a long time were unmolested, are now kept more on the alert, but they hold an impregnable position, and the fire of the enemy has ceased to command attention.

Enemy's tactics abortive.

. . . . . . . .

Movements of troops.

A portion of the Rifles—200—are to be brought to camp from Meerut, et un régiment du Punjaub, 700 Bayonettes, les remplaceront, on leur enverra aussi six pièces d'artillerie legère du Punjaub. Ils sont fachés de nous donner les deux cents voltigeurs, mais c'est fort necessaire parce que le Bataillon a perdu 250 men, and numbers no more than 250 rifles, and is no longer to take its place as a Regiment in the field of battle. It is impossible to overrate the excellent conduct of this Regiment. Nothing disturbs their discipline. Received Muir's of the 8th. No rumour of Rampoor Nawab's murder. Doondeh Khan *Kumoneh Wala* has come into Delhi with 500 rabble.

Praise of the Rifles.

City reports of Havelock being in possession of Lucknow. The Nawab Raees has sent a pressing application to the King for aid with Nuzzers, but got no reply. The idea here is that when the Pandies leave Delhi they will take the Gwalior road. I am opposed to the destruction of the suspension bridge over the Hindun.

Nawab Raees applies to the King for aid.

Up to the 10th inst. Rs. 3,22,000 collected in the Paneeput district.

We are well off for everything in camp, even music.

## CCCCXVIII.

BIJNORE.—J. CRACROFT WILSON, C.S. *14th August.*

THE Nujeebabad Nawab turned out by the Hindoos. The army that threatened Nynee Tal has dispersed. Captain Gowan, 18 N.I., is alive, hidden in a Hindoo Zemindar's house, and has written to Nynee Tal. At Delhi on the 12th we took two 9-pounders, one 6-pounder, one 24-pounder Howitzer, and spiked two more.

Nujeebabad Nawab. Naini Tal. Captain Gowan.

## CCCCXIX.

CAWNPORE.—GENERAL NEILL TO COLONEL COTTON.
*12th August* 1857.

(Reply to 6th.)—General Havelock advanced to Lucknow on the 29th ult., thrashed the enemy severely, took 20 guns, but, instead of following up, returned to 6 miles off for reinforcements; got on the 5th half battery more, and Company of 84th, started off, thrashed the enemy on the 6th in great style and *retired* again. There he remains—more men and guns required. The men, 1000, not to be had at present. Yesterday the General intimated that he would recross, to prevent the river rising and cutting off our communications with each other. But after sending over everything, even spare ammunition, he suddenly changes his mind, and again advances;—this morning he engaged, thrashing him, but I have no particulars. He is following him up, and has again been engaged and is following up. On this side we have 4000 and 5 guns at Bithoor, and 8000 and some guns at Futtehgurh.

General Havelock's movements. Force at Cawnpore, etc.

260 in Hospital, and 12 officers. Captain Young of the 4th died yesterday. Lts. Thompson and Delafosse, 53rd, a private Artilleryman, and one of the 84th, only four of Wheeler's force saved.

Captain Young of the 4th, dead. Survivors of Cawnpore.

## CCCCXX.

ALLAHABAD.—C. CHESTER, C.S., TO W. MUIR, C.S.
*10th August* 1857.

HAS no details of troops to report; "nor am I likely to have any for some time to come." Four R. Regiments detained below Benares to check and punish the Dinapore rebels. They are said to be at Sasseram. Electric Tel. and ordinary post to Calcutta

Dinapore rebels.

Communication with Calcutta cut off. are both cut off. The troops at Sooree are reported to have gone. This is not authentic, but probable.

Rebels between Cawnpore and Lucknow. 60,000 or 70,000 armed men between Cawnpore and Lucknow, and they fight better than the Nana's people did. We are jolly and confident here, though the garrison is not 350 strong. Forwarded message to Lean.

Faithful domestics. Please tell Greathed his servants behaved right well. They have saved his plate and horses. His furniture is destroyed, of course.

The first powerful steamer that arrives will be sent up the Jumna to Agra.

## CCCCXXI.

ALLAHABAD.—C. CHESTER, C.S., TO MR. COLVIN, LT.-GOVERNOR.
*Dated* 11*th August*.

Supplies of carriage. (Reply to letter of the 3rd.)—Carriage. From Rewah we get a few camels and carts and great numbers of pack bullocks. Tucker promises elephants from Goruckpoor. Wheeled carriage we can obtain in large quantities in this district and Cawnpore. Anxious to reoccupy Futtehpore, which he could do with (?). Steamer going to make a second attempt to go to Cawnpore. Communication with Calcutta cut off. Both Electric Telegraph and letter dak to Calcutta are cut off. And no reinforcements arrive from east; nor will they for some time to come. This is all due to General ——'s wretched conduct in not disarming Dinapore troops.

Cossids cannot reach Lucknow. Cannot get news from Lucknow. Cossids go and pretend to have delivered letters, but bring back no reply, and disbelieve them.

## CCCCXXII.

CAWNPORE.—GENERAL NEILL TO GENERAL WILSON.
12*th August* 1857.

(Reply to 6th from Agra; Delhi, 2nd.)—Accounts from down country are better, although the dak between Benares and State of country. Calcutta is cut off, and also the Telegraph. Jubbulpore, Seonee, Nagode, Saugor, all quiet. Last threatened by Boondeelas. 12th Irregulars said to be near Jounpore, intending to join the Dinapore Regiments, and attacking Benares. That has failed, as the Dinapore people are being pursued, and bolting to the eastwards. General —— has been superseded;—blamed.

H.M.'s 5th, 37th, 90th, and two batteries of Artillery detained below. Mutineers got a "severe dressing" at Arrah, but are spoiling dak and Telegraph. Arrah.

Troops are pouring out overland from England. The 48th, 71st, 57th from Malta, will be in India by the first mail. Six other Malta Regiments come by the same route. A wing of the 29th just arrived at Calcutta. All China force, Marwar[1] excepted, comes to Calcutta. Arrival of troops in India.

Two Madras N.I. corps, one Cavalry, about to embark for Calcutta. Madras corps.

After two victorious advances and retreats, General Havelock, for the last three days, has been arranging to recross. He fears the rising of the river cutting off our communication with each other. He had intimated his intention of recrossing to-day, but suddenly changed his mind and recalled detachments, escorts, etc.; got back spare ammunition, and this morning attacked the enemy and defeated him. They will go back to Lucknow, and we have no Cavalry to improve our victories with. Our men are in high spirits. Cholera subsided. Eyre's battery did great execution at Arrah. Havelock's movements. Cavalry needed.

I have not heard from Lucknow lately, but they are holding out stoutly, and have an excellent position, against which the enemy make no impression. Allahabad good garrison, but cannot spare men. Mirzapore—2 companies. Benares well held, but can't help. Ghazeepore, European detachment.

Dinapore has 10th, 90th, 37th, 5th—will soon be settled. Madras intelligence good. We have hostages in their families.

## CCCCXXIII.

CAWNPORE.—FROM LT.-COL. B. FRASER-TYTLER, DEPUTY ASST. Q.M.G. *14th August.*

GENERAL HAVELOCK has met and defeated the rebels 8 times, taking in all 66 guns. The last time was at Busheeratgunj, on the road to Lucknow, where they had entrenched themselves. We took two guns only—a fact which delayed our advance, enabling them to carry off the remainder. We should scarcely have succeeded in capturing these two had it not been that so many of the horses were killed that they were disabled. Circumstances have compelled the General to retire across the Ganges and await reinforcements, but no check has been sustained by us. The enemy is too formidable and too well prepared at Havelock's movements.

[1] No doubt, name of a transport vessel.

Lucknow to admit of 900 European Infantry penetrating the City. Reinforcements are coming up country, as the Mutineers from Dinapore have been destroyed or dispersed. Three Regiments will arrive by next overland mail, and the remainder of the China will soon come in. General Grant informed me that at three months from the time he wrote, about the 15th July, 25,000 men would be landed in India, and if thought necessary more would follow. More will not be wanted; with half that number peace would, I believe, be restored in two months.

Reinforcements.

## CCCCXXIV.

CAWNPORE.—FROM H. BRUCE, CAPT. SUP. OF POLICE, TO IKRAM HOSSEN, DEPUTY COLLECTOR, ETAWAH. 11*th August* 1857.

Paper from Cawnpore.

SIR,—I have received your letter of the 6th inst. The one for General Havelock was doubtless answered by some other Cossid, but I can tell you that it was forwarded to him. I will let you know in good time all about the supplies, etc., and I hope very soon to see you. Please to continue to let us hear all that goes on in your neighbourhood.

(*True Copy.*)

PUNDIT BANEE PURSHAUD,
Peshkar of Tehseel.

## CCCCXXIVA.

FROM CAPT. D. GORDON, OFFG. A.D.C. TO GENL. NEILL, TO THE SAME. 13*th August.*

SIR,—Your letter, dated the 9th inst., to General Neill's address arrived this morning. The letter of Mr. Muir's was no doubt forwarded immediately, as all letters are, to General Havelock, and I daresay he has answered it ere this. General Neill has also sent several letters to Agra, and an answer to Mr. Muir's was doubtless among the number. General Havelock's force had another fight with the rebels in Oude yesterday, and took two more guns and killed a great many men. The force at Lucknow have, we hear, provision to last them for some time yet, and they can easily defend themselves. So General Havelock has determined apparently to go and destroy the Furruckabad Nawab's troops before going to Lucknow. A Telegraph station has been formed at Futtehpore, and the wire

Havelock's fights.

Lucknow.

Furruckabad.

will be completed up to this place in a few days. We are very glad to hear that you have laid a permanent Dak Establishment for the conveyance of letters between Agra and Cawnpore, and hope it will succeed. The Peon has not yet come here. Some European troops were to leave Benares to-day for Allahabad, etc. Don't let the village people think that the European soldiers have been plundering the villages, and killing the inhabitants indiscriminately in the different villages they have passed through on their way up. It may have happened here and there through mistake, but such a thing will never be allowed. The innocent will be spared, the guilty punished.

(*True Copy.*)

PUNDIT BANEE PURSHAUD, Peshkar.

## CCCCXXV.

DELHI.—H. H. GREATHED, C.S., TO MR. COLVIN, LT.-GOVR.
16*th*.

**Attack by rebel force.**

THERE has been a lull since the 12th, and the enemy have ceased firing round shot at the stable on Metcalfe's grounds, occupied by a picket. They knocked down a corner of the building, but they would not have been nearer their object if the whole had been demolished, for an attack would still have had to be made on the breastworks, and that is the rub they do not relish. They have mortars in Kishengung. Their mortar is not so good as their howitzer practice. The aim is true enough, but the shells do not burst.

**Nicholson.**

Under the new distribution of the army, Nicholson has the command of a moveable Column, consisting of the 1st European and 1st and 2nd Punjaub Corps. As he is not a full Colonel he could not be appointed Brigadier in supersession of his seniors, and he was too good a man to lose. The arrangement affords satisfaction. Capt. Hodson is out with his Cavalry watching the movements of a detachment sent to levy contributions in Nujjur and Rohtuck. They got 1,60,000 from the Nawab. A party of their Cavalry went to Putowdee and squeezed a few thousands out of the Nawab; they then set to plundering the town, but were beaten off with loss by the citizens, and the King has disavowed their acts. It was intended to send out more Cavalry to raise the country on both sides of the river, but some one

**Hodson.**

**Pataudi.**

suggested it was a device of the Hukeem to betray the place after weakening the garrison. The Sikhs of the several Regiments are formed into two battalions. The real object is not yet known, but the Sikhs obtained the arrangement on a pledge to show the others the way in attacks. All quiet up above. The disarmed Regiments at Lahore are encamped opposite the 81st, and have 12 guns bearing on their camp. Last letter of General Neill's of 1st quoted in Mr. Colvin's. Health of camp better than it would have been in quarters. Cholera disappeared.

Sikhs in Delhi.

Disarmed regiments at Lahore.

## CCCCXXVI.

ALLAHABAD.—C. CHESTER, C.S., TO MR. COLVIN, LT.-GOVR.
*August* 15*th*.

Lord Elgin reaches Calcutta.

LORD ELGIN has reached Calcutta with a large portion of the China Force (number not stated), and the rest is daily expected. "Shannon" and "Pearl" are named among the steam frigates arrived. Steam gunboat "Jumna" was at Benares yesterday. She may be expected here to-morrow, and will be sent to Agra, I hope. Lucknow may yet be saved, if no delays are permitted. God grant it. Mr. J. P. Grant is appointed Lt.-Govr. of the Central Provinces, to comprise Benares, Allahabad, and Saugor Divisions. I have been directed to forward all public letters to Mr. Grant at Ghazeepore after the 16th inst. The Calcutta dak arrives again as usual. General Havelock has recrossed the Ganges and is now at Cawnpore. When reinforced he will again advance on Lucknow, I hope. Bithoor is occupied by rebels, and will no doubt be attacked. People are flocking over from Oudh to Bundelkhund to take service with the Bondela insurgent Rajas. I fancy Osborne at Rewah is keeping a sharp look-out for the Dinapore Mutineers; not a man of them should ever reach Delhi alive.

Lucknow.

Mr. J. P. Grant appointed Lieutenant-Governor of the Central Provinces.

Havelock's movements.

Jubbulpore, Saugor, Rewah, and Nagode remain tranquil, which is really marvellous. Troops at Berhampore and Ghazeepore have been disarmed.

## CCCCXXVII.

CAWNPORE.—GENERAL NEILL TO MR. COLVIN. 15*th August*.

Havelock's movements.

HAVELOCK recrossed on the 13th to Cawnpore, "and contemplates clearing the country of the insurgents collected near

Bithoor and Sheorajpore. His men are very much knocked up from the fatigue and exposure endured whilst in Oudh, and so much reduced, more by disease than the enemy, that any advance now on Lucknow will be madness until he is reinforced." Hospital lists large. Must wait for reinforcements.

From our people in Lucknow no intelligence has been received since the 22nd ultimo. They were then well, and native report has it that they are all right, and that one good result of General Havelock's moving over has been that the siege was raised for a little, as it were; and they got in provisions for another month. 360 European soldiers, composed of portions of Regiments here, and 800 of the 90th, will be up at Allahabad *en route* immediately. The Dinapore Mutineers have gone off towards Calpee. Rewah troops out against them. Lord Elgin and greater part of China troops arrived on the 8th in the Hoogley; remainder hourly expected. Troops from Cape and Mauritius expected; also from Australia. Three Regiments by first mail from Malta—one probably to Bombay and two to Calcutta. 48th, 71st, 37th are the troops from Malta. 40th from Australia. Six Regiments under orders from Malta by overland route. Lucknow. Arrival of China troops and troops from Malta.

Asks about Jewrakhun (?) Singh, Subadar.

Mayne has gone back to Banda with some of the Rewah man's troops. Macnaghten from this goes down to Futtehpore to-day or to-morrow. It is reported that a new man on our account with some Europeans saved from Fr. has set himself up and attacked the Fr. man, taking 2 guns. O. Mayne, C.S. E. Macnaghten, C.S.

## CCCCXXVIII.

### Cawnpore.—Captain Bruce to Captain Nixon.

*17th August.*

Electric Telegraph still out of order to Calcutta below Benares.

The Calcutta daks, after a suspension of three days brought about by Dinapore or Hazareebagh rebels, arrive regularly. Lord Elgin and 1700 more soldiers have landed. Outram gazetted to Dinapore district. J. P. Grant will act as Lt.-Govr. of the Provinces cut off from Agra. Nothing from Lucknow since 22nd ultimo; but native rumour says that they are all well. The Baillie guard is so carefully invested that it is a matter of extreme difficulty getting a communication to the inmates. Lord Elgin and troops landed. Baillie Guard.

Goorkhas still at Goruckpore. 11 fugitives from Calpee will be in to-day. Mr. Griffith, Deputy Collector, and Mr. Passanah (?), are the only two names I know. Havelock moved out with all his force yesterday to Bithoor, and native report says he had no fighting to speak of, and took 2 guns. I believe he will not at present go beyond Sheorajpore at any rate, and then return. 270 of 5th Fusiliers are at Allahabad, and the 90th Regiment daily expected. The gunboat had passed Benares, and will be most useful here. I think you all have exaggerated reports of the Furruckabad man's strength, and the Hindoo feeling is very strong against the Nawab. Hurdeo Doss, to whom a few of the Furruckabad fugitives went, is reported to have crossed the river with a small force accompanied by "some Sahibs," thrashed the Nawab's troops, taking 2 guns, and departed with the promise of repeated visits. This amateur friend may be of use.

Havelock's movements.

Nawab of Furruckabad.

Hurdeo Dass's loyalty.

## CCCCXXIX.

### DELHI.—CAPT. O. H. ST. G. ANSON, 9TH LANCERS, TO MRS. MUIR. *August 17th.*

Captain Hodson.

HODSON had a skirmish with 25 of the enemy's Sowars. They got under some thatched roof, and would not surrender, so he fired the place and killed 23 out of the 25.

Quantity of rain—last 2 days. Sickness is on the increase. The roar of the guns echoes again through the cloudy atmosphere. Two guns at Metcalfe's to support the picket. Enemy opening a new battery on Metcalfe's from the walls of the city. We expect the Ferozepore siege train about the 25th, and are only waiting for it to attack in earnest.

Delhi position.

## CCCCXXX.

### DELHI.—H. H. GREATHED, C.S., TO MR. COLVIN, LT.-GOVR. *August 18th.*

(Reply to 12th.)—The time that will elapse before the arrival of the siege train affords opportunity for the receipt of decided intelligence from the camp below. If it approaches it will be well to wait. If it is still occupied below, I hope the advance from this side will no longer be deferred; the train is accompanied by a thousand waggons laden with ammunition. The eldest son of Golab Singh has succeeded without opposition. He is on

Rajah Gulab Singh's successor sends a Contingent of Cashmere troops.

good terms with Sir J. Lawrence, and has placed 4 Regiments Infantry and six pieces light Artillery at our disposal; according to the intentions of his deceased father. They are on their march to our camp, and the officers who accompany them will be able to ascertain their worth on the way; Sir J. speaks well of them. Sees no object in destruction of chain bridge. Explains difficulties in way of destruction of bridge of boats. (To attack it with cannon we should have to pass over part of our army, separating the two portions.) As long as it exists it would be hazardous to attack Malagurh, as reinforcements could reach more rapidly from the rebels at Delhi than from us. The King has conferred the Sooba of Rohilkhund on General Bukht Khan, Commander Rohilkhund Brigade, and of Guzerat on General Sindhara Singh of Neemuch! The Bareilly Brigade wanted to go across, professedly to recross to our rear, but their object was seen through, and they were not allowed to go. It was supposed they wished to return to Bareilly. There is a sharp look-out at the bridge for deserters from the city; and they leave by the land side. I had a letter yesterday from Mirza Ilahi Buksh,[1] Shahzada, wanting to know what he could do for us; but I shall not involve myself in correspondence. Soon after I came into camp I received a letter from Mohun Lal (of Caubul) giving a detailed account of what had occurred at Delhi up to the 23rd May, when he left it with Wullee Dad (?), having been plundered of his property. Wullee Dad took him as prisoner, and (he ?) escaped during the (encounter ?). Now at Meerut. Recommends being sent to Loodhianah.

King of Delhi appoints officers.

Bareilly Brigade.

Mirza Ilahi Buksh.

Mohan Lal.

The enemy have been quiet for the last few days; they have withdrawn their field guns from the front, and only fire occasionally from Kishengunge. The detachment that has gone towards Hansi consists of 150 Horse Artillery, 900 Horse, and 2 guns. They are inhabitants of Hissar, and are on their own hook. Captain Hodson is out in that direction with a strong party of Horse watching them. He surprised a post of 25 Sowars, and killed 23 of them. I do not desire to see Rohtuck permanently reoccupied just yet. 160 Peshawur Horse are to be added to the Meerut force. General Penny takes a lively interest in Doab politics, and will go as far as is reasonable in securing a good force for Meerut, but he understands que la prise de la ville est l'affaire majeure.

Hodson follows enemy's detachment towards Hansi. Surprises and kills 23 Sowars.

[1] This man subsequently helped us, for instance, in procuring the King's surrender; and lived in honour in Delhi for many years afterwards. —W. C.

## CCCCXXXI.

### DELHI.—BECHER TO NIXON. 20th.

(Reply to 14th.)—Nothing of importance since 17th; the enemy hardly firing at all. Capt. Hodson out to watch enemy at Rohtuck. He surrounded and destroyed a small party in a village on his way out, and had a successful skirmish with rather a large body near Rohtuck. But he has been recalled, as communication with him is very difficult, and from the state of the country it would hardly be possible to send him assistance should he be pressed.

Hodson recalled from Rohtuck.

The rebels still talk of sending a force to Alleepore in our rear, but they are so divided in their counsel, and have but little unanimity of action among themselves, that I do not anticipate their being able to carry out any such project. Dissension and ill-feeling are certainly increasing among them.

Dissension among rebels.

Regarding procuring heavy artillery from Agra with Havelock's force, Brigr. Wilson will not give an opinion. Depends on Agra's means of transport and working the guns. "We have not a man to spare for them; and, to work the train now coming down, have been obliged to withdraw artillerymen from Meerut, where they are wanted."

Mrs. Tuson or Leeson, refugee from Delhi.

Mrs. Tuson [1] [or Leeson], wife of a son of the late Major Tuson of the Irregular Cavalry, came into camp yesterday from the city, where she has been concealed since the 11th May. Her children were all killed before her; one, a baby, shot in her arms, the same shot passing through her own body. She was left for dead, but was rescued by three Peshawaries, who took her to the house of a Moulvie, who has protected her ever since. She lived with his family and met with the greatest kindness. She heard that there were 22 Europeans still in the city, but I do not believe that this can be possible.

Cashmere loan.

Colonel R. Lawrence commands Cashmere Contingent.

Letters from Sealkote mention that camels had been sent to bring in the first large instalment of the loan of 75 lakhs which Golab Singh's son and successor has promised. His force of some 3000 or 4000 men with some guns is coming down under command of R. Lawrence.

All the accounts from the Punjaub continue most satisfactory.

We are anxiously looking out for intelligence of Lucknow and Havelock. We are getting on very well. Sickness not on the increase, and wounded doing well. Chamberlain is getting on famously. Supplies of all kinds.

[1] Given in other correspondence as Leeson.—W. C.

## CCCCXXXII.

CAWNPORE.—J. W. SHERER, C.S., TO CAPT. NIXON. *17th August.*

ENCLOSES Court's and Chester's letters and Nana's proclamation.[1] **Nana's proclamation.**

Havelock yesterday retook Bithoor, which had been occupied by the 42nd N.I. and various other insurgents, and to-day he has moved on to Sheorajpore, where a mutinous Zemindar, Suttee Pershad, has been doing a great deal of mischief. It is not improbable, I think, that Havelock may move on to Futtehgurh, where the Nawab has collected a couple of thousand Mutineers, and has equipped himself with 10 or 15 guns. But no final move can be made without reinforcements up country. We have lost Captain Young, 2nd N.I., and Campbell, 78th Highlanders, by cholera. There has been a great deal in the city; but camp tolerably healthy. **Havelock retakes Bithoor.** **Suttee Pershad.** **Futtehgurh.** **Captain Young, N.I., and Campbell, 78th Highlanders, die of cholera.**

No news from garrison at Lucknow.

## CCCCXXXIII.

MEERUT.—MAJOR WILLIAMS. *18th August.*

AT Bijnore the Chowdries have given the Nawab of Nujeebabad a tremendous thrashing,—taken Bijnore; and by a letter from Bijnore I see that the Rajpoots have 25,000, and the Mahometans (?) only 15,000. The Hindoos appear determined to attack the Nawab, and a deputation of Hindoos came here the other day to ask Goojur (?) Wilson of Moradabad to take possession. He immediately started to river with 16 Sowars. **Nawab of Nujeebabad. Hindoos *versus* Mahommedans at Bijnore.** **Cracroft Wilson.**

"Every native tells me that one Regiment marching up from the eastward would bring the whole affair to a close."

## CCCCXXXIV.

ALLAHABAD.—C. CHESTER, C.S., TO MR. COLVIN, LT.-GOVR. *13th August.*

TELEGRAM from Benares received yesterday reports that 360 H.M.'s were hourly expected there, and would be sent on here at once; a further reinforcement was hoped for after a short interval to be similarly pushed on. As they arrive they will at once march on to join General Havelock—in time, I trust, to relieve Lucknow. If Lucknow is not to be relieved, I conclude

[1] For this see p. 529, *post.*

that General Havelock will march straight to Agra. The Dinapore Regiments are on the right bank of the Ganges. They evaded pursuit of a force sent to attack them from Benares, and are said to be moving on Calpee. I trust they will not enter Rewah and upset order there. Osborne will guard strongly the Kutra and Sohaga passes. Communication with Calcutta is quite cut off, which gives colour to the rumour that the Ramgurh Battalion has mutinied. Mayne is here. He intends to attempt reoccupation of Banda, with the help of Rewah troops, viz.: 800 Infantry, 300 horse and 4 guns. The Kirvee Raos and Nawab Ali Buhadur profess loyalty. Road to Bombay *via* Jubbulpore is open. Nothing new here.

Dinapore Mutineers.

Mayne, C.S.

Kirvee Raos.

## CCCCXXXV.

ALLAHABAD.—MR. COURT, COMMR., TO MR. COLVIN, LT.-GOVR.
*August* 15*th*.

THE Lucknow Mutineers without ammunition. General opinion that Havelock in his retreat is right.

Havelock.

Lucknow garrison.

Report says the garrison at Lucknow were left free by the enemy going out to meet Havelock, and that they succeeded in getting in supplies. If this be true there is no cause for fear. But neither letter nor messenger has been received from Lucknow. Describes Havelock's third attack and retirement, "though from their (enemy's) number the loss is not felt."

Arrah.

A detachment of near 400 soldiers, British and Sikhs, was cut up near Arrah, having fallen into an ambuscade; 14 only got back untouched. Afterwards Eyre with 200 Europeans and two guns relieved Arrah and drove the enemy towards Sassaram. The dak with Calcutta and Benares ceased for 5 days. But a telegraph from Benares yesterday told us that communication was re-established, and gave us the gratifying intelligence of the arrival of Lord Elgin with a large portion of the China force—the rest of whom were daily expected. This will, I trust, enable the Supreme Government to give you the help you require.

Major Vincent Eyre.

Lord Elgin arrives with China troops.

We have been expecting the 90th H.M. here, and a telegraph from Benares told us 390 of them would be here by to-day (15th). All preparations were made to send them off at once, when yesterday a telegram came to say that Colonel Gordon at Benares had, by order of Commr.-in-Chief, stopped all detachments on their way. This is very unfortunate. There are three European Regiments between Calcutta and Mirzapore, besides

10th at Dinapore and 37th at Benares, and these troops are idle and useless at a time when they are particularly required to save Lucknow and give you assistance. The breaking of the telegraph causes these misfortunes. Colonel Outram with supreme authority will, I hope, put all right. He is expected at Dinapore to-day or to-morrow. Grant will be here in 10 days. A Government Gazette places Allahabad, Benares, and Saugor Divisions under him, in consequence of Mr. Colvin being cut off from exercising rule over these Divisions.

Colonel Outram.

J. P. Grant, C.S., appointed to charge of Allahabad, Benares, and Saugor Divisions.

Acknowledges letter of 3rd; contents sent on to Calcutta. Raise money by bills on me. I could raise loan of ten lakhs (try to send money by letters of credit or Hondies, but difficulties; better to draw upon me). Getting prepared estimate of expenditure. Records Agra for 10 lakhs.

Financial arrangements.

Calcutta dak just in. "Shannon" with 1000 Marines and "Pearl" with a force not detailed. The two frigates will strengthen Calcutta amazingly: equal to two regiments.

Marines arrive at Calcutta.

The Kamptee Column has arrived at Jubbulpore, and has left it for Saugor, where affairs are looking a little black. Hamilton went out against the Palum (?) Raja; licked him and took his gun. The Shahgurh Raja came out with 2000 against his little band of 250, chiefly Police, and forced him to retire; but he succeeded in getting back into Saugor with his captured gun.

Shahgurh Rajah.

Sherer is with Colonel Neill at Cawnpore. Willock with General Havelock. Edmonstone here as judge. Mayne here helping me, and getting information regarding his own district.

Posts of civilians.

Affairs thickening rather, owing to my helplessness. Beyond Ganges,—*i.e.* Sooram, Secundra, etc.,—at first the Busna Buretha, etc., sold-up families, clubbed together to take forcible possession of their estates. Police could give no assistance. I have been obliged to let them alone now. Taluqdars of Oudh encroaching.

Dispossessed proprietors rise.

Pirtee Pal Singh, with 3000, is levying in Secundra, and says he intends to be ruler as far as Hosee.

Pirtee Singh.

Runjeet Singh, another Taluqdar, with 2500 and guns, is making similar depredations in Sooram, and I am losing ground. In Khyragurh the people have heard the Delhi regiments are coming that way. The evil-disposed, of whom I am making records, again assembled to attack our Government offices. Ruttun Singh is in great force.

Ranpal Singh.

Ratan Singh.

The Dya Raja undoubtedly called him; made him his Diwan,

in the firm belief that our dominion was at an end, and that he had to conquer or submit to the Manda Raja. He called Ruttun Singh to fight for him, and when he found out his mistake could not get rid of him. Police absconded. (Court has summoned him; given him 15 days, as he has denied (?) a good deal, and called upon him to deliver R. Singh and family, or have his malikana confiscated, etc.).

In the Doab (. . . ?) all are against us. Have disappeared, and are ready for mischief.

"Jumna" gunboat yesterday at Benares; now on way; goes at once to Agra. Well armed with European sailors.

Madras steamer left for Cawnpore two days since. Captain not willing, and likely to come to grief.

Dinapore rebels.

Dinapore rebels, driven to mountains south of Mirzapore, trying to get to Calpee and across the Jumna. Without arms and disorganised. Hopes to cut them up if they come near the Tonse.

Rewah is keeping the Kutra Pass.

## CCCCXXXVI.

### Cawnpore.—Genl. Neill to Mr. Colvin. 19*th.*

Madras Infantry arrive. Naval Brigade under Captain Peel, R.N. General Outram appointed.

Since Lord Elgin's arrival a brigade of Madras Infantry has arrived, and are being marched up country. A Naval Brigade, under Capt. Peel, R.N., is to be sent up to Allahabad. General Outram started from Calcutta some days since, as Chief Commr. in Oudh, and in command of the united Divisions of Dinapore and this. The 5th and 90th are detained, the former at Mirzapore; but I trust that the late arrivals from home will admit of their being pushed on at once.

General Havelock attacks Bithoor. 42nd Native Infantry.

General Havelock moved out to Bithoor on the 14th, and broke up the force there. The 42nd N.I. fought like devils, and were much cut up. Our lads got at them with the bayonet and used it freely, but we have lost many fine soldiers. Cholera and climate have been very severe upon us.

The enemy have appeared on the opposite bank, and a large force is evidently not far off. Boats are reported to be collecting some way down river for a force to cross.

The steamer has been sent down to destroy them.

(*Reply to* 11*th.*)

## CCCCXXXVII.

### ALLAHABAD.—FROM C. CHESTER, C.S. *17th August.*

### (*Mislaid Letter.*)

DINAPORE fugitives making southwards. Seventy-eight of 78th Highlanders had arrived on the "Hoomgalla" steamer. Colonel O'Brien would not permit the "Jumna" gunboat to be despatched here. *Dinapore fugitives.*

## CCCCXXXIX.

### DELHI.—H. H. GREATHED, C.S. COMMR., TO W. MUIR, C.S., SUDDER BD. OF REV., IN CHARGE INTELLIGENCE DEPT. *21st August.*

REPLY to Mr. Colvin's of 13th and mine of 14th, which tells of Havelock's advance on the 4th inst. Disorganisation is on the increase in the City. The authority of Generals Bukht Khan and Lall Khan is set at defiance; and the King is openly taunted in Durbar. A sense of common danger will probably keep them together, and no one wishes them to disperse. There have been no attacks since the success of the 12th, and not much distant firing. Two light guns were placed yesterday in the advanced Metcalfe entrenchment, to dislodge an obnoxious picket, and this drew down a fire from the heavy guns of Selimgurh, which did no damage, and our object was effected without loss. This morning they were trying to send rockets from across the river into the left of our camp, but it is out of range. A detachment, composed of Hurriana Light Infantry, Irreg. Cavalry, probably residents of Hurriana, with 2 guns, have reached the neighbourhood of Hansee. They are most likely acting on their own account, and intend to raise a local disturbance. The party is about 1000 strong. Van Cortlandt will, I hope, be able to deal with them and their friends. He is at Hansee. Capt. Hodson has been out on an expedition in the Rohtuck district with a strong party of horse. He visited Rohtuck, and defeated a band of insurgents of the City and neighbourhood. He is generally well received by the people. Telegraphic intelligence was received this morning of the Loyal 10th Light Cavalry having mutinied in a body at Ferozepore, and attempted to seize the guns. They failed to do this, and took the road to Delhi. It was understood that they had been dishorsed and disarmed, but the message is silent on this subject.

*Affairs at Delhi.* *Generals Bukht Khan and Lall Khan.* *Doings of rebels.* *Mutinous force near Hansi.* *Captain Hodson.* *10th Light Cavalry mutiny at Ferozepore.*

Mrs. Leeson,[1] a daughter of Mr. Collins, Deputy Collector, *Mrs. Leeson, refugee.*

[1] Leeson or Tuson. See CCCCXXXI. *ante.* The name is given in other correspondence as Leeson.—W. M.

arrived yesterday in camp from the City. She was left for dead on the day of the massacre, her infant having been killed in her arms. She was taken up after dark by a good Samaritan, one of the Faithful, and was carefully tended by his family and conducted in disguise to our picket.

W. Edwards, C.S.

Edwards has brought Mozuffernugger into order. There are no open outrages. The roads are safe and the revenue is being collected. The news from Seharanpore and Dera is favourable. Paneeput will soon be ( . . . ?). We have 12 or 13 lacs in the Camp Treasure chest. Mohun Lal is at Meerut; he wishes to join me. But there is no scope here for his intriguing abilities. I have received 2 or 3 messages from Shazadahs, tendering their services and vowing strong attachment. They meet with no response. We have every reason to be grateful for the sanitary condition of the camp. The arrival of the reinforcements has eased the labours of the Force. The Sikhs of the various Regiments in the City have at last managed to be allowed to form themselves into one corps. This is an important incident; as yet they have not evinced the line they intend to pursue. They were able to prevent the Sikh Cossid, who had been arrested, from being executed. He is now in camp. Tell Harry that his Cossid who was shot in the Subzee Mundee has survived, and returns to his house at Seharanpore.

## CCCCXL.

ALLAHABAD.—MR. COURT, COMMR. 19*th August.*

I HAVE no very particular news to give you. Seventy Europeans of 78th Highlanders are the only troops that have come up for some time. Colonel O'Brien has received strict orders not to reduce the force in garrison so low, but to keep it up to safe complement, which has been, I hear, recorded at 600.

Allahabad garrison.

Allahabad district is getting into trouble. Perganahs Soram, Mirzapore, Sikundra, are being encroached upon by neighbouring Talookdars in Oudh.

Oudh Talookdars encroaching.

Pirtipal Singh of Daoodpore has taken 6 villages in Secundra. He has 3000 with him, but chiefly rabble. His great ancestors were kings and governors of Jhoosa, and it is said he aims at regaining that province, and will come to Jhoosa. I hope he will come within reach of the garrison. I may get the means of teaching him a lesson.

Pirtipal Singh aims at Jhoosa.

Isree Singh, on the part of the Budree Thakooram, has set himself up in the south-west corner of Nawabgunge. A party

Isree Singh.

of his men, led on by rebel Zemindars of Chail. crossed the Ganges and attacked a Thannah at Moorutgunge; took Daroga away captive, and wounded all the constables. Cut the wire and ran off with the dak horses. A detachment of Europeans went out on Tuesday to restore communication and inflict punishment. I have got back the Daroga, but I fear the rebels have got back into Oudh also. Mayne went out with the party.

Thannah attacked and plundered.

Mussulmans have been crossing in numbers over the ghats in the Futtehpore district, and caused some uneasiness. From all I can learn they are for Banda, to assist the Nawab there, who sent to Narain Rao for a loan of 5 lacs. The Rao refused. The Nawab sent back word he would help himself. The Mahratta has collected Rs. 10,000, and the Nawab is collecting all he can. This little affair will help us; and the Rao—instead of doubting whether to set up or no—has sent in elephants and camels for carriage. Nevertheless things are thickening round us. We ought to be strong for defence, which we are not, having but 350 men; and in September, out of 3, 2 have always been non-effective.

Narain Rao. Nawab of Banda.

H.M. "Shannon" arrived at Calcutta; 1000 Marines, etc., land, leaving 200 on board. Captain Peel, we hear, comes up here with a Naval Brigade and 68-pounder Howitzers for defence of Allahabad.

H.M. "Shannon" arrives at Calcutta. Captain Peel coming up with a Naval Brigade.

Madras troops have arrived; one regiment goes to Dinapore.

Madras troops arrived.

Outram talks of making an attempt at Lucknow by Fyzabad on the Gogra, whilst Havelock amuses the enemy on the Cawnpore road. The plan is not liked. It is said we make two small armies, and by dividing the forces of the enemy we do for them what they ought to do. Whereas, if the whole army be collected at Cawnpore, and that army be 3000 with Horse Artillery, he can with facility relieve Lucknow. I wish they would do something quickly. We have no news from Lucknow, and I dread to hear of repetition of Cawnpore atrocities.

Plans for relieving Lucknow.

No news of Dinapore Regiments. Attack on Bithoor expected to be made by Havelock.

## CCCCXLI.

CAWNPORE.—J. W. SHERER, C.S., TO CAPT. NIXON.
*August 20th.*

NOTHING has occurred since I last wrote, except the expedition to Bithoor, which ended in the enemy being driven out and

Bithoor attacked and taken.

dispersed, and the only 2 guns they had, taken. But though successful, blame is cast on Havelock for the loss on our side. He had 15 guns and the enemy only 2, and yet he lost upwards of 60 men killed and wounded.

We are thinking of moving out of our entrenched camp, as it is within range of guns from the other bank. At present we shall join Havelock on the parade-ground, till another site for entrenchment is chosen. The 90th still detained below Allahabad.

Captain Peel and his Naval Brigade. Sir Colin Campbell arrives, and Beatson of the Bashi-Bazooks.

Capt. Peel of the "Shannon" is coming up country with a field Naval Brigade of 600 men, and some of the 68-pounders of his ship. Sir Colin Campbell has arrived in Calcutta. And so has Beatson of the Bashi-Bazooks. The former as Commander-in-Chief.

Havelock cannot move till aid comes. He could not turn out 1000 English bayonets. But we have now lots of Artillery. Electric wire works from here to Calcutta. We have heard nothing of the Gwalior Contingent as yet.

## CCCCXLII.

### Cawnpore.—General Havelock to Colonel Cotton.

*August 18th*, 1857.

Havelock describes his victories and capture of guns.

I defeated the enemy at Bithoor on the 16th inst., routing the Mutineers from Saugor and Fyzabad, and taking their guns. Altogether 48 guns have been captured in the field—20 seized at Bithoor, and upwards of 40 recovered in the Arsenal here.

## CCCCXLIII.

### Cawnpore.—J. W. Sherer, C.S., to Mrs. Harington.

*20th August.*

Havelock at Allahabad.

General Havelock is now here. The reinforcements will be very considerable when they come. The 90th Regiment will soon be up. Then Capt. Peel's Naval Brigade of 600 men with 68-pounders will follow shortly. Three more China Regiments are expected within a month.

We are thinking of giving up our entrenched camp, as it is within shell distance of the other bank; and as the enemy's advance guard are encamped there, and we can see them bathing in the Ganges every day, it is not unlikely they might open fire. Of course we could return it; but then, we want a place for the sick and wounded not subject to attacks of the kind.

## CCCCXLIV.

DELHI.—MACTIER TO DR. FARQUHAR. *22nd August.*

OUR worst enemy by far is sickness, which increases by 150 cases a week. Nothing serious, however—chiefly fever. Sickness in camp.

Friend Pandy seems sick of fighting. We have had no Infantry attack worth mentioning since the 1st and 2nd. Our siege train expected about 1st proximo. Then let Delhi look out. Don't be uneasy about us. We are all very jolly here, and could if necessary stay on here for the next 12 months; but I hope a week or two will see us inside the Imperial City. Attacks from the City almost ceased.

We are very short of both Doolies and bearers, and would be glad to get them from Agra.

All quiet in Punjaub.

Some 100 men of 10th Light Cavalry from Ferozepore have bolted towards Delhi on officers' chargers and artillery horses, which they seized. 10th Light Cavalry.

## CCCCXLV.

DELHI.—CAPT. O. H. ST. G. ANSON, 9TH LANCERS, TO W. MUIR, C.S., SUDDER BOARD. *22nd.*

WE are only waiting for the Siege Train to make a ruinous heap of this Babylon, etc.

Hodson to Rohtuck. Nicholson went out as far as Allipore to support, but found the country too impracticable to proceed.

Details of force at Delhi.

| | |
|---|---|
| Dragoons . | 400. |
| Carabineers . | 180. |
| Infantry . | 4500. |
| Goorkhas . | 1000. |
| Artillery of sorts | 600. |

These are all we have to depend upon.

## CCCCXLVI.

DELHI.—H. H. GREATHED, C.S., TO MR. COLVIN, LT.-GOVR. *22nd August.*

(Reply to 16th.)—Disappointed that Lucknow not relieved up to 11th.

The 10th Cavalry, it seems, helped themselves to officers' chargers and artillery horses to the number of 100. Dispositions have been made for their interception. The disarmed regiments at Lahore are encamped in front of the European Mutiny of 10th Cavalry. Disarmed regiments at Lahore.

lines. They are in a sulky, restless state. There appears no other element of anxiety in the Punjaub, except the state of these disarmed regiments. The Pandies have erected a battery across the river opposite the Metcalfe picket. There was a rocket tube, and two 24-pounders. The former became unserviceable yesterday evening. The guns, with a considerable elevation, throw shot across the river; the arrangement is not worth noticing. They appear to apprehend our passing the river, for they have thrown up breastworks near the batteries. There was some intention of attacking the camp this morning, which was not carried out, and a large force was seen this morning returning from the cover of Kishengunge and taking back their guns. Disorganisation is certainly on the increase. The Jhansi Brigade have crossed the Jumna with the intention of going to Malagurh. They have taken their women, wounded, and plunder with them, so we shall see no more of them; they have their 3 guns, 5 Cos. of Infantry, and some of the 14th Irregulars, and a band of Irregular Infantry. Yesterday an Embassy came from the chief Lady of the Palace offering her good offices. She was told we were highly anxious for her personal safety, and for that of all women and children, but that no communication could be received from inmates of the Palace. I am sorry to see that distrust has spread among our people at Meerut of the Seikh regiment that is to be stationed there. It is not shared by General Penny, who concurs in the alterations that have been made. 200 rifles and 100 Artillerymen (Foot) are taken away, and a troop of English H.A., a Seikh Regiment, wing of Beloch Regiment, and 180 Punjaub Horse are added. These troops are suited for the work required of them, and there are a sufficient number of Europeans left as salt to keep them in a wholesome state. I hope our force in the Doab, especially Seharanpore, will not be weakened for the purpose of recovering Bijnore. That appears a measure which can be put off.

*Operations of Mutineer force.* — *Disorganisation on the increase.* — *Jhansi Brigade.* — *Embassy from the Palace.* — *Distrust of the Sikh Regiment.* — *Changes in Meerut force.*

We are getting on well in camp in every way, and I hope the news received to-day from you will determine the General to lose no time.

## CCCCXLVII.

ALLAHABAD.—20*th August*.

*Gunboats on the Ganges.*

(Reply to 10th. Beadon's letter sent on.)—"Jumna" gunboat went up the Ganges on the 19th; likely to be fired on. "Megna" gunboat expected daily, and will be sent to Agra without delay.

No arrivals of troops here. They are detained, it seems, by order of Sir J. Outram, who is said to be meditating a dash on Lucknow from Fyzabad.

But for the critical position of the poor souls at Lucknow, matters would seem to be mending.

**The Goorkhas at Goruckpore.**

Madras troops are marching up to Benares. The Goorkhas will not leave Goruckpore, but they do good service in keeping that country quiet.

Mr. Grant at Rajmehal on 12th. Osborne at Rewah keeps a sharp look-out for the Dinapore Mutineers—and will give them a good thrashing if they try to force that country or to slip through between it and the rivers. If they attempt the Deccan road they will be met by Europeans.

Tried to raise Khyragurh, Barah, and Arail (?) against the Mutineers. They will never reach Delhi.

## CCCCXLVIII.

MEERUT.—FROM F. WILLIAMS, C.S. COMMR. *22nd August.*

**Mutineers going off without arms.**

No news here from Delhi; all quiet there. The Mutineers apparently going off in large bodies of 500 and 800, but generally without arms.

## CCCCXLIX.

CAWNPORE.—GENERAL NEILL TO MR. COLVIN, LT.-GOVERNOR. *21st August.*

OUR men are now dead-beat, and require rest and to be less exposed. We are now getting them comfortable in the best quarters we can, and waiting reinforcements. Must be at least 6000 men between Calcutta and Allahabad.

**Reinforcements from abroad.**

Remainder of 5th Fusiliers have arrived in Calcutta. Brigade of 2 Regiments Madras Sepoys; also a company of 33rd from Mauritius at Bombay—also another Brigade of Madras Sepoys. All the Artillery of the Chinese force.

## CCCCL.

KURACHEE. *13th August.*

P. AND O. steamer from the Cape with troops was seen coming into harbour as the Kurachee steamer left.

All quiet at Belgaum and Dhárwar, but Mahomedan intrigues discovered.

Disaffection at Kolapore. (?) . . . Europeans on the way to Kolapur, where some of the 27th N.I. had shown symptoms of disaffection. On the 2nd, 150 had plundered the Treasury, and took up a position in the town. They fled during the night, and 50 were captured. No official report received, and is not published in papers.

Three Companies 2nd Europeans land at Goa *en route* to Belgaum.

Satisfactory accounts of Nizam. Satisfactory accounts of the Nizam and his Minister having done all in their power to meet any outbreak. It is hoped that tranquillity will be maintained there.

Colonel Stewart. Colonel Stewart's Column of 300 H.M. 86th arrived at Mhow on the 4th. All quiet at Indore.

Panic at Bombay. Panic at Bombay, but on no apparent grounds.

No troops intended to be sent *via* Egypt when mail left.

Five per cent. Loan. 5 per cent. filling at Bombay. Rain relieved fear of famine.

## CCCCLI.

DELHI.—W. H. GREATHED TO MR. COLVIN. *23rd August.*

Baird Smith. BAIRD SMITH "has no turn and no special aptitude for the art of war; but, as you may imagine, he throws himself into his uncongenial duties with his usual ability, and, adhering to his ruling principle of obtaining from every one the maximum of profitable labour, succeeds in creating a general feeling of stability and confidence without much personal effort."

W. H. Greathed. W. H. Greathed has been "Directing Engineer of the left attack for some time past. Lost a horse on the 9th July," the day on which we were so closely beset in falling short of ammunition at Kishengunge.

Up to this time there has been a lurking dread that when we had our Nicholson Column and our siege train, we should still be kept waiting owing to the short time which need apparently have elapsed before Havelock arrived.

Information came yesterday that he was not likely to come. I confess I am glad of the disappointment. I have never done the Mutineers the honour of estimating them very highly as soldiers. I feel we are strong enough to lick any number of them; whilst our Artillery will entirely swamp anything they can bring against us. I look upon our success here as certain, and the speedy release of a large part of the force as assured.

Our men are in good spirits again now. There was a time when under the pressure of great harassment they somewhat flagged. In camp there is a feeling of confidence in our Native troops; and Guides, Goorkhas, 'Cokeys,' and Seikhs are all popular, and I think all smart and useful. In proportion our enemy has lost in courage and vigour. His attacks for the last month have been made without any intention of winning.

**Confidence in our Native troops.**

**Mutineers losing heart.**

## CCCCLII.

COEL.—A. COCKS TO MR. COLVIN. *29th August.*

(THEY re-entered Allygurh on the 28th triumphantly.)

**Cocks has a triumphant entry at Allygurh.**

"Our entry was triumphant. I was surrounded by Thakoor and Jat Zemindars, and arrived some time before the guns and infantry."

Daniell burnt down the residence of Hussun Khan, Ghous Mahomed's Cotwal.

We are now quite established at Coel, and to-day I am going to level to the ground the houses of several principal rebels in the City. Most Mahomedans are quite dispirited, and know not where to turn. Ghous Mahomed got as far as Khoorja with about 100 followers, and on hearing that we did not follow up our victory he returned to Somna, but yesterday again fled on hearing that we really had shown our faces.

**Rebels' houses destroyed.**

**Ghous Mahomed.**

The Mahomedans of the City are mostly absent, but they would have united against Thakoor Gobind Singh, although they give us up in despair. If we keep Allygurh we shall get in revenue from all directions.

**Thakoor Gobind Singh.**

I hope to hear of the occupation of Secundra Rao to-day. I am arranging for Khyr(abad) and Somna and Akberabad.

The jail, as a position in a military point of view, excellent —and far from town.

Probyn wrote to his brother—another gentleman, a Judge,[1] and a merchant, and a lady there.

**G. Probyn, C.S.**

Mr. Gardener, Eta, harassed by Sepoys flying from Futtehgurh.

**Mr. Gardener, C.S.**

The Chittaree Khan (brother of Koer Vazir Ally) behaving well: sending in gunshot to Agra.

**Chittaree Khan.**

[1] No doubt W. Edwards, C.S.—W. C.

## CCCCLIII.

### Delhi.—H. H. Greathed, C.S., to Mr. Colvin, Lt.-Governor.
*26th August.*

Mutiny of the 10th Cavalry at Ferozepore.

(Reply to 20th.)—The mutiny of the 10th Cavalry at Ferozepore is the last incident of the revolt that has occurred above this. The guns were saved by the invalids of the 61st: their officer had heard a whisper of the intentions of the Cavalry, and ordered his men to have their arms loaded. There was little other precaution shown. The accession of these troopers to the rebel force is of little present importance; but I look with anxiety to the future effects of having so many unpardonable mounted rebels about the country when the neck of the rebellion has been broken. Harriana, Rohtuk, Muzuffernugger, Bolundshuhur, are full of the homes of horsemen, and the breach with the Irregulars will estrange us from some of the best families. I was going on to tell you that General Nicholson left this with a Column yesterday morning for Nujufgurh to intercept the Bareilly and Neemuch Divisions, who had left the city with the intention of getting to our rear. News has just come in that he found the Bareilly Division encamped at a serai 2 miles on the north side of the Nujufgurh escape bridge. He attacked them at once, drove them off, and captured 12 field-pieces. Part of them rallied in a village on the way to the bridge, but they were driven out at the point of the bayonet and fled in utter confusion across the escape. All their ammunition, camp equipage, and baggage were captured, and the day was concluded by blowing up the bridge. Our force left at 4 a.m., marched 18 miles over a cross-road much submerged, and came on the enemy at 4 p.m. Lt. Lumsden of Coke's regiment[1] and Dr. Ireland[2] are killed; and young Low of the Guides, who brings the intelligence, computes the other casualties at 40 to 50. The Column will be back to-morrow morning. This signal success, and the certainty

General Nicholson.

Neemuch and Bareilly Brigades thrashed by Nicholson.

Lumsden of Coke's Regiment killed.

Dr. Ireland.

Low of the Guides.

[1] It is remarkable, as recorded by Sir Henry Norman, what a fatality followed this fine Regiment, the First Punjab Infantry. Coke was severely wounded early in the siege operations (23rd July). Eaton Travers then took command: he was killed 2nd August (see CCCXCIII. *ante*). W. H. Lumsden took command, and was killed, as here recorded, on 25th August. C. J. Nicholson was sent from the 2nd P.C. to take command, and he lost his arm at the assault of 14th Sept. Lt. W. H. (now General) Randall, who had probably come to Delhi with General Nicholson, was then attached to that distinguished corps. He afterwards held the appointment of A.D.C. to Lord Lawrence.—W. C.

[2] Dr. Ireland, though dangerously wounded, recovered, and still happily survives.—W. C.

that General Havelock cannot be here for some time, will, I hope, determine the General in not deferring operations. The siege train is at Kurnaul to-day. The Delhi detachment that went to Hissar has fared ill; it has been defeated on three occasions. Capt. Hodson and his party of Cavalry killed 88, chiefly Irreg. horsemen. This occurred at Rohtuk. He had killed 23 at Kharkouda a few days before. Home news of 10th.

Detachment of rebels.

Captain Hodson.

All quiet in the Punjaub.

## CCCCLIV.

AJMERE.—COLONEL G. LAWRENCE. *27th August.*

IN distress about his wife and children at Aboo. Has not heard from them since the 19th. By express yesterday I received a letter from Monk Mason, Jodhpore, enclosing one from P. Conolly, Erinpoora, of the 22nd, calling on him for assistance in troops, as he found the men of the Legion were about to mutiny. He said the Resaldar in command near Anadra had sent him an intercepted letter from the men of a company lately sent on command, who wrote—"We have fought the few Europeans, and are securing ourselves; join us quickly with the guns." Thirty of the 100 men at Aboo had been withdrawn, and of the 50, many sick; while there were 120 of the Legion; and Bazaar filled with Budmashes. A squadron of Lancers marches to-morrow for Erinpoora—though, if there was to be an outbreak, it will have been long since over. Deesa from Aboo is only 50 miles, and aid might have reached.

Monk Mason, Joudhpore.

Legion about to mutiny.

But want of intelligence disheartening. Only 7 or 8 gentlemen with many ladies and children there.

## CCCCLV.

UMBALLA.—G. BARNES, C.S. COMMR., TO G. F. EDMONSTONE, FOREIGN SECRETARY. *16th August.*

ALL quiet here in the Punjaub. 230 men of H.M.'s 8th Foot leave to-day for Delhi; 7th Punjaub Foot goes to Meerut; and the rest of the 60th Rifles proceed to Camp. We shall then have before Delhi—

All quiet in Punjab.

Troops before Delhi.

7 Cos. H.M. 8th Foot.
52nd, 60th, 61st, and 75th Regiments.
1st and 2nd Bengal Fusiliers.
9th Lancers, and squadron of Carabineers.

The Native Regiments are—

The Sirmoor and Kemaon Goorkha Battalions.
1st and 2nd Punjaub Infantry.
4th Sikh Regt.
Guide Corps.
Wings of 1st and 2nd Punjaub Cavalry.

There are six Troops of H.A.; three reserve Companies, European and Sikhs; a third-class siege train in camp, and a second-class siege train on the road.

Estimate of Rebel forces.

The rebels have 24 regiments Regular Infantry, 3 regiments Regular Cavalry, and 3 regiments Irregulars, 400 miscellaneous horse from various regiments and Contingents, and an armed rabble of fanatics. They have also 30[1] H.A. guns, with the Delhi Fortress and Magazine.

## CCCCLVI.

UMBALLA.—G. BARNES, C.S. COMMR., TO GEO. EDMONSTONE, FOREIGN SECRETARY, CALCUTTA. *19th August* 1857.

ALL well in the Punjaub and Cis-Sultej Estates.

Mutineers send a force to Hansi.

The Mutineers are tolerably quiet, but a force of two Battalions Infantry and one Regiment Irregular Cavalry and four guns has passed Rohtuck *en route* for Hansi. They will give General Cortlandt some trouble and unsettle the country.

The siege train has arrived at Sirhind, and will be here on the 21st August, and at Delhi about the 1st Sept. 500 carts of ammunition have arrived here in advance of the train. The assault will be deferred till its arrival. The troops are in good health. The rains are lighter and mornings getting cool.

Number of Mutineers in Delhi.

The Mutineers in and around Delhi are computed at 12,000 Infantry and 4000 Cavalry, exclusive of new levies and fanatics.

The third batch of sick and wounded from Camp—160 men —will arrive here to-morrow.

## CCCCLVII.

MEERUT.—FROM R. H. W. DUNLOP, C.S. *23rd August.*

REPORTS that they are prohibited from going at Malagurh.

Expresses alarm for our friends at Belowna. Their three guns taken. Golab Singh (punished?); Hopper and Gurhmukhtesur taken.

[1] Query: 12 of those taken on 25th?—W. M.

"I have written a friendly letter to Bukht Khan, and Mirza Mogul opened it. This occurred yesterday in Delhi."

My revenue is being realised most satisfactorily in every Pergunnah except Barut and Moradnuggur. **Revenue being realised.**

Have now $3\frac{1}{2}$ lacs.

## CCCCLVIII.

MEERUT.—J. CRACROFT WILSON, C.S., TO THORNHILL, SECY. TO GOVT. *23rd August.*

GURHMUKHTESUR.—Thirty odd men crossed the Ganges at this place from Delhi on Thursday last. They got as far as Gugroulah. The Mewattees then induced them to start for Moradabad, and plundered them of 1200 rupees! They complained to the Rampore Nizam, who came to Wilson. The Mewattees brought Wilson 620 rupees they had taken from the Sepoys. He told them to keep the cash and kill the Sepoys; and he believes they will do it, if they cannot catch them alive.

## CCCCLIX.

ALLAHABAD.—MR. COURT, C.S., TO MR. COLVIN, LT.-GOVR. *25th August.*

(Reply to 15th.)—Has 9 lacs, and expects 15 more. Reports general combination against our Government. **Revenue coming in.**

Talukdar (?) of Shumspore, Isree Bukhsh, with 3000 men and guns, entered Nuwabgunge. A steamer sent up obliged to return. Police Thannah at Nuwabgunge fell back on Soram. Pirtipal Singh, joined by Benee Buhadur Singh of Secundra and the Tisaee Rajpoots, threaten Phoolpore, Sikundra, and Jhoosa. Dinapore Mutineers escaped, and Rewa is shaking. Osborne ill. Hinde writes despondingly. If Rewa goes we shall be surrounded. **Rebellion rife.**

## CCCCLX.

ALLAHABAD.—C. CHESTER, C.S. COMMR., TO C. THORNHILL, C.S., SECY. TO GOVT. N.W.P. *24th August.*

No steamer to be sent up the Jumna. Benares steamer arrived yesterday with the munitions of war, but no troops. "Mirzapore" with 500 or 600 of H.M. 90th daily expected.

Captain Peel left Calcutta on 18th, and should be at Allahabad by 15th proximo.

Gunboat has a fight.

"Megna" gunboat had a brush with the Oudhites 40 miles up the Ganges; our loss 1 Lascar killed, 1 seaman mortally wounded, and 2 Fusiliers slightly. Their loss unknown. They fought from a jungle, and got heavy guns to bear on the steamer.

Grant expected in a day or two. Report that Lucknow is provisioned for six months.

Dinapore Mutineers.

The Dinapore scoundrels are hanging about the south-east frontier of this district.

## CCCCLXI.

CAWNPORE.—J. W. SHERER, C.S., TO CAPT. NIXON.
*26th August.*

Position at Cawnpore.

HAVELOCK on parade-ground. Cholera prevalent, but stopped on moving men into the stables of 2nd Cavalry. There is no enemy near us now. Oudh fellows come down to bathe, but cannot cross. Dinapore troops in Allahabad district, but have no

Lucknow.

guns. "The Belee guard is still holding out, and it is reported can do so for 15 more days. I am afraid it will be impossible to send relief from this quarter till reinforcements come. 200 Highlanders are this day half-way between Allahabad and here, and, on the 24th, 300 of the 5th Fusiliers had landed at Allahabad. 290 sick, wounded, and disabled start for Allahabad to-night;

Strength of Cawnpore garrison.

and I should say we had about 800 Europeans left fit for duty, including the garrison. Guns and ammunition we have in abundance.

Depression chronic at Allahabad.

## CCCCLXII.

CAWNPORE.—MACBEAN TO CHALMERS. *27th August* 1857.

WE have been quiet here since our fight at Bithoor, which was our tenth action. Are sending 350 sick back to Allahabad.

Sir Colin Campbell. Lucknow.

Sir Colin Campbell is coming up. Cholera diminishing.

From Lucknow we have news yesterday—good—all well, and can hold out another month. We do hope soon to hear of the fall of Delhi.

## CCCCLXIII.

### LAHORE.—(SIR R.) MONTGOMERY, JUDL. COMMR., TO C. RAIKES, C.S. 18*th August.*

UNDER Providence, the Electric Telegraph saved us. We heard on the 12th of May of the massacre at Delhi—Sir John being away—and I summoned a Council. I proposed that we should ask the Brigadier to disarm the 4 corps at Meean Meer. I went out with Macpherson, and he agreed. It was done the next morning. This was the *turning-point of the whole, I think.* The evening of the 13th was fixed for a rise. The Ferozepore troops broke out into mutiny that night, and Sealkot and Jullundur were watching. All our officers were after that on their guard. Our treasure was despatched to places of safety, and we took up an attitude against the Sepoys. A great many corps were disarmed. I advocated its being done at once *throughout.* Officers had confidence in their men (the old story!); gradually they gave in. Gradually the bad spirit began to break out. In some places the disarming was delayed, and they then broke out. All have now been disarmed but 2 Infantry and 2 or 3 Irregular Cavalry Regiments. I urge that they be not excepted. The Infantry Regiments are at Peshawur, and perhaps can do little harm. Still, I would not leave them. They are all bad, and only want the opportunity. **Sir R. Montgomery's account of disarming at Lahore.**

It is marvellous how well the people of the country have behaved, and the excellent spirit that prevails. Our officers have been very active, and we have been very severe. Any one who talks treason is *instantly* hanged; we will not allow it to be *breathed*; and we have men mixed with the population to report it. Our five rivers with their ferries give us great advantages, and no Poorbeah can show his face without being instantly seized. If a Sepoy deserter, or Mutineer, he is tried on the spot and *hanged.* The Sikhs *hate* them, and if a Regiment breaks and runs the whole population is after them. The Sepoys are strangers in a strange land. They have no sympathy from the people, and are not protected or concealed. **Loyal attitude of the people in Punjab.** **Measures for suppressing disaffection.**

Our work has always gone on as usual, but it is *slack*, and trade has suffered.

There is every prospect of Delhi falling by the middle of September, whether aid comes from below or not.

With 2500 of Golab Singh's there will be nearly 15,000 before Delhi.

Describes his efforts to raise troops.

I am turning a soldier in my old age. I have raised and sent 5 Ressalas of horse to Hodson. If you hear of them, remember they are "Montgomery's Horse." I have sent 500 fine old Sikh Khalsa soldiers to the Bhuttiana territory to replace the rascally burkandazes that deserted and went to Delhi. I am raising 500 more for Ford for service in Rohtuk and Goorgaon. They got 6 rupees per mensem. You should draw on us for Sikh burkandazes. They will not play so false if you let them have Jemadars of their own. Don't put Poorbeahs over them.

Recommends Sikhs for service in N.W.P.

## CCCCLXIV.

### Cawnpore.—Colonel Neill to Colonel Cotton.[1]

*27th August* 1857.

(A reply to letter of 20th.)—Since my last there has been little doing here. Only, I am happy to say the health of the men improving. We hear of reinforcements coming from all quarters. H.M.'s 33rd and a company of Royal Artillery from the Mauritius arrived at Bombay. The China force pouring into Calcutta. The low country free of insurgents. The troops no longer delayed, but pouring up the country. Sir C. Campbell, the Commander-in-Chief, sent out to succeed General Anson, is most energetic. Martial law proclaimed in Calcutta. A battery of Artillery added to the Calcutta Volunteers. The European Yeomanry Cavalry being rapidly organised; recruits pouring in. The battalion of Marine Light Infantry brought on the Bengal Establishment under Capt. Peel, R.N., are on their way up river to be stationed at Allahabad; they have ten 68-pounders with them. The Madras Native Infantry Brigade is marching up the Grand Trunk Road; also part of H.M.'s 53rd. 400 men have left Allahabad for this; the 5th and 90th are following hard upon them. I heard from Hill about Hyderabad, dated the 13th August; all right up to then, but he has not confidence in his Contingent if called upon to act. The subsidiary force at Secundrabad in great efficiency, and the Nizam's Government all right; 270 H.M.'s 12th Lancers were expected in 4 or 5 days. The moveable column from Bangalore towards Kurnewul has prevented mischief there. The column from Nagpore to Jubbulpore is also doing its work well. Here we have the road open to Allahabad, but off the Trunk Road civil power not entirely re-established. We want military posts to

Reinforcements.

Captain Peel, R.N.

Hyderabad.

[1] Mr. Lowe's writing.—W. M.

support the civil power. There is no detachment at Futtehpore yet. On your side Sherer's Thannahdars have been murdered in Bithoor and Sheorajpoor, and no civil authority there, because we have no troops to support him. I had organised a military police here, which we have exercised; and Capt. Bruce, as Military Police Superintendent, has had his powers extended through Bithoor and Sheorajpoor Pergunnahs merely as a temporary measure. There is a vagabond at Calpee on the Jumna doing much mischief. A brother of the Nana's is now with him. He has in his possession some uncovenanted service men and their families. He is playing a fast-and-loose game; has several times promised to send them in, but has failed as yet. I have told him that if a hair of their heads is hurt, neither himself, his family, or estate will be spared. The news from Lucknow is most cheering. The enemy had assaulted and been repulsed with vast slaughter. The Ghazees brought to lead the assault were much punished—200 killed and many wounded. They and the troops there now declare that if Lucknow holds out for two years more they won't attempt to storm it again. This is authentic. We are there scarce of provisions for Europeans, but on ½ rations have them for long; but they have no end of wheat and grain. They are, I now consider, all right, and will be saved when reinforcements come up. The fellows on the opposite bank are throwing up earthworks, but we can turn them; I would have a surprise some fine night. A Nawab fellow who is with the Nana at Lucknow, and whose son there commands four Regiments before the place, left their women-kind in the serai here; threats, etc., etc.

**Military posts required to support the civil power.** **Thannahdars murdered in Cawnpore District.** **Military Police.** **Prominent rebel at Calpee.** **Lucknow.** **Ghazees.**

Colonel Otter of H.M.'s 61st supersedes Colonel O'Brien in command of Allahabad. Mr. J. P. Grant is expected there to-day. Sir J. Outram will soon be up here, followed by the Commander-in-Chief in time.

**Colonel Otter.** **Mr. J. P. Grant.**

## CCCCLXV.

MEERUT.—F. WILLIAMS, C.S., TO MR. COLVIN, LT.-GOVR.
*29th August* 1857.

LETTER of 23rd received.

The Neemuch and Bareilly Brigades, which attempted to get to the rear of our camp, were overtaken by Brigadier Nicholson at Nujufgurh on the 25th at 4½ p.m. He took all their guns, 13 in number, all their camp equipage, and everything they had with them, killed and wounded some 500 of them, and utterly

**Nicholson's victory at Nujufgurh.**

defeated them. Fugitives who got to Delhi in the night said our whole force must be out, and the "Pahar" empty. About 10,000 men without guns turned out from the city in this hope, and attacked our position, briskly at first, but they were received so warmly that the attack soon fainted away. They lost 700 (about) there. It is calculated by some that in the two affairs the enemy must have lost about 1500 killed and wounded. Our loss was small—about 100 killed and wounded in both actions. The Jhansi Brigade, "with its women, wounded, and plunder," is out on our side (of the Jumna), but I am getting up a demonstration to send them flying from Malagurh, to which place, it is said, they are bent.

Severe loss on rebels' side.

Jhansi Brigade.

Bijnore Talookdars, I am afraid, are being ruined for want of help.

## CCCCLXVI.

ALLAHABAD.—C. CHESTER, C.S. COMMR., TO C. THORNHILL, SECY. TO GOVT. *27th August.*

Reinforcements.

ON 25th inst. "Ch. Allen" steamer arrived with Headquarters and 300 men of H.M. 64th. The same day 160 men marched from hence towards Cawnpore; to-day a detachment of the same strength will proceed upwards. The 90th [1] are overdue here, but we know not when they will arrive. Detentions and counter-orders perplex us.

The Dinapore Mutineers are in the Pergunnah of Khyragurh, stopped by high floods of the Tonse river. The Rewa troops have not arrived to nobble the scoundrels, and our Rajahs are unable to do so.

Central Provinces.

Rewa, Jubbulpore, Saugor, and Nagode are still all right.

Ramgurh battalion.

The Ramgurh Light Battalion and the local troops at Bhaugulpore have gone.

Osborne writes to me that there has been a row at Bangalore, and that the 27th and 28th Madras Native Regiments have mutinied. I trust this is not the case.

Action of Oudh rebels.

Jounpore and Azimgurh have been farmed to Chuckladars by the Oudh folks, and they are seizing on the Trans-Gangetic Pergunnahs of this district.

Revenue collections small.

Little Revenue—none from Banda or Hamirpore; next to nothing from Futtehpore and Cawnpore; a little from this district.

[1] In his letter of the 24th August, Chester said that the "Mirzapore" with 500 or 600 men of the 90th was daily expected.—W. M.

Mr. Grant is expected here every day. On his arrival I go west.

Wynyard and Paterson have evacuated Goruckpore, with the Goorkhas, and been suspended in consequence.[1] Goruckpore.

Bird held on alone, aided by friendly Rajahs, like a man. Bird.

## CCCCLXVII.

DELHI.—COLONEL BECHER TO CAPT. NIXON. *August 28th.*

YOU will be glad to hear that on the 25th Nicholson's Column marched from this at 4 that morning, attacked and defeated the enemy at Nujufgurh; taking 12 guns and all their baggage and camp equipage. Our troops had a most harassing march, the whole country being under water, but at 4 p.m. came up with the enemy's camp, when Nicholson at once attacked them and drove them from the position. They were apparently surprised, and could not take up quite the position they intended to. Their artillery fire was rather heavy, but they could not stand the steady advance of our troops on the Serai, which was the centre of their position, and fled, leaving all their guns but two on the field. A very large quantity of ammunition was found and destroyed, and our native troops got plenty of plunder of every description. Our loss, about 20 killed and 40 or 50 wounded. Nicholson's victory at Nujjufgurh.

The force consisted of 380 1st Fusiliers, 420 H.M. 61st, 800 1st and 2nd Punjaub Infantry, 3 troops H.A., 100 Lancers, the Mooltanee Horse, and some of the Guides. His force.

Lumsden of Coke's corps was killed. Lts. Gabbett and Elkington, 61st, both dangerously wounded—the former since dead. Dr. Ireland of Artillery dangerously wounded. Casualties: Lieutenant Lumsden of Coke's killed; Lieutenants Gabbett and Elkington died of wounds; Dr. Ireland dangerously wounded.

The force returned to camp on the evening of the 26th.

On that day the enemy, thinking our whole force almost had gone out with Nicholson, attacked our position. They evidently thought they would have an easy business of it, for numbers of women and the riff-raff of the city came out to assist in the plunder of our camp. But they did not take it, and were well thrashed as usual. Our loss small.

The siege train has been delayed at the Markunda river, and will not be here before the 1st or 2nd proximo, when I hope we shall at once commence active operations.

All quiet in the Punjaub. Report of Runbeer Singh's murder quite unfounded.

[1] Shortly restored.

Force at Meerut.

All well at Meerut. 7th Punjaub Infantry arrived there on the 25th. The Beloch Battalion will go over after the arrival of the siege train. Dawes' troop of H.A. is joining them also from Jullundur.

Nusseree battalion. Seharunpore quiet.

The Nusseeree Battalion is at Seharunpore. The district is quiet.

Cortlandt's force at Hissar defeats a rebel force.

A portion of Cortlandt's force at Hissar drove back a body of the enemy who had been sent from Delhi to try to discover the family of some man attached to the King. They killed about 350 of them. Cortlandt is, I believe, still at Hansi, but we hear very little of him.

Ricketts hangs men of the 10th Cavalry.

Ricketts, at Loodhiana, has caught and hanged some of the 10th Cavalry. The main body is not heard of. There is a good deal of sickness in camp, I am sorry to say, and it is on the increase; chiefly fever. Wounded all getting on very well.

*P.S.*—From all accounts the enemy's loss in Nicholson's fight was not very heavy, as our troops could not follow them. A good many were drowned in the swamp in trying to escape.

## CCCCLXVIII.

DELHI.—DR. MACKINNON TO DR. FARQUHAR. *30th August.*

Sickness very prevalent.

THE siege train will be here in 5 or 6 days, and I should suppose the trenches would be opened by the 10th at latest. We should be masters of Delhi by the middle of the month, unless we are disabled by sickness. At present nearly one fourth of our numbers are sick, but if they don't increase we have force enough to take the place from those . . . who now hold it.

## CCCCLXIX.

DELHI.—H. H. GREATHED, C.S., TO MR. COLVIN. *29th August.*

Preparations for bombardment.

(Reply to 21st, 22nd, and 23rd.)—The intelligence they convey will, I believe, only expedite the fulfilment of the object for which this force has assembled. If an auxiliary force had been approaching the siege might have been delayed. Now the General, being left to his own resources, has no reason for delay. The arrival of the train has been delayed by rain at the Markunda, but that difficulty has been overcome. All are impatient for the day. Volunteers have been called for from among officers of infantry and cavalry to serve with artillery in the trenches, and an important work has been commenced.

—— (has asked Penny if Meerut is in any danger). Judging from all that has occurred, I think it highly improbable that the Pandies when retreating from this will attack a well-defended post.

General Mansfield to be Chief of the Staff. General Mansfield.

The health of the force is still good, and I don't hear of any bad result from the exposure and privations to which the column under Nicholson was exposed on the 25th.

The Sikhs, Punjaubies, and Goorkhas continue to do admirable service, and the best understanding exists between them and our men. We have no Hindoostanee soldiers at all in camp. Good service of Native troops. No Hindoostanee soldiers in camp.

The Barout insurgents have sunk the ferry-boat at Baghput. They are not in any great number—not above 200 or 300—but they can do as they like just now.

## CCCCLXX.

DELHI.—H. H. GREATHED, C.S., TO MR. COLVIN, LT.-GOVR.
*August* 30, 1857.

(Reply to Mr. Colvin's of 25th to General Wilson.)

The General's reply (in Greek)—

"I have received your message by Cossid of the 25th inst. Finding that I have no chance of immediate assistance from the Cawnpore force, I have determined, on the arrival of the siege train, to batter and attempt an assault on the city. This will require the energies of every man in camp, and of course all minor considerations must give way to it." General Wilson resolves to assault Delhi.

(Greathed had not put the question before), "but it was quite plain to me" (Greathed) "that the course he has now declared had been taken, and I know him to be firm as well as cautious. I have always looked upon the preservation of our cantonment at Meerut as of as great importance as if it had been a regularly fortified post, and I believe that has always been provided for. The General has diverted some more Punjaub horse to Meerut. There will be 480 horse, and with this force performing its duty here the troops at Meerut will be able to perform a good part, being effective for the work that will be allotted to them." Greathed. Meerut.

## CCCCLXXI.

CAWNPORE.—CAPT. GORDON TO CAPT. NIXON. *29th August.*

(Reply to 23rd.)—The Regiments here are 1st M. Fusiliers (with Enfields), H.M. 64th, 78th, and 84th (the latter with a Force at Cawnpore.

Regiments very weak. few Enfields). All the Regiments are *very, very* weak. The 90th, with Enfields, are expected soon, but we have not heard of their having reached Allahabad. Sir J. Outram at present (here?), suppose he will move upwards. On the arrival of reinforcements another advance on Lucknow is expected.

Lucknow. Last from Lucknow is the 21st. Full rations till 10th proximo; they were on half-rations to last longer. Under 3000 Mutineer Sepoys, and about 10,000 country people, between L(ucknow) and C(awnpore).

Troops from England. English mail to July 15th. Eight Regiments and six Cos. Artillery were under embarkation *via* Cape steamers. Lord Ellenborough urged Artillery horses being sent.

Things settling down in Cawnpore. Things are settling down here, and police stations are being established in the District. No Calcutta dak in for three days, owing to heavy rain.

Regiments below Allahabad. Cape and New South Wales Regiments expected soon—5th, 10th, wing of 29th, 35th, 37th, and 53rd all below Allahabad.

*P.S.*—Authentic news has this moment come in from Allahabad that 1500 men leave that on the 5th proximo for Cawnpore.

## CCCCLXXII.

CAWNPORE.—CAPT. BRUCE TO CAPT. NIXON. *1st Sept.*

Details of reinforcements. BUSY re-establishing police, and troops being rested. One reinforcement came in yesterday.[1] Another will be in to-morrow.[2] There will follow the 5th Fusiliers,[3] and after them the 90th. General Outram has the latter corps with him, and has passed Benares. The troops we have here are the 64th, 78th, 84th, armed with old muskets; Madras Fusiliers with Enfields, and Sikhs with muskets. The other corps have Enfields. H.M. 53rd and a Madras Brigade are marching up the Grand Trunk Road.

Mutineers hanged. Twenty-five men of the Guzerat (Regiment?) had mutinied. Twelve hanged. 150 of the 27th N.I. at Darwar did the same, and 50 were taken. The 28th N.I. is very shaky, but of course these partial outbursts were to be expected.

[1] 200 Highlanders half-way between Allahabad and Cawnpore on 26th Aug. (Sherer, 26th August.)—W. M.

[2] On 25th, 160 men marched from Allahabad; 27th. do., do. (Chester, 27th.) (H.M.'s 64th, 300 men, arrived 25th.)—W. M.

[3] On the 24th, 300 5th Fus. landed at Allahabad. (Sherer, *ut supra.*)—W. M.

Nana offered his services to Oudh rebels. They were declined. His "Mama"[1] died. Jussur Singh also died of wound received at Oonao. Nana. Jussur Singh dies.

Hearsay asked N. Regiments to volunteer. 70 done so. Four men with Hurdeo Buksh opposite Furruckabad. Probyn,[2] wife and three children; Edwards;[3] Mr. Jones, merchant; Mr. Sutherland, ditto, with another Zemindar. Hurdeo Buksh protects English officers and others. G. Probyn, wife and children; W. Edwards; Jones, merchant; Sutherland, do.

## CCCCLXXIII.

DELHI.—H. H. GREATHED, C.S., TO MR. COLVIN, LT.-GOVR.
*31st August.*

SENDS duplicate of General Wilson's message. Very considerable progress was made on the night of the 29th in clearing away the right front, and the covering party drove the enemy out of their breastworks into Delhi; and the work proceeded without interruption. A 6-gun battery was at the same time constructed at the head of the trench, two hundred yards in advance of the advanced posts. (Baird Smith struck by a splinter from a rock; went out too soon, and festered.) There is strong report in camp that the detachment of Rifles took Bigrowl and Baroti *en route* to Shamlee, and captured some of Sah Mul's family and relations. The grandson, who had excited another insurrection on a small scale, fled into Delhi; and our post comes on by Baghput. Nawab Koodrut-oollah Beg, son of Nawab Mehndoo Khan of Lucknow, came into Delhi on the 29th with 1000 followers, and brought 1¼ lac of rupees. On the same day Aga, the son of Yàcoob Ally Khan, a relation of the Rampoor Nawab, arrived with a band of men and presented 10,000 rupees to the King. They have ill chosen the time for their visit, for their own interests. One of my spies returned yesterday evening from the bridge beyond Nujjuffgurh; two Regiments had been there, but hearing of the advance of our troops—a reconnoitring party under Hodson—on the 28th they returned to Delhi. On his way he met a man carrying two "lifafas"[4]—and brought them to me. They are roznamchas[5] from one Zabtuh Khan Thannahdar of Busunt Serae to the Delhi Foujdar. Batteries pushed forward. Baird Smith wounded. Nawab Koodrut-oola Beg of Lucknow enters Delhi with 1000 followers. Aga presents 10,000 rupees.

[1] Probably "mother's brother."

[2] George Probyn, C.S.

[3] William Edwards, C.S.

[4] Envelopes.

[5] Diaries.

## CCCCLXXIV.

BENARES.—H. C. TUCKER, C.S. COMMR., TO W. MUIR, C.S., SUDDUR BOARD OF REVENUE. *26th August* 1857.

Outram's plan for relief of Lucknow.

" OUTRAM intended to make a dash from Benares *via* Jounpore and Sultanpore on Lucknow, to pick up the garrison, take the defences on the Jounpore road in the rear, and join Havelock with the whole force. But the Commander-in-Chief has ordered the 90th and 5th and every available European to go straight *via* Allahabad to Havelock, so that this expedition of Outram's, for which we were collecting mussucks, etc., is knocked on the head. Mr. Grant, Outram, and these two Regiments are expected here to-day."

Wynyard and Paterson leave Goruckpore.

Wynyard and Paterson suspended for abandoning Goruckpore and coming away with the Goorkha Force. But their proceeding borne out by a letter to Wingfield from Supreme Government in For. Depart.

Tucker had a wigging (from Grant) for having advocated the pushing forward to Allahabad *sharp* the whole body of Goorkhas to help Havelock when we first heard of his retreat. This was duly reported to Supreme Govt., who took no offence.

I feel anxious for Bird, who was abandoned in Goruckpore, which is now in the hands of the Insurgents. I trust he has escaped. He was not well treated by Paterson and the others, who were vexed at his holding on when they had determined to go.

The whole 3000 are to halt at Azimgurh for further orders, and the officials have been ordered to rejoin.

. . . . . . . .

H. C. Tucker approves Punjab system. Civil Courts must be thrown overboard.

In reorganising districts I wish only one district officer with his subordinates, as in the Punjaub, to do substantial justice. Our Civil Courts must be thrown overboard bodily. They have collapsed since the commencement of the row.

Jounpore disorganised.

Jounpore is totally disorganised, and overrun with Oudh bands, who are too strong for any of the resident landholders.

Ross, C.S.; his excellent administration of Ghazeepore.

Ghazeepore, strange to say, has gone on beautifully. Ross has been very active and energetic, and sticks at no responsibility. His revenue is all collected, and his district rather better than usual.

Benares; fort built.

Benares is very quiet. A very strong fort has been built, armed, and partially provisioned at Rajghat.

I have told him (Havelock) plain that as he has got the troops instead of Outram, the whole responsibility of relieving

Lucknow in time rests with him now. I think he will move quick, as the last accounts say that the mines were beginning to tell on our defences.

Mirzapore is going on beautifully under St. G.,[1] who has great credit for the brave manner in which he has acted all through. He tried to intercept (. . . ?) Mutineers 20 miles from Mirzapore. But he only killed four—they ran off so fast on the road towards Khyragurh, where they are now stopped by the Tonse. **Mirzapore under St. G. Tucker.**

Chunar (?) has been strengthened and fully provisioned. **Chunar.**

Asks after Mr. A. H. Spense, Royal Engineers, who escaped from Delhi in Rood's (?) company.

## CCCCLXXV.

CAWNPORE.—FROM J. W. SHERER, C.S., TO W. MUIR, C.S., SUDDUR BOARD OF REVENUE. *30th August* 1857.

. . . . . . . .

They have plenty of money at Allahabad. Court has 8 lacs, and 4 more on their way from Shahabad and 10 from G. Treasury. **Cash supplies at Allahabad.**

At Cawnpore little. Military chest ½ a lac; Sherer has 10,000, and hopes to get in two lacs of revenue within a month. Two and a half lacs balances for June, and about 1½ lacs in Futtehpore, which is quieting down, and in which all Thannahs but one restored. The three Thannahs immediately in the vicinity of Cawnpore are given to the Military for the present, and Sherer has only one other Thannah in the Mofussil. But the turn is rapidly coming, and I hope order will soon be restored. **At Cawnpore.** **Police stations in Cawnpore District.**

Suttee Pershad beginning to feel uncomfortable, and putting out feelers for reconciliation. He has been told to deliver up the Nana. **Suttee Pershad.**

"The Nana has come back from Lucknow dispirited. Brijus (. . . ?) will have nothing to say to him; and he is now at Jursa Singh's Fort at Futtehpore Chourassee. But Jursa Singh is dead, and his sons are said to be cool toward their guest, and to wish themselves well rid of him." Nawab of Furruckabad carrying on his game of cruelty and fanaticism. A native Christian reports that Mr. Bridges, an indigo planter, his wife, mother-in-law, and daughter, who was a Mrs. Eckford (?), captured in Mofussil and blown away from guns. **The Nana.** **Jursa Singh.** **Nawab of Furruckabad.** **Reported barbarous treatment of the Bridges family.**

Nasir Ally all right; but Deputy Collector of Humeerpor **Nasir Ally.**

[1] St. George Tucker, Henry's brother.—W. M.

took an active part in the rebellion; and suspicions of Sheopershad.

Salamut Ally. Duryao Singh. Salamut Ally Moonsiff of Hutgaon found true (?). Superintended (?) police there with the assistance of Duryao Singh, who keeps the road open (his son-in-law was in open rebellion). Inactive. Havelock pitched on parade. Neill near canal. The Soane Engineers (?), etc., live in the entrenchment. Cholera quite disappeared.

Cossids' pay. Not to promise more than 25 rupees to each cossid.

Ikram Hoosen writes he is quite right. I question it very much.

Cooper commands the Artillery. Cooper commands the Artillery. Yule is here too.

Fears for Lucknow. Two hundred Highlanders will be here to-morrow, but unless reinforcements come quicker it is impossible not to fear for Lucknow. The garrison have managed to send word that they can hold out till the 10th of September. But a spy describes the batteries as only 150 yards off now. This must make it awful work inside.

## CCCCLXXVI.

### DELHI.—COLONEL BECHER TO CAPTAIN NIXON. *2nd Sept.* 1857.

"WE are all preparing for the grand finale of this tedious business, which, please God, will soon take place. The siege train is to-day at Lussoulie, and will, I hope, be in camp on the 4th. Wilde's corps—4th Punjaub Infantry, and a wing of the Beloch Battalion, will come on with it. Colonel Hogge, of Artillery, came in to-day as Commissary of Ordnance. Letters have been received from Hansi up to the 27th inst.; nothing definite is known of their doings there.

Approach of siege train. Its convoy.

Cashmere Contingent. The Cashmere Auxiliary Force ought to be here on the 6th. They will be useful *in a way* in our final operations. When they commence I will endeavour to send cossids daily.

Letter just come in from Cortlandt dated 30th; all well.

## CCCCLXXVII.

### DELHI, 27th.—"*Lahore Chronicle*" *of 29th August.*

Nicholson's losses at Nujjufgurh affair. Guns captured. TOTAL loss in Nicholson's Brigade on the 26th (25th) is 71 killed and wounded. The guns captured are—one 24-pounder Howitzer; two 12-pounder ditto; two 9-pounder guns; four 6-pounder ditto; four 3-pounder brass guns of native manufacture. *All* the guns of Mackenzie's troop and Kirby and De Tessier's batteries secured. On the 26th we lost 8 killed and

12 wounded. The enemy suffered—37 being counted dead in one place. Cavalry well punished with grape from our heavy guns.

Bukht Khan's force consisted of 18th, 28th, 29th, 68th, and 3 Regiments N.I. and 8th Irregular Cavalry; detachments of 13th and 14th (?), and 18 guns, with all arms, ammunition, etc., from Bareilly. **Bukht Khan's force.**

A portion of the Neemuch Brigade was also probably present, as the Mackenzie guns belonged to it. **Neemuch Brigade.**

51st N.I. broke out yesterday, 28th, at Peshawur, and made an attempt to seize the arms of one of the new Sikh Regiments while the men were at dinner. The Mutineers, however, repelled with loss. They were broken and dispersed. **51st Native Infantry break out at Peshawur.**

Thirteen of the 10th Light Cavalry hanged at Loodianah on the 28th, and 13 of 26th and 46th ditto ditto at Jullundur. Latter seized and sent in by Raja of Chumba. 200 of 50th and 60th at Umballa ordered into confinement. In attempting to escape, 100 (?)[1] were killed, 25 seized, and rest being pursued. **Executions of rebel soldiery at Loodhianah and Jullundur. Rajah of Chumba. *Emeute* of 50th and 60th at Umballa.**

## CCCCLXXVIII.

PESHAWUR.—LAHORE, 30*th August*.

GENERAL COTTON reports that of 871 of the 51st, 785 are accounted for. Missing men being brought in by the villagers in twos and threes. **Mutinous 51st accounted for.**

Pasham (Tosham ?) in Hurriana sacked and plundered by Mahomed Azeem, who cut up 50 or 60 of the Bikaneer horsemen.

Force beaten at Nujjufgurh composed chiefly of Neemuch Brigade and fanatics. Rohilkhund Brigade 4 coss off, and unable to support.

## CCCCLXXIX.

DELHI.—FROM LT. GREATHED, R.E. 2*nd Sept.*

WE have been quiet since I last wrote. Our engineering preparations are complete, and the excitement of expectation of active work on the arrival of the siege train has now settled down to resolution to carry out that course which we feel assured the General has accepted and determined. Removed from the field of speculation, it becomes a matter of business which is calmly and deliberately undertaken, and must be carried through. **Preparations for bombardment complete.**

[1] A note says 130 killed.

. . . No one doubts the result, though ignorant of the means which will be employed. The guns may be in on the 4th probably, and the contents of the siege train unpacked and arranged in park on the 6th. Fever is setting in, and our European (indeed too our native) numerical strength diminishes, but prospect of active employment will bring all but bad cases out of Hospital. The cool nights and mornings which we are already enjoying will enable the troops to endure the increasing heat of the day.

Fever setting in.

## CCCCLXXX.

ALLAHABAD.—C. CHESTER, C.S., TO CAPT. NIXON.
*28th August.*

Movements of troops: 5th—700 90th—900 ½-37th—350

(Answer to 15th and 19th.)—5th, 37th, and 90th detained hitherto by change of plans.

On the 24th, 300 of the 5th Fusiliers arrived: they and 90th armed with Enfields.

. . . . . . . .

Dinapore Mutineers. Central India. Rewa.

The Dinapore Mutineers have crossed the Tonse. Central India is still quiet, but Osborne at Rewa tells me that matters are beginning to look ugly. The Rewa Durbar is not friendly, though the Raja remains wonderfully staunch.

Duryao Singh.

Desires to raise a native body of troops in connection with Duryao Singh—might be promised restoration of Talooka Khass.

Mozuffer Hoosain.

Mozuffer Hoosain is an adherent of the King of Oudh.

## CCCCLXXXI.

DELHI.—H. H. GREATHED, C.S., TO MR. COLVIN, LT.-GOVR.
*3rd September.*

Siege train.

(Reply to mine of 28th.)—Siege train at Raee to-day all safe, and will be in to-morrow or next day. We receive with it an accession of 350 European soldiers. Wilde's Regiment of Punjaub Infantry is immediately in the rear; and the Cashmere Contingent of 4 battalions and 6 guns and some cavalry are with it. The latter are accompanied by Capt. R. Lawrence, but they serve under their own officers. They are said to be serviceable soldiers, and will at all events occupy ground. We suppose that General Outram will get the Nepal troops to co-operate.

Captain R. Lawrence accompanies Cashmere Contingent.

It is fortunate we are independent of aid from the eastwards. The measures to be adopted after the fall of Delhi are under consideration; but nothing definite can be settled until the line of retreat of the Mutineers is known. They will be affected also by the movements of the Gwalior troops. Lawrence requires one Regiment of Europeans to return to the Punjaub.. 785 of 871 of the 51st destroyed at Peshawur. Great execution of Mutineers at Peshawur.

Van Cortlandt at Hansi cannot do all he wishes, and has not yet attacked Jumalpore, the stronghold of the rebels. The Bikaneer troops are not worth much. The town of Tosham has been plundered. After the fall of Delhi, proposes to remain with General Wilson's force. Asks for official letter of appointment, and entertainment of 40 Sowars of Jan Fishan Khan. We have near 3 lacs in the military chest. The Jhansi Brigade are fortifying themselves at Bolundshuhur. These cobwebs will soon be swept away after the great event. Van Cortlandt at Hansi. Tosham. Cash at Delhi. Jhansi-brigade.

## CCCCLXXXII.

### DELHI.—H. H. GREATHED, C.S., TO W. MUIR, C.S., SUDDUR BOARD.

ALL are in great spirits in camp; and there is the best feeling among our Native troops. Fever patients come in and go out of Hospital, but the sick-list is on the increase. Active work will act as a tonic. I was on the top of Hindoo Rao's the other day when a body of Pandies marched out on some duty. Their listless slovenly way of moving was remarkable. The pay question occupies the minds of the soldiers, and leads to violent altercations in Durbar. The money levied from Soukars has been embezzled by the Shahzadas. They don't seem to have any idea of what is in store for them. Good feeling among Native troops. Sick-list on the increase. Mutineers' financial difficulties.

## CCCCLXXXIII.

### DELHI.—CAPT. O. H. ST. G. ANSON TO MRS. MUIR. Mrs. Muir.

WAS to start at 11 on the night of the 2nd—to escort the siege train in. Would bivouac on night of 3rd, and bring in train on the 4th. Great sickness amongst the 61st; upwards of 250 in Hospital, and men are dying like rotten sheep of disease. Principally cholera of a very virulent type. Goolab Singh's troops are expected on the 9th or 10th. Then we proceed to the assault of the city. Batteries to open 400 or 300 yards from the walls. Great sickness amongst 61st.

## CCCCLXXXIV.

HATRASS. *September 8th.*

Allygurh. Gobind Singh works well.

GOOD accounts. Allygurh all right—shops open; people satisfied. Gobind Singh working well.

Two big guns coming in, and a Howitzer (without a trunnion) brought in before—(9 altogether).

Rs. 10,000 sent in on 7th.

Rs. 6000 collected at Allygurh.

Tekum Singh will pay 1000 or 1100.

## CCCCLXXXV.

CAWNPORE.—GENL. NEILL TO LT.-GOVERNOR. *4th September.*

Sir J. Outram moves from Allahabad.

(Reply to 25th and 27th.)— . . . I had a letter this morning from Sir J. Outram from Allahabad, and he expects to leave that to-day or to-morrow with 730 of the 90th, 420 Fusiliers, and 168 of the 64th with Eyre's battery, which will enable them to go to Lucknow in style. He will accompany the force merely in his Civil capacity as Commr.; he observes it would be unfair to deprive Havelock of the merit of relieving Lucknow.

Outram and Havelock.

Rewah.

Chester writes to me from Allahabad that the Rewah country is going, though the Rajah is all right. Part of the Dinapore Mutineers, the 40th N.I. and Ramgurh Battalion, with Budmashes about 8000, under Konwur Singh, are moving on Mirzapore; but there is a strong European detachment there which will keep them out of that. The other portion of these vagabonds is about to cross the Tonse river into the Doab. A gunboat has, however, gone up to the ferry, and will, I hope, be in time to prevent them. (Complains of delay and want of energy in employing the gunboats.)

Dinapore Mutineers.

Troops from below.

All is, however, well down below at Benares, etc. A Brigade, wing H.M. 53rd, 27th Madras N.I., and a battery of artillery, have left Ranee Gungê to march to Benares and Allahabad. More China troops have arrived. 270 of the Mounted Land Transport Corps will make good Dragoons.

China troops.

Mr. Edwards. Mr. and Mrs. Probyn. Hurdeo Buksh. Major Robertson. Feeling among the Hindoo population.

Mr. Edwards, Collr. of Budaon, and Mr. and Mrs. Probyn, of Futtehgurh, with the children, have come in safe.[1] They were protected by Hurdeo Buksh at Dhurumpore. Many Europeans are still in hiding about the country. Major Robertson of the Artillery is lying wounded near there, and will be safe ere long. The feeling among the Hindoo population is for us entirely, but

[1] See p. 501 (notes).

all are waiting to see who is to gain the day,—we or the Delhi king. Much would be done with the Hindoos when the turn comes, and more particularly at Furruckabad the Hindoos would rise on the Moslems there when we approach it.

At Lucknow our people get on stoutly. Six days since, they sprang a mine they had driven under a house outside, but near the works from which the enemy galled them much, and blew up nearly 200 rebels. They then sallied and spiked one of their large guns. The enemy there are much discouraged, and their forces diminishing. **Lucknow. Successful explosion of mine.**

Mr. Edwards says: "Sepoys coming away from Delhi unarmed, in parties of 2 and 3, were passing through where they were. The Zemindars and country people on the look-out to murder them for plunder. The feeling of the ryots against them is most deadly." **Sepoys leaving Delhi. Zemindars' attitude to Sepoys.**

## CCCCLXXXVIa.

MEERUT.—F. WILLIAMS, C.S., TO C. B. THORNHILL, SECY. TO GOVT. N.W.P. *2nd September.*

Is raising Sikh and Wilaitee Horsemen; Goorkha and Sikh footmen to fill vacancies. **Raises Sikh and Pathan horsemen; Goorkha and Sikh footmen.**

"I shall in 15 days, I hope, have 300 or 400 good horsemen."

Accepted Sir J. Lawrence's offer of 200 Sikhs, for whom he is getting horses at Meerut. **Sir J. Lawrence offers 200 Sikhs.**

Is raising Sikh and Afghan horsemen, and mixing them with the Irregular Cavalrymen that remain.

## CCCCLXXXVII.

NAINEE TAL.—MR. ALEXANDER, C.S., TO MR. COLVIN, LT.-GOVR. *August 20th.*

No fresh reports of occurrences in Rohilkhund.

The war between Mahomedans and Hindoos "has apparently subsided—for a time only, I must suppose."

Khan Bahadur Khan is reported to be weeding his rabble, and so slightly reducing his nominal array. **Khan Bahadur Khan.**

"At Moradabad and in that district improvement is, I learn, taking place. Revenue is coming in, and disturbances are fewer." **Moradabad improving.**

The Hindoos discomfited by the Nawab of Nujeebabad's forces. **Nawab of Nujeebabad.**

Nawab of Rampore.

Believes Rampoor Nawab to be staunch; expects his man there in the next two or three days. He supplies our bazaar well.

"All are doing well here."

## CCCCLXXXVIII.

### JYEPORE.—*7th July* 1857.

Good accounts from Jyepore.

"I AM despatching 75,000 Rs. to Agra to-day with Sobajee. He will see you.

"We have had a few very pleasant days with the Kotah Contingent officers, who talk of leaving to-morrow. The Nusserabad officers and party leave that place to-day."

Delhi to fall on the 9th.

## CCCCLXXXIX.

### DELHI.—H. H. GREATHED, C.S., TO MR. COLVIN, LT.-GOVERNOR. *4th September.*

Offers of service by Delhi Princes. Strange offer by them.

(Reply to 29th.)—The offers of service on the part of some of the Princes which were rejected by me were made again to the General in a somewhat altered form. There was a distinct offer to destroy the bridge and to enlist the services of the cavalry, and, with their aid, to put an end to the infantry, on condition of favour being shown to the Royal Family. General Wilson refused positively to entertain any communications from the Palace.

Siege train arrives.

The train came in all safe this morning. The supply of shot and shell seems inexhaustible. It was escorted by 230 of the 8th Queen's and a wing of a Beloch battalion. The detachment of Rifles and Foot Artillery comes on to-morrow. Each of the guns was drawn by 2 elephants. Lt.-Col. Hogge has arrived from Meerut. He is appointed Commissary-General of Ordnance, and is admirably suited for the post.

Lieutenant-Colonel Hogge, Commissary-General of Ordnance.

Wilde's Punjab Infantry. Delhi.

Wilde's Punjaub Infantry are at Paneeput to-day. We shall not wait the arrival of the Cashmere troops; they do not march quickly, and have no great fancy to take the front.

H.M.'s 8th claims the post of honour.

My brother's regiment, the 8th, claims the post of honour, being the senior Regiment in camp. Our troops are animated by the best feeling. Too much cannot be said in favour of the Sirmoor Battalion; they have served at the main picket at Hindoo Rao's ever since we arrived, and have lost half their numbers in action. They insist on having their sick and wounded in the upper storey of Hindoo Rao's house. Traverses

High encomium on the Sirmoor battalion.

have had to be erected opposite the windows to keep out round-shot, and only yesterday a 10-inch shell carried away a corner of the roof. Major Reid has never been in camp. He is our watchman. The corps should bear the motto of "Vigil et tenax." Major Reid.

I have received a letter from Rao Toolaram of Rewaree. I believe he has been setting up for himself, and his name is often mentioned in our news-letters as in correspondence with the Palace. He implicates the Nawab of Furrucknugger. Their real deeds and misdeeds will soon be known. There has been much disturbance in the City and Palace about the payment of the troops. The King was unable to give out more than one rupee to each Infantry and 2 to each Cavalry man. The 4 Hindoostani guns taken by General Nicholson have been given to the Putiala Rajah by Sir J. Lawrence. He purchased them at a valuation, as they were prize of war. Rao Toolaram Rewaree. Nawab of Furrucknugger. Financial difficulties in the Palace. Guns taken by General Nicholson given to Patiala Rajah by Sir J. Lawrence.

All is quiet above.

The Zemindars of Soneput and Paneeput appeared yesterday at the Durbar and apprised the King of the approach of the siege train, and offered with assistance to capture it. The project was referred to General Bukht Khan. Hostile action of Zemindars of Soneput and Paneeput.

Ford, 1st inst., reports the treason of the Moslems in the Putiala Army. No harm has been done. W. Ford, C.S.

Herat evacuated on the 27th July. Herat.

## CCCCLXXXIXA.

DELHI. *5th September.*

It is confidently expected that the ball will open on the 7th, Monday. The Artillery force is the healthiest in camp. Fever is prevalent among the Infantry, and the admissions to Hospital among the Europeans are about 100 a day. Cholera has appeared among the 61st. Sickness in Delhi camp.

All well in the Punjaub.

## CCCCXC.

NYNEE TAL. *23rd August.*

MORADABAD.—Peace kept. But Revenue not collected as it should be. So expenses much larger than income. The Nawab works out, as effectually as under the circumstances could be expected of him, the object which he has always had in view, namely, keeping his own turbulent Puthans from going in any Good accounts of Nawab of Rampore.

numbers to Delhi, and keeping us up here well supplied with provisions, and with such intelligence as he can obtain; at the same time maintaining order in Moradabad, and defending Ramsay's Bhabur and Huldwani against incursions. On our going down he will, I believe, join us at once, and will know whether he can bring any reliable force with him; but it is evident that he would hardly trust a man with us now if we went down without Europeans to retake Bareilly, and if the green flag were hoisted before their eyes.

Shakespear expects a force from Williams to re-enter Bijnore; thinks he ought to have been consulted.

Hindoos of Bijnore. Kazim Ali Khan.

The Hindoos of Bijnore, when they applied to Meerut and Nynee Tal for help, simultaneously applied to Kazim Ali Khan, the Nawab's brother, "our foe, and the very man whom the Nawab has the greatest difficulty to manage. This man has horse and guns, and is said to be casting guns. He is just now at Sumbhul occupying for the Nawab, but a constant cause of anxiety to him; and his last message to the Nawab was that he would go to Bijnore. On the other hand, the Nawab of Nujeebabad sent to the Nawab of Rampoor for aid, which the latter, acting on the cue I had given him, refused. The only reason the Hindoos could have had in applying to Kazim Ali Khan must have been founded on his known hostility to the Nawab, his brother; but they equally knew that he is *our* foe, as well as his brother's."

So if we went over we might find Kazim Ali Khan's Puthans joining the Bijnore Puthans against us. Rampoor Nawab will be probably able to prevent this, but it shows that we cannot go to Rohilkhund trusting solely on Hindoos, *without a force*.

## CCCCXCI.

ALLYGURH.—FROM A. COCKS, C.S., TO MR. E. A. READE, CH. COMMR. 10*th September*.

Jats as soldiers.

SPEAKS well of Tekum Singh. Recommends Jats to be raised for our troops; they drink wine and eat chickens.

## CCCCXCII.

MEERUT.—FROM F. WILLIAMS, C.S. COMMR. 4*th*.

DAWES' troop of 250 Cavalry and 200 Sikhs, for whom I have some horses ready, will be here directly. We shall be ready to astonish Pandy then.

Rs. 1,40,000 in from Edwards to-day. Above 5 lacs in hand now. **Revenue paid.**

All quiet above. A war of creeds threatening in Rohilkhund. **Religious dissensions in Rohilkhund.** Wilson, Superintendent of Commission for Suppression of Mutineers; he would hunt them out better than any man in India, and prevent hundreds and thousands becoming Dacoits and bothering us. **Cracroft Wilson.**

## CCCCXCIII.

MEERUT.—FROM F. WILLIAMS, C.S. COMMR. *7th Sept.*

OUR H(issar) Demonstration (?) force is, I fancy, to-day engaged in paying off some insurgent villagers who gathered to defend a village Pilkŭa, about 7 miles from H(issar), where their videttes watching the Delhi road were fired on. The South-west and West is in the hands of rebels, as we have not a man to send into that part. Sirdhana is threatened by 5000 or 6000 men. **Hissar.**

Palmer on the east border of Mozzuffernugger is threatened, if he has not been attacked, by 1000 or 2000 Goojurs; so the Meerut district is in what may be called open rebellion. **Meerut district in open rebellion.**

G(reăthed) says "the Bareilly Brigade looks to Rohilkhund as their line of retreat." So if you do not hear for some days do not be unhappy. We have from 8000 to 12,000. **Bareilly brigade.**

Seharunpore is quiet, and all right in the Punjaub.

## CCCCXCIV.

DELHI.—FROM LT. GREATHED[1] TO MR. COLVIN, LT.-GOVR. *6th Sept.*

(Reply to 30th.)—The siege train arrived on the 4th, and Hogge, who has come over to administer, reported himself ready yesterday. We have been so for some days, so that it has remained for the General alone to decide when he would begin, . . . . . . . . . . A wing of the Beloch Battalion, dressed as if for the stage, accompanied the train; as did also 230 of the 8th, a very seasonable refresher to the Regiment, hitherto very weak. Some 200 Rifles (60th) and 100 Artillery have marched in. Ten guns will open the morning of the 8th, if all goes well, from sufficiently near position. Thirty-six more next morning, after which I expect that it **Arrival of siege train.** **Preparations for breaching wall.**

[1] Probably a mistake for Colonel Greathed of 8th Queen's. See next letter.—W. C.

will be short work with my friends in the city. Their courage appears to flag, and they are very quiet in their demeanour just now. Nor do we hear of the preparation of any unpleasant contrivances in the city to obstruct our advance. My next letter will, I trust, be dated "from out the Palace of the Cæsars." Prize agents are being appointed, which can hardly be soothing to the feelings of the opposition, and a universal feeling of strength and anticipation of success pervades our force. We stay our hands and make no effort to destroy the bridge, that we may retain it for our own use; whilst at the same time we can punish those who would cross it from their own bastions in the city. We have a great deal of work upon our hands in our brigade, and few hands to do it with. Lt. Warren lost his left arm the other week, but is, I am happy to say, doing capitally. Lt. Walker, Bombay Engineers, who was wounded on the 14th July, after recovering from his wounds was attacked with cholera, in whose clutches he was held in the jaws of death well-nigh a week. He is now, I am thankful to say, out of danger, but Col. Baird Smith is a great invalid, living on medicine, by the aid of which he bears up against his wound capitally. . . . . . . . . . . Capt. Taylor is a most capital officer, of great military capabilities. We have several such men. Lts. Greathed,[1] Stewart, Genesti, Lindsay, Carnegie are all *hors de combat*, while Brownlow and half a dozen more have made a compact with the doctor to do anything he likes eventually, if he will only bolster them up for a week.

Prize agents being appointed.

Lieutenant Warren.

Lieutenant Walker.

Colonel Baird Smith.

Captain Alex. Taylor, R.E.

Engineer officers.

The breach between us and the gentry is indeed irreparable, except in rare isolated cases. From this will spring a military class of men who have earned their title to fortune by their own acts and not by help of caste.

## CCCCXCV.

Delhi.—From H. H. Greathed, C.S. *7th Sept.*

Force at Delhi.

(Reply to letters of 1st and 2nd Sept.)—General Neill's letter of the 27th reassures us very much. Refers to his brother's letter. He is in charge of the left attack, and his home from this evening will be the trenches. We have 7 Regiments Europeans, and 6 of natives, and a magnificent array of guns. The strongest regiment of Europeans mustered yesterday 480

[1] Brother of H. H. Greathed.—W. M.

effective soldiers. The sick and wounded are numerous, but all goes on well, and the enemy has not an idea of our design.

Promises a daily letter. Is at a loss whom to send to Rohtuck: thinks a military officer.

## CCCCXCVI.

HATRASS.—FROM A. H. COCKS, C.S., ALLYGURH. 12*th Sept.*

ALL natives who write or come from the "elaquah" seem to agree as to Wullee Dad Khan having hidden himself since Pilkooa was plundered by the Meerut force. Wullee Dad Khan.

. . . . . . . .

A sentry was fired at by some budmash last night. I am trying to get a clue— probably the miscreant was some Moslem from Coel, but it will be some time before we shall be quite safe from individual acts of revenge and fanaticism.

Aligurh is all quiet, but people's minds will not be quite settled till the final stroke at Delhi. Allygurh.

Letters from Khoorja just in, corroborating the disconsolate state of Mahomedans at Malagurh, and reporting the sound of heavy firing at Delhi for 2 days past,—that is 9th and 10th. Malagurh.

## CCCCXCVII.

DELHI.—H. H. GREATHED, C.S., TO MR. COLVIN, LT.-GOVR. 8*th Sept.*

THE first steps in the siege have been successful. Koodsia Bagh and Ludlow Castle were occupied yesterday evening; and No. I. Battery on the right was constructed and armed during the night without a shot being fired. The enemy were in perfect ignorance of the plan of attack, and had withdrawn their outposts on our left front. A heavy fire from our ridge batteries on our right occupied their attention during the night. It was replied to from all the city bastions, their shots flying far over the heads of the parties working at the Battery, and their first notice of its existence was a shot from it this morning. It is armed with 10 heavy guns. All were placed in the Battery during the night, and 300 rounds per gun were stored in the Magazine. Four guns were on their platforms by daylight, and Koodsia Bagh and Ludlow Castle occupied. No. I. Battery.

two more have been placed in position since then; and the remaining four will be brought into action by evening. Eight hundred camels were employed in taking down fascines, etc., and 300 in carrying the ammunition. The Battery is only 650 yards from the Moree. It had to sustain a heavy fire this morning, which is already much reduced. Lt. Hildebrand, Artillery, and Bannerman, Belooch Battalion, have been killed; and Lt. Budd, Artillery, wounded. There are about 30 other casualties. There was an attack upon Ludlow Castle from the Cashmere Gate this morning, and there was a sharp fire, but it did not last. My two brothers are quite well. They do not return to camp until the siege is over. The Cashmere troops came in this morning. They are about 2000 of all arms. They look as good as the Sikhs used to in Runjeet's time. The horses are poor; they are under their own . . . and officers. The General rode out to receive them. Capt. R. Lawrence is in political charge. There has been a petty disturbance at Murree. We have received General Neill's letter of the 27th. All quiet elsewhere in the Punjaub.

Lieutenants Hildebrand and Bannerman killed. Lieutenant Budd wounded.

Arrival of Cashmere Contingent.

Captain R. Lawrence. Disturbance at Murree.

## CCCCXCVIII.

DELHI.—FROM COLONEL BECHER. *9th September.*

Bombardment commenced.

I AM happy to say that our siege operations have at last commenced. We broke ground the night before last, and erected 2 large batteries on the right, below, to the left front of Hindoo Rao's, about 750 yards from the Moree Bastion, which, with the Cashmere Gate, they are intended to silence, while we erect our breaching batteries.

Koodsia Bagh.

On that night we also took possession of Koodsia Bagh (Custom House Cutchery) (old), a large walled enclosure 300 yards from the city walls on the banks of the river. Within this, masked batteries which will contain heavy guns and large mortars are being completed. A very heavy breaching battery is also in course of construction in front of Ludlow Castle. This, with those in the Koodsia Bagh, will open to-morrow morning. We have a strong picket on Ludlow Castle.

Breaching battery.

The batteries on the right kept up a heavy fire all yesterday, and have damaged the Moree Bastion a good deal. The firing is steady and good to-day. Our loss in these operations has been, comparatively, wonderfully small—18 killed and 57 wounded, including 2 officers killed—Lt. Hildebrand, Artillery, and Lt.

Casualties.

Bannerman, Bo. Army, with Beloch Battalion. Our progress thus far has been most satisfactory.

The Jummoo force under Capt. Lawrence joined us yesterday, —3 Regiments of Infantry, 4 guns, and some Cavalry. Altogether a well equipped and efficient body of men. Detail of Cashmere Contingent.

The Jheend force came in the day before. Lt.-Col. Dunsford, with several officers, are attached to them. Jheend Contingent. Colonel Dunsford.

We hope that Delhi will fall on the 12th at latest.

All is well in the Punjaub.

There was a slight disturbance at Murree on the 2nd, caused by the villagers attacking the station. They plundered two houses, but did no other harm. Several were killed. Troops had gone up from Rawal Pindee. All was quiet again. Our news from all parts very satisfactory. From Calpee, 30th August.

## CCCCXCIX.

### SIÁLKOT.—FROM MAJOR DRAKE TO COL. ELD. 31*st August.*

A PAPER was found yesterday posted in the city calling on the Sikhs to rise in favour of the Jungee Lord Maharaj Shere Singh. I believe it to be a Mussulman production, emanating very probably from a discharged official; but if similar papers are found in other places it will be unpleasant. With it another paper was found addressed to the Feringhees, giving them notice to quit the country they had wrongly held for the last 10 years. Seditious papers.

## D.

### DELHI.—FROM H. H. GREATHED, C.S., TO MR. COLVIN, LT.-GOVR. 9*th Sept.*

WHEN I revisited the Ridge in the afternoon, the 10 guns of the battery erected 650 yards from the walls on our right centre were in action and playing with great effect on the Moree and Cashmeree bastions. The enemy had 2 light guns and rockets in Kishengunge, and sought to enfilade the new battery, but they did not touch it. During the night 12 five-and-a-half-inch mortars, and 6 eight-inch, and 4 ten-inch were put in position on the left. Fire will not open from these mortars Progress of bombardment.

until all the other guns on the left are in position. All will be ready by the morning of the 11th.

Spirit of troops.

Every one is perfectly well satisfied with the appearance of affairs. The troops are getting more and more elated at the hourly proofs of our powers of destruction; and the enemy has apparently no notion how to offer any effective opposition to the approaches. I do not hear of any material desertions from the city, which is well. The effect produced on the public mind in Delhi has not yet developed itself. Since yesterday one sergeant has been killed and 3 men wounded. The admissions to hospital are fewer among the men beyond the ridge; fever has been prevalent, but every one appears of opinion that we have every reason to be thankful that it has not assumed a more dangerous type—it is not of a fatal character. Lt. Somerville of Artillery died of brain fever; Lt. Tyler, 61st, of cholera. All quiet in the Punjaub. Van Cortlandt finds it best to act on the passive system just now.

Casualties. Sickness in the force. Lieutenant Somerville. Lieutenant Tyler.

## DI.

### Delhi.—Capt. O. H. St. G. Anson to Mrs. Muir.
### 10 *Septr.* 1857.

Customs House Battery.

The Customs House was occupied last night, and by to-morrow a breaching battery close to it will open at less than 300 yards, and the Engineers say that 3 hours will suffice to smash the wall.

The working and covering parties have been most zealous and assiduous, and have elicited a complimentary order from Wilson. The place, *D.V.*, will certainly fall by the 15th, if not sooner.

Lieutenant Hildebrand.

We have had a number of casualties in the trenches. Poor H(ildebrand) had his head nearly taken off by a 3-pounder from the wall.

There is a very heavy fire of musketry going on to-day, for we are working away between 300 and 400 yards from the wall. The enemy's fire, however, is not very destructive, for they fire without aim or tangible object.

They say Sunday the 13th will be *the* day of dire retribution.

Bull-dogs *en avant*, and looting gentry behind. Thermometer 96 degrees now at noon.

## DII.

### DELHI.—CAPT. A. D. DICKENS TO CAPT. CHALMERS.
10 *Septr.*

I HAVE been here since the 2nd, and am equipping a flying column, which will start in pursuit directly Delhi falls. **Preparation for Flying Column.**

Since yesterday morning our batteries, now advanced to 600 yards of the walls between the Cashmere and Moree bastions, have been firing salvos of 6 guns continually. Both their bastions are much damaged, and I heard that on the former the heavy guns had been dismounted by our fire. The Moree still occasionally fires a gun, but it is few and far between. **Progress of bombardment.**

Our grand battery ought to be finished by this evening. This is within 250 yards of the wall, and should surprise them not a little. A mortar battery is being constructed, and will open at the same time. **Grand Battery.**

The grand battery is to have 20 heavy guns in it; the other, 10 mortars, 5 10-inch.

The firing is incessant, and at present a great deal of musketry going on.

Day before yesterday Pandy made a feeble attack on our right, which ended in the usual result—utter discomfiture. He has light guns out in the direction of Kishengunge, endeavouring to enfilade our right, and advanced batteries, but they don't do much harm. **Mutineers attack besieging force.**

The Cashmeree levies made their appearance on the 8th. They are not bad-looking Irregulars, but have a downcast, dissatisfied look about them. On the 8th we had, too, an explosion in camp of waggon with loose ammunition and five shells. It killed 6 drivers and wounded three Europeans. Yesterday our casualties were fewer—4 or 5 in all. It is surprising that with so much firing the loss is so small. Everything shows we are approaching the end of the "last act," and that Pandy's reign is coming rapidly to an end. Strange to say, he does not even molest us in constructing batteries! He potters away in feeble style with musketry, which does little harm. **Cashmeree Contingent.** **Feebleness of Mutineers' defence.**

I believe our Column will make its way down to Agra. I fancy it depends upon which direction the rascals take. A fat Pandy was caught asleep by some Goorkhas and brought in. He was "accounted for."

## DIII.

DELHI.—H. H. GREATHED, C.S., TO W. MUIR, C.S., SUDDUR BOARD.
11*th Septr.*

IT was part of the original plan to withdraw four 24-pounders from the left of No. I. Battery when advanced Battery No. II. was ready to be armed. This was to have been done yesterday evening, but the movement was accelerated by the Battery, composed entirely of fascines, catching fire from our own firing. Everything was removed without loss of life or stores, and the right Division of the Battery, being 150 yards off, did not suffer, and continued to play on the Moree. As the Engineers would not allow No. II. to open, we had only six guns in action below the ridge from 2 p.m. yesterday till 10 a.m. to-day, and the enemy seemed to acquire confidence, but not enough to induce them to make any telling attack. Their grounds for confidence were cut away when the mortars and No. II. opened this morning. The gunners in the Cashmere Bastion could not stand the direct and vertical fire combined, and were quickly obliged to cease firing. During the two hours I was looking on, the figure of the bastion changed a good deal. The Custom House Battery will probably open this afternoon, and must soon destroy the Water Bastion, as it is only 180 yards from it. It was certainly an audacious step to erect a battery at such a short distance without first destroying the defences. The whole plan is an audacious one, suited to the occasion, but contrary to rule. Baird Smith is cool, clear, and determined, and he has good aids in Taylor and my brother. There was a good deal of firing all last night from the city, and we had probably some loss. The only officer hit was Gillespie of the Artillery. The Pandies talk of erecting a Dumdummah near the Magazine. They do not appear to have formed any plan of retreat. The Neemuch force has disbanded itself. The pounding will, I believe, be continued for 2 or 3 days more, and then I hope the city up to the Palace gates will be taken without much loss of life.

*Progress of bombardment.* *Custom House Battery. Water Bastion.* *Colonel Baird Smith.* *Gillespie.* *Neemuch force.*

*Nicholson.* Nicholson will command the pursuing force.

*Williams.* I wish a Military Governor to be appointed over the city with supreme authority, and should like Williams, or whoever is to be permanent Commr., to relieve me as soon as military operations are at an end.

*Dunlop in Meerut.* Dunlop writes in good spirits about Meerut. The band who were to have attacked Sirdhana were driven back by the Police.

I have got your letters of the 5th and 6th with news about the Indore force. You will see that the pace of operations here can scarcely be quickened. No force could be inspired with higher zeal. The appointment of Prize Agents will, I hope, prevent an indiscriminate pillage. But the Punjaub troops are inveterate plunderers. One of Coke's men shot a Pandy yesterday from the Battery, and a number rushed out to plunder the corpse, and a volley of grape from the city knocked over most of them. There is no restraining these fellows, and the sooner they go back to the frontier when the work is over the better. The Guides Infantry is admirable. They have only 160 left out of the 600 who came down. They have been all along in the advanced posts. The Battery is going on bravely. It is a fine sight, especially at night.

**Prize Agents.**

**Plundering propensities of the Punjab troops.**

**Guide Corps. Their severe losses.**

## DV.

DELHI.—COL. (?) BECHER TO CAPT. NIXON. 14*th Sept.* 1 p.m.

THE assault on the city took place this morning. The troops entered at the breach near the Cashmere Gate without serious opposition, and gained possession of the large buildings in its neighbourhood, and advanced along the ramparts to the Moree Bastion and Cabul Gate, in progress to which the resistance was very obstinate, and the loss consequently has been severe. But we are advancing gradually within the city.

**Assault delivered.**

Large bodies of the enemy have been seen retreating both in the direction of the Kutub and over the bridge. Arrangements are making for batteries to be made in the city, and their heavy guns have been turned on them. You shall hear again to-morrow.

**Retreat of the enemy.**

## DVII.

BULLUBGURH. 17*th Septr.*

MADE three bastions from Lahore to Calcutta Gate.

. . . . . . . .

The army is now out of city and fort; only King's servants inside.

**The army out of city.**

The King has broken the bridge to prevent the army fleeing. No supplies. Great scarcity.

. . . . . . . .

## DVIII.

### DELHI.—COL. (?) BECHER TO CAPT. NIXON. 17 *Septr.*

Progress of troops in city.

ON the day of the assault we took and held from the Cashmere to the Cabul Gates on the right, and the College on the left.

Magazine taken.

Yesterday morning the Magazine was taken with 150 guns in it, and vast quantities of shot and shell. The small arms had been all removed.

Rifles.

To-day the Rifles occupy the Bank House.

Some further forward movement will be made to-morrow; but we hear the main body are leaving the city, and intend to go towards Gwalior *via* Muthra. The King is in the Palace with some 2000 or 3000 men, who declare they will fight to the last. The Palace, however, is being well shelled to-day, and that may and probably will make them change their minds.

The King.

Losses in Assault.

Our loss on the 14th was above 800 killed and wounded, and 50 officers. Since then our loss has been trifling.

## DIX.

### MEERUT.

Meerut.

WE tried to [illegible]n the direct road to Delhi by Moradnugger this morning, and c[illegible] off the rebels there, employing the Puthan horse. They killed 4[illegible] [illegible]r 50 of the rebels.

## DX.

### SOMNA (16 miles north-west of Allygurh).—SALAMUT RAY, DEPUTY COLLECTOR, SOMNA. 22*nd of September.*

Retreat of fugitive force.

A MESSENGER had been to near Delhi about the 20th. Saw at Fureedabad, 12 coss from Delhi, 500 Sowars. At a Serai 3 coss from Delhi met an immense force with 10 guns, each drawn by 6 horses. The people said, including camp-followers, etc., there were some 20,000. They said they had been 5 days without supplies and food.

They were to be at Pulwul on the 22nd.

This would probably bring them to Hodul or Cosee on the 23rd, and to Muthra on the 24th or 25th.

Salamut adds that Wullee Dad was said to have been captured, and Khoorja burnt. Cocks does not allude to this.

## DXI.

MUTHRA.—FROM IMDAD ALLY. *23rd Septr.*

REBEL army said to have reached Hodul with 3 guns and 6 tumbrils. Would be at Kosee to-day. Coming to Muthra to get money from Seth. Rebel army in retreat. Seth, Muthra.

## DXIII.

MUTHRA. *23rd Septr.* 9 p.m.

THE fugitive force is at Chata, one "pultun," and some at Cosee, and some at Hodul. A Sowar has seen it. All will arrive at Muthra on the 28th. They have guns. 2000 rebels are coming. Retreat of fugitive force.

## DXIV.

SOMNA. *23rd Septr.*

*23rd.*—Salamut Ray reports that 1000 men (500 Cavalry, 300 foot, and 200 camp-followers) have crossed at Sultanpore and Belochpore Ghat. 1000 more to cross, and guns—some say 6—behind. Retreat of fugitive force.

500 Cavalry and Infantry crossing at Goorwaolee Ghat, taking road by Jewar and Khoorja to Bareilly.

## DXV.

UMBALLA ?—G. BARNES, C.S., TO G. F. EDMONSTONE, C.S., FOR. SECY.

THE Sikhs among the rebels are deserting to our side. Sikhs deserting Mutineer force.

Nicholson was wounded in the chest, rib fractured, and cavity of chest laid open. Nicholson.

## DXVI.

DELHI.—CLIFFORD TO WIGRAM. *16th Sept.*

GREATHED, Metcalfe, Saunders, Richardes, Loch, Clifford, civilians, at Delhi. Civilians at Delhi.

## DXVII.

DELHI. *20th Sept.*

TOLARAM left Delhi on Sunday. The bridge is still up; but as the English batteries are opposite it, no one can go that way. Swam across. Passed parties, 200, 300, 400, and 500 Sepoys with muskets, running away from Khoorja towards Ramghat, Anoopshuhur, and Deba. Moradnugger raid mentioned. Tolaram. Retreat of fugitive force.

Ghazeenugger (?) Tehsuldar (Mussulman?) led (?).
8000 or 10,000 Sepoys between Delhi and Furreedabad.

## DXVIII.

King retires to Humayoon's Tomb. Retreat of fugitives.

CAMRROODDEEN reports that a man left Delhi on Monday the 21st. King had gone out to the Tomb of Hoomayoon. All city in our possession. 3000 or 4000 fugitives at Hodul; but in the manner of plunderers and camp-followers. Some said "Go to Bareilly," some "Go to Cawnpore," others "Go to Dholepore and breathe a bit there."

## DXIX.

*25th Sept.*

MARK THORNHILL reports that yesterday the mutineer Sepoys ordered a bridge of boats to be put up, and that about 100 crossed the Ganges in boats.

## DXX.

MEERUT.—F. WIGRAM TO VERE. *22nd Septr.* 1857.

Expedition to Thannah Bhowun.

A FORCE of Sikhs, Rifles, Carabineers, and 4 guns and mortars, with a few of the Khatries, started early this morning for Mozuffernugger. They are to punish Thannah Bhowun, a town the Mozuffernugger people tried to polish off a few days ago. They got in, captured the enemy's guns, but the Sikhs and Goorkhas failing to follow the first party, they were forced to retreat, leaving the guns they had taken, and losing 12 men killed and several more wounded.

Three Regiments are said to be out on this side of Delhi.

## DXXI.

DELHI.—*22nd Sept.* 1857.

King and Begum prisoners. Three Princes shot by Hodson.

ALL is going on wonderfully well here. The King and the Begum Zeenut Muhál are close prisoners, and to-day the princes Mirza Moghul, Abu Bucker, and Khizzar Sultan were brought in by Hodson from Humayoon's Tomb, and shot at the Delhi Gate. Their bodies are now lying at the Kotwalie, where so many of our poor countrymen were murdered, and exposed. A pursuing Column, under Col. Greathed of H.M. 8th Regiment, leaves this to-morrow morning to go in your direction. It consists of 1600 infantry, 18 guns, in three troops, and 600 Cavalry. They

Greathed commands pursuing Column. Details of Column.

will soon join you, I trust, and render complete the effects of the fall of this city. The city is a perfect picture of desolation: completely abandoned. A vast amount of property left behind, which our native troops are possessing themselves of with great gusto, but with very demoralising effect. There are a great number of city Budmashes and others collected near Humayoon's Tomb, but it is to be hoped our Column will meet them. Last night "Her Majesty the Queen," proposed by the Conqueror of Delhi, was drank with all honour, in the Diwán Khass, by the Headquarter Staff.

Plundering in Delhi.

Dinner in Diwán Khass.

Never has the old building re-echoed with any sound half so fine.

The cheer was taken up by the gallant Goorkhas of the Sirmoor battalion, who form the General's personal guard. All is well in the Punjaub and elsewhere.

Sirmoor battalion.

## DXXII.

DELHI.—COL. (?) BECHER TO CAPT. NIXON. *20th Sept.*

DELHI is ours. We occupy the Palace and all strong places. The rebel army is in full flight. Where the rebels will go to it is as yet impossible to say. Little or no loss. The King and all his people have decamped.

## DXXIII.

MEERUT.—F. WILLIAMS, C.S. COMMR., TO C. B. THORNHILL, SECY. TO GOVT. N.W.P. *22nd Sept.* 1857.

GENERAL WILSON writes to the General here that he can send no Column to this side.[1] This is not in consequence of any loss in the final capture of the city, for the Mutineers evacuated. . . .

The Thannah Bhowun Mahomedans have raised the green flag and plundered that Tehseelee. They then attacked Shamlee, and killed the Tehseeldar of that place; and the Tehseeldar of Thannah Bhowun, who had taken refuge there, and nearly all the native officers of the Shamlee Tehseelee. Edwards, with a small force, attacked Thannah Bhowun. His party punished some of the rebels severely, but it was too small to take the place, and they retired to Mozuffernugger. The Baroti and Prasoulee rebels subsequently joined the Thannah Bhowun people, and we have been obliged to recall the force from Haupper to send it against Thannah Bhowun. With Edwards'

Thannah Bhowun Mahommedans proclaim Jehad.

Tehseeldars murdered.

Edwards attacks Thannah Bhowun.

Force sent against Thannah Bhowun.

[1] *i.e.* Meerut side of Jumna.—W. M.

party there will be a large body of troops with 8 guns, and order will, I hope, be restored in 2 or 3 days, but we cannot go at Malagurh yet.

## DXXIV.

### Captain Murray (?).

Nimbhera.

We have only just returned from Nimbhera, which place we captured on the 19th. We had 2 killed and about 20 wounded. Two officers wounded—Dr. Miles, H.M. 83rd., and Mr. C. Burton, Volunteer. We took three guns, ammunition, elephants, horses, etc. The insurgents have fled to Mundessor. They are reported to have had 50 killed and wounded.

Dr. Miles and Mr. C. Burton wounded.

## DXXV.

### Saidabad.—Extract of Letter from Capt. Fanshawe.

*Oct. 2nd.*

Greathed's action at Boolundshuhur.

News just in from Greathed's Column, which was at Boolundshuhur on the 29th ult., where they had a sharp fight with the rebels and licked them, capturing two guns, 25 barrels of powder, and a lot of small-arm ammunition. 150 said to have been killed on the part of the enemy; and some 50 killed and wounded (6 officers among the latter) on our side. The Moveable Column consists of two European and 2 P.I. Regiments, the 9th Lancers, 3 Native Cavalry corps, 18 guns. They are going to Allygurh *via* Anoopshuhur, so that they will not reach the former, I take it, much before the 4th or 5th.

Details of Moveable Column.

Showers' Column.

There is another Column, under Showers, marching in the Muthra direction.

## DXXVI.

### Kuraolee.—From Kanheya Lall to N. Parsick, Dy. Collector, Agra. 30*th September* 1857. Evening.

Honoured Sir,—I sent some information to-day, morning, by Kishen Singh's man, but I do not know how he did not reach you before you wrote to me this note. Yesterday morning at noon nearly 100 Sowars came down from Muthra *via* Achneyra to Kuraolee; and from Kuraolee they went towards the Singharpore bridge, and crossed the Nuddee there, because the water towards the village of Moree was deep. From Singharpore they went to Dholpore by Mullikpore, Kheyra, and Kheyra Bakunda. Among these, most of them were wounded, and their faces were all pale, and very bad, as they have been running to

Fugitive Sowars

save themselves, and they told the villagers not to come near them.

On the night of the 28th nearly 40 Sepoys came *via* Achneyra to Kuraolee, and remained at Kuraolee Sarae at night; and in the morning of the 29th they also went to Dholpore by the same way as the Sowars. They had no pills, and gunpowder for firing the muskets; neither the Sowars had. **and Sepoys.**

. . . . . . . .

Without the Thannah and Tehsil I cannot stop here. All people know me, and they say in their minds when they see me that I am a "mookhbir"[1] like.

. . . . . . . .

Your most obedient servant,

KANHEYA LALL.

## DXXVII.

GWALIOR (?)—FROM LALLA JOOGUL KISHOR. *30th Sept.*

**Gwalior Mutineers.** THE Morar Mutineers have changed their minds. Now they want to go first to Duttiah, Jhansi, and Julaun to ask them to join. If not, then to take from their Rajas certain sums. Then they will go by Calpee. This is what they are talking about. The Vakeel of the Nana of Bithoor is still with them. **Vakil of Bithoor.**

Yesterday the Mutineers were all in full dress, and gave a salute to the above Vakeel. In return the Vakeel granted rank of Brigadier Major, Brigade Major, Captain, and Ensign to some Soobahdars and Jemadars, and has promised that when they will arrive at Cawnpore they will then get pay, and batta, and "enám." **His pretentious proceedings.**

The guns and army which were put out for the Morar Mutineers are still at the same place; and will remain there till the Mutineers start for Morar. The 4 Cos. 6th Regiment, who were in Asseergurh, and one Coy. 5th Regiment, which was at Boorhanpore, were disarmed by Colonel H. M. Durand. They first came to the Lushkar and asked for service. H. H. refused them on account of Col. Durand's order. Now they are with the Morar Mutineers. **Colonel H. M. Durand disarms troops.**

## DXXVIII.

CAWNPORE.—FROM J. W. SHERER, C.S. *27th Sept.*

(My letter of 21st reached before the evening of the 26th.)

Please tell Col. Fraser we have not heard a word from

[1] Spy, or informer.

Lucknow. Our last intelligence was that they were at Begumpore on the night of Tuesday (23rd). We cannot effect a communication, the road being stopped by a few Sowars at Nawabgunge. Wire and dak with Calcutta regular.

. . . . . . . .

Nagode party saved.

No further news from Rewa. The Nagode (?) ladies arrived safe at Mirzapore.

## DXXIX.

DELHI.—CAPT. HALSTED TO CAPT. NIXON. *1st October* 1857.

(Reply to 23rd.)—We are now working hard to get matters settled here and in the district. Brigadier Showers returned yesterday with a small force with which he had been to the Kootub. He found great numbers of Delhi people at Humayoon's Tomb and at the Kootub, and drove them away. They are scattered all over the surrounding country, and in the greatest misery.

Showers' Column.

Another force under Brigadier Showers will march to-morrow towards Goorgaon, and will visit Rewaree and other places. I go with this force. The road must now be open for the dak.

## DXXX.

GWALIOR.—LALLA JOOGUL KISHOR TO MAJOR C. MACPHERSON. *3rd Sept.* 1857.

Gwalior Contingent delayed by Scindia.

ALL safe now since Delhi. On the 2nd inst. all the officers of Morar Mutineers came to Phool Bagh and said that they are going to Cawnpore through Jhansi, and want their pay for the month of September. The Vakeel of Nana Sahib is still with them, and hurrying them to march. But they cannot go without getting as much conveyance as they have asked, and we will take care to check them by this means.

Nana's Vakil.

We, by receiving the news of the grand victory of Delhi, are all well and happy.

## DXXXI.

LUCKNOW.—GENERAL OUTRAM TO CAPTAIN BRUCE. *26th September.*

Victory at Alumbagh.

I HOPE you got my letter of the day before yesterday, telling you of our victory on the previous day at Alumbagh over hosts of the enemy,—seizure of guns as usual.

Telegraph to Governor-General for me. "Yesterday General

H.'s force, numbering about two thousand of all arms, the remainder being in charge of sick, wounded, etc., occupying the Alumbagh, forced their way into the city under serious opposition. After crossing the Char-Bagh bridge the troops skirted the city to avoid the enemy's defensive works, prepared through the entire length of the main street leading directly to the Residency. Still, much opposition had to be encountered ere we attained the Residency in evening—just in time, apparently; for now that we can examine the outside defences, we find that two mines had been run under the garrison's chief works, ready for loading, which, if sprung, would have placed the garrison at their mercy. Our loss is severe. Not yet correctly ascertained, but estimated at from 400 to 500 men killed and wounded. To-day the troops are occupied in taking the Batteries bearing on the garrison, which have been held till assaulted, and continued till then to fire on the Residency, since our junction with the garrison last night. Many thousands of the enemy have deserted the city. The late King's sons have fled to Fyzabad. General Outram's wound very trifling. J. Anderson, the Fayrers, Ogilvies, Gubbins, Banks, and Ommaneys—widows and families, Miss (?) Hayes, the Coupers. Previous letter alluded to had not been received."

Outram's account of the First Relief of Lucknow.

Names of officers and others at Lucknow.

## DXXXII.

THE names of additional parties at Lucknow: Brigadier Gray and party, and the Atkinses, Major Burrell, H.M. 90th, Lt. Preston, ditto.

## DXXXIII.

### A PROCLAMATION PUBLISHED BY THE NANA AT CAWNPORE.[1]

(*Translation from Urdu.*)

### NOTICE (ISHTIHAR).

A TRAVELLER now staying at Cawnpore, who had come from Calcutta, brings the news that after the distribution of the cartridges Government considered how to take away the faith and religion of Hindustanis. The members of Council decided that, as this was a case of religion, seven or eight thousand white soldiers and Englishmen will be used, and fifty thousand Hindustanis will be killed; then all Hindustanis will become Christians. A petition to this effect was sent to Queen Victoria.

[1] These words, in Mr. Muir's handwriting, are on the face of the original lithographed sheet which is pasted into MSS. Vol. V.—W. C.

Sanction came from England. Then a second meeting of Council was held, and English merchants were also included as members of the Council. It was resolved that for help so many English soldiers should be asked for as there were soldiers in the Native Army, to prevent any risk of defeat when the strife waxed high. When this petition was read in England 35,000 white soldiers were with great haste embarked, and went off to India. The news of their despatch came to Calcutta. The Sahibs of Calcutta then issued the order to distribute the cartridges, the real object being to make the Hindustani army Christian. It was considered that when the army became Christian it would not be long before the people of the soil were made Christian; and on the cartridges there was a mixture of the fat of pigs and cows. This circumstance became known through the statements of Bengalis who were employed to manufacture the cartridges, and so one of the people who revealed this was murdered, and the rest were all sent to jail. Here these fellows were concocting their schemes;[1] then the Turkish ambassador sent this news from London to the Sultan of Turkey, that 35,000 white troops had started for Hindustan to make the Hindustanis Christians. The Sultan-i-Rum, Khaladullah Malikah, issued a firman to the Padshah of Egypt, the tenor of which was this: "You are co-operating with Queen Victoria; this is not a time of peace, for I hear from my Vakeel that an army of 35,000 white men has left for India in order to Christianise the people and army of Hindustan. In these circumstances opposition is now possible; if we miss the opportunity, with what countenance shall we appear before the Almighty? And this day is coming for us too some time, because if the English convert the Hindustanis they will desire my country also." When the order of the Sultan-i-Rum reached the Padshah of Egypt, that chief, before the English army arrived, arranged to collect his troops in Alexandria, for that was the way to India. On the arrival of the English army the army of the King of Egypt began to fire guns from 4 sides, and completely broke up and sank the ships, so that not one English soldier of them was left. The English in Calcutta, after the issuing of the order for biting the cartridges, and after the disturbance and fighting had reached a height, were expecting the help of the troops from London, but God Almighty, in the exercise of His omnipotence, had then already made an end of their scheme. When news arrived of the destruction of the London

[1] The tone seems intentionally depreciatory: "Yahán yih apne tadbîren karte the, wahán yih khabar Sultan-i-Rum," etc.—W. C.

army the Governor-General was very vexed and sorrowful, and beat his head—

> "Early in the evening massacre and plunder began,
> In the morning neither had the body a head, nor the head a crown :—
> After one revolution of the blue sky
> Neither Nadir remained in his position, nor his kingdom."

Printed by order of the Peshwa Bahadur, 13th Zul Q'adah 1273 Hijre.[1]

## DXXXIV.

### Extracts (Translation from Urdu) from the "Ashruf-ul-Akhbar," a Lucknow Newspaper, dated 28th March 1857.

*Irân.*—A fresh rumour prevails in all directions that in Arabia, Turkey, and Turkestan those valiant for the faith, and believers jealous of its honour, at their own expense have prepared the material of a "Jihâd." Every one, rich and poor, by exhortation and preaching of the learned in the faith and of the guides in religious matters, is ready for "Jihâd." Every person is continually fixed in this thought, that to give one's life in God's cause is the good way; every one is enthusiastic for "Jihâd," and is bent on defeating in some way or other the army of the infidels. Set up the standard of the faith (they say) in the battle-field; accordingly, many warriors for the faith having entered Irân with purpose of fighting the ungodly, having desired help of the Shah, are hopeful of his kind help.

And this also all said unanimously, in presence of the Shah (the refuge of angels): "The Russians are enemies of the faith: "faithless infidels, it will never do to ask their assistance. In "matters of faith the partnership of unbelievers is unseemly. All "we Musalmans are subject to orders: we are ready to surrender "our lives when the order comes. War material is not necessary; "we do not ask you for any pecuniary assistance, we have our-"selves got ready cannon balls, gunpowder, etc. Thousands of "Ghazies, strong as elephants, and trained soldiers capable of "breaking through the lines of any enemy, are collected in one "place. If it is the will of God, soon we will overcome the "enemies of the faith; we will exhibit Ispahâni and Khorasâni

[1] Corresponds to 5th July 1857 A.D. The massacre at Cawnpore occurred 27th June.

"skill in the day of battle." This strange arrangement has also been made, that the women should sew clothes for the faithful warriors, grind flour, make bread; and let the men, from boy of 12 to man of 40, show their bravery in the day of battle. From this solemn trial let them not flinch; and the weak and old let them arrange for the supplies, so that the brave fighters in this war suffer no want of food and water. Prepared in this matter they stand ready for "Jihâd." They only await the order of the Shah. Our correspondent writes that zealous Maulcevies and revered preachers have raised this enthusiasm for "Jihâd" in the hearts of the people. Everywhere gatherings for admonitions and sermons are going on. Every one hearing the virtues of "Jihâd" is devoted to the way of God. It would not be surprising if the people of Afghanistan also joined them. In matters of faith they should not refuse.

*Afghanistan.*—In these days Nur Khan, the Commander-in-Chief, bringing a brave and countless army, has set out to seize India. He has arrived at Ghazni without opposition, and probably he will soon arrive in the neighbourhood of Kabul; and a great body of men, which is lying outside it, also is advancing daily. Russians in the garb of Iránis go about in every back street with merchandise, and by this device they get information.

*Ditto.*—Some days ago an ambassador of the Shah of Persia arrived with 700 Sowars and footmen; now gradually about 2000 men have assembled, and daily 10 or 20 horse and foot come in. On being questioned, they say that preparations are being made for a "dawk," hence these arrangements.

*Ditto.*—Russian and Persian soldiers, coming by Khiva and Kokan, etc., have arrived on the borders of Yarkand. It appears as if after the snow has melted a great military operation would take place. In this Dost Mahomed Khan has a secret understanding with Persia. Thousands of Afghans have gone towards Herat to take service with the Shah, and are going now. The road is no ways closed.

*Ditto.*—It appears from the pages of "Subah Sadiq" that the Shah of Persia sent a friendly letter to the President of the United States. The President on receiving it was much pleased. It is conjectured that the Shah may have applied for assistance. The President sent an immediate reply, and dismissed the ambassador with great honour.

## DXXXV.

### ARZI FROM RAJA NAHR SINGH (OF DEHLI) TO HIS HONOUR THE LIEUTENANT-GOVERNOR, AGRA.

CHERISHER of the poor, the just of the age, Nawab whose prayer is accepted by God; holder of lofty titles, your Honour, Lieutenant-Governor of Agra, may you ever prosper:—

After paying my respects and bowing, I beg to inform those persons present at the Durbar that I received a kind letter from Mr. Harvey in reply to one I had sent him, and learned its contents. The Sahib Bahadur writes that it would be a pleasure to him if I would send him the Dehli news. Your Honour, all the buildings I possessed in Dehli have been confiscated by the King, and the soldiers of the disloyal army reside in them, and have turned out my servants. Indeed, there is no person in Dehli who could write the news of the place, but to please your Honour, but I have engaged two or three men as servants to bring news; and in such way as it may be possible I will collect and send in your blessed service news of the city of Dehli, and of the Fort, and of the scattered army. But it will be very hard to get the news conveyed to you daily: it will reach you every third or fourth day. At an expense of Rs. 200 I have employed twenty runners as paid servants, simply to bring news and send it on. A paper of news[1] is forwarded to you in the cover with this "arzi." It will pass under your pure glance.

The Sahib Bahadur has dismissed this humble servant's Vakil. So he begs to represent that it really does not signify, if it is considered inexpedient, that his Vakil should remain inside the Fort. Let the order be given that he remains in the city. If the Vakil remains in attendance at Agra, petitions and newspapers will through him easily reach your Honour's presence. It is a great honour for me that my Vakil should remain in attendance. Let this my petition be granted.

For the future, till Government secures victory, my petitions will be written on this kind of light and thin paper, and sent without a kincob cover (kharita). This is contrary to custom, but cannot be helped;—let it be overlooked. After victory is secured they will be again sent, in accordance with the custom of past times, with "kharita."

May the sun of victory and conquest ever shine on you.

[1] No doubt, alludes to No. DXXXVI.

This is the petition of Raja Nahr Singh, Bahadur, written Kowar, baddi doádsi, S. 1914.[1]

## DXXXVI.

### Account of the Mutiny at Dehli, by Raja Nahr Singh.

(*Translation.*)

The true statement of the facts is that on the 16th day of the month Ramzán, in the year 1233 A.H., at 8 o'clock in the day, all of a sudden a clamour was raised that some mutinous infantry and cavalry were coming to Dehli from the direction of Meerut. As soon as the Sahib Collector Bahadur heard of this, he summoned the City Kotwál in order to make arrangements. Although the latter presented himself immediately at the call of the above-mentioned officer, the defence of the city gates could not be satisfactorily arranged for. Just then five horsemen entered the city through the Calcutta Gate, and went towards Darya Gunj, began to set fire to the houses and bungalows, and put the European officers to the sword. After that, other mounted men arrived. In the meantime the City Kotwál hid himself in the house of Hakím Abdul Haq, and most of the European gentlemen went off as they best could. In the evening the cavalry mounted a gun on the gate, directing it towards the magazine; but the officer exploded a mine from the inside, and all of a sudden the bastion on the side of the ghat (ferry) was blown up, and this created a shaking like an earthquake. In short, after the explosion of the bastion three Englishmen were made prisoners from the inside, and they alleged that if they had had but three hours they would have blown up the whole of Dehli. Those Englishmen were killed. After three or four days it was ascertained that some English troops had come from the direction of the Hindun. On hearing this piece of news, Mirza Abu Bakr, in company with son of the Heir-apparent, went towards the river towards these troops, but they were thwarted and had to bear a lot of disgrace and shame. The English forces moved from the Hindun towards Alipur. A mendicant (or beggar) came and took up his quarters in the city, and the troops thought it was Mr. Lawrence. He was found and killed. After some days the English forces

[1] Corresponds to 15th September 1857, the day after the assault of Delhi. —W. C.

left Alipur, and remained at the Mithai Bridge. At this time there were only three regiments in Dehli, but they looked like a large number, so the English troops fell back, and took up their position on the Ridge, and made entrenchments The hostilities continued, and one day a severe fight occurred towards Alipur. The English captured 12 guns, and many men were killed. After that, one day the Purbia forces went at night to make entrenchments at Dr. Patton's house, which is situated outside the sewer gate, and with the cavalry and artillerymen went to sleep. The English soldiers came at the dead of night, thrashed them well, and took away their arms; some four or five hundred men were killed on this occasion. After this, the Indian troops made an entrenchment on the Mithai Bridge. At night the English made an attack, but the Indian troops were vigilant, and saved themselves. After that, all the forces and the King's Bachera regiment made an attack. The number of casualties on both sides was 100 or 125; three men from the King's Bachera regiment were killed. After that, the Nimach Force came to Dehli and halted for some days, and afterwards went to Alipur *via* Najafgarh. The fighting there was very severe, and all the camp was lost. It was heard afterwards that the number of casualties was only 500, and the English soldiers captured 12 guns. The Bareilly Force returned, but the whole of Najafgarh was plundered, and the tents were all looted. Next day the English soldiers made a night attack, and nearly 80 men were killed, including both sides. After that, the English soldiers made entrenchments on the road, below the Ridge, at a distance of about 400 paces from the walls; a hot engagement took place, and shot flew about. Afterwards the English soldiers moved towards Kudsia Bagh, and made entrenchments under the wall. Another fierce engagement took place, and the crown of the rampart was broken down, but the Indian troops repulsed the British force. The guns were left there, neither taken away by the Indians nor by the English. After that, 5000 English troops delivered an attack, and entered the Kashmiri Gate. There was severe fighting. The number of casualties, including both sides, was about 4000. The present state of affairs is that the Indian troops have made entrenchments inside the Kashmiri Gate. Let us see what happens in the future In Dehli the number of infantry and cavalry is about sixty thousand. Mirza Moghul and Mirza Khizr Sultan and Mirza Mendho, and his son Daundi Khan, keep with the army whenever there is fighting. They, as well as Mohamed Bakt

Khan, etc., are the managers. The Purbias are greatly oppressing both the common people and the gentry of the city to a degree which defies description. They plunder and arrest them, and force them to make entrenchments, and say, "Fight with us." The public is helpless, and they do not allow any one to go out. They shut the gates, and the King is vexed beyond description. And to-day it has been rumoured that 5000 English soldiers, in three divisions, entered the city from three sides by the ramparts and took possession of the Shah Burj. The gates of the city had been closed, and a hot engagement took place. The details are not to hand as to what the result was, but the slaughter and bloodshed is beyond description.

(Seal of Raja Nahr Singh, Bahadur.)

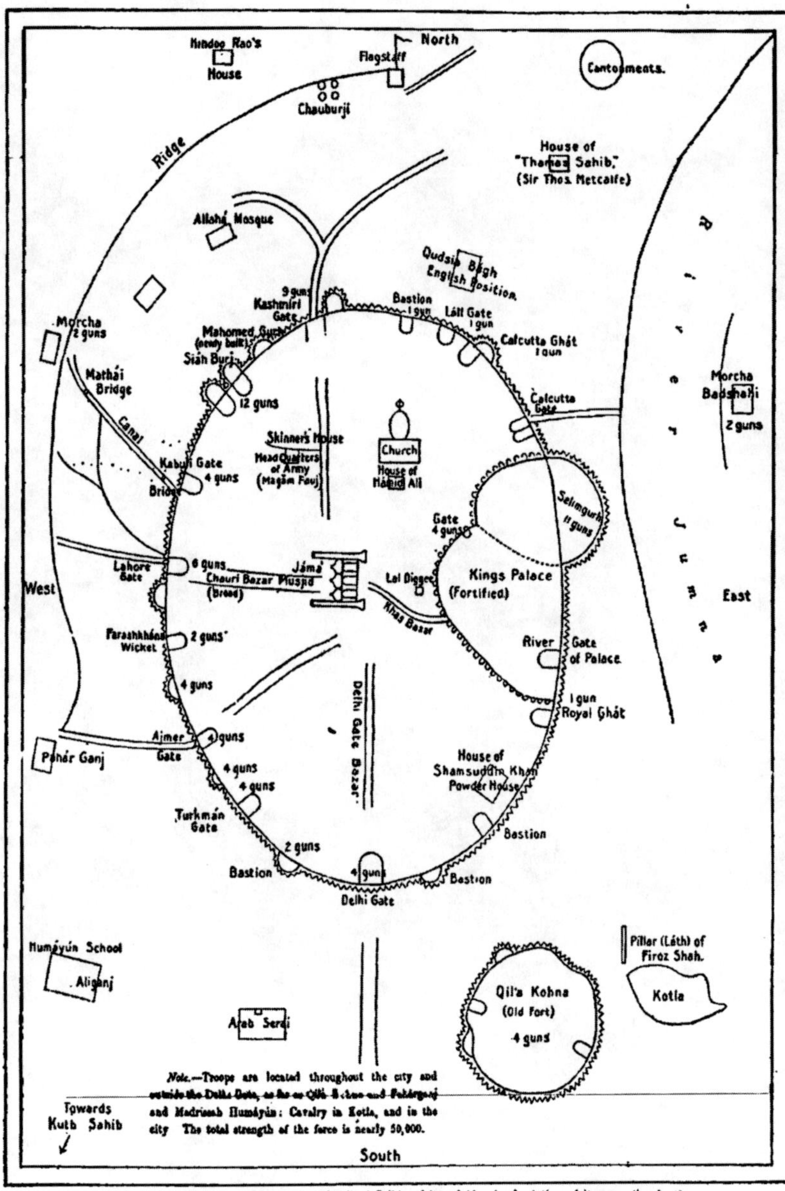


Copy of rough sketch (with names translated) of Delhi and its neighbourhood, at time of its occupation by the Mutineers, furnished by Raja Nahr Singh (annexed to his Report No. DXXXVI.), and probably sent along with his petition. (No. DXXXV.) W. COLDSTREAM.

# INTELLIGENCE DEPARTMENT, AGRA.

MSS. VOL. V.

*EIGHTH SERIES.*

# COPIES, EXTRACTS, AND ORIGINAL LETTERS

FROM

# CAWNPORE, ALLAHABAD, ETC.,

**In September 1857.**

(*This Series is at the other end of the MSS. Vol. from Seventh Series.*)

## *EIGHTH SERIES.*

### DXXXVII.

BENARES.—H. C. TUCKER, C.S. COMMR., TO MR. COLVIN, LT.-GOVP. 1*st September.*

THE Goorkhas are at Azimgurh, and 2000 of them with 5 lacs of Goruckpore treasure are marching on Jounpore. I think Wynyard will be made District Officer of Azimgurh, and Lind of Jounpore with full powers, as neither —— nor —— is compêtent to remodel a district. Goorkhas at Azimgurh. Wynyard, C.S. Lind, C.S.

Bird has escaped in safety to the eastward, after bravely remaining at Goruckpore when all the rest went away. I hope to get a Madras Regiment and some Goorkhas and drive out the new Nazim, so soon as we know what becomes of Lucknow. Escape of Mr. Bird.

. . . . . . .

Koer Singh and the Ramgurh Mutineers are in the back-woods, near Bijeygurh, threatening Mirzapore; but will not dare to attack it. St. George will give a good account of them if they do. Ghazipore and Benares are perfectly quiet. Simson will take Moore's place at Mirzapore. (All drafts will be honoured. Draw on Allahabad and Benares in preference to Mirzapore.) Koer Singh. Ghazipore. Benares. Simson, C.S

Five hundred Europeans coming up the Grand Trunk Road, besides the Madras Column; and the Madras Regiment by steamer, and Peel's battery of heavy guns and sailors.

### DXXXVIII.

ALLAHABAD. *September 2nd,* 1857.

GENERAL SIR J. OUTRAM arrived late last evening on "Kolodyne"; immediately following him are steamers having 90th and 5th Regiments on board. A strong Column, not less than 1200 Europeans, will march towards Cawnpore on 5th inst., and we may yet hope that with God's assistance Lucknow will be relieved. It will be a most difficult operation, though; all Oudh is in arms against us, and the village matchlockmen fight better than the Sepoys. All Goruckpore is in possession of the Oudh General Sir J. Outram. Movements of troops. All Oudh in arms. Goruckpore.

Mahomed Hussen. Bird.

people, Mahomed Hussen being Nazim. This uncovers Bengal. Bird would not abandon his post when Wynyard and Paterson went away with the Goorkhas, and I fear he has been murdered.

I have not heard from Osborne at Rewah for some days, and there is small doubt but that country is in rebellion against the Rajah.

Dinapore Mutineers.

The Dinapore Mutineers are crossing, or have crossed, into the Doab at the Rajapore ferry, and the gunboat left this at dawn to-day to assist their arrangements.

Rewah in rebellion.

Colonel Hinde (?) was to have intercepted them in Rewah, or this district, but internal rebellion in the Rewah State compelled Osborne to recall the whole force and concentrate on the capital.

Mr. Grant is ailing, and detained at Benares.

## DXXXIX.

### Cawnpore.—Capt. Macbean to Capt. Chalmers.
*2nd September.*

W. Edwards, C.S. G. Probyn, C.S.

We have been quiet here since I wrote by your former Cossid. Sent 300 sick away. Got 350 men. General Outram is expected to leave Allahabad with 1500 men about the 6th. We shall then be strong enough to try over the water again, and shall start sharp. W. Edwards, Probyn, wife and 2 children, came in on 31st from near Futtehgurh. It is strange to see a lady again. Cholera has not quite left us, but we are very jolly.

Reward offered for the Nana.

Rupees 50,000 have been offered for the Nana, and there are some hopes of boning him.

Crommelin, R.E.

Crommelin is our Engineer, and we are making an entrenchment that will defy all India, if we are driven back. We have one steamer here. More cannot get up. Some three of the

Bombay regiments mutinied.

Bombay Regiments have mutinied, but been punished. Madras troops are coming up. Some are at Dinapore.

## DXL.

### Cawnpore.—Capt. Gordon to A. Hume, C.S. *3rd September.*

Dinapore Mutineers.

I wrote you on the 31st. From news received this morning there is reason to fear that the 5th and 90th Regiments have been again detained because the Dinapore Regiments have approached to attack Mirzapore.

Lucknow.

There is good news from Lucknow this morning,—that the

garrison is doing very well, and that they have provisions. The atta is bad, but they have plenty of wheat, and a few mill-stones. Former report confirmed about spiking the large gun and blowing up a house with 100 men. The Sweeper garrison of Bithoor is answering capitally. **Sweeper garrison of Bithoor.**

The 8th Cavalry, Madras, have refused to embark for Calcutta. **8th Cavalry, Madras.**

We had grand races and games here yesterday and the day before. **Races and games.**

Sherer was there in a carriage and four.

## DXLI.

ALLAHABAD.—COLONEL O'BRIEN TO MR. COLVIN, LT.-GOVR.
*4th September.*

A FORCE of about 1200 European Infantry, together with Eyre's Battery, are going up to Cawnpore, which, joining with Havelock's force, will march against Lucknow. The 1st Division will march hence on the morning of the 6th for Cawnpore. The 2nd Division will march on the 7th. They may reach Cawnpore in 6 days. With Havelock's force and this force there will be three batteries,—Maude's, Olphert's, and Eyre's, and a couple of heavy howitzers. It is supposed they will be able to relieve Lucknow. **Details of force for relief of Lucknow.**

## DXLII.

ALLAHABAD.—C. CHESTER, C.S. COMMR., TO W. MUIR, C.S., SUDDUR BOARD. *4th September.*

(Reply to 20th.)—Been ordered to send Agra 10 lacs on first safe opportunity.

"James Hume" and "Calcutta" arrived yesterday with men of H.M.'s 5th and 90th. "Mirzapore" is close behind. To-morrow a strong Column will march, and another on the following day. With God's blessing these reinforcements will reduce the relief of Lucknow to a certainty, if they can but hold out for another fortnight. **Relief of Lucknow.**

I hope to get away and overrun F. with that . . . . Durriao Singh; he and I were always great friends, and I can trust him implicitly. He says he can give me 500 men stout and staunch. H.M. 37th and 10th are in an odd frame of mind, positively infuriated against the natives, to such an extent **Durriao Singh.** **Strange spirit in H.M.'s 37th and 10th.**

as to induce them to disregard discipline and act mutinously and disrespectfully to their officers, when rebuked by them for murdering and plundering.

## DXLIII.

### CAWNPORE.—FROM J. W. SHERER, C.S. *6th September.*

Lucknow.

A MAN has just come in from Lucknow—bringing news from thence of the 2nd Sept. The Belee guard was all right. The rebels had managed to get two heavy guns very close, and some damage to the walls had been effected; but our side directed continual fire on the guns themselves, and they have been rendered useless, and the rebels can neither fire them nor move them.

We cannot learn anything certain about their food; but the message says it is well known that they have secret friends in the city, and so we must hope that they will be able to hold out till the old General gets there—which may be by the 20th, or perhaps a day or two earlier.

The Nana. Jarsa Singh.

The intelligence is confirmed of the Nana being in durance at Futtehpore (?) Chowrassee; but I question whether Jarsa Singh's son, being a Thakoor, will give up a guest, though I daresay he will bully him.

## DXLIV.

### CAWNPORE.—J. W. SHERER, C.S., TO CAPT. NIXON. *5th September.*

ARMY waiting for reinforcements, "which may be expected (I hope) by 10th inst." The Futtehgurh refugees report that "Major Robertson and a Mr. Churcher, Jr., are concealed in Oudh, about 8 miles from Futtehgurh; the former is badly wounded." A letter has been received from Capt. Gowan, Adjutant of one of the Bareilly Corps. He says that numerous Europeans are concealed by the Thakoors in Rohilkhund. They (the Thakoors) are much enraged with the Mussulmans, who have taken to killing cows, etc. They have had one or two slight engagements, in which the Thakoors have been victorious. An attack on Bareilly was talked of.

Major Robertson and Mr. Churcher concealed in Oudh. Captain Gowan. Europeans concealed in Rohilkhund. Thakoors attack Mussulmans in Rohilkhund.

Capt. Gowan says that with 300 or 400 Europeans, and power to raise 2 or 3 Regiments of Thakoors, the whole of

Rohilkhund could be easily put in order. He says that the Mussulmans are superior (to the Hindoos) in Artillery. Otherwise they might be at once thrashed (by them).

Feared that no other Europeans escaped from Futtehgurh.

Messrs. Griffiths and Passana have come in from Calpee. The Raja has so far behaved well that he has saved their lives, . . . . The N(ana) Sahib is still at Futtehpore Chourassee. **Messrs. Griffiths and Passana.** **Nana Sahib.**

Dinapore insurgents at Banda *en route* to Delhi. The Nawab wished to detain them, but they refused, being ill-found with ammunition. **Dinapore insurgents.**

## DXLV.

ALLAHABAD.—C. CHESTER, C.S., TO CAPT. NIXON.

*3rd September.*

THE 5th and 90th will be at once advanced on C(awnpore), with details of 78th and 84th and Madras Fusiliers still here. Havelock on their arrival will have 2000 British bayonets, 3 batteries of Artillery, and 400 Sikhs. **Havelock's force.**

One thousand Goorkhas will remain at Azimgurh and 2000 at Jounpore. The Madras troops are coming up by the Trunk Road marching, and H.M. 53rd in waggons. Dinapore Mutineers began crossing the Jumna at Rajapore, suddenly changed their plans, and marched south on Tirohan in Banda district. **Goorkhas garrison Azimgurh and Jounpore.** **Dinapore Mutineers.**

Ramgurh battalion is in the Mirzapore district. These scoundrels keep the country in a ferment. **Ramgurh battalion.**

Some men of the 67th N.I. on leave in this district are behaving well; they have come forward to say they would fight against the Oudh people, who have invaded and seized our Transgangetic Pergunnahs. General O(utram) sent me a message addressed by him to H(avelock), in which he says he will not take the command and the laurels from Havelock, but will serve as a volunteer if his military aid is required. Sir J. Outram goes with the army as the Chief Commissioner of Oudh. This is very fine and self-denying. **Loyalty of some men of the 67th N.I.** **Outram resigns command and laurels to Havelock.**

Treasury at Allahabad well supplied.

The Sodas in Lucknow (a peculiar sect of men, famed for extravagance and honesty as guardians of property) are said to have taken offence at the insurgents and to be fighting for us. They number some 5000 men. We *cannot* get a letter from Lucknow. The last man we sent had his head cut off. **Sodas in Lucknow.** **Lucknow messenger murdered.**

## DXLVI.

### Cawnpore.—From J. F. Tytler[1] to Col. Becher.

*7th September.*

My Dear Becher,—We received last night the intelligence of Nicholson's success over the rebels. It ought to influence events at Delhi very decidedly—the loss of 12 guns, ammunition, and camp equipage, together with the disgrace of the Brigade, is a serious check to the rebels. Outram will join between the 11th and the 14th with 1500 Europeans, including Eyre's battery. He brings two 8-inch Howitzers. We shall immediately cross the river with two thousand six or seven hundred Europeans, two hundred Sikhs, and 18 or 20 guns, and hope to be at Lucknow by the 22nd or 24th. What we are to do then I can't say. Were it left to General Havelock we should recross and march up country, unless Delhi fall in the meantime; but as Outram accompanies us as Commissioner of Oudh he will direct our movements, and I fear we shan't leave Oudh to join you. I do not apprehend difficulty in our operations—our strength (being) four times what it was, not in numbers, but in efficiency. Our eighteen guns were half manned by infantry soldiers, and we had few artillery officers. In our last engagement we had only one efficient and two disabled officers for 13 guns. The Enfield rifle will also in a great measure be substituted for the old musket. The 5th and 90th are trained men in its use. All is quiet round about us. The garrison at Lucknow holding more than their own, and their enemies dispirited. The rebels assaulted the work on the 17th, and were driven back with loss. On the 24th our men exploded a mine under Jacob the shopkeeper's house, from which the enemy annoyed them much by musketry, having also a heavy gun on its flank. The house was reduced to a heap of ruins and the guns spiked by a sally party. On the 20th the rebels brought two guns into the Belundah Bagh and kept up a fire for a day and night, but on the morning of the 27th our batteries opened and silenced and dismounted the guns. Since then the fire on the part of the enemy is very slack. The rascals declare that should the garrison hold out for two years they won't assault again: for once I believe them.

Outram. His force. Enfield rifle. Lucknow. Successful sortie.

European stores are scarce, but wheat is plentiful—so we have nothing to fear, I believe, on their account.

[1] The writer is, no doubt, Lt.-Col. J. M. Fraser-Tytler of the 37th Bengal Native Infantry, who was Commandant of the 9th Bengal Irregular Cavalry. He returned from furlough, and was attached to Havelock's force, and was present at the first relief of Lucknow as Assistant Quartermaster-General.

## DXLVII.[1]

CAWNPORE.—FROM J. W. SHERER, C.S., PROBABLY ADDRESSED TO MR. COLVIN, LT.-GOVR. *Sept.* 2 (?), 1857.

(LETTER incomplete.)—Showed him your letter, and I telegraphed your message to Lord Canning. On the whole, matters are looking much brighter every day. θε ρεεναν ανδ γναλιορ clouds a little threaten the horizon; but, please God, all will be well.

Our entrenchment here has been much strengthened. It is a little open to shells on the river side,—but where are the shells to come from when Havelock crosses the river? Cholera has almost disappeared; the last case was Capt. Sheehey, 81st Queen's, on duty with the Volunteer Cavalry. **Captain Sheehey.**

**Ahmud Buksh.** Ahmud Buksh has written to me to say he has reached home, and would like to join us here, and make himself of use. What do you think of him? I am employing mostly Hindoos in all offices, to the exclusion of Mahomedans. **Hindoo *versus* Mahommedan employees.** I think the latter, if they have really gone through the temptation of the "Mahomdee Jhunda," and have *resisted* it, may be safely used, —and the old Mahomedan prestige gives them an influence which Kayuths, etc., cannot easily obtain. You will be glad to learn that Umr Nath, Tehseeldar of Ghazeepore—now with me—is distinguishing himself very much in every way. **Umr Nath, Tehseeldar.**—Believe me, my dear Sir, with much esteem, faithfully yours,

J. W. SHERER.

## DXLVIII.

CAWNPORE.—FROM GENERAL HAVELOCK TO W. MUIR, C.S.[2] 9*th*.

**Havelock gives a good account of himself.** I HAVE to thank you for your various communications. Your Cossid spake not the truth when he said I was sick. God be praised, I have neither been sick nor sorry since I started on the expedition, though the work and weather have both been trying.

I expect my reinforcements up shortly, and will then go to work again.

## DXLIX.

FROM GENERAL HAVELOCK TO COL. COTTON. 15*th Sept.* (?)

MANY thanks for your information regarding the Contingent, which is very valuable. I regret to say that it is but too

[1] On thin paper about $2\frac{1}{2} \times 4$ inches.—W. C.

[2] Written, like all the Cossid letters of the day, on tiny thin paper, to be secreted about the body lest seen by the Mutineers on the road.—W. M.

Mr. Ommaney killed.

certain that Mr. Ommaney, C.S., was killed during the siege. Sir Jas. Outram brings me up reinforcements. upon which I must go to work again.

## DL.

ALLAHABAD.—C. CHESTER, C.S. COMMR., ALLAHABAD, TO THE HON. MR. COLVIN, LT.-GOVR. *7th September* 1857.

MY DEAR MR. COLVIN,—A cossid has this moment given me your letter of the 27th ultimo, with its enclosures to Lord Canning, Gen. Outram, and Dr. Irving; they will be duly forwarded. The post has also brought Capt. Nixon's letter to me of the 30th ult., and its enclosures from Delhi up to the 24th idem. They will be sent to Mr. Grant with request that he will forward them to Calcutta. We are striving to raise a low-caste Police, horse and foot,—it can be done, I think. At Bithoor the Thannahdar is a hangman, and his officers are sweepers; they prove efficient. West of this we hold the ground we stand on; and nothing more. No revenue is got from Banda or Humeerpoor; next to none from Futtehpoor, or Cawnpore. In Allahabad the collections for the June kist amount to Rupees 176,492, out of a total demand of Rupees 468,603. Sir J. Outram marched out at head of H.M. 90th Regiment at 9 p.m. of the 5th instant. Yesterday a company of H.M. 58th arrived in waggons, and went on again at night. With these reinforcements General Havelock's army should number fully 2000 British and 400 Sikh bayonets, and three full batteries of Artillery, besides some heavy guns and howitzers. From and after the 10th inst. we expect to get daily detachments, 80 strong, of H.M. 53rd. "Mirzapore" steamer went down this morning to Dinapore to pick up "Gamma" (?) Flat with Naval Brigade; she will return between the 15th and 20th instant. How are the 68-pounders to be moved when they arrive here? Bird has escaped from Goruckpore; the report of his murder was false. I heard from Tickell of the 73rd this morning; 8 Officers and a few good men in the Regiment had hitherto held in check the majority, who were ripe for mutiny: 3 plots to murder the Officers had been discovered and defeated. The Dinapore Mutineers are reported to be at Banda on their way to Delhi; I hope they will not cross over to the Doab. Osborne has succeeded in quieting Rewah and nipping in the bud an incipient rebellion against the Rajah; and is now endeavouring to arrest the march of the Ramgurh battalion at the passage of the Tonse. We send him tents and money, but cannot co-operate with men,

Low-Caste Police.

Revenue not coming in.

Allahabad collections.

Sir J. Outram leaves Allahabad.

Movements of troops upwards.

Bird, C.S.

73rd Native Infantry.

Dinapore Mutineers.

Osborne at Rewah.

Ramgurh battalion.

and I doubt if his troops can stop the mutinied Sepoys. I wanted to reoccupy Futtehpore with Durriaow Singh's assistance, but Mr. Grant does not approve of the scheme. I am sorry for this, as there is no present prospect of getting any soldiers. Every man is wanted for the army of relief. The "Jumna" gunboat was unable to stem the current of the Jumna river near Mhow; she had been ordered to Rajapoor to prevent the Dinapore men from crossing into the Doab at that Ghat, and could not get there. Luckily, the rebels changed their plans and did not cross. I am glad to see that more of my letters are arriving than used to be the case.—I am, my dear Sir, yours very sincerely, **Durriaow Singh.**

C. CHESTER.

THE HONBLE. J. R. COLVIN,
Lt.-GOVR.

## DLI.[1]

CAWNPORE.—FROM J. W. SHERER, C.S. *9th Sept.* 1857.

MY DEAR SIR,—News was received yesterday evening from Lucknow, dated the 2nd of Sept., that the garrison was all right and could hold out till the end of the month. As we calculate with God's assistance the reinforced Column will reach Lucknow by the 25th at latest, I trust we may consider our dear friends as in imminent danger no longer. You will be pleased to learn that your movements in the direction of Allygurh have been felt at Furruckabad. A letter received this morning states that on the news reaching that city that the English had arrived at Allygurh, the regular troops—understood to be portions of the 1st, 53rd, 56th, 41st Infantry, 2nd Cavalry, and 18th, 3rd, and 14th Irregulars, but not in all more than 1200 or 1500 men—decided to disperse. So the Nawab will be left with his wretched new levies, his unpopular name, and his black heart, to make the most of his half-dozen guns. **Lucknow.** **Furruckabad.** **The Nawab of Furruckabad.**

The Dinapore gentlemen are at Bandah, and will, I fancy, try to go up country, crossing either in the Futtehpore district, or at Calpee. They don't seem much to incline to fighting, as it is said they have no caps, and are more in search of loot. They will do much harm passing up north, of a temporary nature, disturbing arrangements, and setting all the budmashes in a ferment again; but it cannot be helped. This district could soon be got right if we had a few military outposts—one at the Esur Nuddee, one towards Calpee, and a third at Bithoor. But Futtehpore will give more trouble, as there are several villages **Dinapore insurgents.** **Futtehpore.**

[1] On thin paper about 4 inches square.—W. C.

and Zemindars so thoroughly addicted now to loot—as a profession, you may almost say—that their condign punishment alone will put matters straight. At the same time, we have got *all* the Thannahs restored in Futtehpore, and only two as yet here. Futtehpore was much quieter a week ago. But it is boiling over again a little now. However, the road is kept clear. The mails are going daily, and the wire communicates with Calcutta.

General Neill telegraphed the victory at Nujjufgurh cut.

. . . . . . . .

Watson's narrative.

I beg to enclose a copy of Act XI. I am having a copy on small paper copied for you of *The Cawnpore Mutiny*, a narrative compiled from different accounts by Watson of the Engineers.

(*Letter incomplete.*)

## DLII.

ALLYGURH (probably).—A. H. COCKS, C.S. 15*th Sept.* 1857.

Civil cases.

THE great bulk of cases which we shall eventually have to try and dispose of are of dispossession by former Zemindars of present holders of estates. I have petitions from auction purchasers and such-like by hundreds,—even in the well-disposed pergunahs of Hatrass and Sassna. What will be the number elsewhere? We shall in many instances have to resort

Restoration of property.

to harsh measures to give back possession, and as for punishing all who have acted in this way it will be a labour of years. In the same way with complaints of loot, scarcely a village has not its case.

## DLIV.

CAWNPORE.—J. W. SHERER, C.S., TO CAPT. NIXON. *Sept.* 11*th.*

The Nana.

No news. The Nana has made up his quarrel with Jursa Singh's son. But is still at Futtehpore Chowrassi.

Dinapore rebels. Erskine takes Jhansi.

Dinapore rebels still at Banda. A letter received yesterday from Calpee says Erskine has taken Jhansi and levelled the Fort of Banpore, but this requires confirmation. Some of the Oudh blackguards have had the impertinence to cross over into the Futtehpore district near Hulgaon; but the Munsiff is holding on, and has persuaded Sir J. Outram to send some men and guns to drive them back across the Ganges. (This may delay the 90th a day.)

We are recovering healthiness, and this windy weather seems to blow disease away.

## DLV.

### ETAWAH.

ONE hundred and fifty Sowars of the Gwalior Contingent passed through this town on the 12th inst. *en route* to their homes, and several parties of the Contingent Sepoys on the 12th and 15th inst. were also seen going to their homes. **Men of the Gwalior Contingent going to their homes.**

The Dutiya Raja said to be at war with the Ranee of Jhansee.

## DLVII.

CAWNPORE.—FROM CAPT. BRUCE TO CAPT. NIXON. 13*th Sept.*

(Reply to 5th.)—We have written news from the garrison at Lucknow up to 2nd, and we have heard by scouts up to the **Lucknow.** 5th. They were all well, and I hope will very soon be relieved now. Capt. Inglis writes cheerfully, and the native portion of his force behave nobly, as of course all the rest do. On the latter day an attack was made on the Baillie guard, but through **Attack on Baillie Guard fails.** some mismanagement a mine was sprung at an unfortunate time by the rebels, and they blew up, it is said, 400 of their own people! The garrison then made a sortie and completed their discomfiture. Outram will be here on the 14th, with a battery, 100 Cavalry, and 1500 Europeans; and I trust by the 24th Lucknow will be relieved. There are at present only 18 guns, **Estimate of Rebel force.** and 6000 or 7000 men between this and Lucknow; but I hope they will flock out when our force crosses, for the more we can catch outside the city the better. Deducting the force left here, Outram (or rather Havelock) will have about 3000 men and 20 **Havelock's force.** guns. The former will not, he says, deprive the latter of the honour of relieving Lucknow by assuming military command until after the place falls. Neill goes on in command of a wing. **General Neill.** I believe Col. Wilson and the 64th Foot will remain here, but this may be altered. The Naval Brigade, 500 strong, will be at **Naval Brigade.** Allahabad on the 20th, which will release a like number of soldiers to be pushed up here. Other reinforcements are tumbling into Calcutta daily, and by December we shall be very strong all over India.

Outram.

Outram has polished off some Oudh Zemindars with guns who crossed, but this will not detain him, for he made a double march to do it.

## DLVIII

CAWNPORE.—FROM GENERAL NEILL TO MR. COLVIN, LT.-GOVR.
*7th September.*

Losses of men at Cawnpore.

We have lost fearfully—316 men since Havelock left Allahabad; 3 officers and 57 men killed by the enemy included.

Lucknow.

The intelligence from Lucknow is excellent. I do believe that brave garrison will almost itself raise the siege and investment of the place. The enemy have signally failed; they are quarrelling among themselves, and I believe from all the accounts we have that the Sepoys in particular are walking away to the villages. The great mass of the besieging force are matchlock-men. We will have very few regulars to contend against, and I believe, with the exception of 300 or 400 men, the road to Lucknow is unoccupied, and the bridges are unoccupied. We hope in a day or two to get accounts direct from our own people there, but this may be relied upon as strictly true: "On the 3rd inst. they were all hearty and well. Provisions for some time The enemy's 2 large guns, which they have got up so close to the works, have both been disabled, and the enemy can't resume them." From all we can learn there is a large party of the influential men of the country in our favour, and I anticipate little if any resistance in our next advance.

Dissensions among rebels. Sepoys going to their homes. Besieging force are matchlock-men. Road to Lucknow nearly clear.

Feeling in favour of British Government in Oudh.

. . . . . . . .

Mr. Edwards, Collector and Magistrate of Budaon, will leave in a few days for Allahabad to meet Mr. Grant.

. . . . . . . .

English officers and families saved. Captain Orr. Mr. Thornhill. Gowan.

A great many of our officers are yet alive and safe in Oudh. I have to-day heard of Capt. Orr and Mr. Thornhill, with their wives and children, safe at Mahouly from Seetapore. Capt. Gowan or Lt. Gowan, somewhere near Rohilkhund, wrote to General Havelock.

. . . . . . . .

## DLIX.

HATRASS. *September 19th.*

We have caught a Sapper and Miner and a Sepoy of the 57th. Both very insolent and defiant, especially the latter. They will be disposed of by Court-martial.

The news from Khoorja, Atroulee, and Anoopshuhur, all tend to show that the enemy is flying from Delhi, and a roznamcha from Jamma Ka Pul (between Anoopshuhur and Coel, over the Canal) states that it is said the Jats of Kosee have surrounded some 400 or 500 Sepoys on their way to Gwalior. Jats attack Delhi fugitive force.

## DLX.

CAWNPORE. *15th September.*

THE accompanying note from Macnaghten gives a good account of a very brilliant affair in Futtehpore. About 400 Oude blackguards, with 2 or 3 guns, came over near Hutgam to break up the Thannah—and their end is related in Macnaghten's note. We have got a 24-pounder battery on a high bank near where I am encamped.

. . . . . . . .

The steamer has most provokingly got aground in the middle of the river.

There was a swell down on the bank yesterday on horseback—in a red coat—giving a great many orders. But a 24-pounder shot interfered very much with the execution of his little arrangements.

## DLXI.

CAWNPORE.—LETTER TO DUMERGUE. *September 13th.*

THE 5th Fusiliers and detachments of 67th, 78th, 84th and 1st Madras Fusiliers came in on the 15th. Sir J. Outram with 90th, Eyre's battery, and 200 Cavalry, consisting of Volunteers and 100 12th Irregulars, on the 16th. Troops arrive at Cawnpore.

Two days ago, hearing some guns firing between them and the river, Eyre was sent with two guns and 150 bayonets, and a few Cavalry, to see what the matter was. They found 300 Oude men (Sepoys) with 4 guns; attacked them, and obliged them to take to their boats. The men with the Enfield Rifles doubled after them, and managed to prevent their working their boats, until Eyre came up with his guns, which, depressed 15 degrees, blew the scoundrels out of the water Two boats were sunk with the guns, and 250 men. One boat got away. An Oudh Raja, who had, it is said, crossed with the view of interrupting Major Eyre attacks Oudh men.

our communication between Calpee and Allahabad, retired precipitately on hearing this.

Movements of troops.

Three hundred more of the 33rd have arrived from Mauritius at Bombay. The Land Transport men—250, mounted on horses of 8th Madras Cavalry—are to come up shortly. The 53rd Foot with some Madras N.I. must be near Benares.

We have a bridge of boats ready, but not yet run across. This morning we with two 24-pounders destroyed an embrasure the rebels have had the impertinence to erect near the opposite bank. One shot killed a few of them and sent them flying.

The 82nd, 23rd, and 93rd expected hourly at Calcutta. Sir Colin has had fever, but is better.

## DLXII.

FUTTEHPORE, CAMP MULWA.—E. MACNAGHTEN, C.S., TO J. W. SHERER, C.S. *13th September.*

I AM now with the 2nd Division of the Force under General Outram. We arrived here this morning. The 1st Division under Major Simmons is one day's march ahead of us; and will most likely be at Cawnpore on the 15th. Major Eyre's expedition was a most successful one. About 150 or so of the Oudh marauders were polished off. The 30 men of the 12th Irregulars did good service. They galloped up and fired on the Oudh scoundrels just as they were pushing off. The Oudh fellows, in the eagerness to return the fire, neglected to manage their boats' steering, and a strong wind across the river drove two of them right into the teeth of Eyre's guns, which had arrived and taken up a commanding position on the bank. A third boat in which was their magazine was left on the bank, and the powder being set alight either by them, or the carelessness of some of the 5th, five of that Regiment and a lot of camp-followers who had gone to loot were lifted into the air. Two of the 5th were much scorched—the Doctor says, however, they will get all right. No one was killed. Two others of the 5th were wounded, one by a ball, the other by a tulwar. Major Eyre came across country, and joined us at Futtehpore.

Major Eyre's expedition.

FUTTEHPORE. *21st September.*

Futtehpore.

FUTTEHPORE is getting reinhabited. We left in the Tehseeldaree tents for 400 Europeans. They will, I suppose, be there soon now. There will be lots of work for the fellows then.

If the General can get "khubur" of the whereabouts of Jodar Singh, and information of his retainers being as numerous as is stated, he will, I think, send out against him to-morrow. **Jodar Singh.**

The men are all jolly and in capital pluck. The 90th march much better than could have been expected.

Koer Singh has forced his way into Rewah, and forced the Raja to leave his capital. **Koer Singh attacks Rewah.**

## DLXIII.

CAWNPORE.—FROM J. W. SHERER, C.S. *22nd September.*

GENERAL OUTRAM arrived last night, and to-day preparations are actively going on for crossing. We commenced our embarkation by dropping one gun into the river, but have succeeded in fishing it up again. No news except that through Osborne's influence the Rewah people have resented Koer Singh's invasion, and they have kicked him out. **Outram arrives at Cawnpore.** **Rewah repels Koer Singh.**

## DLXIV.

ALLAHABAD. *September 15th.*

(Reply to 7th.)—Small detachments of 90th and 53rd Regiments arrive here daily. They are sent to Futtehpore, which will be held shortly by 500 Europeans. They had become absolutely necessary. The Oudh people were beginning to overrun the district, and would soon have interrupted our communications. **Futtehpore held by Europeans.**

Osborne has weathered the storm at Rewa. He did not fly to Dumoh, as he at first intended. **Osborne at Rewah.**

Koer Singh's followers heard exaggerated reports of the preparations made to receive him, and went down the Ghats again. They will now march on Banda. The Ramgurh battalion is not with Koer Singh. They are some marches below. The 40th N.I. are with Koer Singh. **Koer Singh.** **Ramgurh battalion.** **40th Native Infantry.**

No fresh arrivals of troops at C——. Several ships with soldiers are due, and daily expected. The Naval Brigade ought to be here on the 20th.

## DLXV.

CAWNPORE.—FROM J. W. SHERER. *30th August.*

WE are yet without news from Lucknow; but we conclude from a body of men having come from the Oudh side and **Lucknow.**

Bithoor Thannah attacked and driven in. Serishtahdar killed.

attacked Bithoor, that the rebels are now fugitives. Bruce's Thannah was driven in—and his Serishtahdar, who had gone out to take charge of matters during the Dusserah, was killed, and 13 Sowars' horses carried off. Pursidh Narain (Bruce's man) seems to have been culpably careless: he was drunk, and they had had a nautch. They were taken by surprise, and of course could do nothing.

# INDEX

## VOLUME I